Hollywood Diva

Hollywood Diva

A BIOGRAPHY OF

Jeanette MacDonald

EDWARD BARON TURK

UNIVERSITY OF CALIFORNIA PRESS

Berkeley · Los Angeles · London

University of California Press
Berkeley and Los Angeles, California

University of California Press, Ltd.
London, England

First Paperback Printing 2000

Library of Congress Cataloging-in-Publication Data

Turk, Edward Baron.
      Hollywood diva : a biography of Jeanette
   MacDonald / Edward Baron Turk.
            p.   cm.
      Includes bibliographic references and index
      ISBN 0-520-21202-9 (cloth : alk. paper)
            0-520-22253-9 (pb. : alk. paper)
      1. MacDonald, Jeanette, 1903–1965.
      2. Sopranos (Singers)—United States—
   Biography.   3. Motion picture actors and
   actresses—United States—Biography.   I. Title.
   M420.M135T87   1998
   791.43′028′092—dc 21
   [B]   97-44792

Printed in the United States of America

08   07   06   05   04   03   02   01   00
9   8   7   6   5   4   3   2

The paper used in this publication meets the minimum requirements of ANSI/NISO Z39.48-1992
(R 1997) (*Permanence of Paper*). ∞

To David E. Lapin,
for awakening me to MacDonald

As if to filter out all hypocrisy, today's movies ruthlessly
subordinate illusion to undiluted realism. The sweet
fragrance of discreet romance, as personified by the heroine
of *The Love Parade, The Merry Widow,* and *Smilin' Through,*
has all but evaporated. That should not prevent
Jeanette MacDonald from assuming her rightful place
among Screen Immortals. More than just nostalgia,
she offers us the scent of subtle pleasures.

THE EDITORS, *Ciné Revue* (Paris), April 1980

Contents

PART FOUR. ECHOES OF SWEET SONG

Preface

> Nightingales and forests are for ever romantic, and it is
> merely cowardice to be afraid of saying so.
>
> VIRGINIA WOOLF, "Romance
> and the Heart," 1923

My love affair with Jeanette MacDonald started eighteen years ago. Boston's old Nickelodeon Theater, then a great house for movie revivals, had scheduled a double bill of *Maytime* and *Sweethearts.* These are two of MacDonald's most lavish musicals from the late 1930s, both costarring her famous MGM singing partner Nelson Eddy. At the time, I was recovering from complicated surgery but was well enough to venture out a few hours each day. I had never seen a Jeanette MacDonald picture, so I wasn't sure what to expect. My friend David Lapin, executive director of the Community Music Center of Boston, urged me to go and watch these films with an open mind. He also advised firmly, "See *Maytime* before *Sweethearts,* not the other way round!"

The first ten minutes of *Maytime* had me stumped. Was that frail old lady on-screen actually Jeanette MacDonald? The answer came with the flashback, when elderly Miss Morrison metamorphoses into radiant young Marcia Mornay, emerges from a glistening carriage, and proceeds to enchant the entire court of Louis Napoléon with her glorious songs For the rest of the picture I sat transfixed and transported. I understood at once why MacDonald's gorgeous looks, brilliant singing, and total conviction had uplifted millions of Depression-scarred moviegoers throughout the 1930s. This beguiling songstress was recharging my spirit as well as my recuperating body. David, by the way, was right about the order. *Maytime* gives us MacDonald as pure movie goddess, inhabiting a black-and-white fantasy world beyond mortal grasp. In *Sweethearts,* she bursts from the screen in dazzling Technicolor, portraying a bubbly, modern-day Broadway star so like our hope of what the "real" MacDonald might be that she almost persuades us the Ideal is within reach.

My newfound ardor was, I soon learned, woefully naive and unschooled. According to most film gurus, the MacDonald worth hankering for was not the diva who sang enthrallingly of great love with Nelson Eddy but the earlier comedienne in delectable lingerie who charmed Maurice Chevalier before censorship clamped down on sex in the movies. I also found out that goose bumps were not the correct response to MacDonald's lyric soprano. Her crisp, gleaming, and elegantly inflected singing voice, the music critics argued, was too small and calculated to merit a serious claim on one's passions. MacDonald's fluky success, in this view, was owed mainly to the electronic wizards in the Paramount and MGM sound departments. Little matter that in the 1940s and 1950s MacDonald went on to become a major presence on the U.S. recital-hall circuit and that for a vast constituency she was the very model of an American concert artist.

Throughout a performance career that spanned half a century, Jeanette MacDonald was an original—utterly fascinating and bewitching. On stage, screen, radio, and television, in concert halls, opera houses, and Las Vegas saloons, she ignored prevailing notions that pitted High Art against mass-consumed entertainment. She remained unshakable in her advocacy of a democratic culture, never losing faith in the civilizing value of music that is unashamedly accessible and driven by beautiful melody. She punctured pretense wherever she saw it, and never lost the ability to laugh at herself as readily as at others.

I began this project with a sense of mission. An important woman of American film and music had never been the subject of a full-scale biography, and the few existing books on her were either flimsy rehashes of previously published material or outlandish fictions steeped in hearsay. A gap in the story of the performing arts in America needed to be plugged, and I wanted to be the one to restore *all* of MacDonald's achievements to their rightful place in the history of music and motion pictures. I also thought that an accurate account of MacDonald's multifaceted career might result in a subtler understanding of the complexity of cultural taste in twentieth-century America.

The exhilaration I felt while writing this book, however, had less to do with my earnest intellectual concerns than with the impact of MacDonald's life-affirming personality. As a biographical subject, MacDonald pricks the dreary clichés about Golden Age movie stars and their penchants for self-destruction. Her life was in large part light, lucky, and fun-loving—much like her motion pictures. MacDonald's early crises and disappointments endowed her not so much with neurosis as with muscle for tackling later challenges. Nicknamed "the Iron Butterfly" by studio wags, MacDonald never let celebrity wreck her personal life. This book, therefore, is in some ways a celebration of splendid health and normalcy—an oddity for a star biography, and a refreshing boon for a writer's state of mind.

Still, preparing *Hollywood Diva* also aroused feelings of loss and regret. I was constantly aware that many of the shining values inherent in MacDonald's life and art are nearly alien to contemporary sensibilities. MacDonald wagered on the public's instinct for responding to quality and refinement, aiming to give audiences something to aspire to, something to ignite their dreams and imaginations. In a way, her movies and music were an experiment in cultural democracy, for they tested the degree to which mass society might respond to a vocal repertoire traditionally associated with a social elite. To her lasting credit, MacDonald carried out this program without succumbing to facile vulgarity or longhair conceit.

I am fortunate to be the first writer with full access to MacDonald's private papers, including an unpublished autobiography written a few years prior to her death in 1965. When I first read MacDonald's memoir, I was struck by its absence of self-congratulation and self-deceit. Quietly, it revealed the intelligence and self-awareness that enabled MacDonald to take on the role of fearless diva without mislaying her sense of humor, honesty, dignity, and femininity. If my own telling of her life conveys to readers a measure of these qualities, I'll consider myself successful.

In today's world, connecting with MacDonald calls for a shifting of gears. You have to let beauty, grace, and gallantry reenter your scheme of values. You need to acknowledge the redemptive power of romantic yearning and heartfelt sentiment. You must submit to the caressing intensity of soprano lyricism. And you need to respond to an erotic charge that perfectly balances sensuality with modesty, passion with restraint.

The rewards, I think, are ample and well worth the effort. I trust the following pages make clear the reasons why.

Acknowledgments

While preparing this book I had the pleasure of conversing with many show-business veterans who knew MacDonald personally and agreed to let me tap their memories. My gratitude goes to Ted Allan, Ann Torri Arndt, Edward Ashley, Lew Ayres, Cecil "Teet" Carle, Thomas Cassidy, Imogene Coca, J. J. Cohn, Leslie Cutler, Elinor Donahue, Ralph Edwards, Jean Fenwick, Chet Forrest, Albert Hackett, Kitty Carlisle Hart, Helen Hayes, Dwayne Hickman, Claude Jarman, Jr., Allan Jones, John Kenley, Leonid Kinskey, Jack Lee, John Pfeiffer, Diana Lewis Powell, Samuel Marx, Leo B. Meyer, Joseph Newman, Cecilia Parker, Harold Prince, Amy Revere, Ginger Rogers, Cesar Romero, George Schaefer, George Sidney, William Tuttle, Maurice Vaccarino, Emily Wentz, Fay Wray, Robert Wright, and Joseph C. Youngerman.

I also interviewed spouses, children, and other relatives of those who were part of MacDonald's story but who are now long deceased. Warm thanks to Virginia Eddy Brown, Sidney Franklin, Jr., Vera Schoenbaum Gebbert, Frances Gershwin Godowski, Mrs. Walter Jurmann, Betty Lasky, Nicola Lubitsch, Dina Merrill, Mrs. Edmund North, Carol Stothart Perkins, Dorshka Raphaelson, John and Donna Ritchie, Mrs. Richard Rodgers, Robert Stack, Herbert Stothart II, Lawrence Tibbett, Jr., Richard Tibbett, and Margaret Whiting.

I learned much about MacDonald's artistry by speaking with singers and musicians who worked closely with her. These included Gene Akerman, Samuel Albert, George Archer, Robert Armbruster, Hubert Head, Louis Kaufman, Virginia Majewski, William B. Marky, Robert L.

McLaughlin, Carl K. Meltzer, Nan Merriman-Brand, Bob Mitchell, Dorothy Porter, and Pamela Randall. Collins Smith, MacDonald's longtime accompanist, was particularly lavish with his time and insight. Other singers, musicians, and composers who spoke to me about MacDonald's vocal legacy are Robert Atherton, Marshall Barer, Lynette Bennett, Richard Cassilly, Patricia Craig, Marthe Errolle, Michael Feinstein, Mary Cleere Haran, Jack Harrold, Verna Hillie, Elizabeth Howell, Rose Inghram, Hugh Martin, Vince Morton, Marni Nixon, Henrietta Pelta, David Raksin, Gale Sherwood, Ira Siff, Nicolas Slonimsky, and Alice Wellman.

Of the many people in the entertainment industry who provided information and leads, I owe special debts to Robert Arthur, Larry Austin, Richard Barclay, Peter Bergman, Harry Caplan, Saul Chaplin, John W. Freeman, A. R. Gurney, Jr., George Hurrell, Ann Jillian, Roddy McDowall, Larry Merritt-Maranville, Herbert Nusbaum, Francine Parker, Charles Pierce, Ken Richards, Lillian Burns Sidney, Robert M. Vogel, and Robert Wise.

I had the good fortune to win the confidence of MacDonald's husband, Gene Raymond, who hitherto had declined to cooperate with authors writing on MacDonald. Gene consented to speak candidly with me about his life with Jeanette, and I am grateful for his trust. I am also beholden to Clara Rhoades and Tessa Williams, chief officers of the legendary Jeanette MacDonald International Fan Club, for facilitating my access to MacDonald's private papers and for bringing new and invaluable primary sources to my attention.

While the bibliography acknowledges the many published sources that have guided my work, the following experts in movie and music history lent a personal hand in shaping my research. For their kindnesses, I thank Charles Affron, Rick Altman, Rudy Behlmer, Peter Bergman, Virginia Bortin, Lance Bowling, Leo Braudy, David Chierichetti, Bill Coffman, Dorothy Crawford, Neal Gabler, Herbert Goldman, Robert Grimes, James Harvey, Stephen Harvey, Roy Hemming, Charles Higham, Henry Jenkins III, Gavin Lambert, Edward Maeder, John Francis Marion, Martin M. Marks, Richard Mohr, Bill Morin, James Robert Parish, Bill Park, William Paul, Vivian Perlis, Lawrence J. Quirk, Frank Ries, Thomas Schatz, David Shepard, David Thorburn, Gerald Turbow, and Mark A. Vieira.

For sharing their reminiscences of MacDonald's childhood in West Philadelphia, I am grateful to Rosemary Arters, Louise Horner, Mrs. J. W. Hundley, Anne Kotkin, Ruth Molloy, and Helen Wright (Mac-

Donald's cousin by marriage). Sally Ruth McCorkle, whose mother was MacDonald's schoolmate, helped me search out these folks. Mrs. Geraldine Brown kindly allowed me to experience firsthand the domestic space occupied by the MacDonalds on Arch Street.

I also thank Dr. Michael DeBakey, former senator Barry Goldwater, and former president Ronald Reagan for their assistance and good wishes for this project.

Librarians, archivists, and curators are a biographer's most precious allies. I salute the staffs of the following, and mention in parentheses individuals who assisted me beyond the call of duty. *In California:* American Society of Cinematographers (George Turner); Directors Guild of America; Doheny Library, University of Southern California (Ned Comstock); Max Factor Museum (Randy Koss); Film and Television Archive, University of California, Los Angeles (Bob Gitt); Margaret Herrick Library, Academy of Motion Picture Arts and Sciences (Sandra Archer, Stacey Endres Behlmer, Barbara Hall, Alison Pinsler, Howard Prouty, and above all Samuel A. Gill, who got me started); Institute of the American Musical (the peerless Miles Kreuger); Local 47 of the Musicians Union (Bill Peterson, Carmen Fanzone); Louis B. Mayer Library, American Film Institute; San Francisco Opera (Koraljka Lockhart); San Francisco Performing Arts Library and Museum (Kirsten Tanaka); Regional History Center, University of Southern California (Dace Taube); Special Collections and Theater Arts Library, University of California, Los Angeles (Brigitta Kueppers); Turner Entertainment (Cathy Manolis, Richard P. May, Roger Mayer). *In Massachusetts:* Harvard Theatre Collection (Joseph Keller); Spaulding Library, New England Conservatory of Music (Tom Scheuzger); Special Collections, Boston University (Howard B. Gotlieb). *In New York:* BMG/RCA Music (Bernadette Moore); Carnegie Hall (Gino Francesconi, Jill Vetter); Margo Feiden Galleries (David Leopold); Film Study Center, Museum of Modern Art (Charles Silver); Metropolitan Opera Association (John Pennino); Museum of Television and Radio (Jonathan Rosenthal); New York Public Library for the Performing Arts (Robert Armstrong, Richard M. Buck, Barbara Cohen-Stratyner); Oral History Research Office, Columbia University (Ronald J. Grele); Washington Irving High School (Mary Ann Calega, Howard Schumacher); President's Office, Ithaca College (Cheryl Drake); Julia Richman High School (Judy Serfaty); Rodgers and Hammerstein Theatre Library (Tom Briggs); Shubert Archive (Maryann Chach, Reagan Fletcher, Mark Swartz). *In Pennsylvania:* Academy of Music, Philadelphia; City Archives, Divorce Index, and Deeds Office, City Hall, Philadelphia; Free Library of Philadelphia (Geraldine Duclow); Historical Society of Pennsylvania; Olivet Covenant Presbyterian Church, Philadelphia; Pedagogy Library, Board of Education, Philadelphia; Personnel Department, Philadelphia Municipal Services Building (James Kimpson); Philadelphia Tax Review Board; Register of Wills and Clerk of Orphans' Court of Delaware County, Media; Urban Archives, Temple University; Vital Records, Department of Health, Commonwealth of Pennsylvania, New Castle. *In Rhode Island:* Providence Public Library (Jeanne Richardson). *In Texas:* Oral History Program, Southern Methodist University (Ronald L. Davis, Tom Colpetter). *In Wisconsin:* Wisconsin Center for Film and Theater Research (Don Crafton). *In France:* Archives Départementales des Alpes-Maritimes, Nice; Bibliothèque de l'Arsenal, Paris; Bibliothèque du Cinéma, Cinémathèque Française, Paris; Hôtel du Cap-Eden-Roc, Cap d'Antibes; Théâtre le Rex, Paris (Martine Martineau). *In England:* British Film Institute, London; British Museum, London.

For helping me track down additional data and sources, I am indebted to Kim Beaty, John Reeves Begley, John Cocchi, Irene Daligga, Norman Dewes, Karen Kettering Dimit, Elsa Dik Glass, Rosalind Hall, Milton Kenin, Ron Kirchhoff, Roger Kolb, Mary L. Komidar, Katya Krivinkova, Frieda Lapin, Jonathan Lapin, Harry Locke, Gail Lulay, John Martin, Norma S. McDaniels, Frank C. P. McGlinn, Leslie C. Perelman, Perry Pickering, Chris Pomiecko, Margarita Schelps, Robert Wolf Scull, Donald Violette, and Mary Frances Penney Wagley. A team of ultrasharp MIT and Wellesley undergraduates—Lia Abbate, Joanna Chouls, Brian Elder, Teresa Helsten, Nic Kelman, Jonathan Roorda, and Frederika Turner—gleaned all references to MacDonald as they appeared over a span of four and a half decades in issues of *Variety, Motion Picture Herald,* and *Billboard.* My mother, Elsie, also proved herself an eagle-eyed research assistant by combing relevant tidbits from current New York dailies.

Financial grants from the offices of MIT's Provost and Dean of the Humanities and Social Science greatly aided my travel and research. An MIT prize for innovative scholarship in the humanities, established through a gift from James A. Levitan, allowed me to finish writing in a timely fashion. Isabelle de Courtivron—friend, colleague, and department chair extraordinaire—was forever supportive.

Old friends and new made work on this project a labor of shared love. I benefited from the warm hospitality of Albert Sonnenfeld and

Noel Riley Fitch during my Los Angeles sojourns; of Edward Feuerstein, Walter Jaffe, and Paul King in New York; and of Alain Hardel in Paris. Eleanor Knowles Dugan and Vera Schoenbaum Gebbert were priceless, selfless sounding boards. Alexandra Yu kept me on course by never failing to decry the hole in the story of American culture which this book aims to fill. Philip Cobb and Annette Insdorf sustained my spirit—as always.

Aside from MacDonald herself, the paramount presence behind this book has been David E. Lapin, a lifelong devotee of the Iron Butterfly. David introduced me to MacDonald's films and recordings, and urged that I channel my enthusiasm into a full-scale biography. For his inspiration and wise critique of every draft, I dedicate *Hollywood Diva* to him.

PART ONE

Born to Sing

CHAPTER ONE

"Now everybody's got to clap!"

Jeanette comes from Philadelphia, but her voice has nothing
in common with the Liberty Bell. She can hold a high C
for fifty-five seconds without cracking!

CECIL B. DeMILLE, *Lux Radio
Theatre*, 1937

SHE EXCELLED IN STUNNING ENTRANCES, and her birth was no
exception.

Jeanette MacDonald loved to recall her mother's story of how she
wriggled into the world from the upstairs quarters of the family's row
house in West Philadelphia: "She used to say she should have known
better than to go into the bathroom after the deep labor pains began.
When it happened, Father was racing to the corner drugstore to telephone the doctor." The physician, it turned out, was on another call.
Frantic, Daniel MacDonald sped home. He bolted into the kitchen,
scrubbed his hands and forearms, and filled the kettles on the iron
stove. Next he flew up the staircase to comfort his wife, who by then
had crawled back to their bedroom and lay on the floor, howling with
pain. It was Daniel, not the doctor, who delivered the infant. In the
years that followed, Daniel often teased his youngest daughter about
her debut: "You always were impatient, Jeanette. You couldn't even
wait until the doctor arrived!"

June 18, 1903, may well have been the last time Jeanette MacDonald was early for anything. She grew up to become a chronic insomniac
and allergy sufferer, exasperating directors and costars with her point-
blank refusal to do early-morning shoots. Yet no one would remain

angry for long. It was impossible to stay mad at this "fabulous creature," as the writer Anita Loos dubbed her. Even as a child, Jeanette had charm and wit in spades, making most people, men especially, feel relaxed and vibrant in her presence.

The third week in June 1903 was unseasonably cool for the City of Brotherly Love. But a restless populace blithely ignored the lag in temperature. Crowds jammed Independence Hall to welcome home the Liberty Bell, recently loaned to Boston. Citizens flocked to Valley Forge to commemorate Evacuation Day. A new holiday, Flag Day, fueled the patriotic spirit as people awoke on June 14 to find Old Glory flying everywhere. Ethnic separation was also starkly evident. White Protestant males chanted "Hail, Pennsylvania" at the University of Pennsylvania's 147th commencement exercises. Fireworks and a parade greeted the Junger Männerchor, a German-American singing society that had just returned triumphantly from vocal combat in Baltimore. Near Columbus Hall, on South Eighth Street, Italian immigrants launched their annual street festival in homage to San Nicandra. Mother Jones, the redoubtable Irish-born labor organizer, led hundreds of textile workers in a fiery demonstration at City Hall Plaza. Clara Barton, the founder of the American Red Cross, rallied new graduates of the Philadelphia School for Nurses to care for black and immigrant children in the city's northern slum wards.

The Philadelphia Orchestra, created in 1900 by millionaire patricians for other wealthy Main-Liners, also concerned itself with bettering the masses. Fritz Scheel, the orchestra's first conductor, was a German autocrat who staunchly resisted pressure from subscribers to add cozy Viennese waltzes to his symphonic programs. Yet Scheel recognized the social need to provide American youth and factory workers with concerts at nominal fees. When Leopold Stokowski began his legendary tenure as conductor in 1912, he massively built on Scheel's initiatives. Even Philadelphians who had never been to a concert proudly embraced the charismatic Stokowski and his orchestra as the city's most prominent ambassadors since Ben Franklin.

For music lovers that third week of June 1903, the chief attraction was Victor Herbert and his orchestra under the stars at Willow Grove Park on Thursday. Ordinarily, the family living at 5123 Arch Street would have packed a picnic supper and taken the special excursion train northward to hear the famous composer, who was scheduled to perform selections from his newest success, the operetta *Babes in Toy-*

land. But the MacDonalds were otherwise engaged. They were attending to the early arrival of the baby girl who, as fate had it, would grow up to be the best-known exponent of Victor Herbert's melodies from *Naughty Marietta* and *Sweethearts,* American operetta classics the maestro had yet to compose.

Jeanette's father cut a refined, almost dandyish figure. He had elongated hands, closely cropped reddish gold hair, and high cheekbones on an oval face whose green eyes glittered under hooded lids. A strong, wide chin and an impeccably trimmed mustache gracefully offset his long, straight nose. Daniel's broad and generous smile exposed a set of naturally perfect teeth. Though all three of Daniel's daughters inherited some of his coloring and features, the new baby was the spitting image of her father.

A staunch Republican, Daniel had supported William McKinley for president, and he revered Teddy Roosevelt, who was residing in the White House at the time of Jeanette's birth. But Daniel never quite met his own ambitions. As a child, he aspired to become a physician. His carpenter father, however, lacked the means to put any of his five children beyond grammar school. Jeanette recalled how Daniel sometimes sprouted a Vandyke beard, which to her eyes made him look "very distinguished," like pictures she had seen of Czar Nicholas of Russia. For Daniel, the makeover provided the slender ego boost of being addressed by the family, even if only in jest, as "Dr. MacDonald."

As an adult, Jeanette occasionally told people that her father had been "one of Philadelphia's leading contractors." The reality was less grand. Daniel was a decent and reliable salesman for Mantels & Co., a small factory that made windowsills, door frames, and mantelpieces. By 1910, Philadelphia had nearly a hundred manufacturers of lumber and timber products, producing an output valued at over $7 million. But Daniel's company never fully recovered from the national recession of 1907, and when Jeanette was six, Daniel found himself laid off. "We had our share of ups and downs," she reminisced. "In those days, I doubt whether Father ever made more than $20 a week. When he got a $5 raise, we celebrated by having electric lights installed to replace the gas. Father was forever sitting down at the kitchen table with Mother to work out a new budget—so much for food, for coal, for new clothes and visits to the doctor—wondering whether he could afford to buy a whole ton of coal at a time, which was cheaper in the long run."

Jeanette eventually learned that Daniel had "silently prayed for a strapping son" throughout his wife's third pregnancy: "Father walked around with a perpetual grin, as if he'd had some 'advance word' the third time was definitely going to be his lucky charm." When the event proved otherwise, Daniel determined that, lacking a son, he would encourage his daughters, especially the youngest, to pursue the American dream that was eluding him. Jeanette quickly became her father's favorite. Yet she never shook the feeling that she let him down by being born a girl. Years later, MacDonald referred to her impromptu birth as "Father's final feminine disappointment."

Daniel's social status had improved somewhat over the years. When his first daughter, Elsie, was born in 1893, he was working in the Philadelphia mills as a weaver. At that time, the family lived in cramped downtown quarters on Brandywine Street, a few blocks east of the Schuylkill River. Two years later, with the arrival of Edith, quickly nicknamed Blossom, the household moved to a larger space across the river, at 3313 Wallace Street in West Philadelphia, but still, as Blossom bluntly put it, "near the railroad tracks." Seven months before Jeanette's birth, in November 1902, Daniel purchased the four-bedroom house at 5123 Arch Street, where his third child would be born and raised.

West Philadelphia had become a part of the Quaker City as a result of the 1854 Act of Consolidation. The area grew rapidly during the next half century, partly because of the University of Pennsylvania's relocation from Ninth and Chestnut Streets to its imposing new site on Woodland Avenue, partly because of the exodus of upwardly mobile, white Protestant families away from the increasingly immigrant and black neighborhoods. Compared with central Philadelphia, West Philadelphia's streets were broader and sunnier, and much of this sprawling expanse took on a certain cachet for its well-to-do inhabitants.

The MacDonalds' new home was in the forty-fourth ward, a distinctly lower-middle-class neighborhood a quarter mile west of the gardens protecting the world-renowned Pennsylvania Hospital for the Insane. The dwelling was one of a block-long row of tidy, identically constructed two-story houses. Each had seven rooms, hardwood floors, and a tiled bathroom; each had an oak porch, a red-brick front, and a minuscule patch of yard in the rear. Across the street, the row houses were just as uniform, but they were three-story and slightly more expensive. Nonetheless, Daniel liked to boast that the odd-numbered side of Arch Street had a natural advantage: a neat line of chestnut trees to temper Philadephia's muggy summers.

Daniel had been twenty-three when he married Anna May Wright, two years his junior, on February 23, 1893. The wedding took place at Philadelphia's Olivet Presbyterian Church, the Reverend Loyal Y. Graham officiating. Anna was the daughter of a Philadelphia teamster named William, and she worked as a forewoman in a factory warehouse. Her own mother, Mary Ann, had died when she was just six, and Anna feared that fate might dispose of her, too, in an untimely fashion. Anna was of Welsh, English, and Dutch descent. She was slightly thickset, with a large, roundish face, and her best feature was her clear, satiny skin. Jeanette's earliest memory was of her mother's hands, "well cared for, small hands with beautiful fingernails, though she did all her own housework. I remember her singing to herself around the house, tunefully but no particular song. I think the only melody she sang clear through was the nursery jingle she rocked me to sleep with: *'Bye, baby bunting, / Papa's gone a-hunting, / Gone to catch a rabbit skin / To wrap the baby bunting in.'* She had a clear, fresh voice like a young girl's, and I used to touch her lips as she sang." In later years, to avert comparison with her illustrious daughter, an increasingly self-conscious Anna rarely warbled, even in private. Yet the lilt and timbre of her speaking voice were so close to Jeanette's that callers regularly mistook one for the other on the telephone.

In temperament, Daniel and Anna made a complementary pair. She was reserved and practical. He was extroverted and mischievous, often at Anna's expense. One day the Arch Street plumbing went on the blink. To take her bath, Anna had to lug a huge wooden laundry tub to the kitchen and heat up water on the stove. Just as she was about to crouch down, she heard a great rattling of tongs at the back door and a gruff voice that hollered, "Iceman! Iceman!" Anna, who was terribly nearsighted, shrieked, "Don't come in! You'll have to come back later!" The door continued to creak. The rattling got louder. Flushed with embarrassment, Anna tried in vain to shrink behind a washcloth. When the entrance opened up wide, the "iceman" turned out to be Daniel. Daniel also routinely alarmed his spouse by faking an impulse to slap the bare back of any woman in a low-cut dress. If the wife of one of his fellow Knights of Pythias paid a visit to the house, he would whisper to Anna: "What a lovely back she has! I don't think I can resist it tonight." According to Jeanette, Daniel never carried out such threats—much to his young daughter's chagrin.

For most of her life, Jeanette MacDonald covered up her precise year of birth. By the time she reached twenty and found a niche for herself on Broadway, MacDonald was savvy enough to discern the bias among theatrical producers against older women, regardless of looks. To take out insurance on her still fledgling career, she became elusive about her birth date, placing it at first in 1904, then in 1905. When she attained international fame in the early 1930s, she gave her birth year as 1907—the year specified on her passports and the one that remains the official date according to her wishes. Although the Philadelphia City Archives have no official record of her birth, MacDonald's true birth year of 1903 can be found in the *Register of Baptisms, 1888–1911* of Philadelphia's Olivet Presbyterian Church and in the *Thirteenth Census of the United States: 1910.*

Jeanette MacDonald's name also shifted slightly over the years. The original spelling was *Jeannette Anna McDonald.* By the time she was four and singing professionally, her parents dropped one of the *n*'s from *Jeannette* for simplicity's sake. And to advertise unambiguously her father's Scottish roots, the *Mc* became *Mac,* a change that also made the surname a touch more pleasing to the ear. Jeanette's Christian name derived from her paternal grandmother, Jannette Johnston. The Johnstons had been dairy merchants in Balfron, a Scottish hillside village not far from Glasgow, whose children—according to legend— were once eaten by wolves. The Johnstons had migrated to Pennsylvania in the 1840s to escape the less fanciful dangers of poverty and unemployment. They settled in Pottsville, where Jannette met and married a plucky young carpenter, Charlie McDonald. Charlie's parents, Archibald McDonald and Margaret McCoy, were natives of Reading, Pennsylvania, and were also of Scottish descent. Daniel and Anna objected when relatives began to call their youngest daughter "Jessie," since that had been the nickname of Grandma Jannette McDonald, who died young. Instead, they called her "Jennie," though Jeanette, perhaps to please Daniel, took on male-sounding pet names like "Jimmee" and "Jammie"—the latter derived from her initials. "I've often wondered," the tomboy later wrote, "if my parents had an ulterior motive in naming me Jeanette Anna MacDonald. . . . I was usually getting into some sort of JAM."

Daniel's father, Charlie, was a stout, white-bearded Freemason, who declined to raise his children within the Presbyterian church. Anna had refused to marry Daniel until he got baptized, and the diffident fiancé complied with her demand in January 1892. Charlie attended neither the baptism nor the marriage, but he stayed on friendly terms with his son, and when Jeanette was two years old he moved into the Arch Street house. "Grandpop" usually started his day with a jigger of rye, leaving the last few drops for Jeanette, who would drain the glass and then skip down the staircase to inform Anna that she and Grandpop had imbibed "our morning drink." Relishing kisses and hugs as much as his liquor, Grandpop lavished affection on Jeanette while taking little notice of Elsie and Blossom. Such partiality distressed Anna, who tried never to show favoritism among her three daughters. Jeanette, however, was a born flirt, and she wallowed in Grandpop's gallantry.

A Civil War veteran, Charlie loved to spin tales of prodigious adventure and romance. One of his best concerned forbidden love between a Pennsylvania mountaineer and a nubile Indian maiden. Jeanette adored these stories and invented a kind of reverse Scheherazade game. Whenever it looked as if Grandpop's yarns were about to end, she would pay a special "tariff" to make him continue: a kiss on each of his cheeks. Invariably, the old man would resume his fables, but not before returning his granddaughter's kisses. In a household where children were trained not to wear their hearts on their sleeves, Grandpop Charlie made Jeanette feel good about strong, spontaneous feeling.

Daniel and Anna were caring parents. But, unlike Grandpop, they rarely showed deep emotion. Their restraint especially upset Jeanette once she began to perform: "I was constantly pestering my parents for praise, but it was always cautiously given. I never once was told that my singing was 'wonderful.' 'Pretty good' was as far as Mother and Father would let themselves go. Father, in his canny, Scottish way, was so thrifty with his praise that I was never more than half-satisfied. After a song, I'd nag him: 'Wasn't that *good*?' He'd cautiously comment, 'That was pretty good,' or else, 'No, I didn't like that. You can do better.'" Early on, Jeanette realized she was "an extrovert, who needed people to watch and applaud me as much as I needed food and drink." Her parents' reluctance to indulge that addiction "only served to make me try all the harder for compliments."

Anna eventually became Jeanette's best friend and constant companion. Joan Crawford is said to have envied MacDonald her mother, observing that Jeanette's exuberant self-confidence and generosity of spirit were in large part the result of Anna's benevolence and trust. Yet

throughout girlhood and adolescence, Jeanette misperceived the depth
of her mother's capacity to love. Gauged by the child's romantic imagination, Anna and Daniel appeared to be the polar opposite of a couple
bonded by passion. Only years later did Jeanette comprehend that her
parents' love was none the less profound for being private and quiet.

By age fourteen, Elsie could play Chopin waltzes and Schubert im-
promptus. Daniel and Anna fantasized that she might grow up to be a
concert musician. But Elsie, ten years Jeanette's senior, was the family
rebel. One afternoon she returned from school, sat down at the upright
in the parlor, and started to pound out "Bill Bailey, Won't You Please
Come Home?" From that moment on, she badgered Daniel about stopping her classical lessons. Elsie enjoyed the role of teacher, however,
and under her tutelage Jeanette progressed from simple versions of
Stephen Foster chestnuts to such Gay Nineties waltzes as "Sweet Rosie
O'Grady" and "In the Good Old Summer Time." Jeanette's singing
voice was clear and bright, and she had an instinctive sense of phrasing. Unfortunately, Elsie had a domineering streak that sometimes
overwhelmed her youngest sister. Only the toddler's drive to please enabled Jeanette to meet Elsie's exacting standards for cue response, pos-
ture, and curtsies.

Under Elsie's watchful gaze, Jeanette made her first public appearance at age three, singing the hymn "O That Will Be Glory" at Tennent
Memorial Presbyterian Church. She had memorized three full verses,
and she even sustained the long high notes without gasping for air.
Convinced she merited applause despite the sacred setting, the wily
songstress literally took matters into her own hands: "I paused ever so
slightly and then, when I realized they needed prodding, I promptly
began clapping my hands, and said to the startled congregation, 'Now
everybody's got to clap!' " To her immense satisfaction, they agreed.

At home on Arch Street, Jeanette's favorite spots were the back
pantry and the front porch. On weekdays, the tiny pantry doubled as
Anna's laundry room. On Saturdays it became a canine beauty salon,
with Jeanette responsible for sponging Trixie and Toodles, the family's
white miniature poodles. Best of all were the summer evenings when
the pantry was converted to a magic place where peach ice cream
"Philadelphia style" was concocted—no starch, no mixes, just fresh
cream, eggs, sugar, and mashed fruit. Armed with his wooden freezer,
salt bucket, and paddle, Daniel became a gentle sorcerer to Jeanette. In
other seasons, father and daughter gratified their palates at Schilling's

Ice Cream Parlor, on Paxon Street just below Haverford. Like so many Philadelphians, Jeanette grew up suspicious of ice cream made in other cities.

The front porch, which stood just five steps above street level, had oak pillars and a balustrade. Between April and November it became the towering stage from which Jeanette serenaded neighbors at the top of her lungs while accompanying herself on a two-octave toy piano. Except for Grandpop, Jeanette's biggest early fan was George Maetrick, a retired butcher who lived next door with his wife, Eleanor. "Old" Mr. Maetrick was an invalid, and he would sit for hours in his wooden wheelchair and applaud Jeanette as she picked out tunes and sang for him. Passersby invariably stopped to smile at the little show woman, and their usual compliment was that Baby Jenny sang like a bird. Mr. Maetrick generously compared her to "the Swedish Nightingale" of the previous century, dubbing her "Baby Jenny Lind." It was a nickname that soon gained currency throughout the neighborhood.

Jeanette's porch recitals were a mix of genuine songs and improvised arias. Her inspiration for the latter came from Joseph and Elizabeth Nelson, neighbors who owned a talking machine long before the MacDonalds could afford one. Little Jeanette paid frequent surprise calls on the couple to listen to their recordings. She would kneel by the Victrola, her ear glued to the sound box, and listen to the likes of Nellie Melba, Emma Eames, and Johanna Gadski. She would then dart home, sit at her tiny piano, and string together phrases from these vocal selections in a gibberish vaguely inspired by Italian, French, or German.

Just after she turned five, Jeanette sang a Scottish ballad and danced a Highland fling at the Twentieth Century, a nickelodeon above Freihofer's Bakery. Charlie Wright, Jeanette's cousin on her mother's side, recalled that she was one of the few contestants that night for whom nobody shouted, "Get the hook!" "Eventually," Charlie continued, "only Jeanette and a magician were left, and when the manager put his hand over Jeanette's head, there was no question as to the winner. The applause fairly rocked the place, and some people even whistled and stamped their feet." Years later, Anita Loos would weave a similar scene into her screenplay for MacDonald's film *San Francisco*. But in 1908, what most impressed little Charlie was his cousin's prize: "Five whole dollars! For just singing a song and doing a dance. Some men didn't earn as much as that in a week!"

While singing for pay at neighborhood lodges of Masons, Elks, and Knights of Pythias, Jeanette discovered she could make people laugh by doing impressions of the era's popular stage singers. Her best takeoffs were of Eva Tanguay, vaudeville's brassy I-Don't-Care Girl, and Irene Franklin, the cherub-faced redhead from whom Jeanette borrowed the showstopper "It's Awfully Hard to Try to Be a Lady." "I could imitate any musical comedy star of the day," she recalled, "although I'd never seen them. I don't even know where I got the idea, but I made up versions of how I thought they should sound and act." MacDonald never lost this talent. Hollywood publicist Cecil "Teet" Carle related that her bravura caricature of Mae West was "the knockout" of many a Beverly Hills party in the early 1930s.

In time-honored fashion, Anna prompted her daughter from the wings. The only snag, Jeanette recollected, was that her mother identified too intensely with the performance: "When my memory failed, hers went blank, too. As a prompter she was hopeless, so at last I discovered you didn't really have to know the words—you could make them up." Anna's knack for costumes was more appreciated. In one comic number, Jeanette wore a knee-length white satin swimsuit and a bright green bandanna, tied Mack Sennett style. For gender-bending songs, she donned a man's pinstriped summer suit, with all the masculine accessories.

The first smell of big success came in the classiest of high-toned milieus. Philadelphia's Academy of Music was the oldest and, for many, the most resplendent concert hall in the nation. On Monday of the week beginning February 15, 1909, the Academy presented the Boston Symphony, with Ignace Paderewski as guest pianist. Tuesday saw the Metropolitan Opera's production of *Tannhäuser,* with Carl Burrian and Olive Fremstad in the leading roles. On Thursday, Geraldine Farrar, Antonio Scotti, and Karl Jörn (replacing an indisposed Enrico Caruso) sang in Massenet's *Manon.* Friday afternoon and Saturday evening, violinist Mischa Elman was guest soloist with the Academy's permanent resident, the Philadelphia Orchestra. Amid this musical splendor, on the evening of Friday, February 19, the Academy saw Miss Jeanette MacDonald, at age five and a half, give her first major public performance.

The vehicle was *Charity,* a juvenile opera staged by local dance instructors James and Caroline Littlefield to benefit the crippled children of Philadelphia's Samaritan Hospital. Elsie and Blossom had been taking lessons with the Littlefields for several years, but they were only in *Charity*'s chorus line. Jeanette, because of her voice and tender age, landed three solo spots, performing "A Real Scotch Song by a Real Scotch Lassie," "The Plight of Old Mother Hubbard," and a virtuoso star turn, "Maybe It's a Bear." The last number earned her a rave review in the local paper:

> The real wonder of the opera is produced by Jeanette MacDonald, a tiny miss only four [sic] years old. She occupies the entire foreground of the stage while singing "Maybe It's a Bear." The scene is one in which twenty-eight children in nighties are sleeping before the Old Shoe of Mother Goose fame. The children are surprised by Clem Harris Congdon, the bear, who does a bit of artistic pantomime work equal to the best ever seen on any stage. The children, frightened, crawl slowly off into the darkness of the stage. At this point little Jeanette, with the limelight thrown upon the bear on the other side of the house, in semi-darkness sings her song and accompanies it by most exquisite dancing and bits of real acting. Her work is really marvelous.

The next morning Anna tried valiantly to shrink her daughter's ego, but nothing worked. Jeanette was euphoric for days. As she later confessed, that triumphant night at the Academy "marked" her for life. So did the review: "When I grew older, newspaper critics weren't always so kind. Sometimes, I thought their cruel words were justified. Usually, I wanted to spit in their eyes."

CHAPTER TWO

Scandals

I was lucky. I had ideals and philosophies
and the strength of a good home life as weapons.

JEANETTE MACDONALD, 1961

NOT LONG AFTER THE ACADEMY OF MUSIC TRIUMPH, a
MacDonald family scandal brought home the narrow-mindedness of
Arch Street.

Jeanette idolized her sister Elsie, in part because she was the little
girl's teacher. But there was another reason, according to MacDonald:
"I had a quirk about people's looks. They had to be pretty if they were
women, or handsome if they were men. Otherwise, I couldn't possibly
like them." Dazzled by Elsie's "golden" blonde hair and "big, wide
blue eyes," Jeanette decided early on that her eldest sister was the
"prettiest member of our family." In truth, Elsie was not exceptionally
attractive, and young Jeanette simply may have found everyone she
liked to be good-looking. Either way, Elsie secured her ardent devotion.

For over a year Elsie had been dating Earle Schmidt, a handsome boy
who lived in one of the imposing three-story row houses across the
street. Daniel and Anna were never keen on this friendship, since Earle,
who worked in a baking powder business with his father, was five years
older than Elsie. Moreover, the Schmidts deemed Elsie beneath their
son's station and scoffed at the MacDonald girls' flirtation with show
business. No shrinking violet, Elsie made it clear to her parents she was
entitled to pick her own companions. After all, she now helped Daniel
pay the household bills by working full-time at Hanscom Bakeries.

On the morning of Decoration Day 1909, shortly before her sixth birthday, Jeanette stood sulking as Elsie prepared a picnic basket in the kitchen. She knew she wasn't invited, and she ached to be sixteen, like Elsie. "You're always so mean to me," Jeanette grumbled. "Why can't I come?" "You just can't, that's why," her sister blurted. "But why not?" insisted Jeanette. Elsie was losing patience: "Oh, for heaven's sake! Earle, will you please make her stop bothering us?" Earle fished a quarter from his pocket: "Will you be a good girl, and stay home if I give you this?"

Clutching Earle's quarter made Jeanette feel better about being left out. She certainly wasn't above bribes. But when it was discovered that Elsie and Earle took the picnic basket and headed straight for Maryland to get married, Jeanette regretted surrendering so easily: "Perhaps if I'd kicked up a bigger fuss, it wouldn't have happened, at least not as they'd planned. But I was bribed, and Elsie eloped, and it brought unhappiness to us all for a long time afterward."

To forestall the wrath of their parents, the lovers concealed their marriage for months—until Elsie could no longer hide her pregnancy. The truth nearly crushed Anna. Her oldest daughter "had deceived her, and to make matters worse, the 'news' set all the neighbors' tongues wagging." Anna was certain that Elsie's waywardness was due to her own shortcomings as a mother. Why, she wondered, had Elsie been unable to share her feelings? Was it because Anna herself rarely talked about love? Or because she and Daniel could never speak openly of sex? Was that wrong? Was it an error for parents to keep their private affairs private? In the end, Anna remained convinced that her principles were true and that, in any event, she could not alter who she was. But she worried about the example Elsie had set for her sisters. Blossom's interest in boys was budding, and Jeanette, though just six, was alert and impressionable. Further domestic scandal had to be quashed.

With Daniel by her side, Anna summoned her daughters to the parlor and sat them on the horsehair couch. Cloaking her embarrassment, she sketched the moral duties of proper young women. She surprised even herself as she expounded on the woeful effects of uncontrolled romantic entanglements, especially with older men. Finally, she made Jeanette and Blossom take an oath: "I want you to promise me one thing. Whatever else you do, you must promise you will never do what Elsie has done. If you want to get married when you grow up, we won't try to stop you. But don't do it without letting us know." Jeanette felt very adult for being included in this solemn forum. She was also terribly confused. Elsie's secret affairs were all rather thrilling, much like the stories of clandestine love that Grandpop told. What Anna called disgraceful, Jeanette found tantalizing. Wasn't the neighbors' back-fence chatter proof that something important had taken place on humdrum Arch Street? Weren't their excited reactions just the thing Jeanette aimed for when she sang and danced?

The neighbors had more to gossip about in the year that followed. Although the Schmidts allowed Elsie to move in with them, their feeble attempts at cordiality made her feel like a pariah. She decided, after the birth of Earle, Jr., to bring her husband and baby back across the street to live with the MacDonalds. But when Elsie discovered the gun Earle had started keeping under his bed pillow, she was shocked and frightened. Often absent without explanation, Earle soon stopped coming home altogether. Divorce proceedings started, and again the neighbors tittered. Marital breakups may have been acceptable in chic circles, but for most Americans in 1910, divorce was sure cause for ostracism. Jeanette later observed: "On Arch Street . . . we weren't sophisticated people. In our neighborhood, a man and woman who loved each other were married and stayed husband and wife for the rest of their lives, with children to bless them if they were fortunate enough. That was the belief I was brought up in. I've never changed."

A nasty custody battle ensued, with the Schmidts alleging that the MacDonalds were too poor and too loose to provide a decent home for Earle, Jr., and the MacDonalds arguing that a man who had abandoned his child was unfit to be a father. When the MacDonalds won the case, no one was more overjoyed than Daniel. At last he had the son he always wanted—albeit a generation late and acquired with bitterness and tears. To help erase harsh memories, Daniel convinced Elsie to drop "Junior," as well as the final *e,* from the baby's first name. Earl soon took to calling Daniel "Pappy."

One evening shortly after the divorce, the adult MacDonalds went to a nickelodeon, placing Jeanette and baby Earl in Blossom's care. Blossom was a touch flighty, and she decided to step out for a few moments, leaving Jeanette in charge. Always eager to emulate Elsie, Jeanette felt the full weight of this new responsibility, especially when Earl started to bawl: "I patted him, tickled him, sang to him, but he only sobbed louder. I didn't know how else to comfort him, until I thought of something I'd seen his mother do. With great effort, I lifted him out of his crib and sat him on my tiny lap. Then I carefully unbuttoned the front of my dress and pressed his lips against my bare, bony chest. That was how Blossom found us when she came home. Little Earl was serenely content, and so was I."

At the newly built Thomas Dunlap School, on the corner of Fifty-first and Race Streets, Jeanette quickly earned a reputation as Peck's Bad Girl. She never seemed to finish a semester without pulling some prank that sent her off to Miss Sallie Morley, the principal. Jeanette especially infuriated Morley with a vocal trick that had nothing to do with high Cs. Most days after lunch, she bought a penny sour pickle at the corner grocery. By swallowing air and placing pressure on her stomach, she could then belch at will for much of the afternoon. Exasperated teachers scolded her for these disruptions. Classmates begged for encores.

Like other Philadelphia public schools, Dunlap was enjoying a resurgence in music instruction. Dr. Enoch Pearson, the system's director of music education, envisioned a new generation of young Americans sensitive to "that which is truly excellent in art" and for whom "living in an atmosphere of good music will be as common among us as good food, pure water, fresh air, and the universal enjoyment of God's own sunlight." Pearson developed a curriculum in vocal sight-reading required of all the city's three hundred thousand students. In the early grades, pupils did unison work on songs by such American originals as George Whitefield Chadwick and Amy Cheney Beach. In the middle grades, they practiced part-singing of works by world-renowned European composers. In high school, the syllabus expanded to include anthems and choruses from operas and oratorios. By the time they finished their senior year, pupils were expected to be familiar with nearly three hundred compositions. Through phonographs, they learned to identify the voices of such luminaries as Nellie Melba, Enrico Caruso, and Alma Gluck.*

While not a terrific student generally, Jeanette excelled at music appreciation. After just one listening, she could repeat the melodies from Dvořák's *Humoresque,* Mendelssohn's *Song Without Words,* and Sibelius's *Valse Triste.* These, she was told, were important pieces with

---

*In the first half of the twentieth century, Philadelphia spawned an abundance of great singers, both classical and pop. Contemporary with MacDonald, two girls from South Philadelphia who also benefited from the progressive, high-minded cultural climate in Dr. Pearson's schools were Dusolina Giannini, the future operatic soprano, and Marian Anderson, the budding contralto. (Anderson went to William Penn and South Philadelphia high schools.)

permanent value, unlike the Tin Pan Alley songs that Elsie so enjoyed. Jeanette felt an affinity for two American composers, Edward Mac-Dowell and Charles Wakefield Cadman, who, according to her teachers, were the nation's most revered. Her favorite by Cadman was "From the Land of the Sky-Blue Water," inspired by an Omaha Indian love song. She enjoyed the lilting melody and, even more, the sentimental notion of a young Indian brave forbidden to associate with his lady-love except through music.

Jeanette's first piano teacher, after her sister Elsie, was Miss Rilla Williams, who lived on Fifty-first and Chestnut Streets. Jeanette's initial goal was to become proficient enough to accompany herself when she sang at lodge meetings or religious events. But after several years of lessons she became more accomplished than anyone had expected, mastering Rachmaninoff's Prelude in C-sharp Minor and Paderewski's Minuet in the advanced version. Daniel and Anna again entertained the hope that one of their daughters might turn into a serious musician. Yet their choice of vocal teacher was odd, to say the least. Mrs. Jessie Marsano was a middle-aged eccentric who shared a house at 3116 North Eighth Street with Mrs. Cora Cox, a psychic. To offset the modest expense of lessons, Daniel and Anna agreed to have Jeanette sing during Mrs. Cox's Sunday evening séances. Jeanette's job was to warble exotically while the medium did her best to commune with ghosts. The more satisfied the flesh-and-blood clientele, the greater their contributions to the kitty; the larger the take, the greater the young singer's cut.

Daniel and Anna deposited all of Jeanette's earnings from Mrs. Cox's séances into a savings account. Jeanette quickly grasped the difference between principal and interest—neither of which she was permitted to touch. But she spent hours gazing at the cramped penned entries of her bankbook. She imagined that the growing sum would one day allow her to dress like Aunt Sally McElroy, Anna's widowed dressmaker sister.

Aunt Sally had panache. When she visited Arch Street, neighbors peeped from windows to take in her flouncy silk skirts, her huge spreading hats heaped with artificial flowers, and her long-fringed parasols. Actually, Sally's taste bordered on the gaudy. But for the naively romantic Jeanette, Aunt Sally was the epitome of fashion: "She looked so radiantly beautiful that I'd gasp for breath at the sight of her. Some of my costumes came from her workroom scraps. I used to think they were as elegant as anything you could see the rich ladies in Rittenhouse Square wearing. I wanted to look like Aunt Sally, hats and all."

Clothes were important because Jeanette considered herself ugly. She didn't mind her flaming red hair, since that made her stand out. But she hated her pale, freckled complexion. She thought her feet too tiny and her limbs gangly. Reaching her full height of five feet five inches by the time she turned twelve, Jeanette was always taller than any girl or boy her age. "I was constantly struggling to make myself pretty," she recounted. "I used to sit with my finger poked into my cheek trying to make a dimple like my sister Blossom's; it didn't work. I had good, straight teeth, and I scrubbed them three times a day with Ivory soap to keep them white. I used to sluice mouthfuls of peroxide around my gums, too, believing I could bleach my teeth even whiter. But I was never satisfied."

Jeanette's thin and shapeless legs caused some of the girls at school to taunt her with the nickname "Broomsticks": "I used to come home in tears about that. I was forever doing exercises to develop some calves by standing on a pile of books, toes close to the edge, alternately raising on tip-toes and lowering my heels." Anna thought that rubbing Jeanette's shanks with mutton fat might help, but nothing worked. "I had no more calves than a mosquito bite," she sadly conceded.

The Broomsticks moniker did little to undermine Jeanette's feeling that "you couldn't trust girls." Selma Crandall's mother once asked Jeanette if she wanted a pair of shoes her daughter had barely worn and that were now too small. Jeanette accepted, only to find out that "Selma started going around telling our girl friends that I was taking her castoffs." On another occasion, Jeanette and one of her first crushes—"it must have been Jack Graugh or Raymond Scott"—joined a group of kids for sodas. Laura Bradshaw, who proclaimed herself Jeanette's "best friend," drew the boy aside and whispered, "Won't you give me a call on our new telephone? But *don't tell Jeanette.*" The incorruptible youth did pass the word, fueling Jeanette's disillusionment with her own sex. "The truth is," she later wrote, "I've had trouble with women all my life. As I grew older, the hurtful things I suffered were mostly at feminine hands."

During one of her many jobs as a five-dollar songstress, Jeanette was spotted by a charismatic showman named Al White, who in the next few years would groom her talent as much as all her previous music teachers combined. White had emigrated from England as a boy, and he began his dancing career improvising buck-and-wing steps aboard New Jersey ferryboats and hoarding the pennies that passengers tossed his barefoot way. An original member of Philadelphia's famed Dumont Minstrels, White toured the Keith vaudeville circuit with Gus Edwards, the Four Cohans, and Eddie Cantor. In 1907, he staged dances for two Hungarian-born twins, Janszieka and Roszicka Deutsch, soon to gain fame as the beauteous Dolly Sisters. He was also a mentor to Ed Wynn, the giggly, lisping comic from Philadelphia. In 1908, White established a dance studio on South Thirteenth Street, where Blossom, having outgrown Mr. Littlefield's classes, took lessons. "Professor" White convinced parents to send their children to his school as much for social as for vocational uplift. "Dance doesn't necessarily mean a career," he maintained, "but it does mean poise and proper carriage of the body; it is a personality builder."

Jeanette impressed White with what he called, in vaudeville argot, "a swell pair of pipes." He also liked her "snap and sparkle," that priceless ability to capture an audience and quicken its pulse. To nurture her gifts, White offered Jeanette a weekly salary and steady bookings with his kiddie act, the Six Sunny Song Birds, that played small-time vaudeville houses between Harrisburg and Atlantic City.

Anna's reflex was to reject the offer. This was understandable, even though B. F. Keith and E. F. Albee had cleaned up vaudeville so tidily that entertainers joked they were now working the "Sunday-school circuit." Anna admitted that such houses were no longer marketplaces for "lascivious attractions and salacious seductions," as a local Presbyterian minister once raged. But Al White's Song Birds played in unregulated theaters independent of the main circuits, and Anna felt Jeanette was too young to mingle with people still reputed to be lax and wild. Her resistance was no match, however, for Jeanette's relentless nagging and Daniel's pragmatism: the fatter her bankbook, he reminded his wife, the more secure their daughter's future. Anna ultimately gave in, but not before extracting a concession from White that she would chaperone all of the Sunny Song Birds.

Jeanette rolled off her lips the mythic-sounding names of the theaters she was about to play: the Lyric, the Criterion, the Empire, the Broadway. Once on the road, she discovered "the most complete happiness, the most stupendously glamorous, the most satisfying excitement I possibly could have imagined." There was just one problem: she was always getting carsick. On terra firma, Jeanette could barely watch a kite without feeling queasy. Now she had to manage long trips on trolleys and trains that set her reeling with nausea. Making matters worse, Jeanette came down with frequent colds and earaches, even in summer. Many such episodes were allergic reactions to ragweed, per-fume, chocolate, and fresh black pepper, but it took years before they were correctly diagnosed. A rare photo portrait of Jeanette with her fel-low Song Birds shows puffiness and dark circles beneath her eyes, al-though more intriguing are the seductive stance and come-hither gaze that appear so natural and effortless despite Jeanette's mere nine years. In any event, the fledgling trouper never missed a show on her debut tour: "It gave me a sense of importance and pride to 'go on' in spite of my ailments. I . . . sang over, under, and around them. . . . I was super-confident. I was equal to anything."

Traveling with the company was Mrs. Ida Kephart, whose daughter, Mildred, was the other female Song Bird. Mrs. Kephart had been a schoolteacher, and it was understood that she would keep the children current in their studies on days when they couldn't return to Philadel-phia in time for the next day's classes. Mildred, however, soon left the act and was replaced by Bessie Cole. Bessie's mother was also an "intel-lectual." But because Mrs. Cole spoke only Polish and Yiddish, the Song Birds were left practicing stage stunts when they were supposed to be doing American geography.

The group was a sensation: four boys and two girls who sang, danced, played instruments, and did comic routines. One reviewer called them "vaudeville's best juvenile act" and singled out Jeanette as "the real 'prima donna' of the troupe." Her solo was a French song just translated into English, "A Little Love, a Little Kiss." Decades later, Jeanette would sing this number on-screen in *Smilin' Through* as a dreamy serenade. Al White, however, taught her to deliver the tune in a slightly naughty, co-quettish style that suggested the chanteuses of Parisian music halls. It is to White's credit that he was the first to recognize and promote Jeanette's affinity for things French. He also taught her to capitalize on her feel for roguish comedy. The trick, he explained, was to temper sauciness with self-deprecation. Always guide that mischievous glance to the side, he told her, and you flatter the public into feeling that they, too, see the archness of the routine. White's teachings stuck.

Joining the Sunny Song Birds put Jeanette on even shakier ground with Dunlap's principal, Miss Morley. At school, Jeanette often befriended the other underdogs, such as Bessie Ditton, a stutterer, and Rachel Weinberg, the Jewish immigrant tailor's daughter. One day in class, a hulking bully named Joseph Armstrong scribbled a note that acciden-tally landed on Jeanette's desk. "Dear Rachel," it read, "Your father is a SHEENIE." Outraged, Jeanette immediately wrote back, with probable dead-on accuracy: "Dear Joe, Your father is a BASTARD!" The teacher, Miss Richards, unfortunately grabbed the reply before Jeanette could pass it on, and she sent the troublemaker to Miss Morley's office. Morley, who attributed Jeanette's foul mouth to the contemptible theater folk she fraternized with after school, placed her on immediate suspension.

Jeanette, too terrified to give her parents the suspension notice, feigned illness for three days. When the ruse was discovered, Daniel came to his daughter's defense in front of Miss Morley. After explaining the note's context, he said: "Miss [Morley], there are things chalked up on fences and walls around this school that are far worse than anything Jeanette has ever heard in the theater." The principal lashed back: "A child's place is here in school, not traipsing around the countryside for a lot of *theatrical* performances. You may as well understand, Mr. MacDonald, that I shall do everything in my power to teach you, as well as Jeanette, that the theater, and its environment, and child labor of any kind have no part in my philosophy. I am a dedicated woman!"

Grudgingly, Miss Morley reinstated the delinquent pupil.

That night, Anna demanded that Daniel give Jeanette a good spanking, not for the suspension but for lying about it. After marching her into the bathroom, Daniel shut the door, took down his leather razor strap, and whispered: "Now when I whale the bathtub, you've got to scream like mad." Always the scene-stealer, Jeanette overacted shamelessly. Within seconds, Anna raced up the stairs, shouting: "Dan, I said to *spank* her, not *beat* her!" Opening the door, she uncovered the trickery. As Jeanette scurried into the hallway, she overheard her mother admonish Daniel: "I think you have made a fool of me in front of her!" Daniel answered: "No, Annie, don't you see, I couldn't have spanked her for the trouble she got into at school. If I had been in her place, I'd have done the same thing myself."

Only once did Jeanette see her gentle father "in a mood to kill." When Mr. Maetrick died, the house next door was sold to Mrs. Kerr, who rented two of her upstairs rooms to lodgers. Jeanette's bedroom faced one of them and was separated only by the narrowest of alleys. One early evening, while doing homework at a desk near the window, she noticed a light come on in the boarder's room. Jeanette returned to her reading but soon became aware of something moving close by: it was the lace curtain in the lodger's window being slowly pulled aside. "For a moment the thought crossed my mind that the man was going to wave or speak to me. In that same instant, I saw he was stark naked. I sat there, not moving a muscle, staring at what he was doing, realizing instinctively that this was something shockingly wrong. In a minute or two, he left the window and threw himself onto his bed. As he moved, the stillness inside me suddenly stirred."

Jeanette ran to her mother's bedroom: "There's a man next door, and he hasn't any clothes on!" Anna hurried downstairs to fetch Daniel, who stormed up to Jeanette's room "like a god of vengeance": "[He] flung open the window and shouted across the alley: 'Pull down your shades, you filthy bugger!' . . . If a gun had been handy, I think my Father would have shot him there and then. Anger flushed his face until it was as red as his moustache." Bolting out of the house, Daniel next hammered on Mrs. Kerr's front door and roared: "There is a man in your room facing Jeanette's! I WANT HIM OUT OF THERE BY MORNING!! If he isn't, I'm going to the police to report him *and* you!" By sunrise, the sex offender was gone.

Jeanette's own brand of mischief went on undiminished. For nearly a year, her buddy Tommy Culpepper had been goading her and a bunch of friends to pocket half of their Sunday collection-plate money to spend on sodas after the service: "So long as my parents didn't find out—and they never did—it was great. I felt sure God wouldn't miss my nickel, and if He did, He didn't seem to care." But she couldn't be sure. When the deacon of Tennent Presbyterian Church asked Jeanette to give a Sunday Bible class for toddlers, she agreed—at least in part to repay her secret debt. It also gave her a captive audience.

Of the many Dunlap instructors she loathed, Jeanette most enjoyed needling Miss Held, the grouchy cooking teacher she rechristened "Miss Hell." At the end of each unit, Miss Held's pupils were expected to consume their culinary masterpieces in silence, with ladylike decorum. On the day they made cupcakes, the sight of fourteen girls solemnly stuffing their faces with devil's food struck Jeanette as ridiculous. "Isn't it funny," she said in a stage whisper, "how you can always find your mouth without looking for it?" This droll thought caused the girls to snicker, but Miss Held snarled and kept Jeanette after class to write five hundred times, "I must not talk in cooking school." Confident that the ogress would not scrutinize every line, Jeanette sprinkled her page with variants like "I love to talk in cooking school" and "I hate Miss Hell in cooking school." Miss Held, it turned out, had the eyes of a weasel. After circling each infraction in red, she labeled

Jeanette a "brazen, objectionable child" and sent her once again to Miss Morley, who lectured her on the virtues of grim decorum.

In 1914, Jeanette graduated from the Sunny Song Birds and joined the Seven Merry Youngsters. Although the others in this act were age fifteen or over, Jeanette, who was barely eleven, fit in because of her ostrichlike height. The Seven Merry Youngsters played bigger theaters and larger towns than the Six Sunny Song Birds did. Their gutsy manager was Elwood Wolf—a name not designed to calm Anna MacDonald's anxieties.

That fall, the kids were slated for a full week's run at Loew's Greenley Square Theater in midtown Manhattan. Jeanette was on pins and needles. She had never been to New York, but she knew that for show people it was the mecca of glamour and opportunity. The booking also meant a reprieve from school and a week's stay at a theatrical boardinghouse. For Jeanette, nothing could possibly be more fun than breaking bread in Gotham with a gang of ventriloquists, contortionists, female impersonators, and donkey trainers.

As the Seven Merry Youngsters pranced offstage at their first matinee, the dream became a horror show. Two men in derby hats were standing in the wings. One pointed to Jeanette and grunted, "There she is." The detectives marched into her dressing room and brusquely asked for her age. Panicked, Jeanette turned to her mother, who said: "You know you must tell the truth." "I'm eleven," she declared, her thin legs quaking. "This child is under age, ma'am," the second detective blurted out in a thunderous voice. "A complaint has been lodged against you. Here is a summons to appear in court."

The document confirmed Anna's worst apprehensions. The Gerry Society of New York City, which protected children from commercial exploitation, was in receipt of a telegram alleging that the parents of Jeanette Anna MacDonald were guilty of child abuse. The Society refused to divulge the source of the telegram, but the MacDonalds knew it was Miss Sallie Morley, the school principal. Mortified, Anna blamed herself for having brought on yet another family scandal. It was sheer moral weakness to have let Jeanette join this act and to have been less than candid about her age. Now Anna contemplated the shame of receiving a huge fine and maybe even a prison sentence.

Three days later, Anna, Daniel, and Jeanette appeared before a New York City magistrate. After questioning each of them, the judge examined Jeanette's bankbook. When he saw that there had never been a withdrawal, he determined that exploitation had not occurred and that further legal action was uncalled for. Anna and Daniel breathed again. Jeanette, however, had little reason to celebrate. The judge ordered her to quit the Seven Merry Youngsters and return to Thomas Dunlap at once. That same week, Miss Morley conducted a full review of Jeanette's academic standing. Because she was below par in several subjects—worst of all, mathematics—the principal ordered her demoted by one semester. Such extreme punishment devastated Jeanette: "To a proud and sensitive child, this was a tremendous humiliation. I crept out of her office certain that every kid in school would laugh at me as a dunce. Father attempted to talk her out of her decision, but she was adamant. I had to be taught that singing was by no means the biggest thing in my life."

In all likelihood, the principal's motive for calling in the police was caring. Miss Morley certainly did not object to genteel singing of the kind advocated by Dr. Pearson and studied in music appreciation classes. Jeanette, who had kept up her voice lessons with Mrs. Marsano, was more than capable of performing such music, and she loved doing so. Yet her one attempt at redeeming herself in the principal's jaundiced eyes turned disastrous.

That winter, the school held a sauerkraut supper to raise funds for a new flagpole. Miss Edna Clear, an English teacher who played piano and sometimes sang at assembly, suggested that Jeanette entertain the parents and teachers with "The Jewel Song" from Gounod's *Faust*. Jeanette knew the music, having heard it over and over on recordings. But the only lyrics she knew were in her private nonsense language. Within five days, kindly Miss Clear taught Jeanette to sing the piece in phonetically passable French.

The supper took place in the school cafeteria, where the tables were arranged in a large U. At the center was an upright piano from which Miss Clear announced Jeanette. Even though she felt a cold coming on, Jeanette was eager to impress the audience with her very first performance of music from an opera. Walking toward the piano, she kept repeating to herself: " 'The Jewel Song' is just like any other song. Higher perhaps. But I can handle it." As Miss Clear played the first bars of the introduction, Jeanette noticed Miss Morley standing against a far wall and gazing at her with tight lips and frigid eyes: "Her disapproval shot invisibly across the room at me with the force of some mysteriously devastating lethal ray." Jeanette's knees began to shake. Her throat constricted. Her gut went hollow. When she missed the opening phrase,

Miss Clear repeated the entire introduction. This time Jeanette caught the cue but raced through the aria, mangling the music and butchering the words. When she finished, there was a smattering of polite applause.

Filled with shame and distress, Jeanette ran from the stage. Miss Clear tried to comfort her, but the girl was unconsolable. "It was inconceivable," she later reflected. "I had never been even close to losing my poise before. I had never been afraid. I had never lost control of my faculties even for a moment. I couldn't understand why it had happened." This disaster began MacDonald's lifelong struggle with stage fright: "Motion pictures were different, because only technicians, in the broad sense of the word, were listening and I knew they were my allies." Gradually, Jeanette learned to live with "the bewildering, newfound knowledge that you could simultaneously love to sing, yet be in an agony when standing up to do so."

During the following two years, Jeanette made a good-faith effort to comply with Miss Morley's standards. She curbed her antics. She devoted more time to her studies and performed less frequently. She even contemplated the possibility that Miss Morley was right, after all.

Her uncertainty vanished one spring night in May 1917.

On Fifty-second Street south of Market stood West Philadelphia's leading vaudeville house, the Nixon Theater. For Jeanette, the Nixon was an oasis. Seating eighteen hundred people, this grandly decorated Beaux Arts building had a vaulted interior lobby with marble wainscoting and a central row of chandeliers. At the hub of its cove-lit auditorium was a huge crystal chandelier whose tiered lamps radiated various shades of gold light. Ascending with slow majesty from the orchestra pit was a three-keyboard Moeller organ framed by a wide balustrade of polished marble.

That Friday evening, the Nixon's main attraction was a singing sister team called Those Tailored Italian Girls. The curtain rose to find twenty-year-old Rosa Ponzillo seated at a grand piano in the center of the forty-two-foot-wide stage; her older sister, Carmela, stood next to her. Both young women wore navy blue pleated skirts and white silk blouses. As Carmela made her way to the bend of the piano, Rosa played a long arpeggio that launched them into the "Barcarolle" from Offenbach's opera, *Tales of Hoffmann.* Never had Jeanette heard such gorgeous, voluptuous singing. Next came Carmela's solo of "Musetta's Waltz" from Puccini's *La Bohème,* followed by a duet of "Comin'

Thro' the Rye" with intricately harmonized runs and trills. Other duets ensued, including "O Sole Mio!" in Neapolitan dialect and, for their finale, a special arrangement of the prison scene trio from *Faust*.

The power, compass, and flexibility of their singing made Jeanette's skin ripple. She wasn't sure if she preferred one sister over the other, but she identified with the younger, higher-voiced one, who under the name of Rosa Ponselle would soon become the greatest American-born dramatic soprano of her generation. When Rosa held, seemingly forever, the high note of the final phrase in Victor Herbert's "Kiss Me Again," she brought the Nixon's awestruck audience to its feet.

Jeanette floated home exultant: "I was too excited to sit down, too keyed up even to look at the dish of ice cream Mother was serving as a going-to-bed snack. I stood still for a second, opened my mouth, sang a few notes in the usual fashion. Then I started to let my voice go free, first low, then high, higher than I'd ever sung before. . . . not with the clear, little girl's voice I'd had up to then, but with richer, higher tones, the way that grownups could sing." Dazed by the splendor of Rosa's voice, Jeanette was nonetheless mindful that, like herself, Ponzillo was a vaudevillian untrained by conservatories on either side of the Atlantic. That night, as she prepared for bed, Jeanette no longer doubted that what she most wanted in life was to entertain others with glorious song.

Rosa's vaudeville career would last only until her Metropolitan Opera debut in November 1918. Yet like Jeanette, the soprano's impulse to thrill popular audiences survived for decades. In the mid-1930s, Ponselle briefly pondered a transition to Hollywood. Without a trace of irony, Paramount executives advised the onetime Tailored Italian Girl that if she was really serious about a foray into motion pictures, she would do well to study scrupulously the work of . . . Jeanette MacDonald.

CHAPTER THREE

Twinkling Stars and Four-Leaf Clovers

CLARK GABLE:	Well, sister, what's your racket?
MacDONALD:	I'm . . . I'm a singer.
GABLE:	Let's see your legs.
MacDONALD:	I said I'm a singer.

MGM's _San Francisco_, 1936

CONGRESS DECLARED WAR on the Central Powers on April 6, 1917. Philadelphia's large German-American community justly took offense at the proliferation of venomous cartoons depicting "Huns" as atrocious savages. Nationwide, acts of persecution struck German and Austrian artists with particular force. Karl Muck, conductor of the Boston Symphony Orchestra, was accused of anti-American acts and wound up interned as an enemy alien. Soprano Johanna Gadski, known to Jeanette from her many Wagner recordings, was hounded from the Metropolitan Opera, where sung German was banned until the 1920s. Fritz Kreisler, the Austrian-born violinist, withdrew from the concert stage when his pacifist views incited public furor. In spite of many similar individual injustices, the Great War was a powerful force for unifying the country. It brought volunteers into the army, money into government bonds, and a fighting spirit into civic enterprise. The Quaker City, with its industrial and commercial might mobilized for war production, redubbed itself the Arsenal of Democracy. Plastered throughout Philadelphia was the slogan Give Till It Hurts!

While American doughboys fought for democracy on Europe's western front, much of the country went about its business largely unaware
of the extent of the bloodletting. Jeanette completed her last term at
Thomas Dunlap and moved on to West Philadelphia High School for
Girls, where she matriculated in the commercial course. It was here
that she met the school's courageous music instructor, Virginia Henderson. In spite of the current Germanophobia, Miss Henderson continued to teach that the works of Beethoven and Brahms were sacrosanct.
She also led the girls in popular songs that were all the patriotic rage:
Irving Berlin's "Oh, How I Hate to Get Up in the Morning"; George M.
Cohan's morale booster, "Over There"; and Zo Elliott's sentimental
"There's a Long, Long Trail" (a song MacDonald would repopularize
on the eve of World War II).

Although she spent only three semesters at West Philly, Jeanette
thrived on the enthusiasm of her teachers and classmates for her musical gifts. At the start of her sophomore year, the music club voted her
Girl with the Best Voice and chose her for the role of Yum-Yum in *The
Mikado,* "a part usually given only to girls in the senior class." By encouraging musical diversity, West Philadelphia High School (the boys'
and girls' wings would not be fused until 1927) provided a congenial
atmosphere for budding musicians who in one way or another would
later be devoted to the notion that serious music and popular culture
can be soul mates, not adversaries. Among the school's other distinguished alumni were opera composer Marc Blitzstein, pianist Eugene
List, baritone Wilbur Evans, and a conductor whose career would one
day mesh with MacDonald's, Robert Armbruster.

As Jeanette's self-confidence climbed, her father's plummeted. The
war brought a severe curtailment to private home construction, which
was Daniel's bread and butter. Although the War Department placed
huge orders for domiciles to shelter thousands of workers drawn to the
city's shipbuilding industry, Daniel's small woodworks company received none of this business, perhaps because of cost inefficiencies, perhaps because of inadequate political pull. In any event, by the summer
of 1919 he again found himself unemployed.

In her memoir, MacDonald asserts that by this time Daniel had will-
ingly left sales for a municipal government position as "the official assessor in our district of Philadelphia." But an examination of Philadelphia's municipal employee records between 1915 and 1920, as well as
the archives of the Philadelphia Tax Review Board (the agency that utilized assessors), offers "no evidence that Daniel MacDonald worked

for the city in any capacity." It is likely that Jeanette, in reconstructing her cherished father's past, sought to minimize the humiliation Daniel felt at being without work. As she poignantly wrote: "He was in his prime, yet he hadn't found any great success in life. Now even his prospects were dark."

Jeanette's father tried to keep faith with Prosperity, the great new American god. But eroding his trust were the postwar economic realities of strikes and work stoppages, competition from returning soldiers, and the need to support a family in a period of runaway inflation. After fruitless job searching in September and October, Daniel got a lead on a position in New York City. Although reluctant to pull up his Philadelphia roots, he was desperate enough to make the two-hour train trip almost immediately. As a special treat to Jeanette, he spent the extra fare to take his favorite daughter along for the day.

On Al White's recommendation, Blossom MacDonald had recently found chorus work in Manhattan, where she shared a tiny apartment with another dancer, Anna Poulson, at 125 West Forty-ninth Street. The plan was to leave Jeanette in her sister's care while Daniel went to his eleven o'clock interview down by Union Square. Upon his return, they would lunch at the Automat and then catch a four o'clock train home.

But Blossom had her own agenda.

The instant Daniel exited, Anna Poulson began to transform Jeanette's face with powder and makeup. Blossom hurried to the closet, ordered Jeanette to remove her middy blouse and box-pleated bloomers, and shoved her into a holly green sheath and size three pumps. Only as the young women sprinted up Broadway did Blossom fully explain the scheme. There was an opening in the Capitol Theater's chorus line, and in fifteen minutes Jeanette was scheduled to audition for Ned Wayburn, the show's director and choreographer.

Pittsburgh-born Wayburn was a pioneer in the new stage genre known as the *prologue,* a live extravaganza designed to precede a feature-length film. Unlike other impresarios in New York's so-called Frivolity Fraternity—notably Florenz Ziegfeld and the Messrs. Shubert—Ned Wayburn did not have the reputation of a Casanova. His main interest in women was to redefine the American showgirl, replacing the Rubenesque fleshpots of yesteryear with a bevy of young, slim, well-proportioned women who had "an inborn air of refinement about them." Wayburn's new breed was meant to appeal not to the lascivious in men but "to the romantic and the beautiful." To launch his *Demi Tasse Revue* at the Capitol, he ran a high-profile search for a Beauty Brigade of Chorus Girls that nabbed Blossom and Anna Poulson.

As Blossom and her kid sister raced to the stage entrance on West Fiftieth Street, Jeanette's adrenaline skyrocketed. With one ear she listened to Big Sister's advice on how to behave in front of Wayburn. But she was just as attentive to the whirling array of marquees and billboards that advertised *Irene* at the Vanderbilt; Marilyn Miller in *The Ziegfeld Follies of 1919* at the New Amsterdam; *Sinbad* with Al Jolson at the Winter Garden; and *Apple Blossoms,* featuring two young Wayburn protégés, Fred and Adele Astaire, at the Globe. One never would have guessed that an Actors' Equity strike had virtually shut down Broadway just weeks before.

Inside the Capitol, Blossom introduced her sister to a corpulent six-footer with a booming voice and squinty eyes that peered through ultrathick rimless glasses. Wayburn rarely hired girls not already enrolled in his Studio of Stage Dancing at Columbus Circle. Nonetheless, he liked Jeanette's flair and thought she might be good in comic skits. Her training with Al White, a fellow Pennsylvanian esteemed by Wayburn, also worked in her favor. Within minutes, the man who took credit for teaching Will Rogers to twirl a lasso and getting Eddie Cantor and Al Jolson into blackface offered Jeanette MacDonald her first job on Broadway.

The near-perfect timing of the day's events makes one wonder whether doting Daniel was privy to Blossom's conspiracy all along. Early that evening he met with Wayburn, who guaranteed that Jeanette would attend a New York public high school in the mornings and be finished in time for afternoon and nighttime shows. Although Daniel felt the final word had to be his wife's, he agreed to Wayburn's proposal that Jeanette remain in the city for a two-week trial period.

By November 17, Jeanette found herself simultaneously in the commercial program at Washington Irving High School and the chorus line of the world's most lavish performance palace. At Washington Irving, she studied stenography and bookkeeping. At the Capitol, where her name appeared on the program as "Janette McDonald," she impersonated an Indian Girl in one of Will Crutchfield's rope-spinning numbers and a Twinkling Star with electric lights wired to her dancing shoes in "Come to the Moon," a new Gershwin tune.

Between matinees and evening shows, MacDonald found time to take lessons at Wayburn's school. A proponent of modern dance, Wayburn revolutionized Broadway choreography by codifying a precision format for routines, which he structured around the physical size of his female dancers. At five feet five inches and 115 pounds, Jeanette was a Wayburn *squab*. Shorter girls were *ponies* or *thoroughbreds;* taller ones were *peaches*. Only the very tallest were Wayburn *showgirls,* and these beauties barely moved. Inspired by principles of expressive gesture codified in nineteenth-century France by François Delsarte, Wayburn required that all of his dancers study pantomime and tableau posing. The heightened expressivity of face, hands, and torso that MacDonald would later bring to her movies, and which so often seemed to hark back to silent pictures, actually was rooted in her training with Wayburn.

Jeanette's modest success coincided with Daniel's further degradation. His New York job interview, as well as renewed searches in Philadelphia, proved fruitless. No longer able to meet his mortgage payments, Daniel put the Arch Street house up for sale. Shortly after Thanksgiving, he, Anna, and the poodles Trixie and Toodles were forced to move into the two-room New York apartment on West Forty-ninth Street, now occupied by Jeanette, Anna Poulson, Blossom, and Blossom's Boston terrier, Roughneck. Of the close-knit MacDonald clan, only Elsie, recently remarried, stayed in Philadelphia. "For Mother and Father," Jeanette later noted, "it meant the end of life as they had known and loved it, and they entered carefully into a strange and uncertain future. I've always thought this uncertainty was too much for Father."

Daniel spent whole days taking the dogs for long walks through Central Park. Anna, who now prepared meals on electric plates stored in the bedroom closet, mastered the etiquette of bathroom clotheslines. Somehow, the family and three dogs managed to live on Blossom's salary alone, with Jeanette's weekly earnings of forty dollars going into a family emergency fund. Daniel's humiliation at having to be supported by the MacDonald women only increased his wife and daughters' efforts to cushion him emotionally. But nothing spared the entire family from the knowledge that a prolonged period of unemployment at the Capitol would mean financial ruin for everyone.

When *Demi Tasse* closed in late December 1919, the main beneficiary was Al Jolson, who incorporated its hit tune, "Swanee," into his show at the Winter Garden. Jeanette stayed on at the Capitol through mid-January, appearing as a dancing Four-Leaf Clover in *Song Scenes,* a new stage prologue. Unfortunately, the Capitol had not yet found an optimal balance between live shows and feature films. Shaken by negative publicity surrounding its ushers, who had gone on strike in December to demand the right to accept tips, the operation was losing money steadily. A turnaround would occur in June 1920, when S. L. Rothafel, better known as "Roxy," was brought in to supervise the house. Through weekly radio broadcasts on the NBC Blue Network, Roxy would eventually make the Capitol the most famous entertainment shrine in the nation. It would also become the flagship house of the Loew's theater chain and, after switching to a movies-only policy during the Depression, the site for the New York premieres of Hollywood's flagship diva, Jeanette MacDonald. In the winter of 1920, however, MacDonald's modest goal was simply to graduate from playing Twinkling Stars and Four-Leaf Clovers.

At the Capitol, Jeanette cashed in on her dancing abilities and her comic timing. But after just two months in New York, she began to fantasize a different persona for herself, one that might lead to roles calling for subtle allure, social polish, and even a dash of mystery. Prodded by this urge for self-improvement, MacDonald transferred in February 1920 to Julia Richman High School for Girls, then on West Thirteenth Street. The school's principal, Michael Lucey, had just begun a character-building campaign called the Personality Idea: "While we strive to pay due regard to courses of study and scholastic requirements . . . we hold that scholarship, happiness, health, charm, service, and character may walk hand in hand." Jeanette appreciated the concept, and in later years gave similar advice to aspiring young singers. But intoxicated by the Great White Way, she found herself focusing on happiness and charm to the near exclusion of scholarship. One result was that she flunked English that spring with a final grade of 50.

Impressed by MacDonald's showbiz drive, Ned Wayburn arranged for her to replace a dancer who had fallen ill during the out-of-town tryouts of his latest show. *The Night Boat*, which opened on February 2, 1920, at the Liberty Theater on West Forty-second Street, was a Charles Dillingham production, with book and lyrics by Anne Caldwell and music by Jerome Kern.

In retrospect, the combination of Jeanette MacDonald and Jerome Kern seems inevitable. So many of Kern's suavely elegant and vaguely nostalgic melodies matched MacDonald's refined, sentimental soprano. Kern's efforts to give the American public more complex forms of lyric theater also corresponded to what would become MacDonald's own hopes for movie musicals. As a screen star, however, MacDonald was associated with only one Kern vehicle, *The Cat and the Fiddle,* her first film for MGM in 1934. In 1935, MGM commissioned Kern and Oscar Hammerstein to write an original operetta for "la Jeanette," as Kern affectionately called her. Its plot concerned a sophisticate, MacDonald, who takes refuge from her problems in a mountain retreat only to find romance in the person of Nelson Eddy. Kern wrote several compositions for *Champagne and Orchids,* the working title for this picture that never got filmed. According to his daughter, Betty, Kern "felt terrible" about the studio's decision to drop the project.

The Night Boat became the second strongest musical of the 1919–20 Broadway season, rivaled only by Harry Tierney's *Irene.* Musically, it didn't produce the standards of Kern's other hit that year, *Sally* ("Look for the Silver Lining," "Wild Rose"). But it did leave audiences humming the joggy "Left All Alone Again Blues," sung by Stella Hoban in the role of a wife whose husband justifies his nocturnal skedaddlings by alleging he is the captain of a Hudson River night boat to Albany. A farce about the pleasures of adultery and liquor (Prohibition had just gone into effect), *The Night Boat* won praise from *Billboard* for its "commendable absence of offensiveness," while the *New York Sun-Herald*'s critic reveled in its being "a bit naughty." MacDonald stayed with the show through August and understudied Stella Hoban and Louise Groody—both of whom gloried in infallible health.

Rumor had it that MacDonald's hasty departure from *The Night Boat* stemmed from her refusal to play house with one of the producer's assistants. The truth was that Jeanette tired of the chorus and wanted a meatier role. In a stroke of good timing, she auditioned for one of the road companies of *Irene,* got cast as the second ingenue lead, and toured with the company for nine weeks at Boston's Wilbur Theater and then six at Philadelphia's Chestnut Street Opera House.

Louise Horner, a classmate at West Philly High, recalled that Jeanette paid a visit to her old school and sang *Irene*'s beguiling "Alice Blue Gown" at a special assembly in the auditorium: "She impressed all of us students by having gotten so far so quickly." Jeanette's own most vivid memory of the tour occurred in Boston and had nothing to do with rapid development—on the contrary: "I was invited with two other girls to a dance at the Massachusetts Institute of Technology. I took along an extra pair of silk stockings, rolled them up, and tucked one into each half of my bra. That gave me a shape almost as good as the other girls; but not so permanent. Every so often, I had to excuse myself, return to the powder room, roll up my two extra stockings, and restore them to their proper positions." At seventeen, Jeanette was terribly concerned that for lack of substantially well-rounded bosoms, she did not possess what was then referred to as "flash."

Following her stint with *Irene*, MacDonald returned to New York, temporarily without income. Daniel, now over fifty, had all but resigned himself to permanent unemployment. But the combined savings of Jeanette and Blossom allowed the family to move to a more comfortable apartment at 383 Central Park West, just below 100th Street. With two bedrooms, a living room, dining room, and kitchen, the new dwelling helped salvage some of Daniel and Anna's shattered self-image.

Being jobless gave MacDonald a chance to repair her spotty education. Although she had no desire to return to Julia Richman High, which she quit after one semester, Jeanette was determined to study whatever fields might further her career. New York's cosmopolitanism raised her awareness of things European. France was now the social elite's point of reference for sophistication and modernism in the arts (Picasso and Cocteau) and fashion (Chanel and Patou). To plug into this vibrant current, MacDonald started French lessons at Berlitz. She also renewed dance classes with Ned Wayburn and studied voice with Wassili Leps, the Russian-born founder of the Philadelphia Operatic Club, who saw students every Tuesday in Manhattan. She even squeezed in riding lessons three mornings a week and soon became an excellent horsewoman. "Had it been necessary for me to study trapeze techniques, I would have done that too," she later said of her self-tailored curriculum.

To help pay for classes, MacDonald took jobs modeling clothes, especially furs. Enveloped in mink and chinchilla, she perspired through the summer of 1921, modeling in photo shoots for Bergdorf Goodman at forty dollars per session. One day in mid-July, Jeanette ran into an agent on the corner of Broadway and Forty-sixth. When Jeanette mentioned she had just come from a fur shoot that left her swimming in perspiration, the smart aleck gibed: "I bet you sweated plenty last night when you made it with the guys who own those coats." Without missing a beat, Jeanette swung from the ground, busted the man in the jaw, and knocked him out cold.

That September, MacDonald landed a replacement role in *Tangerine*, a musical starring Julia Sanderson, the petite songstress who had introduced "They Wouldn't Believe Me" in Jerome Kern's inspired rewrite of *The Girl from Utah*. When *Tangerine* opened in early August, *Variety* predicted a run of no more than eight weeks. But the show turned into a hit, in spite of behind-the-scenes lawsuits involving producer Carle Carlton, a backer, and the backer's chorus-line protégée. Playing at the Casino Theater through May 1922, *Tangerine* was the season's leading draw among less expensive musicals and gave MacDonald her first stab at creating a character she would play to perfection in many of her best movies: a cunning female doing battle with the opposite sex. As Kate Allen, she was one of a trio of divorced wives whose alimony-dodging ex-husbands flee to Tangerine, a fanciful Polynesian isle where native women abjectly obey their men—a condition the thoroughly modern divorcées scheme to reverse.

With the Nineteenth Amendment just ratified, most critics agreed with Heywood Broun of the *Tribune* that *Tangerine*'s tang lay more in its sharp social satire (the book was authored by Guy Bolton, Jerome Kern's collaborator on the landmark Princess Theater shows) than in the sprightly but penny-ante tunes composed by Monte Carlo and Alma M. Sanders. When a *Tangerine* road company was set up in the spring, Carle Carlton offered MacDonald a contract. Taking her lead from the hard-boiled females she observed doing business with influential men in the fur trade, Jeanette said she'd accept only on condition of an immediate salary hike. Such gutsiness did not sit well with Carlton, who the next day put her on notice.

Unemployment meant once again haunting the offices of agents, managers, and producers. It also gave MacDonald an opportunity to satisfy her curiosity about the huge dirty yellow brick building on Broadway between Thirty-ninth and Fortieth Streets. Her mother was with her as she climbed to the standee section at the top of the Metropolitan Opera House. Neither had ever attended a full opera, but both had heard about the glamorous Moravian soprano whose debut, earlier that season, had taken New York by storm. Through binoculars, Jeanette scrutinized every movement of Maria Jeritza as she performed Puccini's *Tosca*. Here was a soprano who broke the stereotypes. Young, beautiful, and reasonably slim, she not only sang exquisitely but also acted persuasively. Moreover, Jeritza had the physical prowess of a tiger. When she sang "Vissi d'arte" in a prone position, Jeanette throbbed with emotion—and more than a touch of envy. It caused her to wonder whether trying to succeed in second-string musicals was a total waste of time.

Along the Rialto, MacDonald's apparent innocence was stirring the libidos of numerous stage-door Johnnies and seasoned showmen. Yet Jeanette's game plan never included exchanging sexual favors for career advancement. Even affairs of the heart could prove risky, as Elsie's scandal had so vividly shown. Possessed by ferocious independence and self-control, MacDonald simply would not allow anyone to control her. Later, she would seek the allegiance of men—invariably good-looking ones—who could accommodate themselves to her career without compromising their self-esteem.

The first serious pretender to this princely role was Jack Ohmeis, a New York University architecture student. Jack was thoroughly unaffected. The son of a wealthy bottle manufacturer, he shared Jeanette's interest in horses and riding. Both liked to poke fun at pretentious social mores. Jeanette fascinated Jack with stories of backstage life along Broadway's "roaring Forties." Jack furnished Jeanette with regular entrée to the magnificence of Manhattan east of Fifth Avenue—the grand hotels, the private clubs, the sumptuous parties.

It was at one such party, in the ballroom of the Hotel Astor, that Jack and Jeanette first met. The event was the annual Beaux Arts Ball, a high-society masquerade benefit for needy students. Although MacDonald looked terrific in a rented Second Empire gown and mask, she couldn't help feeling like a gate-crasher out of *Irene*. Her self-absorbed blind date didn't make matters easier. Even worse, everyone seemed to be speaking French with a fluency that put her Berlitz skills to shame. The Astor ballroom had been transformed into a replica of Paris by Night, and Jeanette spent much of the evening alone, wandering among the attractions. After midnight there began a lavish procession of *tableaux vivants* depicting great moments in architectural history. When the Construction of the Pyramids passed by, Jeanette riveted her gaze on a young man dressed, or more precisely *un*dressed, as an Egyptian slave. Sporting little more than a loincloth, this muscular, make-believe Egyptian was six feet five inches tall and had pale blue eyes and a slicked-back shock of honey blond hair. Before the party ended, Jeanette made it her business to get introduced to this sexy giant.

Jack Ohmeis soon became Jeanette's regular escort in New York nightlife. At one soiree, she decided to test her tolerance for bootleg rye: "I wanted to prove myself to Jack in some lunatic way, and I wanted to see how I'd feel." After imbibing for an hour, she went to the powder room and became so sick that Jack had to pick her up, carry her out to his Pierce-Arrow, and attempt to drive without churning her stomach even more. "I learned my lesson," she later reflected. "If I couldn't drink intelligently, I'd be damned if I'd drink like a fool."

Jack's family at first suspected Jeanette of gold-digging. But after a weekend at the Ohmeis summer estate on New Jersey's Lake Hopatcong, she convinced them she was not the scheming vamp they imagined. Herbert Ohmeis, Jack's younger brother, remembered Jeanette as a "nervous but well-possessed young lady of nineteen" who especially won the heart of his mother. Mrs. Ohmeis saw Jeanette as replacing a daughter she had tragically lost years earlier. She even let Jeanette use her charge account at Jaeckel's on Fifth Avenue in order to buy a first mink coat, asking for repayment in whatever weekly installments the working girl could manage.*

MacDonald cleverly played the frugality card when, after another summer of modeling, she was hired to replace a featured singer in *A Fantastic Fricassee,* a Greenwich Village revue that had just opened to tepid reviews. Her weekly salary was seventy-five dollars plus 5 percent of the take, but she also had to supply her costumes. Reluctant to dip into her own purse, she searched the phone book for addresses of Seventh Avenue wholesale houses. At the first one she visited, she grandly proclaimed: "I am going to star in a show at the Greenwich Village Theater. If I can get program credit for you, will you let me have a couple of evening dresses—my selection?" The merchant bought the idea, and MacDonald became two gowns richer.

Part slummy, part genteel, Greenwich Village was then considered New York's Montmartre, and by all accounts *A Fantastic Fricassee* was a bargain-priced bohemian stew or, as the *New York Evening Post* unkindly put it, "an uncooked mess." The recipe mixed folksy strains from Village troubadour Bobby Edwards; a Grand Guignol poetic

---

*In an ironic reversal of fortunes after the Great Crash of 1929, Jack Ohmeis turned to MacDonald for a business loan of $2,500, which until the 1950s he was unable to repay. It was soon after meeting Jack that MacDonald devised a strategy for becoming wealthy on her own. Rule 1: Pay cash, avoid credit. (By writing a check or handing over hard currency, she reasoned, the greater the opportunity to reconsider a purchase.) Rule 2: No matter the size of a weekly paycheck, 10 percent must go into savings. (If agents could lop off a tenth, surely she could do the same for herself.) Rule 3: Never ignore the Scottish adage It Is Better to Be Bent on Economy than Broke on Extravagance.

drama, "The Master Poisoner," penned by Maxwell Bodenheim and future *Front Page* writer Ben Hecht; and a grotesque Japanese death song culminating in simulated hara-kiri as performed by Jimmie Kemper, a youthful baritone fresh from Kansas City. By the time MacDonald joined the company, the death song was mercifully dropped, and Kemper joined her in the less morbid Franke Harling number, "Waiting for You." For her solos, MacDonald sang "A Heart That's Free," wearing her new peach evening gown, and "Maman, dites-moi," for which she donned French peasant garb à la Lexington Avenue.

A Fantastic Fricassee brought MacDonald her first notice in a trade paper. After lambasting the revue's revised version as "all gravy and no meat," Patterson James, with astonishing foresight, wrote in the November 11, 1922, issue of *Billboard*:

> There is one girl in the show, however, who is worthy of the attention of uptown managers. Her name is Jeanette MacDonald. She has a winsome manner, she sings fairly well, though slightly flat at times; she is very pretty, and she looks as if something might be made of her by an intelligent coach or director. Anyway, she deserves a chance. If she gets it, *A Fantastic Fricassee* will not have been in vain.

The potpourri ran for an impressive 124 performances, probably because the unlikely question "But will it play in Ossining?" made it a minor cause célèbre in the annals of stage censorship. On Sunday, November 19, MacDonald and the *Fricassee* company traveled up the Hudson to perform for the inmates of Sing Sing Penitentiary. When they arrived, the warden rescinded his invitation due to last-minute pressure from the Prison Reform Association, the Jewish Welfare Board, and the Catholic Welfare Council—all objecting to the scantily clad dancers in the revue's pièce de résistance, "Virgins of the Sun." As described by Alan Dale of the *New York American*, this number was a bungled homage to Diaghilev's Ballets Russes set to music sounding like "Debussy gone sour" and displaying "sinuous young women who wiggled their shapes, tossed their manes, and behaved altogether like sufferers from delirium tremens" in their lust for an Adonis-like sun worshiper.

The notoriety of *A Fantastic Fricassee* attracted, among others, veteran actress-turned-playwright Zelda Sears. Sears was at work on a new musical for producer Henry Savage, and she thought MacDonald perfect for a supporting role. The show was to star the very popular and eternally youthful Mitzi, a diminutive Hungarian singer-dancer-comedienne famous enough to discard her last name (Hajos). At her audition, MacDonald flubbed the high A in a song from *Fricassee*. But Savage, who had recently masterminded a hit revival of Franz Lehár's *The Merry Widow,* liked the lightness of her voice and found her "cute as a bug's ear"—even though Jeanette was a full head taller than Mitzi. A week later, Savage signed MacDonald to play the lead ingenue in *Minnie and Me,* the working title for what eventually became *The Magic Ring.*

Minnie and Me tried out in Connecticut and Massachusetts. The show was in some ways a family affair: Mitzi's leading man was Boyd Marshall, her real-life husband; and Zelda Sears, constantly tinkering with the book, was married to Lou Wiswell, Savage's longtime business manager. Traveling solo, MacDonald quickly became the object of lewd advances from a very persistent dance director, Julian Alfred. In confronting the first real moral crisis of her adult career, she decided to stick with principle even if it jeopardized her most important role to date. "I wanted men to look at me and like what they saw," she explained. "But if any man thought I must be 'easy' because I was in the theater, then I fought like a hellcat." In this instance her obstinacy only further aroused Alfred, who said he would get her fired if she refused to engage in what was quaintly referred to in the vernacular as "misbehaving."

MacDonald's uncustomary edginess surprised Boyd Marshall, who persuaded MacDonald to confide in him. Against her wishes, Marshall disclosed the harassment to Henry Savage. Savage was a former Harvard classmate of Teddy Roosevelt and, like the late president, a champion of the so-called little man. He went to bat for MacDonald beyond anyone's expectations, firing Julian Alfred on the spot. The producer did, however, ask a favor in return. The show was scheduled for a summer hiatus, and in the fall Savage planned a publicity campaign that would advertise MacDonald as That Girl with the Red-gold Hair and Sea-green Eyes. But for his taste, Jeanette was unacceptably scrawny. He therefore urged her to spend a few weeks at Dr. Rheinle's Sanitarium and Milk Farm in Summit, New Jersey, and gain ten pounds on his expense account. MacDonald agreed, without foreseeing the genuine health problems she was about to encounter.

To put an end to her coughs and laryngitis, Jeanette took the advice of a New York doctor and had her tonsils removed at a downtown clinic. What was supposed to be a routine procedure, however, resulted in damage to one of the muscular pillars of her throat and substantial hemorrhaging that left her with a serious case of pleurisy. Ordered to stay in bed for a month without speaking, Jeanette feared she would never be able to sing again. It was more than likely she would lose her job with the new show. Worst of all was the prospect that she and her parents would once again slide into poverty. Frail and emaciated, MacDonald left New York for a three-week stay at Dr. Rheinle's Sanitarium. Under orders to "chew" a glass of whole milk every half-hour and ingest several pints of ice cream at meals, she put on thirteen pounds. Because she had lost weight during her illness, however, she was still below Henry Savage's prescribed gain.

The Magic Ring proved to be a variation on themes from Cinderella and Aladdin. It opened to decent reviews at the Liberty Theater and ran for ninety-six performances before embarking on a two-year nationwide tour. In addition to MacDonald and a live monkey named Minnie, the show featured two other future movie personalities: actor Sydney Greenstreet, playing a soused antique dealer; and set and costume designer Gilbert Adrian (born Adolph Greenberg), who would become—divested of both his real and his faux first names—Jeanette's brilliant couturier at MGM.

Within hours of the premiere, MacDonald savored her first New York press mentions. The *Times* cited her "appearance and voice" as one of "the merits of the evening." The *American* spoke of her "pleasing voice and pellucid personality." The *Herald* found her "pretty and refreshingly naive." More expansive was the *Tribune*: "The blonde beauty of Jeannette [*sic*] MacDonald is one of the glowing things to be commemorated like the keepsakes of which she eloquently sings. It was understandable that only a resort to necromancy could [release] the handsome hero from her legitimate charms."

MacDonald learned from Mitzi that the authentic verdict on a performance comes from the paying audience. But she was always open to honest criticism. Most reviewers of *The Magic Ring* felt that MacDonald was less forceful in act 1, where she appeared with an all-female chorus, than in act 2, where she led a corps of dancing men and virtually stopped the show. One critic noted it was "the first time in history a male chorus took a curtain call." This was a lesson MacDonald would bring to the movies, always preferring her foils to be men rather than women.

A second press ripple had a more immediate effect. A number of commentators paid greater attention to MacDonald's legs than to her voice. By contrast, Phoebe Crosby—who played Jeanette's buxom mother—was consistently singled out for a "voice of unusual quality," showcased in act 2's hilarious opera parody. In the wake of her disastrous tonsillectomy, MacDonald counted herself blessed simply to be working. But she hated to be perceived as a dancer who also just happened to sing. One day she confided her ambitions to Crosby, who had a good deal of concert and opera experience. Phoebe listened as Jeanette gave an earnest but awkward rendition of "The Jewel Song," which she had not sung for anyone since that traumatic day back in grammar school. "Look," Phoebe told her, "you have a pretty voice but it is such a little voice that you ought to do something about it. I wish you'd come to see my teacher, Torriani. I think he's the greatest."

Ferdinand Torriani was a tall, dark-haired Italian whose good looks were spoiled by one unfocused eye. He lived and worked in studio 301 of the Carnegie Hall Building. Torriani's father, Angelo, a noted European conductor and voice teacher, was said to have trained Adelina Patti, unrivaled for her purity and beauty of tone. The all-consuming passion of the younger Torriani was to keep alive his father's secrets of voice production.

Legend holds that when Torriani first met MacDonald, he exclaimed, "Lei è come un venticello primaverile!" (You're like a breath of spring!). After she nervously sang the Gounod aria, Torriani decided: "I can do a lot for your voice. I know exactly what it needs. Your throat has contracted. You must learn control so that it will expand itself automatically." Jeanette was suspicious. She had encountered a plenitude of quacks amid the New York vocal scene. But as Torriani expounded his ideas, MacDonald was taken by his tranquil presence of mind: "A voice is no more and no less than a vibration of air, like the sound produced by any other musical instrument. My work must therefore be considered not vocal but instrumental. This is basic. To perfect the instrument God has given you, this requires exercise and will power, not voice exercises but anatomical, muscular exercises. See." Torriani stretched out his chin and stroked the muscles of his throat. He continued: "The windpipe is surrounded by muscles. There are more muscles extending all the way from the diaphragm to the lips. All of them are involved in the voice. They must be made to operate not involuntarily, as yours do now, but under the command of your will. You will acquire this control by concentration, together with a certain feeling of vitality, of *élan*. Then you will find that if you produce the true sound *in your mind*, the tone will follow automatically."

MacDonald negotiated a course of three lessons per week at five dollars an hour, half of Torriani's customary price. The sessions, she recalled, were always exacting: "There were no phoney airs about Torri, no glass of sherry poured to while away part of your hour's instruction. He worked you hard every minute." To avoid unsightly grimaces that interfered with tone, Torriani had MacDonald practice in front of a mirror. A stickler for enunciation, he insisted that her lips be kept off her teeth and that each syllable be shaped and sounded to perfection. What most set Torriani apart from other teachers was his lack of interest in breath control and diaphragm development. Instead, he emphasized *vitalità,* or "vitalization" of the muscles at the tip of the chin, a kind of mind-body connection that a tenacious student might fully attain only after years of intense concentration.

When MacDonald finally mastered Torriani's brain-muscle link, some music critics, like Patterson Greene of the *Los Angeles Examiner,* chided her for indulging in what looked like "an unhinging and excessive stretching of the jaw." But in 1923 what most mattered to Jeanette was that within weeks of starting to train with Torriani, she sensed her voice change in small but basic ways. Her tone seemed clearer, more silvery, and placed more forward: "To hear this was like seeing some wilting plant brought to life. Suddenly, one day, I knew I'd have a full, strong voice again."

Around this time, Jack Ohmeis gave MacDonald a diamond ring and a proposal of marriage. While he was eager to elope, Jeanette remembered her parents' heartache over Elsie. She was also unsure about the compatibility of wifehood and a career. To put off a major decision, she accepted Jack's ring but convinced him to wait until the following year, after he graduated, before setting a marriage date. Jeanette also knew that for better or worse she and he would be going separate ways during most of the waiting period, since she was about to embark with Mitzi and company on her first transcontinental tour.

Known as a top road-show moneymaker, Mitzi raked in record receipts as *The Magic Ring* journeyed from Pittsburgh to Tacoma to Los Angeles to Chattanooga. By the tour's end in Bridgeport, Connecticut, MacDonald had worked out what she half seriously called "a geography of the laugh and the tear." People west of the Mississippi, she decided, had an overdeveloped sense of pathos and were easy to make cry. Easterners, by contrast, were more sophisticated and responded better to comic nuance. For all its crudeness, this theory was borne out

in the early 1930s, when MacDonald's best movie bedroom farces fell
flat for much of rural America.

In the course of touring, MacDonald and Mitzi became very fond of
each other. Although Mitzi had enough jewelry to beggar a maharaja,
it was not because of the promiscuity many suspected. "Very early in
my career," Mitzi explained to Jeanette, "I made it a rule to give myself
an I-Owe-Me present every year. An *expensive* one. That way, no dirty
old man will ever have an I.O.U. on me!" MacDonald admired Mitzi's
devotion to her fans and well-wishers. Following her lead, she spent
hours perfecting her signature—in the hope there might someday be a
demand for it.

Jeanette's penmanship had always been free and bold, but now she
made it fly even higher and wider across the page. Her small *e* was unusual for replicating the graceful shape of a capital script *E*, which one
graphologist later interpreted as the sure sign of a "cultured, discriminating taste." MacDonald's sprawling signature, with its wide *t* bar
springing upward and forward, led another specialist to deduce—to no
one's surprise—a personality full of "purpose," "determination," and
"bubbling vivacity."

When *The Magic Ring* road company went on summer break, Jeanette,
now twenty-one, spent most of her time at Lake Hopatcong with Jack
Ohmeis and his sister, Lee. One Friday morning at about four o'clock
she awoke with a start: "In the darkness I was filled with an immediate
certainty that there was someone moving about the room." Her mind
turned back to Mrs. Cox's séances, of which she had been so skeptical,
and she remembered her father telling Anna, "She'll never believe in all
that bunk; she's got too much sense!" After ten or fifteen minutes of
sleeplessness, Jeanette heard Jack, who rapped on the door and rushed
over to her bed: "Jimmee, I have something I wish I didn't have to tell
you . . ." "Father died," she said with certainty.

Jeanette rushed home to comfort Anna and then insisted on a few
moments alone with Daniel, who had succumbed to a heart attack:
"He lay with his mouth open, cold and unreal, in the bed in which he
had died. It wasn't the gold bed I'd promised as a child. I was sorry
about that. I was sorry, too, that I'd gone in to see him. I would rather
have remembered him the way he used to be." Later that morning,
when Blossom emptied Daniel's wallet, she found it contained but one
photograph—of Jeanette.

The funeral took place in Philadelphia on August 4, 1924. Jeanette recollected: "I followed Mother up to the coffin for a last sight of him. She stooped, kissed him gently, then whispered, 'Goodbye, my darling.' Through all the years, I had never heard that word between them. I had never seen any display of the intense love that was there. Until that moment my own grief had been deep but dry-eyed. Now I was overcome in a flood of emotion."

Daniel's estate was valued at $1,400—barely four times Jeanette's weekly salary in *The Magic Ring*. MacDonald would later say that her "greatest regret" in life was that her father did not survive to see her attain truly outstanding success.

CHAPTER FOUR

A Fair Princess on Broadway

MACDONALD: I'm *no one's* fiancée.
FRANK MORGAN: Let me congratulate you. It's a delight
to find a beautiful woman who's
modern.

MGM's *The Cat and the Fiddle*, 1934

MACDONALD HELD THE SUPERSTITION that the third of anything brings misfortune. When asked to sing "Oh, Promise Me!" at the wedding of her fiancé's brother, she hesitated. She had just sung at a friend's nuptials in Philadelphia, and before that for her sister Blossom, who in September 1926 married her new vaudeville partner, Clarence "Rocky" Rock. Jack Ohmeis's brother would make three. Ignoring her premonition, she gave in to the request, but, sure enough, bad luck followed. Three weeks after the ceremony at University Heights Presbyterian Church in November, she and Jack broke their engagement.

The decision took place in the lobby of a small East Side hotel, where Jeanette and Jack often met to talk freely without the constant presence of Anna, now living with Jeanette at 100 West Fifty-fifth Street. Jack longed for a conventional life. He wanted an at-home spouse, not one who worked nights or spent months traipsing around the country with a band of actors. For Jeanette, marriage could only be entertained in tandem with a career. This conflict had been patched over throughout their engagement, which was itself a kind of make-do arrangement. "It would be unfair to go on," Jeanette told Jack as she returned his round-cut diamond ring.

In the wake of her breakup with Ohmeis, none of MacDonald's relationships proved more intense than her involvement with Grace Adele Newell, the longtime accompanist and associate of Ferdinand Torriani. When Torriani died of cancer in 1925, Newell dedicated herself to perpetuating his technique and took on several of his more promising students, including Jeanette. Many suspected that Newell, who stayed single all her life, had been in love with Torriani but refused to admit it for fear of jeopardizing the maestro's marriage. Born in Providence, Rhode Island, in 1874, Newell was the sister of Florence Newell Barbour, a respected composer of chamber and vocal music and the wife of a Brown University president. Grace's stern, bony exterior conformed to stereotyped notions of New England spinsters, and when the director Ernst Lubitsch set eyes on her in Hollywood, he supposedly quipped, "Well, you must be Jeanette's morals teacher." Newell, however, was her own woman. She was not averse to cracking off-color jokes, and she had a passion for racetracks, gin rummy, and Early Times bourbon. While urging Jeanette to stick with weak tea and lemon, she never missed late-afternoon cocktails, referring to them as "mother's milk."

Newell was an unremitting taskmaster in imparting Torriani's baffling principles. Among her celebrity pupils were Irene Dunne, Bebe Daniels, Allan Jones, and Jane Powell. Yet only MacDonald submitted religiously to Newell's near-sadistic requirements. At every lesson the two would scream and quarrel—and end in an embrace. Decades after MacDonald became a star, she continued daily lessons with Newell. In a birthday note written in the early 1960s (Grace died in 1966 at age ninety-two), Jeanette wrote: "For all the years of hard work, sweat, and tears you and I have suffered thru, I want you to know that every moment has paid off in love and gratitude for you and your friendship and understanding."

Choreographer Albertina Rasch was another gutsy woman from Manhattan to have lasting impact on MacDonald. An alumna of Vienna's Imperial Ballet School, this darkly handsome danseuse gained New York's attention in 1925 by mixing classical pointe work with modern interpretive dance in her ballet staging of Gershwin's *Rhapsody in Blue* at the Hippodrome. In musicals such as Harry Tierney's *Rio Rita* and Sigmund Romberg's *My Princess*, Rasch replaced the familiar Ned Wayburn style of precision tap formations with more complex and subtle routines that drew on ballet and American jazz. In an era when male dance directors dominated Broadway, New York producers made an exception for the "Czarina," as she was known, because of her business sense and her grasp of the public pulse.

MacDonald enrolled at Rasch's studio in the Steinway Building on West Fifty-seventh Street shortly after her stint with *The Magic Ring*. While less stalwart pupils were intimidated by the instructor's accented bellow, thumping cane, and scalding sarcasm, Jeanette took instantly to her demands for discipline, stamina, and consistency. Bicoastal Rasch, who married the Hollywood composer Dimitri Tiomkin in 1926, would later create the dances in many of MacDonald's MGM musicals. Her comments on MacDonald's verve in 1937 apply as well to Jeanette's fiber during these formative New York years: "MacDonald is never satisfied with her work, no matter how near it approaches perfection. When we started rehearsing the Spanish numbers for *The Firefly*, it was physically painful for her at first to return to the steps I had taught her when she began musical comedy work. . . . But she kept it up, four and five hours every day, in addition to her song recording, until she was as good as any professional, and better than a lot of them."

An emancipated European, Rasch believed that the United States offered the greatest promise for democratizing the female body politic. In dance, she insisted, if a woman's body is "lithe and resilient and perfectly controlled," and if she possesses "an abundant vitality," she will project, regardless of her actual social stratum, the manners and mental attitudes Europeans typically associate with aristocratic breeding. MacDonald was an exemplar of this philosophy. She learned from Rasch how to tone down her chorus-girl prance and walk across a stage with stately grace in an American manner, without affectation. Rasch also believed that classical art forms had to be adapted to a New World context. She argued for American ballet and opera geared not to an intellectual elite but to the general populace, in much the same way as baseball and motion pictures have mass appeal.

For MacDonald, still uncertain about how to reconcile her vocal ambitions with her work in Broadway shows, Rasch's ideas offered new, if somewhat abstract, terms for thinking about the future. They certainly harmonized with the astounding talents of the composer of her next show.

Only twenty-seven years old, George Gershwin had already electrified concert audiences with his jazz-symphonic *Rhapsody in Blue* and, with his lyricist brother, Ira, had composed a string of commercial hits for their 1924 musical, *Lady, Be Good!* MacDonald's taste in popular songs, along with Dame Fortune, helped her win a featured role in the Gershwin brothers' second full Broadway undertaking: "The day I called to see the producers [Alex A. Aarons and Vinton Freedley] about this one, my luck was in. George Gershwin, who had written the *Tip-Toes* score, happened to be sitting in the office. We got to talking and found we were both great Jerome Kern fans. Gershwin played the piano while I sang 'Left All Again Blues' from the Kern hit *The Night Boat*. Imagine having Gershwin as your accompanist! No wonder I landed the part."

Tip-Toes was about a female vaudevillian who has to trap a Florida millionaire in marriage. The title role went to Queenie Smith, the original "Ida, Sweet as Apple Cider" girl and the actress who later played Ellie in the 1936 screen version of Kern's *Show Boat*. Smith introduced *Tip-Toes'* most enduring song, the hankering "Looking for a Boy (To Love)." MacDonald played Sylvia Metcalf, a Palm Beach society flapper. The role was slender, but "Nice Baby!," her bouncy act 1 duet with Robert Halliday (who went on to create the male lead in Romberg's *The New Moon*), gave New Yorkers a tantalizing glimpse of her flair for comic sexual sparring. Cutting her macho husband down to size with Ira Gershwin's incisive lyrics, Mac-Donald made clear that his ideas were, to her modern mind, fairly "twisted."

When *Tip-Toes* opened at the Liberty Theater on December 28, 1925, it broke the house record for first-week receipts and went on to a run of 192 performances. Most reviewers joined the *World*'s Alexander Woollcott in marveling at the hotly syncopated "Sweet and Low Down," notable for the entire company's frenetic blowing on slide kazoo-trombones. Lyricist Lorenz Hart, fresh from his success with Richard Rodgers in *Dearest Enemy,* sent congratulations to Ira Gershwin, whom he had yet to meet, for offsetting the "brutally cretinous" nature of most lyrics written for musical comedies. Mac-Donald got excellent notices. *Billboard* found her "unusually ingratiating." The *New York Times* called her "truly beautiful." Walter Winchell (who would later give MacDonald headaches over what he perceived to be her secret married life) also singled out her beauty in his rave for the *Graphic*. But an alert critic for the *Newark Star* put his finger on an issue MacDonald had yet to confront head-on: "And Jeannette [*sic*] MacDonald, with nothing at all to do, makes you glad she's there anyway." Ira Gershwin voiced a similar thought years later: "Beautiful and true as her voice was, she really didn't belong in musical comedy."

The truth was that MacDonald's floating lyric soprano was better suited to the soaring melodic lines of operetta than the more angular, bluesy, and hard-shelled quality of musical numbers in the new Gershwin style. A huge resurgence of operetta was in fact taking place on Broadway, bringing new or greater prominence to such singers as Mary Ellis, Evelyn Herbert, Tessa Kosta, Dennis King, Robert Halliday, and Howard Marsh.* MacDonald, however, kept her distance from the playing field. In part, she didn't want to tamper with a sure thing. Musical comedy song and dance came easily to her. She had moved from chorus girl to supporting ingenue fairly swiftly, and she was determined to rise higher. For all their renewed popularity, operettas were still just a fraction of the musical theater scene, and the competition for plum roles was notoriously fierce. Operettas also entailed more exacting vocal demands, and MacDonald knew she still had a long way to go in her training with Grace Newell. She herself told aspiring singers years later: "Perhaps the greatest mistake the average student makes is in thinking that one may succeed in light opera with less natural voice, or with less thorough training than would be required for grand opera."

Above all, MacDonald was nervous about cutting herself off from what was starting to look like a reliable source of income. Her economy was already notorious among theater insiders. Amy Revere, a featured player in *Tip-Toes* and MacDonald's sometimes roommate in the mid-1920s, recalled an incident that took place when the Gershwin show was trying out at Newark's Shubert Theater:

> One afternoon on our way to New Jersey from the Upper West Side of Manhattan, we found ourselves on the wrong side of the subway station, heading uptown instead of down. This was not a station where you could get to the other side of the tracks for free, and Jeanette refused to walk outside, cross the street, and pay the extra nickel to reenter on the correct side.

---

*Rudolf Friml and Herbert Stothart's brilliantly melodic *Rose-Marie* (1924), with a book by Otto Harbach and Oscar Hammerstein II, was a staggering hit at the Imperial Theater. Sigmund Romberg's *The Student Prince* (1924) had a phenomenally long New York run and spawned nine national road companies. Friml's *The Vagabond King* (1925), overflowing with romantic love songs, played for nearly two years at the Casino, as did Romberg and Hammerstein's *The New Moon* (1928) at the Imperial. Gershwin and Stothart's *Song of the Flame* (1925) and Harry Tierney's *Rio Rita* (1927) showed that American-born composers usually associated with crisp musical comedies were just as inclined to have a try at the expansive, sentimental lyricism of operetta. In perhaps the most important breakthrough in Broadway musical history, Jerome Kern and Oscar Hammerstein created the first totally Americanized operetta with *Show Boat* (1927), which ran at the Ziegfeld for 572 performances. Well-attended foreign imports included Hungarian-born Emmerich Kalman's vibrant *Countess Maritza* (1926) and Britisher Noël Coward's plaintive *Bitter Sweet* (1929).

Instead, she insisted we take the uptown train all the way to Ninety-sixth Street, where you could change directions at no charge. I was furious with her! And that was in 1925, when she was making about $400 a week!

MacDonald's first crack at a leading role was one part fluke, two parts calculation. In late summer 1926, H. H. Frazee was stalled in his efforts to secure a female protagonist for *Yes, Yes, Yvette,* a spin-off of his previous blockbuster, *No, No, Nanette.* Working out of Detroit, the producer sent a troubleshooter to Boston, supposedly to check out Cleo Mayfield, who was headlining in *Bubbling Over,* a New York–bound musical that pitted Mayfield's gold digger against Mac-Donald's ingenue. The buzz on Frazee's new show was that the title role had to go to a fresh young face percolating with zest. MacDonald suspected that Frazee was actually curious about her, not veteran Mayfield.

Bubbling Over was in the thick of rewrites because raven-haired Mayfield was coming off as unsympathetic, while MacDonald was bewitching audiences with the show's best songs, including the rousing title tune. With the cards in her favor, Jeanette willed herself to give the standout performance of her life, projecting a vitality and allure beyond anything that Mayfield, six years her senior, could possibly pull off. Duly impressed, Frazee's deputy persuaded Jeanette to leave *Bubbling Over* (which never did make it to Broadway) for a trial run with *Yes, Yes, Yvette* in Detroit and Chicago.

Mayfield's resentment at having been so brazenly upstaged put a strain on those last days in Boston. But MacDonald left a glowing impression on another cast member, a tiny, wiry eighteen-year-old from Philadelphia who had just arrived as a replacement in the role of the goofy maid. Imogene Coca, who would not become a major celebrity until pairing with comic Sid Caesar in television's early years, recalled: "In those days I was very shy and, being new in the show, *very* insecure. Jeanette seemed to sense this and always helped me to feel more at ease. . . . I watched her every performance and for me she really was a STAR—beautiful, charming, gifted."

At twenty-three, MacDonald was on the brink of becoming a leading lady on Broadway. She also became a hot press item. One reporter tied her name to that of a celebrated female writer who would later help define MacDonald's movie career: "And what a pretty darling of a girl Jeanette MacDonald . . . is, proving that Anita Loos knew a thing or two when she celebrated [in *Gentlemen Prefer Blondes*] the golden-haired daughters of today. . . . Miss MacDonald is certainly slated for the favor of the gods. I don't know when I have seen so altogether fascinating a 'lady.' " When journalists queried her on the place of women in contemporary society, MacDonald usually made a case for "wifehood and motherhood and home-making" so as to promote the old-fashioned values at the heart of *Yes, Yes, Yvette*. But she always hastened to dispel mistaken inferences about her own life: "I do not mean that women will suddenly relinquish the strides they have made in the commercial and artistic worlds. There still will be a goodly percentage of us who will find that fate or inclination has placed us in a niche outside the home."

MacDonald reveled in the newfound celebrity. Amy Revere recalled: "One evening when we were trying out in Baltimore, Jeanette and I went to dinner at the Belvedere Hotel. In the course of the meal, Jeanette had to go to the bathroom rather urgently. She was wearing a colorful, long-fringed embroidered Spanish shawl. There was an exit right near our table, but she refused to move until the orchestra went on break. She then got up from the table and paraded casually across the huge empty dance floor to reach an exit on the far side of the room. When I asked her afterward why she did that, she answered, 'At times like this, I think I'm the most beautiful thing in the world—and beauty is something that shouldn't be kept private.' "

While out-of-town audiences loved the show, *Yes, Yes, Yvette* lasted but forty performances at New York's Sam H. Harris Theater. All the principals—including Charles Winninger, who within weeks would abandon his role as Yvette's father to create *Show Boat*'s endearing paterfamilias, Cap'n Andy—got favorable press treatment, as did Sammy Lee's acrobatic choreography. Critics were unanimous in judging *Yes, Yes, Yvette*'s witty, sophisticated book, based on the hit play *Nothing But the Truth*, superior to *No, No, Nanette*'s. Yet its sister show had left the nation humming and spooning to Vincent Youmans's "Tea for Two" and "I Want to Be Happy." The score of *Yes, Yes, Yvette*, composed by Philip Charig and Ben Jerome, was eminently forgettable. According to Irving Caesar, lyricist for both shows, Harry Frazee "wanted Youmans to compose the score for *Yvette*," but unwisely refused to meet the composer's increased financial demands.

MacDonald was still asleep when Frazee left a phone message with Anna the morning after the New York opening: "If Jeanette would come down a little early to the theater tonight, she'll see something that might interest her." When dusk arrived, Jeanette had her taxi circle Broadway and West Forty-second Street again and again—and again. There in electric lights, for the first time on a marquee, were all seventeen letters, six feet high: J-E-A-N-E-T-T-E M-A-C-D-O-N-A-L-D.

That same night brought more surprises. While dancing a furious Black Bottom with actor Jack Whiting, MacDonald broke a shoe strap, causing her *peau-de-soie* slipper to fly from her foot and into the lap of a distinguished gentleman seated fourth row center. Finishing the number half shoeless won MacDonald extra applause and much goodwill. In her dressing room at intermission, the unwitting target of the torpedoing footwear introduced himself as the marquis Henri de la Falaise. He then presented his theater companion and new bride, whose world-famous face had just missed getting scraped by the shoe. To the relief of Jeanette and the management, Gloria Swanson and her third husband were all graciousness and smiles—a far cry from MacDonald's tangles with European and Hollywood aristocracy in the years to come.

Yes, Yes, Yvette shut down on Saturday, November 5, 1927. Two days later, MacDonald signed with the Shubert Theater Corporation, the nation's biggest and most powerful show-business empire. J. J. (Jacob) and Lee (Levi) Shubert, sons of an eastern European immigrant peddler, were as legendary for their dislike of each other as for earning millions by producing the tried, true, and trite. At the time they signed MacDonald, the notoriously stingy Shubert brothers owned or had extended leases on about 150 theaters throughout the country and controlled the booking of 750 more. Their personal relationship had become so nasty that Lee kept offices in the Sam S. Shubert Theater on the north side of West Forty-fourth Street, while J. J. moved to separate quarters across the street in the new Sardi Building, which the brothers had just built. To further reduce the frequency of their squabbles, a division of labor placed J. J. in charge of musicals and made Lee responsible for straight plays, or what his more philistine brother once called "lousy dramatic shows which nobody else wanted and nobody cared about." Against J. J.'s advice, Lee had recently produced Noël Coward's *Hay Fever* and J. M. Barrie's *What Every Woman Knows*—not quite Strindberg or O'Neill, but comedies several notches above the Shubert average.

Of the two brothers, MacDonald preferred Lee, the more polite and reserved scoundrel: "My association with J. J. was unpleasant, and I did not hesitate to tell him so, because I'm afraid I was not given to tactfulness or diplomacy in early youth. . . . However, Mr. Lee and I were good friends, [and] I would go to Mr. Lee with a little list of questions or complaints during my couple of years with the Shuberts. . . . Then he would try—I'm sure obviously with malice aforethought—to divert me by talking all around the subject I had come in about. But my little papers always brought me back on to the subject. Later on, he teased me about it and said . . . 'I always knew when the papers came out that I was going to be pulled right back onto the complaint again.' "

MacDonald's contract went to September 1, 1928, and gave the Shuberts an option for a nine-month renewal. It guaranteed her twenty-five weeks of work at $700 per week during the first term and $900 per week in the event of a second. She would appear only in new productions intended for New York City, not in revivals, nor in theaters west of St. Louis, and never in one-night stands. The contract granted MacDonald "featured artist" status, stipulating that should she appear in attractions with other featured artists, her name must always be printed in equal type size and, in the case of other *female* featured artists, always ahead of them. It also made clear that without the Shuberts' written consent she could not perform on radio or in motion pictures. Absorbed by the immediate reality of steady work and good income, MacDonald did not fully appreciate this last proviso, which was a preemptive tactic against Hollywood poachers of the rich Broadway talent within the Shubert stables: ". . . and should you attempt so to do we shall have the right to apply to any Court having competent jurisdiction for an injunction restraining your appearance, and you now agree that . . . your services are extraordinary and unique and that you cannot be replaced."

Strictly speaking, MacDonald was still not a genuine star. In Broadway parlance, a star was that rare player—a Marilyn Miller, Beatrice Lillie, or Fanny Brice—whose name consistently got placed above a show's title. To prevent nasty rivalry of the kind she herself had elicited from Cleo Mayfield in *Bubbling Over,* MacDonald executed a kind of preemptive strike of her own. The final clause of her Shubert contract originally read: "We agree to provide you with No. 1 dressing room unless some outstanding star shall be a member of the cast." In her own pen, and initialed in the margin by her and J. J. Shubert, she revised this to read, "We agree to provide you with No. 1 dressing room—ALONE."

Full of optimism, MacDonald rushed to Philadelphia's Chestnut Street Opera House to replace the weak soprano lead in tryouts of *The Studio Girl,* a quasi-operetta version of George Du Maurier's famous novel *Trilby.* Here at last was a part Jeanette could get excited about: a young concert singer who jump-starts her career thanks to the sinister, mesmerizing Svengali. The production, however, was a complete disaster. A *Variety* reporter wrote: "The cast is about as disappointing as the play, except for Jeannette [*sic*] MacDonald in the title role. With a much improved voice and a warmer personality, Miss MacDonald charms by her work . . . It wouldn't be a bad idea to keep Miss MacDonald and at least a part of the score and start all over to make a really good operetta out of *Trilby.* It could be done." The Shuberts disagreed. They folded the show three days later.

As Ginette Bertin, a Parisian flower-shop girl in *Sunny Days,* MacDonald finally headlined a moderately successful musical. The show's fourteen-week run at the Imperial Theater attracted the cream of New York society, from Mayor Jimmy Walker to Russian émigré Prince Alexis Obolensky (a basso cantante who occasionally gave recitals). A musicalization of the 1925 comedy *The Kiss in a Taxi* (which had future movie star Claudette Colbert as the romantic innocent), *Sunny Days'* galloping plot found MacDonald the object of lecherous schemes by a philandering middle-aged financier, and of tender wooing by a young, flamboyant novelist. It was a show that let MacDonald poke fun at her ingenue image in ways that forecast her early self-mocking Hollywood persona. Act 1 had a male chorus sing her praises as "Gin*ette,* the *pet* / of all the Rue de la Paix," only to have her coyly respond that these dancing boys would do better to cool off and think of her simply as a "pal." In act 2, Ginette teasingly conspired against those who placed her among the "loose language, lipstick, and lingerie" crowd, the better to expose in act 3 the "humbug, hot nights, and hypocrisy" of aging, cheating husbands.

Supervising this exuberant confection was Hassard Short, a producer-director whose technical trademarks—brightly colored sets, crisp, stunning costumes, sharp lighting effects—helped raise public enthusiasm for That Girl with the Red-gold Hair and Sea-green Eyes. Soon MacDonald's full-page portrait graced the *New Yorker* in soap ads carrying the caption: "*'I'm so glad to have Lux Toilet Soap. It keeps my skin* *petal smooth'*—JEANETTE MacDONALD." (Actually, MacDonald followed a self-devised complexion regimen that called for avoiding soap whenever possible and indulging in warm olive oil massages at bedtime.)*

The *New Yorker* photo makes clear what reviewers meant when they described MacDonald in *Sunny Days* as "beautiful," "easy on the eyes," and "command[ing] an orchidlike daintiness." Wearing a satin and tulle evening frock that heralds 1930s couture, MacDonald projects all-American freshness and modernity. Low-angle lighting, employed to soften her strong jaw, conceals the eloquence of her aquiline nose, which in the movies would help define MacDonald's patrician look. Here, spotlighting accentuates the broad oval of her face, with its spacious forehead, ample cheekbones, wide and lively eyes, and full, sensuous mouth. The parted, smiling lips disclose large, flawless teeth whose brilliant luster harmonizes with the impeccable smoothness of her complexion. Black-and-white photography unavoidably eclipses the sheen of her soft green eyes, which appeared blue at a distance, and her honey-copper tresses, which here are fixed to resemble a bob but which MacDonald in fact kept unfashionably (and girlishly) long.

Competing with such smash musicals as *Funny Face, Show Boat, Rosalie,* and *Good News, Sunny Days* quickly fell behind at the box office. To keep the show afloat, the Shuberts issued reduced-price tickets and slashed the salaries of the cast. In apprising MacDonald of her 20 percent wage cut, the management added, with a twist of the dagger: "We shall provide you with additional work above the guarantee of twenty-five weeks . . . until you have received an amount equal to the total amount of such deduction." Outraged, MacDonald put up a fight. She ordered her attorney, J. W. Ashley, to draft a letter to J. J. Shubert stating she'd be "very happy" to accommodate a salary drop on condition that at the end of her run with *Sunny Days* she receive "the amount of money that has been deducted" *without* a single day of extra, uncontracted work.

Three days later, J. J. agreed to MacDonald's demands. His acquiescence came less from magnanimity than from a wish to prevent Mac-

---

*Two pages later in the same *New Yorker* issue (May 19, 1928) is a second Lux ad, this time featuring singer Vivienne Segal, then appearing opposite Dennis King at the Lyric Theater in Rudolf Friml's *The Three Musketeers.* This is the earliest evidence of an overlap in the two women's professional lives. Segal, who grudgingly played a supporting role in MacDonald's 1934 film *The Cat and the Fiddle,* would later bitterly blame MacDonald for edging her out of the fuller celebrity she felt she merited.

Donald from initiating a breach-of-contract suit. Prodding him was an announcement in that week's *Billboard:*

> Jeanette MacDonald has been notified by Henry Russell, former director of the Boston Grand Opera House, the Théâtre des Champs Elysées, in Paris, and Covent Garden, in London, that he has procured an offer for her to sing with the opera in Monte Carlo and the Opéra-Comique in Paris upon the termination of her contract in *Sunny Days,* at the Imperial Theatre, New York. Russell is now trying to induce Miss MacDonald to begin work at once upon Italian and French direction and the vocal study of Mimì, Butterfly, and Manon.

Although nothing came of this overture, the Messrs. Shubert saw opera as a definite threat to their claims on MacDonald. Moreover, Paramount Pictures, Inc., in the person of rugged screen actor Richard Dix, had already begun to court the songbird.

Dix was scheduled to make his first talkie, *Nothing But the Truth,* from the same property that had inspired MacDonald's *Yes, Yes, Yvette.* Paramount chief B. P. Schulberg envisioned MacDonald as the ideal female lead, and Dix himself urged her to take a screen test. Jeanette was only mildly intrigued. She wasn't much of a movie fan, and she was still hopeful that her future lay with opera. She also knew that sound reproduction in current talkies was abysmal. When she showed up at Paramount's Astoria studios in Queens, however, she received star treatment. Her makeup was the best she had known. Her costume fit to perfection. And the cameraman was Dix's personal lighting expert, Eddie Kronjaeger. The results took MacDonald by surprise: "In the darkened projection room, I sat thinking, 'Oh, boy, I'm *beautiful!*' My morale soared. Singing in the test, I sounded as I usually did. But speaking, I had a voice surprisingly deep. Somehow I thought of Sophie Tucker. And my face, which to me was usually no more than okay, my face was absolutely gorgeous. I hugged myself with joy. Then I remembered what I owed to the cameraman."

Equally enthusiastic was B. P. Schulberg, who ordered contract negotiations to start immediately. But J. J. and Lee were hell-bent on keeping MacDonald under their sway. "Why should we help the movies when they are ruining us?" J. J. bluntly told her. On April 7, 1928, the Shuberts exercised their option and extended MacDonald's services through June 1, 1929. MacDonald accepted the Shuberts' obstructionism stoically—and with good reason. Time was on her side. Talkies were as yet unproved. Her readiness for opera was dubious.

Above all, she was unprepared to relinquish the financial stability her association with the Shubert organization guaranteed.*

Yet MacDonald did not remain set in her ways for long. A seductive, charismatic man who had just entered her life would cause her to revise her self-image radically.

It was the first Saturday in April 1928, and MacDonald had just made a splendid entrance down the red-carpeted staircase that plunged into the Ritz-Carlton's posh Crystal Room. The occasion was a Mayfair Club party. Designed by and for a glamorous clique of theatrical folk, the Mayfair Club parties reversed the usual protocol of New York's late-night social whirl by barring Astors and Vanderbilts except through invitation.

Suddenly a radiant man in his early thirties swaggered toward Jeanette's table with the self-assuredness of someone expecting to inherit the entire Ritz chain. His name was Robert George Ritchie, and he was a Wall Street representative for the New York investment firm of Cassatt & Company. Ritchie very much wanted to meet the honey-haired stunner whom his pal, Elliott Spurber, was squiring that night. Physically, Bob Ritchie was a riper version of Jack Ohmeis. He was tall, blond, and athletically built, but he had a tougher, more ruggedly chiseled demeanor. Jeanette found him tremendously appealing and promptly abandoned Spurber to spend the rest of the evening dancing with this debonair stranger. The following Monday, Ritchie made a surprise appearance at the Imperial's stage door. He encountered little resistance from *Sunny Days*' leading lady, and he managed to see Jeanette steadily during the remainder of that week. Soon he was the only man she dated.

Bob Ritchie claimed to be the son of a fallen millionaire. Born in Newark of English stock, he supposedly paid his way through Penn State by pushing a dockyard trolley car, traveling the seas on a cargo boat, and embarking on a screen-acting career that aborted when he played a love scene so ardently he caused the picture's female star to fracture a rib. It was true that Bob's father, James, had been a well-to-do Philadelphia stockbroker who lost his fortune through compulsive gambling. But Bob Ritchie neither matriculated at Penn State nor

---

*The Paramount screen test has not survived. *Nothing But the Truth* (1929), directed by future MacDonald collaborator Victor Schertzinger, was a hit, with Wynne Gibson playing opposite Dix and "boop-boop-a-doop" girl Helen Kane singing Bud Green and Sammy Stept's "Do Something."

played in a movie. After graduating from East Orange High School, where he was the football captain, he worked as a stevedore on the Edgewater, New Jersey, docks and then became a purser for the Grace Line. During World War I, he spent a year in France as a first sergeant in an engineering corps.

MacDonald was too cagey to be deceived by Ritchie's tall tales. But she liked the way he moved with equal ease among the old social registry, the new café society, and Broadway bigwigs. Ritchie, like Mayor Jimmy Walker, embodied the brash exhibitionism of 1920s New York City, where the line between ostentation and propriety had all but evaporated. A regular at the best speakeasies, he introduced Jeanette to the set then frequenting the Sutton Club, Ciro's, and the Mirador. When they didn't go nightclubbing, Jeanette visited Bob at the Murray Hill apartment he kept with his roommate, Steve Kroeger. For the first time in her life, MacDonald wanted to violate old rules: "I knew what I should be doing, but was irresistibly drawn to what I shouldn't be doing. I was ripe for anything, crawling farther and farther out on a precarious limb. One shake of the tree and I would have fallen all the way."

Jeanette's mother did not approve of Ritchie. She found him snobbish, reckless, and, at age thirty-two, too old for her daughter (who was then twenty-four but already pretending to be younger). Anna also saw Ritchie as a threat to her own influence. In the years following Daniel's death, Anna's bond with Jeanette intensified. Lyricist Irving Caesar, who casually dated MacDonald in these years, was convinced that she "never indulged in sex until she was married" because of Anna's ever-present shadow: "Once, after *Yes, Yes, Yvette* had opened in Atlantic City, I asked her for a date to go riding in one of those wheel chairs along the boardwalk. She accepted and we rented one chair—and her mother rented another and rode right beside us all night! Jeanette's mother *never left her side!* She was our chaperone, I guess. I had the feeling that Jeanette's mother watched over her too much. . . . [Jeanette] seemed a little afraid. She wouldn't let herself go."

With Ritchie, Jeanette became liberated: "I didn't think my Mother an old fogy, but I did think some of her ideas were too narrow. If this intrigue made me feel so deliciously good, could it be all bad? And if a little bit of wrong-doing was so pleasant, wouldn't more of it be the ultimate?" Crossing her mother's wishes made Jeanette feel deceitful. She was also vaguely disappointed with herself. MacDonald had come to take pride in her conviction that the best way for men and women to relate was through staunch friendships free of emotional entanglement. Now she was racing pell-mell into a sizzling love affair—and thoroughly enjoying the sensation.

Like Mozart's *Don Giovanni*, Bob Ritchie kept a record of the many women he bedded. ("Girls get Itchy / Watching Bob Ritchie," an admiring, envious friend once wrote in his honor.) Ritchie's scorecard shows that he first slept with MacDonald on April 7, 1928, and that there were forty repeats in the course of their seven-year relationship. If his list of names and figures is to be trusted, Ritchie made love to over four hundred different women between 1927 and 1960, including Grace Moore, Hedy Lamarr, Dorothy Lamour, Zsa Zsa and Eva Gabor, Greer Garson, and Nanette Fabray. After World War II, when he was a regular at El Morocco, it was said in the gossip columns that no young lady could make her way among New York café society without first dating the silver-red wolf, Bob Ritchie.

In early October, MacDonald was in Boston for tryouts of her next show, tentatively called *The Queen's Taste*. One Thursday, the morning mail brought a letter:

> Dear Shorty,
>
> By the time you read this, I shall be married. [Gertrude Laird] and I have been engaged for some time. I was engaged to her when I met you, and I have a moral obligation to her. I cannot let her down. She does not know, and she will never know as far as I am concerned, but I hope one day you and she will be able to meet. . . . I want you to know that I shall always adore you.
>
> Bob

In a daze, MacDonald left her hotel and wandered for hours amid the little streets of Beacon Hill and the tree-lined lanes of Boston Common. She felt abused and foolish. Her thoughts raced back to Arch Street and the boy who had seduced and abandoned Elsie. By the time she returned to the Statler Hotel, tears and self-pity had given way to anger. Anna had been right. Bob Ritchie lacked character. He was cruel in his deceit and cowardly for revealing the truth by letter rather than in person. So much the worse for him.

MacDonald performed that night without a trace of her private turmoil. When *Angela* (the new title of *The Queen's Taste*) opened three weeks later at New York's Ambassador Theater, her singing voice was stronger than ever, her line readings were wickedly sharp, and she outdanced the featured hoofer, Peggy Cornell. The show, however, was a quick flop. Chummy first-nighters wildly applauded, but the next day only a dedicated few remained to the end. After Jeanette took her final bow on that second night, she walked to the wings and then froze. There stood Bob with a sheepish smile. Showing no emotion, Jeanette allowed him into her dressing room.

Bob explained that his marriage was being annulled and that he wanted to renew his relationship with Jeanette. No apologies. No remorse. Only an affirmation. Jeanette could feel the hormones clobbering her reason: "Although I could never really forgive him, nor could I ever feel that I would trust him totally, I felt drawn to him once more." She consented to see him again, and she believed in the sincerity of his wish to marry her once his annulment became final. But MacDonald had, as she later put it, "a very feminine desire to get even." On Christmas Eve, Ritchie formally proposed marriage. With avenging pleasure, MacDonald declined: "I could see the hurt look in his eyes, the astonishment of the wounded animal, and I had my moment of getting even and I relished it for an instant, tasted the victory, and then felt absolutely miserable. . . . I cried because we were really in love, but not the kind of love that makes any sense."

In the first play of what was to be a prolonged and often confounding game of hardball sexual politics, MacDonald redefined their friendship on her terms. Ritchie, she told herself, was a Wall Street insider; he had great social savvy; his ambition was as immense as hers. Why not let him become her personal business manager? "Oddly enough," she admitted, "while I hadn't married him because of shaken faith in him, in the matter of money I completely trusted him." Handed an offer that lent new hope to his designs, both amorous and pecuniary, Bob readily accepted.

Ritchie and MacDonald had diverging views on the best course for her career. He saw her future in movies. She was committed to the musical stage. Both agreed that her contract with the Shuberts was not to be renegotiated, for it was obvious that MacDonald's notices were improving in inverse proportion to the quality of her vehicles. *Angela* was a case in point. Overwhelmingly, critics concurred with the *Brooklyn Standard Union* that MacDonald deserved the "unchallenged title" of "prima donna" of "fair princesses" (the plot burlesqued the affairs of Queen Marie of Romania). But they also echoed the *Daily News* in citing her as the "redeeming feature" of an otherwise dreadful show. *Angela* played only three weeks at the Ambassador. Then, to encourage theater parties at discount prices, the Shuberts moved the show to their huge Century Theater on Central Park West. This ploy failed, and two weeks later, on January 5, 1929, *Angela* closed shop.

Broadway was slipping. After years of new theater construction, the number of profit-making attractions to fill the city's houses was in steep decline. Production costs were soaring, and ticket distribution was in disarray. Glorious cross-country tours were a thing of the past. Above all, no Broadway producer had the finances to compete with the movie corporations in outfitting a quality production, especially a musical. In one of his first deeds as her manager, Ritchie convinced MacDonald to make a second screen test, this time for Fox Film Corporation.

The test was a duo affair. It had Jeanette going through a song-and-dance routine with Archie Leach, a handsome, dark-haired Britisher then playing the heavy in her new Shubert show, *Boom-Boom*. MacDonald never saw the footage, but she learned that Fox was unimpressed by both her and Leach. "Thank you," studio representatives wrote back, "but we feel neither of these people has a screen personality." Leach later made a test for Paramount with better results: offered a contract, he moved to the West Coast and made a name for himself as Cary Grant.

In spite of Ritchie's clear-sightedness, the fizzle with Fox strengthened MacDonald's conviction that her best future remained with the stage. Aching to be signed by class producers like Arthur Hammerstein or Alex Aarons and Vinton Freedley, she was desperate to find quick ways to break her Shubert contract. *Boom-Boom* offered several opportunities.

From the moment she was assigned to replace Ann Seymour in *Boom-Boom*'s Newark tryouts, MacDonald's disenchantment redoubled. To start with, she found the book atrocious. Its outlandish Oedipal plot had her inadvertently married to and then divorced from her boyfriend's sex-crazed father. It was the kind of show that gave tired businessmen a nonstop barrage of lame jokes about buxom blondes, French postcards, men's pajamas, strip poker, and making "boom-boom" (a kind of foreplay to "whoopee"). A blackface comedian named, oddly enough, Eddie Nelson had lines like, "Yessah—I likes my girls light—because when I gives them a black eye—I likes to see it!" The show's uninspired score was essentially a string of noisy upbeat dance numbers that denied MacDonald even one vocal solo. Her only interesting musical moment sped by in a brief prologue duet with her leading man. MacDonald found this unacceptable, since her one other duet was the moronic "Nina," a mock-romantic Spanish serenade performed with Archie Leach/Cary Grant in homage to a "Spanish *Queen*," hot as a "Chili *bean*," who doesn't say much with her "*lips*," but "oh, what a language she speaks with her *hips*." After wiggling her torso, MacDonald intoned: "From toes to her *forehead* / This bimbo was *torrid* / I mean this tamale was *hot*"; and Leach responded: "She kissed with such *pash* / That she'd scorch your mous*tache* / And that's hot enough, is it *not*?"

Such material was not going to further MacDonald's goal of Broadway superstardom. In protest, she rushed to the Sardi Building to make her case for being dropped from *Boom-Boom*—and, she hoped, from her contract. For a quarter hour MacDonald harangued J. J. Shubert, trying to balance outrage with civility. Unimpressed, the mogul dismissed her arguments with the patronizing old saw, "Most actors and actresses don't know *what* they ought to do anyway!" Shubert could not have struck a more sensitive nerve. Inflamed and resentful, MacDonald sprang to her feet, looked the little man in the eye, and lashed out: "This is the rottenest show I've ever been in and I know it will flop! If you paid more attention to your actors and believed in *them* more, maybe you wouldn't have so many flops! *Goodnight!*"

A second opportunity to sever her contract stemmed from a managerial oversight. When she arrived for her first tryout performance in Newark, MacDonald found that Ann Seymour's name, not hers, was still on the marquee and the printed playbill. She immediately phoned her attorney, Dudley Field Malone, who advised that she could refuse to perform, since her contract clearly stipulated featured billing; moreover, if the Shuberts replaced her with an understudy while she remained on the premises, the management would be in breach of contract. Within minutes, J. J., just recovered from a heart attack, phoned from Atlantic City, screaming hysterically: "If you don't open tonight, I'll ruin you! I'll run you out of the business!" MacDonald refused to budge from her dressing room. A few minutes later, the phone rang again. It was Frank Gilmore, president of Actors' Equity. Gilmore asked MacDonald not to deprive her fellow actors of work. He said that if she felt there was breach of contract, he would swiftly appoint an arbitrator. Once the management reset the marquee, MacDonald went on. But the incident ushered in a perception that would remain with her for life. The first-page headline of Tuesday's *Newark Ledger* read: "INDIGNANT STAR HALTS SHOW—AUDIENCE WAITS HALF HOUR."

Beneath her picture was the inevitable caption: "Jeanette MacDonald, musical comedy star, has red hair and that means temperament."*

MacDonald's prediction proved right. *Boom-Boom* flopped. Even with cut-rate tickets, the show could not sustain more than a nine-week New York run. Opening night had garnered extra publicity when, twenty minutes into the show, MacDonald's love duet was brought to a halt by the late arrival of Captain George Fried and the lifeboat crew of the S.S. *America,* heroes of the hour who had just rescued thirty-two men from the storm-tossed Italian freighter *Florida.* In a communal display of patriotism, MacDonald led the house in singing "The Star-spangled Banner." At intermission, many in the audience were heard to quip that the rescue of *Boom-Boom* would really have put the good sailors to the test. As usual, MacDonald rose above lousy material. The *Wall Street Journal* wrote the next morning: "Jeanette MacDonald in her quiet way again proves herself one of the most attractive and gifted young women in musical comedy."

April 1929 found MacDonald touring cheerlessly with *Boom-Boom* in Pittsburgh, Cincinnati, and Detroit. By month's end, the show was set for a run in Chicago, with four weeks at the Apollo and then two at the Grand Opera House. After checking in at the Hotel Ambassador, MacDonald went immediately to her eighth-floor room. Seated at the writing table, she penned a letter that made her purr with delight:

> April 29, 1929
>
> Mr. J. J. Shubert
> Sardi Building
> New York, NY
>
> Dear Mr. Shubert,
>
> Please take notice that I am exercising the rights of my contract, which expires May 30, 1929, in terminating my engagement in *Boom-Boom* on that date. This will give you ample time to replace me.
>
> Yours truly,
> Jeanette MacDonald

*As a result of the flare-up, J. J. Shubert never again spoke to MacDonald. A few years later, when she was an international film star and the American stage was foundering, a business associate urged J. J. to mount a new show for MacDonald at the newly constructed Saint Louis Municipal Auditorium. Her name, it was argued, would guarantee a full house at top prices. Unwilling to forget their past skirmishes, J. J. put vindictiveness above profits. The stage producer John Kenley told me that J. J. growled: "No, I don't want her! She's always constipated. I remember her always going from room to room backstage and asking the girls for Ex-Lax!" (interview with Kenley on March 12, 1991).

Apprehension dampened MacDonald's joy. She had no firm offers for the next Broadway season, and she worried that her association with the Shuberts had irreparably tainted her image in the eyes of the more prestigious producers. Several days later, Bob Ritchie phoned from New York with news he hoped would quiet her anxieties. She recalled his saying: "You're going to be invited to have breakfast next Sunday morning to meet Ernst Lubitsch. He's stopping off for an hour or so on his way back to Hollywood. He wants to talk to you about playing opposite Maurice Chevalier. It seems when he saw your test with Richard Dix, he said, 'That's the girl!' "

MacDonald looked forward to her breakfast with the famous movie director more with curiosity than with high hopes. She vaguely imagined what might result if all went well, but she kept telling herself she was too levelheaded to invest in sand castles. She certainly had no inkling that *Boom-Boom* had already marked her farewell to the Broadway stage. A ten-year veteran at age twenty-five, Jeanette Mac-Donald would never again play the Great White Way—except in motion pictures.

PART TWO

Lingerie Queen of the Talkies

CHAPTER FIVE

Lubitsch and Chevalier

In the days of the silents, face and figure were practically the only essentials to screen success. But the girl who looks like a Madonna and talks like a moron hasn't a chance these days.

ERNST LUBITSCH, 1932

I have no voice.

MAURICE CHEVALIER, 1931, when asked
if he was a baritone

THE HEAD CONCIERGE at Chicago's Blackstone Hotel escorted MacDonald to the intimate French Room. The German-born director sprang to his feet, yanked from his mouth a signature Havana cigar, and gallantly kissed the soprano's hand. Short and stocky, with dark, glinting eyes and coal black hair, Ernst Lubitsch spoke a confident but heavily accented English. His manner, more roguish than royal, made Jeanette feel she was about to have breakfast with a Jewish court jester.

Lubitsch flattered MacDonald by repeating what she already knew from Bob Ritchie. After scouring Broadway in search of a new female voice to sing opposite Maurice Chevalier, Lubitsch had wailed to Paramount's East Coast officials: "Show me some old tests *und* then *mein Kopf* I'll blow off!" Jeanette's, the twentieth he saw, caused him to cry out, "Stop! I have found the queen!" Herr Lubitsch lurched back and forth from their table to act out snippets of *The Love Parade,* whose story he and librettist Guy Bolton had just finished outlining in New York. MacDonald, he explained, would be the husband-seeking ruler of Sylvania, a mythic European queendom. Chevalier would play a womanizing count she elevates to prince consort and royal stud. Lillian Roth, the New York "blues" singer from the *Earl Carroll Vanities,* would get the comic maid role. Chevalier's valet would be British music-haller Lupino Lane. Lubricating his throat with coffee, Lubitsch then went through the songs that Victor Schertzinger and Clifford Grey had written for the film. Quite the mimic, he delivered Chevalier's couplets with Gallic bounce and chirped the queen's numbers in a fluttery falsetto.

MacDonald was in stitches as Lubitsch quietly resumed eating. He looked more like a pubescent schoolboy than an internationally acclaimed master of sophisticated film comedy. A self-taught pianist, Lubitsch confessed that his fondest dream as a youth in Berlin was to become a popular band leader. If Jeanette accepted Paramount's offer, he hoped his leading lady would listen to the songs he recently composed. Jeanette was totally won over. For two years the humorless J. J. Shubert had miscast and mistreated her. Now a major creative talent was urgently wooing her.

By breakfast's end, MacDonald had made a verbal agreement to appear in *The Love Parade.* Yet Jeanette had one serious concern: she knew nothing about movies. As they walked through the lobby, Lubitsch held her hand and told her not to worry, that he would be her mentor. But climbing into the taxi that would shuttle him back to Union Station, the director looked up at her and admitted that he, too, had a concern: "*Meine Liebling,* you are much too thin. Before we shoot, gain at least ten pounds!"

MacDonald's enthusiasm for Lubitsch was mighty enough to quell some of her doubts about movies. She also kept in mind the truism, nicely worded by humorist Robert Benchley, that "the only difference between working in Hollywood and working elsewhere is that you are getting a great deal more money for it in Hollywood." She therefore instructed Bob Ritchie to hammer out a contract with Paramount's New York representative Henry Salisbury, reminding Bob that her own financial goal was to pile up $100,000 in savings. Amid a flurry of last-minute counterinitiatives from Metro-Goldwyn-Mayer, Ritchie secured for MacDonald a contract that guaranteed her a weekly salary of $2,500 for *The Love Parade* and gave Paramount the option for a second picture.

While these arrangements were taking place, MacDonald made a brief pilgrimage to Dr. Rheinle's Sanitarium and Milk Farm and foolishly began "chewing" eight quarts of milk per day. Weight gain, however, was not in the stars. A raging case of colitis caused Jeanette to lose as many pounds as Lubitsch wanted her to put on. Physically depleted and emotionally drained, she returned to Manhattan and packed for the cross-country rail trip.

In spite of Anna's unflagging care, Jeanette's outlook was grim that first week in June: "Never in my life did I feel so depressed as the day we left for Los Angeles. Bob saw us off. I was deathly scared, my digestion was revolving like a carousel, and my hay fever was in full bloom. I was entering a new life with nobody to depend on except my wonderful, woefully inexperienced Mother. I was walking like a lamb into an industry allegedly full of wolves. As the train rumbled through the tunnel out of Grand Central, I collapsed from sheer nervous excitement and hysteria. I wept for hours."

Four days of continually applied ice packs did little to relieve MacDonald's puffy face and allergies. When the transcontinental ordeal terminated in Pasadena, Paramount publicity staff rushed into the MacDonalds' compartment, pointed to a small crowd of reporters awaiting them, and furnished a crash course on movie-colony press etiquette. Followed by Anna, Jeanette descended to the platform and for two frantic minutes managed to project the requisite charm, chic, and composure. Journalists fired queries. Newsreel cameras rolled. Still photographers shot away. Jeanette and Anna were then hustled into a limousine that sped toward Hollywood and the Ambassador Hotel.

No sooner had they signed the register than the chauffeur whisked Jeanette off, this time to Paramount's main administration building on Marathon Street, where she was introduced in an assembly-line manner to studio head B. P. Schulberg, a handful of his associates, and a cluster of chief technicians. Just as swiftly she found herself redeposited at the Ambassador, in a suite that looked and smelled like a flower show: "The wonder is that I wasn't immediately hospitalized and put on the critical list with hay fever." Vexed by the impersonal treatment accorded her, Jeanette consoled herself with one thought: she had kept the lease on her New York apartment.

On Broadway, MacDonald had been a favorite among reporters who covered the city's entertainment beat. In Hollywood, she almost instantaneously alienated Louella Parsons, the gossip columnist for the Hearst newspaper chain and a notorious reputation ripper. Parsons's animosity took root at a party thrown by Lubitsch at his Beverly Hills home soon after MacDonald's arrival. "Right and left that night," Jeanette explained, "I offended some of the movies' mightiest names simply because I'd never heard of them. I'd be introduced, I'd smile pleasantly, I'd give no sign whatever of being impressed. The trouble was I wasn't a movie fan. I didn't recognize these celebrities any more than I recognized the hired help at the Lubitsch home." On the heels of the buffet dinner came an impromptu musicale by Carmel Myers, a fading silent screen vamp who would resurface briefly in the early days of television. While Myers sang a few songs in the music room, accompanying herself on a ukulele, MacDonald and some others remained in the dining area. Parsons misconstrued MacDonald's absence as a willful show of condescension by an East Coast culture snob. Always one to hold a grudge, Louella spent the next seven years zestfully slashing her.

Hostilities escalated a few years later when Parsons wanted MacDonald to appear on her weekly radio program, *Hollywood Hotel*. Jeanette made the unheard-of demand that she be paid her usual fee. It was absurd, she felt, to work for free simply to ingratiate herself with a woman she regarded as coarse and shallow. A showdown took place at the wedding reception for Ginger Rogers and Lew Ayres. Amid a crowd of merry guests, Louella walked up to Jeanette, glared, and spat: "I think you're a bitch." Silence chilled the room. "Thank you, Louella," Jeanette cooed sweetly. "May I say that the thought is mutual?"

During her first months in Tinseltown, MacDonald also had a bizarre run-in with Hedda Hopper, the actress who would later co-rule the L.A. gossip coop with Parsons. One Sunday afternoon, Jesse Lasky, the creative impulse behind Paramount Pictures, had a big gathering at his oceanfront house in Santa Monica. MacDonald sat poolside, chatting, when all of a sudden Hopper walked up to her, unintroduced, and proceeded to bury her hands in Jeanette's hair, pulling two adjacent clumps in opposite directions. "I want to see if you're a natural redhead," she stated curtly and then strutted away. MacDonald was aghast until someone explained that Hedda "detested phonies" and was simply "checking" her out. Word soon spread that Lubitsch's canary had passed Hopper's color test.

MacDonald quickly grasped her paradoxical status in Hollywood. On one hand, she had landed a leading role opposite a major star at a prestige studio. Such good luck inevitably provoked jealousy in the City of Angels. Moreover, Jeanette belonged to that roster of so-called legitimate New York actors who, with the advent of talkies, were displacing great silent stars such as Pola Negri and John Gilbert. These screen legends—as well as their fervid supporters, like Louella Parsons and Hedda Hopper—viewed Jeanette MacDonald and her kind as opportunists and arrivistes. On the other hand, compared with many Broadway transplants—Fanny Brice, Sophie Tucker, George Jessel, Will Rogers—MacDonald had yet to prove her mettle on a truly national scale. Adolph Zukor, Paramount's cofounder with Lasky, often said that a movie star was not so much a famous player as an engaging personality. In the summer of 1929, MacDonald was known to the general public as neither. Poised between screen glory and oblivion, her future was riding on the fate of a motion picture that had yet to be made, that would not be released until a half year later, and that was designed for Maurice Chevalier, an established international star.

Hollywood's rituals of welcome made MacDonald see one basic truth: if she was going to be perceived as a prima donna in this land of make-believe, she would have to start acting like one. Accordingly, just days after settling in, she vacated her suite at the Ambassador, close to the studio, and moved westward to the Beverly Wilshire Hotel—more remote, more chichi, and in the heart of Beverly Hills.

MacDonald could not have chosen a riper moment to enter motion pictures. Only in 1929 did the talkies really begin to talk—and sing—to much of America. By the year's end, nearly half of the country's twenty thousand movie houses were wired for sound. After Warner Bros., the pioneer of sound movies, showed a staggering 745 percent increase in annual earnings, all the other major studios hopped on the bandwagon to wipe out silents. When Wall Street collapsed in October, film corporations were among the least affected. That year, the movie industry employed more people than General Motors or Ford; its capital investments exceeded $2.5 billion; and attendance at picture shows reached an all-time high. Nine out of ten Americans were going to the movies at least once a week.

Home to Erich von Stroheim, Ernst Lubitsch, and Josef von Sternberg, Paramount was the most Continental of studios and the leader in worldwide film distribution. Faithful to its early slogan, "If It's a Paramount Picture, It's the Best Show in Town," the company took pride in the elegance, inventiveness, and visual dazzle of its product. It granted gifted émigré directors more artistic control than did Warner Bros., essentially a writers' studio, or MGM, where producers had the ultimate say. With the shift to talkies, it lured name stage entertainers like

Chevalier, the Marx Brothers, Gertrude Lawrence, Walter Huston, and Claudette Colbert. Paramount also hired outstanding composers, lyricists, and musical arrangers for its two music departments in Hollywood and Astoria. Predicting that movies would soon spawn most of the nation's song hits, the company bought a 50 percent interest in the Columbia Broadcasting System and founded Famous Music Corporation, its own sheet-music publishing company. Self-congratulation notwithstanding, no other studio could make the claim boasted in *Variety* on August 7, 1929: "Paramount touches the lives of more people in the world—and more intimately—than any other commercial activity under one management."

To offset the expense and risk of polished pictures, Paramount produced its share of potboilers. But Jeanette MacDonald was to have little part in these. Handpicked by the master of sophisticated farce for his first talking picture, MacDonald was slated to debut in the classiest and most expensive of Paramount's releases for 1929–30. The first romantic operetta written specifically for the screen, *The Love Parade* carried a projected cost of $650,000, outstripping *The Cocoanuts* (the Marx Brothers comedy adapted from Broadway at a cost of $500,000) and *The Virginian* (the Gary Cooper and Walter Huston western, budgeted at $425,000). Paramount was counting on Lubitsch not only to restore the visual grace and vitality that had been taken from movies by the bulky, immobile sound camera, but also to offer an alternative to backstage musicals, those awkward films in which music, lyrics, and dance had virtually nothing to do with action and character.

Her first days on the set infused MacDonald with awe for Lubitsch's painstaking craftsmanship: "When he directed, he acted out every scene, every character. No one could be more intense. You were drilled and re-drilled until you spoke every line, handled every bit of business the way he wanted it. If you laid a piece of paper on a table, you placed it precisely where he told you to. If you crossed a room, you walked his way. He would squat or stoop right under the camera, playing out motion by motion the scene he was directing." Intent on learning the trade, Jeanette barely noticed that the thirty-seven-year-old *Meister* began to take more than a professional fancy to her: "There were no outward signs, at least to me. Lubitsch was a perfectionist, a pixie-devil, a kind-hearted tyrant on the set. I respected him, I was grateful to him, but I didn't 'yes' him. Sometimes the set seemed like a convention of 'yes' men. I never 'yessed' anybody. I was even impertinent. It amused him and intrigued him, and, as I learned later, it attracted him irresistibly. . . . He couldn't figure me out, although it seemed I was a jigsaw puzzle he wanted to put together, and possibly take home."

In the art of ribbing, Lubitsch found a match in his new discovery. One famous prank occurred soon after shooting began. On the backs of the familiar canvas chairs were stenciled the names MR. LUBITSCH, MR. CHEVALIER, and MISS MACDONALD. Because Lubitsch overheard Jeanette say she hated the nickname "Mac," he decided one evening to have her chair relettered, erasing everything but the prefix. When Mac-Donald arrived the next morning, Lubitsch hovered with the expectancy of a jokester who has just handed someone a loaded cigar. Jeanette saw his trick right away but said nothing. Ernst was in agony. He circled around until he could stand it no longer. "You notice your chair?" he asked. "Why no," she replied calmly, "should I?" MacDonald sat down, and Lubitsch looked terribly deflated. As the day went on, Jeanette pondered how best to hoist him on his own petard. At five o'clock, she summoned a prop man and made a request of her own. The following day Lubitsch arrived to find that his chair, too, had been altered. In ever so tiny print it read "Lu," and in giant-sized letters: BITSCH. Faking fury, he rushed over to Jeanette, his arms aflutter, and yelled, "You, you are a bitch yourself!" From then on, MacDonald always called the director "Lu," and he seemed to like it fine.

On another occasion, Lubitsch was in MacDonald's dressing room discussing her lines when he suddenly asked, "Is it true that you're a virgin?" MacDonald looked him straight in the eye and answered, "Mr. Lubitsch, that's none of your business." "I know that, but the word is around that you *are* a virgin." "Who's going to disprove it?" Jeanette replied. "Not me!" retorted Lubitsch, "I wouldn't touch you with a ten-foot pole." Insulted by his attitude more than his remarks, MacDonald was not going to let Lubitsch have the final word: "Let me ask *you* something. When you married your wife, was she a virgin?" Lubitsch stared, flushed, and left the room. "I didn't know then," Mac-Donald later recalled, "that the current Mrs. Lubitsch, blonde and most attractive, had been married before."

MacDonald was a long way from being as self-possessed as she tried to appear. One scene required her character to enter through a door, close it behind her, lean against the frame, and sing a tearful reprise of the ballad "Dream Lover," supposedly after having just quarreled with her consort. The major complication was MacDonald's costume, a fitted silver lamé gown with three trains, one on each side and one at the back. Getting herself and her dress gracefully through the doorway was difficult enough. But maneuvering the trains clear as she shut the door was next to impossible. MacDonald made her entrance ten times and flubbed each try. Either one of the trains got caught in the door, or her foot got tangled in her skirt, or there were problems with the sound or camera. After eleven fumbled takes, her fuse blew: "I stood there berserk, stamping on my dress, tugging at the trains in blind rage. The string of pearls I was wearing promptly snapped, and I went down on my hands and knees to pick them up, crawling around the floor like a lunatic. . . . 'I cannot do this scene!' I howled. 'These damn trains are driving me crazy!' "*

When Lubitsch reproached her for being temperamental, MacDonald dared *him* to do it. She stormed into a trailer, slammed the door, and seconds later tossed the gown onto the dusty studio floor. Twenty minutes later, Lubitsch appeared on the set bedecked in lamé, his lips still clenching a burning cigar. The gown was too long and tight for him, but he enacted the scene with utmost dignity. MacDonald remembered: "He handled the dress as gracefully as any prima donna, like a lady to the manner born. I could never figure how." Not one to be outdone, especially by a mock-transvestite, MacDonald got back into the costume, had her makeup retouched, and succeeded on the very next try.

Still hoping to fatten up his queen, Lubitsch ordered malted milk shakes from the commissary every hour. Because dairy products adversely affected her vocal chords, MacDonald would drink the shakes only on days when she didn't have to sing before the camera. Still, she imbibed enough to keep her weight mounting and to drive costume designer Travis Banton haywire. Banton, who favored the pencil-slim look over Lubitsch's zaftig feminine ideal, was exasperated by the constant ripping and letting out of MacDonald's frocks. He soon placed a standing order with the wardrobe department to sew extra-wide emergency seams into all of Miss MacDonald's clothes.

MacDonald and Lubitsch's shared sense of fun extended beyond the studio. One evening Ernst gave a small dinner party to introduce Jeanette to Greta Garbo. In cahoots with her host, MacDonald pretended to be hard of hearing. "What name?" she asked. Lubitsch loudly restated, "GARBO!" "Garvin?" MacDonald queried, rather un-

---

*Unknown to MacDonald, Lubitsch kept the camera rolling. While viewing rushes the next morning, he showed her the footage to prove her capacity for mustering the "fire" that he felt was lacking in her first few days' work. When you watch the film again, note that the shot of MacDonald's entrance through the door was edited out of the release cut; the scene begins with MacDonald leaning against the door, her back to the camera.

believably. The Swede responded politely, "It's a pleasant evening." "Oh, tennis?" answered Jeanette, "I adore it." Garbo repeated, "I said it's a PLEASANT—" MacDonald inspected her plate and replied, "Really? I thought it was CHICKEN." Lubitsch signaled to Garbo by touching his ear and murmured, "Poor girl!" Garbo whispered to Lubitsch: "But how can she sing when she can't even hear?" "Well, it's like this," MacDonald responded to the muttering from across the table, "I just open my mouth—"

Perhaps on account of MacDonald's prank, she and the silent Swede never clicked. At later parties, Jeanette felt slighted by both Garbo and her intimate female friend, the screenwriter Salka Viertel: "They would get in the corner, and I know they used to tell jokes in German which I couldn't understand. But by their raucous laughter I knew it was a good hot story and I felt a little excluded. It was a little silly, I thought, but it was indicative of her peculiar anti-social attitude."

When she later moved to MGM, MacDonald would have a dressing suite in a complex that housed the studio's other top female stars. MacDonald occupied the first floor, with Norma Shearer and Jean Harlow; Myrna Loy, Joan Crawford, and Garbo were on the second. One morning, MacDonald and Garbo were both due to report to their respective sets at nine o'clock. Just as Jeanette opened her door, she saw the Pallid One descending the staircase. Their eyes met, and Garbo suddenly turned and rushed back to her dressing room. She then sent her maid down to make sure that the smiling American would be gone when she reappeared. Riled by such uncalled-for guardedness, MacDonald informed the maid: "Please send word back to Miss Garbo that I am no more interested in her than she is in me, and to please come down without any worry, as I am not going to stare or snap pictures or even look!"

At MGM, MacDonald would become very friendly with Harlow and Shearer. In these early Hollywood years, she established close rapport with Irene Dunne, Ginger Rogers, and Fay Wray. She also became a good friend of silent screen sweetheart Mary Pickford, who arranged a live sneak preview of *The Love Parade*'s songs to cap a formal dinner party at Pickfair, her twenty-two-room Tudor-style mansion. Yet, as in New York, MacDonald's strongest female friendship was with her voice teacher, Grace Adele Newell. Coaxed west by MacDonald, Grace fell in love with southern California, especially its racetracks. She would later ascribe her longevity to daily walks between her Castle Argyle apartment and her studio on Highland Avenue, a renovated garage crammed with antiques and encircled, as if in defiance of Jeanette's allergies, by an overgrown rose garden.

Newell advised MacDonald to shoot *The Love Parade*'s music scenes in midafternoon, when her "vitalization" level would be at its peak. Audio engineers were not yet certain how best to handle the higher frequencies of the soprano voice. Still, Paramount's sound department predicted that MacDonald, perhaps because of the lightness of her singing, would be extremely "microphonic." Jeanette herself was more worried about looking ugly while singing on-screen. She spent long nights that June and July rehearsing her numbers within eyeshot of oddly positioned mirrors specially installed throughout her Beverly Wilshire suite, including the bedroom. Boudoirs, after all, were about to become MacDonald's concert halls, courtesy of Mr. Lubitsch.

The Love Parade's delectable virgin monarch first appears in lacy, low-cut lingerie with a ruffled satin pillow supporting her queenly head. After two sensuous sighs, MacDonald speaks her first words on-screen: "Why am I always awakened from my dreams?" Before rolling over to clutch the pillow that substitutes for a lover, she caresses her bare right shoulder, throat, and forearm. Violins flutter, and she props herself up, the shape of her breasts now clearly exposed. When the ceremonious matron-in-waiting expresses a hope that the royal dream might come true, the queen responds with skepticism: "No, I'm afraid it will always have to remain a dream." She then sings the verse to "Dream Lover," confiding her longing for a mate from the land of Sweet Romance.

Effortlessly and luxuriously, MacDonald stretches, steps out of bed, and slithers into the sheerest of peignoirs. On the refrain's final prolonged high note, with slight self-mocking vampishness she heads out to an extravagant bathroom of the kind only Lubitsch could decree.* In a medium-long mirror shot she fully disrobes, although four maids discreetly conceal her from our view. Inserted within the deep sunken tub, she assumes the form of Naked Truth posed teasingly in a well. Decorum demands that she deny requests from her retinue for greater explicitness about her dream. With a touch of embarrassment, she concedes that hers is not a "dream for a queen." Yet its meaning is all too obvious. The mateless sovereign of Sylvania is frustrated, and she doesn't quite know what to do about it.

---

*Look for its prototype in the bath scene of Lubitsch's dazzling 1919 German comedy, *The Oyster Princess*.

This is quintessential early MacDonald as inflected by Lubitsch. The scene's decor and acting style, its cinematic and musical direction, could not be more contrived. Yet the artifice is so all-embracing, so passionately executed, that it somehow enhances our identification with the character's feelings and conflicts. Not unlike heroines of classic stage tragedies (of the kind Lubitsch studied and performed in Berlin with director Max Reinhardt), MacDonald's queen is torn between patriotic duty and erotic desire. Consigned to the most ludicrous of comic realms—a fairy-tale operetta kingdom—MacDonald might have played for burlesque triviality or overemphatic sentimentality. Instead, she projects the freshness and earnestness of a modern American woman. For all the surface absurdity of Queen Louise, MacDonald creates a young, independent female searching to reconcile social convention and sex.

Advance publicity made much of *The Love Parade*'s sexual boldness. MacDonald was heralded as Hollywood's answer to Anna Held, the European glamour legend who inspired Ziegfeld to create his eye-popping, beauty-laden *Follies*. It was also claimed that MacDonald's marble and onyx bathroom scene would "outdo Cecil B. DeMille" in sensual opulence. *Variety* spotlighted her wedding-night negligee of baby blue tulle sprinkled with silver stars, describing it as "fragile, fluttery, and every inch a stage queen's." During these Paramount years, MacDonald would sing so many songs in underwear and dressing gowns that music industry insiders soon called her "the boudoir warbler."*

Today, *The Love Parade* astonishes less for raciness than for technical innovation. "Dream Lover"'s reprise, occurring just after the count first kisses the queen, is a superlative instance of Lubitsch inventing fluid and harmonious sound pictures. The scene begins with strains of the waltz as sung by MacDonald, seated alone at a piano behind closed doors. While she sings, Lubitsch's camera gracefully pans the palace garden to disclose sweethearts who dreamily overhear the queen's vocalizing. A complete chorus follows, with MacDonald's soprano alternating and then combining with the courtiers' voices—all accompanied

---

*The film's bath scene, risqué dialogue, and various states of undress caused many self-appointed guardians of public gentility to growl. Pedro J. Lemos, editor of Stanford University's *School Arts Magazine,* solicited protests from citizens in Palo Alto. One of his respondents, Mrs. H. B. Amidon, declared: "I am not a mother, but I shudder for all mothers' children who see such vile pictures" (*The Love Parade,* Production Code file, Herrick Library). Similar views could be heard throughout the country, especially in rural areas.

by full orchestra and climaxing in vigorous, resounding chords. Throughout the song, Lubitsch intercuts shots of MacDonald at the piano, the strolling sweethearts, the queen's cabinet listening blissfully in an antechamber, and the comic maid and valet perched dovelike in a neighboring tree. The result is a uniquely cinematic celebration of shared romantic ideals.

As in other early musicals, most of *The Love Parade*'s songs were recorded simultaneously with the action and with an orchestra positioned just off camera. But "March of the Grenadiers," the elaborate number that shows MacDonald reviewing her troops within a huge palace courtyard, posed novel problems. Lubitsch discovered it was impossible to film panoramic distance shots and at the same time position microphones close enough to pick up MacDonald and her soldiers. Nathaniel Finston, the founder of Paramount's West Coast music department, came up with a trailblazing solution: prerecord MacDonald and the chorus, and then film the scene with everyone mouthing the words and moving their bodies to an amplified drum beat. Another issue reportedly surfaced during prerecording. At the end of the march's first chorus, MacDonald had to hold the final high note for eight full seconds. On each try, she ran out of breath. To the rescue came sound assistant Merrill Pye, who assured Finston he could "stretch" MacDonald's note mechanically. Stories of similar "patch" jobs would circulate through the years and never failed to inflame MacDonald. For this reason she often made a point of singing "March of the Grenadiers" in live concert, holding the high note so long she would catapult adoring audiences into stratospheric frenzy.

With "Dream Lover" on the flip side, "March of the Grenadiers" became MacDonald's first commercial release for RCA Victor, recorded in December 1929. A month earlier, on November 8, she sang the march for her broadcast debut on the CBS weekly *Paramount-Publix Radio Hour*. Twenty-one years later, she would make it the opening number of her *Voice of Firestone* television debut.

The Love Parade rompingly scrambles time-honored sex roles. Traditionally, operetta associates women with waltzes and men with military marches. "March of the Grenadiers" is the kind of spirited action song that baritones like Lawrence Tibbett and Nelson Eddy delivered with particular flair. But here MacDonald performs it in cross-gender soldierly regalia, rousing her infantry to a thunderous display of allegiance to their matriarch. When the military procession starts, Lubitsch cunningly cuts to Prince Alfred, sulking in pajamas as he reads a missive from the queen specifying his day's agenda: morning tennis, afternoon bridge, and a nap to gird him for husbandly labors at night. This sly reversal of convention turns out, however, to be little more than a tease. Having begun as a daring New Woman in an Old World fairy tale, MacDonald's Queen Louise ultimately grants her husband the traditional upper hand. In the film's final moments Louise, simpering and compliant, promises Alfred to remain by his side and no longer view him as her dream toy but as "my King!"

Much like Chevalier's character in *The Love Parade,* Bob Ritchie was viewed by many in the film colony as MacDonald's gigolo. When he came out to Hollywood in the summer of 1929, he, too, checked in at the Beverly Wilshire, and none but the most naive subscribed to MacDonald's claim that he was only her manager. When *Variety* trumpeted that the two were "engaged," MacDonald issued a flat denial: "We are not engaged and are not going to be married." The truth was that MacDonald and Ritchie never had a formal compact of any kind. She simply agreed to supply him with 10 percent of her earnings in return for professional services that mainly entailed renegotiating her contracts. As MacDonald's ready escort, Ritchie also allowed her to keep wolves at arm's length, mix freely at social events, and concentrate on her work.

The strength of their liaison was unsuspected by Richard Rodgers's young wife, Dorothy, who once invited MacDonald to a formal dinner party: "I had just traveled west with our ten-month-old baby, Mary. Dick was renting Elsie Janis's home in Beverly Hills. Jeanette lived nearby and we invited her to dinner. I was a very inexperienced hostess. I nearly died when she showed up with Bob Ritchie. Jeanette had never said a word about bringing a guest. I had planned on serving twelve, and we had exactly one dozen filets mignons. To ease this embarrassment, my mother said, 'Just give me some cold chicken and I'll say I don't eat red meat.'"

Ritchie's ambiguous status in MacDonald's life paved the way for more serious upsets. During the production of *Monte Carlo,* MacDonald's second picture for Lubitsch, the director's eight-year marriage was on the brink of collapse. When Helene Lubitsch sued for divorce in June 1930, she testified that her husband was "ninety-nine percent in love with his work and had no time for home." Helene's percentages notwithstanding, Ernst Lubitsch had found the time to fall madly in love with Jeanette MacDonald, perhaps as early as their first encounter in Chicago.

Halfway through *Monte Carlo*'s production, Lubitsch gave a Sunday afternoon garden party at his beach house in Santa Monica. Among the guests were a host of celebrities, including Garbo, Helen Hayes, and the film's male star, English song-and-dance man Jack Buchanan. At a certain point Jeanette excused herself and went to the bathroom. When she opened the door to leave, she found Ernst standing in the doorway. Before she could ease her way out, Lubitsch entered and locked the door from behind: "He took hold of me, his face dark and intense. 'Jeanette,' he said fiercely, 'marry me! I promise I will be true to you. I promise you this. Just say yes to me.' I stared at him for a moment, and then I laughed in his face. I couldn't help it. This from him, out of a clear blue sky, was almost farcical. The setting was ridiculous. He let go of me, looking utterly crushed. The minute I laughed, he sagged like a sail when the wind drops. I pushed past him, not heeding what he'd said, because it still appeared to be a joke." Only later did MacDonald realize how serious Ernst's words were meant to be, and how cruel and thoughtless her reaction was.

Lubitsch took revenge at the studio. That Monday, he brought MacDonald to tears by savagely picking holes in her duet with Buchanan, "Always in All Ways." On Tuesday, MacDonald showed up with Bob Ritchie for protection. Lubitsch turned rabid. "I am too important a man for you to come marching in with the likes of *him*," he roared contemptuously, and then ordered the good-looking rival to leave the set. For the next two weeks Lubitsch blamed MacDonald each time Buchanan made an error. Unwilling to endure such a beating, MacDonald called for a showdown in her dressing room. She protested Ernst's harassment, saying he so upset her she could barely function. Suddenly Lubitsch turned tender and solicitous: "Don't you understand? Jack is nervous and insecure. When I blame you, it's because I must give him a chance to do the scene better. You've got be a good sport and go along with it."

Lubitsch was projecting his own insecurities onto Buchanan, and MacDonald was not deceived: "Neither [of us] gave a hint of the real truth to the other, that this new treatment meant he was settling the score for my cruelty to him. But from then on, we entered into a healthier relationship, never mentioning our bathroom scene again. We became very close friends. He even brought his woman problems to me for us to talk over. All his life, he was trying to find love, but it somehow seemed to elude him."

In 1934, when Lubitsch was furnishing his new Bel-Air bachelor house, MacDonald bought him a piano, arranging with his decorator for it to be delivered in his absence. When Ernst walked in and saw the gift, he wept. Jeanette recalled: "Ironically, Lubitsch got fewer gifts than most directors because his stars stood in awe of him. They felt he was too great for the customary diamond cuff-links and gold cigarette cases." In 1943, recuperating from his first heart attack in Cedars of Lebanon Hospital, Lubitsch asked that MacDonald be by his side before anyone else. Like high school sweethearts, the two held hands, and the director spoke of his longtime dream to adapt Richard Strauss's bittersweet comic opera, *Der Rosenkavalier.* He wanted Jeanette to play the Marschallin, the worldly princess who comprehends that affairs of the heart seldom last forever. Marlene Dietrich would later recommend the sensitive French actor Gérard Philipe for the role of Octavian, the Marshallin's young lover. Emil Jannings, the great silent screen star, was envisioned as the boorish lovesick Baron Ochs. What Lubitsch hoped would be the most precious jewel in his crown of cinema achievements was never to be. On November 30, 1947, three days after spending Thanksgiving at the home of Jeanette and Gene Raymond, he suffered another heart attack and died. At the funeral, MacDonald sang a slow and expressive rendition of "Beyond the Blue Horizon," the song she introduced in *Monte Carlo,* and "It's Always a Beautiful Day," composed by Lubitsch himself in honor of his young daughter, Nicola, the offspring of an unhappy second marriage. Lubitsch kept two framed photographs in a place of honor on his piano. One was a baby picture of Nicola. The other was of Jeanette MacDonald in *The Love Parade.*

MacDonald's bumpy relations with Maurice Chevalier were more the result of competing egos than romantic entanglement. Still, legend has it that early on Chevalier made unwelcome advances that provoked MacDonald to dub him "the Fastest Derrière-Pincher in the West," thereby gaining a reputation for herself as mistress of the bon mot. The truth is that by 1929, Chevalier's marriage to Yvonne Vallée, a former singer-hoofer, was crumbling. From his male Gallic perspective, blunt rebuffs by a woman apparently having a casual affair with Bob Ritchie smacked of poor taste, if not puritan hypocrisy. Little matter. Marlene Dietrich, whose dressing room was next to Jeanette's, would soon prove more responsive.

When Chevalier wrote his first set of memoirs shortly after World War II, he could not foresee that his Hollywood career, presumed finished in 1935, would later be rekindled. About MacDonald's more durable hold on moviegoing audiences, he explained:

> I've often been asked why Jeanette was the only singer to stay at the top of her screen specialty. The reasons are simple. First, her red-haired beauty, her figure, her unusually rare acting ability for a singer, and on top of all that, a crystal voice, fresh as spring water. It would appear that Jeanette could have been an important star, even without the help of her voice. But with that nightingale talent tossed into the bargain, she became what she became: unbeatable. Moreover, she is a serious woman and performer . . . whose head is planted firmly on her shoulders. She has everything! The others, not everything. Our four films together were experiences to cheer for my having been in such adorable company.

Jesse Lasky had wooed Chevalier to America with the hope that Europe's number one stage attraction would be Paramount's answer to Al Jolson at Warner Bros. Chevalier met Lasky's expectations, and then some. *Innocents of Paris,* his first American picture, suffered from creaky editing, a weak screenplay, and mediocre direction. Yet far more than Jolson, Chevalier projected himself as vividly on-screen as he had on stage. His smile, accent, and antic boyish mannerisms—the shrug, the rolling eyes, the swaying gait—proved irresistible. A consensus arose that, along with Clara Bow, the singing Frenchman with the protruding lower lip most embodied that special magnetism known as "It."

After just one picture, forty-one-year-old Chevalier was crown prince of Paramount. The studio extended his contract for a year and guaranteed him over a half million dollars. Yet Maurice was reluctant to accept the lead in *The Love Parade,* a picture originally conceived for the elegant actor Adolphe Menjou. Born of a poor Parisian family, Chevalier had always drawn on working-class roots for his stock of songs and public image, the trademark straw hat offsetting the tailored tuxedo. In *Innocents of Paris,* he played a junk dealer turned music-hall singer. Never could Chevalier imagine himself as a count, much less a prince consort. Lubitsch thought otherwise and rushed him to Wardrobe, where, looking more debonair than ever, Chevalier was photographed in full Viennese military attire. The next morning, Ernst brandished the photos, exclaiming: "Splendid, Maurice! Marvelous! YOU ARE A PRINCE!" Chevalier agreed.

Lubitsch understood that behind the Frenchman's bubbly image was a timid and troubled man. From his alcoholic father who abandoned the family when Maurice was a child, Chevalier had inherited a predisposition to panic attacks, suicidal fantasies, memory lapses, irritability, impotence, and gastric disorders. Above all, Chevalier suffered from a chronic sense of inferiority that worsened when he came to the United States. Americans perceived him as sophistication incarnate. Even before his arrival, it was a mark of cosmopolitanism to rave about Chevalier. Yet he saw himself only as a comic purveyor of racy *chansonettes* inspired by the lives of Parisian laborers. To complicate matters, Chevalier was fearful of being unmasked by a woman. The only female he loved unconditionally was his mother, Joséphine, nicknamed La Louque. An early romance with the music-hall diva Mistinguett, fifteen years his senior, promoted his phenomenal rise at the Folies-Bergère and the Casino de Paris. But blue-eyed Chevalier then had to cope with allegations that he slept his way to the top. When he and the legendary "Mist" parted company, around 1920, Chevalier found himself attracted only to plain, docile women who could be counted on to soothe his wounded masculinity. After a nervous breakdown in 1923, he got out from under Mistinguett's shadow and broke box-office records in solo triumphs at the Empire Theater and the Casino de Paris.

Jeanette MacDonald could not have been more of an irritant to Chevalier's fragile psyche. Without a trace of neurotic conflict, she, too, was bent on soaring above her humble beginnings. But rather than dwell on her father's failings, she zestfully incorporated his ideals and was not going to let gender weaken her drive to attain them. Others might label her pretentious or insufficiently skilled, but MacDonald almost immediately perceived herself as a legitimate player among Hollywood's elite, and she kept Grace Newell by her side to validate her pedigree. Constitutionally, she was strong. Sexually, she had no inclination for hanky-panky in the workplace. Worst of all from Chevalier's vantage, she was the latest discovery of the revered Ernst Lubitsch, meaning she inevitably would take away some of his glory.

While making *The Love Parade,* Chevalier had little reason to advertise his anxieties about MacDonald. She was clearly *his* supporting actress, and she was working at a fraction of his salary. Although none of the picture's songs became his standards, he got to sing the bulk of them. When journalists around the world began calling Jeanette and Maurice "The Screen's Greatest Lovers," Lubitsch made clear that he arranged his shooting so that "the camera honors them fifty-fifty." Yet in point of fact Lubitsch consistently blocked their duets to favor Chevalier, whose better side—like Jeanette's—was his left. When *The Love Parade* won him an Oscar nomination, Paramount tripled Chevalier's wages for his next two pictures. From then on, his fees for live performances became so exorbitant that London's Dominion Theater billed him as "The Highest-Paid Performer in the World."

Chevalier would manage to coexist peacefully with the budding prima donna until 1933, when the issues of her billing, her salary, and his uncertain future became more prominent. Yet seeds of contention sprouted as early as *The Love Parade*'s release, when *Variety* saw in MacDonald an actress "who all but steals the picture." *Time* bore out Chevalier's hesitation to do the film, finding his "informal and Parisian" technique at odds with the movie's regal setting. The New York press, while appreciative of the Frenchman, found special reason to praise MacDonald. For Richard Watts, Jr., of the *Herald-Tribune,* "Nothing in her past career has given reason for anticipating the skillful and alluring performance [MacDonald] brings to *The Love Parade.* Blessed with a fine voice, a sense of comedy, and a definite screen personality, she registers an individual success that makes her future in the new medium an enviable one." On the West Coast, Edwin Schallert of the *Los Angeles Times* zeroed in on MacDonald's "clear and true voice": "She invokes a great variety of inflections even in her speech, and endows the part in the repartee allotted to her with plenty of brightness. She is withal a fine match for the Chevalier style, and as regards her voice she might well be chosen to appear in the near vicinity of even [operatic baritone] Lawrence Tibbett [about to make his film debut in MGM's *The Rogue Song*]. I am not so sure that she is not the most satisfying woman singer yet heard on the screen." The issue of the new team's vocal compatibility was already being raised—negatively— by certain rural audiences. The owner of the Cozy Theater in Winchester, Indiana, put it this way: "Jeanette MacDonald is no doubt the greatest artist of the talking screen. Maurice Chevalier is also a great artist, but being unable to render spoken English is handicapped."

Regardless of how viewers perceived MacDonald and Chevalier, it is a reflection of Lubitsch's genius to have cast two utterly opposed personalities and vocal styles in a story that pits a seductive, foxy male against a beguiling, forceful female. By film's end, Man is securely Master of his Castle. But the ending in no way obscures the crisis of male sexuality at the movie's crux, highlighted by the spicy lyrics of Chevalier's solo "Nobody's Using It Now." Chevalier is "going to seed" not because *nobody* is using "it," but because only one party, MacDonald, is—and to her advantage. Monogamy, the prince consort seems to be saying, threatens male privilege. Within four years, Maurice Chevalier would make it clear that screen partnership with a woman as tough as Jeanette MacDonald did likewise.

Paramount staged a gala world premiere for *The Love Parade* at New York's Criterion Theater on Broadway and Forty-fourth Street. As MacDonald's train rolled east, she recalled her days in *The Magic Ring* and Mitzi's advice about the annual "I-Owe-Me" present. Upon arriving in Manhattan, she went to Cartier on Fifth Avenue and bought herself an emerald-cut solitaire diamond ring. She couldn't care less that many would construe it as an engagement gift from Bob Ritchie: "What outsiders thought about us didn't interest me. I knew what the score was."

The black-tie opening was set for Sunday, November 19. Tickets sold at the unprecedented cost of eleven dollars apiece. In the wake of the Great Crash that had hurled the country into panic just three weeks earlier, the event was a timely affirmation of the continued vitality of American corporate enterprise. Eight doormen were on duty in front of the Criterion, each garbed as a Sylvanian grenadier. When Jeanette alighted from her car, she encountered a situation that would soon become familiar: kleig lights, public clamor, and police patrol. Escorted into the lobby by two Sylvanians, she was greeted by Major Edward Bowes, the manager of the Capitol when Jeanette danced there as a teenager. While Bowes interviewed her on a radio hookup, MacDonald clung nervously to the arm of silent-movie queen Colleen Moore.

Inside, thousands of French and American flags decorated the theater. MacDonald sat in a side box with Bob, Anna, and her sisters and their husbands. Notables included the French consul general; Mayor and Mrs. Jimmy Walker; Metropolitan Opera board president Otto Kahn; United States Major General J. Leslie Kincaid; and virtually all of Paramount's brass. Conspicuous by his absence was Chevalier, who injured his hand while shooting *The Big Pond* with Claudette Colbert (who *was* in attendance). Chevalier excused himself in a filmed apology that so charmed the public it was repeated at subsequent screenings. The house manager then called MacDonald to the stage. With appropriate brevity and humility, she told the audience how lucky she felt to be a part of this picture and how much she hoped they would enjoy it.

The Love Parade was a sellout for thirteen weeks at the Criterion and did smash business in cities as far-flung as London, Copenhagen, and Buenos Aires. A Sydney radio station broadcast the sound track to Antarctica, where Rear Admiral Byrd and his fellow explorers cheered it. In this country, *The Love Parade* launched what would become a permanent love affair between San Franciscans and MacDonald: as of its ninth week at the St. Francis Theater, "almost one third of the daily attendance was made up of 'repeaters.'" But MacDonald cast her most seductive spell in Paris. *Parade d'amour,* with special French lyrics, played at the sumptuous Paramount Theater on the Boulevard des Capucines, just off the Place de l'Opéra. The French came to see and applaud Maurice. They left swooning over Jeanette. Among the most smitten was a non-Frenchman who happened to be in Paris that winter: King Albert of Belgium.

MacDonald had only just begun to win the approval of Hollywood's ersatz royalty. But in Paris, she had already stolen the heart of a real-world monarch.

CHAPTER SIX

Only a Nose

You have to sense changes in public taste . . . and if you don't
anticipate the changes, well, you're just sunk.

JEANETTE MACDONALD to a reporter, 1940

DURING WORLD WAR II, WALTER WINCHELL gallantly cited
MacDonald as one of the reasons Technicolor was invented. Her Titian
hair, green eyes, and ivory-pink complexion had by then brightened
such movies as *Sweethearts* (MGM's first full-color Technicolor musical), *Bitter Sweet*, and *Smilin' Through*. Yet long before the familiar
three-strip Technicolor process came into being, MacDonald helped
make color picture history. In late summer 1929 she took on the female
lead in Paramount's first complete two-color Technicolor talkie, *The
Vagabond King*. After its release in 1930, this cinematic landmark went
virtually unseen until 1991, when the UCLA Film and Television
Archive unveiled an impeccable restoration of the sole surviving color
print. It is a startling example of the expressive heights attainable by
early Technicolor, which produced only hues of red and green along
with black and white.

The new assignment should have pleased MacDonald. *The Vagabond
King* was to be an adaptation of a proven crowd pleaser, Rudolf Friml's
1925 stage operetta. Its throbbing score would showcase MacDonald's
voice to excellent advantage in romantic songs like "Some Day" and
"Only a Rose." As Katherine de Vaucelles, niece of the medieval
French monarch Louis XI, she would play an impassioned heroine who
nearly sacrifices her life for her beloved François Villon, poet-beggar

and savior of France. As with *The Love Parade*, Paramount conceived of *The Vagabond King* as a superproduction. It was intended to out-class other Technicolor extravaganzas such as Warner Bros.'s *Gold Diggers of Broadway* and MGM's *The Rogue Song*.

Early publicity played up the movie's epic sweep: "*The Vagabond King* will not be merely a photographed stage operetta. Contrasting with the few sets of the stage production, the motion picture will have more than fifty—most of them massive reproductions of architectural splendors." Häns Dreier's sets would indeed prove spectacular, ranging from a shimmering stained-glass chapel in Notre-Dame Cathedral, where MacDonald's character is first discovered in prayer, to the dark and fiery recesses of a beggars' tavern, to an enormous gilded reception room in a fairy-tale palace. Paramount's quest for quality was so in-tense that it spent $200,000 just to obtain the entangled rights to the story, which started as a novel and had two prior screen versions.* For this new incarnation, the plot was to be shaped by the gifted screen-writer Herman J. Mankiewicz, who a decade later would write *Citizen Kane* for Orson Welles. In short, MacDonald was once again in a proj-ect that had an enormous budget, high artistic ambition, and outstand-ing music.

In an era when Technicolor movies were often smudgy, glary, and aesthetically at sea, *The Vagabond King* displayed painterly finish. One critic compared the film to "a series of beautiful pictures, such as one might gaze upon in a gallery of art, rather than look upon merely as a passing entertainment." The combined efforts of costume designer Travis Banton and cinematographer Ray Rennahan (whose genius with color would win him an Oscar for *Gone with the Wind*) made Mac-Donald glow with a poetic delicacy reminiscent of Pre-Raphaelite paintings. In the thrilling montage sequence depicting the climactic bat-tle between the Parisian beggars and the Burgundian villains, MacDon-ald's beauty is literally made transcendent. High above the bloody field of action, a superimposed cameo shot of her face and flowing orange mane flashes three times, intimating that, like some divine inspiration, her exquisite image is spurring Villon to victory. Colorful reproduc-

---

*Fox filmed the property in 1920. United Artists released a 1927 remake, *Beloved Rogue*, starring John Barrymore and Marceline Day, with screenplay by Paul Bern and direction by Alan Crosland. Paramount would star Ronald Colman and Frances Dee in a 1938 nonmusical version, *If I Were King*, with script by Preston Sturges. Kathryn Grayson and Oreste would head the cast in Paramount's 1956 remake of the operetta, di-rected in VistaVision by Michael Curtiz.

tions of MacDonald's face soon appeared in trade magazines to advertise the glories of color film stock.

The fact that she would shine musically and visually as never before did not keep MacDonald from despising her work on *The Vagabond King*. One fly in the ointment was Ludwig Berger, the film's émigré director. Like Lubitsch, Berger had worked with Max Reinhardt in Berlin. He, too, was a music lover, and even had a musicology degree from Heidelberg. But unlike the mischievous Lubitsch, Dr. Berger, as recalled by MacDonald, "was a heavy-handed German who, in outbursts of temper, hurled Teutonic insults and slapped his wooden leg. Compared with working for Ernst, this was like prison." Berger's command of English was so weak that Dorothy Arzner, Hollywood's leading female director, had to be brought in as an unofficial supervisor. While the cast's inflated declamatory style is a good indicator of how American operetta must have sounded on stage in the 1920s, their bombastic dialogue is also the product of Berger's inexperience with the language.

A second great annoyance to MacDonald was her leading man, British-born stage baritone Dennis King. Because he originated the role of Friml's Villon to great acclaim on Broadway, King had Berger and the front office eating out of his hand from the day shooting began. King carried extra cachet for having done Shakespeare on stage, a big plus in the eyes and ears of Hollywood producers. While MacDonald had little choice but to accept his backstairs influence, she refused to put up with King's shameless scene snatching. Ray Rennahan recounted: "After I'd set the lights on them they were supposed to keep their positions on the set and not move unless we were prepared for it. But King would be constantly moving this way and that to get a camera advantage over Jeanette. He'd block her key light by putting a shadow over her face, and just as soon as that would happen, Jeanette would say, 'Oh, no! Wait a minute!' "

MacDonald's guard failed her during the shooting of "Only a Rose." Set in a luxuriant garden, this pivotal moment has Katherine respond in song to the vagabond's ardent pledge to win her love by saving France. Berger had planned the scene so that except for one brief reaction shot of the actor, MacDonald would appear on-screen alone and in close shot until the song's final strains, sung in duet. To make sure King would stay on his mark, Berger placed a hobbyhorse between the singers. Yet the baritone, true to form, spoiled MacDonald's solo shots by prematurely inserting his fingers, nose, and slick pompadour

into her frame. Somehow, the resulting glitch went uncorrected. Mac-
Donald was as much enraged by Berger's negligence as King's hogging,
and pleaded with B. P. Schulberg to order retakes or else drop her name
from the opening credits. Schulberg refused to do either. From then on,
MacDonald sarcastically referred to the song as "Only a Nose."

Lubitsch hit the ceiling when he saw how MacDonald was used in
the picture. The publicity department had promised that the movie
would reveal "the gorgeous beauty and coloring" of "Jeanette Mac-
Donald, pulchritudinous prima donna." It did. Yet *The Vagabond King*
was far more attentive to Dennis King's exposed torso and shapely legs.
To his credit, King's musical moments are electrifying. In "The Song of
the Vagabonds," with upraised hands and blazing eyes, he spurs his fellow sons of France to move onward against the foe. In the soaring duet
"Love Me To-night," he and MacDonald generate a lyric excitement
that would not be equaled in movies until MacDonald's pairing with
Nelson Eddy. Overall, however, the film's leading lady is eclipsed by
Dennis King's grandstanding. Also deflecting viewer sympathy from
MacDonald was actress Lillian Roth, who received almost as much
screen time in her role as the tragic young tavern wench. Roth's rendition of "Huguette's Waltz" disclosed an intense singing style that suggested Lotte Lenya with a Brooklyn accent.

After its New York premiere on February 19, 1930, *The Vagabond
King* broke opening-week records in Chicago, Rochester, and New Orleans. It took London, Buenos Aires, and Paris by storm—although
some French carped at the fanciful twisting of their history in what was
grandly billed as an *opéra cinématographique*. Like *The Love Parade*,
The Vagabond King did weaker business in small-town America. Many
rural exhibitors resented Paramount's hard sell of a product whose so-
called prestige values left them and their patrons cold. Later that year,
Variety tried to assess why screen "musical comedies" invariably
reaped higher grosses than "operettas." The former, it concluded, were
"built for the taste of the public," whereas the latter, exemplified by
The Vagabond King and MGM's *The Rogue Song*, went "over the
heads of the masses—not educated as yet."

In truth, *The Vagabond King* was Paramount's response to an increasing call for cultural as well as moral uplift in movies. Herbert T.
Kalmus, the inventor of Technicolor, urged in 1930: "[The industry]
must offer more pictures above the twelve-year intelligence level, more
unusual pictures, more of subtle romance and less of obvious sex. It
must evidence greater originality and less herd instinct . . . and greater

recognition of a diversified public taste which is trending upward." In its vocal and orchestral artistry, *The Vagabond King* strengthened the case of musicians predicting even loftier unions of music and celluloid. Igor Stravinsky, pointing to the sound film as "the future medium of the music art," imagined "enormous audiences gathered in the big houses where once but small groups attended the concert halls." Bruno Walter, conductor of the Berlin State Opera in pre-Nazi Germany, believed that "grand opera on the talking screen" would make "the great general public . . . educated to operas as entertainment." Oscar Straus, the Viennese operetta composer who would soon contribute to Mac-Donald's *One Hour with You,* argued that as a result of sound pictures "musical genius which otherwise might never blossom, for lack of stimulus and inspiration, will enter upon its heritage and add to the treasury of human happiness."

With the coming of sound, movie producers perceived the cinema more than ever as a bastard cousin of the established arts. So-called serious music, they realized, could either be embraced for its respectability or just as easily ridiculed for its pomposity. Often, the same filmmakers did both. In 1929–30, MacDonald rode the first wave of cultural idealism in Hollywood's new wired-for-sound era. Beyond any other film of the period, *The Vagabond King* reeked of literary, painterly, and musical pretensions. However, this surge of Quality and Prestige fell short of expectations, spelling disappointment at the box office and threatening the future of a movie actress with more than a face to sell.

Still, *The Vagabond King* validated MacDonald as an unusual screen beauty. The marketability of her visual appeal would soon encourage United Artists to launch her in *The Lottery Bride,* a new part-Technicolor operetta, and the Technicolor Corporation would debut its three-strip process in the finale to her first MGM musical, *The Cat and the Fiddle.* Opera and movies never became the perfect partners envisioned by 1930s highbrow musicians. But in Jeanette MacDonald, the color screen found a dream lover made in Hollywood heaven.

MacDonald spent the 1929 holiday season in Manhattan with her mother and Bob Ritchie. When the playwright-impresario David Belasco wooed her to star in an upcoming "romantic drama with music," she had airy thoughts about a return to Broadway. But the Wall Street quake had extinguished too many familiar lights along the Great White Way. MacDonald now had to concede that entertainment's immediate future lay with radio, recordings, and motion pictures. Virtually no Broadway musical star who was salable out west elected to remain in New York. Fred Astaire, Ginger Rogers, and Eddie Cantor would soon leave. Ethel Merman stayed, but only because Hollywood didn't know what to do with her.

While in New York, Ritchie worked out a new two-picture deal with Paramount, as well as an enviable contract with United Artists: one film and a ten-week guarantee of $5,000 per week. MacDonald finally vacated the Beverly Wilshire Hotel and rented a house at 621 North Bedford Drive in Beverly Hills, two blocks above Santa Monica Boulevard. The home had a pool, and MacDonald liked to sunbathe on the diving board, letting the water's reflection intensify her tan. Since French was proving central to her career, MacDonald hired Rose and Henri Coen, a Jewish-Belgian couple, as her personal maid and chauffeur-hairdresser. (The Francophone Coens would remain with her for nearly two decades.) She also resumed formal French lessons, this time with Hollywood's premier language instructor, Georges Jomier, a tall and wiry French eccentric who invited students for candlelit gourmet dinners served at a table draped with the Sunday comics. Mindful of the Latin Americans who idolized her in *The Love Parade* and *The Vagabond King,* MacDonald thought it wise to begin lessons in Spanish as well.

Bob Ritchie, routinely shuttling between New York and Los Angeles, was still the only man in MacDonald's private life. Although his West Coast mailing address remained the Beverly Wilshire, he spent most of his time at Jeanette's and left little doubt that they were living together (along with Jeanette's mother, of course). Paramount publicist Teet Carle recalled: "When Ritchie was in town, he'd give parties for the publicity department at the Beverly Hills home. Jeanette would be gone and we'd all play cards, have drinks, and eat snacks. Ritchie was very personable and we got a lot of support from him. He was really Jeanette's front man. Motion pictures were still new to her and she was busy learning lines, recording, and rehearsing. She relied on Bob to give us items for the newspapers. It seemed pretty clear they were living together, and it never occurred to me that they might be married."

Rumors of a secret marriage surfaced in 1930. To quash them, MacDonald announced in mid-December that she had recently become engaged to Ritchie and that a wedding would take place "in the near future." Five years later, with no nuptials in sight, Louella Parsons cattily enshrined the MacDonald-Ritchie affair as "the longest engagement in Hollywood." Two years earlier, Walter Winchell was so convinced he had proof of a marriage that he wrote in his Broadway column: "Heretofore the rumors had it. Now we know it! That Jeanette Mac-Donald and Robert Ritchie were married in the U.S. at least three months before departing for Paree [in December 1932]. Five Cs will bring them Ten—if they want to wager." Never one to avoid a sure win, MacDonald raised the ante. She cabled Winchell that she would pay him five Gs if he could prove his claim. Winchell never met the challenge.

Half of Hollywood believed MacDonald's denial. The rest preferred to imagine she was covering up a secret ceremony for reasons best known to herself. Her réclame as a prankster made many feel she would enjoy nothing less than confounding movietown's mighty know-it-alls. "So I should," she devilishly told reporter Jack Grant: "It's nearly worth getting married for. Though if I did, the joke might be on me!" To confuse matters further, MacDonald and Ritchie's pet names exuded conjugality. He was her "Popsie." She was his "Mommerino" and "Old Lady." (Bob also called her "Brat," "Shorty," and "Redskin.") When the studio crowd referred to her, often snidely, as "that temperamental Madame Ritchie," MacDonald never openly objected. Chevalier, who felt that Ritchie mistreated Jeanette, confided years later: "He, of course, was not the man for her . . . although I'm sure they were married." Even Ritchie's relatives never dismissed the rumors. His nephew John said: "We always heard in the family that 'Bub' was married to Jeanette and that it was annulled. But there's never been any proof of it. Bub was unbelievably private and he didn't confide in his family."

There is no evidence that MacDonald and Ritchie ever married. Yet their correspondence in early 1931 shows that the engagement was not a simple matter of convenience. In spite of Ritchie's notoriety as a womanizer, MacDonald never doubted the authenticity of his love. She was dubious only of its viability. One of her letters begins:

> I got your sweet sentimental letter today about our "bed of clouds" and I loved it. Sweet, I know you love me—and I love you too dearest—I am just hoping for the day when we can really enjoy our love. Do you think it will ever come? Sometimes I wonder, for things do just seem to keep us apart. I suppose that's why we should take love while we can, for it's a funny elusive fellow. And since we've found it, we must make the most of it.

MacDonald feared that Ritchie might become another Daniel Mac-Donald, a likable father with no means for supporting his children:

> You know why I'm so anxious to have you make some money and get a fine job that will reassure your future. It's that we really should get married soon

or else I'm liable to suffer—you know (morally). As it is, people cannot understand why not. And I can't say 'cause you have no money or job and
there's no future for you in simply taking care of my career. Besides, there's
not much dignity or prestige. And what I want most is for Pop to make
enough so the Old Lady can have a real papoose before old age creeps in
and spoils it.

Although always tender, MacDonald's tone toward Bob was sometimes
condescending: "It's the difficult things that prove most interesting,
Honey. And remember when you're having a good time that all the
people you're having your good times with have jobs and it makes a little difference, you know."

To show his independence, Ritchie sometimes made flashy pur-
chases. In spring 1931, he dropped in at Cartier to buy with his own
money a $7,000 emerald-cut diamond ring for Jeanette. Intended to
mark their third "anniversary," its stone was conspicuously larger than
the one MacDonald had purchased for herself the previous year.
Jeanette accepted graciously, but deep down she worried that Bob was
a spendthrift.

In spite of the Depression, United Artists stayed committed to promot-
ing ambitious films, and MacDonald's one-picture deal held out the
promise of exciting moviemaking. *The Lottery Bride*'s producer was
Arthur Hammerstein, the mighty Broadway impresario whose smash
operettas included Victor Herbert's *Naughty Marietta* and Friml's *The
Firefly* and *Rose-Marie*. Based on a story by Herbert Stothart, *The Lottery Bride* called for an original Friml score and would give MacDonald, for the first time in her screen career, top billing. Her cinematographer was to be the formidable Karl Freund, who had filmed Fritz
Lang's *Metropolis* in Germany. A much-publicized final episode shot in
Technicolor would find MacDonald trudging over expressionistic ice
floes in an Arctic setting featuring the aurora borealis ablaze overhead.
When shooting got under way, Louella Parsons observed backhand-
edly: "They tell me she asked for everything but a platinum stove for
her dressing room at the United Artists lot. That gal knows what she
wants and when she wants it, if all one hears is true."

For all the hoopla, *The Lottery Bride* was a commercial fiasco and
an artistic misfire. It led Arthur Hammerstein back to Broadway and
bankruptcy. MacDonald recalled that the production's "only saving
grace" was "the fun I had emoting with Joe E. Brown and ZaSu Pitts,
who kept the set pleasant with their special brands of hilarity." One of

the film's running gags has rubber-faced Brown retorting "Never mind, let it lay!" after each of his corny jokes fails to click. The critics agreed. *Variety* had reason to write: "Something that even amateurs would be ashamed of. One of the very worst of the really very bad features released since sound."

Let's Go Native, MacDonald's return vehicle to Paramount, was only marginally better. The studio warned its sales agents: "There are songs in the show—good songs. But use your discretion about talking about them." The five tunes by Richard A. Whiting and George Marion, Jr., were in fact gems compared with the lumbering screenplay. After reels of ponderous exposition, a bunch of New Yorkers, including MacDonald as a happy-go-lucky showbiz costume designer, get shipwrecked on a South Atlantic island. Assisted by the isle's female natives, Jack Oakie dispatches the splashy title tune and then woos Kay Francis with a Jolson-inflected rendition of "I've Gotta Yen for You." Perhaps the best reason for viewing this anarchic comedy today is to see and hear Miss Francis join in on the flirtatious second chorus. Another is to chuckle at what was deemed unacceptable in light of the newly established Production Code. Censorship authorities urged Paramount to cut the female islanders' dancing gyrations and to drop the lame one-liner: "As far as I can figure out, this *was* one of the Virgin Islands—but it drifted." For better or worse, Paramount failed to comply.

Still, *Let's Go Native* gives us a glimpse of how MacDonald must have performed in Broadway stinkers like *Angela* and *Boom-Boom*. It's as if she made up her mind to transcend the film's hokey gags and uninspired music and let JEANETTE shine through. Such radiance was not, however, a feat of mere willpower. When *The Love Parade* came out, one New York critic argued that MacDonald's facial features and contours, being "abnormally long," caused her to photograph lousily onscreen. She agreed, and set up an appointment to discuss lighting, camera angles, and alternative shades of makeup with Victor Milner, her black-and-white cinematographer at Paramount. Experimenting on their own time, MacDonald and Milner came up with tricks that guaranteed her a dazzling look in *Let's Go Native*.

The film's director, Leo McCarey, also helped revamp MacDonald's image by making the most of her gift for daffiness. McCarey was responsible for Stan Laurel and Oliver Hardy's silent comedies and within a few years would direct the Marx Brothers' *Duck Soup* and Columbia's *The Awful Truth* with Irene Dunne and Cary Grant.

Throughout *Let's Go Native,* MacDonald exhibits the famous Mc-
Carey "slow burn," remaining gaily oblivious to the havoc surrounding her: at the start, she dallies in bed while a crew of incompetent
movers demolish the furniture her creditors are repossessing; at the
film's end, she lingers to bicker with her boyfriend as the island under-
goes a catastrophic earthquake—portrayed through special effects and
editing as endearingly threadbare as *San Francisco*'s would be awesome.

Let's *Go Native* brought little credit to McCarey and even less to
MacDonald. But their brief pairing in 1930 sets the imagination
awhirl. MacDonald soon became so associated with lavish musicals
that, unlike her soprano friend Irene Dunne, she would never be considered for "straight" romantic comedies. Yet from *The Love Parade*
onward, MacDonald evinced a flair for screwball mischief that cried
out for the right property and director. Had circumstances allowed Mc-
Carey and MacDonald to team up when they both hit their stride, the
singer-comedienne might have found greater favor with critics and historians less susceptible to her vocal charms.

By the end of 1930, MacDonald's movie marketability was once
again suspect. Technicolor was proving too expensive for an industry
in financial crisis, and the public was sick of musicals. Another factor
prompting Paramount to terminate MacDonald's contract was her
"temperament." Many at the studio, including acting chief David O.
Selznick, considered her unreasonably demanding and snobbish. As she
had done with J. J. Shubert, Jeanette often bellyached to Paramount's
top brass about script assignments. When asked to make promotional
appearances without pay, she categorically refused. It didn't help that
Bob Ritchie drove her film crews insane by passing judgment on every
production detail that pertained to her.

Friction with the bosses was not, however, the main reason Mac-
Donald was dropped from *Paramount on Parade,* the studio's all-star
cavalcade. As early as October 1929, the press department announced
MacDonald's participation in this crazy quilt of skits and musical routines, whose roster of warblers included Chevalier, Dennis King, Lillian
Roth, Helen Kane, and "It girl" Clara Bow. Soon thereafter, MacDonald filmed a comic episode entitled "It's Tough to Be a Prima Donna,"
a lengthy medley that drew on Luigi Arditi's "Il Bacio," Gilbert and
Sullivan's *The Mikado,* Green and Stept's "That's My Weakness Now,"
and Gershwin's *Rhapsody in Blue.* But when copyright issues arose re-
garding the Gershwin piece, scheduled for use in Universal's *King of*

Jazz, the front office decided not to wage a legal battle on MacDonald's behalf but to remove her episode altogether. While legend has it that she survived as mistress of ceremonies for the picture's Spanish-language version, *Galas de la Paramount,* in point of fact it was Rosita Moreno who filled that function. MacDonald did apparently show up in some editions of *Galas de la Paramount,* performing Newell Chase and Sam Coslow's "Music in the Moonlight" in a Venetian gondola setting. Regrettably, the footage of both "It's Tough to Be a Prima Donna" and "Music in the Moonlight" has been lost.*

Like *The Love Parade, Monte Carlo* has become enshrined as a master-work of the early film musical. Although MacDonald lived to see some of her films exhibited in universities and museums, she did not always share the connoisseur's reverence. Once, when she attended a screening of *Monte Carlo* at New York's Museum of Modern Art, her laughter at all the wrong moments so irritated the audience that an attendant had to be dispatched to quiet her. Putting blame on the marcelled hairdos she sports in the film, Jeanette whispered: "I'm sorry, but one more wave and I'll drown!" In fact, MacDonald almost never made *Monte Carlo.* David O. Selznick, thinking her not yet enough of a name to carry the picture, wanted her off the project. Lubitsch, however, refused to shoot his second talkie with any other actress and managed to have Selznick reverse his veto.

Monte Carlo clinched MacDonald's reputation as Lingerie Queen of the Talkies. Its most celebrated sequence is "Beyond the Blue Horizon," a duet for soprano and locomotive with peasant chorus obbligato. Countess Helene Mara (MacDonald) has just hopped onto the Riviera Express after narrowly escaping marriage to the asinine Duke Otto von Liebenheim (Claud Allister). Having jettisoned her wedding gown as well as her groom, the runaway bride rushes into a compartment and sheds her chinchilla coat to expose nothing but bare skin and silk undergarments. In the company of her maid Berthe (ZaSu Pitts),

---

*At the summer 1995 Cinecon Convention in Los Angeles, UCLA restorationist Robert Gitt presented a restored and reconstructed silent Technicolor print of the English-language *Paramount on Parade,* minus the first reel. When the episode that has Nino Martini steering a gondola as he sings "Torna a Surriento!" began, a collective murmur of surprise and delight shot through the hall: "There's Jeanette!" The cognoscenti had spotted MacDonald in long shot seated in Martini's gondola. A subsequent close-up, however, displayed an entirely different actress sitting mute and admiring the lover seated beside her. The hoary mystery of MacDonald and *Paramount on Parade* still awaits a complete solution.

the financially strapped countess chooses Monaco as her destination, where luck at the tables might help her stay single. The train's whistle launches a twelve-bar introduction for strings, percussion, and smoke-stack. Simultaneously, a rapid montage of the surging engine, wheels, and pistons sets up a propulsive chug-chug-chug-chug rhythm. Mac-Donald, peering blissfully out the window, intones the verse and cho-rus, bidding farewell to things that bore her and anticipating the joy that awaits her elsewhere. She then lowers the window to discover dis-tant field hands waving at the train and chanting the second chorus. Through an ingenious blend of visual editing and prerecorded song, Lubitsch makes this train ride a beguiling ode to MacDonald's conta-gious playfulness. Composed for her by Richard Whiting, W. Franke Harling, and lyricist Leo Robin, "Beyond the Blue Horizon" would re-main, along with "San Francisco," the most "modern" of MacDon-ald's signature songs. Its optimism would carry meaning beyond the film and past Depression America. It was reportedly John F. Kennedy's favorite tune after "Hail to the Chief."

As in *The Love Parade, Monte Carlo* finds MacDonald torn be-tween social convention and sexual desire. Her suitor, the wealthy Count Rudolph (Jack Buchanan), disguises himself as a hairdresser after bungling several flirtatious overtures—including movie history's first love duet via telephone, "Give Me a Moment Please." MacDonald soon holds him indispensable, not for his dexterity with shears and comb but for his headache-curing massages that prompt her to gush forth the melody "Whatever It Is, It's Grand." Eager to gratify her "Al-ways in All Ways," the sly coiffeur hands over 200,000 francs he pre-tends to have won on her behalf at the casino. His reward is a deep kiss suddenly interrupted by MacDonald's ingrained sense of propriety. Making a swift exit to her bedroom, she locks the door, places the key in a locked dresser drawer, the drawer's key in a locked jewelry box, and the key to the box under her pillow. When MacDonald and Buchanan quarrel the next morning, sex and social class become so jumbled that he construes her patronizing insult—"To me you're not a man at all!"—as a blow to his virility. Buchanan's revenge is a deliber-ate rape manqué. Stomping over the sitting-room divan, he locks the hall door, strips off his blazer, and slips sneeringly into a robe. Even as he manhandles her, the sighing tone of MacDonald's voice undercuts her threat to phone the police. A long and passionate kiss follows, with Buchanan sweeping her into his arms and carrying her to the daybed— only to plop her down like a sack of *pommes de terre*. Photographed mouth agape, MacDonald stares in astonished frustration as Buchanan leaves her to herself.

The rest of the film plays out the Lubitschean fantasy of Woman Crawling for Man's Favor. The conclusion takes place at a gala performance of André Messager's *Monsieur Beaucaire,* the operetta about a prince of France disguised as a barber and rejected by a noblewoman on account of his lowly station.* This art-mirrors-life device conveniently frees Buchanan from having to admit he lied about himself and obliges MacDonald, now enlightened, to beg for his forgiveness. She does, he grants it, and the movie ends with their reprising "Beyond the Blue Horizon" aboard the Riviera Express.

Paramount had hoped that Buchanan, an established English song-and-dance man with only one prior movie credit, would burst on the screen with the manly charisma of Chevalier. Instead, he reinforced stereotypes associated with real-life hairdressers, his prissiness tempered only by comparison with the even greater mincing of Claud Allister (another Britisher) as the abandoned groom. If the near-rape episode manages to stay inoffensive, it's because the notion of Buchanan actually inflicting sexual violence on MacDonald seems as absurd as his giving her sexual pleasure. "I was frequently challenged to prove my manhood in my own country, particularly as a trembling youth," Buchanan once confessed. Following *Monte Carlo,* Buchanan returned to England and retook his place among a theatrical set that included Beatrice Lillie, Noël Coward, and Gertrude Lawrence. Despite his hope that he and MacDonald might pair in a London stage show—"I felt a very arresting part could be built for her, as her range of talent was so considerable"—their careers never again coincided. Buchanan played in many British films but wouldn't make another American musical until twenty-three years later, when Vincente Minnelli shrewdly cast him as the temperamental aesthete in MGM's *The Band Wagon.*

Monte Carlo brought MacDonald strong notices. *Variety* acknowledged: "If it were not for Jeanette MacDonald, there would have been no picture." At a time when musicals carried scant favor with the general public, *Film Daily* recognized the quality of her performance, placing it alongside Walt Disney's *Silly Symphonies* series and Josef von Sternberg's direction of *Morocco* as one of 1930's "Meritorious Deeds."

---

*Messager's operetta, from the Booth Tarkington novel, spawned two other Paramount versions, the "serious" *Monsieur Beaucaire* with Rudolph Valentino in 1924 and a burlesque remake with Bob Hope in 1946.

She also made a terrific impression on a young stage actor who saw the picture in Chicago. Raymond Guion, touring with his first Shubert play, *Young Sinners,* was feeling low the day his show was to open. To relax, he took in a matinee screening of *Monte Carlo.* Years later he would recall that watching MacDonald on-screen "took me out of the doldrums"—an effect she exerted in real life when he, renamed Gene Raymond, would become romantically involved with her in Hollywood.

MacDonald's move from Paramount to Fox baffled even industry mavens. Fox was downscale. It lacked Paramount's swank, MGM's grandeur, and Warner Bros.'s excitement. The Fox product tended to be folksy. Its stars—Will Rogers, Janet Gaynor, Charles Farrell—embodied down-home American values at odds with MacDonald's high-toned glitter. The studio, however, was short on female players, and production head Winfield Sheehan and general manager Sol Wurtzel felt that MacDonald might inject just the right dose of stylish naughtiness—and profitability—into Fox movies to help keep the company solvent.

The alliance was a disaster. No period in MacDonald's early Hollywood years more assaulted her self-esteem. Unlike Lasky and Lubitsch, the Fox brass had little patience for prima donnas. In a hollow effort to gain favor with Winfield Sheehan, MacDonald volunteered to serve as a property scout, bringing him plays and novels she deemed adaptable. The chief was unresponsive, and Jeanette moaned half seriously to Bob Ritchie: "When I count the doors I have to go through to see Mr. Sheehan, I bet that when I die, if I've been good, I won't have to pass as many doors to get to see God—nor as many secretaries." Manager Wurtzel was no less off-putting. Even by movie-mogul standards, this honcho was notoriously crude and tough. Only a facial tic that curled his mouth into a nervous smile released him from a near-perpetual scowl. It was said that the sole person Wurtzel revered was his New York boss, William Fox, because only Fox was more unlikable than himself.

MacDonald's unhappiness was immediate, and it led to physical distress. She confided to Ritchie in late February: "I am awfully tired again. I don't sleep well and it's all because I'm not content. My life seems all chopped up and so damned uncertain. I can't relax and my back aches. I need a treatment."* In early March, just as an intestinal

---

*Wary of medications because of side effects on her voice, MacDonald discovered during her New York years that body massage "treatments" helped relieve symptoms of stress. They became a lifetime indulgence.

disorder was making her gaunt and cranky, family problems cropped up to compound her troubles. In the wake of vaudeville's sudden demise, her sister Blossom was out of work. At Paramount, MacDonald had managed to wangle a small role for her in *Fighting Caravans,* a Gary Cooper western. But her efforts to open doors at Fox's Movietone City proved futile. With Blossom and her husband now forced to live on meager savings, Jeanette was hard on herself for not being able to find them more work. An additional worry was Elsie, who recently sent word that she was divorcing husband number two and would raise her son, Earl, by herself.

While grappling with these woes, MacDonald filmed *Oh, for a Man!,* the most sexually explicit movie of her career. Marketed by Fox as "the subtlest, sexiest, super-sophisticated, smartest . . . succession of stirring sequences that the silver sound screen has shown in many a season," this ribald farce was light-years from the cunning innuendo of her Lubitsch-Paramount films. MacDonald played Carlotta Manson, a vain and headstrong opera star whose undisguised carnal cravings find satisfaction in a brutish jewel thief portrayed by the rugged British actor Reginald Denny. This odd twosome marry, quarrel, separate, and reunite—less under the sign of Cupid than of Lust. At the close of their first bedroom scene, Denny gives MacDonald the longest, roughest kiss she would ever receive on-screen. Censorship boards in New York, Massachusetts, and Ohio green-lighted the embrace but deleted the final half of Denny's exit line: "Aw, don't get sore, Baby. *I might have taken a lot more than a kiss.*"

As of her first week at Fox, MacDonald waged war against the music department. "What the people at this studio knew about music," she asserted, "could be played with one hand on a toy piano." The opening sequence of *Oh, for a Man!* called for her to sing the "Liebestod" from Wagner's *Tristan und Isolde.* She protested to Wurtzel, explaining that her lyric soprano was totally unsuited for *hochdramatische* utterance. Such niceties eluded the boss, who insisted she chirp Wagner. MacDonald rushed to study the piece without the aid of coach Newell, then in New York. A lot was at stake, since her voice was not going to be prerecorded and the scene would mark her debut at performing opera in a movie: "I sweated blood learning the ['Liebestod']. I rehearsed my German pronunciation, but I was a nervous wreck when I played the scene because I knew I shouldn't have been doing it." MacDonald rose to the occasion and gave, on the very first take, a more than creditable rendition of one of the most demanding pieces in the German repertoire: "The musicians must have been as amazed as I was; they broke into applause, and I took a bow."

The next morning, however, Wurtzel ordered director Hamilton MacFadden to cut the bulk of the scene and retain only the final passages. Infuriated, MacDonald again barged into Wurtzel's office and scolded him for daring to toy with the integrity of a classic *Kunstwerk*. Her highfalutin proclamation left Wurtzel unmoved. He reminded his nightingale that *he* ran the studio and *he* knew what the public wanted. *Monte Carlo,* he insisted, proved that people didn't want much music in pictures: "We had a report from San Diego, from one of the theaters down there. When you started to sing that song on the train, a bunch of sailors in the audience had tin cans in their hands. And you know what they did with them? They threw those cans at the screen. Does that prove they don't want music or doesn't it?"

Jeanette wanted to sock the philistine in the eye. She spat back: "It proves to me, Mr. Wurtzel, there were a lot of disorderly sailors just waiting for a chance to throw tin cans. Why else would they have brought the cans with them?" MacDonald's reasoning made sense. But Wurtzel was on the mark in gauging current moviegoer taste, or lack thereof. Her next two pictures for the studio would not be musicals.

MacDonald found an ally at Fox in cinematographer Charles G. Clarke, an ingenious experimenter who would later work with her at MGM. Clarke respected MacDonald for her lighting savvy, and he often conspired in her schemes to outwit the studio: "She liked to go home at six, so she'd look at me and I'd say, 'I guess we'd better quit. She's getting rings under her eyes.'" During the shoot of *Oh, for a Man!*, MacDonald led Clarke to a major technical innovation: "I found that to make her appear at her best I had to use a light right over the camera which produced a flat and flattering source of illumination. This was no problem for her individual close-ups, but when we did an over-the-shoulder shot with someone in the foreground, that person, being closer to this front light, received too much light." To alleviate this problem without a forest of scrims cluttering the set, Clarke had the metal shop make him a small barn-door device that fit directly onto the front light and blocked the unwanted illumination. This device so impressed his colleagues that similar ones were soon in general use at all the studios.

Unfortunately, Clarke was not assigned to MacDonald's second Fox feature, *Don't Bet on Women,* and it shows. "There is no question," she confided about this talky chamber piece, "it is not *my* picture—and I look very unpretty most of the time." MacDonald did get to wear two evening gowns, a riding outfit, and the obligatory gauzy negligee. Yet neither the direction nor the lighting capitalized on her beauty. Although she got second billing on-screen, immediately under and in equal height with that of leading man Edmund Lowe, print publicity put her name in type almost as minuscule as that given supporting players Roland Young and Una Merkel. Worst of all, many reviewers held, with justification, that Merkel gave the film's strongest performance.

Unhappy over the so-so reception of *Don't Bet on Women,* MacDonald was in no mood to suffer the latest indignity Fox had to offer. Right before the release of *Annabelle's Affairs,* a sharp comedy of remarriage, the studio decided to rename it *She Wears the Pants.* "Over my dead body!" MacDonald ranted, wondering how the front office could not see the lunacy of a title that had nothing to do with the story. Moreover, she suspected Fox executives of a nasty inside joke, since the new title encapsuled the way many in Hollywood saw her relationship with Bob Ritchie. If, on the other hand, the studio seriously hoped to package her as a cross-dresser worthy of competition with Garbo and Dietrich, it would have to do it, she maintained, with the flair and expense lavished on them by MGM and Paramount. MacDonald in fact begrudged Fox for having recently fired, in a petty cost-saving move, her friend, the costume designer Sophie Wachner. When Wurtzel refused to budge on the title issue, MacDonald threw caution to the wind and fought back in a way that would set a pattern: she went over the boss's head. At a special meeting of Fox's board of directors, she managed to get the matter reversed in her favor.

As irony would have it, *Annabelle's Affairs,* the only MacDonald film for which no known print survives, was her finest Fox picture. *Time* called it "hilariously funny . . . of a sort rarely seen in cinema"; beneath its photo of MacDonald in an eye-catching negligee, the magazine wrote: "She undresses well." *Variety* declared the picture "a shock for the boys who didn't think Jeanette MacDonald is a light comedienne," hailing her as "a splendid *farceur*" and "the best among the femme contingent now on the Coast."

In spite of the accolades, *Annabelle's Affairs* was weak box office. Word soon had it that MacDonald was slipping and slipping fast. Musicals were out of favor. Her straight comedies were not catching on with the vast public. Studio heads were branding her a troublemaker. Her options in Hollywood were dwindling. In addition, her Fox films were about to trigger a sea of trouble in Europe that would threaten her moral repute.

Still, MacDonald refused to give up.

CHAPTER SEVEN

Vive la France!

I've been to Paris, France, and I've been to Paris,
Paramount. I think I prefer Paris, Paramount.

ERNST LUBITSCH to Garson Kanin

IT BEGAN WITH A CAR CRASH in August 1930. On a highway near
historic Bruges—the Belgian city of lace, canals, and medieval
churches—a seriously injured couple was rushed to a nearby hospital.
Officials kept the pair's identity secret. Two nights later, the gentleman
was transported to a private train. The following morning, the lady
vanished. It was soon whispered that he was Prince Umberto, heir to
the throne of Italy. It was hinted that she was Jeanette MacDonald, the
prince's favorite movie star.

For nearly a year, similar rumors ran riot throughout Europe, each
variant more bizarre than its predecessors. One story had it that Mac-
Donald had been murdered by Belgium's Princess Marie-José, recently
married to the Italian royal. When the irate consort uncovered her husband's affair, she shot MacDonald to death in a bedroom on the French
Riviera, where *Monte Carlo* was supposedly being filmed. Others asserted it was not a pistol but sulfuric acid that Marie-José aimed at the
screen siren's face, leaving her grotesquely disfigured. That's why there
was no singing in *Don't Bet on Women,* the latest MacDonald movie
to reach Europe: the leading lady was actually Blossom, doubling for
her maimed sister. Speculation mounted that MacDonald had taken her
own life. Before the suicide, according to one account, she gave Charlie
Chaplin, then at nearby Juan-les-Pins, her love letters from the prince.

With utmost discretion Chaplin passed this packet to an English duke, who in turn conveyed it to the prince's father, Victor Emmanuel III. The Italian monarch was so relieved that he hastened to sign an Anglo-Italian naval treaty, long bogged down in negotiations.

The scandal raged through the spring of 1931. Spokesmen for the Italian and Belgian thrones issued flat denials despite evidence that the prince and princess were not ideal honeymooners: Umberto was said to be homosexual. In both countries the official press divulged with fanfare the *real* identity of the Bruges crash victims: he was a prominent banker from Milan; she was his mistress, an Italian dressmaker with an uncanny likeness to MacDonald. None of this convinced Continental journalists and their readers. If Jeanette MacDonald was alive and had nothing to hide, why, they asked, was she not confronting the rumors head-on?

The claims were ridiculous. Yet MacDonald faced potential disaster. A wave of puritanism was again enveloping Hollywood. The "cleansing" of Fatty Arbuckle in the early 1920s had found a recent echo in Clara Bow, whose career fell apart after the tabloids detailed her alleged sexual excesses. If the public were to perceive MacDonald as tainted, her career, too, might be over. Lubitsch thought the predicament worthy of his comic operettas and wryly told his pet: "I am afraid that now since associating with royalty, you probably won't speak to *me* any more." *Time* gave details of "the preposterous story" and noted that "no name of scandal attaches to able Actress MacDonald whose chief talent . . . has seemed to be an aptitude for undressing before the camera quickly and almost completely with becoming grace and without embarrassment."

Despite similar nonchalance from the rest of America's press, Mac-Donald needed to guarantee Hollywood that her pictures would do well in foreign markets. Already there was talk of theaters abroad threatening to boycott her movies. Even Europeans who discounted the rumors were offended by what they took to be a high-handed publicity stunt with political fallout too complex to be fathomed by "infantile" Americans. Belgians denounced MacDonald for having "tarnished a Belgian Princess in the eyes of the French." The French indicted her for mocking the royal clans of two friendly nations. An "Open Letter to Mademoiselle Jeanette MacDonald" from the editor of *Comoedia,* France's leading entertainment journal, bristled with rancor:

Mademoiselle,

. . . Paris can very well do without the smile—and how ironic that smile must be!—of the beautiful protagonist of *The Love Parade*. LOVE PARADE on screen. LOVE PARODY in real life. . . . America must not take us for what we are not. We are more than willing to lend an ear to the financial advice of your statesmen. . . . But when it comes to art pure and simple, when it is clear that you have gone beyond the limits of honest fun, we say, "STOP!" One of our great sculptors has given America a magnificent Statue of Liberty. Do not imagine that what we need in return is a Statue of Indecency! . . .

Jean de Rovéra

Bob Ritchie pressed Jeanette to view her plight as an opportunity. The challenge, he insisted, was to go to Europe and convert notoriety into popularity. The bonus, he predicted, would be increased respect at home. Europe's media had already furnished colossal free publicity. Henri Privat, a pioneer in French radio and a best-selling author of pulp fiction, was about to publish a novel based on MacDonald's life. Word had it that France's top film magazine, *Cinémonde,* would soon dub MacDonald "Queen of Mystery" and rank her as the equal of Chaplin and Garbo in mass fascination. If ever there was a time to take the bull by the horns, it was now.

Persuaded by Bob's pleading, Jeanette instructed him to arrange a European concert tour for the late summer and fall. The strategy would be three-pronged: dispel the sex rumors; smother the notion that she had been assaulted and disfigured; and spread the news that the diva was indeed a seductress, but not necessarily in bed.

The *Ile-de-France* docked at Le Havre on August 7, 1931. Armed with State Department letters, impressions of her fingerprints, and affidavits testifying that she had never before stepped foot on European soil, the supposed Jezebel allowed a handful of reporters from the best papers to come aboard and conduct an interview in her lacquered stateroom. All others had to wait until she settled into her suite at Paris's Hotel George V.

"*Non, non, et non!!*" MacDonald shouted at hounding journalists as she stepped off the train at the Gare Saint-Lazare. The mayhem was unprecedented. It took twenty minutes to wade through frenzied crowds before reaching the car that swept her to the Champs-Elysées. The next morning's headlines compared the drama of her transatlantic journey to that of Botticelli's painting *The Birth of Venus*. Her entry into Paris was called the greatest sensation since aviator Charles Lindbergh had landed there four years earlier. But neither Venus nor Lindbergh was lucky enough to have had Bob Ritchie as a promoter. It was no coincidence that MacDonald's *Oh, for a Man!*—with an equally provocative French title, *L'Amant de minuit* ("Midnight Lover")—was slated to open at Paris's Olympia Theater on August 9.* Nor was it chance that prompted the Théâtre des Capucines to schedule a reprise of *Monte Carlo*.

Posters everywhere announced MacDonald's two-week run at the Empire Theater. Located in the shadow of the Arc de Triomphe, the Empire was Paris's largest music hall, seating three thousand. The house had showcased only a handful of American stars—Fatty Arbuckle, Jackie Coogan, Sophie Tucker—and none of them had had all-out success. Part of the problem was that French vaudeville was more worldly and yet more isolated than its British and American counterparts. If Jeanette hoped to transform her wicked repute into acclaim, she would have to make this engagement the show of a lifetime.

On the day before opening, MacDonald invited the critics for caviar and champagne at the George V. The atmosphere in the Art Deco *salle de réception* was strained and chilly. Journalists are paid to be suspicious, and many believed that this extravagant woman, whom no one had yet heard sing, was simply posing as Jeanette MacDonald. Even if their hostess turned out to be who she claimed, the fact was she had upset two royal families. MacDonald worked the room, mixing respectfulness with intimacy, until everyone felt taken into her confidence. The reception started at five o'clock. By six, she had the entire press corps in her thrall. The *Candide* critic gushed to his readers:

> In under fifteen minutes we all lost interest in what was true or false in the rumpus over her identity. We just wanted to watch and admire that beautiful, refined, distinguished face with its dazzling sunset-colored hair. And— what a surprise—here was a movie star who did not play *the* star. . . . Most amazing was that when we left, none of us had anything nasty to say about her. Not even the women, and that is rare. All she had to do was appear, smile, and flash her eyes. She conquered us all—including those who arrived filled with mistrust and hostility.

The next morning MacDonald awoke to an incipient cold and some dreadful news: Mussolini's henchmen were threatening a terrorist at-

---

*Within weeks of MacDonald's arrival in France, Paul Castelle published *L'Amant de minuit*, his novelization of *Oh, for a Man!* (Paris: Editions Jules Tallandier, 1931). It was prominent among the fall season's pop fiction releases.

tack on the Empire Theater. For the Italian Fascists, her identity was beside the point. What mattered was that some woman had dared to humiliate their prince in public. MacDonald, they decided, would have to pay the price. With the help of the American ambassador, Ritchie arranged for plainclothes policemen within and outside the house. MacDonald became so panicky that a doctor had to be called to examine her pounding heart. The physician ordered her to suck on a piece of sugar soaked in ten drops of tincture of aconite. Fearful that the herbal medicine would harm her voice, MacDonald opted to let Rose Coen give her a full-body massage. Yet nothing kept her from obsessing about the bomb that might go off the moment she walked on stage.

The only explosion that Friday night was the roar of audience adulation. At the sight and sound of Mademoiselle Jeanette, the crowd melted. Had anyone trumpeted, "But it's *not* her," a riot would surely have broken out. As the curtain rose, the orchestra played strains of "Dream Lover." One by one, twenty-four dancing girls flitted into position before a black velvet drop. When MacDonald's first notes floated forth from a spot offstage the audience erupted into applause. When she stepped out from the left wing in a drifting Molyneux gown of orange crepe de chine, she literally set the theater aglow. Artfully hesitant, she moved to stage center. Her song finished, the audience went into a frenzy.

This was Jeanette MacDonald *en personne.* This was the actress who had captured the hearts of Maurice Chevalier and France. She was real. She was alive. She was theirs. MacDonald next sang *The Vagabond King*'s "Some Day" in near-perfect French. The theater echoed with "Brava! BRAVA!!" As if to quash any doubt about her feelings for *la douce France,* she followed "Beyond the Blue Horizon" with "Reviens" ("Return"), a French-language torch song from the Belle Epoque. For her closing number she appeared in blinding white military attire to intone, again in French, *The Love Parade*'s "Marche des Grenadiers." A specially built runway enabled many of the fans to touch their *adorée.*

The demands for encores were deafening. Shrewdly, MacDonald gave none. After five curtain calls, she made a little speech: "Merci, merci. Mille fois. Vous êtes gentils. Vous êtes merveilleux. JE VOUS ADORE." The house went wild. Tears trickled down Mistinguett's cheeks. Morris Gest, the international producer who gave New Yorkers their first exposure to Chekhov, had never seen such an ovation for an American in Paris. He became so excited he threw his trademark fedora into the air and lost it.

The following day MacDonald went to hospitals in Neuilly and Beaujon to offer patients the bouquets showered on her the night before. Later that week she was seen on horseback with Bob in the Bois de Boulogne. She also served as "starter" for the annual Grand Prix walking race. At the Place de la Nation, amid throngs of working-class Parisians clamoring "Jeanette, Jeanette, voilà Jeanette!" she led a hundred thousand Frenchmen in "Marche des Grenadiers" and then waved a flag that set the race going.

Her one misstep was a radio appearance on Paris-P.T.T. The quality of the transmission was so poor that rumors resurfaced claiming that the real Jeanette MacDonald was actually dead.

The MacDonald–Prince Umberto scandal stands as one of the more ludicrous yet spectacularly successful publicity coups in show-business history. To this day, it is impossible to gauge the precise extent to which Ritchie's scheming prolonged the impact of the original rumors.* But one thing is certain. MacDonald's Paris adventure gave new life to a phenomenon many believed had been destroyed by the talkies: international stardom. At year's end, *Variety* named Chevalier, Dietrich, and MacDonald the sole Hollywood celebrities whose names were "a practical assurance of success" in Europe. Chaplin, by contrast, was viewed as slipping. Garbo was impeded by the unexpected timbre of her voice. Yet the abiding paradox of Jeanette MacDonald was that her popularity was greater abroad than at home.

For the French, MacDonald's seductiveness resulted from a rare blend of voluptuous looks and cultured vocalism. If her singing failed to meet the standards of some cognoscenti, especially those for whom volume was the mark of quality, that very "handicap" heightened her attractiveness as a woman. As the critic Henry Fleurance observed: "The moment this radiant female appeared on stage, she created a sym-

---

*A satirical French journalist named André Ransan published in *Fantasio* an account of his imagined interview with MacDonald, in which he identified himself as the anonymous press agent who supposedly started the rumors. His account perpetuated the image of MacDonald as a scarlet woman. "Our interview," he wrote, "was intimate, intoxicating, sensual and delicious. She let me go as far as I liked. I cut off a lock of her hair. I counted the 25 lashes she has on each eyelid. I breathed on the down of her neck. I ran my little finger along her bare arm. I measured her calves. I tickled the palm of her hand." MacDonald, not amused, sued Ransan for having "offended her modesty." She won the suit but was not awarded the 200,000 francs sought in damages; the judge simply ordered the journalist to apologize. Excerpts from Ransan's bogus account were published in translation by the *Chicago Tribune* and the *Pittsburgh Post-Gazette* on July 13, 1933.

pathetic and reciprocally admiring bond between herself and the audience. Her voice is small—far less powerful than her mechanically amplified recordings had led us to believe. But it is an ardent, luminous voice, whose timbre is intoxicating. She has the voice of a rose, if roses could sing." By denying the rumors of hanky-panky and at the same time parading athletic Bob Ritchie as her *"manager et fiancé,"* MacDonald cagily flaunted both her propriety and her availability—the combination that had made her so alluring to Lubitsch. Another French journalist rhapsodized: "Jeanette MacDonald is not a woman of ordinary dreams and ordinary adventures. She is not a heartless beauty holding out a tired promise of vague possibilities. Everything in her delicate being hints of real sensual delight and urges you on to ecstasy. . . . Call it sex-appeal, if you must. But she has so much more. Her bewitching qualities transcend vulgarity. They elevate dreams and exalt desire."

Sopranos often elicit extreme responses in men. When MacDonald first made it known she was alive and uninvolved with Prince Umberto, she was deluged with marriage proposals. Among the more bizarre was a letter sent to the editors of *Cinégraph:*

> Plombières-les-Bains
>
> October 7, 1930
>
> I hereby declare my intent to marry Jeanette MacDonald because I am a defrocked priest devoted to the Devil and I wagered for her in a pact with Satan. I'd delighted to have her endure the agony other movie stars have caused me. This woman, whom I've recently seen in *The Vagabond King,* instills me with a ferocious desire for revenge. I have every hope of one day torturing her in a Black Mass. In the meantime, I salute her with all Satanic gallantry.
>
> E. G.

Another Frenchman displayed chivalry of a more orthodox sort. So as not to steal MacDonald's thunder at her Paris debut, Maurice Chevalier delayed showing up until her second evening performance. Jeanette was touched by his presence and sang "Reviens" directly to him. The prince of the boulevards needed no further prompting. He leaped from his box to the stage, kissed MacDonald on the mouth, and then stood pensively for a moment, as if to assess the kiss. With mock astonishment, he exclaimed: "Yes, this is *her! Mais oui, c'est elle!* Oh-oh-oh, this is DEFINITELY my pal Jeanette MacDonald!" Pandemonium shook the house. The next morning an old rumor hit the papers. Were these two an item?

In less than a month, MacDonald had become the toast of Paris. She then crossed the Channel for a two-week stint at London's Dominion Theatre, endearing herself to the English as much as she had to the French. Jack Buchanan, her *Monte Carlo* partner, threw a welcoming reception at the Savoy. The gathering drew the likes of Ambassador Andrew Mellon, musical comedy greats Gertrude Lawrence and Anna Neagle, and Charlie Chaplin, who was rather cool over having been linked to the Prince Umberto affair. Later that week, Jeanette took tea with Prime Minister Ramsay MacDonald at 10 Downing Street. She went for morning rides in Hyde Park, where she found herself signing autographs for lords and ladies. One afternoon she presided over the inauguration of the *jeanette,* a bubbly cocktail created by the bartenders at Dorchester House. In Paris, MacDonald had kept her champagne glasses filled with ginger ale. In London, she could not escape sampling this new concoction.

Someone had the good sense to make a sound movie of MacDonald's dress rehearsal at the Dominion. Lamentably, it is lost. On September 25, she made four recordings with Ray Noble's orchestra for His Master's Voice at Kingsway Hall. They are reliable indicators of her vocal prowess during this early period of international celebrity. In addition to "Reviens" and the Albert Von Tilzer waltz "Dear, When I Met You," she put to disc two delightful numbers from Paul Abrahám's new operetta, *Viktoria and Her Hussar:* "Good Night" and "Pardon, Madame." All disclose purity of tone, charming diction, and an ability to eschew sentimentality for romantic élan.

On October 7, MacDonald, along with her mother, Bob, and a huge puppy courtesy of Ye Olde English Sheep Dog Society, set sail for Canada on the *Empress of Britain.* The crossing was rough, and mother and daughter were seasick all the way. The pup did just fine, earning for himself the name Captain. Jeanette, too, had a new moniker. Viewed as the epitome of New World glamour, she was hailed on the Continent as La Belle Américaine.

Despite his display of affection for her on the stage of the Empire, Maurice Chevalier felt threatened by MacDonald's European triumph. Chevalier's private life was in shambles. The death of his adored mother in 1929 had left him devastated. Yvonne Vallée, furious over what the tabloids called a "close friendship" between Dietrich and her spouse, wanted a divorce. With Marlene's libido already directed elsewhere, Maurice was drawn to Kay Francis, who had only a mild interest in men. As for MacDonald, Chevalier began a vain campaign to distance himself personally and professionally. He resented Jeanette's love affair with Paris. He begrudged her the contract she had been offered to play *The Merry Widow* at Paris's Gaîeté-Lyrique Theater—the first time an American was asked to headline a French-language stage musical. Only a new Paramount offer at twice her former salary forced Jeanette to decline the stage *Widow,* as well as a planned engagement at Berlin's Kabaret der Komiker.

Chevalier had made it known that he wanted actress Carole Lombard, a nonsinger, for the female lead in his next movie, *One Hour with You.* Lubitsch, who was producing and directing the musical, insisted on pairing Maurice with his *Liebchen* Jeanette. He and scriptwriter Samson Raphaelson had conceived the screenplay (a remake of Lubitsch's 1924 American silent *The Marriage Circle*) with *The Love Parade*'s winning team in mind. Both Jesse Lasky and Adolph Zukor agreed with Lubitsch, and MacDonald was signed. Lubitsch was especially excited about directing Sylvania's queen and prince consort in a non-fairy-tale context. But as editing for *The Man I Killed* (his pacifist message film and a commercial flop) fell behind schedule, he reluctantly handed *One Hour with You* to George Cukor, a young import from the New York stage.

MacDonald got along smashingly with Cukor. She found him bright and extravagantly funny, yet he could also be tough, gutsy, and stubborn—qualities she admired in Lubitsch. She also liked Cukor's willingness to weigh her ideas about a scene before ordering the cameras to roll. Chevalier, by contrast, viewed the German-Jewish New Yorker as an effete intellectual whose cultural pretensions made him, a Parisian of the faubourgs, feel inadequate. Years would pass before Chevalier felt comfortable around those he once described as "men so bizarrely made they are compelled to seek out . . . sensations with others of the same sex." MacDonald, on the other hand, was relieved that Cukor didn't pressure her with unwanted advances, as Lubitsch and Chevalier had done. In fact, Cukor became one of the rare persons to whom MacDonald confided her misgivings about Bob Ritchie. He later said: "From my observation of them, I don't think Jeanette would have been very happy with Ritchie for long."

Even by Lubitsch standards, *One Hour with You* was a provocative picture. It exploited Chevalier's gift for making male spectators feel like accomplices to his sexual escapades. Throughout the film Chevalier, an urbane Parisian doctor, steps out of the story, looks directly at the camera, and charmingly asks the audience for advice—sometimes in prose, sometimes in song. MacDonald tries to overturn Chevalier's male prerogatives, hinting that she too has committed—and has a right to—an extramarital affair. Yet at film's end Lubitsch and Raphaelson reinstate the old double standard: men can be Don Juans, but proper wives wander only in dreams. Cukor, who would soon be saddled with the label of "woman's director"—a subtly negative term to describe his gift for guiding actresses through complex emotional scenes—was a perfect choice for such a plot. The problem, as Chevalier rightly saw, was that the future director of *The Women* and *My Fair Lady* might make Mac-Donald come off too sympathetic or, even worse, victorious in her challenge to the Frenchman's star status.

Happily for Chevalier, studio chief Ben Schulberg disliked the early rushes. At a tense conference in Schulberg's office, Cukor agreed to let Lubitsch handle directorial matters whenever he wanted. Soon Lubitsch was overseeing rehearsals, lighting setups, and actual shooting. Cukor was unfazed until the matter of screen credit cropped up. Lubitsch, whose contract was due for renegotiation, demanded director's billing and suggested that Cukor be listed as "dialogue director." Cukor, who was eager to leave Paramount and join David O. Selznick, now at RKO, filed suit against the studio, claiming that his imprint as director was visible in every scene.

An out-of-court settlement gave Cukor credit as "assistant director" and enabled him to break with Paramount immediately. To pacify Lubitsch, the studio ordered that all advertising for *One Hour with You* include his name in print "as large as Chevalier's and at least two-thirds as large as the title." MacDonald's name was to appear in type no more than "three-fourths as large as Chevalier's." When work on *One Hour with You* ended, Maurice offered Jeanette a gift expressing his deepest sentiments: a pair of boxing gloves. Cukor wanted to do likewise for Lubitsch, but his lawyer restrained him.

There has been endless speculation about Cukor's actual contributions to *One Hour with You*. It's tempting to imagine him responsible for the fluid "girl talk" sequence in which MacDonald catches up with her school pal turned home wrecker (Genevieve Tobin). Never again would MacDonald appear so at ease on-screen with another featured actress. It's also likely that the ring of her speaking voice—more polished, confident, and conversational—owes much to Cukor. In her memoir, MacDonald gave an account for the seemingly contradictory claims of Lubitsch and Cukor: "Maurice and I made two versions of *One Hour with You,* one in French with Lili Damita as 'the other woman' and George Cukor directing, one in English under Ernst's direction with Genevieve Tobin as the third member of the eternal triangle." *Une heure près de toi* was a major event in France. It was one of the few Hollywood musicals to be entirely reshot with a totally Francophone cast and French-language screenplay. To Chevalier's chagrin, the French distributors gave MacDonald equal-size billing with his own, and the Paris critics praised her acting over his.

Playful, sparkling, and effervescent, *One Hour with You* was nominated for a Best Picture Oscar, although the prize went to MGM's *Grand Hotel.* It was the only musical to make the *New York Times* annual Ten Best Films List. Technically it was a tour de force. Its smooth shifts from underscored dialogue to partially sung rhyming couplets to full song made this intimate operetta a landmark in the fusion of character, story, and song.* At a time when it was feared that a picture's sound quality would suffer if printed on tinted film stock, the dialogue and music stayed razor sharp even though the nighttime exteriors were bathed in lavender and the interiors in gold.†

The April issue of *Photoplay* cited MacDonald, along with Chevalier and Tobin, for the month's Best Performances. The *New York American* ascribed the exceptional feel of *One Hour with You* to the film's two costars, whose "charm and magnetism distinguish each from all others in Hollywood." MacDonald won special individual notice from the Massachusetts Board of Censors, who found fault with the scene in which she answers the phone in an extremely décolleté undergarment. These wicked shots, the Bostonians ordained, had to be cut from all *Sunday* showings.

Shortly after the cast had dispersed, Lubitsch decided to do retakes on the final shots of *One Hour with You.* Maurice was in New York, negotiating his Palace stage debut. Jeanette was in Beverly Hills, now renting at 711 North Linden Drive. Invitations had just gone out for a Valentine's Day extravaganza she was throwing in honor of Bob's thirty-sixth birthday. The studio had to take sides. Would they shoot

---

*The introduction of rhymed-and-rhythmed dialogue in film musicals is often attributed to MacDonald's subsequent movie, *Love Me Tonight* (1932), directed by Rouben Mamoulian. In fact, Lubitsch had already utilized this playful device in less conspicuous ways in both *The Love Parade* (1929) and *Monte Carlo* (1930).

†Film preservationist Robert Gitt has restored *One Hour with You* to its original tinted version, housed in the UCLA Film and Television Archive.

on Long Island or in Hollywood? MacDonald was ordered to depart for the East Coast immediately. Although the official reason was expedience, Lubitsch and Chevalier took private pleasure in seeing Ritchie's evening of merriment sabotaged. Louella Parsons dutifully advertised the party's cancellation in her column.

In New York, Earl Carroll, the producer of Broadway's naughty *Vanities,* courted MacDonald and Chevalier for his new stage musical, *Rendezvous.* Yet the last thing both wanted was to perpetuate themselves as a team. MacDonald was hopeful MGM might renew its earlier overtures toward her. Talk had it that Irving Thalberg, Metro's head of production, wanted to pair her with Ramon Novarro in *The Merry Widow.* Others said MGM would consider her for the part only if she played opposite Chevalier. MacDonald hated the uncertainty.

It was not just musicals but the whole future of movies that was in a state of confusion. The industry's immunity to the Great Depression had broken down. Paramount-Publix was especially hit, slumping from a profit of over $18 million in 1930 to a deficit of nearly $16 million in 1932. B. P. Schulberg and Jesse Lasky were soon forced out of a bankrupt company that went into receivership. Earlier, Schulberg had criticized his colleagues for having risked too much on sophisticated movies: "The industry has . . . listened all too often to the articulate minority and all too often has overlooked the inarticulate majority. The result has been many pictures brilliantly done and praised by the articulate few but without mass appeal. . . . The public wants simple, homely, heart-interest pictures that it can believe and understand. . . . The industry must think of mass appeal; otherwise it cannot survive." Adolph Zukor outlasted the purge and later became chairman of the board of the newly reorganized Paramount Pictures, Inc. But in early 1932, Zukor ignored Schulberg's advice to abandon class for mass— and with reason. Two of his swankiest stars, MacDonald and Chevalier, were raking in $5,000 and $10,000 per week, respectively, even though they were between pictures. Lubitsch, whose huge contract had yet to be renewed, was playing politics, telling New York reporters that he wanted to leave movies to direct soprano Maria Jeritza in a new Broadway operetta. At his wit's end, Zukor turned to Rouben Mamoulian, the stylish director who had just completed *Dr. Jekyll and Mr. Hyde* with Fredric March.

Their meeting was like a scene lifted from a George Kaufman and Moss Hart farce. Zukor, the squat and steely Hungarian émigré who virtually invented the U.S. movie business, shed tears as he begged Mamoulian, the tall, suave Russian exile famous for avant-garde opera direction, to bail out his failing studio: "Do anything you want, forget about the money. Any story you like, any way you want, just say you'll do it! You know, I'm an old man. . . . Do it as a friend, PLEASE!" (Zukor, then 49, lived to be 102.) Mamoulian resented Zukor's emotional blackmail, especially since *Dr. Jekyll and Mr. Hyde* had left him physically exhausted. But carte blanche to do what he wished with the king and queen of Lubitsch musicals was an offer not to be turned down. Mamoulian said yes.

Rouben Mamoulian was an alumnus of the Moscow Arts Theater and a rebel against naturalism. In 1927 he mesmerized Broadway with his production of Du Bose and Dorothy Heyward's *Porgy,* and he would later mount the premiere of Gershwin's opera, *Porgy and Bess.* Mamoulian's first two movies—*Applause* with Helen Morgan (1929) and *City Streets* with Gary Cooper and Sylvia Sidney (1931)—mixed sound and visuals in ways that expanded the medium's capacity to portray human experience. "Art for art's sake," he liked to say, "is not satisfactory; art should be for life's sake."

Mamoulian turned to French playwright Léopold Marchand to create the MacDonald-Chevalier story, which was to be a combination of Sleeping Beauty and "Cinderfella." Broadway's Richard Rodgers and Lorenz Hart composed songs that would become their biggest hits to originate in Hollywood: "Lover," "Mimi," and "Isn't It Romantic?" But Mamoulian alone was responsible for *Love Me Tonight*'s overall concept. This movie, he decided, would be an illustrated musical score. In a reversal of convention, his writing team developed the screenplay only after Rodgers had composed all of the film's music and after Hart had penned the rhymed-and-rhythmed dialogue. The remaining action and dialogue were then fitted to this preexisting blueprint. Like *One Hour with You,* this elegant, witty picture would be a model for the integration of song and story, tone and style, that Rodgers would achieve a decade later on Broadway with Oscar Hammerstein II in *Oklahoma!*— directed by Rouben Mamoulian. Vincente Minnelli and Kurt Weill are among those who have judged *Love Me Tonight* to be the perfect film musical.

For MacDonald, the production took off badly. She found Mamoulian pesky and humorless. The crew, mainly Lubitsch veterans, shared her feelings. Rebellion soon broke out. One morning, an electrician dropped a lamp perilously close to the director. That afternoon, a sound man inserted a sneeze into the track. These blatant taunts cut Mamoulian to the quick, and he sought Jeanette's advice. "Rouben," she told him, "we are supposed to be making a comedy, a gay picture full of laughter. But it's almost impossible in the funereal atmosphere you're creating. There you have it. Now don't hold it against me for letting truth be known." MacDonald's straight talk worked. Mamoulian soon took the lead in encouraging cast and crew to relax. But there still remained one source of tension the director could not smooth over. Bob Ritchie was hanging around the set and constantly giving Jeanette hints from the sidelines. Mamoulian's temper eventually blew, and he ordered Ritchie barred from the set.

Mamoulian used his blank check to borrow Myrna Loy from MGM. Loy played Countess Valentine, the nymphomaniac cousin of Princess Jeanette. (In a wink to the audience, the Chevalier and MacDonald characters were named—Maurice and Jeanette.) Loy had been in scores of grade B melodramas, mainly as slinky Oriental vamps. Mamoulian wanted *Love Me Tonight* to disclose her flair for smart comedy, a gift that would ripen when she starred opposite William Powell in MGM's *Thin Man* series. Stories have circulated about MacDonald's supposed irritation when Mamoulian expanded Loy's role in midproduction. Joseph Youngerman, who was prop man on the film, saw things differently: "I think Myrna was just a little bit jealous of being in a supporting position—although she didn't show it much." Loy did have some of the picture's best laugh lines. When the princess suddenly faints, the spendthrift cousin (Charlie Ruggles) rushes to awaken the countess, found napping in the salon: "Valentine, can you go for a doctor?" "Certainly," she quips, "bring him right in." MacDonald herself sets up Loy's best retort when the two are on horseback outside the château stables:

> MacDonald [*in a condescending tone*]: Tell me, do you ever think of anything but men, dear?
> Loy [*nonchalantly*]: Oh yes.
> MacDonald [*slightly exasperated*]: Of what?
> Loy: Schoolboys. [*She rides off.*]

Perhaps because he was infatuated with Loy, Mamoulian did not fully tap the sensual playfulness MacDonald radiated in *The Love Parade* and *One Hour with You*. When Jeanette and Maurice share their first passionate kiss in a bower, the scene plays awkwardly: she is a novice; he is a social impostor; their show of ardor is a bit forced. The title song follows, and though the lyrics proclaim the immediacy of their fervor, the duet takes place not in the here and now of the garden but in the far-and-away of a dream sequence.* This tug between intimacy and distance reaches a climax in the film's final, frenzied episode. Superimposed over Maurice, who is seen from afar as he boards a train, are extreme close-ups of Jeanette, agonizing in solitude. Suddenly strains of "Love Me Tonight" provoke her to join the tailor and flee with him, his plebeian station be damned. Racing on horseback, her shoulder-length hair wafted by the wind, heroic Jeanette overtakes the train, leaps from her steed, and positions herself smack in the center of the railroad tracks. With Amazonian force of will, she brings the locomotive to a halt, Maurice to her arms, and this modern fairy tale to its near gender-bending end. A coda, however, reaffirms sex-role conventions, as Jeanette's three aunts unfurl the needlepoint they've been stitching throughout the film: it shows a valiant knight on horseback rescuing a princess locked up in a castle tower.

Love Me Tonight forever identified MacDonald with great Rodgers and Hart standards. She introduced "Lover" as a brisk syncopated waltz, interspersing fanciful thoughts about an unknown lover with commands to the frisky horse drawing her carriage.† MacDonald's rendition of "Isn't It Romantic?" anticipated the ripe romanticism that was to become her stock-in-trade at MGM. Chevalier launches the tune in his tailor shop as a jaunty portrait of domestic life: he imagines a partner who will "scrub the floor," "cook me onion soup," and "kiss me every hour." The infectious melody then travels through time, space, and musical styles. It journeys from Maurice's customer to a roving taxi driver, from an itinerant musician to a platoon of marching soldiers, from campfire gypsies to, at last, the solitary Princess Jeanette. The soprano steps onto her balcony. The fox-trimmed sleeves of her clinging velvet nightgown shimmer in the moonlight. Her tones glisten. She rolls her *r*'s. Delivering the song as a poignant ballad, she invokes "music in the night," "a dream that can be heard," and the longed-for "sweet lover of my fancy." Mamoulian claimed that MacDonald "took

*MacDonald gave a deliciously seductive rendition of "Love Me Tonight" in a promotional one-reeler for the picture: feline style, she crawled to the foot of a tufted satin bed and sang provocatively to the camera. This promo became part of the compilation film *Hollywood on Parade* (No. 5, 1932), a print of which is housed in the UCLA Film and Television Archive.

†MacDonald never recorded "Lover" for commercial release. But like other songs from her films—"Beyond the Blue Horizon," "Indian Love Call," "Maids of Cadiz," "Lover, Come Back to Me," "Donkey Serenade"—it became a favorite among jazz musicians, including guitarist Les Paul and singer Peggy Lee.

the whole thing very seriously . . . not realizing the humorous tone behind it." Yet her performance transcends simple notions of authenticity
and self-parody. Her vocal fervor is so at odds with the tongue-in-cheek
contrivances—the setting, the preceding statements of the song, indeed,
Mamoulian's overall direction—that MacDonald becomes a radiant
icon of romantic yearning.*

Love Me Tonight cost Paramount nearly $1 million. Like MacDon-
ald's other early prestige vehicles, it did better business abroad than at
home. Reviewers in this country admired it as a "director's film," but
many found Mamoulian's inventiveness unrelenting. Small-city moviegoers, who would shortly embrace the kid-next-door antics of Ruby
Keeler and Dick Powell, were tired of Continental sophistication. The
hinterland and Bible Belt were downright hostile to Chevalier, calling
him "washed up," "a headache," "a flop." Yet when the nation's theater owners ranked the ten biggest box-office draws in June 1932,
Chevalier appeared on 40 percent of the lists. MacDonald was on only
5 percent. Another survey, conducted in August for RKO, graded the
moneymaking power of 133 screen performers on a downward scale
from "AA" to "H." Chevalier and Garbo were the only ones to make
"AA" status. MacDonald received a "D"—as did Tallulah Bankhead at
Paramount and Loretta Young at Warner–First National. These rank-
ings upset Jeanette. It was no consolation that Irene Dunne and Barbara Stanwyck were "Cs," and Carole Lombard an "H."

Still hungry for popular approval, MacDonald decided to make another, more protracted trip abroad. A recent British poll placed her
popularity just beneath Garbo's and right above Crawford's. In France,
the journalist Paul Achard was about to publish an entire book on her
life and films. MacDonald was convinced that if Chevalier could carve
out a career in America, she could do likewise in Europe, where her talents, beauty, and esprit were more compatible with prevailing tastes.
Before departing, she told the press that if she should return to American pictures, it would be for straight dramatic parts. She also declared

---

*In the early 1960s, composer Hugh Martin (*Best Foot Forward, Meet Me in St. Louis*)
and librettist Marshall Barer (*Once Upon a Mattress*) conceived *A Little Night Music,* an
elaborate musical intended to mark MacDonald's return to Broadway and Liza Minnelli's Broadway debut. Its inventive score contained a haunting countermelody to "Isn't
It Romantic?" titled "Wasn't It Romantic?" MacDonald was to sing it in duet with her
screen self of three decades earlier. She declined to do the show, but "Wasn't It Romantic?" got recorded and was much performed in the 1980s by singer Michael Feinstein.
The musical, entitled *Happy Lot!,* had its world premiere in concert format on February
21, 1998, at Theatre West, Hollywood. The production was "dedicated to the memory
of Jeanette MacDonald" and starred Betty Garrett, Feinstein, and Melissa Converse.

that her underwear days were over: "I don't think my career of risqué roles has really hurt. I just feel I have gone far enough in lingerie. . . . I'm sure that people must say about me, on the screen, 'Good gracious, is Jeanette MacDonald going to take off her clothes—*again?*' "

Three days before Christmas 1932, MacDonald arrived on the French Riviera aboard the new Italian liner, the *Conte di Savoia*. Her entourage included Anna, the factotums Rose and Henri Coen, a trilingual secretary, Captain (no longer a pup at eighty-five pounds), and Captain's companion, Stormy Weather, a tiny Skye terrier. Ritchie was already on French soil. When MacDonald disembarked at the violet-tinged port of Villefranche-sur-Mer, reporters assailed her with questions about her impending marriage—to Chevalier! A few months earlier, Maurice had finally divorced Yvonne Vallée. When news broke that he was inviting Jeanette to spend the holidays at La Louque, his villa near Cannes, rumors of an imminent wedding mushroomed.

The gossip disgusted Bob Ritchie, who was furious with Jeanette for not having declined outright the Frenchman's last-minute offer of hospitality. One goal of this European tour was to showcase MacDonald independent of Chevalier. Bob construed Maurice's generosity as a Machiavellian ploy for holding Jeanette's fame hostage to his own. To keep plans on track, Ritchie ushered Jeanette and her retinue to Antibes and the Hôtel du Cap. This luxurious hotel—a haven for European royalty, American industrialists, and filmdom's haut monde— would be fictionalized the following year in F. Scott Fitzgerald's novel *Tender Is the Night*. Former New York mayor Jimmy Walker and his latest mistress were currently vacationing there.

MacDonald remained on the Côte d'Azur for the next two weeks. On Christmas Eve, she was guest of honor at a dinner hosted in the Restaurant des Ambassadeurs by the Marquise de Meyronnet de Saint Marc, the former Eleanor Wain of Philadelphia. Asked about the alleged engagement, Jeanette answered: "Marriage to Monsieur Chevalier is quite out of the question for the simple reason that I am engaged to Mr. Robert Ritchie." Congratulations followed. Bob greeted them with a smile that barely camouflaged his wearied sense of déjà vu. Four days later, Jeanette played the international diplomat. She went to La Louque—without Bob—and thanked Paul and Henriette Chevalier, Maurice's brother and sister-in-law, for preparing the house even though she would not be staying there. The threesome then cabled

Maurice, at work in Hollywood: "ALL TOGETHER THIS EVENING THINK
OF YOU AND DRINK TO YOUR HEALTH HEARTBROKEN DESPITE GREAT
DESIRE PUBLIC OPINION PREVENTS LA LOUQUE SOJOURN. PAUL HENRI-
ETTE JEANETTE."

Cannes was not yet the sister city of Beverly Hills, nor the site of the
great film festival. Yet Mayor Gazagnaire honored Jeanette with an official city hall reception, a gesture previously accorded to only one
actor, Charlie Chaplin. She also visited Monte Carlo, where she disappointed some by being drawn not to the gaming tables but to the new
International Sporting Club.

The next few months were as much a test for Ritchie as for Jeanette.
The European press kept fishing for news on the elusive wedding. Mac-
Donald's usual response was to say she considered marriage and a
movie career incompatible. The untold story was that Ritchie had still
not proved his worth as an independent moneymaker—her requirement for legalizing their union. Bob had wonderful schemes. With his
associate Edwin "Ned" Marin, he planned to make Europe an international base for the production and distribution of high-toned films. He
would establish a new company, Jeanette MacDonald Productions.
Mervyn LeRoy was to direct Jeanette in a London-based picture; Lubitsch would do another with her in Paris. Ramon Novarro, whose European concert tour Bob was already handling, would be launched into
French films. Ritchie and Marin would acquire world rights to the
movies of producer-director Alexander Korda, who had just bailed out
the British film industry with *The Private Life of Henry VIII.* Ritchie
would also furnish Dietrich and Gloria Swanson with new personal
management. He would represent directors René Clair, Fritz Lang, and
G. W. Pabst in the States. And he would team Jeanette with the English
actor Herbert Marshall, fresh from Lubitsch's *Trouble in Paradise,* in a
British & Dominions Film Corporation picture, possibly *Bitter Sweet,*
to be directed by Herbert Wilcox and released through United Artists.

None of these plans materialized. Yet the main purpose of this self-
imposed exile was to show off Jeanette's popularity to those with
power back home. And here, the MacDonald-Ritchie partnership hit
the jackpot.

In Paris, MacDonald moved into a princely double suite at the George V.
Each afternoon, she combed antique stores near Saint-Germain-
des-Prés and around the Place Vendôme in search of historical fans.

On her earlier trip she had gone to Fontainebleau to visit retired vaudeville star Jennie Dolly, who gave her an amber fan that had once belonged to Empress Joséphine. When MacDonald learned that Jennie's gift had extraordinary monetary worth, she started a fan collection of her own and eventually acquired specimens once the property of Empress Eugénie, Maria Theresa of Austria, and Jenny Lind. To practice her skiing, MacDonald spent a few days in Saint Moritz, Switzerland, where she joined Gloria Swanson, Harold Lloyd, and Clara Bow at the Palace Hotel. Back in Paris, she gave an informal concert at a country home for crippled war veterans. When she showed up at a gala screening of René Clair's new film, *July Fourteenth,* she snatched the limelight from Annabella, the picture's young star.

Eager to be better known in Paris music circles, MacDonald struck up a friendship with Gustave Charpentier, who thought her lyric fluency would make her the ideal heroine of his opera *Louise.* She also became friends with Reynaldo Hahn, the Venezuelan-born composer who had been Marcel Proust's lover. Hahn's 1923 operetta *Ciboulette* had sealed his reputation as the embodiment of elegance in French musical theater. Like MacDonald, Hahn was drawn to the tradition of French *romances*—simple sentimental songs reminiscent of 1890s parlor music. His special gift was to make such music sound fresh rather than merely antique. It was a talent many ascribed to MacDonald as well.

The huge white-on-scarlet letters R-E-X descend from the top of an Art Deco facade that dominates the Boulevard Poissonnière. The theater's interior is a witty mix of Deco, Moorish, and Byzantine. Massive by French standards, the house seats thirty-three hundred. The stage, framed by a scarlet-lit arch, is broader than that of the Paris Opéra. The Rex was the brainchild of Jacques Haïk, the Jewish-Tunisian movie producer who had introduced Chaplin to France and dubbed him "Charlot." Within days of its opening on December 8, 1932, the Rex equaled the Eiffel Tower and Sacré-Coeur as a must-see Paris attraction. Jeanette MacDonald was its first international star. While Franklin D. Roosevelt was shaping a New Deal for Americans, France was just starting to feel the impact of the Wall Street disaster. Nonetheless, MacDonald demanded and got the startling sum of $35,000 for two weeks of personal appearances, four times daily, at the Rex.*

*In today's currency, $35,000 is the equivalent of about a half million dollars.

On February 3, telegrams from Hollywood and New York flooded her dressing room. Well-wishers included Claudette Colbert, Joan Crawford and her husband Douglas Fairbanks, Jr., Laurel and Hardy, Tallulah Bankhead, Chaplin, and Lubitsch. One cable came from a singer who was Hollywood's bridge to a realm MacDonald still longed to be part of, opera: "ANOTHER SONG ANOTHER TRIUMPH MAY IT ALWAYS BE YOUR LOT TO MAKE THE WORLD MELODIOUS. — LAWRENCE TIBBETT."

The Rex program was more adventuresome than the Empire show, if only because MacDonald sang and spoke entirely in French. Her songs, performed over a forty-piece pit orchestra, included selections from *The Merry Widow,* two numbers from *Love Me Tonight,* and Jean Lenoir's popular waltz "Parlez-moi d'amour" ("Speak to Me of Love"). For openers she sang "Aimez-moi ce soir" ("Love Me Tonight") while reclining on a white canopied bed that glided slowly downstage. Later, dressed in black satin, she burst forth from an immense red heart for "N'est-ce pas poétique?" ("Isn't It Romantic?"). For an encore, she sang the song all Europeans thought of as hers, *The Love Parade*'s "Marche des Grenadiers," this time joined by a regiment of twelve Rex Appeal Girls and sixteen Rhythm Dancers supplied by her old Broadway mentor, Ned Wayburn.

MacDonald again electrified Paris audiences, and French chauvinism once more colored the reviews. One journalist wrote: "[MacDonald] gave the Parisians a gift of that voice whose every note is like a star plucked from a firmament all sweetness and sensitivity. . . . There is no one in France who can resist it. If it were not for that delicious accent, nothing would be less American than Jeanette MacDonald. Her charm, like her first name, is French." She was just as triumphant in Lyons, Marseilles, Lille, Strasbourg, Amsterdam, Rotterdam, Geneva, Lausanne, and Zurich.

Her boldest stroke came in Brussels, where the Belgians made up for the animosity shown her during the Prince Umberto scandal. When she arrived at the Gare du Sud, five thousand fans broke through police lines and set off a full-scale riot. Her opening at the Alhambra Theater was a charity benefit for wounded Belgian soldiers. King Albert did not attend, but he sent Lieutenant-General Biebuyck to extend his regal congratulations and to present MacDonald with a gift showing that all was forgiven: "I was handed a tiny Griffon Bruxellois, a dog no bigger than a teacup, who promptly wet right down the front of my immaculate white 'March of the Grenadiers' costume." A more fitting finale to the farcical feud could not have been preordained.

When musicals went out of vogue in late 1930, Lubitsch declared that the public was "sick of the tripe, not the music." Now times were changing. Dance director Busby Berkeley was preparing *42nd Street*, a gutsy backstager for Warner Bros. Fred Astaire was about to make his screen debut in MGM's *Dancing Lady*, with Clark Gable and Joan Crawford. Vincent Youmans was writing an original score for RKO's *Flying Down to Rio*, which would star Dolores Del Rio and Gene Raymond and would team Astaire with Ginger Rogers for the very first time. At United Artists, Al Jolson was due for a comeback with *Hallelujah, I'm a Bum*. More than ever, MacDonald sensed the time was right for *The Merry Widow*. MGM's Irving Thalberg, who had produced the 1925 silent version, felt the same.

Jeanette and Bob planned strategy. Thalberg was on a sabbatical in Europe. At age thirty-four, MGM's vice president in charge of production was recovering from an exhausting power play with studio head Louis B. Mayer, a heart attack suffered at Christmas, and a tonsillectomy just undergone in Bad Nauheim, Germany. Word had it that Thalberg and his wife, "Queen of the Lot" Norma Shearer, would be vacationing at the Hôtel du Cap in April. It was essential, Jeanette and Bob agreed, that a personal rapport be established with them prior to any business talk. Bob swiftly left Paris for London, while Jeanette and her mother drove to the Riviera in their black custom-built Packard, shipped from California. They checked in at the Hôtel du Cap one day before Irving and Norma's scheduled arrival. When they met, the MacDonalds and Thalbergs laughed at the amazing "coincidence."

The actresses, who barely knew each other, fast became friends. They swam and exercised together. They shared diet tips. Norma confided in Jeanette about her mother's ambition to see her become a concert pianist. When Norma's hairdresser became indisposed, Jeanette loaned her Henri Coen. Had this been Beverly Hills or Santa Monica, MacDonald and Shearer most likely would have been competing for attention. But in Cap d'Antibes, they were two ambitious North American girls—one from Philadelphia, the other from Montreal—who found that their patrician manners played just as convincingly in a country that had guillotined its real nobility as in their native land of immigrants, parvenus, and movie fans.

Irving Thalberg found MacDonald's humor and optimism a tonic for his ailments. He, in turn, captivated Jeanette with his soft-spokenness and princely aura. Physically, Irving was the antithesis of the kind of man that ordinarily appealed to her. At five-foot six and barely 120 pounds, he was slight of build and not at all muscular, and his black wavy hair crowned a high pale forehead. Yet MacDonald was moved by the intellect and sensitivity of a man whose congenital heart deformity led him to live with ferocious intensity, not for pleasure but for achievement. She was relieved that Bob Ritchie was six hundred miles away. Bob's robust humor was a shade too common, his social graces a tinge too abrasive. He would have appeared crass in such company.

Thalberg spoke vaguely of Metro's plans for *The Merry Widow.* He also told MacDonald that Rodgers and Hart, now at MGM, were at work on a score for *I Married an Angel,* a fantasy musical he could see as another vehicle for her. He talked about the industry's financial crisis and his conviction that when Americans endure hardship they must be rewarded with entertainment of exceptional appeal. He spoke of his chronic insomnia and how his best ideas for fine-tuning a picture came to him in the wee hours of the morning.

With their perfectionism and insomnia out in the open, MacDonald and Thalberg were hooked on each other. Yet neither one made any commitments at Cap d'Antibes. MacDonald's plan was to move cautiously and without compromise. She was convinced that MGM needed her as much as she wanted them. Accordingly, she left the Riviera to join Bob in London, where plans for a British picture were still afloat.

Her aloofness paid off. Louis B. Mayer's London proxies had been sending out feelers through Ritchie. MacDonald now understood the symbolic weight Mayer and Thalberg individually attached to getting her signed to the studio. For ten years, the twosome had been regarded as the most formidable production team in the history of movies. Mayer, the fierce studio chief, fought money battles with Nicholas Schenck, president of MGM's parent company, Loew's, Inc. Gentle young Thalberg supervised productions with an unfailing instinct for smoothness and polish. Mayer claimed to love Thalberg as a son. However, by late 1932 their special alliance had soured. Mayer construed the admiration of MGM's producers, writers, and directors for Thalberg as a challenge to his own authority. Thalberg, whose contract was expiring, demanded higher compensation for a job that, to his mind, was more important than Mayer's. Schenck, fearful of losing both men to other studios, made liberal adjustments to their contracts. But in a stunning Judas kiss, Mayer seized upon Thalberg's convalescence in Europe as cause to relieve him of his duties as vice president in charge of production. He divided Thalberg's responsibilities between himself and his son-in-law David O. Selznick, reluctantly wooed from RKO. Henceforth Thalberg would run only a small unit within the huge studio. King Louis would be absolute monarch.

When Thalberg stopped off in London shortly before returning to the States, he left word with MacDonald at Dorchester House that he wanted to talk business with her and Ritchie. Jeanette's instinct told her that Irving was the right man to tailor pictures for her, just as he had done with Shearer, Garbo, and Helen Hayes. But Ritchie, who was keeping tabs on the MGM shake-up, pleaded that she not alienate L. B. Mayer. She would be a fool, he said, to let anyone but the top boss take credit for getting her signed by the New York office. He reminded her that she could always maneuver herself later into Thalberg's camp.

MacDonald bowed to Ritchie's stratagem. For nearly a week she avoided Thalberg's calls and ignored his telegrams. When she finally learned of his voyage homeward, her guilt was brutal: "I felt like a hypocrite. . . . That night I had my first attack of asthma. The doctor called it psychosomatic. I called it Hell."

CHAPTER EIGHT

Mr. Mayer and the Widow

If there is one thing that I insist upon, it is quality.

LOUIS B. MAYER, at the opening
of Metro-Goldwyn studios, 1924

JEANETTE MACDONALD COOED HER WAY TO DIVADOM upon Louis B. Mayer's lap—it was said. MGM's chief had a definite weakness for beautiful, slim women who projected virginal freshness, high moral standards, and devotion to their mothers. In Jeanette, he found the embodiment of his Jewish fantasy of the clean-cut American shiksa. When Mayer's wife, Margaret, had a hysterectomy in late 1933, she became depressed and physically remote. Mayer, only forty-eight and in need of female companionship, found Jeanette's infectious vitality enthralling. At their first meeting, he urged her to think of him as "your friend, counselor, and guide"—his standard line to all valuable female newcomers. Within a short time, the mogul and his star singer developed an authentic friendship. Soon no one on the lot doubted that Jeanette MacDonald was the boss's "favorite."

Many at Culver City resented the special status Mayer accorded MacDonald. Sam Marx, who headed the story department, recalled: "One day I had to see L. B. at about 4:45 P.M. to get his approval to buy an expensive property. His secretary, Jeanette Spooner, told me he had someone in his office and that I'd have to wait. In bounced MacDonald, who said to Spooner, 'I must see Mr. Mayer.' The secretary noted that I was first in line and that my yes-or-no question would take only a minute of Mayer's time. Seconds later, L. B. opened his door, ushered someone out, and MacDonald VAULTED in ahead of me, looked back, and said, 'Sam, I promise not to be more than a half hour.'" Marx never forgave MacDonald's rudeness: "I knew Jeanette from my New York days as editor of *Broadway Amusements,* and I had a helluva time accepting prima donna pretensions from someone who had starred in *Boom-Boom.*"

Mayer indulged his pet in a superstitious ritual each time she started a new film. Over full costume and makeup, MacDonald would wrap herself in her lucky garment, an old Mother Hubbard cloak and hood, and burst into Mayer's inner sanctum, interrupting whatever conference he was having. In a teasing, breathy voice that never failed to make L. B.'s pulse quicken, she would then whisper, "Mr. Mayer, you simply *have* to wish me my good luck!" The studio patriarch would rise from his horseshoe-shaped desk, pat her on the shoulder, and proclaim assuringly, "Jeanette, it's going to be a *great* picture."

Both MacDonald and Mayer had fathers who had failed in business. This core disgrace, the root of much of their ferocious ambition, led each to determine never to reexperience poverty or impose it on loved ones. Mayer's favoritism toward Jeanette was paternalistic and overbearing, yet it satisfied her compulsive need to be rewarded lavishly for hard work. MacDonald and Mayer also served each other's claims to refined taste. Mayer was a businessman who craved legitimacy and social approval. One of his proudest early achievements took place in 1912, when as a young theater operator in Haverill, Massachusetts, he brought the Boston Opera Company to town for a production of Puccini's *Madama Butterfly.* Twenty-one years later, as he struggled with Irving Thalberg to seize credit for MGM's artistic loftiness, Mayer saw Mac-Donald's incorporation into the MGM family as confirming his sense of cultural mission. The soprano, in turn, viewed Mayer as her key to winning the hearts of Americans who had resisted her Paramount image.

Mayer was hardly a cultural barbarian. He enjoyed opera and ballet. He reveled in operetta. But he made no pretense of connoisseurship. "L. B. Mayer was a guy who probably knew the 'Toreador Song' from *Carmen* and 'Un bel dì' from *Butterfly,*" said Johnny Green, who would later become MGM's general music director. "But I doubt that he would know what you were talking about if you mentioned 'Mi chiamano Mimì' from *Bohème.*" When *The Great Caruso* was in pre-production, Mayer instructed Green: "None of this remote stuff. Don't forget the public. They don't have to know the title; they don't even have to know what opera it's from; but give them the chance to pat themselves on the back and say, 'Oh, I know that aria!' " Tenor Allan Jones, MacDonald's leading man in MGM's *The Firefly*, later observed: "You can say what you like about the Louis B. Mayers and the heads of the studios in my day. They were not educated, they were pretty crude, but they wanted to improve themselves and they wanted to improve the public."

One thing Mayer did not think well of was MacDonald's liaison with Bob Ritchie. Leery of sophistication, Mayer championed loyalty to kin, civic service, and dignified, almost puritanical restraint in one's private life. No one ever accused Bob Ritchie of the last. As MacDonald's business manager, Ritchie was tough and effective. He got Metro to set her starting salary at $4,000 per week, then the equal of Joan Crawford's and only a thousand below that of Her Royal Highness Norma Shearer. But Bob's efforts to carve out an independent career for himself continued to go nowhere. Shamelessly, he told outsiders he was now an important MGM producer. He even sweet-talked the ladies of the switchboard into taking messages for him while he was "away" from his nonexistent office. Bob soon became an embarrassment to Jeanette, and Mayer decided to set things right. With a view both to cleansing her image and to promoting his own quixotic dream of winning her heart, Mayer placed Ritchie on the company payroll—overseas. Through 1939, Bob worked as a talent scout in Europe, helping MGM recruit Luise Rainer, Greer Garson, and Hedy Lamarr. At the peak of his association with Metro, Ritchie earned $4,000 a month.

Mayer's ploy had mixed results. Rumors of MacDonald's secret marriage quickly evaporated. She began to be seen socially with a variety of escorts, thereby pleasing the publicity department as well as Mayer. She soon made the distinguished attorney Louis Swarts her principal business adviser. She also felt freer to cement her friendship with Ida Koverman, Mayer's executive secretary. The formidable Koverman, a former assistant to President Herbert Hoover and a major force in the California Republican Party, disliked Ritchie, whom she considered a schnorrer, or parasite. Jeanette, Ida urged, would do far better to depend on her and L. B. when trouble threatened. MacDonald often did. But Koverman and Mayer underrated Jeanette's staunch fidelity to friends, lovers, and protectors. For years to come, she and Ritchie would remain emotionally and professionally close.

MacDonald's ascent at MGM coincided with the studio's Golden Age. Metro-Goldwyn-Mayer was the only major picture company to survive the Depression unscathed. It never abandoned the "controlled extravagance" Thalberg had set up as a guiding production principle during the 1920s. For moviegoers, Metro meant Glamour: ultrapolished pictures built around ultraglossy stars. For the industry, Metro meant an unrivaled corps of technicians and a house policy that encouraged rewrites, retakes, previews, and reedits—regardless of cost. For MacDonald, Metro meant the promise of lavish musicals tailored to her particular talent and charisma. It also meant assurance from Mayer and Thalberg that the studio would risk losing money on one or two MacDonald pictures if that would help crystallize her image.

Her first film at Metro was supposed to be *I Married an Angel,* a Thalberg project. There was vague talk that a strapping baritone named Nelson Eddy, just signed to the studio, would play opposite her. Thalberg had grabbed Richard Rodgers and Lorenz Hart from Paramount in late 1932 and asked them to join Moss Hart in concocting a sophisticated screen musical based on a Hungarian comedy by János Vaszary. Within a few months, the story and songs for *I Married an Angel* were almost completed. Sam Marx recalled that in the late afternoon of March 10, Rodgers and Hart were so elated at having completed the title song that they had him come to their tiny music department office for a private performance: "Seconds after Dick struck chords on the piano and Larry opened his mouth to sing, the huge earthquake of '33 started. A terrific crash shook the building and the three of us abandoned ship through a minuscule window—in hindsight, a terrific metaphor for that picture's destiny!"

The actual force of nature to rip apart *I Married an Angel* was Louis B. Mayer. Vaszary's satirical play had been a huge hit in Hungary, a very Catholic country. But in the United States this tale of a heaven-sent angel who marries an earthling and loses her wings in their nuptial bed was potentially explosive. Back in 1930, the Motion Picture Producers & Distributors of America, Inc., had called upon its president, Will Hays, to draft a code of ethics to regulate screen depictions of sex and crime. For the next three years the so-called Hays Office was fairly lax in enforcing the Code. By 1933, however, many public watchdogs—especially Catholic prelates—were decrying the "indecency" of current movies, taking special aim at Paramount's Mae West. Mayer, a Republican, feared federal controls by the new Roosevelt administration, and he called upon the industry to exert stricter self-censorship. The Code specified that pictures must uphold "the sanctity of the institution of marriage and the home" and that "no film or episode may throw ridicule on any religious faith." By such standards, *I Married an Angel* was doomed. A letter to Mayer from Joseph Breen, Hays's West Coast administrator, judged the entire plot to be "blasphemous and sacrilegious . . . offensive and profane." Mayer soon deep-sixed the project, thereby ending a major Thalberg initiative.

MacDonald's challenge was to get launched at Metro without antagonizing either Mayer or Thalberg in the process. She expected the shelving of *I Married an Angel* to hasten the start of *The Merry Widow,* another Thalberg venture. But Mayer again intervened, urging her to consider *The Prisoner of Zenda,* a musical remake of the 1922 adventure story, with David O. Selznick as producer and the untried Nelson Eddy as her leading man. Even though she wanted to patch up old differences with Mayer's son-in-law, she roundly rejected *The Prisoner of Zenda* after reading the script: "I just think that's a man's story and I don't see a part in it for me." She opted instead for *The Cat and the Fiddle,* adapted from Jerome Kern and Otto Harbach's recent Broadway success.

Budgeted at $843,000, *The Cat and the Fiddle* would be the fourth costliest of Metro's forty releases that year. The project was slated for producer Bernie Hyman, a lesser bigwig than Thalberg or Selznick but solidly in the former's camp. MacDonald would share star billing, above the title, with Ramon Novarro. Jeanette considered the Mexican-born heartthrob a "safe" partner. On one hand, Novarro's public appeal was slipping: his stardom had peaked in 1927 with *Ben-Hur.* On the other hand, Novarro had made a graceful transition to talkies with *The Pagan,* baring not only his familiar torso but also a sweet singing voice that introduced "Pagan Love Song." Novarro's light, reedy tenor and ever-boyish looks were more gentle than arresting, and there was little chance he would overpower MacDonald in the manner of Chevalier at Paramount.

The screenplay for *The Cat and the Fiddle* was by Samuel and Bella Spewack, who would later write Cole Porter's *Kiss Me Kate* with MacDonald in mind. The story opens in contemporary Brussels with American Shirley Sheridan (MacDonald) and Romanian Victor Florescu (Novarro) accidentally meeting in a taxi. Both are students at the Music Conservatory—she composes jazz-inflected pieces, he, operetta—and they quickly fall in love. On the eve of Shirley's reluctant marriage to the impresario Daudet (Frank Morgan), she learns of Victor's plight: his operetta, *Le Chat et le violon* (*The Cat and the Fiddle*), is in peril because his leading lady (Vivienne Segal) has quit the company. Shirley rushes to the theater and with barely a hint of rehearsal saves the show. The lovers' final duet is photographed in three-strip Technicolor, still in its trial phase, as MacDonald's Mercurochrome hair and painted doll's rouge attest.*

The censors urged Eddie Mannix, Mayer's chief lieutenant, to modify the central Paris episode that shows MacDonald and Novarro living together in sin. The studio disregarded this advice. At the same time, they green-lighted MacDonald's lingerie scenes—one in her boudoir, another at the theater—perhaps because these were by now expected of her. They also let pass some playful bedroom dialogue concerning Novarro's body:

> MACDONALD [*in bed; she awakes, stretches, her eyes are closed; she sighs*]:   Ahhh. I had such a lovely dream. I dreamed of you all night.
> NOVARRO [*seated on the bed; tenderly*]:   Tell me.
> MACDONALD [*eyes still closed*]:   I dreamed we were so rich you went around in a golden jacket.
> NOVARRO [*flirtatiously*]:   And nothing else?
> MACDONALD [*opens eyes very wide*]:   I don't think so. [*She laughs; they kiss.*]

A moment such as this is reminiscent of MacDonald's sexy Paramount-Lubitsch pictures. But it also heralds her MGM image, as yet not fully formed. MacDonald's Paramount men—Chevalier, Dennis King, even Jack Buchanan—resisted her romantic charm the moment it threatened their machismo. Her Metro partners—Nelson Eddy, Allan Jones, Lew Ayres, Gene Raymond, Robert Young, even Clark Gable—ultimately relax their male egos and submit to her almost maternal brand of idealized love. In the preceding scene, a sure sign of the transition is Novarro's willingness to be as much the object of MacDonald's erotic fantasies as she is of his.

The Cat and the Fiddle opened to good reviews without becoming a box-office hit. It lost $142,000. *Dancing Lady*, MGM's earlier musical venture that year, sold many more tickets. But that Joan Crawford picture was basically derived from Warner Bros.'s *42nd Street*. The MacDonald feature, by contrast, brilliantly transposed to the screen Kern and Harbach's stage concept of an integrated music drama, thereby

---

*Although the new three-strip Technicolor process had been used in Disney cartoons for more than a year, this was its first application in a live-action feature, predating RKO's 1934 live-action three-color short, *La Cucaracha*.

opening up a whole new direction for MGM musicals. It also confirmed the studio's lead in two areas crucial for MacDonald's rise to superstardom: sound technology and musical vision.

In these matters, three talented Metro men lent MacDonald their support. One was Norma Shearer's brother, Douglas, head of the studio's sound department and a researcher in novel ways to eliminate distortion from high-frequency sources, including sopranos. A second wizard was Mike "Mac" McLaughlin, MGM's chief sound mixer. McLaughlin had a reputation for blending more cocktails than acoustic tracks, but he inspired great confidence in MacDonald, who had him oversee her West Coast radio broadcasts at her own expense. Yet the person second only to the singer herself in making MacDonald's MGM musicals unique and inimitable was Herbert Stothart, music director for all her Metro films.

Stothart was a towering, fair-haired Wisconsinite who reminded Mac-Donald of "a bluff sea captain." On Broadway, he had co-composed *Wildflower* with Vincent Youmans, *Rose-Marie* with Rudolf Friml, and *Song of the Flame* with George Gershwin. Along with his flair for operetta, Stothart had a talent for comic novelty numbers, his best known being "I Wanna Be Loved by You," cowritten with Harry Ruby and Bert Kalmar. As a music student, Stothart had spent a year in Germany copying Richard Wagner's autograph scores, which sparked his interest in leitmotifs and in weaving diverse melodies to express dramatic tension. In his musicals (Stothart won an Oscar for *The Wizard of Oz*) as well as in his dramatic films (he was nominated for *Mutiny on the Bounty, Marie Antoinette,* and *Madame Curie*), Stothart believed that "a musical episode must be so presented as to motivate a detail of the plot, and must become so vital to the story that it cannot be dispensed with."

In *The Cat and the Fiddle,* Stothart reworked Kern's original score so as to leave barely a moment of silence on the music track. Some of the film's most striking musical moments are "effects" rather than numbers: a taxi-horn montage as Novarro dashes about the streets of Brussels; rain rhythmically dripping into MacDonald's garret during the reprise of "The Night Was Made for Love"; windblown chandeliers that tinkle ghostly melodies as MacDonald wanders heartbroken in her elegant boudoir. It's little wonder that MacDonald's pictures are underrepresented in compilation films like *That's Entertainment.* Unlike lyricist-producer Arthur Freed (from *Babes in Arms* in 1939 through *Gigi* in 1958), Stothart does not lend himself to easy anthologizing. In Stothart musicals, the vocal solos, duets, and ensembles are part of a musico-dramatic continuum that demands context for full impact.*

Like Mayer and MacDonald, Stothart regarded popular films as the perfect medium for bringing excellent music to the masses. One woman who disagreed was Stothart's wife, the daughter of a famous New York theatrical agent. Mary Wolfe Stothart never broke with the legitimate theater's disdain for movies and movie people. Herbert Stothart II remembered: "My mother used to make fun of Jeanette MacDonald. She considered Jeanette *schmaltz*. My mother was a woman who always tried to be 'with it,' on the cutting edge of the avant-garde. The kind of filmmaker she prized was Robert Flaherty, the documentarist. Music-wise my mother was into Stravinsky at that time and she considered what Jeanette and Herb were doing as old-fashioned. I remember Jeanette giving my father a pink tea set one Christmas, and my mother made fun of it. She was really very jealous of Jeanette MacDonald. They represented different points of view."

MacDonald also triggered animosity in *The Cat and the Fiddle*'s supporting actress, Vivienne Segal. Until her death in 1992, Segal maintained that MacDonald plotted with Mayer to have her role sharply reduced. She reported that Jeanette's first words to her on the set were, "Hello, Viv, have you seen your part? It stinks!" Segal also hinted that MacDonald led a conspiracy to get her so shabbily photographed that "no one would cast me after that."

It's possible that MacDonald lobbied Mayer to get Segal's role abridged. But the alleged taunt would have been wholly at odds with MacDonald's notion of star propriety. Segal's rancor was probably a matter of sour grapes. Six years older than Jeanette, she had enjoyed a Broadway career in more prestigious and successful shows than Mac-Donald's, all the while honing her operatic potential with Estelle Liebling, Beverly Sills's future voice teacher. Although she starred in a cluster of early musicals churned out by Warners and First National,

*In the television documentary *Herb Stothart: A Forgotten Legend* (produced by Laura Greenfield for City-TV, Santa Monica), the musicologist Bill Rosar noted: "You might say that Stothart wrote his music in pastels whereas [Max] Steiner or [Alfred] Newman worked more in oil colors. His was a subtler kind of art than the Big Hollywood Sound. . . . He doesn't pull out all the stops. He works at a subtler, more psychological level. He himself said he didn't think in terms of definite melodic material or themes but in trying to evoke psychological impressions. . . . He had a particular feeling for pathos, which he constantly strived to find ways of expressing in the orchestra, certain orchestral colorings and musical devices. He was a specialist in sad and sentimental things."

Segal soon found herself lacking not only MacDonald's international fame but also her youth. Louella Parsons, in her Halloween column of 1933, added public salt to a gashed ego: "Vivienne Segal is in a terrible panic; she has had her nose done over and now she is afraid that she will be sent for retakes on *The Cat and the Fiddle*. What can a lady do in a case like that?" Segal never made another movie.*

Allegations of MacDonald's haughtiness usually came from lower-echelon associates at Metro who envied her talent or were unaware of the special needs of singers. Many construed her ever-present entourage—voice coach Newell, personal maid Rose, studio maid Marie, hairdresser Olga, practice pianist Maggie Hart—as a female phalanx shielding their Sovereign Majesty from intruders. Like Garbo, MacDonald declared her sets off-limits to unapproved visitors. She rarely ate in the commissary, preferring to lunch quietly in her dressing suite on brought-from-home vegetables. In the morning MacDonald's energy level was usually low, and she needed to be alone and "off" as much as possible. The constant jovial racket coming from Myrna Loy's suite, directly above hers, never failed to unsettle her. If she arrived to find that a wardrobe person had disturbed that day's costume or wig, she would go into a tailspin. Makeup artist William Tuttle recalled: "After *The Cat and the Fiddle,* Jeanette started wearing wigs made by Max Factor, both for period and modern-dress films. That allowed her to avoid sitting for an hour under a dryer each morning. One day, a new wig was brought over from the shop and she didn't like it. I saw her throw it on the floor, stomp on it, and scream, 'I DON'T WANT IT!' But Jeanette had a facility for getting over temperamental moments rather quickly."

Others have attested to MacDonald's thoughtful regard for MGM's crew and contract players. According to Kitty Carlisle, "She was so kind to me. When I got to Metro for *A Night at the Opera,* she left a note for me at Makeup saying that my mouth was too big, too much like a bow, and that I should do such and such. Well, I was no fool. Jeanette MacDonald was a big star, and I followed her advice to the letter." The violist Virginia Majewski, MGM's first female musician, also recalled MacDonald's considerateness and good humor: "There was an oboe player named Phil Memoli who had a tremendous crush on

---

*After returning to Broadway, Segal attained her greatest success in 1940 with the role of Vera Simpson, the callous, past-her-prime matron in Rodgers and Hart's *Pal Joey,* which she revived to much acclaim in 1952.

Jeanette. Each time she showed up for a recording session, Phil would smile bashfully and Jeanette would throw a glance his way, to show she knew. Phil was married, but he loved it. MacDonald earned respect from all of us because she was always perfectly prepared. Only Judy Garland was her rival on that score."

The last thing MacDonald wanted at MGM was to produce the bad vibes she had generated at Paramount. Yet woe to those who dared trample on what she took to be her rights and privileges: "One of the bits of advice I was determined to live by at MGM was delivered by Wallace Beery, that hulking, kindly bear of a man who was one of the studio's top money-makers in the thirties. 'Remember, it's the squeaky wheel that gets the grease,' he told me. I remembered!"

Among the many deviations from the stage version of *The Cat and the Fiddle*, MacDonald thought the reunion scene at the movie's end "particularly absurd." She complained to producer Bernie Hyman, who responded "in a patronizing manner": "Maybe you're right, maybe wrong. Here's what we'll do. Let's make it my way first. If you don't like the result, we'll do it your way. I give you my word." Jeanette found the rushes "awful." When she then suggested starting on her idea (an adaptation of the stage version's "Poor Pierrot" episode), Hyman stonewalled her: "Trouble is that the budget won't stand it. We'll have to let the present ending ride." Not if MacDonald could help it. She trotted straight to Eddie Mannix's office and raised Cain.

Mannix, a former bouncer at New Jersey's Palisades Park, was MGM's executive patrolman over all operations. He was tough, but extremely evenhanded. Many likened him to a battered Irish boxer "with a cauliflower ear for a face" and "no nerves in his body." After listening to MacDonald's charges of injustice, Mannix phoned Hyman: "The hell with budget, Bernie. You made a promise. You've got to live up to your word. You do it."

Hyman shot the "Poor Pierrot" sequence according to Jeanette's wishes. Then, with avenging glee he scrapped the footage and used his earlier version for the final cut. Still, MacDonald had given fair warning that she was no one's patsy. In years to come, she would often rely on Mannix to pass judgment on her disputes. He was once heard to grumble, "The trouble with Jeanette is that she's too damn conscientious." Mayer, on the other hand, cheered MacDonald's high-mindedness (at least at the beginning), seeing it as further cause for placing her on a pedestal.

One spring evening in 1934, Mayer hosted a banquet for the sultan of Johore, a Southeast Asian protectorate. From his great star roster, the MGM chief chose Jeanette for the seat of honor beside this head of state. Three days later, MacDonald received a coy note from Mayer:

May 12, 1934

Dear Jeanette:

I have ordered some flowers for you because I wanted an excuse to send you a note and quote you from a letter Mr. Murdock [a State Department official] wrote me—

> "You know I do not know of anyone you could have put next to the Sultan who would have made a more charming impression than—"

No, I have changed my mind and have decided I won't quote the rest of the letter after all. You have had enough bouquets handed to you anyway, and besides even Scotch heads can swell. I don't know just why Mr. Murdock felt that he must make you such flowery compliments, except that perhaps being Scotch himself he felt the call of the clan.

While I have controlled myself as to quoting Mr. Murdock's letter, unfortunately it is too late to cancel the flowers.

Faithfully yours,
Louis B. Mayer

Miss Jeanette MacDonald
912 North Rexford Drive
Beverly Hills

For Mayer, MacDonald was as royal as any American could be. She was his Lady—even his Queen, as Lubitsch had dubbed her five years earlier. There would be fights, feuds, and awkward reconciliations. But ever the Knight doing honor to his unattainable *belle dame,* L. B. would cling to this romantic ideal until his dying day.

MacDonald appreciated her prominence in Mayer's plan to bring wholesome sentiment to America's Depression-plagued populace. Yet she still ached to star in Thalberg's production of *The Merry Widow,* a property that oozed worldliness and could hardly be turned into family fare. Nonetheless, she knew better than to ruffle L. B. when he proposed his favorite operetta, *Naughty Marietta,* as the project to follow *The Cat and the Fiddle.*

At a meeting with the boss and Herb Stothart, she explained that she admired the Victor Herbert score but was not convinced the vehicle suited her. Mayer reminded her that Crawford and Shearer flourished only because they had followed his instincts over their own. He wondered aloud whether Jeanette was actually up to the job, since some perceived her as icy and holding back feelings: "When you play Marietta, you will need great heart, great warmth, great emotion in your voice. You have to reach out from the screen to move your millions of devoted admirers to laughter—or to tears." Mayer then fell to his knees and intoned—half Job, half Jolson—"Eli, Eli," the Hebrew song of lamentation. MacDonald knew a dramatic cue when she heard one. She bent low and whispered, "Thank you, I'll do it. I'll be happy to make *Naughty Marietta*. I put myself completely in your hands."

Jeanette eluded Mayer's grasp for the time being, since plans for *The Merry Widow* were starting to fall into place. Thalberg tapped Ernst Lubitsch, on leave from Paramount, to direct the long-awaited picture. The director and producer agreed that Chevalier, recently signed to a multipicture deal with Metro, would be the perfect male lead. With MacDonald already on board, it looked as if the famed threesome would re-create their spicy Paramount magic at Culver City. But while *Good Housekeeping* was glorifying the MacDonald-Chevalier pairing as an alliance "made in heaven," the *Los Angeles Times* was depicting the Frenchman as preferring a vacation in purgatory to playing opposite MacDonald. Reports also surfaced that Chevalier was deeply unhappy with Lubitsch for straitjacketing him in "boudoir conqueror" roles.

Rarely did Hollywood in the thirties go public with genuine dirty linen. Yet Lubitsch was so enraged by Chevalier's apparent display of ingratitude that he vented his rancor to Louella Parsons in the *Los Angeles Examiner*: "I can only think . . . that [Chevalier] was afraid of [MacDonald's] great popularity abroad. *The Love Parade*, in which Miss MacDonald was his leading lady, grossed more than any other of his pictures and her ovation in Europe equaled his in its enthusiasm. I know that Chevalier's feelings toward Miss MacDonald are not rumor. . . . *The Merry Widow* has been the dream of Jeanette's life. Who is a better choice? If Metro-Goldwyn-Mayer intends to keep Franz Lehár's music and really make a musical play, there should be someone who can sing."

Under pressure from Thalberg to cease fire, Chevalier cabled the producer from Paris five days later: "I COULD NEVER SAY ANYTHING AGAINST ERNST LUBITSCH OR JEANETTE MACDONALD. I HAVE THE GREATEST ADMIRATION AND RESPECT FOR BOTH OF THEM. . . . AND A DEEP APPRECIATION OF MR. LUBITSCH'S WORK WITH ME. . . . AS YOU KNOW, IT IS NOT UP TO ME TO SAY WHO SHALL PLAY IN THE MERRY WIDOW. I AM ONLY GRATEFUL THAT I AM IN IT." In an unusual show of pique, Thalberg reprimanded Lubitsch in a statement printed in the *Examiner* and the *Times:* "I am greatly surprised that a swell fellow like Ernst Lubitsch, in an interview, would jump in and issue statements based only on idle rumors and gossip. Jeanette MacDonald is a talented and charming actress with a beautiful singing voice, who has had many successes on both the stage and screen. She is being considered, among several other players, for the feminine role. The ultimate selection, however, will not be influenced by controversy or backstage intrigue, but will be decided in favor of the person best suited for the success of the production."

Chevalier unquestionably did not want to make a fourth film with MacDonald. But there is evidence that Bob Ritchie, in an effort to gain public sympathy for Jeanette, may have leaked and exaggerated Chevalier's disinclination to the press. A few days before the brouhaha started, Chevalier wrote to Ritchie:

> September 16. 1933
>
> Mr. Robert Ritchie.
> Beverly-Wilshire.
> Wilshire Blvd.
> Beverly Hills. Calif.
>
> Painfully surprised to receive such a letter from you.
>   Never said things of that kind about anybody in my career, and very upset to be accused of starting now.
>   Just agreed with M.G.M. heads when they told me that they thought we had been teamed enough with Miss J. MacDonald and that they should find a woman to play *The Merry Widow* who has not yet played with me.
>
> Maurice Chevalier

Over the next five months, the casting of the Widow became Hollywood's hottest topic of guesswork. Alternatives to MacDonald included French opera star Lily Pons, vengeful Vivienne Segal, the fading Gloria Swanson, and *Dancing Lady*'s marginally musical Joan Crawford. One day Crawford sat in on MacDonald's voice lesson with Grace Newell. Afterward, she fixed her rueful eyes on Jeanette and asked: "You have only one teacher? I have two—one for my high voice and one for my low."

A more serious contender was Grace Moore, the tough and salty Metropolitan Opera soprano. Moore was Chevalier's first choice, and she later claimed to have wanted the part so badly she would have worked for free. Thalberg, however, had reservations. Although Moore possessed a youthful figure and pleasant face by opera singer standards, she was given to plumpness and had problems adjusting to the camera. One unkind critic compared her on-screen movements to those of a "moose." Back in 1930 she had made two films for Metro, the Jenny Lind biopic, *A Lady's Morals,* and Romberg's *New Moon* with Lawrence Tibbett. Although they offered some of the most glorious singing of the early sound era, these films were commercial flops. In addition, Moore was now on the outs with L. B. Mayer, who was said to have had an unrequited crush on her before he took up with Mac-Donald. Louella Parsons, a Moore devotee, kept slinging unfounded barbs: "Time for Jeanette MacDonald to get busy and diet; too bad, with her looks and voice, if she continues to ignore her figure." Yet the December issue of *Vanity Fair* gave evidence to the contrary. It featured slim Jeanette in a sensual pose photographed by Edward Steichen, and it extolled her "amiable worldliness, her beautiful legs, and the best soprano voice now in the films."

Thalberg decided to go with MacDonald. He knew that Lubitsch wanted her, and he believed that only she could guarantee the picture an international appeal. But there still remained a ticklish matter. Mac-Donald's contract gave her the right to top billing, a condition Chevalier found unacceptable. The second week in February 1934, Thalberg summoned Jeanette to his office. Mayer, now resigned to deferring *Naughty Marietta* and eager to get *The Merry Widow* under way and finished, counseled her beforehand: "No matter what Irving says, don't refuse to do the picture. Maybe that's exactly what he wants you to do. So grit your teeth if you have to; bite your tongue. But be nice!"

At five o'clock, Jeanette entered Thalberg's back-lot bungalow for a conference that lasted three hours: "He really gave me the works, a sermon on my art and the unimportance of billing, mingled with a hint or two that left no doubt in my mind that I wasn't forgiven for signing through L. B. Mayer and not him. But I have never been more fascinated by the brilliance and great powers of persuasion of this remarkable genius. I was almost ready to do the picture on any terms, but had to keep reminding myself of L. B.'s advice. Anyway, I did *The Merry Widow* with my name once again appearing beneath Maurice's."*

---

*Marlene Dietrich, according to her daughter, reacted with scorn and disbelief to *The Hollywood Reporter*'s announcement that MacDonald would get the role. Although Maria Riva explains in her 1993 biography that "my mother had never liked Jeanette MacDonald," her verbatim account of Dietrich's supposed tirade rings suspicious, because it could only have been inspired by MacDonald's post–*Merry Widow* films: "Now you tell me how all that affected sweetness can sell tickets? Those awful rosebuds on everything, the trills through ever so slightly parted lips—the 'flutter,' the 'little steps' in

Principal photography for *The Merry Widow* began on Friday, April
13, and ended on Friday, July 13—a total of thirteen weeks. Jeanette
had long considered thirteen her lucky number, since *M,* as in Mac-
Donald, was the alphabet's thirteenth letter. Now that she was at a studio whose logo had two *M*'s, MacDonald turned the letter into a fetish:
in each of her subsequent pictures she would insist that a capital *M* figure in the name of her character: Marietta, Rose Marie, Mary Blake,
Marcia Mornay, Gwen Marlowe, Marianne de Beaumanoir, and so on.

Embassy balls and secret emotions. Resplendent uniforms and political
intrigue. The most sensuous Viennese waltz ever composed. These were
just a few of the delights found in Franz Lehár's *Merry Widow,* first
seen and heard at the Theater an der Wien on December 30, 1905.
Considered revolutionary by turn-of-the century standards, this operetta took a widow, not a virgin, for its heroine and chose a philan-
derer, not an idealist, as its hero. Lubitsch, who pushed back the action
to the earlier bustles-and-gaslight era of 1885, aimed for what he called
"a hundred percent romantic picture" with timeless appeal: "It tries to
combine the European court ritual of a generation ago with a very
modern flavor."* While editing the footage, Lubitsch got wind of horrible news: the Nazis planned to revoke his German citizenship on the
grounds that he was a "dangerous" Jew. Seven years later, Lubitsch
would boldly satirize Hitler's regime in *To Be or Not to Be,* a black
farce with comedian Jack Benny. In 1934 he chose to keep *The Merry
Widow* good-natured, with just a hint of melancholy in MacDonald's
otherwise scintillating character. "It is unfortunately true," Lubitsch
explained, "that great events of our time have been marching so fast
that we are too busy with politics, national crises, and all kinds of
'isms' to devote enough time to enjoying life, to being happy in the
careless gaiety that used to be. In former times . . . people made love in

---

satin slippers—ever so dainty! People can't believe all that! *She* . . . is *big* box office?
Chevalier says he can't stand her. He told me she smells of cheap talcum powder, and I
said 'In what place did you smell it?' So, of course, he was stuck—and couldn't answer!"
(*Marlene Dietrich,* p. 264).

The Merry Widow was first adapted to the screen in 1907, as a fourteen-minute
Swedish short. Reliance-Majestic produced an American one-reeler in 1912, followed by
Essenay's two-reeler in 1913. Erich von Stroheim's 1925 MGM silent, with Mae Murray
and John Gilbert, gave the property a dark Freudian tinge. Metro's 1952 edition cast
Lana Turner and Fernando Lamas in sumptuous Technicolor. In the mid-1970s, Ingmar
Bergman announced his intent to make yet another film version, but his plans have not
materialized.

a romantic way because its glamour made them happy. . . . But despite all this, people have not changed at heart. . . . [R]omance still lives, but in another form. It is the suppressed desire of the people of this day."

From *The Love Parade* onward, MacDonald was Lubitsch's vehicle for expressing romantic desire. In *The Merry Widow,* their only period costume piece, she is the embodiment of that fragile, gentler era the gallant Lubitsch longed to preserve, whose passing he mourned, and whose beauty he celebrated not through nostalgia but through irony and sly wit.

Although Lehár's score furnishes MacDonald with beguiling vocal melodies, it is dance, not song, that becomes the movie's principal metaphor for romantic coupling.* The film's most spectacular episode begins on the terrace of the Marshovian embassy in Paris, where Captain Danilo (Chevalier) has been ordered by his impoverished king to engage in "diplomatic relations" with Madame Sonia (MacDonald), a Marshovian who is also the world's wealthiest widow. Following a spat, he and Sonia are about to part when strains of "The Merry Widow Waltz" emerge from within the palace. Irresistibly, Danilo clasps Sonia, and the two glide along the parterre. Scores of other waltzing couples pour out through French doors, giving the transported twosome sole use of the huge ballroom. As Stothart weaves the carefree "Melody of Laughter" theme into the slightly menacing "Waltz," Lubitsch alternates between overhead shots of the swirling masses and the solitary couple. The tempo builds as throngs of waltzers, dressed in black or white, form stunning visual patterns that multiply when, as in a kaleidoscope, lines of couples twirling six abreast surge through a narrow mirrored corridor. This fantasia in black and white—perhaps symbolic of the intertwining of innocence and deceit, of the Widow's impulse to life and her flight from death—ends with MacDonald and Chevalier whirling back to temporary repose on the terrace.

The film's first statement of "The Merry Widow Waltz" occurs in a scene equally memorable but poles apart in scale. MacDonald, disguised as "Fifi," a lady of the evening, is lured by Chevalier to a private

---

*This *Merry Widow* points up the basic mismatch of MacDonald's mellifluous soprano and Chevalier's happy-go-lucky rasp: it denies them even one singing duet. More than her prior Lubitsch pictures, *The Merry Widow* makes palpable the solitary dimension of MacDonald's emotional yearnings. Early on, when she intones "Vilia" from her moonlit balcony, MacDonald hears her lilting song echoed by a tender male voice she presumes to be Chevalier's; in actuality it is that of his gawky orderly (Sterling Holloway, lip-synching to a playback by studio tenor Allan Rogers) in cahoots with Chevalier to con the widow.

upstairs dining room in Maxim's. When she emits mixed signals, the infuriated rake protests: "I don't mind a little teasing. . . . But this is absolutely demoralizing!" He almost walks out on the "girl" but returns when she asks if he'd like to dance. Sulking, Chevalier sits at a table in the room's center. Suddenly the "Waltz," moderato cantabile, is heard. MacDonald, standing, gently sways. She then bends, lifts the train of her gown, and proceeds to dance in a clockwise circle around Chevalier—sweeping, dipping, gliding. This is Jeanette MacDonald at the peak of romantic yearning, abandoning herself to the sensual pleasures of music and motion. Chevalier, unable to resist, rises to join her. Together they waltz, now counterclockwise. Spellbound and spellbinding as she moves, MacDonald sings a solo rendition of the "Waltz" to new lyrics by Lorenz Hart. Her kiss with Chevalier brings to a voluptuous end one of the great moments in movie musicals.

Neither of these dizzying routines required undue rehearsal by the costars, who were experienced dancers. Joseph Newman, Lubitsch's assistant director, recalled: "They picked it up very easily, although Maurice was starting to gain weight and was a little paunchy by then. We had his clothes tailored to camouflage that." When Chevalier got tired after multiple takes, he would rest on the pink upholstered leaning board MacDonald always kept on the set in order to relax without creasing her costumes. "Jeanette kidded Maurice a lot about that," Newman remembered.

The Merry Widow tested the Hays Code by depicting Maxim's as a deluxe whorehouse. Before shooting started, Joe Breen examined the screenplay and ordered the deletion of Chevalier kissing MacDonald on both shoulders, pulling down her shoulder straps, and starting to unhook her dress. He also succeeded in transforming Chevalier's line "May I have the honor of putting on this shoe—or the pleasure of taking off the other one?" to a decorous "May I put it on?" After viewing a rough cut in mid-August, Breen still found the private-room episode offensive and called a meeting with Thalberg and Lubitsch. As originally filmed, Chevalier lifted MacDonald and placed her reclining on the sofa following their waltz. "Mr. Thalberg," Breen wrote in a memo after their meeting, "will reshoot this entire scene with a view to getting away from the 'horizontal.' The scene will not be played with Danilo and Sonia lying on a couch." In the film as we know it, however, the scene is played *very much* on the horizontal. The studio defended itself to Breen by affirming that MacDonald and Chevalier both had their feet on the floor while the cameras were rolling. Why take anyone to task, they cagily argued, just because in the final product the actors' legs are cut from viewers' sight?

Such artful dodging led Code authorities in late October to threaten "serious strictures" for other Metro films if this scene was not modified before the picture went into general distribution. Thalberg stuck to his guns, claiming to have worked with the Code Association "in the best of faith" and to have already spent over $100,000 in retakes. In a *New York Times* interview, Lubitsch was more blunt: "I am on the side of everybody who fights vulgarity in the cinema. But this present campaign, I must admit, has caused me to worry about the future. . . . The effect . . . will be to force artists to see life through pink glasses. The films will be just as bad as before, only in another direction." Lubitsch also responded to the charge that films like *The Merry Widow* are a corrupting influence on children: "To ask that films be produced for the amusement of children is to work a terrible injustice upon adults. If people who worry about the cinema were to worry, instead, about their children, the campaign would be more plausible to intelligent people."*

Production Code squabbles may actually have saved MacDonald's life. She had planned to join Kitty Marin, the wife of MGM producer Edwin Marin, and Mrs. Arthur Stebbins, the niece of Nicholas Schenck, on a trip to Yosemite Park in late August. When Breen's grumblings prompted Thalberg and Lubitsch to call for additional retakes, MacDonald was forced to cancel her vacation. On their return trip, her friends' Chevrolet crashed into a truck. Marin's daughter suffered grave injuries, and Stebbins's two children were killed. On September 4, MacDonald attended their funeral at B'nai Brith Temple, realizing that but for Breen and the grace of God, she too might have been among those being mourned that Tuesday. Bob Ritchie was a pall-bearer.

"Boys, I'm on my own!" Jeanette exclaimed to reporters at Grand Central Station after stepping unescorted from the Twentieth Century Limited. These bombshell words triggered juicy headlines in the minds of

---

*Foreign audiences got to see a slightly racier movie. Lubitsch simultaneously shot two versions of *The Merry Widow*, one in English and the other in French, both starring MacDonald and Chevalier but with different supporting casts. All prints of *La Veuve joyeuse* retained the more "adult" shot of Chevalier carrying MacDonald to the couch at Maxim's. In deference to British and Belgian royalty, special foreign editions demoted cuckolded King Achmed and promiscuous Queen Dolores of the American version to cuckolded General Regent Achmed and his promiscuous wife Dolores.

New York journalists itching for new MacDonald gossip that late September. But Jeanette dashed their hopes by explaining that Ritchie, still her fiancé, would soon be flying in for *The Merry Widow*'s world premiere at the Astor Theater on October 11. In the meantime, she said, she planned to congregate with old Gotham friends, catch Moss Hart's *The Great Waltz* on stage at the Center Theater, and visit Radio City Music Hall, the supercolossal movie palace just opened at Rockefeller Center.

Among her less publicized doings was a quick trip to Philadelphia, where she helped Elsie polish a speech for Overbrook High School's French Club entitled "The Part That the French Language Has Played in the Screen Success of My Sister." She also went up to Riverdale to see Jack Ohmeis's mother. According to Jack's brother Herb, she confided that her engagement to Ritchie was "purely a matter of convenience and that she was neither in love with him nor had any intention of marrying him." Nonetheless, when Bob got news of his father's death on October 3, Jeanette was steadfastly by his side.

The Merry Widow's premiere was vintage glitz. Overhead arc lamps threw a blue mist visible up and down Broadway. Mounted policemen restrained cordoned-off crowds on all sides of the Astor Theater. Major Bowes interviewed a host of arriving celebrities over WHN radio. With Chevalier absent, the night belonged to MacDonald, who proved Lubitsch and Thalberg had been right all along. MacDonald's Widow was a performance for the ages: beauty encased in irony, sincerity at the edge of self-parody. The British photographer Cecil Beaton aptly compared the film's luxury, invention, and technical perfection to those of "the Easter eggs of Fabergé" and judged MacDonald to be "the apotheosis of the widow herself."

Reviewers were unanimous in their enthusiasm. Even Parsons conceded that MacDonald now made past contenders "seem like amateurs." For Regina Crewes of the *New York American, The Merry Widow* brought to fruition MacDonald's metamorphosis from "the cool chrysalis of earlier films" to "the gorgeous, pulsing, palpitating butterfly, alive with love and life." Perhaps L. B. Mayer's lesson in the art of emoting paid off. A more plausible explanation is that MacDonald was at last in a movie that capitalized equally on her looks, voice, and comic abilities. "What I'm most pleased by," MacDonald said of the picture, "is the opportunity I was given to attempt a real characterization, something I haven't had much occasion to tackle before on any real scale." Screenwriters Samson Raphaelson and Ernst Vajda deserved much of the credit. But so did Lorenz Hart and Gus Kahn for sharp new lyrics; Oliver Marsh for luscious lighting; Adrian for plush gowns; Stothart for dazzling musical adaptation; Albertina Rasch for dreamy choreography; Cedric Gibbons for Oscar-winning sets; and of course Lubitsch, for knowing just how naughty MacDonald could be while still remaining nice, and just how nice she had to be in order to get away with being naughty.

MGM spent prodigiously to promote *The Merry Widow,* which at $1,605,000 was Hollywood's most expensive musical yet made. Throughout the nation, dance schools ran Merry Widow Waltz contests, stationers stocked Merry Widow diaries and blotters, and beauticians advertised Merry Widow hairdos featuring MacDonald's revival of "Langtry bangs." Shoe stores displayed stills of Chevalier provocatively placing MacDonald's evening pump on her foot. At the State Theater in New Orleans, male patrons were handed sealed envelopes marked "DON'T SHOW THIS TO HER!"; inside were flirtatious notes in Jeanette's handwriting. Even though MacDonald hated live promo stunts, she showed up in San Francisco, where socialites hosted teas in her honor and drove their guests to the Warfield Theater in turn-of-the-century carriages.

Widowmania did not, however, sweep the entire country. Predictably, exhibitors in the Midwest found the picture "out of step with modern America" and pleasing to only "the few high-brows we got to see it." From Ohio to Oregon, moviegoers complained about Chevalier's impenetrable accent. The owner of the Majestic Theater in Nampa, Idaho, decried the film's Eurocentrism: "Let me again assure the producer that the public won't stand for operetta, let alone opera. Will somebody kindly send some steamer tickets to Vienna, Budapest, London, Rome, and Paris and ask the producers to come back to America, and all will be forgiven!" The picture, as expected, did sensational box office in South American and European countries—except Germany. Hitler's *Vaterland* had its own screen operetta tradition, featuring the singing sweetheart teams of Willy Fritsch and Lilian Harvey, and Jan Kiepura and Marta Eggerth. Although the Führer himself had great affection for Lehár's *The Merry Widow* (in spite of the fact that the librettists and the composer's wife were Jews), he banned the Lubitsch-Thalberg-Mayer adaptation. When Lehár's support of Fascism became known in late October 1934, MGM dropped the title card that had dedicated the movie "To the Beautiful Melodies of Franz Lehár."

The Merry Widow had its West Coast premiere at Grauman's Chinese Theater on November 29. After the screening there was a huge party at the Trocadero. Five days later, MacDonald and Chevalier returned to the Chinese and in front of a paying audience sank their hands, feet, and signatures into wet cement slabs that had been wheeled onto the stage. Their gray-tinted imprints were then transported to the theater's Forecourt of the Stars, where they remain to this day. It was a fitting ceremony to mark the end of an era in motion-picture history. Industry censorship and public breadlines had conspired to sign the death warrant of Continental sophistication. Boudoir musical farce was finished, as was Chevalier.

The Frenchman was hardly keen on being immortalized alongside his ambitious costar. Yet he was able to take some comfort in the fact that Grace Moore had just surprised everyone with her successful *One Night of Love* at Columbia. In fact, Thalberg now offered to pair him with Moore in Oscar Straus's operetta *The Chocolate Soldier.* Her loan-out, however, called for top billing. At age forty-six, Chevalier preferred to abdicate his claim to Hollywood royalty rather than be listed beneath a woman. Amicably, he dissolved his MGM contract and sailed home on the *Ile de France.* With the exception of *Folies Bergère,* produced by Darryl F. Zanuck for 20th Century in 1935, it would be twenty-three years before he'd make another Hollywood musical.

Some say that Chevalier, in 1958, agreed to do MGM's *Gigi* on one condition: that director Vincente Minnelli not cast Jeanette MacDonald in the role that ultimately went to Hermione Gingold. Ah, yes, he remembered her well.

PART THREE

Hollywood Diva

CHAPTER NINE

An All-American Team

It's ter-rific. MacDonald and Eddy are the new team
sensation of the industry. Their duet of "Sweet Mystery
of Life" is the grandest thing ever recorded!

ED SULLIVAN, *Daily News,* April 1935

Musicals . . . should be the big money films. They should be
the pepper-uppers, the builder-uppers, the spice.

VARIETY editorial, April 1935

THE PAIRING OF MACDONALD WITH NELSON EDDY may have
been music's most profitable marriage since Gilbert and Sullivan. "No
question about it," Jeanette declared, "the timbre of our voices blended
beautifully, his baritone and my soprano. We liked each other; we enjoyed working together; we were enthusiastic about [*Naughty Marietta*]. Evidently all this came through on screen."

Metro, however, took a risk by giving Eddy costar billing. In early
1933 Mark Sandrich, the future director of Astaire and Rogers musicals, had pitched Eddy to RKO as "another Lawrence Tibbett." Executive Merian Cooper skeptically responded, "*Must* there be another
Lawrence Tibbett?" and hired pop band leader Phil Harris instead.
Eddy found a more effective champion in MGM's Ida Koverman.
Mayer's gal Friday had been to a Philharmonic Auditorium concert
where the baritone, barely known on the West Coast, pinch-hit for the
indisposed soprano Lotte Lehmann. Eddy's Viking looks and resonant
singing voice seduced Koverman, who lobbied successfully for his sign-

ing with Metro. Still, for the next eighteen months, Nelson Eddy was
Culver City's forgotten man. His cameos in three pictures (*Broadway
to Hollywood, Dancing Lady,* and *Student Tour*) totaled under seven
minutes. The publicity department hailed Eddy as the Great Blond
Hope. But most reviewers failed to notice him.

Eddy's love of opera made him ambivalent about movies. In
Philadelphia and New York he had sung in *Aïda, I Pagliacci, Tann-
häuser,* and the American premiere of Richard Strauss's *Ariadne auf
Naxos.* He played the Drum Major in a historic 1931 performance of
Alban Berg's *Wozzeck* at Carnegie Hall under Leopold Stokowski.
Even after his success in *Naughty Marietta,* Eddy fulfilled a commitment with the San Francisco Opera Company to sing Amonasro
opposite Elisabeth Rethberg's Aïda. But Eddy's voice coach, Dr.
Edouard Lippe, doubted he could sustain a major opera career in the
face of competition from fellow American baritones Lawrence Tibbett, John Charles Thomas, and Richard Bonelli. Lippe therefore encouraged Eddy to carve a niche for himself on the recital circuit. The
appeal of Hollywood lay mainly in Eddy's hope that screen celebrity
might lead to higher concert fees and increased bookings. Eddy made
sure that his seven-year Metro contract would allow three free
months each year for concertizing. Nevertheless, his first pictures so
demoralized him that he begged to break with the studio for good.
When Mayer refused, Eddy, in the Chevalier tradition, brooded and
turned cranky.

MacDonald first met Eddy at Irving Thalberg's wrap-up party for
the cast and crew of *The Merry Widow.* The slot for *Naughty Marietta*'s male lead was still up for grabs when Jeanette viewed the screen
tests of several hopefuls and was struck by Eddy's: "I remember seeing
Nelson for the first time and thinking he fulfilled most of my requirements in a man: he was tall, blond, goodlooking—but was awfully self-
conscious about his acting."

Mayer's first choice for the role was Broadway, concert, and operatic tenor Allan Jones, but he finally settled on Eddy. Within hours of
the decision, MacDonald sent a congratulatory telegram to her partner-
to-be. Eddy replied by handwritten letter:

517 N. Elm Dr.
Beverly Hills, Cal.
November 7, 1934

Dear Miss MacDonald,

Thank you for the wire. It was terribly sweet of you and I appreciate it more than I can tell you.

Some day I hope to get up courage enough to tell you I think you're the grandest person in the world.

Very gratefully yours,
Nelson Eddy

Ten days later, MacDonald watched Eddy in live performance at the Shrine Auditorium, where he was appearing in Ermanno Wolf-Ferrari's one-act comic opera, *Il segreto di Susanna*. She found both him and the opera delightful but considered her presence a professional obligation, not a voluntary night at the theater. Accordingly, she entered the evening's expenses, including a new gown, among her 1934 income-tax deductions.*

On the first two days of shooting *Naughty Marietta,* Eddy kept his distance. MacDonald's reputation for being difficult, along with her much higher salary, intimidated the thirty-three-year-old novice. By the end of day three, however, Eddy walked over to her with a sheepish grin and confessed: "I was all prepared not to like you. I heard you were pretty tough to work with—you'd try to crowd me out of every scene. I want to apologize. I know you've been throwing scenes my way." As filming progressed, Nelson's jitters dwindled. He and Jeanette soon inaugurated a habit of running over lines together in her portable dressing room. It was MacDonald who suggested that Eddy be given "'Neath the Southern Moon," a song intended for her in the film, although originally composed for a mezzo-soprano voice. Along with "Tramp, Tramp, Tramp" and "The Owl and the Bob Cat," that made three ostentatious Eddy numbers early in the picture. Jeanette did not feel upstaged—on the contrary. She had always believed that the worth of a movie depended as much on the quality of the other players' performances as on that of her own. Nelson's credibility as a love interest,

---

*MacDonald's tax records for that year list as "studio-requested appearances" thirty-two other such events, including a birthday party for President Roosevelt, hosted by L. B. Mayer (January 30), the opening of Garbo's *Queen Christina* (February 9), a Theater Owners Ball at the Ambassador Hotel (April 12), the Screen Actors Guild Rodeo (May 18), Marie Dressler's funeral (July 31), Nelson Eddy's performance at the Hollywood Bowl (August 2), an MGM luncheon for the Japanese prince (August 30), the Max Reinhardt stage production of *A Midsummer Night's Dream* (September 18), and her own performance for the Symphony Society Civic Dinner at the Biltmore Hotel (November 13).

she realized, hinged on her capacity to register convincing ardor, even in silence while *he* sang.

When it premiered in 1910, Victor Herbert's *Naughty Marietta* marked a turning point in American stage operetta: its eighteenth-century New Orleans settings looked refreshingly novel by contrast with the make-believe kingdoms then dominating the genre. A quarter century later, the original book by Rida Johnson Young seemed silly and out-of-date. Producer Hunt Stromberg demanded a total revision of plot and characters. The assignment went to Albert Hackett and Frances Goodrich, the husband-and-wife screenwriting team, and to John Lee Mahin, who penned the Jean Harlow vehicles *Red Dust* and *Bombshell*. The result was a brisk saga of high adventure that starts in Paris under Louis XV and moves through episodes depicting the voyage of prospective brides to the New World, their capture by pirates and rescue by mercenary scouts, and the Louisiana romance of Captain Dick Warrington (Eddy) and Princesse Marie de Namours de la Bonfain (MacDonald), a fun-loving, democratic aristocrat who masquerades as her serving girl Marietta to escape marrying an effete Spanish grandee.

Stromberg's choice of Woody Van Dyke II as director initially seemed downright perverse. Unlike Lubitsch and the Europeans, Van Dyke claimed not to give a damn about film as art: "I resent simpering idiots who babble about the Artistic Urge in a director's job—a director's job like mine anyway." Tall, lean, and military tough (he was a captain in the Marine Corps Reserves), Van Dyke gauged a movie's success by the money it made. Among his early blockbusters were exotic adventure films like *White Shadows of the South Seas* and *Tarzan, the Ape Man*. Prior to directing *Naughty Marietta,* he had launched another stellar team, William Powell and Myrna Loy, in *The Thin Man* mystery series (also scripted by Hackett and Goodrich). Even though he directed Lawrence Tibbett in *The Cuban Love Song,* Van Dyke boasted no affinity for music and liked to say that his favorite "aria" was "Pushin' Up the Daisies." His outstanding gift for shooting pictures under budget and in record time gave rise to his famous nickname: One-Take Woody.

Van Dyke's quickie tactics at first caught MacDonald off balance. One afternoon she estimated a half hour's wait before being needed, and so meandered from her trailer to view the previous day's rushes in a nearby projection room. She hadn't been gone five minutes when Woody called for her. Informed of his star's disappearing act, Captain

Van Dyke lost his cool. "Well, that's just dandy," he barked. "I'm holding up an entire company while my leading lady is enjoying a movie!
. . . THAT'S ALL FOR TODAY. COMPANY DISMISSED!" Moments later,
MacDonald returned to a deserted sound stage, where an anxious
watchman related what had happened. Van Dyke, Jeanette realized,
wanted to prove from the word "go" that he would not put up with
temperament from singers. Eddie Mannix advised her to do some "fast
apologizing." Instead, MacDonald placed a call to Harry Albiez of the
property department.

At 8:55 the following morning, four brawny stagehands trudged
onto the set carrying an immense doghouse. Van Dyke fumed as he
watched the unordered prop being placed at his feet. Suddenly a slender bare arm slinked from the house and shoved a shiny red apple at
his face. Another limb followed with a bouquet of sweet peas. Finally,
Jeanette's head popped out and she asked, eyes aflutter: "Now may I
come out, please, hmmm, Mr. Boss Man, may I please, hmmm?" The
crew rolled with laughter, the director most of all. In a single stroke
MacDonald both ratified Van Dyke's authority and sealed his allegiance as her number one fan.

One evening in midproduction, Woody took his leading lady to
Ciro's for dinner and dancing. "When he reached my front door,"
MacDonald recalled, "he twisted me around to take me in his arms. I
instinctively stiffened. That was enough for Woody. He politely kissed
the cheek I offered him and drove home." The next morning, MacDonald found a huge bouquet of yellow roses in her dressing room.
Woody's card read: "To Naughty Marietta—P.S. Not so naughty."
"That established our relationship," Jeanette later commented. "Good
friends, but no nonsense"—except for the usual goofy gags.

MacDonald's big solo in *Naughty Marietta* was "Italian Street
Song." Marietta's emphatic "La, la, la! *Ha, ha, ha!* Zing! Boom! Aye!"
gave the public its first occasion to hear MacDonald sing coloratura.
Jeanette had worked tirelessly on the prerecording, and Van Dyke
knew it. The day of the shoot, he made sure she felt at ease, asking
twice if she was ready for the take. Jeanette replied, "Yes." Woody
hollered, "QUIET, PLEASE! TURN 'EM!" and winked to one of the sound
men. Just as the star opened her mouth to pick up her voice on the
playback, high-pitched Chinese vocal music blared from the speakers.
MacDonald, usually unflappable, was struck dumb.

Van Dyke's principal challenge was to get Nelson Eddy to act. Much
was riding on "the Team"'s success, including Mayer's eminence as a

casting director. The truth was that Nelson felt awkward and foolish before the camera. Three weeks into production, his impassivity prompted Van Dyke to utter what became a classic showbiz put-down: "I've handled Indians, African natives, South Sea Islanders, rhinos, pygmies, and Eskimos and made them act—but not Nelson Eddy!" Days before the film's release, many of Eddy's scenes had to be reshot. The trick, Van Dyke discovered, was to keep him in motion, never at rest. An unkind joke soon spread through the industry. Question: How did Woody Van Dyke make Nelson Eddy a star? Answer: By putting the camera on Jeanette MacDonald.

The picture's preview at Grauman's Chinese laid to rest anyone's remaining doubts about Eddy's or Van Dyke's talents for operetta film. This *Naughty Marietta* was modern in tone, feel, and sound. Van Dyke's get-on-with-it touch helped the film's pacing and made Mac-Donald's vivacity all the more engaging. The confidence with which she wore Adrian's period costumes made them look lived-in, not fake. Frank Morgan as the bumbling colonial governor and Elsa Lanchester as his nagging spouse gave spirited comic relief. Major advances in audio recording caused the music and dialogue to sound crisper and more vibrant than ever. Almost everyone who previewed the picture agreed that its most compelling feature was MacDonald and Eddy's singing—a sensual blend of pulsating voices, the likes of which had never been heard in movies.

Following the preview, Mayer threw a mammoth party at the fashionable Trocadero nightclub. When he took the floor, Mayer derided the doomsayers who had harped on the fact that *Naughty Marietta*'s dream melody, "Ah! Sweet Mystery of Life," was also the theme song of Forest Lawn Cemetery. He turned to MacDonald: "They told me you were through—washed up. I didn't believe them. I had faith. After listening to you in *Naughty Marietta*, I want to tell you you are greater than you ever were." He then acknowledged MacDonald's strapping silver-blond costar: "They told me you could sing, but you couldn't act, that I would be foolish to put you in this picture. I didn't believe them. After seeing the picture, I want to tell you they were wrong. You can act as well as sing."

For Metro's top brass, *Naughty Marietta* showcased state-of-the-art Hollywood craftsmanship unburdened by European artiness. Appropriately, Mayer chose Washington, D.C., for the picture's world premiere on March 8, 1935. In attendance at Loew's Fox Theater were congressmen and senators, Supreme Court justices, aides to President

Roosevelt, and ambassadors from Austria, Greece, and the Soviet Union. Prior to the midnight screening, Captain Van Dyke hosted a VIP banquet and saluted American movies as "a potent force" for international understanding. That spring, the president enjoyed a private showing of the picture at Hyde Park.

It was perhaps to be expected that "Italian Street Song" and "Ah! Sweet Mystery of Life" would elicit resounding ovations when *Naughty Marietta* opened at New York's Capitol Theater. Yet something new was percolating in the backwaters of Depression-era America. From Flomaton, Alabama, to Lebanon, Kansas, to Sumas, Washington, the picture generated more passion than any movie musical before it. "Excellent, that's the word, excellent," wrote S. H. Rich, who owned the Rich Theater in Montpelier, Idaho. "You have a picture here that's in a class by itself. It should make money for every situation." Ingmar Oleson, proprietor of the Sons of Norway Theater in Ambrose, North Dakota, saw the film as marking an upward tilt in American moviegoers' taste: "The public is getting to appreciate more and more the better class of musical shows. This is a picture you will enjoy 'hearing' the second time, and there are not many in that class." MacDonald applauded the shifting tide: "Suddenly I had a different set of fans, who forgot about the sophisticate I'd portrayed in *The Love Parade, Monte Carlo,* and *The Merry Widow.*" One woman astonished Jeanette with a report that she had seen *Naughty Marietta* sixty-four times. "I wanted to write and ask her if she was an usher," Jeanette commented, "but I didn't dare."

Naughty Marietta quickly established itself as the movie sensation of the year. People asked not "Have you seen it?" but "How many times have you seen it?" Shot in half the days and at less than half the cost of *The Merry Widow,* it reaped $407,000 in profits, won an Academy nomination for Best Picture, and grabbed the Oscar for Best Achievement in Sound. It was the first musical to receive *Photoplay*'s Gold Medal for Best Picture, outstripping in viewer popularity *Mutiny on the Bounty, David Copperfield,* and *The Informer. Film Daily*'s Critics of America Poll ranked it fourth in the Best Feature category, placing it above such musical competition as *Top Hat, Broadway Melody of 1936,* and *Roberta.*

The picture also gave America a new brand of male romantic singing star. Theodore Paxson, Eddy's longtime accompanist and close friend, reported that when Eddy gave a concert in Dallas shortly after *Naughty Marietta* opened, "the women got so thick around the stage door . . . that almost 500 of them fought for his coat buttons." Eddy stood apart from tenorish crooners like Ramon Novarro and dashing Continental lovers à la Chevalier by projecting a boyish idealism that made his gawkiness come off as endearing. His strong, muscular baritone made him palatable to American men who equated male operatic singing with effeminacy. For many women, Nelson Eddy was just waiting to be smothered with kisses. One female viewer in New Haven compared "he-man" Eddy with his Gallic predecessor: "I am glad that, in cleaning up the movies, the producers are also breaking up a few of these screen teams. The best thing they did was to separate MacDonald and Chevalier. His croaking [was] an insult to her glorious voice. . . . If [Chevalier] is what they call effervescent, then I'll take ZaSu Pitts." For Metro's featured player Kitty Carlisle, Nelson elicited feelings that were not so much sexual as nurturing and almost maternal: "I think what attracted women to Nelson Eddy was that he was unthreatening. He had a beautiful manly voice, which was an extra added attraction, but he aroused the mother in them, or the sisterly. It wasn't Gable or Valentino, who aroused totally different feelings. Nelson was a nice-looking fellow. He looked like every American mother's dream of her son. A nice, clean-cut, good-looking boy."

While Eddy was *Naughty Marietta*'s revelation, MacDonald was its miracle of transformation. Never before had Jeanette looked so radiant, acted with such ease and verve, and sung so gorgeously. Her role—a runaway princess disguised as her own servant—was a comic-opera stereotype. Yet MacDonald invested the portrayal with a conviction that made the entire picture come alive. In spite of the new censorship, there was still room for MacDonald's tongue-in-cheek quips and innuendo. For months Production Code officials fretted over the implied avowal of prostitution when MacDonald, to avoid being auctioned into marriage, implores the colonial governor: "Oh, but surely here in New Orleans you have room for a girl who doesn't necessarily wish to become a housewife, but who—[*brief pause, pregnant with suggestion*]—likes to be charming and pleasant." Yet *Naughty Marietta*'s radical originality was to suffuse movie-musical characters with romantic yearnings so intense that physical consummation became irrelevant. The film's famous climax, which finds MacDonald and Eddy intoning "Ah! Sweet Mystery of Life," glorifies the union not of two bodies but of two full-throated singing voices. Just as the song's lyrics celebrate a love that repays enormous longing, yearning, and striving, so the entire film invites moviegoers to prize rapturous vocal pleasures over sex.

"Together they're a world rarity!" crowed audio engineer Mike McLaughlin, who was responsible for balancing Eddy's round, powerful tones with MacDonald's clear and intensely pressurized high notes. The offshoot was a sonic mix that mesmerized filmgoers the world over.

MacDonald credited Van Dyke's laissez-faire attitude with the blossoming of her new screen image, "more human, more sympathetic, and warmer than the girl Ernst Lubitsch had created." "Ernst," she explained, "believed in studied perfection; Woody in what he called 'spontan-eye-ity.' He left your portrayal very largely up to yourself. . . . Instead of the cold, stylized, calculating woman Ernst had manufactured, I was myself and I reveled in it." For the first time in her career, MacDonald added, "I liked myself on the screen. . . . In *Marietta,* I could sing as I felt, giving my best to the mood of the songs and concentrating all my attention upon interpretation and delivery." Her playful numbers, such as "Chansonette" and "Italian Street Song," revealed a bright, fluid soprano brimming with infectious joie de vivre. "Ah! Sweet Mystery of Life" throbbed with vibrancy because MacDonald trusted the music. She neither strained nor condescended to the melodic line. As a result, she furnished millions of filmgoers, most for their very first time, with the kind of thrills one associates with a great night in the opera house.

Naughty Marietta placed MacDonald at the top of Hollywood's pecking order and on the A-list of elite party hosts. She was a frequent guest of the Basil Rathbones, the Harold Lloyds, and the Irving Thalbergs. One night Elsa Lanchester and her husband, the actor Charles Laughton, were at a party given by the Thalbergs in their Santa Monica oceanfront home. Lanchester strolled down to the shore and discovered that the beach was covered with grunion—small silvery fish that spawn at high tide in wet sand and then, their instincts gratified, "stand on their tails, twiddle round, and go back to deep water." With her evening dress yanked to her knees, Lanchester dashed barefoot into the house and roared: "The grunion are running! The grunion are running!" The only ears to prick up were Laughton's and MacDonald's. Within seconds, filmdom's Henry VIII, Merry Widow, and Bride of Frankenstein could be seen splashing in the Pacific and luxuriating in the feel of grunion massaging their bare legs.

Since Bob Ritchie was now frequently abroad, MacDonald had a small pack of ready escorts for social rounds, including Nelson Eddy.

Although their "dates" were mostly publicity appearances engineered by the studio, MacDonald liked Eddy's company and enjoyed his combination of gentlemanly reserve and playful humor. Jeanette often expressed feelings of friendship by making gifts of animals, and soon after meeting Nelson she gave him an enormous sheepdog named Sheba. Eddy, who was born in Providence, Rhode Island, came of age in Philadelphia and, like MacDonald, retained strong ties to the city and its musical life. Jeanette flooded him with questions about how best to prepare herself for work in classical concerts and opera. For his part, Nelson was staggered by Jeanette's adeptness at maintaining a private life. He wittily compared her "unbelievable personal strength" and "feeling for living life smoothly" to "a silver spoon cutting into frozen custard." MacDonald, in turn, likened Eddy's earnest thoroughness to that of "a platinum-plated steam shovel." Obviously, the two did not think of each other in amorous terms. Joseph Newman, *Naughty Marietta*'s assistant director, recalled: "They were always friendly, but not overly friendly."

Unlike MacDonald, Eddy never took to Movieland's social circuit. The rumor mill linked him romantically to actresses Cecilia Parker (who played a bit part in *Naughty Marietta*) and Alice Faye. But Eddy resented MGM's early efforts to depict him as a man about town, and he stuck tenaciously to uncomplicated bachelorhood. His only profound relationship at this time was with his divorced mother, Isabel—a situation that led to gossip about his sexuality. Some speculated he was homosexual. Others whispered he was impotent. His immediate family later claimed that he was sterile. Nelson's half sister Virginia, twenty-five years his junior, explained: "Dad [Nelson's father, William] told us one day after I had my own children that he was saddened because there was no one to carry on the Eddy name. Dad informed us that Nelson, when a youngster, fell out of a tree, and the way he landed resulted in what today can be willfully brought about by a vasectomy. . . . Nelson adored my kids and once told my parents that I had done the one thing he could never do, have children."

Jeanette had no reason to know of Nelson's condition. Isabel Eddy and Anna MacDonald, who regularly played cards and mah-jongg together, briefly thought of their children as potential mates: "One day Mrs. Eddy buttonholed Mother and confided, 'Nelson for the first time is talking about what fun it must be to be married. I have my own ideas about what he means, haven't you?' I think Mrs. Eddy and Mrs. MacDonald may have done a little happy daydreaming and matchmaking."

When fans began to have similar fancies, MacDonald and the MGM publicity department nipped the illusion with an ironically titled article in the June 1935 issue of *Hollywood,* "So I'm in Love with Nelson Eddy!" It began: "Perhaps I should not be telling this story at all. Doubtless the people who start these absurd rumors of Hollywood romances—and somebody must be the first to gossip—will seize upon my words as new evidence of my 'interest' in Nelson Eddy. But I don't mind. We both think it is very funny." To wipe away all ambiguity, MacDonald spelled out an awful truth that some obsessive fans refused to accept: "Just because two people play love scenes on the screen is not an indication that they are in love." Years later, in her memoir, she confessed: "The truth of the matter was that whatever attraction Nelson and I might have had for each other was interrupted before it ever got started. Another man appeared: a tall, handsome, fun-loving fellow who fitted exactly my prescription for what a man should amount to."

MacDonald had met Gene Raymond at a party in the spring of 1935. The two arrived simultaneously on the doorstep of Roszika Dolly's house in Beverly Hills. When Rosie greeted them, she raced to a conclusion: "Darlings, how nice of you to come together!" Jeanette later admitted to being instantly attracted by Gene's "young god's physique." On this night, however, she was the object of Howard Hughes's advances, and the twenty-six-year-old Raymond seemed captivated by Loretta Young. A few days later, Jeanette went to a Sunday brunch at the home of her lawyer, Louis Swarts. She was about to ring the doorbell when she heard a wolf whistle emanating from the driveway. "Do you always turn around when the boys whistle?" asked the perpetrator—again Gene Raymond, also Swarts's client. It was getting to be a comedy routine, but MacDonald could not help feeling "that mysterious tingle, that something that meets in space" between two unsuspecting people. About a week after, there was a sneak preview of *Les Misérables* at Grauman's Chinese. As MacDonald retrieved her ticket from a press table in the forecourt, a voice piped up from behind: "Well, I seem to be meeting you on doorsteps all the time!" It was Gene Raymond. He and Jeanette sat together, applauding Fredric March and Charles Laughton. During the movie, Gene whispered: "Look, we've been meeting so often on these doorsteps, whoever it is that ordains these things seems to have something in mind. Why don't you have dinner with me tomorrow night?" Jeanette accepted, on the condition that it be one of her mother's informal meals at home. The menu, it turned out, featured eggplant, Gene's least favorite vegetable.

Gene Raymond had been a professional actor since age five. He came to movies from his native New York, where he was known by his given name, Raymond Guion. Blue-eyed, platinum blond, and preppy, Guion established himself as the Rialto's "perfect juvenile" in such Broadway hits as *The Potters, Young Sinners,* and *Cradle Snatchers.* Film director George Sidney remembered him from this period as "the most gorgeous thing the world had ever seen." Guion continued to turn heads in Hollywood, where he signed with Paramount in 1931 and was rechristened Gene Raymond. Jesse Lasky's daughter, Betty, recalled: "He was always around our beach house and was almost like a member of the family. I remember his large biceps and very developed chest. He wore tight T-shirts, so you were conscious of his muscular build. He was very attractive, very sweet, and very young."

Gene was a natural athlete who excelled in gymnastics and tennis. He also had a flair for repartee, jokes, and storytelling. Yet according to MacDonald, he was "an introvert in a business where extroverts abound." Raymond was one of the rare actors of the early 1930s courageous enough to criticize the movie business for not, as he put it, "living up to expectations." Fiercely self-reliant, he turned down long-term studio contracts and managed to stay afloat as a freelancer, claiming to enjoy "bucking against the entire industry." Raymond demanded—and got—script rewrites before signing with Columbia for *Brief Moment,* opposite Carole Lombard, and with Metro for *Sadie McKee,* opposite Joan Crawford. It came as no surprise to Raymond that in his RKO picture *Flying Down to Rio,* the dance routines of two supporting players eclipsed him and his costar Dolores Del Rio. He later commented that Fred Astaire and Ginger Rogers were the only ones in that picture who "knew what they were doing."

Raymond set high standards for himself. He made a string of grade B comedies with Ann Sothern for RKO—*Walking on Air, The Smartest Girl in Town, There Goes My Girl*—that brought decent returns. But he found artistic gratification only in the unconventional leading roles he played in independent pictures made for Lasky at Fox, such as the animal lover in the atmospheric *Zoo in Budapest,* with Loretta Young, and the sensitive puppeteer in *I Am Suzanne!,* with Lilian Harvey. Around the time he met Jeanette, Gene went public with his ambition to fill the void left by Douglas Fairbanks, Sr., and bring swashbuckling heroes back to movies. He never met this goal.

Jeanette and Gene's first formal date was at Ciro's on June 17. As the radiant duo strolled into the supper club, the orchestra struck up

"All I Do Is Dream of You (The Whole Night Through)," the Arthur Freed and Nacio Herb Brown song Gene had introduced in *Sadie McKee*. During dinner Jeanette kept looking at her watch. Gene asked pointedly, "Are you so bored that you can hardly wait to go home?" Jeanette smiled: "If you just wait a *little* while longer, I'll tell you what I'm waiting for." At midnight she blurted: "It's my birthday!" Gene ordered a cake, candles, and champagne. Jeanette was elated to learn that Gene's birthday, in August, fell on her lucky number—13.

In the weeks that followed, the twosome went dancing at the Mocambo, the Cocoanut Grove, and the Miramar. They spent afternoons riding at the Riviera Country Club. "Jeanette was the only woman I knew in Hollywood who rode sidesaddle," recalled Gene, whose own equestrian specialty was hurdle jumping. "And that impressed me." Jeanette did not reveal that the horsehair and dust were playing havoc with her summer allergies: "I had to stay on a routine of pills and injections to look pretty for him, which was real evidence of my affections." They soon invented joke names for each other: "G. McGillicutty" and "Hunky" for Gene, "Flora MacIntosh" and "Bunko" for Jeanette.

One reason MacDonald felt comfortable with Raymond was that "not wanting marriage was something we had in common." Gene portrayed himself for the fan magazines as "indifferent to girls" and "addicted to solitude": "I don't see how a man who is undergoing all the painful processes of a career can make a go of a happy domestic life." This was not a case of playing coy. Gene Raymond was the product of a broken home and was genuinely fearful of marriage. He never erased the painful memory of huddling in bed with his younger brother, Leonard, while his parents quarreled viciously. If Gene grew up to be a man of wide acquaintanceships but few intimates, it was because, as Jeanette soon came to understand, in boyhood he and his brother were "forced to protect themselves against the raw emotions around them." Shortly after they started to date, Gene told Jeanette that his parents divorced when he was eleven and that his father was dead.

Gene's handsome, honey blonde mother, Mary, had the same brilliant sky blue eyes as her elder son. She was a would-be writer whose fascination with numerology led her to conclude that "Kipling" was a more auspicious moniker than either her maiden or married names. Each year Mrs. Kipling spent six months with Gene in Los Angeles and the other six in Manhattan. Whether near or far, she kept a protective eye on her son's activities. Mary Kipling did not like Jeanette MacDonald.

That year Basil and Ouida Rathbone were hosting a charity White Ball at Perino's, the chic Wilshire Boulevard restaurant. Gene and Jeanette committed to a table for ten. Two days later, Gene announced that his mother had already reserved a table of her own. Jeanette, who took for granted that she would be among Mrs. Kipling's party, thought nothing of changing their arrangements. Embarrassed, Gene said: "I'm afraid she hasn't included you. She's invited Janet Gaynor for me." Jeanette kept her cool.

On the night of the ball, Norma Shearer raised eyebrows by wearing bright red instead of the obligatory white. Dietrich scored points by arriving, with Doug Fairbanks, Jr., in resplendent, but by now familiar, tails and top hat. But it was MacDonald who stole the show as she sailed into Perino's dressed in orchid satin and sporting on either arm Hollywood's most eligible bachelors, housemates Jimmy Stewart and Henry Fonda. "It was a glittering evening for sure," she recollected, "but I burned with a mixture of jealousy and hurt pride, particularly when I saw Gene dancing with Janet. So I played it à la Pagliacci. I said the right sentimental things at the sight of Robert Taylor and Barbara Stanwyck dancing as though nobody else existed. I exchanged the correct platitudes when Gene stopped at my table to meet Hank Fonda and Jimmy. I visited Mrs. Kipling's table to pay my respects; she couldn't have been more cordial. I was determined to let nobody realize my feelings."

The next morning she and Gene went horseback riding and avoided discussing the ball. Jeanette convinced herself that the previous night's trial "had done more to bring us together than to keep us apart."

Gene Raymond embraced Los Angeles as a City of Homes, perhaps because he was haunted by memories of constant moves from one Brooklyn boardinghouse to another. During his teens, Gene, like Jeanette, was the household breadwinner, and he, too, developed a no-nonsense feel for finance. He especially mistrusted stocks and bonds. "Being wealthy," Gene once told a friend, "means nothing if you can't write a check." When he met Jeanette, Gene was having rebuilt a lavish eleven-room Colonial-style house on Benedict Canyon Drive in Beverly Hills, just above Sunset Boulevard. He called the house Monterey, and it was intended for himself, his mother, and his brother, Bob. (Numerology had moved Mrs. Kipling to demand that her second son, an aspiring actor, change his name from Leonard Guion to Robert Marlow; Kipling openly admitted she had little affection for Bob because he looked too much like his father, whom she despised.)

To celebrate the completion of Monterey, Gene threw a party. In advance of the housewarming, Jeanette sent a service of silver flatware—"a gift I thought was in keeping with my financial ability and my high hopes of making friends with Mrs. Kipling." When she arrived at the gathering with her mother and Bob Ritchie, a scowling Mrs. Kipling snapped, "How dare you send such an extravagant gift to Gene!" Jeanette rationalized that Mrs. Kipling was a doting mother who clung to the belief that no girl was good enough to keep company with her son. Having won over the Ohmeis and Ritchie families, she was certain she could convince Gene's that there was no cause for alarm. Anna MacDonald, who observed Kipling's rudeness in silence, was less optimistic.

As the end-of-year holidays approached, Gene and Jeanette exchanged Christmas presents: a gold-and-jade charm bracelet for her, an Irish setter for him. Mrs. Kipling was dead set against having the puppy in her house, but Gene prevailed, and he named it Tray, after the "old dog" in the Stephen Foster song. On Christmas Eve, Jeanette went a-caroling through Brentwood and Beverly Hills with Jimmy Stewart, Kay Francis, and Allan Jones. After stops at the homes of Woody Van Dyke and Ralph Bellamy, the group went to Gene Raymond's. They were singing "We Three Kings of Orient" when Mrs. Kipling's silhouette appeared at one of the upper bedroom windows. Soon her voice could be heard detonating in the foyer downstairs. Moments later, Gene opened the front door and strained to be hospitable. The carolers sensed his agitation and promptly moved on to serenade Grace Moore and her husband, Valentin Parera, the Spanish actor.

Rose Marie, the second MacDonald-Eddy opus, had required its stars to spend nearly a month on location in the Sierra Nevadas, along with two dozen pack mules loaded with cameras, reflectors, sound equipment, makeup boxes, portable toilets, and other paraphernalia. Hours after she arrived at Chambers' Lodge, on the west shore of mile-high Lake Tahoe, MacDonald wrote to Bob Ritchie, then in New York: "The scenery here is simply marvelous. My cottage overlooks the lake and the sun is just now setting. The reflection on the mountains is a glowing rose—quite lovely. We will no doubt be here for three or four weeks (if we're lucky). I do hope it doesn't run on for weeks beyond. But I don't think it will, as they say it'll be snowing any day now."

The threat of a mid-September blizzard drove Woody Van Dyke to keep the cast and crew moving at breakneck speed. They beat the snow, but uncompliant weather twice brought Hollywood's great out-door musical production to a near halt. The setting for MacDonald and Eddy's "Indian Love Call" was an isolated cliff overlooking a steep, verdant valley. Van Dyke's instinct told him that this tender love duet—

> When I'm calling you . . . oo . . . oo . . . oo, . . . oo . . . oo . . . oo!
> Will you answer true . . . oo . . . oo . . . oo, . . . oo . . . oo . . . oo?

—demanded a few high clouds. On their first try, he and the company reached the remote site only to remain under solid blue skies until evening. Woody also thought that a ripple on the lake should accompany the title song, Eddy's serenade to MacDonald while they glide together in a canoe. One-Take Van Dyke lost four days as actors and technicians marked time waiting for a sustained breeze. The false starts at Emerald Bay made MacDonald, never comfortable in small boats, queasy and out of sorts. Exasperated, she wrote to Ritchie: "That 'Rose Marie' song is a jinx!"

A 4:30 A.M. wake-up siren discouraged even the most rambunctious from seeking nighttime amusements in Reno, a two-hour drive. As a result, evenings at the lodge were jovial. Jimmy Stewart, who played MacDonald's outlaw brother in the picture, entertained with his accordion. (According to Jeanette, newcomer Stewart's knees "shook so much" in his scene with her "that he could scarcely speak.") The Rose Marie Rhythm Kings, a group of cameramen and prop assistants who loved western music, also loosened up everyone with their cowbells, sticks, and whistles. At one evening's Amateur Hour, Jeanette and Nelson conspired to sing comic songs so horrendously that the boisterous Rhythm Kings were guaranteed first prize.

For all the frolic, MacDonald was on edge for most of the location shoot. "One morning," recalled assistant director Joseph Newman, "it was 9:45 and I sent Walter Strohm, my assistant production manager, to see why Jeanette still wasn't ready. Strohm poked his head through the door to her cottage, and said, 'Miss MacDonald, we're all waiting for you.' Jeanette didn't say a word. She just threw a wig in his face."

At the root of MacDonald's distress was the eternal triangle. Bob Ritchie, in a letter from England that summer, had hinted he still wanted to marry Jeanette. When he returned to New York in September 1935, Ritchie publicly announced he was headed for Lake Tahoe to join his fiancée. These maneuvers caught MacDonald off guard. She had been dating Gene Raymond for several months, and she considered her engagement charade with Ritchie to be over. Bob's renewed advances made her realize that "in all the time he'd been my friend and manager, [Ritchie] regarded himself as being on probation." Once and for all, the ambiguity of their liaison, convenient for so many years, had to be laid to rest.

Weeks earlier Harry Warner's daughter, Doris, had asked Jeanette how she managed her little "design for living," a none-too-subtle reference to MacDonald's presumed ménage à trois with Bob and Gene. Such gossip didn't faze Jeanette. What troubled her was how to avoid hurting either of these men. Ritchie may not have been a faithful consort, but his devotion through the years was profound. Jeanette still had deep affection for him. On the other hand, her relationship with Gene Raymond had yet to be defined: "This romance hadn't quite reached the seriously romantic stage. . . . We simply recognized that we liked each other, perhaps more than we should."

At Lake Tahoe, MacDonald accepted nightly phone calls from both suitors. The pressure of trying to stay noncommittal caused her to lose sleep, appetite, and peace of mind. To cushion the inevitable showdown with Bob, she wrote him on September 16: "Well, it won't be long now, Pop. And I'm warning you, you're in for a couple of shocks. One is the way (weigh) I'm looking. . . . I love you dear. Just remember that no matter what else comes about—I love you very dearly!"

Two weeks later, Ritchie arrived at Chambers' Lodge accompanied by a cunning Bedlington terrier, a gift for Jeanette. If Bob hoped the fleecy dog, groomed to resemble a lamb, might placate its mistress, he was right. Jeanette was unable, or unwilling, to give Ritchie his walking papers in Tahoe. Yet the calls from Gene Raymond kept coming. One day Gene phoned just as Jeanette and Nelson finished some canoe shots on the lake. As Nelson dug deep with his paddle, he quipped: "Fine thing. Me working like a dog to take you back to talk to Gene Raymond. *That* one! Just tell him for me that I've been making violent love to you." "Don't think I won't," Jeanette replied. "It might have a good effect on him."

MacDonald tested Raymond's emotions while trying not to pressure him unduly. In one letter from Lake Tahoe, she wrote flirtatiously: "Here I sit in the car overlooking Cascade Lake, a most picturesque spot—highly romantic, etc., and instead of taking in its splendors I'm getting into a bad habit! YOU'RE the cause of that my friend, I HATE writing letters ordinarily and yet it would seem that I'm doing this quite voluntarily. So what do you make of it?" One hour after finishing the scene in which she devours a plate of beans at Eddy's mountain camp site, she wrote Gene: "I am *so* full of baked beans I can hardly move. Long shots, medium shots, and close ups, all eating beans ravenously and it was before lunch so it should be convincing. Strangely enough *you* crept into my mind cause it made me think of that Sunday at my house when you all were kidding me about the beans being too salty. These today weren't nearly so good—they were just Heinz's." (MacDonald seldom cooked, but she prided herself on her baked beans casserole à la MacDonald, covered with bacon or pork chops and served with steamed brown bread.)

Jeanette was forthright with Gene about her predicament with Ritchie, but her candor did not always prevent awkwardness: "Bob arrives tomorrow at noon—and so I shan't talk with you—tho I may call you Thursday—unless you'll be out—if so don't hesitate to wire me, *not* to call—or better still—if I do call and you're out I'll be *big* about it—you know me—the understanding type!" After several sleepless nights during Ritchie's stay, Jeanette wired Gene: "OH MORPHEUS MY MORPHEUS WHEREFORE ART THOU MORPHEUS. ALSO MY SENSE OF HUMOR. JULIETTE."

Over the next few months, MacDonald's affairs of the heart kept the gossip columnists stumped. Parsons wrote on October 8: "If report [is] true that Jeanette and Robert Ritchie, her manager and former boy friend, are expecting to finally marry, then she and Gene [Raymond] are permanently parted." On December 11, Walter Winchell tooted: "Robert Ritchie and Jeanette MacDonald have clinched, again—all is now serene." Four days later, from Parsons: "Hollywood is completely mystified over the Jeanette MacDonald–Robert Ritchie situation. Robert is leaving for England almost immediately and if looks mean anything, he is the most depressed soul in Hollywood. Apparently he and Jeanette have struck a snag in their romance. . . . Gene Raymond makes no secret of his adoration of Miss MacDonald and she apparently shares his feelings."

In fact, MacDonald was still undecided. It was not until after the phenomenal release of *Rose Marie* in February 1936 that Jeanette told Bob she wanted a complete break:

Wednesday

Dear Bub,

They're just now singing [on radio] "A Little Love, a Little Kiss," and I'm crying! It's funny how miserable it makes you to lose it! . . .

Bub, I've just *got* to *be* and *feel* entirely free and cut loose from you before I'll ever know if I can care for you (that way) again. Do you know

what I mean? Men (most of them) are a bit diffident about seeing me
because they feel you're still head man. And so unless I am free and clear,
I'll never feel I've had a chance to interest others and so will never know by
comparison if you are or not *the best!* You've really left me in a pretty bad
position and you are the only one to relieve it, you know!

There was another article in Reid Kendall's column last week saying that
before you left you'd assured everyone everything was just the same
between us. But they were still wondering, since I'd been seen out with
Henry Fonda, who seemed to be cutting in on G.[ene] R.[aymond]'s time.

You see, Bub, it isn't quite fair to me, 'cause a girl can never be the
aggressor—whereas you can do all the dating and chasing you want to. And
so I wish you'd make it clear from your end. The easiest way is to establish
it as "sometime ago." Then there is no possibility of anyone's thinking you
were cut out while away. That's why I said in one of my letters to you that
I bet you wouldn't say "It was really established on a different basis two
years ago"—that's about the time you first went to Europe alone. Also, that
takes the curse off your having stayed at 912 Rexford when you returned.

Oh hell! It's all very confusing. And as you can guess, it's had me terribly
worried and upset and I now weigh *110 lbs!* So thin that everyone is
commenting on it and I am rather unhappy over the entire situation as
I feel whenever I go out people are speculating as to whether or not I'm
cheating on you etc. . . .

I am ok except for dreadful nervousness and sleeplessness. Conscience
I guess! . . .

Ever,
The Old Lady

With the New Year, MacDonald and Eddy's box-office appeal skyrocketed. "They touched your heart in *Naughty Marietta* . . . They'll win it
in *Rose Marie!*" went one of the catchlines for selling the picture. "The
Singing Sweethearts are back again!" touted another. The studio was
betting that the romantic yearning glorified by MacDonald and Eddy
in their first joint effort could be resurrected with even greater intensity
the second time around. MGM was right on the money. *Rose Marie* affected moviegoers like no musical before or since. There were drench-
ing rains in Pittsburgh, subzero temperatures in Chicago, flooded roads
in Des Moines, icy streets in New York, and a flu outbreak in Los Angeles. Yet nothing that winter of 1936 could keep viewers away from
the new *Rose Marie.** Even women in advanced states of pregnancy

---

*Joan Crawford and James Murray had starred in MGM's 1928 silent version, directed
by Lucien Hubbard; Ann Blyth and Howard Keel would grace Mervyn LeRoy's Cinema-
Scope and Ansco Color edition of 1954. These versions were more faithful than the
MacDonald-Eddy picture to the plot of the 1924 Friml-Stothart-Harbach-Hammerstein

were willing to stand for hours on ticket lines several blocks long, and some commemorated the event by naming their newborn daughters Rose-Marie.* The picture amassed profits of $1,488,000, making it MGM's second-biggest moneymaker of the year, exceeded only by MacDonald's *San Francisco.* These two movies together accounted for over one-fourth of the studio's 1936 returns in a year that saw forty-five Metro releases.

Audiences were captivated by the expanded breadth of MacDonald's acting. As Marie de Flor, alias Rose Marie, she moved convincingly from the broad stereotype of a temperamental opera star to the nuanced portrayal of a woman torn by emotional conflict. In appearance, too, MacDonald was more expressive than ever, looking glossy-metallic in the early glamour sequences and creamy-natural in the rustic ones that followed. The image of Jeanette MacDonald in boots, camping slacks, and flannel shirt was unexpected. It ingratiated her with moviegoers previously unresponsive to Powdered Princesses and Merry Widows. "We had the boys from the sawmill applauding!" reported a movie-house owner from Arkansas.

Rose Marie also unveiled a new dimension to MacDonald the soprano. Shortly before the production started, Jeanette shared with Bob Ritchie her anxiety over the film's opera sequences:

[August 24, 1935]

Popsie my sweet,

Just got some more script on *Rose Marie* and it looks promising. Of course I'm very thrilled about the music. I am going to sing the *Romeo and Juliette* aria ["Juliette's Waltz Song"] in the first scene and the Execution Scene (last scene, last act) from *Tosca.* I sing them both very well. Hunt [Stromberg] was thrilled to death today. I sang Juliette for him. Only, of course, you must not breathe it to a soul because someone else is liable to beat us to it and take the edge off it. "Juliette['s Waltz Song]" is one of the few good lyric arias left and I'd hate for G.[race] M.[oore, originally slated to star in *Rose Marie*] to beat me to that one too. So hold your fingers crossed that I get this in first. I know you're wondering where Grand Opera comes in in

---

stage operetta *Rose-Marie,* which showcased Mary Ellis and Dennis King and remained Broadway's biggest moneymaker until Rodgers and Hammerstein's *Oklahoma!* (1943). In the early 1960s, *Little Mary Sunshine,* Rick Besoyan's off-Broadway hit musical, merrily spoofed the MacDonald-Eddy films and featured a duet titled "Colorado Love Call."

*In an advance publicity stunt, MGM offered $2,000 to the parents of the first set of female twins born after January 1, 1936, and christened "Rose" and "Marie." The prize went to Mrs. Owens of Fort Smith, Arkansas, who was presented with a check by the town's mayor on behalf of MacDonald and Eddy.

Rose Marie, but this is a picture version of *R. M.* and nothing like the stage play. Thank goodness! . . . Incidentally, L. B. told me he's trying to swing *Maytime* to me now. It seems he's sore as a boil at Grace Moore. (NEVER TELL THIS TO A SOUL.) She sent him a snotty wire, in effect: "Understand you are releasing my old pictures. This is a shabby thing to do and unworthy of you and Metro. Unless you stop, I have no intention of fulfilling my contract with you. G. M." It burned him up. . . . Of course, I don't know what will come of it. But SAY NOTHING. I may wind up the winner after all!! . . .

All my love,
Mommie

And win MacDonald did. It was one thing for a *Variety* reporter to place her "at the head of the singing moving picture prima donnas." It was another for W. J. Henderson, New York's dean of music critics, to write in the *Sun:* "It is not too much to say that in tone, formation, attack, equality of scale, breath control, intonation, and diction," MacDonald and Eddy in *Rose Marie* "hold their own with any other artists of this day. Young persons studying voice ought to listen to them and consider carefully how they do it." For MacDonald, this tribute validated years of study and sacrifice. It was also a slap in the face to her only true rival, Grace Moore. With *Rose Marie,* Jeanette MacDonald became Hollywood's undisputed diva.

Nelson Eddy, whose challenge following *Naughty Marietta* was to maintain his appeal as a singing matinee idol, smelled a threat in Allan Jones. Now under contract to Metro and fresh from the Marx Brothers' *A Night at the Opera,* Jones sang opposite MacDonald in *Rose Marie*'s opera sequences. "For the death scene from *Tosca,*" Jones recalled, "I originally sang the aria 'E lucevan le stelle.' After Nelson went to a preview in Pasadena, he rushed to L. B. Mayer's office and said, 'If you don't cut Allan Jones's aria out of there, I'm going to go on strike; you'll have trouble with me.' So they took it out."

If Jones spelled competition for Eddy, it was less in voice than in dramatic élan. When Van Dyke greeted Eddy after his overnight triumph in *Naughty Marietta,* the director asked, "How does it feel to be a star, kid?" Nelson truthfully replied, "I don't know how to act." To which Woody bluntly added, "You're telling me!" As *Rose Marie*'s Sergeant Bruce of the Royal Canadian Mounted Police, Eddy stretched credibility. Yet the public didn't care. When Nelson burst on the screen chanting "The Mounties," women squealed and men cheered. Nelson Eddy in his Mountie hat became an instant pop icon. No matter what else he did in movies, Eddy would forever be etched in filmgoers' consciousness as Sergeant Bruce, the stoic, morally upright singing Mountie who gets his man—and Jeanette MacDonald.

MacDonald once joked to singer Patti Paige: "[Nelson and I] never needed a psychiatrist's couch; we just needed a love seat." A careful look at *Rose Marie* suggests otherwise. Marie de Flor's loyalty to her murderous brother comes across as no less passionate and obsessive than her love for Sergeant Bruce. The latter appears more committed to tracking his man than wooing his woman. On top of this, the picture culminates with the soprano's nervous breakdown and her retreat to a sanitarium. These psychological undercurrents, not found in Friml's stage operetta, are disturbing and unresolved. They give the lie to the hoary notion that MacDonald-Eddy musicals are squeaky-clean. On the contrary, in a cycle of pictures where physicality is repressed, the erotic often ends up all the more insistent—which just may account for the hypnotic pull these films continue to exert on so many viewers. In Astaire-Rogers musicals, overt physical playfulness is essential to courtship. In MacDonald-Eddy pictures, sex behaves differently. Channeled through song, it becomes as disembodied as Indian spirits echoing sweet love calls throughout the Canadian Rockies.

CHAPTER TEN

The Iron Butterfly

I hear the trained soprano. . . .
[She] convulses me like the climax of my love grip.

WALT WHITMAN, mid-1800s

Heaven is a city much like San Francisco.

TONY KUSHNER, 1991

HOLLYWOOD'S UNDISPUTED QUEEN OF SONG became Mac-Donald's new title just two years into her association with MGM. Of all the singing personalities who had deserted vaudeville and the music halls during the first wave of talkies—Jolson, Cantor, Chevalier, Buchanan, Fanny Brice—MacDonald alone remained at the top. Without the complexes that afflicted so many other stars, she reveled in the international celebrity she had vigorously labored to possess. From thirty-fifth place prior to *Naughty Marietta*'s release in 1935, MacDonald shot up to *Motion Picture Herald*'s Top Ten Money-Making Star List of 1936. By early 1937, *National Box Office Digest* would rank her number one in drawing power of all screen actresses. Her potency abroad remained colossal. In Paris, MacDonald's only female competition came from French natives Danielle Darrieux and Annabella. In the United Kingdom, her popularity was stronger than it had been at the time of *Monte Carlo*. Her sole rival at MGM for the foreign market was the increasingly costly and elusive Garbo.*

---

*Even in China, MacDonald was hailed as the outstanding "screen idol." Dr. Lin Yu-tang, special correspondent to the *New York Times*, reported on November 8, 1936, that

Yet MacDonald wanted something more. She wanted to choose her pictures and costars. Following *Rose Marie,* nothing would have been easier than to heed Mayer's urging and move directly into *Maytime,* the Sigmund Romberg stage confection being adapted especially for her and Nelson Eddy. But it was not in MacDonald's nature to let the expectations of others block her own agenda. She was unwilling to be locked into an exclusive pairing with Eddy. She wanted formats other than operetta. And she was hell-bent on showing herself able to carry a picture without a male singing partner.

Many have rightly perceived MacDonald as one of the great "ladies" of Golden Age Hollywood. She was adept at flattering Mayer and his cronies with rapt attention. She nodded sympathetically when they offered sage counsel. However, she was not going to let the old-boy system destroy her independent spirit, as it was doing to Jean Harlow. The woman who began her MGM career by refusing *The Prisoner of Zenda* and by jockeying for the lead in *The Merry Widow* was now set to play hardball with the company men—even Mayer's bosses in New York. "Halfway ambition," she once proclaimed, "can be a dangerous thing. If you've a burning desire to be something, do something."

Robert "Hoppy" Hopkins was the great lovable oddball on the MGM lot. As resident "gagman," he furnished producers and writers with quick lines to perk up scenes that were flagging. Hoppy was a tall, disheveled Leopold Stokowski look-alike, who was as addicted to four-letter words as he was to caffeine. He also had a gift for the High Concept. When MacDonald was making *Naughty Marietta,* he nabbed every executive in sight and screamed like a madman: "San Francisco! Earthquake! MacDonald and Gable! You son-of-a-bitch, don't you see it? She's a singer. He's an operator. Spence Tracy is a priest. Atheist becomes religious. DON'T YOU GET IT?"

MacDonald got it, and she began to lobby Eddie Mannix, who in turn lobbied Irving Thalberg, who had Herman J. Mankiewicz draft a scene. Hoppy's writer pal Anita Loos, a fellow native San Franciscan, then developed the concept into a full-blown screenplay. Loos, who started in pictures writing titles for D. W. Griffith, had recently scripted

---

"young people are playing 'The March of the Grenadiers' on their harmonicas at camping parties in the way people used to sing Peking operatic airs from *The Three Kingdoms* at public baths."

for Gable in *Hold Your Man* and Tracy in *Riffraff,* two Harlow vehicles. The challenge of imagining this manly duo with MacDonald, whom she considered "a woman of great strength and ambition," fired Loos's creative juices as never before.

Like Loos, Clark Gable was attuned to MacDonald—which is precisely why he wanted no part of the project. According to Jeanette, Gable told Mannix: "Hell, when she starts to sing nobody gets a chance. I'm not going to be a stooge for her while she sings in a big, beautiful close-up and the camera shoots the back of my neck!" Gable refused to read even an outline. He made it clear that once he wrapped up *Mutiny on the Bounty,* he would take his vacation and return to Metro only in assignments already agreed upon and scheduled.

Ida Koverman, MacDonald's devoted ally in Mayer's office, urged Jeanette to cozy up to Gable socially. Obsequiousness, however, was not MacDonald's style. Uplift was. Jeanette wanted the King of the Lot to realize he would be missing a blue-chip opportunity by not doing this picture. To prove her commitment to Gable and the project, MacDonald did the unthinkable—for Hollywood. She took an unpaid leave from the studio, thereby putting *Maytime* on hold and opening the way for her schedule to mesh with Gable's. To reduce Clark's fear of playing opposite a singer, she prodded Loos to beef up the ruggedness of his scenes. She also issued statements to trade papers about the need for greater "realism" in pictures with music. "Filmgoers today want *credibility*—believable stories," she told *Film Weekly.*

MacDonald's boldest strategy was to appeal for support from the East Coast offices of Loew's, Inc., MGM's parent company. This maneuver had the potential for alienating Mayer, who jealously guarded his privilege as the studio's sole conduit to New York. On March 20, 1935, MacDonald sent a special delivery letter, typed on personal stationery, to Felix Feist, MGM's general manager of sales and distribution:

Dear Felix,

This will probably be the beginning of a big romance by correspondence between you and me. In any event I shall expect an answer, but be careful, for I may hold it against you!

But to get down to business, I am appealing to you because I believe you and your Department of the organization have more influence on what this gang out here shall do than anyone else. I feel a bit like a little girl telling tales out of school, so if you get the same impression, remember I have already labelled myself.

The situation is something like this:—Some months ago I was approached about a story (based on an original idea) by one Hopkins out here, momentarily called *San Francisco* to be done with Clark Gable. The idea is a swell one with great dramatic background, punch, but happily not a musical comedy or operetta, but with music opportunities and scope so great that unless I am entirely crazy, it is a natural. In its present embryonic state it fits Gable and me like a pair of gloves: he being the King of the Barbary Coast and I being the girl who comes to sing in one of his joints.

Just last week I turned down *The Life of Johann Strauss [The Great Waltz]* for various reasons, one being that it is not the kind of part I like playing, and secondly that I am not convinced of its popular appeal. It is definitely not the type of thing the shop girls will go for, although in all possibilities [it] would be an artistic success.

On the strength of *Marietta* (I am keeping my fingers crossed), which I think has such strong romantic appeal that it will definitely intrigue the shop girl type of trade as well as the high-brows, I am more than ever determined that I want to continue making my appeal to this former type of trade who comprise the majority of audiences.

Having turned down the Strauss story brought on further negotiations resulting in my granting the studio ten weeks' extension on my contract (dam' decent of me I say) so that they can concentrate on *San Francisco* to replace *Johann Strauss* as the next vehicle for me. Now I am told Gable will not be available for *San Francisco* and a list of assignments will prevent his being teamed with me. Who they will put with me I do not know. This is not a singing part so that precludes the possibility of Eddy. The role demands a *fine, virile* actor, otherwise the whole story goes to pot. The entire outlook was so perfect, the whole setup so 100% box-office, with a brand new team from the public's viewpoint, also Metro's, that I am heartbroken and at the same time furious that such an opportunity is going to be missed. Isn't there anything the Sales Department can do in having one of Gable's other assignments postponed so that this picture can be made as great as it should be with him in it? . . . Shouldn't it be intriguing for the public to see me with him instead of a musical comedy man like Chevalier or Novarro? Remember how everyone has said what a tremendous sensation *The Merry Widow* would have been if Gable had played it instead of Chevalier? And shouldn't it be intriguing by the same token for the public to see Gable with me instead of again with Crawford or Harlow? Doesn't it offer to you fine possibilities from a selling standpoint?

Please don't get the impression that I am trying to run your job, but I am interested in making myself, if possible, the outstanding personality on the screen, to make my appeal to all classes, music lovers, non–music lovers, the layman and his wife, etc. I know sometimes out here they lose sight of lots of possibilities in their hectic endeavor to fill in their quota of pictures to send to you.

So there! Now it's up to you to get a Gable-MacDonald special for your early Fall release.

Oh, by the way, I haven't forgotten the picture and frame I promised you, but I don't dare send it just now. It might look like a bribe, but of course there is nothing to prevent my sending it for a reward!

Love and kisses,
Jeanette

Two days later, Feist responded by telegram:

MY DEAR JEANNETTE [*sic*]: NOT ONLY ARE YOU BEAUTIFUL AND TALENTED BUT YOU ARE GEEDEE [goddamn] SMART. AND FOR MY COMPANY'S INTERESTS AS WELL AS MY GREAT ADMIRATION FOR YOU I WILL LOOK FOR A SPOT TO GET IT OVER. BEYOND THAT OF COURSE I CANNOT GO. MARIETTA IS SUPERB AND EARLY INDICATIONS GIVE PROMISE TO AN OUTSTANDING SUCCESS. IN MY OPINION YOU NEVER WERE PHOTOGRAPHED BETTER LOOKED PRETTIER SANG AS DIVINELY OR GENERALLY DID SUCH A WONDERFUL JOB. WE ADORE YOU. AM WORKING FOR YOU. REGARDS. FELIX.

It was around this time that Hoppy Hopkins coined a new nickname for his favorite actress. Most people used it only in a whisper behind her back, but MacDonald was tickled pink to be known as—the Iron Butterfly.

Waiting for Gable gave MacDonald more time to spend with Gene Raymond. Jeanette had just moved to Carmelina Avenue in Brentwood Heights. After a night at the Mocambo, she and Gene returned to her rented Colonial-style house and for the first time gave in to their mutual passion. "I literally felt the world leap off its bearings and spin around like a carousel," Jeanette recalled. It was an indulgence long overdue. For years, Bob Ritchie's philandering had caused MacDonald to guard against deep romantic feelings. Now Raymond's tenderness played havoc with her crumbling defenses.

Gene soon gave another party at Monterey. When most of the guests had left, Gene's mother, Mary Kipling, invited Jeanette to view the doll collection in her bedroom. As MacDonald walked over to the figurines, Mrs. Kipling locked the door and tucked the key in her bosom. "Why are you trying to take Gene away from me?" she asked sternly. Jeanette felt like the "other" woman in a Joan Crawford picture. "But I don't know what you mean. You don't *take* anybody. I mean, Gene and I are just good friends—" Mrs. Kipling interrupted: "No. You are a sophisticated woman with a dubious reputation, and my son is infatuated with you. Why don't you marry Bob Ritchie, instead of trying to break up my home?"

Kipling demanded a promise that Jeanette would not marry her son. Jeanette kept repeating that she and Gene had no thought of marriage. Like a woman possessed, Kipling paced back and forth. To appease her, MacDonald delivered the line usually reserved for her own mother: "I can only promise you that I'll never marry without letting you know."

A few days later, Gene and Jeanette drove out to Mount Rubidoux in Riverside. On a stone bench near the mission shrine, Gene confessed he had lied about his father being dead. Roy Guion was alive. He explained that Roy, as a provider, was unable to meet his wife's inflated expectations. Mary had therefore saddled Gene with her hopes for fabulous prosperity, shoving him on stage at an age when all he desired was a regular boyhood. Gene still resented his parents' divorce, which prompted a custody battle that awarded him to Mary and his brother to Roy. Gene had not seen his father in over a decade. Mrs. Kipling now had an irrational fear that if her more successful son married, she would wind up penniless.

Since Gene doubted his mother could ever accept any woman who wanted to be part of his life, he asked Jeanette if she could possibly endure such a situation. After a long silence, MacDonald responded with total conviction: "Why don't we pray a little? Maybe the answer will come to us. Maybe in some way we'll be guided." Anita Loos would write no better lines for the spiritual Mary Blake in her emerging screenplay.

Gable was impressed that MacDonald had given up pay on his account. Still, he remained unyielding in his refusal to play Blackie Norton to her Mary Blake. MacDonald was equally obstinate when the front office proposed William Powell and Robert Young as substitutes. Finally, Felix Feist and the New York crowd pressured Mayer into rallying around MacDonald's cause. After months of resistance, Gable grudgingly took on the part—but only after Mayer threatened him with suspension and Jeanette found herself "$140,000 poorer."

San Francisco went into production on Valentine's Day, 1936. Word spread that the picture's earthquake sequence would be a knockout technical achievement without precedent. Irving Thalberg, preoccupied with *The Good Earth* and his failing health, tossed the project to producer Bernie Hyman, his right-hand man. Hyman, however, was not on speaking terms with MacDonald, who still held him responsible for

Figure 1.   Jeanette's parents: Anna May and Daniel.

Figure 2. Jeanette at four months; her father had hoped for a son.

Figure 3. Already a seasoned performer—Jeanette at age five.

Figure 4.   Jeanette (bottom, left) on the vaudeville circuit with Al White's Six Sunny Song Birds, circa 1912; the other girl is Bessie Cole.

Figure 5.   Ferdinand Torriani, who in 1923 began retraining MacDonald's singing voice; with his associate, Grace Adele Newell, who later became MacDonald's lifelong coach.

Figure 6.   MacDonald (front, left of center) introduces the wailing "Sweet and Low Down" in George and Ira Gershwin's *Tip-Toes* (1925), on the stage of the Liberty Theater.

Figure 7.   MacDonald as the title character in the Broadway musical *Yes,
Yes, Yvette* (1927); though her puckered lips say *yes, yes*, the pillow says *wait,
wait*.

The New York stage agrees with Hollywood

"Lux Toilet Soap for smooth skin"

SATINY, smooth skin! The stage world knows its value. Stars give it wisest care—with Lux Toilet Soap.

Personal interviews recently obtained reveal that an overwhelming majority of the New York stars are using it.

Leading theatres all over the country have placed it in the dressing rooms in response to requests from their players.

In Hollywood, too, 9 out of 10 stars use Lux Toilet Soap. All the great motion picture studios have made it the official soap in their dressing rooms.

Order some today. Instead of paying 50c or $1.00 for a cake of French soap, you can now have the same luxury for just 10c.

JEANETTE MacDONALD

In "SUNNY DAYS" at the Imperial Theatre this sparkling, titian-haired young prima donna delights New Yorkers with her dazzling smile, her enchanting voice and the nimble gaiety of her dancing.

Nickolas Muray

"I'm so glad to have Lux Toilet Soap. It keeps my skin petal smooth." — JEANETTE MacDONALD

Figure 8. The Broadway star of *Sunny Days* endorses Lux and a well-scrubbed, all-American look in 1928.

Figure 9. MacDonald with Bob Ritchie—for nearly a decade her manager, escort, and sometimes fiancé.

Figure 10. On the Paramount back lot, prankster MacDonald copies her mentor Ernst Lubitsch—a giant firecracker standing in for his cigar.

Figure 11.   In *The Love Parade* (1929), the queen's vulnerability surfaces during this tense boudoir scene with her prince consort, played by Maurice Chevalier.

Figure 12.   MacDonald in the garden scene in *The Vagabond King*, with
baritone Dennis King, who hogged the frame as she sang "Only a Rose,"
1930.

Figure 13.   Keeping up the public's view of her as the "Lingerie Queen of the Talkies," MacDonald poses alluringly to promote *Oh, for a Man!* (1930).

Figure 14.   Poster for MacDonald's Paris stage debut at the
Empire Theater, 1931.

Figure 15.   MacDonald and Chevalier fox-trot to the title song of *One Hour with You* (1932); seated on either side of the camera are George Cukor and, with trademark cigar, Ernst Lubitsch.

Figure 16. Princess Jeanette (MacDonald) falls for the tailor Maurice (Chevalier) in *Love Me Tonight* (1932).

Figure 17.   Crowds gather for the opening of MacDonald's show at Paris's Rex Theater, 1933.

Figure 18.   The bedroom scene with Ramon Novarro in *The Cat and the Fiddle* (1934), MacDonald's first musical for MGM.

Figure 19.   Ernst Lubitsch, reflected in mirror, supervises this photo of
MacDonald and Maurice Chevalier as they dance to "The Merry Widow
Waltz" in 1934.

Figure 20.   With Sid Grauman looking on, Maurice Chevalier assists
MacDonald, who immortalizes her footprints in cement for the Chinese
Theater forecourt on December 4, 1934.

Figure 21.   MacDonald is all eyes and ears for Nelson Eddy in *Naughty Marietta* (1935).

Figure 22.   Jeanette parades with her MGM men: (l. to r.) Herbert Stothart, Nelson Eddy, Woody Van Dyke, Hunt Stromberg. (*Rose Marie* © 1936 Turner Entertainment Co.)

Figure 23.   Gene Raymond, a stunning
Hollywood newcomer, circa 1931.

Figure 24.   As the sophisticated opera singer obliged to traverse the Canadian
Rockies in *Rose Marie* (1936), MacDonald envies Sergeant Bruce (Nelson
Eddy) his feast of beans; the scene was shot on location at Lake Tahoe in the
fall of 1935.

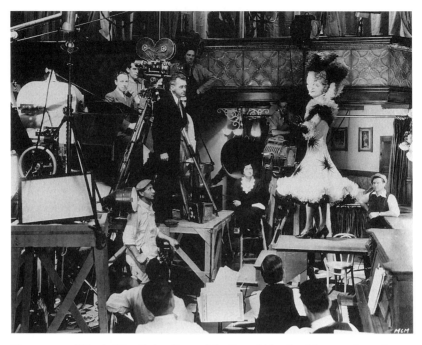

Figure 25. Woody Van Dyke directs MacDonald in the title song from *San Francisco* (1936).

Figure 26. On the set of *Maytime* (1937), MacDonald checks a lyric with the prompter before shooting the Page's scene from *Les Huguenots*, the opera by Giacomo Meyerbeer. (*Maytime* © 1937 Turner Entertainment Co.)

Figure 27.   MacDonald records Léo Delibes's "Les Filles de Cadiz" for *Maytime*; note the chair that keeps her at a steady distance from the microphone.

Figure 28.   MacDonald with Clark Gable and Jean Harlow, 1936.

Figure 29.   The celebrity wedding party of the decade, June 18, 1937: (l. to r.)
Nelson Eddy (soloist), Allan Jones (usher), Helen Ferguson Hargreaves (bridal
attendant), Richard Hargreaves (usher), Blossom Rock (matron of honor and
sister of the bride), Robert Marlow (best man and brother of the groom),
MacDonald (the bride), Gene Raymond (the groom), Fay Wray (attendant),
Harold Lloyd (usher), Ginger Rogers (attendant), Warren Rock (usher),
Mrs. John Mack Brown (attendant), John Mack Brown (usher), Basil
Rathbone (usher).

Figure 30. The newlyweds in their living room at Twin Gables, 783 Bel-Air Road, in 1937.

Figure 31. Playing with Nick, Tray, and Stormy Weather on the lawn at Twin Gables; Jeanette once said, "A MacDonald home without dogs is like ham without eggs."

Figure 32. Jeanette tests the water in her jagged-edged, free-form swimming pool, a gift from Gene for their third wedding anniversary; in rear is the "playhouse," which Jeanette redecorated as her present to Gene that year.

Figure 33. The honeymooners on the north side of Oahu, 1937;
photographers kept their distance—but not enough to please the newlyweds.

Figure 34.   On the set of *The Firefly* (1937), director Robert Z. Leonard (left of center) observes MacDonald's dance step.

Figure 35.   MacDonald models one of the boldly accented ensembles Adrian designed for her to wear in *Sweethearts* (1938). (*Sweethearts* © 1938 Turner Entertainment Co.)

Figure 36. MacDonald and Wagnerian tenor Lauritz Melchior follow the advice set forth in Gene Raymond's new composition, "Let Me Always Sing!," published by Schirmer in 1939.

Figure 37. The Raymonds open Twin Gables to Hollywood's music elite at a garden tea party on August 6, 1939, to honor soprano Lily Pons and her husband, conductor André Kostelanetz; seated (l. to r.), MacDonald, Miliza Korjus, Pons, Rosa Ponselle, Irene Dunne; standing (l. to r.), Lew Ayres, Allan Jones, Nino Martini, Igor Gorin, Douglas McPhail.

Figure 38. On July 17, 1939, MacDonald signs her most lucrative contract with MGM; executives Nicholas Schenck (l.) and Louis B. Mayer (r.) look on.

Figure 39.   Standing apart from masked jitterbugs and jazz musicians,
MacDonald intones Tchaikovsky's "None But the Lonely Heart" in Busby
Berkeley's spectacular finale to *Broadway Serenade* (1939).

Figure 40.   Jeanette's mother visits her on the set of *New Moon* (1940).

Figure 41. MacDonald rehearses the breathtaking "Zigeuner" sequence for *Bitter Sweet* (1940).

Figure 42. On an army camp tour in 1942 MacDonald, dressed as if in a concert hall, comforts a wounded soldier named, by coincidence—Gene Raymond!

Figure 43. The Raymonds pose for this portrait shortly before Gene leaves for Army Air Force combat overseas, in spring 1942; the year before, in the picture *Smilin' Through*, they played lovers separated by war.

Figure 44.   A crew member takes a light reading of MacDonald on the set of *I Married an Angel* (1942); note the brace supporting her massive wings. (*I Married an Angel* © 1942 Turner Entertainment Co.)

Figure 45.   On stage with tenor Armand Tokatyan for MacDonald's opera debut in *Roméo et Juliette*, on May 8, 1943, in Montreal.

Figure 46. With soprano Lotte Lehmann, MacDonald's opera and art-song teacher, in Santa Barbara, July 13, 1944.

Figure 47. Louis B. Mayer congratulates MacDonald after her Hollywood Bowl debut, August 9, 1945; with Gene in uniform.

Figure 48. MacDonald returns to MGM in September 1946 to shoot *Three Daring Daughters* (1948), a Joe Pasternak production.

Figure 49. MacDonald with Margaret Truman, celebrating the young singer's twenty-fifth birthday at Washington's Mayflower Hotel on February 17, 1948.

Figure 50.   Being chummy with Lassie, MacDonald's costar in *The Sun Comes Up* (1949). (*The Sun Comes Up* © 1948 Turner Entertainment Co.)

Figure 51.   Greeting fans after her second Carnegie Hall recital on
January 16, 1953; at right is Emily Wentz, MacDonald's gal Friday,
who holds Jeanette's platinum mink coat.

Figure 52.   MacDonald heads a show-business delegation to the presidential inaugural festivities of January 1953; in front (l. to. r), Guy Lombardo, Fred Waring, Elivera Doud (the president's mother-in-law), MacDonald, Mamie Eisenhower, President Dwight D. Eisenhower, Lily Pons, George Murphy; Lauritz Melchior is behind Lombardo; Esther Williams and James Melton are behind Mrs. Eisenhower; Gene Raymond is in rear, left of American flag.

Figure 53. MacDonald bares her legs in a dance routine that brings down
the house at the Sands Hotel, Las Vegas, October 1953; with dancer Bill
Alcorn.

Figure 54.   On May 30, 1953, Leonard Job, president of Ithaca College, confers the degree of doctor of music upon MacDonald for her many contributions to the field of music.

Figure 55. MacDonald as Mrs. Anna Leonowens, with Leonard Graves as the King, in *The King and I*, Starlight Theater, Kansas City, Missouri, August 1956.

Figure 56.　On the set of MGM's *Gigi* in September 1957, Maurice Chevalier gives surprise guest MacDonald a slice of his birthday cake.

Figure 57.   The Singing Sweethearts again join forces on Patti Paige's TV show, *The Big Record*, September 25, 1957.

Figure 58. Outside the Thalberg Building in Culver City, MacDonald (center, in pants) poses with members of the Jeanette MacDonald International Fan Club to mark the Club's twenty-fifth anniversary, in June 1962; front row, second from left, is Clara Rhoades, chosen by Jeanette that year to be the Club's president, and serving in this capacity ever since.

Figure 59. MacDonald, in her last formal portrait sitting (1959), wearing
ivory and gold satin; the clips on her pearl necklace and matching earrings are
made of white and canary diamonds.

Figure 60.   Gene Raymond was a dashing presence well into his golden years.

The Cat and the Fiddle's botched ending. Mayer intervened and granted coproducer status to John Emerson, Anita Loos's partner in what she once described as a marriage of *in*convenience. Emerson's know-how as a moviemaker was minimal. But with MacDonald's sanction, this unusual chain of command allowed Loos to function— through her husband and in complicity with Jeanette and Hoppy—as the picture's de facto supervisor. Woody Van Dyke directed.

Gable and MacDonald's initial scene together set the tone for the entire shoot: Clark's breath so reeked of garlic that Jeanette could barely get close. After a week's work, she wrote to Ritchie: "Gable is a *mess!* I've never been more disappointed in anyone in my life. It seems (according to Mayer) he's terribly jealous of me and acts very sulky if I get more attention on the set than he. The third day of production, he and Van had quite a blow-up and it all came out in Mayer's office that evening. I like Tracy very much. There's as much difference between the two as day from nite. Gable acts as tho' he were really too bored to play the scenes with me. Typical *ham*."

For the next six weeks, the two costars kept up a show of cordiality. Margaret Irving, who played the weakly camouflaged madam in Blackie's lusty life, remembered a commissary lunch at which Clark and Jeanette displayed "good friendship and companionship." But Gable and MacDonald never entirely clicked off-camera. Joseph Newman, whose work on the picture brought him an Oscar nomination for Best Assistant Director, described the nub of their friction as a "mismatch in routine": Gable liked to start shooting at nine sharp; MacDonald needed an extra hour before feeling ready; and when Van Dyke granted her that hour, Gable stewed with resentment. Clark and Jeanette would soon see a lot of each other socially, since Gable was a pal of Gene Raymond, with whom he had worked on *Red Dust*. But the King of the Lot's usual warmth evaporated when he was around the fun-loving but strong-willed diva. "They were not kindred spirits," concluded MGM publicist Emily Torchia.

One day Clark pulled up a chair close to Jeanette's and asked bluntly, "Why did you want me so badly?" MacDonald avoided a straight answer. "If I'd told him the honest-to-God reason was that I considered him a great actor and exactly right for the part," she reminisced, "I could perhaps have made a friend. But my memory of Ida Koverman's advice wouldn't let me tell the truth. I looked him square in the eye. 'Because you have sex appeal,' I said. The minute I said it, I could have cut out my tongue. He grunted and walked away, repulsed and insulted."

Spencer Tracy was totally at ease with MacDonald, and was the one person on the Metro lot in whom Jeanette confided details of her affair with Gene Raymond. Gene had recently taken his mother on a trip to Florida in the hope that a change of scenery might bring a change of heart. It was now several weeks since Jeanette had heard from Gene, and she feared the worst. As her appetite waned, her face became emaciated, and costume designer Adrian had to compensate with extra-broad hats and collars. One day MacDonald leaned her head on Tracy's shoulder and asked: "How do you suppose I can discover if Gene is serious or just making a fool of me?" Spence replied: "I think you will find he is testing himself, even more than you. When *he* finds out, *you* will find out." A few days later, Jeanette received a one-word telegram from Gene: "BORED." That single adjective spoke more eloquently than a thousand other words could ever have done. Jeanette started to eat with regularity again.

MacDonald was nursing a dreadful cold when Van Dyke and Joseph Newman directed the earthquake scenes. This awesome sequence, done with full-scale buildings atop hydraulically operated rocker platforms, made *San Francisco* the measure of all disaster films to come. Jeanette was so eager to watch the earth split open—a spectacular effect devised with assistance from engineers at the California Institute of Technology—that she fled her sickbed and raced to the studio. No one, however, was allowed onto the quake stage without a preauthorized pass, including the film's ailing star. When two electricians saw her wrangling with a guard, they escorted her on the sly to a high catwalk. Wheezing, sniffling, and dizzy from the perspective, Jeanette took in the scene. She then hurried home, feeling wretched.

The next day, MacDonald's impatience with the dragging cold overrode her fear of heights and motion. She arranged to be flown in Amelia Earhart's private plane to Palm Springs for a recuperative sundrenched weekend. Jeanette returned, tanned and rested but still underweight, to film her scenes from the operas *Faust* and *La traviata*. "Your face is getting too gaunt," scolded the cinematographer Oliver Marsh, who mistakenly thought she was dieting.

Weeks earlier, Jeanette and Grace Adele Newell had huddled together in a recording room and listened to the playback of Marguerite's "Jewel Song." Thirteen years—again, the lucky number—had passed since MacDonald ineptly sang the Gounod aria for Phoebe Crosby, the Broadway friend who had led her to Ferdinand Torriani and Newell.

This time Grace squeezed Jeanette's hand, saying that now the maestro would approve.

MacDonald's greatest ambition, to move from films to opera, seemed on the verge of becoming a reality. Maria Jeritza, the mesmerizing Tosca of Jeanette's first visit to the Metropolitan Opera House, was now in Hollywood to be close to her future husband, Winfield Sheehan, Jeanette's old enemy at Fox. After viewing *Naughty Marietta,* the stage diva urged MacDonald to consider opera. Lily Pons, the Metropolitan's leading coloratura, also lent encouragement. Following *Rose Marie,* a reviewer in *Musical America* wrote: "One wonders why she is not actually in grand opera. Many singers far less well endowed are doing great things in the lyric theatres." Wilhelm von Wymetal, the Metropolitan regisseur hired by MGM to direct MacDonald's operatic sequences, worried that her voice was "a little bit too thin" to sustain an entire role in the opera house. Wymetal thought, however, that "continued training might give it the necessary stamina." Grace Newell boasted: "She's had many offers to go into opera . . . but Jeanette has always wanted to wait, and go in at the top."

One musical moment in *San Francisco* placed MacDonald at loggerheads with Woody Van Dyke. For the mission scene, she was supposed to have sung the Bach-Gounod "Ave Maria." Van Dyke rightly feared that the largo tempo at which the piece had been recorded made for meager contrast with the following scene, a talky encounter between MacDonald and Tracy. Stothart agreed to rerecord at greater speed. MacDonald protested, arguing that the increased tempo would undermine the hymn's spirituality. After much dispute, Van Dyke dropped "Ave Maria" and substituted a version of Stephen Adams's "The Holy City" ("Jerusalem, Jerusalem"), a popular anthem that MacDonald had to learn from scratch.

Along with memorable renditions of arias and anthems, MacDonald introduced two popular songs in *San Francisco* that became instant standards: "Would You," the tender waltz by Arthur Freed and Nacio Herb Brown, reprised on-screen by the dubbed Debbie Reynolds in *Singin' in the Rain* (1952); and the rip-roaring "San Francisco," a triumphant slice of musical Americana composed by Bronislaw Kaper, Walter Jurmann, and Gus Kahn—native sons, respectively, of Poland, Austria, and Germany. "An American composer would be a little embarrassed to write this kind of corny song," Kaper later said. "So I wrote it very sincerely and honestly. . . . And, as you say, pompously, 'The rest is history.' "*

In *Rose Marie,* MacDonald's haughty diva fails pitiably at "hot" renditions of "Dinah" and "Some of These Days" in the backwoods honky-tonk. Her reward is Nelson Eddy's sympathy. In *San Francisco,* opposite Gable, MacDonald is never short of complete confidence. Mary Blake, the parson's daughter from Benson, Colorado, may be temperamentally averse to "heating up" the title tune as Blackie Norton orders. But in a world filled with designing Blackies, this plucky working girl cannot afford to bungle a challenge. On her first night at the Paradise, Blackie's gaudy cabaret, she brings to "San Francisco" an unfaltering ragtime vigor that sets the crowd cheering. At the Chickens' Ball, on the fateful early morning of April 18, 1906, her rendition leaves no stops unpulled: she teases, vamps, descants, and soars through the number while, at her bidding, a frenzied audience joins in on the second chorus. With perfect melodramatic irony, this delirious tribute to San Francisco ("the heart of all the golden west") takes place just moments before the Great Earthquake erupts.

When *San Francisco* opened throughout the nation in late June 1936, it jolted the movie business from its annual summer slump. In New York City alone, the picture shattered Loew's booking and box-office records at the Capitol and State on Broadway, the Metropolitan in Brooklyn, the Valencia in Jamaica, and the Paradise in the Bronx. With gross receipts totaling $5,273,000 worldwide, *San Francisco,* which cost $1,300,000 to produce, became MGM's greatest moneymaker before *Gone with the Wind* (1939) and has remained one of its most durable hits through reissues, TV showings, and videocassette sales. The film earned six Academy nominations: Best Picture (the fourth MacDonald movie to be nominated), Best Actor (Spencer Tracy), Best Director, Best Assistant Director, Best Original Story (Hoppy Hopkins), and Best Sound Recording (won by Douglas Shearer).

While the national conventions of the Democratic and Republican Parties were wringing their hands over the country's economic plight, *San Francisco* offered Depression-weary Americans a portrait of people rescued from calamity through faith in God and their own resourceful-

*The Kaper-Jurmann-Kahn "San Francisco" almost never made it into *San Francisco.* As late as mid-January 1936, the studio was considering the merits of another "San Francisco" (song no. 3131) with words by Harold Adamson ("Manhattan Serenade") and music by Walter Donaldson ("Carolina in the Morning").

ness. "We'll build a *new* San Francisco!" shouts a youth when the Tent City survivors learn that the fires are finally extinguished. The sight and sound of MacDonald, alive, first comforting a grieving family with the hymn "Nearer, My God, to Thee" and then leading Gable, Tracy, and a cast of thousands in "The Battle Hymn of the Republic," lent a majestic air of uplift to the movie's ending.

In the fall of 1936, the director of recreation at New Jersey State Prison in Trenton ran *San Francisco* for his inmates. "At the close of the film," he reported, "the men rose as one, paid a momentary tribute of silence, and then broke into the loudest and longest burst of applause we have ever known."

Over the decades, *San Francisco*'s inspirational pull has remained impressive. Ten days after the lethal quake of October 17, 1989, World Series baseball fans, unconcerned by the lingering potential of aftershocks, packed into Candlestick Park, home to the San Francisco Giants. Following a solemn minute of homage to the dead, they proceeded to extol their city's gutsy vitality with a spirited chorus of "San Francisco." Fifteen years earlier, San Franciscans sparred bitterly over which song would be their official civic anthem, MacDonald's footstomping "San Francisco" or Tony Bennett's sentimental "I Left My Heart in San Francisco." The MacDonald song eventually won out because, as one inhabitant said, "We are *not* mawkish and insipid and maudlin; we are *alive,* vibrant, raucous, bawdy, with a 'who-gives-a-damn-about-earthquakes' spirit."*

Judy Garland was MacDonald's only legitimate successor as Queen of Musicals at MGM. More than a decade after her tempestuous reign ended, in a Carnegie Hall concert of April 23, 1961, Garland acknowledged her lineage with a special rendition of "San Francisco." An introductory verse by Roger Edens, her associate producer at Metro, went: "I never will forget / Jeanette MacDonald; / Just to think of her / It gives my heart a *pang;* / I never will for*get* / How that brave Jea*nette,* / Just *stood* there / In the *ru*ins / And *sang* / A-a-and—*SANG!*" After pronouncing MacDonald's name, Garland paused for three waves of audience laughter and applause. Composer Hugh Martin, who was present, remembered seeing "a glint in Judy's eyes that tipped me off that there

*Today, San Franciscans diplomatically acknowledge the Bennett tune (by Douglass Cross and George Cory) as the city's official *ballad,* whereas the MacDonald melody remains its official *song.* In *Tales of the City* (1978), the novelist Armistead Maupin divides San Franciscans into two broad categories, based on how they envision the city's spirit: "Jeanette" types and "Tony" types.

was venom in the offing. I felt stupid as I realized how angry it was making me, especially since my devotion to Judy exceeded even my devotion to Jeanette. But to make fun of anything as seemingly pure as Jeanette aroused my ire in a way that quite surprised me."

As Lingerie Queen of the Talkies, MacDonald had been party to a sophisticate's view of humanity that often trivialized sentiment. Even in *Naughty Marietta* and *Rose Marie,* drenched as they were in post-Code virtuousness, MacDonald managed to inject ironic doses of self-parody. But with *San Francisco,* MacDonald completely abandoned her armor against sentiment and combated Gable's machismo with the new, double-edged sword of romantic love and religious piety. In years to come, MacDonald's increased identification with opera, art songs, and music allegedly "good for the soul" alienated her from audiences with more down-to-earth tastes. Judy Garland and her first steady costar, Mickey Rooney, were light-years away from MacDonald and Eddy, not to mention MacDonald and Chevalier. Still, sophisticates who felt betrayed by MacDonald's abandonment of bedroom farce, as well as youngsters resisting cultural uplift, found common pleasure in Judy and Mickey's adolescent antics. These audiences often poked fun at MacDonald, claiming she gave their hearts more burn than pang.

Garland's tribute to MacDonald at Carnegie Hall was both a salute to her great predecessor and a wink—in the manner of the pre-Code Jeanette—to those who summarily dismissed the diva as sentimental and kitschy. When she learned of the Garland rendition, MacDonald joked to a friend: "I think I should get some royalties on that!" But in 1936 MacDonald was virtually unassailable. *Time* magazine, then inclined to flippancy, took her to task for "acting with her teeth" in *San Francisco.* Yet overall the press lauded MacDonald as the most versatile singing actress in movies. "It is impossible to conceive of anyone else in the part," raved the *Hollywood Spectator.*

The *New York Times* astutely assessed MacDonald's capacity to bridge opera and cabaret as "a near-perfect illustration of the cinema's inherent and acquired ability to absorb and digest other art forms and convert them into its own sinews." The response of American moviegoers was less cerebral. Jeanette MacDonald was simply great entertainment.

MacDonald's MGM contract was up for renegotiation in the summer of 1936. Her shrewdness in bringing about *San Francisco* so impressed Mayer and the New York office that Jeanette was able to wield considerable muscle. Her top priority was to avoid being forced into pictures she did not want. Accordingly, she rebuffed a proposed long-term arrangement in favor of a nine-month contract for two films at a salary of $125,000 per picture, with the option of this contract being extended, at a higher salary, for another nine months if both she and the studio could agree on properties. Among her specific demands, all granted, were rejection of *The Vagabond King, The Prisoner of Zenda,* and *The Student Prince*—vehicles that would favor male costars; the right of refusal to appear in more than *one* film in which Nelson Eddy would also appear; and a right to do radio broadcasts any time she wanted.

For years MacDonald had been seeking greater financial control of her recorded voice on the airwaves. In late 1934, she joined Al Jolson, Eddie Cantor, Fred Astaire, and opera stars Mary Garden and Lucrezia Bori in founding the Society of American Recording Artists (SARA). SARA called for performers to receive "five to fifteen cents, depending on a radio station's power" for each use of their recorded music. MacDonald's early contracts with MGM prohibited her from making live radio appearances while filming unless they served the studio's promotional interests. Commercial broadcasting, in under ten years, had become a major U.S. industry that expended over $60 million annually in live talent. Jeanette wanted a slice of that pie for herself.

On June 29, 1936, MacDonald made a major live national broadcast. It was a *Lux Radio Theatre* presentation of *Irene,* hosted, narrated, and directed by the virtuosic showman Cecil B. DeMille. *Lux Radio Theatre* was one of the most popular weekly shows in radio history, attracting audiences of over forty million listeners. The *Irene* program, fifth in the new series, was unique in the fact that MacDonald was being starred *singly*—her nonnegotiable requirement for doing the broadcast.

When DeMille, in his stentorian voice, introduced her as "the prima donna with a sense of humor," MacDonald stepped briskly on stage. She wore a simple white sport dress with a red-and-green fishnet scarf knotted carelessly around her neck. She took her spot behind a music stand and, to the astonishment of the studio's viewing audience, positioned horn-rimmed glasses atop the bridge of her nose—a first ever for myopic MacDonald in public. As DeMille told listeners how he had once refused to give Jeanette a part in a picture at Paramount because he didn't think she had "anything," she looked at him from across the mike, wrinkled her nose, and stuck out her tongue. The studio audience roared.

If any preconceptions of her being hoity-toity remained, she squelched them at the end of act 1. Sinking into a chair, her arms and legs sprawled in all directions, Jeanette mimed a "Whew!" and mopped her brow—gestures that further endeared her to the crowd. Throughout the broadcast MacDonald's readings were brisk and colloquial, her singing, strong and clarion. Near the show's close, she said that aside from performing at the Metropolitan Opera, her only unrealized ambition was to dance "just once" in a picture—"because just once is perhaps all the public will stand for!" Her lack of pretension caused listeners in kitchens and living rooms around the country to respond to MacDonald in a new way. Hollywood's diva was also a regular gal.

Eleven days earlier, MacDonald celebrated her birthday with Gene Raymond on a long horseback ride in the hills above Los Angeles. When they dismounted for a rest, Gene took Jeanette's hand and teased: "I've been waiting for you to propose to me for a long time. Since you won't, I guess I'll have to." Jeanette was flustered. She was in love with Gene, but she had not thought seriously about marrying him. Following her instincts, she accepted his proposal on the spot. Heeding her brain, she asked for a lengthy engagement.

If MacDonald was now willing to contemplate marriage, it was largely because Gene Raymond was in many ways the polar opposite of Bob Ritchie. Gene was able to envision marriage as a wedding of people, not of careers or fortunes. He recognized that his stardom was less luminous than Jeanette's and would probably remain so. But unlike Ritchie, Gene had amassed substantial personal wealth. To Jeanette's mind, there was little risk he would ever descend to the fate of her beloved father and become dependent on her for support. Gene also brought out measures of warmth and tenderness in Jeanette that she had never known. As a lover, he was as sensitive and considerate as Ritchie had been self-centered. Moreover, Gene was not a womanizer. Had she married Bob, Jeanette would inevitably have found herself competing with other women. Further still, Gene shared Jeanette's feelings about offspring. Bob Ritchie had often spoken desirously of children, and when Norma Shearer had her second child, Jeanette confided to him: "Lucky dog. She always manages to get what she wants, doesn't she?" Yet Jeanette could not imagine herself giving a child "a square deal in time, attention, and affection." As Gene Raymond later confided: "It would be most unsatisfactory to bring a child into our life and have one brought up by nannies."

In public, MacDonald increasingly advocated progressive, unsentimental views on marriage and divorce. She decried the double standard that permitted husbands more freedom than wives: "I believe a man and woman should stand on the same level. One should not be looked down upon as though she were inferior; the other should not be looked up to fearfully or conciliated as if he were a human devil." At the very moment when national publications were gushing over her affair with Raymond, the Iron Butterfly asserted: "It is unwise to stake all you have on love. Nor do I think it was ever intended that love should be everything in life for us, for in that case work wouldn't enter into the scheme of things. I place everything I hope to get out of life on an equal basis." In Raymond, MacDonald found a man secure enough in his masculinity not to feel threatened by such ideas. She and Gene were also forward-looking in their rejection of the custom that husbands should be older than their wives. Soon Ginger Rogers, Joan Crawford, Norma Shearer, and Rosalind Russell would follow MacDonald's lead in taking a younger mate.*

It was the era when screen celebrities with marriage on the mind flew in secret to a dusty courtroom in Yuma, Arizona, said their "I do's," and then had publicists break the story to the media. Lengthy formal engagements were the height of eccentricity. Nonetheless, on August 21, 1936, Anna MacDonald hosted a tea at the Beverly Wilshire Hotel to announce her daughter's intent to wed Gene Raymond. Among the guests were the Harold Lloyds, the Mervin LeRoys, Fay Wray and her screenwriter husband, John Monk Saunders, Ida Koverman, Nelson Eddy, actress Anita Louise, Laura Van Dyke (the director's mother), and a cockeyed romantic who once hoped he would be the bridegroom at just such an occasion, Ernst Lubitsch.†

Usually MacDonald declined to wear spectacular jewels, because she thought it "inconsiderate to flaunt jewelry in these days" of economic Depression. On this occasion, however, she brandished with pride a platinum-set emerald-cut sapphire solitaire, notable for its nine and a half carats and, in light of the event, its absence of diamonds. Gene had

---

*Gene Raymond was born on August 13, 1908. Although MacDonald claimed only one year's age difference, she was in fact five years older than her fiancé.

†At the party, Fay Wray was visibly pregnant with her first child. As an example of MacDonald's "great sense of fun," Wray recalled for me, in July 1991, that the day after her daughter's birth in September 1936, "every hour a small bouquet from Jeanette arrived until the number equaled Susan's weight, six pounds thirteen ounces."

a flair for jewelry design, and he hired William Ruser of Beverly Hills to construct the engagement ring to his specifications. When the fiancé chirped, "I am the happiest person in the world," Jeanette, beaming, corrected him: "You mean *we* are."

Gene's mother, in a dark cloche and veil, attended the event. Yet with apparent malice aforethought, she arrived too late to hear Anna's little speech voicing affection for Gene. A few days afterward, Mrs. Kipling entrained for New York—but not before mailing letters, sending telegrams, and placing personal calls to Bob Ritchie, Gene's lawyers, and the MGM brass. Her theme never varied: That dissolute older woman is stealing my son and it must be stopped!

Kipling sent a particularly vicious letter to Louella Parsons. For seven years, Lolly had been slinging barbs at MacDonald, mainly because the singer refused to honor her on bended knee. Jeanette's fabulous success was an unwelcome reminder of Parsons's inability to break genuine talent. But even Louella's vindictiveness had limits. She found Mrs. Kipling's letter so revolting that she immediately phoned Helen Ferguson, MacDonald's publicist. "This could really wipe up the ground with Jeanette MacDonald," she told Helen, "but I think it's below the belt." Parsons said she was burning the letter as they spoke.

Ferguson relayed the news. At last, Parsons merited MacDonald's allegiance. Jeanette arranged a lunchtime tête-à-tête at the Vendôme, on Sunset in Hollywood. The women had not met alone since their catfight three years earlier—at the wedding reception for Ginger Rogers and Lew Ayres (now headed for divorce). When MacDonald entered the restaurant, she found Parsons strategically planted on a corner banquette. Sliding into her seat, Jeanette extended her hand and asked matter-of-factly: "When would you like me to go on your radio program?" Louella protested that she did not mean to elicit such a response. Jeanette interrupted: "So far as the hatchet is concerned, it's buried long since. I'll do the show for you not in payment for what you did for me, but because you're a good, decent woman, and I like you very much." For her first Parsons broadcast, MacDonald sang excerpts from *Maytime* with Igor Gorin—gratis.*

---

*Suddenly MacDonald became the apple of Louella's eye. In her column of October 24, 1936, she divulged a few MacDonald scoops with hardly a shadow of the old bitchiness: "Nothing short of screen grand opera is to be the reward of golden-voiced Jeanette MacDonald, who has had the most phenomenal turn in her career since *San Francisco* broke box-office records all over the country. MGM has not only acquired the lovely Massenet opera *Manon,* but the novel *Manon Lescaut* as well. What a thrilling procession of prima donnas Jeanette will follow as Manon—Geraldine Farrar, Melba, and Grace Moore

No one was more disgusted by Mrs. Kipling's shenanigans than Gene. When Jeanette gave him a deluxe edition of *The Rubáiyát of Omar Khayyám,* Kipling, a devout Catholic, construed the gift as further evidence of her future daughter-in-law's sinfulness and "vicious influence." Vehemently anti-Semitic, Mrs. Kipling also insinuated that Jeanette, and even her son, shared her bigotry. Gene felt powerless to combat his mother with moral arguments. Instead, he targeted her pocketbook:

October 18, 1936

I am engaged to marry, and I am going to marry, the girl of my choice, Jeanette MacDonald. Because you do not approve of this fact, you persistently and constantly malign, slander, and libel both my fiancée and myself. . . . I ask the privilege that life gives every man; the right to live my own life, make my own decisions, marry according to my own choice, in accordance with my highest sense of right, honor, and self-respect. In pursuing this inalienable right, I am forced to abandon my hope that you and I will see things in the same light. . . .

Now that your recent correspondence to me has forced me to the reluctant conclusion that you are just staying in New York for the purpose of maligning my fiancée and me "to teach me a lesson" and to "ruin my career if necessary," I am discontinuing the generous allowance I made when you left California. I am moving out of your house [919 Benedict Canyon Drive] on November 1. I will await your occupancy—or you can rent it for a very substantial sum. That, of course, is for you to decide. You have the house, the $30,000 in cash, and the check I gave you to buy a new car. I cannot continue what amounts to the financing of a campaign designed to wreck my happiness. If your good judgment persuades you to abandon your activities against me and Jeanette and you return to your home, I shall, of course, provide for your comfort as I always have.

Mary Kipling did not return to California at this time. Instead, she wrote more poison-pen letters. Even after Jeanette and Gene married, she refused to acknowledge MacDonald as her daughter-in-law and referred to her always as "that woman." In rare direct correspondence, she addressed her as "Miss Jeanette MacDonald," never "Mrs. Gene Raymond." When she was not bombarding Gene with pleas to escape

---

among the most famed. *Manon* is scheduled to follow *The Firefly,* and that comes immediately after *Maytime.* With all these pictures piling up I pity Jeanette's chances for trousseau shopping for that three-month's honeymoon starting June 17. Both Gene Raymond and Jeanette have permission from their respective studios to leave immediately after their wedding for the Orient and then on to Europe." The *Manon* project never materialized.

from "that woman's" supposed claws, she planted rumors of their imminent divorce with Winchell, Hedda Hopper, and Jimmie Fidler.

Early on, Anna MacDonald encouraged Gene to call her "Mother."
But Gene preferred "Maw," a term that did not evoke the rage he felt
each time he thought of Mrs. Kipling.

Irving Thalberg's death from pneumonia on September 14, 1936, put
Maytime, MacDonald's new picture-in-progress, on indefinite hold.
Two weeks after the tragedy, Jeanette announced her plans for a June
wedding and then traveled east for a ten-day vacation. To minimize
publicity, she registered at New York's Hotel Ambassador under the
name of Helen Ferguson. In the course of this vacation, she went to see
Helen Hayes emote in *Victoria Regina* and Ray Bolger prance in
Rodgers and Hart's *On Your Toes.* She made a brief trip to Philadelphia to visit her sister Elsie, whose rented house Jeanette had purchased
for $11,000 a few months earlier. Elsie had recently decided to capital-
ize on her sister's fame by establishing the Elsie MacDonald School of
Dance in Upper Darby, Pennsylvania, which already had two hundred
students. MacDonald also stopped off in Newark to chat with Bob
Ritchie's mother, whose affection was as abiding as was Mrs. Kipling's
contempt. One evening Steve Kroeger, Ritchie's best friend, pleaded
with Jeanette to reconsider her break from Bob. Kroeger made the
bride-to-be cry, but he could not make her change her mind. MacDonald also renewed her friendship with the contralto Emily Wentz, an old
buddy from her Broadway years who had sung at the Roxy Theater
and, more recently, at Radio City Music Hall. Emily helped organize a
"bachelorette" party for Jeanette at the Colony and promised to journey to the West Coast for the wedding.

When MacDonald returned to Los Angeles, Phi Beta, the women's
national music and drama sorority, awarded her an honorary membership for embodying "the true artistic standard in motion pictures." The
lesser-known musical talents of Gene Raymond, then at work on the
score and libretto of a full-scale operetta, gained public attention with
the release in November of RKO's *The Smartest Girl in Town,* which
featured Gene singing his own composition, "Will You," to Ann Sothern. In early December, Jeanette and Gene found themselves in amateur
competition. The occasion was the annual Los Angeles Dog Show, one
of southern California's grander social events. Gene's Irish setter, Tray,
the gift from Jeanette, won two ribbons. Jeanette's Bedlington terrier,
Sunny Days, the gift from Bob Ritchie, did better, winning three rib-

bons and a gold cup. The outcome could have been a measure of the two's box-office power. Unperturbed, Gene gave Jeanette a Newfoundland pup for Christmas. They named it St. Nick.

Gene's break from his mother made him more relaxed. He decided to launch the 1936 holiday season with a dinner-and-dance soiree for two hundred in the new English-style house he and his brother were now occupying in Bel-Air. Amid heaps of poinsettias and Yuletide greenery, Gene, assisted by Helen Ferguson and Mrs. Johnny Mack Brown, greeted Irene Dunne, Randolph Scott, Mary Pickford, Fredric March, Cary Grant, Jimmy Stewart, Joan Bennett, Jack Oakie, Anita Loos, Max Steiner, Nacio Herb Brown, the Jack Warners, the Darryl Zanucks, the William Goetzes, the Ernst Lubitsches, the David Selznicks, and scores more of Hollywood's crème de la crème. Jeanette was Gene's most special guest, and, as befits a queen, she arrived very late.

On New Year's Eve, Jeanette and Gene joined a small group of celebrity friends in a "progressive dinner," a ritual that involved traveling course by course from one person's home to another. The evening began with fruit cup and soup on the just-laid floor of Ginger Rogers's new house, still under construction in Beverly Hills. It ended at three in the morning with coffee and dessert at Doris and Mervin LeRoy's.

New Year's Day 1937 was spent at the races, and Jeanette did exceptionally well with her two-dollar bets. It was a winning start to what would turn out to be the most eventful year in the Iron Butterfly's life.

CHAPTER ELEVEN

Hollywood Diva

[Jeanette MacDonald] has done more, perhaps, than any one
individual to develop an appreciation of good music
throughout the land, having brought light and grand opera
into the lives of millions.

LILY MAY CALDWELL, music critic,
Birmingham News, 1940

Art is simply fine in Hollywood—if it pays dividends.

LOUELLA PARSONS, 1935

MACDONALD'S VOCAL SUCCESSES in *Rose Marie* and *San Francisco* magnified her desire to sing at the Metropolitan Opera. By 1937, the Met's general manager, Edward Johnson, as well as his hard-pressed financial angels, had good reason to eye Hollywood and its star soprano with interest. Vexed by fiscal crises and the legitimate fear that he would soon lose many of his singers to war in Europe, Johnson proposed a radical hiring plan. Its aim was to cast homegrown, physically attractive young artists who, as Johnson put it, could "look and act their parts, as well as sing."

While MacDonald was filming *Maytime,* a picture that had more operatic music than any Hollywood movie before it, rumor spread that Johnson was considering a contract for her. The talk, however, was premature. Two decades after Rosa Ponselle's debut, no other American soprano had successfully exorcised the Metropolitan's bias against singers who had not trained abroad. MacDonald's movie-star status was also a stumbling block, since the Met's board of directors had little wish to compromise their institution's elitism through association with an icon of mass culture.

Still, in her impact on the popular consciousness, MacDonald was increasingly perceived as a bona fide successor to the legendary European divas who had taken America by storm in the nineteenth century. A cousin of Adelina Patti paid tribute to MacDonald by presenting her with the great singer's snuffbox. When the contralto Ernestine Schumann-Heink died in 1936, one of her sons sent MacDonald, "in deepest admiration for your glorious voice," the rosary his mother had clasped in her hand before every performance. The Metropolitan's two biggest box-office draws of this period, the Wagnerians Kirsten Flagstad and Lauritz Melchior, were unabashed MacDonald fans. Flagstad, shortly before making *The Big Broadcast of 1938* for Paramount, requested and received an audience with Jeanette, and the sopranos were soon observed "chatter[ing] like schoolgirls together." Melchior, who would bring cultural cachet to MGM's second-string musicals following World War II, became a lifelong friend.

Along with the standard requests for autographed photos, Hollywood's diva was inundated with questions from ambitious young singers about how to nurture a voice. For these devotees, in 1937 she wrote a four-page brochure entitled "No Royal Road to Song." Within three years, MGM's publicity offices had fifty thousand copies in circulation. On top of the study of vocal technique and music history, MacDonald prescribed "breadth of human understanding," "definite feeling for the dramatic," and facility in "several languages." The pamphlet's cautionary tone echoed MacDonald's own history: "The idea that song is a heaven-sent gift, and somehow automatically furnishes its own knowledge and training, has done more to injure aspiring singers than anything else. . . . Given a voice, the girl who wants to become a singer must . . . be possessed of a determination to succeed that consumes her every other thought."

At the beginning of *Maytime,* a hopeful young singer, not unlike the girls writing to MacDonald, implores the elderly Miss Morrison for advice on whether she should place her career ahead of romance: "I just want the chance to become a famous singer like Tetrazzini or Jenny Lind—or *Marcia Mornay.*" To the lovesick adolescent's shock, frail Miss Morrison—played faultlessly by MacDonald in pearl gray wig, rubber facial overlays, and lead-filled heels—reveals that *she* was the great Marcia Mornay. Marcia's flashback account of how devotion to art deprived her of personal happiness becomes the film's narrative frame, a story as grandiose and poignant as any in opera.

The Metropolitan Opera may not have been ready for Jeanette MacDonald in 1937. But with *Maytime,* the year's highest-grossing movie worldwide, MacDonald immortalized herself as the silver screen's *prima donna assoluta.*

When *Maytime* went into production during the summer of 1936, it was going to be MGM's first three-color Technicolor movie. Moss Hart had adapted the bittersweet plot of Sigmund Romberg's 1917 American-set operetta, a story of two star-crossed lovers who cannot marry but whose grandchildren do. Romberg himself was brought to Culver City to compose four additional songs for the picture. Direction went to Edmund Goulding, an Englishman who could be as moody as he was talented. Goulding quickly took advantage of producer Irving Thalberg's deteriorating health and broke with house protocol, tinkering with the screenplay as he shot.

Assistant director Joseph Newman had the chore of racing each morning to Santa Monica to get Thalberg's verdict on the previous day's rushes. Newman recalled: "Thalberg envisioned a romantic comedy with music such as had never been done before. Goulding was aiming for a British music-hall style of movie. It was a terrible mess." Nearly half of the picture was shot by the time Thalberg died, at age thirty-seven in mid-September. A few days later, Mayer appointed Hunt Stromberg to take over the production. As Stromberg pored over the footage, his stomach turned. "The scenes themselves and the characters within them," he noted in a memo, "are so dreadfully unreasonable as to nullify any chance for sentiment, tenderness, or any of the fine emotions that should belong to a beautiful love story." Stromberg decided to scrap all of Goulding's work. It was a gutsy move that cost the studio an estimated $800,000.

During the shoot of this aborted *Maytime,* MacDonald's health went haywire. In early August, an intestinal virus forced her to delay by two days the recording of her romantic duet with Nelson Eddy, "Will You Remember?" ("Sweetheart, sweetheart, sweetheart, / Will you love me ever?"). A few weeks later, MacDonald lost her usual tolerance for sunlight and wound up with a swollen face, burned eyelids, and an infected lower lip following a weekend boating excursion with Gene. In agony, she showed up at the studio on Monday to rehearse the dance routine for the minstrel-like "Jump Jim Crow." But Jeanette's condition ruled out work in front of the camera, and she threw the company's schedule off.

Of the music MacDonald recorded for the Thalberg *Maytime,* only "Will You Remember?" survived into the Stromberg version. Three numbers were dropped: the act 2 murder scene from Puccini's *Tosca,* which included MacDonald's rendition of the aria "Vissi d'arte"; a soprano-baritone duet from act 4 of Verdi's *Il trovatore;* and "Farewell to Dreams," a Romberg waltz specially composed for the film's stars.

MacDonald and Eddy recorded "Farewell to Dreams" for RCA during a weeklong studio session that began on the afternoon of September 17. The day before, Jeanette had attended Thalberg's funeral at B'nai B'rith Temple, where Grace Moore, not MacDonald, was asked to sing. The Thalberg tragedy thrust MGM out of gear, and for several days Mayer maneuvered to consolidate his power base. But it was business as usual at Hollywood Recording Studios on Sycamore Avenue. To the accompaniment of Nathaniel Shilkret's twenty-two-piece orchestra, MacDonald and Eddy also put to disc that week "Will You Remember?," "Song of Love," "Ah! Sweet Mystery of Life," and "Indian Love Call." The last two, issued back-to-back, eventually won a gold record for sales of over a million copies and was RCA Victor's earliest Red Seal label offering to attain this vaunted status. These were the only commercial releases featuring MacDonald and Eddy together in their prime.* Eddy would soon sign an exclusive contract with Columbia Records, where he sang duets with Risë Stevens, Dorothy Kirsten, and Eleanor Steber—singers who came to personify Edward Johnson's America First policy in the 1940s.

Anxiety was intense when principal photography for the "second" *Maytime* began in late October. Hunt Stromberg, impatient to prove himself worthy as Thalberg's successor, supervised the writing of an entire new screenplay and music score in under six weeks. Legend has it that twenty-four-year-old Noel Langley, recently arrived at Metro, wrote the new scenario in just three and a half days, thereby incurring the jealousy of the entire story department. In fact, Langley did not start from scratch but built upon detailed directives from Stromberg and prior drafts by veteran MGM writers Alice Duer Miller, Claudine

*"Song of Love," from Romberg's *Blossom Time,* would not be issued until 1965, on the RCA album *Jeanette MacDonald and Nelson Eddy.*

West, and Jane Murfin. After submitting a full draft the last week of
October, Langley was then required to do substantial rewrites for the
next month and a half.

Stromberg wanted this new *Maytime,* now set in a black-and-
white Paris, to be a "drama of idealism" that would capitalize on the
MacDonald-Eddy screen chemistry. The challenge, he wrote, was to
give moviegoers "undisputed evidence" of "a love great enough to endure through eternity" while keeping the story free of "sexual consummation or remembrance of ecstasy." One of *Maytime*'s central
episodes takes place at a May Day festival in the rustic Paris suburb of
Saint-Cloud. Its lavish images include MacDonald in a vine-covered
swing being pushed by Eddy to intoxicating heights; moments later,
the two of them dance gaily in a leafy pavilion as flower petals spill
fabulously through the air. In notes on this exhilarating sequence,
Stromberg specified: "Both MacDonald and I thoroughly understand
the *romance* and *soul* that has been awakened [in her] by this first and
only contact with vital youth and all the excitement it implies."

With production costs for the two *Maytime*s now predicted at over
$2 million, Stromberg fired Goulding and replaced him with Robert Z.
Leonard. "Pop" Leonard was a Falstaffian figure whose warm, booming voice betrayed his early experience as an operetta baritone.
Leonard, who was as methodical as Van Dyke was nonchalant, had a
solid track record with big-budget MGM musicals. Among his credits
were *Dancing Lady* and *The Great Ziegfeld,* the extravaganza that
beat *San Francisco* in the race for Best Picture Oscar of 1936. While always deferring to Hunt Stromberg's guiding artistic hand, Leonard ran
the *Maytime* company with amiable efficiency. MacDonald considered
him "one of the most loveable men I've ever had the joy to work with."

Pop was adept at handling Jeanette's temper, and he jokingly baptized her "The Red Volcano." One scene in *Maytime* called for her to
make an especially grand entrance, and Pop instructed, in a very emphatic tone, that she was to "come *sweeping* into the room." On the
first take, Jeanette entered on cue—dutifully wielding a janitor's
broom.

Stromberg had agreed to produce *Maytime* on the condition that the
bulk of the existing score be discarded. He loathed Romberg's music
and found "Jump Jim Crow" offensive. Romberg's contract, however,
stipulated that no other living composer could be credited in an MGM
film entitled *Maytime.* Herbert Stothart found a clever way out of this
predicament by filling the movie with a profusion of music by dead

musicians. Aside from Romberg's "Will You Remember?," which would become one of their signature melodies, MacDonald and Eddy's only complete duet was "Carry Me Back to Old Virginny," by the African-American songwriter James A. Bland. In addition to the Page's scene from Meyerbeer's rarely performed *Les Huguenots* and a swift montage of excerpts from Donizetti, Verdi, Gounod, and Wagner, Mac-Donald got to sing her favorite chanson, the flirtatious "Les Filles de Cadiz" by Léo Delibes—a number she probably sang better than anyone else—and Robert Planquette's rousingly patriotic "Le Régiment de Sambre et Meuse." These were showy pieces for which she was exquisitely suited, by both voice and temperament.

For MacDonald and Eddy's fervent on-stage reunion in New York seven years after their May Day rendezvous, Stothart composed a twelve-minute operatic pastiche called *Czaritza,* based on themes from Tchaikovsky's Fifth Symphony. It's a telling sign of MGM's estimate of the general public that this imaginary Russian opera was sung in Russian and French, without titles.* Clearly, *Czaritza* was ersatz opera. But it disarmed the critics and enthralled the Singing Sweethearts' legions of fans. MacDonald and Eddy's twelve-second kiss at its emotional climax—the most passionate in their eight films together—also disarmed the Production Code Administration, which pleaded with Mayer "to cut to the minimum all physical contact." This was the only time MacDonald and Eddy would play at singing opera together on-screen.

An amazingly glib and talented duo crafted *Czaritza*'s libretto, as well as the droll lyrics for *Maytime*'s reworked operatic material—which included a rhapsody on ham and eggs to a takeoff on "Caro Nome" from *Rigoletto*. Bob Wright and Chet Forrest had come to Hollywood after performing underage in cheesy Miami cabarets. Barely twenty years old and nicknamed "the Boys" for life, they were assigned to be Stothart's factotums, helping with words and music for whatever special material *Maytime* required. A day after they landed the job, MacDonald summoned the Boys to her dressing suite. They trembled as the star declared: "You may as well know a very important fact. I sing only *open.* Do you know what that means?" Chet took a stab: "You mean you only sing on the open or pure vowels—*ahh, ohh*, and such?" "Exactly," Jeanette replied, "and it's essential that most of your

---

*It helped that *Czaritza*'s plot mirrors the lovers' offstage plight and could thus be easily grasped by viewers.

lyrics be open for me." The Boys told her not to worry and left. Minutes later, Nelson Eddy ordered the youngsters to his suite. "What did Miss MacDonald tell you?," he inquired suspiciously. "She said she sings only open," answered Bob. "Good," shot back Nelson, "because I sing only *closed.*"

For the next six years, the Boys concocted countless *ah*'s for Jeanette and a multitude of *ee*'s for Nelson. MacDonald's emphasis on open sounds reflected her training in the Torriani method. But Wright later noted that "by sticking to open vowels Jeanette knew she would look more gorgeous in close-up, displaying her beautiful teeth and smile." MacDonald's physical allure was also, according to Wright and Forrest, at the root of a major musical decision concerning *Maytime:* "Hours after Stothart asked us to come up with an idea for the interpolated opera, he telephoned and said, 'I've just been talking to Cedric Gibbons about the kind of opera we should write. Gibbons says the one thing we've never seen Jeanette wear is one of those inverted heart-shaped Russian headdresses, which he thinks would be lovely for her face.'" The Boys relished the concept. They convinced Stothart that a Russian setting cried out for Tchaikovsky and that "the most passionate and irresistible Tchaikovsky would be the Fifth Symphony."

Little did the Boys know that *Czaritza* would set the pattern for their own adaptations of late romantic composers for Broadway over the decades: *Song of Norway,* from music by Edvard Grieg, *Kismet,* from Alexander Borodin, and *Anya* from Sergei Rachmaninoff. In the 1990s, Wright and Forrest were still going strong, contributing music to Tommy Tune's *Grand Hotel.*

Slavko Vorkapich was the Yugoslav master of montage who conceived the kaleidoscopic opera scenes that chronicle Marcia Mornay's rise to international fame. Vorkapich always worked with his own crew. But on the day he set up a shot from an angle MacDonald thought too low, she raised a howl and demanded that her pet cinematographer, Oliver Marsh, be rushed in to oversee Vorkapich. At issue was the MacDonald chin line. When shot from below, it could appear heavy and jutting. MGM's lighting wizards had long determined that positioning the key light very low and shooting from slightly above made MacDonald more photogenic, widening the bottom half of her face and enlarging her eyes. Marsh, who lit her films from *San Francisco* onward, also succeeded in bringing out a creamy, almost liquid glow in MacDonald's skin with strategically placed bulbs filtered through silk. Jeanette preferred this richly glamorous look to the crisper, more metallic sheen William Daniels had given her in *Naughty Marietta* and *Rose Marie*. As with Wright and Forrest's lyrics, MacDonald did not hold back from venting her opinions on technical matters when the real issue was controlling her screen and sound image.*

John Barrymore, however, was beyond Jeanette's control. With spine-chilling credibility, the Great Profile played Nicolai Nazaroff, Marcia's insanely jealous manager and husband. When Stromberg assigned him to the picture, Barrymore, a chronic alcoholic, gave assurances he was on the wagon. One day Joseph Newman caught a whiff of his breath and asked, "John, you're not drinking now, are you?" "I'm *not* drinking," the fifty-four-year-old actor snarled; "I just have a few bottles of beer, but I don't drink any *alcohol*." MacDonald dreaded the stink when she had to submit to his impassioned kiss. "It's been a nightmare," she confided hours later to Ritchie. "Barrymore got so plastered today we had to quit early as he was in no condition to work. It's disgusting."

In their first scene together, MacDonald and Barrymore had to exit from a carriage and walk up a grand stairway to be presented at the court of Louis Napoléon, with Barrymore all the while instructing his protégée in proper etiquette. "Unfortunately," MacDonald reminisced, "Barrymore couldn't remember his lines. I'm afraid he was at the stage where his somewhat misspent life was catching up with him, and he blamed his failing memory on everything and everybody." Pop Leonard was more patient than Van Dyke would ever have been, and he arranged to have the actor's lines written on off-screen blackboards along the staircase. Still, the self-destructing actor raised hell. "You stupid S.O.B.'s are trying to make me nervous," he'd shout at the prop men holding the boards. "It was an exhausting day for us all," MacDonald recalled, "up and down, up and down that long stairway, and me toting my fifty-pound hoop skirt." The next day, when she and Leonard saw the rushes, they were stunned. "It's the darnedest thing," Pop whispered to Jeanette. "That fool's performance comes over as though he had the most perfect poise and assurance!"

Barrymore had little fondness for MacDonald, especially when she

---

*Jack Dawn, head of the studio's makeup department, created a plaster mask of MacDonald in order to experiment on how best to make her look like an octogenarian in the film's early and closing sequences. William Tuttle, Dawn's longtime associate and eventual successor, told me in August 1990 that he still uses that mask to instruct his makeup students at UCLA, "because of its classic proportions." The year *Maytime* was released, Cecil Beaton remarked that MacDonald had "the eyes of a puma and the flat ram-like profile essential to film photography" (*Sir Cecil Beaton's Scrapbook*, p. 51).

sang. One story had it that he barged onto the May Day set and urinated against a cardboard tree while she and Eddy were duetting "Will You Remember?" Another tale reported him spitting venom at MacDonald after discovering on his marriage night that twenty-year-old Elaine Barrie, the fourth Mrs. John Barrymore, brought to her lovemaking a "skill and enthusiasm" that bespoke far more experience than he imagined she had. When the chafed groom appeared on the *Maytime* set the next morning, he supposedly growled to his leading lady: "If you wave that loathsome chiffon rag you call a kerchief once more while I'm speaking, I shall ram it down your gurgling throat."*

Still, MacDonald's charms did not leave Barrymore unstirred. During the court banquet scene, Jeanette had to remove her wide skirt and hoops in order to sit comfortably at the long dining table. As the cameras rolled, Barrymore's hands, she later divulged, were "busy roaming" under the table and atop her navy-colored trousers.

When *Maytime* hit the movie houses in March 1937, it outdid even *San Francisco* in setting records. The picture gave Manhattan's Capitol Theater a prosperous Holy Week for the first time in nearly a decade. When a New York clergyman cited *Maytime* in his sermon as "a good and powerful influence for marriage," his words were picked up by the wire services and printed in newspapers nationwide. Within days, countless pairs of impressionable young sweethearts exited movie theaters and rushed to exchange wedding vows, cheerily ignoring the fact that Marcia Mornay's unwise marriage leads to abject emptiness and murder. Throughout the spring, "Will You Remember?" vied with Hoagy Carmichael's "Little Old Lady" and Gershwin's "They Can't Take That Away from Me" for top place in the sheet-music market. Beauty salons pitched Gabrieleen Glo-Tone as the permanent wave to duplicate MacDonald's *Maytime* hairstyles. In department stores, Max Factor illustrated makeup talks with stills of Jeanette as the diva Mornay. School principals promoted May Queen contests among fledgling sopranos.

Reviewers were unanimous in praising *Maytime* as a milestone in the fusion of opera, song, and cinema. All agreed that MacDonald had once again surpassed herself in both singing and dramatics. "It is a

---

*A Freudian could have a field day with the form, content, and displacement of Barrymore's rage. However, there's a problem with this anecdote, repeated by virtually all of Barrymore's biographers over the past quarter century: MacDonald and Barrymore never had a scene together in which she holds or wears anything resembling a kerchief.

temptation to hail a new Jeanette MacDonald, for this is unquestionably her greatest performance," trumpeted the *Hollywood Reporter.* "She does a job of acting that a Bernhardt or Duse wouldn't refuse to applaud," crowed Louella Parsons, adding that "*Maytime,* I would say, entitles her to Academy award attention." Some, however, were begrudging in their appraisal of MacDonald's vocal repertoire, which, as one critic put it, "comes just a little this side of being too good for popular consumption." A few took direct aim at her voice, claiming that the "miracle" of MacDonald's pure soprano was the work of "bright young men at the sound controls."

Highbrows continued to raise eyebrows. *The American Singer,* the first major book on opera to devote a chapter to the movies, deigned to mention MacDonald only as a "film actress," not a "soprano." Other pundits decried her alleged tampering with the classics, resulting, they claimed, in an upsetting "hodgepodge of arias." Among those embarrassed by the forcefulness of her delivery, adjectives like "syrupy" and "overdrawn" cropped up for the first time.

To be sure, not everyone in 1937 was willing to buy into the fantasy of MacDonald and Eddy eternally postponing physical love only to be united as singing ghosts in a blossom-drenched afterlife. "A pain in the neck to those that only got as far as the fourth grade!" was how one theater owner described customer response in Westby, Wisconsin. "Too much Italian [*sic*] opera!" complained another in Cogswell, North Dakota.

Nevertheless, *Maytime* was generally judged to be the most polished of the early MacDonald-Eddy films. Its enormous popularity—plus an Oscar nomination for Best Musical Scoring—convinced MacDonald and her MGM colleagues that she and her pictures were elevating the taste of mass audiences. Visually resplendent, musically sumptuous, and emotionally stirring, *Maytime* marked the zenith of the operetta genre in American movies.

Maytime brought MacDonald a Screen Actors Guild award. For the rest of her life, she cited it as her favorite film. Shortly before her death, she reflected: "More than a part, [Marcia Mornay] represented my justification in striving to be a dramatic actress." Although *Maytime* gave Nelson Eddy the best movie notices of his career, the baritone harbored no special love for it. When Eddy switched on the TV and by accident saw himself in *Maytime* years later, his attention mainly fell on his costume, which he dismissed as "one of those silly suits with frills at the cuffs": "My reaction was simple and direct. I whistled and said, 'Get him! Ain't he pretty?' "

By the time of her wedding, MacDonald had become an industry within the Industry. Epic productions like *Maytime* and the forthcoming *The Firefly* made her directly responsible for the employment of more writers, sound engineers, musicians, singers, dressmakers, wig designers, carpenters, cameramen, electricians, and extras than almost any other star on the MGM lot. Simultaneous with her film commitments came radio broadcasts, recordings, public appearances, singing lessons, and daily physical workouts. In the midst of this frenzy, MacDonald found time not simply to get married but to take the leading role in planning Hollywood's biggest wedding of the decade.

With the same meticulousness Thalberg and Stromberg lavished on her musicals, Jeanette organized the details of her nuptials, even to the point of dividing the 915 celebrity invitees into two categories: the chosen 10 percent, powerful or dear enough to merit front pews, and the rest.

The invitation read:

> Mrs. Daniel MacDonald
> requests the honour of your presence
> at the marriage of her daughter
> Jeanette
> to
> Mr. Gene Raymond
> on Wednesday, the sixteenth of June
> at nine o'clock in the evening
> Wilshire Methodist Episcopal Church
> Los Angeles, California

MacDonald had wanted to hold the ceremony on June 17, the second anniversary of her first big date with Gene. But the Wilshire Methodist Episcopal Church, just blocks away from her and her mother's current home at 401 North June Street, was only available on the preceding day. This picturesque church, which boasts neo-Romanesque arches and an imposing tower modeled after the Moorish La Giralda in Seville, had coincidental tie-in value for *The Firefly*, MacDonald's picture-in-progress, set in Spain. It was not by chance that the

MGM publicist assigned to the wedding was John Woolfenden, son-in-law of the church's minister, Dr. Willsie Martin.

Ever since carnival antics marred the gargantuan wedding of silent stars Vilma Banky and Rod La Rocque in 1927, Hollywood marriages had tended to be small and private. MacDonald, however, refused to let a legacy of mayhem crush her desire for a large church affair. She found a sympathetic ally in Dr. Martin, who since 1919 had been urging movie stars to see themselves as public servants above reproach. Martin wanted the MacDonald-Raymond nuptials to show the world that movie idols did not lack the "human ideals" held to by everyday Americans. Jeanette would later point to her wedding as "the most sacred event of my life." Still, the media seized on it as "Hollywood's most colossal social event in history."

In an article carried by the Hearst newspapers, Robert Z. Leonard had recently cited Jeanette MacDonald and Nelson Eddy as the "Princess and Prince Charming" of modern times. For fans unwilling to set aside fable from reality, MacDonald's marital plans were an act of betrayal. How could Jeanette have been so heartless, they grumbled, as to abandon Nelson for Gene? Eddy, who received an avalanche of sympathy notes, tried to straighten the record: "From the beginning, at the studio, we have been as close as—well, as close as the covers of a song. Outside the studio, it so happens that we haven't seen much of each other."

When Jeanette asked Nelson to sing at the ceremony, he replied tongue in cheek:

Hotel Statler Detroit

Apr. 15

Dear Jeanette,

Sure I'll sing at the wedding. Kindly select numbers from the following:

    1. Ciribiribin [Grace Moore's number]
    2. One Night of Love [ditto]
    3. In the Still of the Night [Nelson's number]
    4. Vive l'opéra! [ditto]
    5. All I Do is Dream of You [Gene Raymond's theme song]

Love,
Nelson

As the date drew near, Isabel Eddy joined the mothers of Joan Crawford, Jack Oakie, Ginger Rogers, Darryl Zanuck, and Anita Louise in giving Jeanette a linen wedding shower hosted by Helen Ferguson's mother, Emelie. Harold Lloyd threw a stag party for Gene. Asked if he was going to be loaned out for another picture soon, the groom, who had just finished RKO's *The Life of the Party,* quipped "Yes, on June 16, I'm being loaned out to Jeanette MacDonald!" Gene and Jeanette wowed 250 guests at Basil and Ouida Rathbone's costume ball when they marched into the Restaurant Victor Hugo dressed as Romeo and Juliet. (Gene's formfitting tunic was made to order, while thrifty Jeanette borrowed and altered Norma Shearer's screen outfit.) At MGM, *The Firefly*'s cast and crew halted work to present the couple with a silver flower basket and a silk-bound book containing all their names. When the film wrapped, there was yet another party at which MacDonald gave an off-the-cuff rendition of "Carry Me Back to Old Virginny." "It was the most moving, beautiful singing we ever heard her do," said Chet Forrest. "There were no cameras, no machines, no acoustical flaps. It was just Jeanette and a piano, and it was perfect. We all cried."

Nine days before the wedding, Hollywood broke into tears over the grim news that Jean Harlow, only twenty-six, had died of uremic poisoning. MacDonald and Harlow had formed a special bond. After Marie Dressler had passed away in 1934, Jean Harlow inherited the older actress's MGM dressing suite, adjacent to Jeanette's. For the next three years, the painfully shy platinum Venus from Kansas City took the flaming redhead from West Philadelphia as a confidante.

Harlow had started in feature pictures as an extra in MacDonald's *The Love Parade,* and she was now sick to death of playing dumb comic broads. Her hotly reported affairs and three disastrous marriages—the most notorious being the brief one to MGM producer Paul Bern that ended in his suicide—left her desperate for affection. By 1935, Harlow developed what MacDonald tactfully described as "a kind of crush" on her. Although the official love of Harlow's final years was William Powell, the actress was reluctant to marry him. She told the press in 1936: "I am much more matured [*sic*] in thought and experience than I was a few years ago. . . . I can't convince myself that this is the time for me to consider giving up my work, my career." Anita Loos may have been closer to the truth when she said of Harlow: "She was rather like a boy. . . . She had this tremendous effect on men, but I've noticed that most of the girls of that type are inclined to be completely sexless, and that she was."

For MacDonald, Harlow was basically "a young, naive, nice girl, who was being exploited by the studio." For Harlow, however, MacDonald was the very model of the emotional stability she desired for herself. Jeanette recounted the turning point in their relationship: "I invited her to a cocktail party and apparently she had a great admiration for me, which was very flattering, but in front of everybody she rushed up to me and kissed my hand. I nearly died, because, you know, that's an awfully embarrassing thing. I'm sure it wasn't thought out. It was not an act, not put on." Suddenly MacDonald realized she was being seduced into playing Lady to Jean Harlow's Tramp: "I represented so much that was so different from what she represented." MacDonald discussed *l'affaire* Harlow on only one occasion, in 1959: "It was just an impulse, a sweet young impulse." This terse observation suggests that Jeanette had learned to deflect Harlow with far more skill and tenderness than she exhibited with Ernst Lubitsch back in 1930.

MacDonald reluctantly consented when Jean Bello, Harlow's mother, asked her to sing at the funeral. It was a mistake. As Jeanette sang Rudolf Friml's "Indian Love Call," the peculiar choice of Mrs. Bello, she broke down weeping. MacDonald was rescued—for once in real life—by the stalwart Nelson Eddy, who helped her complete the song. In a moment worthy of medieval allegory, Romantic Yearning bade farewell to Sensual Abandon.

For all her grief, MacDonald was not going to allow Harlow's death to upset her marriage plans. To avoid public attention, she and Gene made a late-night visit to the home of Rosamond Rice, chief clerk of the Los Angeles County Marriage License Bureau. Nonetheless, a couple of reporters caught them in the act and spilled the nocturnal goings-on in next morning's papers. Like MacDonald's birth certificate, her marriage license application has inexplicably vanished.

Bob Ritchie, who still assisted Jeanette with tax-free foreign investments, was a gallant loser. Two days before the wedding, Jeanette wrote to him at London's Savoy Hotel:

Dear Bub,

Your letter came as a pleasant surprise as I was beginning to think I was off your list and you were not going to write. . . . It made me very happy and yet a little sad, for I believe whole-heartedly that you meant everything you wrote and it was sweet.

I have had fears and qualms, but lately none at all. And as the date approaches I feel more relaxed and certain I am not making a mistake. I am going to try and make this go as I have always with everything else. Wish me luck as you have in everything else!

I wish you a great deal of happiness and success and feel that at last you are well on the way to achieving something really splendid—Heaven knows you do deserve it.

This is Good-bye. But with it goes much love and all the fine thoughts any girl could have for a fine fellow. Let's always think of each other kindly.

Ever,

Jen

P.S. Mother sends her love.

The day before the big event, Gene and Jeanette exchanged personal wedding gifts. On a little card accompanying the diamond cufflinks she gave Gene, Jeanette wrote:

My dearest one—

With this gift goes my devotion, my love, and my complete faith in you—

I hope I will make you happy. Anyhow—you won't hate me for trying will you?

The wedding was Hollywood's answer to the civil marriage, thirteen days earlier, of the former king of England and Mrs. Wallis Warfield Simpson. It also dispelled the pall cast by Jean Harlow's death. Under a perfect full moon, a throng, estimated at fifteen thousand, jammed Wilshire Boulevard. Automobiles choked every adjacent street for blocks. Several women fainted. As each limousine pulled up, surging fans threatened to break through ropes barely held in place by a phalanx of L.A.P.D. officers. The demonstration outdid not only the Banky–La Rocque hullabaloo of a decade earlier but every movie premiere within memory.

Lily Pons, who was invited to sing but had to remain in New York, asked CBS to arrange for her voice to be piped directly into the church, as well as over the airwaves. When MacDonald learned of this plan just hours before the ceremony, her blood boiled. She groused to Dr. Martin: "I don't blame Lily, but I hate the commercial aspect of it, with the sponsors seeing this as a ready-made way to get a fat audience." The minister agreed, and he banned the hookup.

That evening, the Wilshire Methodist Episcopal Church was a luminous arbor of pink Joanna Hill roses. Six candelabra, each bearing seven slender tapers, burned in the chancel. Soaring trellises blanketed with blossoms framed the altar. At every seventh pew on both sides of the center aisle, tall, softly glowing lamps were nested in roses and linked to one another with pink satin ribbons. Basil Rathbone, Harold Lloyd, and Jeanette's leading man in *The Firefly,* Allan Jones, were among the full-dress ushers who led guests to their seats. For years afterward, Jones would be teased for trying to steal the show because his new patent-leather slippers squeaked.

The official reason for delaying the ceremony a full half hour was snarled traffic. The real cause was Gene's mother. The capricious Mrs. Kipling had publicly announced her intention to be present, and Jeanette thought the wedding might bring an end to her senseless animosity. But when Gene sent a car to Kipling's hotel, she had already checked out. As Nelson Eddy intoned "I Love You Truly," the unwilling mother-in-law was en route to San Francisco.

Anna MacDonald, wearing gray lace and white orchids, sat in the front left pew with her daughter Elsie and her sister Sally. Gene and his brother, Bob, who served as best man, appeared from the front right antechamber and joined Dr. Martin at the altar. When the "Wedding March" from *Lohengrin* rang out, all eyes turned to the rear for an Adrian-designed fashion extravaganza. First came the bridal attendants—Fay Wray, Ginger Rogers, Helen Ferguson, and Mrs. John Mack Brown—in pink mousseline coats over Grecian-style pink crepe gowns and little caps edged with pink baby's breath. Next came Jeanette's sister and matron of honor, Blossom Rock, in pale blue mousseline.

Gasps of admiration greeted MacDonald's solo entrance. Here was a storybook princess come to life, but with a contemporary twist. Instead of white, the copper-toned redhead broke with convention and wore flesh-pink organza over matching taffeta. Her princess-line gown, edged with Adrian's signature tucks and loops, had modified leg-of-mutton sleeves and a high-neck collar trimmed with lace and a tiny spray of roses. MacDonald's hands held a single rose and a pink satin prayer book with the initials "G" and "J" embroidered in gold. An eighteen-foot double tulle veil trailed her steps.

As she walked down the aisle, unaccompanied, Jeanette tried to stay oblivious to everything except the radiant groom waiting at the altar. With each step she took, however, one dark thought nagged at her brain: "This taffeta underskirt is making so much *noise!*" MacDonald was later informed that Walter Winchell violated her ban on photographs and had a keyhole camera hidden under his jacket. But to the bride's delight (and the foxy newsmonger's lasting dismay), the candlelit church proved too dim to get usable shots.*

Because Jeanette and Gene both believed that a woman's subjugation to her husband was unacceptable, their single-ring ceremony parted from tradition by omitting the word "obey." Eternally binding romance, however, was a notion that appealed to them greatly, and a day earlier Jeanette had vowed to Gene in private that she would never remove her platinum wedding band—which, unknown to everyone in the church, had the groom's secret love message engraved inside.† The brief service culminated with Dr. Martin's benediction and a medium-long kiss by the principals. Before the final prayer, Nelson Eddy sang the hymn "O Perfect Love."

As the newlyweds sprinted up the aisle to strains of Mendelssohn's "Wedding March," cynics were already predicting the marriage would not survive six months. One catty gossip wondered in print whether the new marrieds would "wait up all night for the morning newspaper reviews." Other journalists took jabs at the ceremony's "super-musical comedy" trappings and estimated the event's cost at $25,000. For months afterward, MacDonald had to defend what she called "really a simple wedding" and a price tag she put at "less than $5,000." "I simply cannot imagine," she told *Life,* "how anyone *could* spend $25,000 on a wedding without thoughtless extravagance, and I cannot abide such extravagance—I am, you must remember, a MacDonald!"

For the thousands of well-wishers outside the church and the tens of millions who followed the event on radio and in the papers, expense was beside the point. Jeanette MacDonald and Gene Raymond were playing out an idyllic love story that resonated with the aspirations of everyday Americans, and *that* was what mattered to the vast public. As Louella Parsons exulted the next morning: "This is no usual Holly-

---

*Seated in the middle and rear of the church were, among others, Fred Astaire, Ralph Bellamy, Mary Boland, George Cukor, Sam Goldwyn, Howard Hawks, Al Jolson, Gus Kahn, Carl Laemmle, Jr., Rouben Mamoulian, Fredric March, Dick Powell, Eleanor Powell, Sigmund Romberg, Victor Schertzinger, David Selznick, Barbara Stanwyck, Max Steiner, George Stevens, Jimmy Stewart, Gloria Swanson, Robert Taylor, Spencer Tracy, Sophie Tucker, Walter Wanger, Loretta Young, and Vincent Youmans. In front pews reserved for close friends, amicable rivals, and industry heavyweights sat Pandro Berman, Marion Davies, Janet Gaynor, Will Hays, William Randolph Hearst, Anita Loos, Jesse Lasky, Mervyn LeRoy, Ernst Lubitsch, Louis B. Mayer, Jack Oakie, Grace Moore Parera, Mary Pickford, Albertina Rasch, Joseph Schenck, Norma Shearer Thalberg, Harry Warner, Jack Warner, and Darryl Zanuck.

†Since MacDonald never took off her wedding ring, she had to camouflage it while making pictures, sometimes covering it with flesh-colored tape, sometimes placing a larger ring over it. Neither Gene nor Jeanette ever disclosed the secret message.

wood marriage, but a union based on real love and as exciting a romance as any girl and boy might have in the ordinary walks of life."

A reception for 250 took place at the home of Jeanette and her mother on June Street. The bride, now in white, wore a splendid diamond necklace, her wedding present from Gene. Aunt Sally, in mauve lace and still glamorous at seventy, stood next to the ninety-pound pink wedding cake flown in from Freihofer's Bakery in West Philadelphia. Sally told everyone how she used to make costumes for "Baby Jenny Lind." Among the gifts on display were a full service of sterling silver flatware and dinnerware from Nicholas Schenck and Louis B. Mayer, a crystal Madonna from Norma Shearer, and a pair of lamps from Nelson Eddy.

Parsons, who arrived with a portable typewriter concealed beneath her silver fox cape, set up shop in a second-floor bathroom. When Jeanette found out, she pounded on the door with fury: "Louella, you and that typewriter come right out here!" The embarrassed reporter exited, only to have the bride lead her to a worktable equipped with telephone, a glass of champagne, and a piece of cake.

Jeanette expected to spend her wedding night at a rented seaside bungalow. As the newlyweds set off, driving west along Sunset Boulevard, Gene took an abrupt right turn at the east security gate to Bel-Air. "It's in case anybody is following us," he explained. Moments later, Gene brought the car to a halt in front of an enormous Tudor-style mansion at 783 Bel-Air Road. The fourteen-room house, built mainly of stone with a steep and rolling shingled roof, was part of a two-acre hilly estate set off by dense shrubbery, giant redwoods, and towering eucalypti. The home shimmered with lights, but no other car was in view. Perplexed, Jeanette inquired, "Whose house is this?" "It's ours," said Gene. "I bought the house, and I furnished it, and it's ours." "I don't believe it," retorted Jeanette, almost angry. When she realized Gene was serious, she uttered softly, "How much did you pay for it?" In no frame of mind to mix finance with high chivalry, Gene trotted over to Jeanette's side of the car, enveloped her in his arms, and lifted his bride through the double-gabled threshold of their new abode, aptly named Twin Gables.

Even by Hollywood standards Gene had pulled off a daring masquerade. When he purchased Twin Gables for $85,000, he had the paperwork done under Helen Ferguson's married name in order to guarantee secrecy. It was clear from the outset that this long-empty site—adjacent to the estate of oil millionaire Alfonzo Bell, the founder of Bel-Air—needed extensive repairs. For over six months, Ferguson fronted for Raymond as he executed a plan, devised with architect Kenneth Albright, to remodel the house, the furnishings, and the grounds.

"I thought it remarkable," remembered Fay Wray, "that Gene could feel so confident about doing this without even consulting Jeanette." The resourceful fiancé, using the alias "John Morgan," would visit the work-in-progress incognito, wearing dark glasses, a high muffler, and an oversize fedora yanked down to cover his telltale blond mane. Neighbors whispered that a Chicago gangster had bought the place. Three hours before the wedding, Gene entrusted Sylvia Grogg, Jeanette's private secretary, and Rose Coen, her maid, with the covert delivery of his wife-to-be's personal effects. "My mouth sagged open," Jeanette recalled. "My dresses, shoes, books, records, keepsakes, wedding presents, all were in place as though we'd been living there for months. . . . I dreamed all my life of a place I'd call home. I found it [that] night."

Next morning, soon after sunrise, Gene guided Jeanette from the main house to a nearby annex, converted from guest quarters into a new music studio housing two Baldwin grand pianos, "one for each of us." Then they toured five levels of terraced gardens that offered magnificent views spanning to the Pacific. Giverny, Claude Monet's country home, was the inspiration for Twin Gables' landscape. The grounds teemed with fig, cherry, plum, peach, and citrus trees, with azalea, begonia, cyclamen, and narcissus blossoms, and with honeysuckle and trailing lantana vines. An inscription above an arched trellis read "LE JARDIN DE MA PRINCESSE" (My Princess's Garden). Gene next led Jeanette down to the kennels, which had customized compartments for each of their five dogs. A special surprise awaited her in the new stables, built with a shingled roof to match the main house. Alongside Black Knight, an Arabian horse Jeanette had given Gene for his birthday the previous August, stood a magnificent snow white Arabian mare. This was Gene's birthday present to his bride. They named her White Lady.

That Monday, MacDonald was obliged to report to the studio for retakes on *The Firefly*. But the next Saturday, June 26, the "MacRaymonds," free of all responsibilities, sailed on the *Lurline* for a Hawaiian honeymoon. Also aboard were Mary Pickford and her young husband of several hours, actor Buddy Rogers. Another passenger was Mrs. Spencer Tracy, who was traveling without her spouse. After a tumultuous *aloha* on the dock in Honolulu, Jeanette and Gene, dripping with leis, sped to a hotel, where they gave a radio interview, and then went to a beach house on the northern side of Oahu. This hideaway, however, did not prove secluded enough for the newlyweds' comfort, for fans and reporters ceaselessly intruded on their privacy. When the couple reentered California on August 5, Gene spoke for himself and his bride in beefing to the press: "If the Governor of the Territory of Hawaii wants to confiscate all the candid cameras there, that's perfectly all right with me."

One day after Jeanette Raymond's return home, *The Firefly* had a glittery West Coast premiere at the Four Star Theater on Wilshire Boulevard. Four weeks later, the picture opened at New York's Astor and generated the kind of electricity usually reserved for a Metropolitan Opera gala. Vying for top fashion honors were Broadway first-nighters Dorothy Hammerstein, Kitty Carlisle, Fannie Hurst, and Hope Hampton. Their sense of occasion was fitting, for *The Firefly* was no ordinary movie. It was an unprecedented attempt to break new ground by merging two ordinarily separate Hollywood film genres: the historical war epic and the musical.

MacDonald's *The Firefly,* except for its music, had nothing in common with the original Rudolf Friml operetta of 1912. Ogden Nash, the popular poet for the *New Yorker* and the *Saturday Evening Post,* joined Frances Goodrich and Albert Hackett in discarding the operetta's comic libretto, set in pre–World War I America. Their new inspiration was *On the Road with Wellington,* a historical novel about the Peninsular War and the 1813 defeat of the French in the Battle of Vitoria (Spain). All three screenwriters were sympathetic to the ongoing Republican struggle against Fascism in the Spanish civil war, which had erupted in July 1936. They conceived of *The Firefly* as a protest against dictatorial oppression. For MacDonald, they created Nina Maria—a Spanish spy who lures Napoleon's officers through flirtatious dances and ultimately makes possible the liberation of Spain.

Nina Maria would be the most dramatically complex of MacDonald's screen roles. It also required her to dance as much as sing. Jeanette was eager to display once again the talent that had fueled her early ascent on Broadway. For two months prior to shooting, she made daily morning visits to the La Brea Avenue studio of the Spanish dancer Paco Cansino, Rita Hayworth's father, where she labored tirelessly to get her body into top form. With Cansino, she studied the intricacies of fandango, bolero, and flamenco, all the while practicing the picture's original choreography, devised by Albertina Rasch.

When filming began in March, MacDonald was still revitalizing muscles and tendons not used since those Broadway years: "I reported every morning for a 90-minute workout with Albertina before the 9 o'clock call on the set. The *barre* was backbreaking, the exercises . . . exhausting, and I had no double. Any dancer will sympathize with me; by the time that 9 o'clock call came, I was ready to go back to bed."

Metro budgeted nearly $1,500,000 for this sprawling epic, whose sets and costumes rivaled those of *Maytime* in opulence. The spangled beading on the gown and mantilla MacDonald wears in the "Love Is Like a Firefly" number was said to result from two weeks' work by a team of Guadalajaran craftswomen. For her tour-de-force rendition of "He Who Loves and Runs Away," designer Adrian, never a slave to fashion history, looked to the androgynous images of Aubrey Beardsley and fin de siècle Art Nouveau: he dressed MacDonald in a tight-fitting black velvet costume slit up the side, with jeweled tendrils embroidered in a line from neck to hem; a two-cornered Napoleonic hat cocked on her head; and a sleek ebony cane to offset the curve of her raised train.

In these two cabaret scenes, one set in Madrid, the other in Bayonne, Pop Leonard had the camera make elaborate 360-degree sweeps as the glowing "Firefly" whirled amid her military admirers—a bold mise-en-scène that was closer to the experimentation of a filmmaker like Jean Renoir in France than to standard Hollywood practice. For the Bayonne sequence, the property department purchased an 1801 crystal chandelier from the United States Embassy in Vienna and had it wired with sixty flame-shaped bulbs. Along with Oliver Marsh's chiaroscuro lighting for night scenes and Jack Dawn's novel mixture of genuine gold dust with powder for MacDonald's makeup, a new sepia-platinum tint known as "Metrocolor" made the movie glisten like an Old Master painting. In fact, the nightmarish shots depicting French brutality took inspiration from the Spanish artist Francisco de Goya, just as the picturesque highway scenes were influenced by the genre paintings of Bartolomé Murillo.

At L. B. Mayer's MGM in 1937—the year of such high-minded movies as *The Good Earth* and *Captains Courageous*—*The Firefly*'s ambitious cinematography, its use of authentic historical materials, and its allusions to revered artworks certified the film as a lofty project. Like fireside classics, Jeanette MacDonald musicals, far from being only entertainment, were now expected to advance the cultural life of moviegoers and strengthen the studio's faith in its own respectability.

The front office hired Rudolf Friml to lend further artistic legitimacy, but the Czech-born composer wound up suing the company for $5 million. Friml claimed to be "in love" with MacDonald, who had brought his *Vagabond King* and *Rose-Marie* to the screen with "so much charm." His opinion of Herbert Stothart was less gracious: "I gave him a chance to be a conductor, but he went too far. He . . . grabbed my music and put his name on it!"

Friml's hostility peaked on the day Allan Jones recorded "The Donkey Serenade," an elaborate adaptation by Stothart, Forrest, and Wright of a 1920 Friml piano piece, "Chanson." Minutes after Jones completed a first take, Stromberg called his fellow MGM producers to the recording stage. Jones's catchy lament of a lovesick fool serenading his señorita's mule delighted the men, who rightly predicted the number would become *The Firefly*'s runaway hit. Friml, informed of the goings-on, stormed into the hall just as a fifth take began. Drowning out the marimba, maracas, and Mexican guitars, he bellowed, "ZOT IS NOT FRIML!" and stalked out. The next day, he slapped MGM with a copyright suit. An out-of-court settlement satisfied Friml, but from then on he was persona non grata in Culver City.

A Friml hex may have touched off the mishaps that nearly shut down the location shoot of "The Donkey Serenade" at Lone Pine, in the vicinity of Mount Whitney. The first calamity took place when the thin Sierra Nevada air brought on a heart irregularity in Robert Z. Leonard, who had to be rushed away by ambulance. Then Allan Jones's Arabian horse, Smoky, got pinned between an artificial rock formation and MacDonald's mule-drawn stagecoach, resulting in an injury to Jones's foot. Filming went forward with Joseph Newman replacing Pop Leonard and Allan Jones hobbling about on crutches. For all the turmoil, the gentle interplay of Jones's earnest wooing and MacDonald's feigned indifference resulted in an endearing, witty sequence. Subsequent revivals of the stage operetta almost always incorporated this number into the score. (Woody Allen included Jones's rendition of the song in the sound track of *Radio Days*, his 1987 tribute to an earlier era's pop culture.)

MacDonald hoped that *The Firefly*, the first picture to give her sole billing above the title, would propel her friend Allan Jones beyond Nelson Eddy's shadow. She was pleased to be playing opposite a singer who could act with grace and subtlety. "The first day on the set," Jones recalled, "Jeanette turned to Ollie Marsh and said: 'I want you to understand one thing from the beginning. Allan Jones is my costar. I want him to have as many close-ups as I have, and I want you to treat him the way you treat me.'" According to Jones, MacDonald felt this change of male partner enabled her to do "her best work" in *The Firefly*. Not all critics agreed with *Film Daily* that "Jeanette MacDonald was never more perfectly cast." Some felt cheated by a musical whose serious topic did not allow her to be "lightly amusing." Still, virtually all who applauded MacDonald also acknowledged Allan Jones as a major presence, "dashing and manly."

Variety was impressed by *The Firefly*'s "size" and "class," calling it a screen adaptation that "emerges from Metro as a screaming eagle." The influential National Screen Council honored the picture with a Blue Ribbon Award for Outstanding Merit. Yet even some enthusiastic reviewers faulted the movie for its "pretentious" folding of a heavy subject into the operetta mold. Rural exhibitors, especially, found the picture "excessive" and "a little high-class for the hillbillies."

Although *The Firefly* went on to become the fifteenth-biggest-grossing picture of Hollywood's 1937–38 season, its net profit of $163,000 was barely a tenth of its huge production budget. In a year when MGM lost three-quarters of a million dollars on its costliest movie, *Marie Antoinette* with Norma Shearer and Tyrone Power, studio executives began to question the commercial viability of lavish screen epics, musical and otherwise. MGM's *Love Finds Andy Hardy*, a typical-American-family story with incidental songs from fifteen-year-old Judy Garland, cost only $212,000 to make, yet it brought in whopping profits of $1,345,000.

Political turmoil abroad made *The Firefly* vulnerable to foreign censorship. France cut dialogue harmful to its cherished image of military preparedness. Nazi Germany squelched references to a secret police. Imperialist Japan deleted all scenes portraying rebellion. In the United States, mainstream critics downplayed the picture's contemporary relevance, while the left-wing press grumbled that the romantic format weakened *The Firefly*'s symbolic references to the plight of Loyalists in the Spanish civil war.*

*James Francis Crow, writing in *The Hollywood Citizen News* on July 21, 1937, typified the downplaying response: "The factual matter of the story is curiously and sharply significant in this day when Mussolini is assuming the Napoleon role in the despoliation of Spain. But the [film's] Spanish struggle, however interesting it may be in the light of current events in Europe, is only incidental to the primary business of the picture." "R. W.," who reviewed the movie for *New Masses* on September 14, 1937, exemplified the contrasting, left-wing view: "What seems to have the most interest (at least for a large sec-

There's no question that *The Firefly* was an impressive chronicle of international war and intrigue and that it transcended many operetta conventions. MacDonald's portrayal of a heroic nationalist sacrificing personal sentiment for patriotic ideals infused the picture—to a degree perhaps greater than any film musical before or after—with the exalted feel of Italian tragic opera. Yet even producer Stromberg, who held that "the great essential is to give every picture something that will make it stand out among all others," knew that *The Firefly*'s political and cultural ambitions had to be kept within limits. Originally Stromberg had the film end with a sermonette on the horrors of war and the virtues of peace, featuring a dizzying montage of French, British, and Spanish flags, troops, and heroes. Audience response at previews, however, made Stromberg drop this coda. Instead, after a dramatic climax with emotional twists worthy of Verdi's *Il trovatore*, *The Firefly* concludes with MacDonald and Jones in a mule-drawn covered wagon, oblivious to history, and blithely reprising "The Donkey Serenade" and "Giannina Mia."

Of all her MGM epics, *The Firefly* is today among MacDonald's least remembered and appreciated. This sad turn reinforces the mistaken notion that by the late 1930s Jeanette MacDonald was no more than half of the MacDonald-Eddy musical team. As for Allan Jones, his reward for competing with Eddy was banishment from L. B. Mayer's stable of active stars. Jones went on to make *The Great Victor Herbert,* opposite Mary Martin, for Paramount in 1939. He would abandon Hollywood musicals altogether after starring in Universal's lightweight *Honeymoon Ahead,* released in 1945.

---

tion of the audience) is the feeling of a unified people in arms resisting an aggressor. The emphasis on traditional musical comedy–melodrama material casts a pall over everything else."

CHAPTER TWELVE

Middlebrow Muse

It's always easier to educate down than it is to educate up.

JEANETTE MACDONALD, on her first
U.S. recital tour, 1939

If a public is given a chance to discriminate,
the tendency is always upward.

OLIN DOWNES, *New York Times*
music critic, 1954

"RADIO, IN MY OPINION, is one of the finest musical influences history has seen," MacDonald asserted in November 1937, after two
months of hosting her own CBS music show, *Vick's Open House.*

That autumn, nearly twenty-five million American households were
tuning in to a medium that, even more than sound pictures, revolutionized people's access to music. For most listeners, "live" music meant
the smooth harmonies of pop-tune bandleaders like Eddie Duchin and
Guy Lombardo, whose broadcasts from dreamy hotels and fancy dance
halls delivered a night on the town for the price of a mere flick of the
dial. Yet "longhair" music was also plentiful. Enthusiasts could hear
Eugene Ormandy and the Philadelphia Orchestra on Mondays, the
Metropolitan Opera on Saturday afternoons, and the NBC Symphony
Orchestra, with Arturo Toscanini conducting, on Saturday nights. CBS
broadcast the New York Philharmonic every Sunday afternoon.
Wednesdays brought "light" classics from the André Kostelanetz Orchestra, courtesy of Chesterfield cigarettes. "That there is a market for

all this melody where none existed before," noted MacDonald, was proof of "the rising musical taste of the nation."

Vick's Open House aired on early Sunday evenings, opposite NBC comedian Jack Benny. Its music was unapologetically middlebrow. In a typical program, MacDonald mixed favorites by Romberg, Kern, and Rodgers; a Scottish or Welsh folk song; and a familiar French aria. Late in the season she risked a heavier duet from *Il trovatore* with Wilbur Evans, her baritone for the yearlong series. *Variety* called the show "a treat for all who love rich vibrant singing," but it faulted the producers and writers for not allowing MacDonald to be "her natural self," saddling her with "some of the most asinine chatter that ever threatened a dignified artist's dignity."

MacDonald savored the added exposure and income that came with weekly coast-to-coast broadcasts. But her fear of being in poor voice led to acute anxiety attacks: "All day Sunday, with its hectic rehearsing and last-minute changes of program, I'd be fine. Then, as air time drew nearer, tension clenched me like a vice and my heart pounded like a triphammer." Mike McLaughlin, her trusty sound engineer, would then walk MacDonald up and down Santa Monica Boulevard "like a trainer exercising a racehorse." This brought results, but it embarrassed Jeanette, who remembered the therapy as "a grim experience."

Stage fright also weakened her immune system. MacDonald's sign-off line was "And don't catch cold!," yet just before Christmas she came down with a bronchial infection that spread to her ear and forced her to miss several programs. The Vick Chemical bosses panicked, since their products were supposed to bring speedy relief to upper-respiratory ailments. To save face, Vick reported that its star, recuperating in Palm Springs, had suffered "an attack of ptomaine poisoning."

Nicholas Schenck, the CEO of Loew's, Inc., and the man L. B. Mayer scoffingly renamed "Mr. Skunk," was suspicious of MacDonald's independent radio work. He rightly viewed *Vick's Open House* as a potential drain on the Sunday-evening movie market. To avert further competition from his own MGM employees, Schenck reversed his long opposition to the rival medium and entered the radio business in partnership with General Foods. *Good News of 1938,* sponsored by Maxwell House Coffee, debuted over NBC on the first Thursday of November 1937. *Variety* called it "the greatest development in the history of high-priced big time, de luxe, transcontinental radio." The premiere episode was a behind-the-scenes "visit" to Culver City. It began by stringing together Eleanor Powell, George Murphy, Judy Garland,

Buddy Ebsen, and Sophie Tucker. The second half showcased MacDonald in scenes from *The Firefly*, which was to open nationwide the following day. During an intermission segment, Mayer hyped *Good News* as a "complete merger of radio and motion pictures."

Still, L. B. did not achieve his and Nick Schenck's hidden goal: the taming of their diva. MacDonald had consented to appear on the inaugural broadcast only after fighting tooth and nail for a fee befitting her standing as a movie *and* radio star. Then, to taunt Mayer and Schenck with her mindfulness that the real issue was not the Loew's payroll but who was going to call the shots, she donated her $2,000 earnings to the Community Chest of Greater Los Angeles.

Jeanette's nine-month MGM contract was up for option that November, and she nearly tied Schenck's hands. A *Fortune* survey had just ranked her, after Norma Shearer and Shirley Temple, America's "favorite actress." *Variety* was soon to name her the industry's "top musical magnet." Readers of *Screen Guide* elected her Queen of the Screen for 1937. Abroad, MacDonald's popularity remained unassailable. Schenck did not want to forfeit this golden goose to another studio and therefore resolved not to press the issue of MacDonald's right to broadcast at will. Loew's stood firm, however, on an equally sensitive point. MacDonald wanted guaranteed time off for personal appearances. Why, she asked, should Nelson Eddy have the chance to earn $200,000 in yearly recital tours and not she? From the company's perspective, the answer was plain: Eddy was a compliant employee who had entered into a seven-year contract with Metro, whereas MacDonald continued to spurn long-term arrangements. Schenck felt no remorse in refusing to grant the prima donna special leaves.

MacDonald's self-reliance finally took some of the bloom off Mayer's infatuation with her. "I could feel the temperature falling," Jeanette remembered. "L. B. still gave me his good wishes when I went in to see him on the first day's shooting, but something had gone wrong between us." When *The Firefly* was in production, Mayer arbitrarily revoked a policy that had given MacDonald the right to dub her own singing voice in French- and Spanish-language versions of her pictures. Aggrieved, she repeated the ploy that had worked so well for her with *San Francisco*. She bypassed Mayer and called upon her allies at Loew's in New York to arrange a closed-door meeting with Schenck: "I went to argue that, contrary to what the studio wanted, I couldn't permit anyone but me to sing my songs in foreign languages . . . since my singing voice was my stock-in-trade." Schenck sided with MacDonald.

Mayer, forced to give in, stewed over what he took as Jeanette's back-handed trump.

Another wrinkle in MacDonald's rapport with Mayer arose from the casting of her next film, *The Girl of the Golden West*. The story, based on the 1905 play by David Belasco, required a romantic male lead who could convincingly portray a masked desperado terrorizing California in the days of the gold rush. MacDonald rightly thought that Nelson Eddy, Mayer's choice for the role, would look ridiculous toting a six-shooter and holding up stagecoaches. She lobbied instead for Allan Jones, a top-notch horseman whose dramatic caliber in *The Firefly* had allowed her to avoid the overacting she sometimes employed to offset Eddy's shortcomings.* Mayer, however, disliked cocky Jones. He pointed to *The Firefly*'s restrained profits as evidence that the public wanted more MacDonald-Eddy. Eddy himself issued another ultimatum to the front office. "You're going to have trouble with me if you give Jones any more pictures," he told Mayer.

Eddy got the part, and Jones was a poor loser. He facetiously boasted to everyone on the lot that he was training his horse to stomp on life-size Nelson Eddy cutouts. The story got twisted by the time it reached Nelson, who angrily confronted his rival: "I heard you put a picture of me behind Smoky and when he shits, he shits all over my picture." "Nelson," replied Jones, "I've got six horse's asses in my stable. What in the hell do you think I'd want with another one?!"

Rumor soon had it that MacDonald and Eddy were feuding. Some of the gossip stemmed from Jeanette's preference for Jones. Much of it came from the same adoring fans who had claimed, months earlier, that Jeanette and Nelson were madly in love with each other. No costars in movie history had followers more passionate than did Mac-Donald and Eddy. A mere hint in Parsons's column that the team might be headed for a split provoked howling enthusiasts to swamp the MGM mail room with protests. Many of the fans were rabidly partisan. Eddy zealots wailed that MacDonald received too much screen

---

*MacDonald voiced similar qualms when MGM proposed to costar her with Eddy in *Robin Hood,* from the operetta by Harry B. Smith and Reginald De Koven: she thought Jones far more suitable as the heroic marauder of Sherwood Forest. The debate became academic when MGM scrapped the project after Warner Bros., in 1938, released *The Adventures of Robin Hood* with Errol Flynn and Olivia de Haviland. Joan Crawford, always eager to show off her singing abilities, reportedly wanted to do *The Girl of the Golden West* before the role went to MacDonald. It's tempting to fantasize the screen chemistry that would have resulted from a Crawford-Eddy pairing.

time. MacDonald devotees shrieked the opposite. Eddy addicts attributed MacDonald's glory to the baritone. MacDonald worshipers derided Eddy for being catapulted to fame on the soprano's high Cs. This operatic cultism flattered the stars, who made light of the gossip. When Nelson had to snap a giant bullwhip around Jeanette's waist in *The Girl of the Golden West,* he kidded: "Come on, now. Let's show the world what one of these Hollywood feuds *can* be like!"

Yet for all their public claims to the contrary, MacDonald and Eddy were not chummy. Vera Matthews, daughter of the MGM cinematographer Charles Schoenbaum, visited the set of *The Girl of the Golden West* and recalled that "the ice between them was thick, cold, and scary": "My father said it was due to jealousy, each wanting to outsing the other, receive more praise and fan mail, and be catered to by the MGM moguls." Bob Wright remembered Eddy's resentment over MacDonald's higher salary: "Nelson was the team's real prima donna. He had this kind of money draw in concerts and in radio, and he would clean up. But at the studio he had to fight for pay raises. In fact, he'd often stay in his dressing room when he was fighting and would gladly have taken suspension for it."*

There's little question that Allan Jones would have made a tougher hombre than Nelson Eddy in *The Girl of the Golden West.* But if the film misfired, it was not because of Jones's absence. Instead of being assigned to Hunt Stromberg, the project went to William Anthony McGuire, the writer-producer who had just supervised *Rosalie,* Nelson Eddy's West Point musical with Eleanor Powell and Ilona Massey. McGuire did not have Stromberg's gift for turning dated stage scripts into fresh and lively movies. Ignoring Puccini's 1910 opera version of the same story, McGuire had Sigmund Romberg compose a set of original musical numbers. He assembled a strong supporting cast: Walter Pidgeon as the sheriff who vies for the Girl's attentions; Leo Carillo as the bandit's comic sidekick, making Eddy look macho by comparison; Buddy Ebsen as the Girl's gentle confidant; and Ray Bolger—ultimately edited out—to perform a song-and-dance routine. With Robert Z. Leonard directing, the sepia-toned production exuded

---

*At the point when Eddy was struggling to get his salary hiked from $4,000 to $6,000 per week, he was astonished to find out that Bob Wright and Chet Forrest were making only $200—further evidence, to his mind, of Mayer's bloodsucking. Wright informed me in our interview of February 1990 that Eddy felt so indebted to "the two young men who have made the difference in my feeling that I can do this thing [movies]," he hired them on the sly to write special material for his radio appearances, paying them $600 per week from his own pocket.

period California flavor. Yet the picture lacked tempo, sharp dialogue, and smooth integration of music and drama. In an unfortunate swerve from formula, MacDonald and Eddy had no extended love duet. Their separate renditions of Romberg and Gus Kahn's "Who Are We to Say?," satisfying by themselves, emphasized the film's overall sprawl.

The Girl of the Golden West was the first MacDonald-Eddy movie to get so-so notices. Almost all reviewers took swipes at Eddy for his torpor, Leonard for mislaid inspiration, and the studio for not having slashed the running time to under two hours. Most gave MacDonald good marks for her polished singing of Liszt's "Liebestraum" and the Bach-Gounod "Ave Maria." Many smirked at the western drawl and jaunty swagger she affected to portray the no-nonsense proprietor of the Polka Saloon. The critics, however, had little impact on moviegoers during the pre-Easter weeks of 1938. *The Girl of the Golden West* was a box-office bonanza. Some houses, like Los Angeles's State, reported grosses higher than any since the Great Crash. Jeanette MacDonald as an unschooled barkeep and Nelson Eddy as a cream-puff bandito may have stretched plausibility, but realism was beside the point. Audiences previously entranced by *Naughty Marietta, Rose Marie,* and *Maytime* wanted nothing more than to submit once again to the spell of heroic MacDonald renouncing her love for Eddy only to get him back in the last reel, this time morally "regenerated."

During the final weeks of 1938, *Ladies' Home Journal* ran a nationwide survey titled "What Are the Women of America Thinking?" It found that a majority of females of all ages and income groups placed *The Girl of the Golden West* among the year's "ten best movies."

In late April 1938 the Raymonds made their first trip together to New York City. It was as much a business journey as a vacation. Gene's new picture, *Stolen Heaven,* was opening at Broadway's Paramount Theater, and he agreed to give a week of personal appearances. The Paramount was already an important venue for pioneering musicians like Tommy Dorsey and Benny Goodman, whose big bands had ushered in the Swing Era. In his own bid to woo the youth market, Gene slipped "Alligator Swing," a number he had just composed, into his song-and-banter act. The effort flopped. "Mr. Raymond's 'getting hot' is barely lukewarm, and the Paramounters know their hotcha," guffawed *Variety.* Some teens were heard to yell: "Come on back, but don't sing!" Gene took the ribbing with humor and kept the audience in his camp.

Around this time, some people began to peg Gene Raymond as envious of his wife's greater fame. Amy Revere, MacDonald's old hoofing friend from *Tip-Toes* and *Yes, Yes, Yvette,* stopped by one night at the Raymonds' suite in the Gotham Hotel on Fifth Avenue. She remembered Gene, who was rehearsing in the bedroom, as "stiff and unsociable": "The three of us went off to Sardi's for a bite to eat and autograph hounds mobbed our cab. I had the impression Gene was annoyed, because all attention was directed at Jeanette, not him." Others who observed the couple over time discount claims of rivalry. "Gene Raymond was very serious about his work, but he had a sense of fun," said Fay Wray, "and that's what made him and Jeanette comfortable and happy together. It was a secure marriage." The actor Lew Ayres agreed: "I think the two of them were a very good match in their interests. I always felt strongly they were a team that was meant to be together."

During much of that first year after the wedding, Jeanette found Gene to be "the most thoughtfully generous man I had known—imaginatively, incredibly so." Every week he gave her an "anniversary" present, a volume of the collected works of her favorite author, Victor Hugo, and inside each was a personal message. One read: "A whole week, and I love you twice as much.—McGillicutty." Still, Jeanette had to adjust to what she called "a kind of secrecy" within Gene that made him "self-sufficient, self-disciplined, and self-centered." "There were times," she admitted, "when I was as much outside his world as if he didn't recognize me. I often wondered what he was thinking. Did he perhaps wish he hadn't married me? That was hard to bear."

Sometimes Gene unburdened his feelings in notes that would suddenly appear on Jeanette's dressing table. The subject was often Mrs. Kipling:

> I'm mighty proud of you and the grace with which you've accepted a most
> difficult mother-in-law attitude. Perhaps other brides have borne the same
> kind of cross—but none so admirably! I love you more each day! I'm
> happy for the first time in my life. And I'm enjoying the prospect of your
> sharing a lifetime of work and play and, I hope, success and the love and
> respect of everyone, with—
>
> Your Old Man

The real drama of Gene's New York stay occurred several weeks before the Paramount appearance. Gene decided it was time to restore ties with his estranged father. Roy Guion lived in the Great Kills section of Staten Island, where he operated an upholstery shop. At the sight of a grown son known only from the movie screen, Guion, stocky and white-haired, turned "radiantly happy." Among his first words to Gene was a plea to forgive and forget Mary Kipling's malice. Such generosity touched Gene deeply. Later that day, Roy Guion went to Manhattan to meet his famous daughter-in-law. Jeanette remembered seeing "a beaten man who, in his fifties, still carried the scars in his makeup that he'd suffered as a husband." Her first gift to Roy was a terrier called Foxy.

Soon Roy Guion came out to the Coast and moved in with his younger son, Bob. Gene arranged for his father to run a gas station, and he spent every free hour fishing, gambling on horses, and drinking freely with him. It was one of the rare periods when MacDonald felt she no longer had to worry about family. Her sister Elsie was about to be married, for the third time. Blossom, who now called herself Marie Blake, was getting bits in MGM pictures, including roles as the switch-board operator in the *Young Dr. Kildare* series and Augusta the cook in *Love Finds Andy Hardy.** But if luck was siding with the MacDonald clan, it quickly ran out on the Guions. Within less than two years, Roy suffered a massive heart attack and died after surgery. Jeanette recalled Gene crouching beside the oxygen tent at Good Samaritan Hospital, crying "*Dad, Dad, Dad!*" as his father slipped away.

For Gene, the loss reopened the great emotional wounds of his child-hood. For Jeanette, Gene's sorrow imparted a renewed sense of duty. She now understood that her husband's well-being turned on having a home free of the tensions he knew as a boy: "I had to try not to make an issue of anything, not to argue. . . . I had to learn early that tears would get me nowhere. There was also one subject I didn't allow myself to pursue, ex-cept in my private daydreaming. The MacRaymonds had no children."

During the late spring of 1938, MacDonald began shooting her fifth film with Nelson Eddy. Their four previous pictures had grossed more

---

*Blossom reconciled herself to Jeanette's greater success with humor and grace. She jok-ingly told a *New York Herald Tribune* reporter on July 12, 1936: "If I took being a film star's sister too seriously, it . . . might do strange psychopathic things to my personality. I am having much too good a time to let that happen." In 1938, Blossom gave a Come As You Think You'll Look in Fifty Years party and dressed as the perennial-ingenue-with-one-foot-in-the-grave. A tombstone attached to her ankle had an epitaph that read:

> As Blossom MacDonald she started in life,
> As Blossom Rock she became a wife.
> For her movie career she was tagged Marie Blake.
> The studio told her to jump in the lake.
> P.S. She did!

than even L. B. Mayer had thought possible. Still, Schenck and the East Coast executives were starting to have doubts. How much longer would the public spend money to watch, yet again, the Singing Sweethearts fall rapturously in love amid historical and exotic locales?

In a kind of apotheosis, the team's new project was Victor Herbert's 1913 operetta, *Sweethearts*. Wisely, Mayer restored Hunt Stromberg to the producer's seat. Stromberg's charge was to bring fresh twists to the duo's romantic image without diluting their alchemy. One strategy was to make *Sweethearts* MGM's first complete three-color Technicolor movie. Another was to display the pair in ultracontemporary dress and settings. A third surprise was to show MacDonald and Eddy blissfully married at the story's outset and then have their union fall apart through hints of adultery and deception.

Screenwriting went to Dorothy Parker and Alan Campbell, a married couple personally familiar with domesticity's ups and downs. Herbert's fairy-tale operetta told of a crown princess abandoned at birth and raised by a laundress. Parker and Campbell, with uncredited help from Ogden Nash and Robert Benchley, relegated this quaint libretto to incidental backdrop. In its place, they devised a snappy modern story about two married actors who star for six years in a Broadway musical—Herbert's *Sweethearts*—and are suddenly tempted by a Hollywood movie contract.

Dorothy Parker knew whereof she wrote. The author of poems, stories, and waspish play and book reviews for *Vanity Fair* and the *New Yorker,* she had gained celebrity in the 1920s as the wittiest of the mainly male quipsters who lunched at the Round Table of Manhattan's Algonquin Hotel. When she moved to Hollywood in 1934, Parker ridiculed motion pictures even as they made her rich. "Writing for films is just like doing crossword puzzles," she said, "except that to do crossword puzzles you have to have a certain knowledge of words." Just prior to *Sweethearts,* she and Campbell scripted David O. Selznick's devastating portrait of the private agonies of Hollywood nobility, *A Star Is Born.* They peppered their *Sweethearts* screenplay with just as many jabs at show business, both on the Great White Way and in Tinseltown. But what was dark and sordid in *A Star Is Born* became sparkling and lighthearted in *Sweethearts.*

Stromberg wanted the picture to be a screwball musical with enough "sophistication," "humor," and "dizzy tempo" to rival his *Thin Man* series for lunatic charm. He instructed Parker and Campbell to aim for a "Noël Coward type of writing." Stromberg's overall concept—realism with Technicolor glamour—was imaginable only at MGM. "Our scenes," he insisted in preliminary story notes, "must have the same authenticity as scenes depicting the life of newspapermen in *The Front Page.* . . . These are not STOCK characters. This is NOT the story of the *Broadway Melodies,* the *42nd Streets,* and the *Big Broadcasts*—in all of which formula prevailed. . . . Our story is entirely different in every single respect, for we BEGIN where all the other stories have ENDED and thus penetrate completely a new field of material."*

Although Cedric Gibbons's impossibly spacious sets bespoke fantasy more than reality, *Sweethearts* did re-create authentic sites: Times Square, Radio City, the RCA Victor Recording Studios. MacDonald's former Broadway boss, Lee Shubert, was a real-life model for Frank Morgan's fumbling producer. Sam Goldwyn inspired the spluttering Hollywood mogul played by George Barbier. The pretentious manners and Francophilia of Reginald Gardiner's Movietown agent were a parody of Arthur Hornblow, the Paramount producer soon to join his wife, Myrna Loy, at MGM. These in-jokes were strictly for showbiz initiates. But *Sweethearts* also gave regular moviegoers their own thrill of "recognition." By making its protagonists the Monarchs of Operetta, the picture shamelessly catered to every fan's most cherished fantasy, furnishing the illusion of a "genuine" look at how Jeanette MacDonald and Nelson Eddy lived off screen. If the picture ultimately portrayed the twosome as idyllically married, so much the better for obsessed idolizers who deemed Eddy a better real-life match than Gene Raymond.

One of the delights in viewing *Sweethearts* is to watch MacDonald spoof her MGM persona. She first appears in pigtails and gingham, as a Dutch girl in scenes from the Herbert operetta. Singing and dancing "Wooden Shoes" with Ray Bolger, she is sprightly, frolicsome, and *relentlessly* cute. When she joins Eddy in "Every Lover Must Meet His Fate," she relies on broad pantomime gestures to take her from sweetness to ardor to anguish, all the while radiating virginal innocence. In these six droll minutes, MacDonald recaps the exuberant mannerisms that caused viewers and reviewers to adore—or loathe—Hollywood's Queen of Operetta.

---

*Dorothy Parker claimed to have no idea what she was doing writing for MacDonald and Eddy. Bob Wright told me that at one story conference she interrupted Stromberg and begged: "Oh, God. Please get those Boys in here. When that one boy sings high [Wright would play Jeanette in falsetto] and the other sings low [Chet Forrest, as Eddy], that's the only time I understand what it's all about!"

During the dressing-room scene that follows, her brio is just as scintillating, but it flares as if by spontaneous combustion. In a nonstop whirl of movement, color, and repartee, MacDonald rushes from the shower, dries her flame orange hair, flaps her wrists, darts her sea green eyes, and molds her cherry red lips from smiles into simpers into pouts into grins. More genial than *Rose Marie*'s hot-tempered diva, MacDonald still hints at an imperious underside. When her vigilant gal Friday denies her a bonbon, she chides half seriously: "If I ever engage another secretary, she's going to be nearsighted and extraordinarily kindhearted." Taken as a look at the "real" Jeanette MacDonald, this backstage scene pricks the self-deceit of moviegoers who imagined the actress as either a monstrous egomaniac or a languishing goody-goody. Throughout *Sweethearts,* MacDonald projects mischief, glamour, and graciousness. The resulting portrait is the closest thing we have to a screen rendition of her genuine vivaciousness.

Stromberg worried that Technicolor would make Nelson Eddy look effeminate. Originally, the producer wanted Eddy's character to be as flagrantly rugged as Gable in *It Happened One Night.* "He would much rather be driving a truck than singing, and God knows it isn't his fault that he has this golden voice," Stromberg asserted during preproduction. An early concept for the "Pretty as a Picture" number had Nelson surrounded by twenty chorus boys in blond wigs and Eddy masks. Mercifully, the producer scrapped the idea. As filmed, this playful sequence hit a fine balance between the romantic sentiment of Eddy's song and MacDonald's tongue-in-cheek parody, delivered partly in swing. In their subsequent waltz, Jeanette's graceful twirls and dips made Nelson seem like the last word in manly elegance. Eddy in fact appeared so relaxed and natural through the film that Walter Winchell proclaimed in his column: "Nelson Eddy comes to life in *Sweethearts*!" As a birthday prank, Jeanette and director Van Dyke had a silver loving cup inscribed to "Nelson Eddy, Waltz King." Nelson tolerated such teasing. But when a snide nickname put his virility into question, he was devastated. Some say it was Ray Bolger who caused Eddy to become known as the Singing Capon.

Since *Sweethearts* was going to display MacDonald in Adrian's first made-for-Technicolor designs, the star and her couturier abandoned the sweep and delicacy associated with the gowns of her black-and-white historical films. With the blessing of Technicolor consultant Natalie Kalmus, they opted for what Adrian called "bold" and "accented" ensembles, many of which exploded the myth that redheads could not look terrific in lemon yellow, dusty pink, or fire-engine red. MacDonald wore these taboo colors with ease and authority.

The idea for building an entire clotheshorse sequence around MacDonald began with Dorothy Parker's offhand quip about Lynn Fontanne, then a Great Lady of the New York stage. When Parker meowed that Fontanne's notion of a vacation was to go on a two-hour shopping spree along Fifth Avenue, Stromberg sensed "a good scene for Jeanette." In addition to the ten drop-dead outfits she models in the boutique montage, Jeanette's eye-popping wardrobe included an enormous rust-colored orangutan muff with coordinated cossack-style turban—for afternoon radio broadcasting; a backless fan-pleated evening gown in shell pink—for high-style nightclubbing; and a cornflower blue morning robe with a single cape-sleeve that trailed riotously to the floor—for at-home packing of one's Hollywood-bound trunks, practicality be damned.

The movie's sartorial climax comes when MacDonald, lodged in a drab backwater hotel reminiscent of an Edward Hopper painting, regrets her separation from Eddy. As if in mourning, she sports a stark midnight blue suit with frilly white lace at the neck. Suddenly, her marital plight is straightened out. Cut to Manhattan. In a dazzlingly bright suit of postman blue and lipstick red, with stylized hat and bag to match, MacDonald storms the office of "villainous" Frank Morgan, who engineered the couple's split. The visual impact is staggering. MacDonald's flashy attire, a herald of 1940s fashion whimsy, boosts the film's modernism to a delirious high, wiping away all lines between chic and outré.

Yet the vision that ultimately triumphs in *Sweethearts* is backward-looking. Returned to the operetta stage and to Eddy, MacDonald reappears at the movie's end in the voluminous, fairy-tale pink tulle confection she wears at its start. Her reprise of the title song assures us that Eddy and she *forever* will stay sweethearts. The paradox is delectable. The sole picture to place MacDonald and Eddy in a contemporary context also pledges to viewers that the team will continue indefinitely and without alteration.

Sweethearts turns out to be much less about the "real" lives of Jeanette MacDonald and Nelson Eddy than about the quality of their cinematic union—timeless, self-contained, and sublimely indifferent to changing fashion.

Released three days before Christmas 1938, *Sweethearts* contributed to the nation's biggest holiday spending splurge since the collapse of Wall Street. Along with *Boys Town* and *Goodbye, Mr. Chips,* it did better box office than all other MGM movies of fiscal year 1938–39. Of Metro's three megamusicals that year—*Sweethearts, The Great Waltz,* and *The Wizard of Oz*—only the MacDonald-Eddy feature turned a profit. It received Oscar nominations for Sound Recording and Scoring. It won a Special Academy Award for Color Cinematography—an apt honor for the film that inaugurated MGM's golden era of Technicolor musicals. Readers of *Photoplay* voted it Best Picture of 1938, making *Sweethearts* the third MacDonald film, after *Naughty Marietta* and *San Francisco,* to reap that accolade.

Sweethearts represented a high-water mark in the way critics wrote about MacDonald-Eddy movies. Nearly all reviewers recognized the picture as state-of-the-art entertainment. Yet many hinted at their discomfort with the film's perceived excesses. "A dream of ribbons, tinsel, Technicolor, and sweet, theatrical sentiment . . . that you never seem to get through unpacking," said the *New York Times.* "It really is too much, a feast composed exclusively of rich dishes," bellyached the *Hollywood Spectator.* "The production numbers are beautifully staged, but there are so many of them," groaned the *Daily News.*

Journalists also grew condescending to those they presumed to be the film's "true" audience. *Life* spoke begrudgingly of MacDonald's "pleasantly coy mannerisms" and the public's "still healthy demand" for her brand of "old-fashioned musicals." For the *New York Sun, Sweethearts* was "all very much like a lollipop; but there are plenty of people who like lollipops."

MacDonald was at a crossroads. A decade's hard work had made her the world's most popular and enduring movie-musical star. Now thirty-five, she was at the pinnacle of her powers as a singer and an actress. Yet as with Maurice Chevalier in 1934, the creative bite of her partnership with Nelson Eddy had reached its limits. Mayer was eager to renegotiate her contract. But MacDonald sensed a growing split between MGM's goals and her own. Mayer wanted still more recycled operettas starring the Team. Jeanette craved straight dramatic films with only incidental songs. The time was ripe to set new challenges away from the studio and its controlling bosses.

Nelson Eddy was also reviewing priorities, mainly about his private life. Four weeks after the release of *Sweethearts,* the thirty-eight-year-old bachelor shocked Hollywood by eloping to Las Vegas with Ann

Denitz Franklin, the ex-wife of MGM director Sidney Franklin. The news stunned millions of women, many of whom were heartbroken that their dream man was now "taken." It also piqued the interest of gossips, who were certain Nelson was gay. Eddy inadvertently fueled this belief by taking for a wife a matronly divorcée four years his senior and then supposedly telling Noël Coward, of all people, that "marriage is the tax on stardom." Coward cunningly promoted the marriage-as-a-front angle, later stating, "[Eddy] didn't want a virgin bride or some insatiable creature. . . . She was satisfied, Eddy was satisfied, the studio was satisfied, the public was satisfied. At least I *assume* Nelson Eddy was satisfied. For his sake, I hope he had a very low sex drive. Or perhaps he was very, very discreet if he did step out."*

Those who knew the Eddys well offer a contrasting perspective. Sidney Franklin, Jr., who was fourteen when his mother remarried, noted that the couple "slept in a double bed the size of a polo field, and I'm sure they had grand times together. . . . My mother was no slouch." Eddy's sister, Virginia, pointed to the pair's mutual fidelity: "Ann was very protective of Nelson. She was supportive, a perfect hostess, and devoted to him. And Nelson was devoted to her. He called her every night when he was on the road. There was never the sense that there was trouble in the marriage." The singer Gale Sherwood, who teamed with Eddy on stage in the 1950s, referred to Ann as Nelson's "Rock of Gibraltar": "She was calm, quiet, stable, loving, respectful—all of the things he wanted but which all the stupid little starlets tittering around him lacked. Nelson needed someone who was a normal person." Eddy confided to Sherwood that when he realized he was in love with Ann, whom he had known since 1933, "it was just like a load was taken off my shoulders. I knew that everything would be all right."

MacDonald was about to take one of the biggest gambles of her career. She had not given a live concert since her trip to Europe in 1933. Her

---

*Hearsay has it that Eddy frequented gay baths and watering holes in New York City. Less disputable is his status as a gay icon. At the popular Greenwich Village bar Julius' in the 1950s and 1960s, Eddy's recording of "Stouthearted Men" from *New Moon* was a jukebox favorite that invariably prompted mass sing-alongs. The 1928 Romberg-Hammerstein song, in its celebration of men boldly fighting shoulder-to-shoulder for "the right they adore," continues to offer an appealing gay subtext that is especially evident when sung by gay men's choruses.

Composer-lyricist Jerry Herman exploited the Eddy rumors in his song "Nelson," written for the 1980 revue *A Day in Hollywood / A Night in the Ukraine*. About her screen partner, Herman's soprano confesses: " 'A pair made in heaven,' the fans love to say, / But each time we kiss I swear that he's gay."

last extended outing on native soil had been in 1929, with *Boom-Boom*. Could she pull off a national recital tour entirely on her own? Would she disappoint audiences by performing sans scenery, lighting effects, and fancy costumes? As a Hollywood celebrity daring to lay claim to the "serious" repertoire, wouldn't she be an easy target for snooty, big-city music critics?

MacDonald's stage fright became so severe that she arranged for some "long, expensive talks" with a hypnotist—still a chic therapy in 1939, even in Bel-Air. The practitioner angered her by his near-total silence during most of their sessions. After weeks of therapy he finally spoke, declaiming with slow emphasis: "When you get out there and see the rows of heads, think of the audience as heads of cabbage." MacDonald gulped. "That's a joke. I can't cut cabbage; it gives me awful indigestion." "Well," answered the good therapist, "heads of lettuce, then."

To reduce the risk of getting crucified by the critics, MacDonald confined her tour to small towns, and launched her odyssey on March 16, 1939, at State Teachers College in Pittsburg, Kansas. There were oohs and aahs when she walked on stage in a floor-length bright green gown with violet shawl. After pausing for a moment, she burst out with uncontrollable laughter. It was an awful faux pas for a recital artist, but MacDonald's old vaudeville instinct saved her. In a loud voice, she addressed the crowd: "You must wonder why I'm laughing. . . . Somebody told me a trick to cure my nerves, to think of you as heads of lettuce. Well, when I first saw you, I thought that was exactly what you looked like!" The audience roared its approval, and MacDonald proceeded to sing "Lehn' Deine Wang an Meine Wang" a German art song by the romantic composer Adolph Jensen. "From that point on," MacDonald realized, "I could have sung 'Waltz Me Around Again, Willie,' and they'd still have loved it. With the audience warmed to me, I warmed vocally to them. I got better as the evening progressed."

For the next two months, MacDonald followed an itinerary that made Rose Marie's trek through the Canadian Rockies seem like a cakewalk. She traveled to nineteen out-of-the-way cities throughout the Deep South, the Bible Belt, and the Pacific Northwest. The response was stupendous. In Stillwater, Oklahoma, state troopers had to calm restive throngs who had driven from towns and hamlets as far as two hundred miles away only to be denied entry to the sold-out auditorium of A&M College. Patrolmen in Rochester, Minnesota, wrangled with scalpers who preyed on shivering ticket seekers camped outside the Mayo Civic Auditorium. In Selma, Alabama, stalkers waited for their idol to finish lunch and then plundered her table for souvenir glass-ware, china, and napkin shreds. Minutes after MacDonald vacated room 609 of the Graham Hotel in Bloomington, Indiana, a male ad-mirer secured the room, ordered the staff not to make the bed or change the sheets, and then slept in her linens for three days.

Some of this ballyhoo was the work of Charles L. Wagner, MacDon-ald's concert manager and constant companion on the trip. A wizard in public relations, Wagner had shepherded humorist Will Rogers and opera singers Amelita Galli-Curci and John McCormack through fabu-lously successful cross-country tours. In packaging the Hollywood diva, Wagner threw the spotlight on her down-to-earthness. "There are two kinds of people," he told one small-town reporter. "Those you can talk to and those you can communicate with. Miss MacDonald is the first singer I have managed since Mary Garden who comes in the sec-ond group."

Jeanette's main goal was to prove herself a bona fide concert singer, not a picture player on parade. She wanted to show that a classical vo-calist trained on American soil could hold her own against those schooled in Europe. She also hoped to demonstrate that an apprecia-tion of elite art did not require elite birth.

Those who came only to hear songs from her movies had to squirm until the encores. She opened almost every recital with lieder by Brahms, Grieg, and Schumann, followed by European and American folk songs. ("To be honest," she later confessed, "I hadn't too much feeling for the German.") Her accompanist, Giuseppe Bamboschek, next performed two pieces by Chopin. She capped the program's first half with a Gounod, Verdi, or Puccini aria. After intermission came art songs by Debussy, Massenet, and Félix Fourdrain. Her concluding set consisted of recent or contemporary English and American airs, high-lighting works by such female composers as Liza Lehmann, Amy Woodford-Finden, and Florence Newell Barbour (Grace Newell's sis-ter). Midway into the tour, MacDonald introduced a new song by Gene Raymond, "Let Me Always Sing." Many of these selections found their way into an anthology published by G. Schirmer in 1940, *Jeanette MacDonald's Favorite Operatic Airs and Concert Songs.*

The stratagem worked. Small-town America was not inclined to de-bate the quality of MacDonald's voice. Most press accounts focused on her personal magnetism, not her artistry. Audiences reportedly thrilled to "the charming way she tilted her head to indicate the end of a song," her "infectious good humor," and her "tête-à-tête manner of confiding the meaning of the words" in her French and German offerings. One of the few in-depth reviews came from Walter A. Hansen, the music and drama critic for the *Fort Wayne (Indiana) News Sentinel:*

> Anyone who keeps abreast of what is going on in the world of music knows that there are singers whose vocal and artistic equipment is far superior to what Miss MacDonald has at her disposal at the present time: but it is as sure as anything can be that the number of those who have a similar ability to win their way into the affections of their listeners is exceedingly small. Miss MacDonald has a small voice of pleasing quality, and it is easy to see that the technical training she possesses rests on a carefully constructed foundation. In all likelihood, her singing will gain in warmth, refinement, and eloquence as her musical education progresses. But even though the readings she offers do not as yet reach imposing heights of artistry, they are imbued at times with something tangibly vital. Her sense of style is in need of further cultivation. In short, it would be doing her a gross injustice to say that she has already achieved undeniable mastery in the art to which she devotes so much time and effort. There is reason to believe that the adulation bestowed upon her by millions of admirers will not cause her to swerve from the path of rigorously hard work which every singer of any significance whatever must constantly pursue.

MacDonald learned to ignore reviews: "It put me into such a state of confusion that I'd find myself—the night after a harsh review—trying to correct the specific fault of one critic, but that only ruined something that might please the next fellow. I was frantic, trying to please each one. Finally, I made up my mind that I'd never be The Critics' Darling. Please the public, they're the ones that pay. The critics *get* paid, and sometimes I'm sure they feel so underpaid they wouldn't like [any performance], even if it were great."

Artistic growth was not the only motive behind MacDonald's recital tour. Also at stake was her independence. When her MGM contract came up for renewal in February, MacDonald needed to show the powers at Culver City that she alone was master of her destiny.

From Indiana she wrote to Howard Strickling, Metro's West Coast publicity chief:

> April 11, 1939
>
> Dear Howard:
>
> Have been intending to write you for ages, but with the customary good intentions all gone to hell. . . .

The tour is surpassing my expectations and surprisingly I do not find it nearly as tiring as I had feared. I must say people everywhere have been wonderfully hospitable and have practically broken in two to please me, even to refurnishing hotel suites in anticipation of my visit. All this, I don't mind telling you, is good for one's ego. You know, after you have been around a studio long enough, you just can't help absorbing some of that "all actors have bad judgement" propaganda, and of course I don't need to tell you, one also gets a feeling that he should be awfully pleased to even have a job! But all this is changed on a tour like this. Looks like I am going to be difficult if I ever come back, doesn't it? But I shan't be.

However, I do think I have found a real value on myself. The press have simply been 100%. . . . I understand Mr. L. B. had a close call [due to pneumonia]. Do you suppose that it will make him more, or less, tolerant and understanding?

Sometime when I return, you and I must have a long serious talk, as I have heard from a couple of sources some things about you that have warmed me considerably. . . .

Fondly,
Jeanette

Before setting out for the provinces, MacDonald drew up the toughest contractual demands of her career. She wanted $10,000 per week, with a minimum guarantee of two pictures per year and fifteen weeks per picture. She demanded approval of director, producer, and story. She asked for sole star billing. She was willing to endure a male costar only on condition that she have veto power over the studio's choice. She demanded a completed script at least two weeks prior to the start of a production. She wanted all her pictures to be shot in Technicolor. She refused to make any film without the services of Adrian, Oliver Marsh, Herbert Stothart, and Mike McLaughlin. She would begin work no earlier than 9 A.M. and quit no later than 5:30 P.M. Above all, she would not make the operetta *New Moon* with Nelson Eddy unless the studio guaranteed her the dramatic property *Smilin' Through*, with Robert Taylor as costar.

Negotiations inched forward while MacDonald traversed the country. At her insistence, Bob Ritchie was brought from England to work with Eddie Mannix in representing the studio. When she learned that Mannix was haggling over her salary and wanted to lock her into a yearly commitment of more than thirty weeks, Jeanette didn't mince words. "Remind them," she instructed her attorney, Louis Swarts, "that [Claudette] Colbert and Norma [Shearer] are each getting ten grand a week, Colbert on a twelve weeks' guarantee, and you can bet if she goes overtime she is not doing it because she is Irene or Edith

Mayer's girl friend." "I beg you to quote me," she continued, "that by giving them any more time than is actually contracted for I am only lessening my earning capacity, and that after looking over the list of executives' income tax returns, I am convinced that the bargaining on salaries should not begin with the actors."

She warned Swarts not to "coax and chisel" in a demeaning fashion: "It would take very little to wean me away from them, so colossal has my ego become." When Mannix contested her right to approve producers and directors, Jeanette informed Swarts: "Tell [Mannix] I am not a sufficient gambler to experiment, and if I were, then I might better experiment with a career and take the bigger cash elsewhere."

Actually, MacDonald had no outside offers to back up her threats. There was vague talk about a move to Warner Bros. There were also hints that she might establish an independent production unit at United Artists. Yet more than hard ammunition, it was her breakaway spirit that wounded Louis B. Mayer. One day Swarts was in Mayer's vast white-on-white office and dared to proclaim himself Jeanette's "confidant, guide, and father-confessor." Mayer sprang from his great chair, slammed his thick fist on the desk, and raged: "*I* am her father-confessor! *I* am the one she confides in, not you! Get out of my office!"

Around this time, Mayer met with Nick Schenck to discuss his own future as studio chief. He threatened to leave MGM if Loew's, Inc., did not meet his demands. "And if I quit," he told Schenck, "I guarantee two-thirds of the stars will go with me." As Mayer named them one by one, Schenck interrupted: "I know two or three who wouldn't leave with you—Myrna Loy, William Powell, Jeanette MacDonald." At the sound of Jeanette's name, Mayer, stung, barked back: "MacDonald? This I don't believe. Prove it to me." Schenck (who could indeed be a skunk) invoked a remark MacDonald had made during their meeting in New York at the time of *The Firefly*. Offhandedly, she had said: "I love to do business with Eddie Mannix. He's always so kind to me; I know that when he says, 'You've got my word for it,' he won't let you down." Schenck distorted MacDonald's meaning to suit his scheme. "She told me," he said to Mayer, "she preferred to do business with Eddie Mannix, not with you." At Schenck's bogus revelation, L. B. collapsed into his chair, whimpering tearfully: "This can't be. I don't believe this." But he did believe it, and he agonized for days.

Mayer, however, never let bruised feelings impair his head for business. The Independent Theater Owners of America had just dubbed two of Metro's top stars, Garbo and Crawford, box-office poison. A huge poll run in January by the *New York Daily News* and fifty other papers crowned MacDonald Queen of the Movies for 1939. The same poll showed that Nelson Eddy was still popular, ranking him third among male stars after Gable and Tracy. Yet Eddy's newest film, *Let Freedom Ring* opposite Virginia Bruce, gave more evidence that Eddy could not carry a picture at the box office without MacDonald. In these circumstances, Mayer and Schenck saw little choice but to try to meet MacDonald's demands.

The contract got ironed out in early summer. One lingering bone of contention, however, was MacDonald's portable dressing room. It was falling apart. The walls had holes and the carpet was stained. The toilet leaked, the furniture was rickety, and the doors refused to close. Although Mannix agreed to make repairs, MacDonald thought it more cost-effective for the studio to purchase her a brand-new trailer. Mannix replied that the studio would cover only costs for repairs. He added that Norma Shearer and Joan Crawford had each spent money out of their own pockets to buy themselves new trailers. "That's showing off, if you ask me," snapped back Jeanette, who submitted to the maintenance department a full list of items to be fixed.

The following week, she settled into a sparkling new trailer with customized double doors allowing smooth access in hoop-skirted period costumes. MGM sprang for the tab.

While MacDonald was off instilling rural America with fine music, her latest picture, *Broadway Serenade,* was flopping in major cities. An American-set variation on *The Cat and the Fiddle, Broadway Serenade* had wrapped in early February under a cloud of uncertainty. Robert Z. Leonard, who produced and directed, let MacDonald down by failing to consult with her early on about the songs for this original screenplay. "I do not hold myself up as a picker of hits," she complained to Louis Swarts, "but I do feel more qualified than practically any of the producers in knowing what has likely possibilities and what has not." The box office bore out MacDonald's worst fears. Business, according to *Variety,* was "sad" in New York, "slow" in Chicago, and "sour" in Los Angeles.

Broadway Serenade presented MacDonald as a New York cabaret singer whose lightning success destroys her private life with Lew Ayres, a struggling composer of "serious" music. The canary gets her big break when producers Frank Morgan and Ian Hunter discover that her bright lyric soprano is pliant enough to deliver a swingy rendition of their showstopper, "High Flyin'." MGM, however, could not align MacDonald exclusively with American pop, since that would deprive moviegoers of the music they expected of her. Hence, an octet of chorus boys, each seated at a grand piano, declares in song that "once the public wanted *sim*ple things, / now they're aiming HIGH," and the centerpiece of her Broadway debut becomes "Un bel dì" from *Madama Butterfly.* MacDonald performs the aria in a spangled kimono while descending a forty-foot, steeply arched bridge. Her rendition prompted Grace Moore, who had sung the Puccini warhorse in *One Night of Love,* to comment tartly that the height of a bridge does not reflect the level of a performance. Moore's sour grapes notwithstanding, MacDonald's reading shines in its simplicity of line and honesty of expression.

Late in the production, Metro executives decided *Broadway Serenade* needed a stronger ending. They therefore hired the inventive dance director Busby Berkeley, formerly of Warner Bros., to concoct a spectacular finale worthier of MacDonald. With manic speed, Berkeley dreamed up a surreal fable whose implied subject was MacDonald's music and the forces threatening its survival. Staged as a dark Freudian psychodrama, this eight-minute sequence unfolds amid oddly angled staircases leading nowhere. It starts with MacDonald, dressed in a Greek-style robe and neoclassic wig, earnestly intoning a special arrangement of Tchaikovsky's setting of a poem by Goethe, "None But the Lonely Heart." Soon, however, MacDonald's voice comes under assault, first by a small army of masked jazz musicians playing syncopated riffs on bleating horns and rackety percussion, then by a horde of frenzied, gyrating jitterbugs, also in grotesque masks. Only when the boogie-woogie and jive all but smother MacDonald's crystalline melody does the macabre nightmare abruptly end. MacDonald, now in modern evening dress, stands atop a thirty-foot white marble pedestal and, to the accompaniment of a traditional symphonic orchestra and choir, brings her song to a majestic end—on E above high C.

Busby Berkeley brilliantly captured the paradox of Jeanette MacDonald's status as an American cultural icon in 1939. She was, according to the polls, the nation's most famous singer and its most popular female movie star. Her populism was imposing and far-reaching. Yet the swing craze—embodied by the big dance bands of Benny Goodman, Artie Shaw, Duke Ellington, and Count Basie—exerted an increasingly firm hold on the general populace, especially among the young. Berkeley himself went on to direct the wildly popular Judy Garland–Mickey Rooney let's-put-on-a-show-in-the-barnyard musicals.

Actor Lew Ayres, an amateur swing saxophonist in offscreen life, had an unexpected response while playing opposite MacDonald in *Broadway Serenade.* Fresh from his success in *Young Dr. Kildare,* Ayres was eager to work with Jeanette in what he later referred to as "a so-called better picture": "I didn't quite have the level of stardom of a Gable, Allan Jones, or Nelson Eddy, and I thought it would be an opportunity for me." Ayres could not have foreseen that he'd become dizzy each time he heard MacDonald's voice on the playback system: "After a few days, I asked Pop Leonard whether the volume had to be so strong, and I was told that that's the way Miss MacDonald gets such perfect synchronization."

The next morning, Ayres found on his dressing table a small package wrapped in fancy paper. It was a carton of earplugs, courtesy of Jeanette.*

---

*MacDonald felt there was something phony about "lip-synching." She therefore always sang full voice while filming prerecorded musical numbers, and she kept the volume high in order to concentrate on how she looked without worrying about how she sounded to those present on the set. Her insistence on authenticity occasionally made the veins in her throat visible to the camera, but she would often conceal them with a hand or, in costume pictures, with a fan.

CHAPTER THIRTEEN

The Soprano Militant

I'm simply working hard these days with my body—but my heart
is only marking time—awaiting the end of this bloody mess
when I hope we'll have much more to live and love for.

MACDONALD, letter to Captain Gene
Raymond, Christmas 1942

JEANETTE AND GENE WERE RELAXING at Lake Arrowhead on
the fateful first day of September 1939 when Hitler invaded Poland.
Two days later, France and England declared war on Germany. Certain
that the United States would become entangled in the conflict, Gene
started flying lessons the very next week. "I want to be up in the air,
dishing it out, not down below getting it," he told Jeanette only half in
jest. Gene's foresight and patriotic fervor did little to stifle Jeanette's
dread of aviation. Days after getting his pilot's license, Gene was doing
lazy eights above Malibu. Suddenly the engine malfunctioned, and he
had to make a forced landing at Santa Monica Airport. His plane set
down with a spurt of thumps. Jeanette, astounded by Gene's imper-
turbability, began calling him "my air fiend."

Gene had recently lost out to newcomer William Holden in a bid for
the title role in Columbia's *Golden Boy*. Rather than accept the second-
rate scripts that kept coming his way, he decided to focus on his flying
and music. Jeanette had another idea: "Like most people in our profes-
sion, where comediennes want to play Lady Macbeth and tragediennes
envy Beatrice Lillie, we had a certain dissatisfaction with what we were
doing at the studios. . . . We talked at great length about [the husband-
wife team of] Alfred Lunt and Lynn Fontanne, because they seemed to

have worked out a combined career for themselves." Bringing her notion to Louis B. Mayer did little to advance the team of MacDonald and Raymond on-screen. Lunt and Fontanne were fine for playgoing sophisticates, Mayer insisted, but moviegoers would reject a romantic picture that starred an actual husband and wife. Better to stick with MacDonald and Eddy in costume operettas like *New Moon*, a project to which Jeanette soon committed herself with routine enthusiasm.

New Moon was a rehash of *Naughty Marietta*. MacDonald's best films relied on caring producers, like Lubitsch, Thalberg, and Stromberg, and savvy writers, like Anita Loos, Dorothy Parker, and Albert Hackett and Frances Goodrich. *New Moon* was produced by Robert Z. Leonard and written by Jacques Deval and Robert Arthur. The Sigmund Romberg score gave MacDonald two of her grandest screen songs, "One Kiss" and "Lover, Come Back to Me," as well as a memorable duet with Nelson Eddy, "Wanting You."* But as Marianne de Beaumanoir, the haughty New World heiress in love with her manservant (actually a revolutionary French duke incognito), MacDonald at times acted as if she was on automatic pilot. By locking her into formula, the writers denied her the high spirits that had made Marietta, Rose Marie, and Nina Maria so vivacious. Deadpan comedian Buster Keaton might have helped offset the story's creakiness with a cameo role, but his footage got scrapped. Pop Leonard knew he had disappointed Jeanette. After a preview in Inglewood, he told her sheepishly: "While I do not think it will ever be a great picture, it at least is not a bad one."

Most critics were indifferent. Yet Mayer's instinct, as usual, was on the money. *New Moon* did terrific business, bringing in profits of $211,000. The picture opened in forty first-run theaters and was held over for second weeks in many. Fans deluged the studio with oaths of gratitude for MacDonald's reunion with Eddy, since many had been as upset by Nelson's pairing with Ilona Massey in *Balalaika* (1939) as they were with Jeanette playing opposite Lew Ayres in *Broadway Serenade*. *New Moon* was also, as *Newsweek* put it, "a welcome antidote for the war jitters." The image of Nelson Eddy trudging through the Louisiana bayou while inciting "Stouthearted Men" to battle for freedom was American corn. But it struck just the right balance with

---

*After a three-year hiatus, MacDonald returned to RCA Victor in September 1939 and recorded "One Kiss" and "Lover, Come Back to Me" on the Red Seal label. She also put to disc that month "Depuis le jour" from Charpentier's *Louise*, "The Waltz Song" from Gounod's *Roméo et Juliette*, and "Il était un roi de Thulé" and "The Jewel Song" from Gounod's *Faust*. All show MacDonald at the top of her vocal form.

moviegoers still ambivalent about going to war once again to defend democracy overseas.

In the years preceding America's alliance with the Soviet Union to defeat Fascism, there was a dress rehearsal in the halls of Congress for the witch-hunts that would erupt in the aftermath of World War II. Martin Dies, chairman of the House Un-American Activities Committee, alleged a Communist infiltration of the movie industry. Reputations got smeared as public confusion grew. Somewhat unexpectedly, MacDonald stepped into the fracas when her next recital tour took her to Washington, D.C., in February 1940. She was the guest of honor at a Women's National Press Club luncheon, where a reporter asked her whether Hollywood was as infested with Communists as Representative Dies believed. She answered discreetly: "As at any focal point, there are some belligerents, but they are no more numerous than in any other community."

Later that day, the prominent lawyer Mabel Walker Willebrandt hosted a reception for MacDonald at the exclusive Sulgrave Club. Willebrandt, famous for defending women's property rights, was a former assistant attorney general who now served as counsel to MGM and the Screen Directors Guild. A high-profile Republican, she arranged for Jeanette to meet Supreme Court associate justices, New Deal leaders, and senators from both political parties—who all joined the crowd of four thousand that packed Constitution Hall the next night to hear MacDonald sing. Jeanette boasted afterward: "The Washington audience was very swank, but Mabel said I broke through their reserve immediately."

Variety now ranked MacDonald the third-biggest draw among female concert artists, just behind Lily Pons and Marian Anderson and well ahead of Kirsten Flagstad and Lotte Lehmann. Out of self-defense, she continued to steer clear of New York, but her second tour brought her to major cities, including Philadelphia, Chicago, San Francisco, and Los Angeles. Sometimes reviewers complained of a lack of "volume" and "emotional depth" in her voice. One critic detected a "strange tonal flurry." Chicago's Claudia Cassidy, soon to become MacDonald's greatest champion among critics, noted that the voice in person was "smaller, less secure, but more sensitive" than the voice on-screen. The Hollywood composer Hugh Martin heard her in his native Birmingham, Alabama, and reported that the size of her instrument was no problem, for she projected "like a million bucks in a terrible old barn of an auditorium."

Singing for celebrities almost never fazed MacDonald. But seated in the seventh row of Baltimore's Lyric Theater on March 1, 1940, was her lifelong idol, Rosa Ponselle. "Damned if I wasn't as nervous as a June bride," she joked in private after blurring the coloratura passages in "The Jewel Song" from *Faust.* Following the recital, Ponselle invited MacDonald for oyster stew and shoptalk. "While I must say she was very kind, it was still and all with reservations," Jeanette confessed.

In mid-May, the loquacious dummy Charlie McCarthy became one of the first female impersonators to "do" MacDonald in public when he mimicked her trill on his *Chase and Sanborn* radio show.* A few weeks later Germany invaded France, and Americans were suddenly less prone to laughter. MacDonald showed her concern by appearing on KFWB radio in Los Angeles to help Sam Goldwyn launch an industry drive in support of the Red Cross. Among the first to respond was Cary Grant, who donated half of his salary from *The Philadelphia Story,* while earmarking the rest for British relief.

When Noël Coward first saw the 1940 MacDonald-Eddy version of his 1929 operetta *Bitter Sweet,* he supposedly wept in horror. When he viewed it a second time six years later, he wrote in his diary: "It really is frightening that the minds of Hollywood could cheerfully perpetrate such a nauseating hotchpotch of vulgarity, false values, seedy dialogue, stale sentiment, vile performance and abominable direction." MacDonald's "insane coquetting" and Eddy's "triumphant lack of acting ability" made Coward liken the experience to "watching an affair between a mad rocking-horse and a rawhide suitcase."

Bitter Sweet started badly when, on May 5, MacDonald's forty-nine-year-old cinematographer, Oliver Marsh, suffered a fatal heart attack while making color tests. The film's producer, Victor Saville, was a big and ruddy transplant from England who was thought to be attuned to the Coward original. But musicals were not Saville's strength. Throughout the shoot he had unproductive tiffs with Woody Van Dyke, who directed. Just weeks before the movie's release, Saville forced a disastrous change in story construction. As filmed, the picture adhered to the stage operetta: it began with a prologue in which the elderly MacDonald is asked to divulge her bittersweet tale of love and

---

*In the postwar decades MacDonald was often the object of camp send-ups. The drag comedian Charles Pierce kept audiences rolling in the aisles each time he lip-synched MacDonald's "San Francisco" while dangling from a *Maytime*-like swing and exposing his bloomers beneath a huge hoop skirt.

loss in order to assist a pair of confused young lovers. On the basis of a few responses from a preview audience, Saville decided this frame-and-flashback device would strike moviegoers as too reminiscent of *Maytime* (whose 1937 story was probably inspired by *Bitter Sweet*). He therefore cut the prologue and shot a new epilogue. As a result, *Bitter Sweet* begins by plunging us into MacDonald and Eddy's tender farewell duet, "I'll See You Again," without sufficient character buildup to be convincing. At the film's close, MacDonald stands at an open window and reprises the melody with the recently deceased Eddy, whose ghostlike head floats among midnight clouds. Photographed in sallow yellow, the effect is more ghoulish than transcendent and is light-years away from the mystic reunion of *Maytime*.

Viewers who remembered the intimate charm of Coward's 1929 original were appalled. Many accused MGM of slaughtering delicate sentiment on the altar of gross extravagance. Some felt MacDonald looked too old to play Sari, the English maiden who escapes a planned marriage and runs off to Vienna with her music teacher. Pamela Randall, who performed the lively "Ladies of the Town" with Jeanette, recalled that the star was "not particularly happy having two singers much younger than she at her sides." At thirty-seven, MacDonald was the same age as Peggy Wood when she originated the role on the London stage. But a Technicolor movie camera is less obliging than a proscenium arch for creating illusions of youth. When Saville killed the prologue, he denied MacDonald a flattering on-screen contrast with her "aged" self. Equally damaging was the story's focus on the everyday woes of penniless newlyweds, the image of Jeanette as a sweet, impoverished housewife too unnatural for MacDonald and all but her most devoted fans.*

Still, "Zigeuner" makes *Bitter Sweet* well worth watching. A wild gypsy opéra-ballet designed entirely in tones of eggshell and copper, this tour de force of Technicolor understatement brought the film an Oscar nomination for Color Cinematography. Adrian dressed MacDonald in an extravagant Russian "peasant" gown topped with rust-colored beads. Busby Berkeley supervised but went uncredited. His

---

*Here's a disgruntled fan's point of view, addressed to MGM on February 23, 1941, by Mrs. Helen Newby of Sewickley, Pennsylvania: "Gentlemen:—Having seen *Bitter Sweet*, I feel I must protest and request. It is neither big enough nor fine enough for Nelson Eddy and Jeanette MacDonald. Can you not give them to us in pictures equaling in beauty and charm their magnificent *Naughty Marietta*? People everywhere seeming not to get enough of it [*Marietta*]. We, having seen it ten times, would gladly double that number."

complicated boom shots took up so much rehearsal time that Berkeley pushed the production over budget. He also wore out MacDonald: "I had to move down an incline, never watching where I put my feet, stopping at intervals for the camera to catch up with me . . . not stumbling or tripping—it was quite a steep slope—never getting out of focus with the camera, and singing all the while as though I had nothing else on my mind." Even after Berkeley put blocks on the incline to guide her, MacDonald repeatedly missed them. On September 9, with one day left to finish the sequence, she phoned in sick, alleging "nervous indigestion."

MacDonald started her next recital tour with egg on her face, but not on account of her singing. It was November 1940, and FDR had just won his third term as president in a close popular vote. During the campaign, MacDonald had kept her support of liberal Republican Wendell Willkie private. "I sing for Democrats and Republicans, black and white, everyone, and I just can't talk politics," she told reporters when she arrived for her concert in Willkie's native Indiana. Still, her personal views got the best of her, and she added impulsively: "There is one thing I will say, though. I think you Hoosiers should be chastized for not upholding Indiana's favorite son." The rebuke was poorly timed. Several journalists enlightened her that just hours earlier the photo-finish Indiana count had been revised in Willkie's favor.

The horrors which the Nazis were now inflicting on Europe plunged MacDonald into grief. "France, at least the France we knew, will have to be just a fond memory," she said. "England, too. I don't think they will ever be the same, at least not in our lifetime." Her sorrow did not, however, cause the soprano to follow World War I precedents and remove lieder by Robert Schumann and Hugo Wolf from her recital programs. "Many things German are too fine to give up in spite of the way we feel about Hitler," she explained without apology.

This new tour took her to Havana, where MacDonald was careful to avoid diplomatic blunders. Germany now banned U.S. films from areas under its control, and Latin America was a crucial overseas market for Hollywood. "De política nada, señores; soy artista" ("No politics, gentlemen; I'm a performer"), she told the Cuban press after arriving, airsick, on a Pan Am clipper from Miami. When she mounted the stage of the Teatro auditorium, she announced she was polishing her Spanish with an eye to a recital tour throughout South America, a plan that delighted the Cubanos.

In December, New Yorkers finally got to hear MacDonald live, but not in Manhattan. Her performance at the Westchester County Center in White Plains drew a crowd of forty-seven hundred in spite of an early snow. Seconds before her first encore, Big Apple admirers seated in the rear became fed up with concert-hall niceties and stampeded forward to revere their pink-chiffoned idol from the edge of the stage. Few New York City papers covered the frenzied event. The *New York World-Telegram* commended her "often engaging readings" and spoke well of her tone and feeling in "The Jewel Song" from *Faust.* The reviewer also hinted that the music establishment's "frozen silence" may well translate into "a still higher form of flattery."

Two days earlier, Jeanette had donned a chinchilla cape—the fur of choice for 1940—and attended opening night at the newly refurbished Metropolitan Opera. Everything shouted a break with the past. The posh Diamond Horseshoe was for the first time filled with paying subscribers, not hereditary box-holders. At the center of the Grand Tier stood a new booth designed for experimental television as well as radio broadcasts. On stage, in Verdi's *Un ballo in maschera,* soprano Zinka Milanov, from Yugoslavia, and tenor Jussi Bjoerling, from Sweden, gave glorious proof of the Met's commitment to a new generation of opera singers.

As always when she entered this great house, MacDonald regretted that the excitement she generated there was strictly offstage and between acts.

In early 1941, MGM finally gave MacDonald a reprieve from operetta with *Smilin' Through,* a classic tearjerker filmed twice before, with Norma Talmadge in 1922 and Norma Shearer in 1932. MacDonald's version would boast Technicolor and nostalgic song revivals from the era of the Great War. Frank Borzage, the studio's master sentimentalist, was assigned to direct. The writer Donald Ogden Stewart, who recalled injecting human "truth" into the "unreal schmaltz" of the 1932 screenplay, also worked on the remake. A budget of $1.1 million assured *Smilin' Through* the gloss and polish of MGM's most prestigious nonmusicals.

Jimmy Stewart was announced as MacDonald's featured male lead. But when Stewart enlisted in the army, Jeanette pressured Mayer into giving the role to Gene Raymond, who by now had returned to pictures and had just finished shooting Alfred Hitchcock's *Mr. and Mrs. Smith* at RKO. The decision to put Gene in *Smilin' Through* was of considerable import, since none of Hollywood's other screen-star spouses—Gable and Lombard, Taylor and Stanwyck, Joan Fontaine and Brian Aherne—had ever played opposite each other. MacDonald acknowledged the potential for doing harm to her offscreen marital relationship: "Any actor or actress is selfish, instinctively selfish. We have to be. We sell *ourselves.* And while we are actively engaged in the business of this high-pressure, personal salesmanship, which is when we are facing those cameras, we are little egos rampant, let's face it. So we are liable to see a little bit of the unnice side of the other fellow. . . . At home, [Gene and I] have so few differences. . . . To risk finding incompatibility in that almost perfect pattern of compatibility [is] chancy stuff."

Smilin' Through called upon Gene and Jeanette to take on difficult dual characters. In her most demanding part since *The Firefly,* MacDonald played Moonyean, a mid-nineteenth-century English bride shot to death at her wedding by a jilted lover (Gene), and Kathleen, Moonyean's twentieth-century niece, who falls in love with the murderer's son (Gene, again) during World War I. Brian Aherne, Hollywood's ideal of a well-mannered Britisher, got costar billing as the grieving fiancé to whom Moonyean's spirit keeps smilin' through o'er the years. Jane Cowl, the stage actress who cowrote and starred in *Smilin' Through* on Broadway in 1919, coached Jeanette and Gene. For their intimate scenes, Borzage kept his instructions brief. "I'm just the 'forgotten man' when it comes to telling you two how to make love," he impishly told the pair. MacDonald agreed: "You can believe love scenes when you see a husband and wife who are in love, making love. The thrill is not manufactured. The glamour is not gelatin. The director does not have to resort to emotional hypodermics."

When the movie previewed, Nicholas Schenck became jittery over one of Gene's best moments. It showed him returned from war, maimed, and falling down the church steps in a desperate attempt to prove he can walk. Jeanette had been struck by the realism Gene brought to the scene, in which he had to cry: "He didn't need any phony stimuli, either, neither glycerin, soft music, nor 'mental suggestion.' He *really* cried. And he made me cry, too." Schenck, however, felt that such a graphic portrayal of a ravaged soldier would be perceived by many as antiwar propaganda, damaging the film's commercial value. To avoid controversy, the president of Loew's, Inc., made a rare order to cut the footage. "I didn't see eye to eye with him, but it was his picture," Gene later stated.

Schenck was probably right. Public opinion was shifting slowly in favor of military intervention abroad. American audiences flocked to see heroic Gary Cooper take up arms in Warner Bros.' *Sergeant York*. But they did not rush to *Smilin' Through*. MacDonald attributed the puny box office to people's reluctance "to face the kind of reality the film portrayed." It didn't help that the movie premiered in Manhattan just three days before Pearl Harbor. The reviews were mainly luke-warm. Many critics scoffed at the picture's full-bodied sentiment and patronized it as a "woman's film." Most refused to take MacDonald seriously as a straight actress, although her performance was heartfelt, her gift for projecting empathy perhaps never more palpable. One male viewer in England, a middle-aged bricklayer, admitted to watching *Smilin' Through* several times over: "Although I saw it during war time, it made me forget war, and lifted my thoughts to higher levels; this was a clean, decent, and elevating film, and . . . sentimentally, yes, upholding that most beautiful of all things, Love."

The tepid American response to *Smilin' Through* caused Jeanette and Gene to give up hope of becoming the movies' Lunt and Fontanne. Around this time, rumors were circulating of marital trouble at Twin Gables. One Sunday Jeanette was sitting on Gene's bed waiting for him to exit the shower. Suddenly Walter Winchell barked from the radio that Mrs. Raymond was on her way to Reno for "you know what." "Did you hear that?" Jeanette shouted. Gene turned off the water. "I'd like to bust him on the jaw," he growled. Jeanette, too, was annoyed. But as her fourth wedding anniversary approached, she was satisfied with the way she and Gene handled malicious gossip. They stuck to two simple rules. When apart, never believe anything said or written about the other until you can speak about it person to person. When together, always kiss before going to bed—no matter how tense the sit-uation. Their most carefree moments away from the rumor mills now took place at Temecula, an out-of-the-way spot in California's River-side County, where they owned a hundred acres of ranch land.

Earlier that year, the Raymonds had come up with the idea of "date leaves" for homesick servicemen. Every other Sunday afternoon, ten sailors and soldiers from nearby camps would be whisked by station wagon to Twin Gables, where coeds from USC and UCLA awaited. They swam, danced the rumba poolside, and chowed down on a chicken barbecue featuring Jeanette's famous baked beans. With Gene at the piano, MacDonald would sing "The Star-spangled Banner" and then lead a sing-along. Jeanette urged other celebrities to open their homes for parties like these. Harold Lloyd and Constance Bennett were among the first to follow suit.

Through much of 1941, the motto of draftees was: Gonna serve my year, then get the hell outta here! To boost army morale, Gene and his brother Bob, who had both enlisted in the air force, cowrote a servicemen's show to be staged at Fort Ord. After six weeks of preparation, *Gold Brickers of 1941* was scheduled for a dress rehearsal on the evening of December 7. By late afternoon, the cast's one hundred soldiers had all been sent to sites along the California coast to guard against enemy airplanes. "I have always thought," Gene said facetiously, "that the only reason the Japs attacked Pearl Harbor was to prevent me from making *Gold Brickers of 1941* a reality!!"

The Hawaiian devastation that left 2,280 dead and brought the United States into the war galvanized Californians, who had every reason to fear a Pacific bombardment. At Long Beach Municipal Auditorium, Governor Culbert Olson called on all citizens to avenge the Pearl Harbor military martyrs, many of whose families were seated in the hall. As a soldier, sailor, flier, and marine placed wreaths at the foot of a huge white cross, MacDonald appeared from the wings in a black dress and black veiled hat. Moving to stage center, she intoned the Bach-Gounod "Ave Maria." At the climax to this solemn service, a curtain opened on a magnificent American flag. Standing before it were the Bob Mitchell Choir Boys and, in front of them, MacDonald, who led the assembly in the national anthem. "That's when everyone got a lump in his throat and pledged to himself that America must go on," one observer remarked.

Gene left for active duty in the Army Air Force on Friday, March 13—once again a lucky date by Jeanette's reckoning. His departing words were, "I'll keep 'em flying, you keep 'em singing." Throughout the war, Gene carried Jeanette's gift of a four-leaf clover wrapped in cellophane.

Hours after their parting, Jeanette wrote her first letter to Gene:

Friday March 13—1942
(your lucky number)

My Sweetheart,

This is simply to tell you once more—I love you! As if you didn't already know—and all the love in my heart and body is with you every minute! Naturally, I shall expect you to take good care of it and remember you're "next to the best" cause even in war you can't get rid of me.

I have a very secure feeling that you're coming back to me all ready to continue with our plans—they're too good to give up—so I'll never stop thinking of them.

Think of all the songs I've sung to the world and what they mean. And now, if I try, I couldn't sing them to you—not with my voice; but with my heart, yes! Maybe they were really meant just for us anyway.

And now, I want you to promise that occasionally you'll write me a silly, sentimental letter and pretend we're just as adolescent as we were 6 or 7 years ago—which I guess we really are—Squirt Face! I hope you will put this little gadget on your key chain [a heart-shaped locket with her picture] so that if "going" ever gets difficult "my heart" will be there to offer you whatever you need of me!

That's all for now, dearest—the rest is all "shut up inside," where even you can't see. A girl 'as gotta have a coupla secrets—don't you know!!

Mrs. "Hunky"

The Iron Butterfly had little patience for self-pity. "It's high time for wives to stop being the Little Woman and be women," she told the press. "Women's place is in the world. . . . Men must fight and women must *work*. There is no time for . . . useless little feminine gestures in this world today." In a letter to one of her daughter's young female fans, Anna MacDonald wrote: "Yes, Jeanette and all of us miss Gene very much, but she has been too busy to sit and mourn."

A few days after Gene left home, MacDonald gave a series of concerts to benefit the American Women's Voluntary Services, of which she was a California state director. In April, Lieutenant Ronald Reagan phoned from Fort Mason to ask that she sing "The Star-spangled Banner" at an "I Am an American" Day observance scheduled for May 17 at the San Francisco Dog Racing Track. MacDonald exceeded the lieutenant's hopes by offering to do an entire program. The future U.S. president later recalled that while Jeanette's music was "of somewhat classical tone," the boys heading for the South Pacific "loved it": "She finally ran out of material, but they were whistling and cheering, and wanted more. In desperation she said, 'I know only one more song that I can sing. It happens to be my favorite hymn.' She started singing 'The Battle Hymn of the Republic'—and then a strange and wonderful thing happened. All over the vast infield men started coming to their feet and, when she finished, seventeen thousand soldiers were standing, singing with her." It was a virtual replay of MacDonald's exhilarating close to *San Francisco*, yet this time the emotions weren't make-believe.

Like many other stars, MacDonald entertained tirelessly in army camps and hospitals. But she was the only celebrity licensed by the

USO to stage an entire solo show. In the torrid summer of 1942, Jeanette made a five-week tour, traveling through blistering heat by bus, car, and jeep, often arriving at stops with barely enough time for a warm-up arpeggio. "Just give me a sound truck and something to stand on," she told the USO. "I'll sing in a field if necessary. I don't want a big stage and fancy lighting effects. I only want to sing for as many boys as want to hear me." Although she dripped sweat and smacked mosquitoes along with everyone, MacDonald dressed for the troops with the same high elegance she displayed in formal recital halls, convinced that GIs deserved no less.

The *New Yorker* had described MacDonald in *Smilin' Through* as a "militant diva," noting that "there is something of the top sergeant in her proud bearing and certainly no artiste today could carry a flag with more style." Yet for hundreds of thousands of young servicemen, her live renditions of "Lover, Come Back to Me" and "Johnny Doughboy Found a Rose in Ireland" made Jeanette a comforting symbol of tender romance. "I'm going to be sentimental for a week," a soldier wrote to his mother after one of her camp shows. Journalists nicknamed MacDonald "The Star-spangled Singer." Many GIs called her "the Army's Best Sweetheart."

While Lana Turner and Dorothy Lamour sold kisses for war bonds, and Bette Davis got Hedy Lamarr to scrub dishes at the Hollywood Canteen, MacDonald hawked songs for the Army Emergency Relief Fund. In September 1942, she began a fifteen-city recital tour to benefit the AER. In addition to donating her earnings, she paid all her own travel expenses. But on opening night in Oklahoma City, MacDonald hatched an idea for raising still more money. Why not auction off the encores? "You give to the Relief Fund," she told the audience, "and I'll sing as long as my throat holds out." In each city, top bidders deposited their money into the caps of roving soldiers who piled the loot at the singer's feet. Final bids usually ranged from fifty dollars to a thousand. When a young girl in Indianapolis offered one dollar for "Ah! Sweet Mystery of Life," MacDonald brought the child on stage and sang directly to her. In Charleston, where Jeanette's voice finally gave out after thirty-six songs, she auctioned her autograph. By the tour's end in Washington, D.C., she raised a total of $94,681.87, the largest cash contribution to come from the efforts of a single entertainer.

MacDonald now had pull with the War Department, and used it to get Emily Wentz released from her job at Douglas Aircraft. Emily had been living on the Coast with her mother since Jeanette's wedding, and, until the war, had worked part-time as a singing extra at Metro and as an assistant to Sylvia Grogg, MacDonald's secretary. Grogg was now about to retire, and MacDonald thought Emily, who was intelligent and quick, and had a knack for diplomacy, should become her new gal Friday. With Gene away, Jeanette also needed a companion. Emily, who now went by the simpler surname "West," soon took up residence at Twin Gables in an apartment above the garage. She would live there for the next two decades.

By May 1942, Gene had risen to the top of his cohort of new pilots at Bolling Field in Washington, D.C. He was then assigned to the 97th Bombardment Group in the European Theater of Operations, stationed in Polebrook, England. This was to be the first B-17 group to engage in precision bombing missions.

Before going overseas, Gene came home on a brief furlough. At the end of his stay, Jeanette stunned him by booking a seat for herself on his return flight to Washington: "Without dramamine—which hadn't been discovered yet—I'd be all shades of green, but whoever worried about such trifles when her husband was off to war?" Their farewell took place in Manhattan, where they dined and danced at the Plaza Hotel. That night, Jeanette gave Gene one half of a jagged-cut sterling silver coin on which was inscribed, "May the Lord watch between me and thee when we are absent one from the other." She kept the matching half.

MacDonald rarely wept. Yet she found it hard to control her feelings as she watched Gene's plane take off the next morning. "Looking around me at the other girls, I wondered if they would all cry themselves to sleep that night as I knew I would. I prayed with all my being for his safe return. But in the depths of my soul I hoped I might have his baby to remember him by in case something should happen to him." Jeanette, however, was not pregnant, and at age thirty-nine had little time left for childbearing. Years later she admitted: "I think I missed having children. That's the biggest order I never filled. It just wasn't in the cards, I guess. I think Gene and I might have given them something. But then we never know about that either, do we?"

Gene's letters from England came thick and fast. He wrote amusingly of his distress at having to ingest Spam and powdered eggs and his pining for old-fashioned American milk. On a brief leave in London, Gene hooked up with the film director William Wyler, now an army major. Two days later he detailed for Jeanette their star-studded night on the town:

Sept 10 1942

Dearest Bunk:

. . . That evening [we] went to see *The Doctor's Dilemma* by George Bernard Shaw, with Vivien Leigh. Though it is old and the plot is highly improbable, the whole thing was very entertaining, and the dialogue was the principal star in the cast. Leigh was good, but didn't think she had the power that the role required. Also, she seemed a little young. Bill Wyler and I went around backstage to see her, and she was quite charming. I don't think she quite realizes the whole broad picture of what is going on in the world today however. There, also, she seemed a little young. In passing, she asked me the somewhat incredible question: "How often do they let you go back home on leave?" I thought she was being amusing at first, but soon found out that she wasn't kidding! I soon enlightened her on the score. She said Larry [Laurence Olivier] her husband is flying in the Fleet Air Arm, and was expecting a two week leave and they were going on a holiday somewhere together—lucky devils!! She's quitting the show for two weeks to be with him while someone else takes her place, then resumes after the holiday is over. Pretty soft!!

Afterwards we walked to The Savoy Grill where, it seems, all THE theatrical people assemble. . . . I don't know if you remember [*The Cat and the Fiddle*'s coscreenwriter] Sam Spewack from Hollywood. I knew him years ago when I did a show with him called *The War Song* with George Jessel. . . . After dining, Bill and I went on to a party which was being given for Commander John Ford, U.S. Navy. He is shooting all kinds of pictures of all the engagements he can and I understand he is doing a marvellous job. . . . He said he had heard some very fine things about me and my work in the field, and complimented me. Said also he was glad to see me so much thinner—"You now have some bone structure in your face!" says he. Well that's fine, and Ford knows what he's talking about. So you see, you were right about the diet!! If he had seen me about three weeks ago he'd probably have wanted to make a screen test of me immediately. Since then, fortunately I've put some of it back on again. . . .

The party broke up about 1:30 A.M. and I went home with Ford who was also staying at Claridges. I got up at Four forty-five A.M. in order to catch a very early train to get back on the post at eight A.M. when I was due. Missed one train, the other was late and I expected to be court-martialed when I finally did arrive at eleven!! But they didn't put me into the jug, so everything worked out okeh. . . .

Oh. That picture you sent me of yourself milking the cow [at Temecula] gave me a tremendous kick!! I've shown it to quite a few of my friends around here and they enjoyed it too. . . . I certainly would like to have the pleasure right now of swinging you back and forth in that hammock up at the Ranch, which I see you are naming Ray's Ranch. Very Cute.

I love you Bunko; I wish there was some possibility of seeing you again sometime in the near future. I have no hopes of it. So I guess we'll just have to go on wishing and waiting. I do miss you something fierce, and it's growing every day—this missing you. Only consolation is the knowledge that the longer we wait, the more happy that day when I arrive on the front step will be. It makes me feel good right now to even think about it!!

I've got to get out of this office and get to bed darling. I hope you don't mind this rambling letter. As Shaw, or somebody said: "I have not the time to write a short one!"

Good-night Sweetheart. I'll try to write again tomorrow.

All my love,
O[ld]. M[an]. R[aymond].

Jeanette, too, kept her letters light and newsy. A few days after Gene flew in the August raids over Dieppe, she described how White Lady, her Arabian mare, had taken on airs at the ranch: "She wouldn't come to [Blossom and me]—in fact ran away from us but after much persuasion [we] finally grabbed her and patted her—she will have nothing to do with the other horses—snob!" Only at the end of her letter did she turn serious: "I just finished a sweet book and in it the writer says, 'No one who is loved is ever alone.' That's good for us to remember, for maybe that's why I don't feel entirely forlorn and forsaken knowing that you love me. Yes, I get pretty lonesome for you, but I don't really ever feel alone, do you? Well, you shouldn't, for you are *never* alone! Remember that always, when you're tired or blue or homesick. Just remember you're loved."

In September, Gene cabled news of his promotion and asked Jeanette how it felt to be the wife of a captain. She wired back: IT FEELS TERRIFIC WONDERFUL MARVELOUS COLOSSAL STUPENDOUS EVEN GOOD CONGRATULATIONS AM I PROUD ALL MY LOVE JEANNETTE [*sic*] RAYMOND. In a later message, however, she let down her emotional guard: "While you think I've been swell and brave and understanding, don't overestimate me. I'm just as hysterical as any Mary Jones at certain prospects, and when those prospects are magnified by the job you find necessary, I keep asking myself (and you): *Why? Why? Why?*"

At the end of her AER tour, MacDonald spent time in New York City. One morning she received a letter from the actor Sam Jaffe, who was chairman of the Artists Front to Win the War. The Soviet Union had just withstood the Nazi onslaught at Stalingrad, and the Artists Front was calling for a speedy opening of a second U.S. military front in Europe to aid the Soviets. Jaffe was planning a rally the following

week at Carnegie Hall. Orson Welles was expected to introduce Charlie Chaplin, the organization's honorary chairman and that night's featured speaker. Also slated to speak were the writers Lillian Hellman,
Carl Van Doren, and I. F. Stone. Jaffe asked MacDonald to add her
name to a list of sponsors that included Lawrence Tibbett, Charles
Laughton, Fannie Hurst, Dorothy Parker, Fritz Reiner, Efrem Zimbal-
ist, Mischa Elman, Vincent Youmans, Bela Bartok, Aaron Copland,
Rudolf Serkin, and Duke Ellington. Jaffe said that MacDonald's accep-
tance would "give this meeting the importance it deserves," assuring
her that "Charles Chaplin and Orson Welles join me in making this
plea to you."

MacDonald did not mince words in her response, written on
Columbus Day:

> October 12, 1942
>
> Mr. Sam Jaffe
> Artists Front to Win the War
> 11 West 42nd Street
> New York City
>
> Dear Mr. Jaffe,
>
> In reply to your letter of October 9th, I most certainly agree that the
> cultural relations of all United Nations must be preserved, and as artists
> of the cultural world we should try to preserve this close relationship. But,
> don't you think it presumptuous for your group to assume the role of army
> leaders and war strategists? Certainly, it would be "musical disaster" for
> General Marshall or General Eisenhower to attempt to conduct
> Shostakovich's Seventh Symphony!
>
> My husband, Captain Gene Raymond, is at present on active duty in the
> Army Air Force, 97th Bombardment Group, in England. He participated in
> the brilliant raid over Dieppe and Rouen, and in all probability in the most
> recent raids over Lille. I am sure he would not want me to lend my
> sponsorship to your group, great personalities that you are, since at this
> distance from the actual theaters of war, you cannot possibly know, or even
> divine, what the problems or plans of our military leaders are. I honestly
> believe it is our duty, as civilians, to give our services and talents in
> whatever capacity we are most qualified for, then earnestly place our
> confidence in the men so capably trained to lead our soldiers to war. Let us
> reassure them of our faith and not try to force them to accept our judgment
> in matters we know little or nothing about. Wouldn't it be wiser not to be
> back-seat drivers?
>
> For Mr. Chaplin's genius as an entertainer, I have such profound respect
> that I have not given up the hope that he will find it in his heart to go to
> England, or even Russia, where he could bring joy and the comfort of

laughter to soldiers returning, half-crazed and exhausted from "under fire." Oh, what "power to save" lies within his grasp!

As for Mr. Welles—I hope he will find it in his conscience to join our armed forces overseas. There he can actively participate in the great second front he so patriotically advocates, and may God's blessings go with him.

Most sincerely,
Jeanette MacDonald

Feeling she had done the right thing, MacDonald sent Gene a copy of her answer. At Carnegie Hall that Friday, Chaplin was reported by the *New York Times* to have hailed the Russian people as "comrades," thus adding to the public's growing perception of his support for Communism.

At the time of Pearl Harbor, MacDonald had been filming her eighth and final picture with Nelson Eddy, *I Married an Angel*. When Mayer shelved this project eight years earlier, Rodgers and Hart reworked their material for Broadway. The result was an enchanting musical that opened in 1938 and starred the dancer Vera Zorina and the baritone Dennis King (Jeanette's costar in *The Vagabond King*). Mayer then bought back the rights and had Hunt Stromberg develop the property once again for MacDonald and Eddy. "This was probably the only time that . . . anybody got paid three times for one subject matter," Richard Rodgers quipped. The new version had MacDonald take on multiple guises. She starts out as a mousy stenographer secretly in love with her playboy boss. She then becomes a winged angel who descends to earth in response to the playboy's mock-serious call for a squeaky-clean mate. In later episodes she's a sophisticated vamp, whose unchaste adventures restore the failing fortunes of her husband's bank.

I Married an Angel was Hunt Stromberg's swan song for MGM. After sixteen years with the studio, he was about to set up an independent movie company at United Artists. Stromberg wanted his final Metro feature to equal in lavishness *The Great Ziegfeld* and *Marie Antoinette*, his most grandiose efforts. Budgeted at nearly $1.5 million, *I Married an Angel* was the costliest MGM production of 1941–42. Even before a foot of film was shot, Stromberg predicted that this musical fantasy would be "one of the greatest pictures of the year."

To no one's surprise, the censors again found fault with the screenplay's "sex suggestiveness." They warned against "any attempt to parallel the loss of the [angel's] wings with the loss of your heroine's virginity." They were also on edge about MacDonald's transformation from angel to "streamlined siren" in the second half. Under pressure from Mayer to keep the story clean, Anita Loos hit on the idea of turning much of the plot into an extended dream sequence. This device allowed Eddy, the roué banker, to awake and realize he must ally himself with Virtue, as embodied by MacDonald's prim stenographer in the "real-life" story that frames the dream. Stromberg could thus assure Production Code officials that "if any story *ever* glorified chastity, and made it appear attractive, it is *this* tale."

George Cukor was supposed to have directed *I Married an Angel*. According to Bob Wright, Cukor "loved the material, the idea, the script, and the score," but when he demanded eight weeks for preparation, the front office carelessly shifted the assignment to Roy Del Ruth, who shot many scenes, and then to Woody Van Dyke, who completed the picture. "Stromberg, Jeanette, Nelson, and Anita Loos did *not* want Van Dyke to direct," Wright emphasized. "*I Married an Angel* was meant to be a sophisticated, advanced, subtle film. Anita Loos had Freud and Surrealism in mind. She was a bright dame, and Cukor would have understood that. Woody's sophistication—as with Myrna Loy and William Powell—was of a different kind." MacDonald and Eddy quickly "turned sour over the Cukor affair," Wright continued. "They felt they weren't being protected as they had been."

Van Dyke was under strain. Recently diagnosed with heart failure, he refused to lighten his workload. For months he had been juggling film duties with his command of the 22nd Battalion Marine Corps Reserves. When assistant director George Sidney showed him sketches for *I Married an Angel*'s musical numbers, Woody closed the portfolio without even a glance at the drawings. "Kid," he told Sidney, "I've used up all my own ideas on this picture, you'll have to use yours." One of Woody's ideas seemed so lame to Wright and Forrest that it prompted them to pack their bags and leave MGM: "The Monday after Pearl Harbor, we were rounding the commissary and Van Dyke came over to us and said, 'Boys, I've been thinking about our movie. When the harpists get there and do that Debussy thing [Metro had bought the rights to "Clair de lune"], I'm going to have billows of smoke pouring out nonstop. *That* would be fantasy, wouldn't it?'" For better or worse, Van Dyke's smoke—along with Debussy—wound up on the cutting-room floor.

MacDonald, who said she "hated" making *I Married an Angel*, called the film "a credit to nobody." Most reviewers agreed. Ed Sullivan ran a postmortem in his gossip column: "The critics really walloped Jeanette MacDonald and Nelson Eddy in *I Married an Angel*.

Did you read Bosley Crowther's summation?: 'The only tolerable part of the picture is when Mr. Eddy gets bored by Miss MacDonald's charm.'" At New York's Capitol Theater, the film had the misfortune of being paired with *New Soldiers Are Tough,* a gritty documentary on the training of combat troops in Allied countries. Metro advertised the film as "Something Different!" Yet wartime moviegoers failed to be stirred by a musical love match set, as the opening title reads, in "Budapest in the gay days not so long ago."

The wonder is that *I Married an Angel* remains a sophisticated, sparkling, and often ingenious social satire. While affectionately looking backward at film operettas with European settings (and above all Rodgers and Hart's own *Love Me Tonight*), it also points to the great Rodgers and Hammerstein musicals of the 1940s and 1950s that integrated songs, dialogue, and dance. Both *Love Me Tonight* and *I Married an Angel* are the cinematic forebears of *Oklahoma!* and *Carousel,* and all are united by Richard Rodgers's great music. Some may object to Stothart's reworking of the original score of *I Married an Angel,* tossing in everything from Bizet and Gounod to "Aloha Oe" and boogie-woogie. Still, Wright and Forrest's adroit additions to Hart's lyrics are wickedly droll.* The uncredited art direction of Vincente Minnelli offers a witty and daring mix of surrealism and expressionism. Nelson Eddy turns in his smoothest performance ever. And MacDonald gives a bravura show, with her spicy sophisticate doing heavy battle with her high-minded angel.

If the film is a wry allegory on MacDonald's star image, pitting her precensorship naughtiness against her post-Code correctness, in 1942 almost nobody got the joke. If they did, they didn't care. A box-office fiasco, *I Married an Angel* was quickly disavowed by Richard Rodgers,

---

*For the nightclub scene in which MacDonald plays the vamp and "apologizes" to the socialites she previously insulted, Wright and Forrest elaborated on the Rodgers-Hart number "A Twinkle in Your Eye" and wrote a mix of normal and rhymed-and-rhythmic dialogue for MacDonald. An excerpt:

BRIGITTA [*spoken, to the obese Mrs. Gabby*]:	Mrs. Gabby, how perfectly en*chan*ting to see you again.
MRS. GABBY [*indignant*]:	Well, that's certain to be an improvement over our last meeting, Countess!
BRIGITTA [*rhythmic*]:	When I implied your starboard side had gone *flab*by, Mrs. *Gab*by, I didn't mean you were *fat.* Not *that!* How could I?, when you have that *per*fect sufficiency of *tor*so the men a*dore* so this season. Uhhuh, Uhhuh. I thought you knew—I said it with a twinkle in my eye.

Anita Loos, and the stars themselves, who were eager to blot from memory what Eddy very mistakenly labeled "a horrible mess."

MGM's basic problem with MacDonald was financial. Though Metro had dominated the movie industry throughout the Depression, as of 1940 its annual profit margin began spiraling downward. High-cost, high-stakes pictures like MacDonald's only added fiscal risk. It simply was not worth MGM's while to remedy an older star's obsolescence when younger models could be promoted more cheaply. Greer Garson, Lana Turner, and Esther Williams earned smaller wages and ate up less overhead. In the year that saw the departure from Metro of Garbo, Shearer, and Crawford, Mayer reluctantly declined to pick up his option on MacDonald. An era of fabled leading ladies had come to a quiet end.

The Iron Butterfly chose to make her break amicably. Mayer was still wounded by her past assertiveness, which he took as a breach of trust. But Jeanette continued to bring out L. B.'s gallantry. With Schenck's blessing, Mayer expressed the hope of renewing their association at some future time. RKO, a studio then short on stars, immediately began to court MacDonald. Its executives, however, also found her too costly for serious consideration. Privately, Jeanette was fed up with studio politics. "These asses of movie magnates aren't worth the so-called gray-matter weight they possess," she confided with bitterness to Gene. Still, one year away from turning forty, MacDonald was not willing to abandon pictures for good, and she let it be known she was eager to read promising scripts. "I didn't dream there could be so many really bad ones," she soon lamented.

Nelson Eddy, seeing no future at Metro without MacDonald, bought out the remainder of his contract and soon signed with Universal for a successful Technicolor remake of *Phantom of the Opera,* costarring Susanna Foster and Claude Rains. MacDonald, who owed MGM one more film, stood by her commitment. Shot in half the time and at two-thirds the cost of *I Married an Angel, Cairo* was a clever spoof of wartime spy thrillers that found MacDonald as a former Hollywood operetta star turned nightclub singer in Egypt. Robert Young played a naive American reporter who mistakes her for the leader of a Nazi terrorist spy ring. When she sings a perfect high C—whose frequency opens a secret door to an ancient pyramid where the real Axis agents hide out—she deters the bombing of a U.S. warship and helps catch the villains. In the manner of Bob Hope–Bing Crosby "road" pictures, *Cairo* is filled with calculated asides, amusing double takes, and

Hollywood in-jokes. When Young asks MacDonald if she has ever been to San Francisco, she tosses back, "Yes, once, with Gable and Tracy, and the joint fell apart."

Cairo opened in movie houses two days before the U.S. invasion of North Africa, as British forces under General Bernard Montgomery were hastening Germany's retreat from Egypt. In the shadow of such epic events, the picture's modesty was almost beside the point. *Cairo* did not make money. Yet it did make a significant contribution to Hollywood history by pairing America's most famous soprano with its best-known black vocalist.

Ethel Waters, as MacDonald's constant sidekick, accepted with no resentment her clichéd role of a maid. (Lena Horne had also been under consideration.) One black commentator justly complained: "I can't imagine any white star of her magnitude that the movie moguls would have dared to offer the role Ethel played in *Cairo,* in support of Jeanette MacDonald." Waters's big number was a swing rendition of Harold Arlen and Yip Harburg's "Buds Won't Bud." Self-contained, it could easily be cut from prints sent to Southern theaters. But a vocal medley in an earlier sequence intermingles MacDonald's parlor songs and patriotic rousers with Waters's hot and growly version of "Waiting for the Robert E. Lee," which MacDonald gamely reprises. The sequence barely raised an eyebrow in 1942, but it did reflect a nascent impulse, promoted by the war, to embrace Negro culture as part of what America was all about.

Cairo brought MacDonald's nine-year reign as MGM's top musical star to an end. It also hinted at new comedic and lyrical directions her film career might have taken had Metro chosen to stick by her.

PART FOUR

Echoes of Sweet Song

CHAPTER FOURTEEN

Battles Operatic

When the final curtain rings down on her "Juliet" it will also
ring down on one of the greatest sagas of determination in
the history of the theater.

JIMMIE FIDLER, Hollywood columnist,
on MacDonald's opera debut

There was enormous pressure on us young Americans to be
measured against all those well-remembered foreign stars.

ROBERT MERRILL,
Metropolitan Opera baritone

WITH HER DEPARTURE FROM MGM, MacDonald resolved once
and for all to see her name on billboards outside the Metropolitan
Opera House. By 1942 she was already a presence within the Metropolitan's social and fund-raising orbit. That November she helped the
Metropolitan Opera Guild launch its annual membership campaign,
and she graced the cover of *Opera News*, the guild's magazine. A few
weeks later, on opening night of the new season, she stole all eyes while
entering the Thirty-ninth Street foyer on the arm of conductor André
Kostelanetz. Out of respect for America's fighting men, MacDonald
kept her apparel subdued, wearing a black velvet gown and an ermine
cape. On stage, Kostelanetz's wife, the coloratura Lily Pons, brought
Donizetti's *La Fille du régiment* to a surprise ending when she brandished the flag of Charles de Gaulle's Free French Forces and led the
company in a stirring rendition of "La Marseillaise."

Edward Johnson, the Met's general manager, asked MacDonald to meet with him in December. A native of Canada, this debonair and handsome ex-tenor was adept in the delicate art of caring for prima donnas. At their meeting, he told Jeanette how much he had liked *Rose Marie* and her scenes from Gounod's *Roméo et Juliette* in that film. He suggested she learn the entire opera for an eventual stage debut. Mac-Donald was flattered, but she made it clear she wanted to qualify for the Met on her vocal and dramatic abilities, not on her reputation as a motion-picture star. Johnson offered an unwelcome strategy. "Why not enroll in the Juilliard School?" he said. "They contribute $25,000 every year to our support—much needed I assure you—and each year, of course, we present one or more of their outstanding singers. It might be a subtle way of coming to us." Annoyed, Jeanette retorted: "Buying my debut is the one way I couldn't accept."

Johnson declined to commit to any course of action but advised MacDonald to start preparing *Roméo*. Meanwhile, he gallantly assured her, he would try to influence the board of directors in her favor. MacDonald later realized she had bungled a platinum opportunity: "Looking back, I realize exactly what I should have done in playing musical politics to achieve my aspirations. But I would have none of it then. I was going to sing at the Metropolitan, and I was going to get there in my own way, honestly, without payoffs in cash or kind to anybody. How wrong I was!"

Relations with the Met became more strained in mid-February. Charles L. Wagner, MacDonald's concert manager, let it be known through a United Press dispatch that she was studying the role of Juliette for a Metropolitan debut the following season. Days later Johnson refuted this statement in the *New York Times,* declaring "there [is] no contract yet." Johnson also asserted, with exquisite artfulness, that the Met would "always be interested in a potential box-office draw." Wagner soon revised his claim and reported, accurately, that MacDonald would tour Canada in *Roméo et Juliette* that spring and thereby "submit her qualifications to a public audition."

Before taking the plunge, Jeanette had one last Hollywood commitment to fill. The 1943 Academy Awards ceremony, the last to include a banquet, took place at the Ambassador Hotel on March 4. The night's theme was Hollywood Goes to War, and the affair opened with Mac-Donald singing two stanzas of the national anthem while Marine Private Tyrone Power and Army Private Alan Ladd unfurled a gigantic service flag with 27,277 stars. L. B. Mayer, Jeanette's dinner partner that evening, was never more proud of his former leading lady. Missing from the festivities was Woody Van Dyke, who a few weeks earlier had died at home in his sleep.

The next day MacDonald left for New York. Since December, she had spent each afternoon dissecting the Gounod score with Grace Newell. Now she needed specialists. Lucrezia Bori, a great Juliette from the 1920s, steered Jeanette to Léon Rothier, a Metropolitan bass and gifted coach. For two months Rothier instructed her in the dramatics of the role, imparting his memories of legendary Juliettes like Bori and Geraldine Farrar. He even managed to enhance MacDonald's considerable Gallic flair. Perhaps Rothier's strongest advice, however, was to encourage MacDonald to sing the part as if she were inventing it. Rothier had Giuseppe Bamboschek, Jeanette's former recital accompanist, drill her daily in the music.

MacDonald's newest East Coast champion was Constance Hope, a public relations executive. Hope was the daughter of the concert pianist Eugene Bernstein, and she numbered Lauritz Melchior, Grace Moore, Lily Pons, and Fritz Reiner among her celebrity clients. Hope and MacDonald were kindred spirits. "When [Jeanette] walked into the room," Hope said of their first encounter, "I was hers! Her beauty in person was even more dramatic than on the screen, with her flame-colored hair, opalescent skin, and sparkling blue-green eyes. Within one hour of conversation we were not star and counsel, but friends. Her knowledge, sincere interest, and determination to acquire all the necessary professional know-how that lay before her to make a successful operatic debut staggered me. . . . She could not, and would not, ever compromise." At Hope's urging, MacDonald studied the artistry of Alicia Markova, the British ballerina who was dancing Juliet in New York with the Ballet Theater. Hope rightly thought that Markova's lightness and purity of line would help Jeanette visualize traits she was aiming for in her operatic depiction of the maiden of Verona.

MacDonald's opera debut took place in Montreal at His Majesty's Theatre on the evening of Saturday, May 8, 1943. "Keep your fingers crossed," she slyly told the press when she arrived in the cosmopolitan city days earlier, not quite recovered from a cold. The house had been sold out for weeks. Most of her supporting cast were Metropolitan Opera regulars. "I knew I was vulnerable," MacDonald explained, "so

I welcomed the idea of being surrounded with a stellar cast. To be surrounded by second-raters would be no test at all." Her Roméo was Armand Tokatyan; Ezio Pinza sang Friar Laurence; Wilfred Pelletier conducted. Adrian designed her costumes.

The night of the performance, MacDonald's lingering ear congestion
made her tense. Nerves got to her in act 1, where she rushed the famous waltz aria and let some notes get caught in her throat. But in the
rest of the opera she sang tunefully and with confidence. Her balcony
love duet won much applause, and the marriage scene in Friar Laurence's cell prompted five curtain calls. MacDonald's Juliette radiated
so much girlish grace that some in the audience were led to feel, like
Shakespeare's young hero, that they "ne'er saw true beauty till this
night." Maestro Pelletier called MacDonald "perfect for the role" and
praised the "purity and tremendous charm" of her singing. When she
refused to take a solo bow, explaining she was just one of the company
and not the star, Pelletier was stunned: "It was a great experience and a
great lesson in modesty to all of us."

While Ezio Pinza injected noble grandeur into the production, he
stirred up memories of Maurice Chevalier behind the scenes. Pinza was
a noted Don Juan, on and off stage, and at their first rehearsal he cor-
nered MacDonald and virtually panted with lust. Jeanette just glared
and said, "Oh, cut it out!" By the time the curtain rose on their first
performance, Pinza no longer held to the notion that a movie star
could not seriously tread the boards of an opera house. MacDonald, he
had to admit, was a true musician.

The Canadian tour was a popular success. From Quebec City to
Toronto to Ottawa, MacDonald attracted many who had never attended an opera and whose frame of reference for Juliet was Norma
Shearer, not Lucrezia Bori. In Windsor, Ontario, where the production
took place in a hockey arena and pulled in large crowds from Detroit,
spectators sat on cushionless chairs and devoured hot dogs and cokes
during intermission. From his office at the Met, Edward Johnson followed reports of these festive happenings with great interest.

In Toronto, MacDonald received a cable from Mark Woods, president of RCA's Blue Network:

MISS JEANNETTE MCDONALD [sic]
ROYAL YORK HOTEL TOR

UNDERSTAND YOUR ROMEO AND JULIET A SENSATION IN
TORONTO AND OTHER CITIES WOULD YOU BE WILLING TO GIVE
PERFORMANCE AT METROPOLITAN OPERA HOUSE FOR BENEFIT

OF GREATER NEW YORK FUND THIS FUND NUMBER ONE NEW
YORK CHARITY AND HOSPITAL DRIVE AM SURE MISTER
JOHNSON WHO HEADS THEATER COMMITTEE WOULD BE
DELIGHTED WILL YOU PLEASE WIRE ME.

She replied the next day:

MARK WOODS
PRESIDENT, BLUE NETWORK CO., INC.
NEW YORK, NY

THANK YOU FOR YOUR NICE TELEGRAM INVITING ME TO SING
ROMEO AND JULIET AT METROPOLITAN FOR BENEFIT OF
GREATER NEW YORK FUND BUT REGRET MY CONCERT
COMMITMENTS WILL CARRY ME THROUGH TO END OF JUNE
AND STUDIO COMMITMENT BEGINS JULY WHICH PREVENTS MY
ACCEPTING YOUR KIND INVITATION HOWEVER IF IN THE
FUTURE I SHOULD EVER BECOME ASSOCIATED WITH THE
METROPOLITAN OPERA COMPANY I SHOULD BE HAPPY TO
CONTRIBUTE A PERFORMANCE TO YOUR MOST WORTHY CAUSE
KINDEST WISHES

MacDonald was stretching the truth. She had no major commitment in July. But this new backdoor invitation insulted her sense of worth as much as the suggestion of a Juilliard detour had. Was she lopping off her nose to spite her face? Yes, she later conceded, her clinging to principle was "one more crashing mistake."

The three-week Canadian tour, while a critical triumph, was a financial bust. Each of the eight performances cost $12,000, yet because of the relatively small seating capacities of most opera houses, there was nearly no booking where sellout ticket sales could have exceeded $9,000. Although MacDonald agreed in advance to forgo a weekly salary of $2,000, by tour's end the operating budget was so overrun that she herself had to finance the company's return to New York. The whole tour cost her $25,000—exactly the "donation" Johnson had implied would buy a Metropolitan debut via Juilliard.

Jeanette stayed philosophical: "I settled the bills, squared my shoulders, stuck out my chin—and added *Faust* to my opera repertoire."

A brief return to the lucrative world of movies fetched MacDonald $25,000 for three days of playing herself in Universal's *Follow the Boys*. This celebrity-packed tribute to the Hollywood Victory Committee featured Orson Welles, Dinah Shore, and the Andrew Sisters, among others. MacDonald performed "Beyond the Blue Horizon," staged outdoors with thousands of GIs hanging on her every note. She also sang "I'll See You in My Dreams" to a blinded young soldier in a hospital ward. No screen moment better captures the consoling, maternal quality of MacDonald's singing than her sweet rendition of this Gus Kahn–Isham Jones ballad.

Following Gene's return from England via Trinidad, he and Jeanette reunited for a few days in New York. Before turning in that first night, Gene chugged a full quart of "real" milk and eyed the empty bottle lovingly. "Darling," he teased, "if I ever leave you I think it will be for a cow!" The Army Air Force shortly ordered Gene to San Antonio for more training and then to Yuma, Arizona, where he instructed bombardier cadets and was soon promoted to major. Jeanette continued to sing for camps, canteens, and military hospitals. Their prolonged separations gradually strained the marriage. "He would be flying back to California just about the time I'd be headed for an engagement in New Orleans, or some such place," MacDonald recounted. "And on rare occasions when we'd manage a couple of days together, we laughingly pretended it was 'like a series of honeymoons,' but it wasn't. It was filled with frustration and anxiety."

Jeanette frequently complained of loneliness on the road, and Gene did his best to raise her spirits in his letters. "It naturally is not the most comfortable life you are leading," he wrote, "but look at any of the lives of any of the artistically accomplished people and you find hardship—in most cases much greater than yours. . . . —a life and lot which few have the opportunity or stamina to grasp, that you have. . . . You are proving yourself an Artist daily—and no one can take that from you." To Jeanette's inquiry about what he wanted for his thirty-fifth birthday, Gene replied mischievously: "You—on toast—will be quite sufficient."

A well-timed furlough in June 1944 enabled Gene to join Jeanette and celebrate their seventh wedding anniversary at Twin Gables. Over the years the Raymonds' social circle remained small, consistent, and loyal. For their anniversary dinner that June 17, the guests included Mary Pickford, Hedda Hopper, Lauritz Melchior, Ernst Lubitsch, and the writer-producer Edwin H. Knopf. Also present were Ann and Nelson Eddy, who scrawled in the guest book, "Many More Happies."

Later that summer, as the Allies liberated northern France and Gene trained dozens of American pilots, Jeanette went incommunicado to prepare Gounod's *Faust*. Constance Hope prodded her into asking

Lotte Lehmann, the German-born expatriate soprano, to coach her in the role of Marguerite. MacDonald could not imagine that the era's most illustrious singing actress would agree to work with her, but in mid-July Lehmann, who lived in Santa Barbara, began an intensive private tutorial, charging Jeanette twenty-five dollars a lesson.

Lehmann expected her new pupil to be, at most, a dilettante: "I was really curious how a glamorous movie star, certainly spoiled by the adoration of a limitless world, would be able to devote herself to another, a higher, level of art." Lehmann's encounter with MacDonald brought what she called "the surprise of my life." "There couldn't have been a more diligent, a more serious, a more pliable person than Jeanette," she said admiringly.

The two women became instant friends. Usually Jeanette drove up to Santa Barbara for lessons at Lehmann's ranch. Other times Lehmann traveled to Twin Gables, where Jeanette put Gene's bedroom, now unoccupied, at her teacher's disposal. The widow of a Viennese insurance executive, Lehmann supposedly had had an affair with Arturo Toscanini during their Salzburg collaboration on *Fidelio* in the 1930s. Yet MacDonald seemed to trigger in the great Lehmann the kind of schoolgirl crush Harlow had professed toward Jeanette eight years earlier. Beyond music, Jeanette and the fifty-six-year-old soprano shared a passion for dogs, outdoor sports, and privacy in their personal lives. Equally congenial were Emily Wentz and Lehmann's live-in companion, Frances Holden.

No one was more impressed by Lehmann's impact on MacDonald than Gene Raymond. "He is convinced that meeting you is the best thing that has happened to me in many years," Jeanette told Lotte a month after lessons began. Lehmann replied:

> . . . There is nothing that could give me more satisfaction than to think that I really help you to develop what is hidden in your soul: I cannot *make* you a great artist if you are not one with all your being. And you *are*: it is almost miraculous how quickly you are able to bring to life what has up till now only slumbered in your heart. You have always much too much been concerned about the technique of singing. And also the fear of "overdo" has held you back. Seeing what you are able to do after such a short time, I don't doubt that the possibilities are almost limitless for you, especially as a concert singer.

On her visits to Santa Barbara, MacDonald often took a bungalow at the secluded El Encanto Hotel, overlooking the Pacific. Minutes after she climbed into bed on the night of July 14, 1944, a prowler leaped from a closet and tried to smother her with a blanket: "I screamed and fought with him when he reached me. Then I felt a terrific blow as he struck me in the face. I continued to fight, and suddenly he turned and ran, when I managed to turn on a light." The attacker, caught by hotel security, was a fourteen-year-old bellboy on probation from reform school who claimed he was "looking for a souvenir." MacDonald didn't fall for his story, but she dropped charges after learning the boy was the sole support of his blind mother. Lehmann, jolted by the news, reproached herself for not having insisted that Jeanette stay at her ranch that night.

Six weeks later, MacDonald did a *Lux Radio Theatre* broadcast of *Maytime* with Nelson Eddy. When the show signed off, Lehmann scribbled a fan letter, her lapses in colloquial English perhaps a sign of the authenticity of her emotion:

> Dearest Jeanette,
>
> It sounded very beautifully. I was proud of you, as if I have made you!!! It was cleverly done, rather touching. Frances and I listened excitedly. Much love from us both to you and Miss Wentz.
>
> Always yours,
> Lotte

At her last lesson before the Chicago debut, MacDonald made some foolish mistakes. When she apologized to Lehmann for being "particularly stupid" and having "forgotten so much," her coach responded with typical warmth:

> 22.10.44
>
> Dearest Jeanette,
>
> . . . Don't blame yourself that you had forgotten something. My lord, who wouldn't??? It is also utterly unimportant if you really do everything we worked out. The main thing is that you got the *spirit* of it. And the freer you will be—the freer of my guidance so to speak—the more your own personality will come through. And is not this the most valuable achievement?
>
> If only we could have more time to work together really for some months—so that everything has become absolutely your own—but we never, never will have the time unfortunately.
>
> My heart is with you on your Tour—and especially in Chicago with your performance of Marguerite. I will be at least as nervous as you. Please, please, don't forget to be very, very simple in the beginning! The first entrance is so difficult—and so damned important. Please memorize that often. Don't make gestures—you easily do here—and it looks very

artificial. And don't forget to turn your face quicker to the audience. They want to see you. I can't blame them, by the way.

Good luck to you. Frances sends very warm regards—and I a lot of my sincere love.

Always yours,
Lotte

Fausto Cleva was the new artistic director of the fiscally ailing Chicago Opera Company. To promote ticket sales, he filled the artists' roster for 1944 with leading lights from the Metropolitan. Bidu Sayao sang *La traviata* and *Pelléas et Mélisande;* Zinka Milanov appeared in *Aïda;* Helen Traubel performed *Die Walküre;* Leonard Warren and Jan Peerce starred in *Rigoletto.* But it was MacDonald who made the really big stir at the Civic Opera House with her U.S. debut in *Roméo* on November 4 and her world debut in *Faust* eleven days later. This time she was in full command of her Juliette. "It takes real flexibility to negotiate the valse arietta of the opening act," wrote Felix Borowski, music critic for the *Chicago Sun,* "and the artist won an impressive victory over its difficulties." Claudia Cassidy, the demanding reviewer for the *Tribune,* spoke of "an exquisite performance."

Cleva, who conducted only *Faust,* mortified Jeanette when he told her she could not have a rehearsal with full orchestra. It seemed that the tenor Raoul Jobin would not reach Chicago until the afternoon of the performance, and since the company had already mounted *Faust* that season with an identical cast save MacDonald, Cleva, mindful of budget, felt a run-through with piano in his office would suffice. Mac-Donald turned paranoid. She was sure the Italian-born maestro wanted to show that a singer trained solely in America had no place in the operatic world. Relief came during the performance, when Cleva established what she called "a beautiful musical rapport": "All my resolve against the agonies of opera melted in a flash."

MacDonald's Marguerite, wrote Cassidy in the *Tribune,* was "beautifully sung with purity of line and tone, a good trill, and a Gallic inflection that understood Gounod's phrasing." Some listeners noted that at the end of "The Jewel Song" she managed to take no breath in the final trill, turn, and high B—an unusual feat long associated with the nineteenth-century diva Adelina Patti. Theatrically, Mac-Donald showed "something more than mere stage presence—a kind of intuition that makes an actor do the right thing at the right time," Cassidy continued. Many reviewers found her confrontation with Ezio Pinza's Méphistophélès in the act 4 cathedral scene especially grip-

ping. The evening's only shortcoming was the botched and needless effort to amplify MacDonald's voice in ensemble numbers. During the
garden quartet, a nest of microphones to the right of the stage picked
up Pinza, not MacDonald. "It's the first time I ever heard it as a bass
solo," Cassidy scoffed.

MacDonald mailed the Chicago reviews to Lehmann, who wrote
back jubilantly:

> I cannot tell you how I feel—proud and blissfully happy! . . . I think it is
> wonderful that the church scene got an ovation: it is easier to have success
> with the aria. And to have an [sic] applause after the trio in the prison is, I
> think, *absolutely unusual*. Dearest, dearest Jeanette: congratulations from
> the bottom of my heart!!!
>
> Keep on. Be convinced that you have the ability to make a wonderful
> career as an opera and concert singer. After years of making movies, a
> sincere artist will be tired of it. There are more satisfying ways of
> expressing oneself artistically. Certainly: the big money will always be
> in the movies. But what really is the advantage of making now so much
> money? You have to pay the dreadfully high taxes—and then what have
> you in the end??? Not as much money as you want to make—and the inner
> feeling: I wish I could be a singer of *only good* music, not only a beauty
> who sings and plays what she has to do. Am I not right—quite entre
> nous???

In a postscript, Lehmann hinted at how much she wanted MacDonald
to play her young rival in Richard Strauss's *Der Rosenkavalier:* "I shall
sing on February 23rd the Marschallin in the Met. [Maestro George]
Szell has changed one high tone which bothered me—in the trio. How
about the Sophie???? Good idea!!!"

MacDonald raced from Chicago to a new round of recitals. Her manager was no longer Charles Wagner, who had grown resentful of Constance Hope's influence and one day referred to her in MacDonald's
presence as a "pushy Jewess." Outraged, Jeanette fired him on the
spot, contending she could not keep anyone in her employ who de-
means another's race or religion. She replaced him with James A.
Davidson of the William Morris Agency.

On the road MacDonald learned that some members of the Metropolitan's conservative board of directors viewed her as an unwelcome
"Hollywood intrusion." When word came that Gaetano Merola, manager of the San Francisco Opera Company, was prepared to make her
an offer, Jeanette was elated. Here was a sign, she thought, that the
Met's bias might still be overcome. However, Merola's deal carried a

stipulation: MacDonald was to sing *Roméo et Juliette* with the company in Los Angeles but not in San Francisco. She demanded an explanation and got a stinging but forthright response: "We believe the [San Francisco] critics may be prejudiced against your background in Hollywood."

MacDonald now wanted a straight answer from Edward Johnson and the Met. "I do not wish to create the impression," her letter to Johnson read,

> that my career has been a series of achievements and applause. Indeed, I've had my share of disillusionments, heartbreaks, setbacks, and damning criticisms, but I've usually been able to find out the "why" and then set about the job of correction and improvement. I am appealing to you now, in the hope that you can supply the "why" in this present crisis—for my career has, of late years, been more than kind to me, and I do not wish to toss it about lightly.
>
> Indeed, I am in a quandary. Should I abandon my idealistic ambitions and continue to make the most of my practical career? Should I continue to turn down the flattering offers to appear in various operettas that are proposed almost weekly? Would it not be foolish for me to accept the numerous offers to sing "any opera of my choosing" in various key cities throughout this country, Mexico, and South America, without the dignity of the Metropolitan's recognition? I feel you are the only one in a position to give me an honest explanation and am, frankly, counting on your doing so.

The Met's general manager remained vague and guarded:

> . . . If external influences could have carried any weight upon our internal problems, it would have been the favorable reports received on your excellent work while on tour. As involved as are the difficulties at the Metropolitan, the decisions are always arrived at for technical reasons and never personal ones.
>
> Hoping to have the pleasure of seeing you on your return to New York, I beg to remain,
>
> Sincerely,
> Edward Johnson

In the end, Johnson seemed no more inclined to hire a movie star than he was to break the company's color barrier—and for the same reason: both risked offending his patrons' sensibilities. Johnson revived *Roméo et Juliette* the next season with twenty-year-old Patrice Munsel, a winner of the Metropolitan Radio Auditions of the Air. In a review, Irving Kolodin wrote: "Patrice Munsel is pretty and well-intentioned, but her other qualifications for this style are limited. Her Juliet had more assurance after a tremolo-ridden, joyless version of the waltz . . . but there was little to nourish the ear. . . . Gounod wrote for singers who lived in an aura of elegant and flawless vocalization."

The turn of events left Jeanette crushed. She had never fallen so short of a personal goal. If her defeat had resulted from her own limitations, she could have found comfort in the fact that she had tried her best. But it was clear to her that she was the target of cultural snobbery grounded in a foolish prejudice. Self-pity, as always, was not an option for MacDonald. As George Cukor once said, she was "too intelligent to let a few disappointments in her life affect her adversely. She was too sensible. She had guts." Yet as 1944 came to a close, the Iron Butterfly was angry and frustrated.

That Christmas, Gene helped soothe Jeanette's spirits with a gift of a silvery Skye terrier. They named him Misty.

Mike Todd's colorful stage production of *Up in Central Park* premiered on Broadway in late January 1945. The following week MacDonald recorded its Sigmund Romberg–Dorothy Fields songs for RCA in Manhattan. Her baritone on the album was the barely known Robert Merrill, a Constance Hope protégé who would soon embark on one of the great Metropolitan Opera careers.*

Merrill, nervous as a jackrabbit, was amazed when MacDonald switched places in the middle of the session to allow him a better view of conductor Robert Russell Bennett: "This lovely star, who was supposedly a holy terror, sensed my insecurity. . . . It was one of the kindest and most unprecedented gestures I have ever seen—and from a soprano!" The two MacDonald-Merrill duets, "Close as Pages in a Book" and "The Fireman's Bride," are touchstones of Broadway vocalism: the first soars operatically; the second jangles brashly, with Jeanette mixing in the robust chest tones of a "belter."

On the Sunday following President Roosevelt's death in mid-April 1945, MacDonald sang "Ave Maria" in a CBS radio tribute. Three weeks later, Germany surrendered to the Allies. The next day, MacDonald joined Frank Sinatra, Charles Boyer, Nelson Eddy, and the Mills Brothers in a V-E Day radio homage to the victorious forces.

---

*When Merrill went Hollywood in 1951 with the Paramount clunker *Aaron Slick from Punkin Crick,* Rudolf Bing, the Met's new general manager, briefly dismissed him from the company.

After her rendition of Edward Elgar's "Land of Hope and Glory," MacDonald spoke to the nation:

> Thank you, ladies and gentlemen. It's a pleasure to take part in the V-E Day observance here in Hollywood. I say "observance" because "celebration" is the wrong word. Yes, we rejoice in this day, but as our President has asked, let it be sober rejoicing. For there's much to be done before the world will know real peace. There's a war against another ruthless enemy to be won. There's a peace to be settled with justice and permanence. That great day will come if we all keep up the fight.
>
> And now I'd like to sing a song which—well, perhaps it doesn't express all the hopes we have in the future—but it comes close to the feeling most of our boys hold for the great day when they can come home for good. For them, there's—"*Beyond* the Blue Horizon."

As she did whenever she sang this trademark number during the war, Jeanette changed the final words to "*shining* sun" so as not to evoke the "*rising* sun" of the Japanese flag.

MacDonald continued her lessons with Lotte Lehmann. She now wanted to expand her recital repertoire and increase her skill in German lieder, Lehmann's great specialty. "When you hear my songs in German you will declare I am a native—Swede!" she warned Lotte. Jeanette often stopped by Ernst Lubitsch's house before tackling a Schumann, Brahms, or Strauss piece. If Ernst could make out her pronunciation of the German lyrics, she knew she was ready to start on the music. Lehmann had strong opinions about which songs suited her special pupil. She found "I Arise from Dreams of You" by the modern English composer Roger Quilter to be a "perfect" choice for MacDonald: "You have only to think of Gene and it will be just breathtaking." But when Jeanette proposed "Love's Philosophy," also by Quilter, Lehmann roared: "I think it is a rather dreadful cheap song—not worthy of you. *Please* don't sing it!" Trashy music was not, however, always verboten for Madam Lehmann. When Lotte suggested they work on "Charming Chloe" by Edward German, she confessed: "I sang it in Australia quite often and the public liked it tremendously. It is not very good; I mean, it is just a cheap little song. But one always has to have something like that on the program."

That summer MacDonald sang *Roméo* and *Faust* to overflow crowds at the Cincinnati Zoological Gardens Pavilion, with Cleva again conducting. Opera in the park brought new challenges, as Jeanette confided to Lotte:

There was at no time any attempt to rehearse the stage business—not a sign of a prop. When I asked the (so-called) stage director what the sets would look like, and where the benches, doors, etc. would be, it was as though I had committed a *faux pas*. The truth of the matter was that he didn't know himself, and it wasn't until the actual performance (before each act) that I was able to find out and look the situation over. I might add that I even took the liberty of placing the furniture for my own convenience. . . .

The church scene of *Faust* was an unholy mess, with the chorus picking up the wrong cue for the prayer, which meant that the orchestra and I were doing one thing and they were singing another. It was pretty ghastly, to say nothing of being very confusing to me. And, since they were singing so loud, I had to stop to be sure that I was with the orchestra. You know how difficult it is frequently to hear the orchestra. The prompter had left his box in order to play the organ back-stage, and the stage manager was in his place. He, in turn, knew no more about prompting than little Mausi [Lehmann's pet dog]. So, all in all, the effect must have been like a cat and dog fight. Ultimately, however, the chorus, realizing I had stopped singing, took their cue and stopped also. I then proceeded with the orchestra alone. At any rate, I won! . . .

Maestro Cleva has treated me very differently this time. Many of the members of the other operas [in the Cincinnati Zoo's summer series] were present, and I have been told by friends who were present that, as a whole, they did a pretty good job of knifing me, which, I am afraid, is prompted by a natural resentment and jealousy.

During intermission at the Cincinnati *Roméo et Juliette,* a note from someone in the audience reached MacDonald's dressing room. It read: "Won't you please sing 'Indian Love Call'?" MacDonald laughed at the irony. For all her striving to do "grand opera," she was destined to be associated forever with the semiclassical music from her movies. Even Lehmann conceded the point: "I am quite sure that Jeanette would have developed into a serious and successful *Lieder* singer if time would have allowed it. But alas, movie contracts had to be fulfilled— and perhaps it was right so: we have now simply more of her exquisite records—songs which nobody nowadays can sing as Jeanette."

On the balmy evening of August 9, 1945, a record-breaking crowd of twenty thousand flooded the Hollywood Bowl. It was one of the largest arenas ever to test MacDonald's infectious magic. Among the notables were California Governor Earl Warren, Army Air Force Major General Ralph Cousins, and Louis B. Mayer.

The program began with maestro Leopold Stokowski leading the Hollywood Bowl Symphony Orchestra in Franz Suppé's pulse-lifting *Light Cavalry Overture.* The guest artist then appeared, swathed in pink organza and looking bronzed and youthful. As she glided to the center of the huge outdoor stage, the ovation was as thunderous as it was heartfelt. Her selections, performed with no amplification, held few surprises: "Il était un roi de Thulé" from *Faust;* "The Waltz Song" from *Roméo et Juliette;* Delibes's "Les Filles de Cadiz"; Herbert's "Summer Serenade" from *Sweethearts*. After the Delibes, Stokowski's tall, graceful frame could be seen bending leftward as he murmured into the ear of his prima donna: "I have never heard this sung more beautifully." MacDonald capped the evening with five encores, all songs from her movies, and the crowd hollered for still more. Nobody wanted to go home.

It was a unique night in Hollywood Bowl history. For this was not Arthur Rubinstein, Jascha Heifetz, or Gregor Piatigorsky "slumming" on yet another stop in a round of summer concerts. Nor was it one more Bowl appearance by the likes of Lily Pons, Lawrence Tibbett, or Maria Jeritza—"highbrow" singers who had Hollywood ties but were not really of Hollywood. Rather, this was the Bowl debut of a Movie-town faithful who for fifteen years had stayed at the top of the picture industry and then had the courage and talent to go back East, make good in the rarefied world of high art, and return home once again. Hollywood was proud of MacDonald's new prestige and basked in the reflection of her increased glory. Hers was a Bowl concert that brought forth collective feelings of esteem, gratitude, and love.

And also of comfort. Earlier that day (Japan time), a nuclear bomb had destroyed Nagasaki. Three days previously, a similar attack had taken place over Hiroshima, ushering in the atomic age. Five days after the concert, Japan would surrender to the Allies, making World War II a closed chapter and giving rise to drastic changes in American society and culture. For many that night at the Hollywood Bowl, MacDonald and her music gave reassurance that some good things were bound to last.

In October, MacDonald returned to Chicago's Civic Opera House and sang better than ever in two more performances of *Faust*—without microphones. According to Claudia Cassidy, her voice showed more "dramatic focus" and "greater freedom and sparkle" than it had the year before: "She was a singing actress of such beauty of voice and form you felt if Faust must sell his soul to the Devil at least this time he got his money's worth."

MacDonald, however, was ready to kiss the opera world good-bye.

In her Ambassador-East suite the night before her Saturday matinee, Jeanette turned out the lights at ten o'clock. But with the Gounod score running endlessly through her head, she failed to get any sleep: "I didn't dare take a sedative, for sleeping pills relax the vocal cords as well as the body and mind, and this would have been fatal." Emily Wentz recalled: "She just couldn't take another night like that. During the performance she had a splitting headache, so I gave her one of my massage treatments. I practically squeezed her head off, but it got rid of the headache. Each time she came off, I worked on her."

Lehmann begged MacDonald to stay with opera. She wanted Jeanette to study Mimì, the seamstress heroine of Puccini's *La Bohème*. That way, Lehmann said, the critics will "cease to talk about that damned glamour business, which would drive me crazy in your place. . . . I love you very much and want the very best for you." But MacDonald never performed Mimì. Except for a brief reprise of *Roméo* and *Faust* at the Cincinnati Zoo and in Philadelphia five years later, she abandoned her operatic calling altogether.

"Opera takes too much time and hard work," MacDonald later rationalized. "Besides, I get a lot more satisfaction out of concertizing and so does the public."

CHAPTER FIFTEEN

A Graceful Exit

Hollywood is the city of youngsters.

French writer BLAISE CENDRARS, 1936

THE AMERICAN MUSIC INDUSTRY was moving in new directions. As big bands dissolved, pop singers like Doris Day, Margaret Whiting, and Peggy Lee carved out independent recording careers. In 1946, Perry Como sold over ten million 78s; Decca issued its pioneering original-cast album of *Oklahoma!*; and the Ink Spots, shored up by the increased vogue for black singing groups, vied with Frank Sinatra for the year's top album. In radio, new local programs were edging out the weekly live-music network shows. Inventive disc jockeys like New York's Barry Gray devoted entire broadcasts to single vocalists and call-in requests. The same season that saw Alan Jay Lerner and Frederick Loewe give fresh hope to American operetta with *Brigadoon* found Ethel Merman electrifying Broadway with Irving Berlin's *Annie Get Your Gun*. Perhaps the boldest new entertainment trend was owed to mobster Bugsy Siegel, who built the Flamingo Casino and made Las Vegas, Nevada, a hub for live musical extravaganzas.

That June, MacDonald set out on a recital tour of the war-ravaged British Isles, her first overseas venture in thirteen years. In keeping with the times, she took one of the first commercial flights from New York to Dublin. Although Lotte Lehmann urged her to try a tincture of strychnine in order to avoid airsickness, MacDonald relied only on Gene's bon voyage gift, a gold bracelet with a medal of Saint Christopher, patron of travelers. The result was nonstop nausea, with Collins

Smith, her pianist and companion for the trip, having to "pass her the bag several times." "I'm a living argument for the fact that man was meant to travel on his own two feet," Jeanette reported woozily after the flight.

MacDonald's appearance at London's Royal Albert Hall was, by most accounts, a historic success, with standees crammed eight feet deep. Jeanette bestowed a patriotic aura to the event by starting her program with a song by Henry Carey, an eighteenth-century English composer credited with writing "God Save the King." After the recital she was presented to Queen Mary, the queen mother confessing she was an avid fan. In a famous show of praise for an American concert artist, the London *Daily Express* hurrahed, on the morning of July 1, 1946: "The problem of the Albert Hall's bad acoustics was solved last night by the film prima donna Jeanette MacDonald. Recipe: 1. Fill the hall (the largest audience this year). 2. Sing (her softest notes were heard in the top balcony). 3. Enunciate (every word was clear)."

The United Kingdom was still suffering from food and clothing shortages. "Londoners have the sturdy courage which we've all heard about so much, but the wreckage . . . is almost too staggering for the mind to encompass," MacDonald noted. Even though she donated her Albert Hall proceeds to St. Dunstans, a charity for the blind, a number of columnists in England and Wales vented outrage over her mountain of luggage—MacDonald's ten hatboxes arousing special fury.

When she arrived in Scotland, however, Daniel's daughter could do no wrong. In Balfron, MacDonald visited the two-story house in Keir Place where her paternal grandmother, Jannette Johnston, had lived as a youngster. "She jist spoke awa' like an ordinary person," crowed the village's oldest woman, who claimed to remember some of the Johnston clan, but "no' o' the generation Jeanette's askin' aboot." In Edinburgh, MacDonald learned that a certain wool fabric she hoped to purchase for Gene was off-limits to foreigners. When the workers at her hotel volunteered to pool their ration points to buy her a few yards, Jeanette, in exchange, surrendered her "sweets" coupons plus a stash of Hershey bars brought from Philadelphia. The barter satisfied everyone.

MacDonald's prewar pictures continued to be enormously popular in Britain. The London reissue of *Maytime* that spring had played to sellout crowds. In existentialist-drenched France, however, the attitude du jour was disdain for nearly everything American. The French organizers of that year's Cannes Film Festival (the very first) cordially invited MacDonald to attend as an honored guest, although her British concert schedule obliged her to decline. Yet the long-delayed Paris release of MacDonald's *Sweethearts* in June mainly prompted snootiness. One typical reviewer called the film "totally without interest," its plot "lamentably imbecilic" and its Technicolor "sickening and aggressive." Not until a decade later, when the movie magazine *Cahiers du Cinéma* exerted a pro-American influence, would the French bestow a more fair-minded look upon MGM musicals, with some pundits finding in their dreamlike exuberance the essence of all movies.

Joe Pasternak, the Hungarian-born Hollywood movie producer, was known for his golden touch. In 1936 he had saved Universal Pictures from bankruptcy by starring teenager Deanna Durbin in cheery Depression-era musicals. He also salvaged the wilting career of Marlene Dietrich when, in 1939, he cast her as the brawling saloon tart in *Destry Rides Again*. Now at MGM, Pasternak wanted to bring MacDonald back to the silver screen, and he boldly offered her the part of a mature divorcée whose love affair and second marriage incite her daughters to rebellion. To lighten the tale's serious themes, Pasternak promised plenty of sunny music and song. At age forty-three, Jeanette agreed to appear in *The Birds and the Bees*, soon retitled *Three Daring Daughters*. "No actress can afford to play young girls indefinitely," she publicly conceded.

Though Pasternak had ultimate say in casting, Benny Thau, the MGM executive who oversaw all acting assignments, was nervous about MacDonald's return to King Louis's domain. Despite his public geniality toward MacDonald since her departure from MGM, Mayer still felt bruised by Jeanette's supposed betrayals. It was essential, Thau insisted, that she and the chief have a private talk to clear the air once and for all.

The meeting took place early one morning in Mayer's new home on Benedict Canyon Drive. After a light breakfast, L. B., who was now living as a bachelor, led Jeanette into the library. With tears trickling down his cheeks, he described the heartache her "disloyalty" had cost him. "Do you know what finally hurt me more than anything else you'd done?" he asked. Jeanette sat silent. "It was when I found out one Christmas that you sent me the same present you gave Eddie Mannix." MacDonald's standard gift for the MGM brass had been a $7.50 box of pears ordered by mail from Oregon. "L. B.," Jeanette countered, "did it occur to you that the box of pears was more than you ever gave *me* for Christmas?" For a moment Mayer stared, then he grinned and answered: "By gosh, I never thought about that." Their peace was made over this absurd tête-à-tête.

MacDonald, with her good-luck Mother Hubbard cloak taken out of storage, returned to Culver City in September 1946 to start wardrobe and sound tests. "It's a wonderful feeling to be back," she confessed to *Silver Screen* magazine. "I hadn't realized how much I missed picture-making until I came back to it. And to add to the sense of being home again, the studio gave me the crew that worked with me on my former pictures." "The only difference," she joked "is the men are fatter." Many familiar faces welcomed her: Ray June in cinematography, Douglas Shearer in sound, Jack Dawn and William Tuttle in makeup, Cedric Gibbons in art. Yet the men who had really shaped MacDonald's vehicles were gone. Van Dyke had died. Stromberg was on his own. Stothart was ailing. Forrest and Wright were composing for the stage. Adrian had left movies to open a private boutique in Beverly Hills. Everyone in Pasternak's unit treated MacDonald respectfully, some even with awe. But the camaraderie she formerly enjoyed with the studio's creative powers was missing, and Jeanette now felt like a guest in a home she had once owned.

Metro still manufactured the world's glossiest musical pictures, but it boasted a new roster of young stars with names like Van Johnson and June Allyson. Although the studio was cranking out more musicals than ever, most of them were built around Esther Williams's backstrokes and Red Skelton's pratfalls. The expansive, haunting love melodies that had been so central to MacDonald's movies in the mid-1930s were not at all to the taste of Arthur Freed, now the studio's top producer. The defining trait of Freed's latest musicals, such as *Good News*, with Allyson and Peter Lawford, and *The Pirate*, with Judy Garland and Gene Kelly, was zingy choreography.

MacDonald's four-year hiatus had no effect on her confidence before the cameras. "She knew what she wanted and she got it," recalled Jane Powell, who played Tess, the eldest daughter. One thing MacDonald knew was not to sing too much. She delivered the old Jolson standard "You Made Me Love You" with quiet, sultry flare. She brought charm to "Where There's Love," her solo arrangement based on lush waltzes from Strauss's *Der Rosenkavalier*. Her nostalgic rendition of "Sweethearts" showed that MacDonald's voice had evolved. In her screen recording of that song eight years earlier, Jeanette's soprano was bright, with its usual penetrating edge. Now it sounded rounder and fuller, even warmer. A touching duet of Edward Grieg's "Springtide" gave petite Powell the distinction of being MacDonald's only singing partner to warble in a range higher than her own. In a symbolic passing of the lyric torch to a new generation, it was Powell who sang an abridged "Waltz Song" from *Roméo et Juliette*—the aria MacDonald had so rightly claimed for herself in *Rose Marie* and in her stage performances of the complete opera.

The myth of MacDonald's virginal persona at MGM never seemed to impress the censors, who had badgered the studios about most of her films from *The Cat and the Fiddle* to *I Married an Angel*. Incredibly, just two weeks before shooting began, the censors attacked *Three Daring Daughters*, labeling it "anti-social." Joseph Breen warned Mayer: "This is exactly the type of story which thinking men and women in all parts of the world, who are concerned for the preservation of family life and the institution of marriage, will single out for serious criticism." Unlike Thalberg or Stromberg, who regularly challenged Breen, Pasternak was in no mood for a fight. The script lost its radical edge, and under Fred Wilcox's direction MacDonald projected a fairly tame image of a well-to-do, single working mom. Even when her character discovers new love on a cruise to the tropics, the story's emotional climate stays as cool as that of a 1950s television sitcom.

MacDonald's purported love interest in *Three Daring Daughters* was concert pianist José Iturbi. "Just between you and me," Jeanette later told Hedda Hopper, "I always felt confident that had Nelson played in *Three Daring Daughters*, instead of Iturbi, it would have rekindled another hot box-office set-up. But as you know, Joe Pasternak was going through such a hero-worship stage that he could think of nothing but how great José was going to be in the picture." Impresario Sol Hurok correctly predicted that Iturbi's movie work would "ruin his concert career." But with MGM planning to launch its own record company, the front office saw the Spanish-born pianist's crossover potential as the perfect middlebrow complement to MacDonald's. The year before, when he played Chopin's Polonaise in A-Flat on the sound track to the Columbia biopic *A Song to Remember*, sales for his RCA recording of that piece zoomed to eight hundred thousand.

In *Three Daring Daughters*, Iturbi coyly appears as himself and moves easily from Georges Enesco's Roumanian Rhapsody—performed at twin pianos with his sister, Amparo—to a boogie-woogie rendition of "(Get Your Kicks on) Route 66." Yet Iturbi was short, chunky, and lacked the charisma expected of a leading man. His amorous moments with MacDonald, who still looked gorgeous in Technicolor and in gowns by Irene, strained credibility. As the *New York World-Telegram* noted: "At one point [Iturbi] snatches a kiss so quickly that it looks as though he was afraid the camera would catch him."

Shyness was no problem for the trio of daughters played by Powell, Ann E. Todd, and Mary Eleanor Donahue. MacDonald was particularly fond of ten-year-old Donahue, who would later shorten her name and gain celebrity as Robert Young's TV daughter Betty in *Father Knows Best.* Donahue remembered Jeanette as "lovely and friendly," though just a bit compulsive, like most singers, around germs: "One day I had a little sniffle. We were doing a scene in bed together, and I was supposed to lie down with my head on her shoulder. Well, she placed her arm on *my* shoulder and kept shoving me downward, because she didn't want to breathe in my germs. The director kept saying, 'Mary Eleanor, stay up there, stay up there!' And of course I couldn't say, 'But Miss MacDonald keeps pushing me down!'"

Loew's held up the release of *Three Daring Daughters* until February 1948. The reviews were mixed. Some found it a weak imitation of *Three Smart Girls,* the Pasternak film that had launched Deanna Durbin a dozen years earlier. Edwin Schallert of the *Los Angeles Times* called MacDonald "amazingly competent in a role that is probably one of the stuffiest ever foisted on anybody." The movie, which had taken a staggering seventy-eight days to make, cost $2,538,000, the largest amount ever for a MacDonald picture. The film was among the studio's top grossers for the fiscal year, but red ink still flowed in the amount of $136,000—a minor bleed compared with Arthur Freed's *The Pirate,* which hemorrhaged over $2 million.

The plight of rising production costs and lagging audience enthusiasm was in fact now commonplace at MGM. The previous year, for the first time in its history, the studio had failed to win an Academy nomination for Best Picture. Metro could still come up with moneymaking musicals: *Easter Parade,* the big-budget Freed film with Garland and Astaire, brought decent returns, and Pasternak's *A Date with Judy,* a modest Jane Powell musical in which Carmen Miranda steals the show with her deliciously manic "Cuanto Le Gusta?," was the studio's top grosser of the year. Nonetheless, MGM was now trailing Paramount, Warner Bros., and 20th Century-Fox in profits.

Mayer was thrilled to have MacDonald back in the fold. But it was clear she was not helping turn the financial tide.

On May 16, 1947, Jeanette and Gene were entertaining at military hospitals in San Francisco. The next morning they returned to Los Angeles and were met at the train station by Emily Wentz, who was standing, pale and somber, on the platform. "Jeanette," Emily said softly, "I have to tell you something terrible. Your mother died last night." Emily explained that a blood clot, stemming from a recent broken ankle, unexpectedly triggered a fatal heart seizure. Though Blossom had phoned for a doctor, Anna died before the physician could get her to a hospital. As Emily drove the shocked couple home, Jeanette dreaded the thought of viewing her mother's corpse: "I remembered Father in bed with his jaw fallen open, and [the poodle] Trixie refusing to go into the room with me. I wanted to remember Mother as she had been in the full, happy life she enjoyed so much."

Private funeral services took place two days later at Forest Lawn. Nelson Eddy sang Schubert's "Serenade." Eddie Mannix was present, not as MGM's representative but as a devoted friend who grasped the immensity of Jeanette's loss. Gene and Jeanette accompanied Anna's remains to Philadelphia, where Anna was buried next to Daniel in Mount Peace Cemetery. Jeanette, in line with her mother's and her own growing ecumenism, asked Monsignor Robert Edwards Moore, a Catholic prelate and family friend, to recite a graveside requiem. The newspapers gave Anna's age as seventy. She was in fact nearly seventy-six.

For the first time in MacDonald's life, she knew unspeakable grief. Anna's soothing voice, knowing glance, and astonishing ability to size up people had always come to her aid. Now this dear friend and confidante was gone, and everything seemed to be called into doubt. In the weeks following the burial, Jeanette took solitary walks late at night in the gardens of Twin Gables.

Gene recalled one early morning when Jeanette's insomnia was especially bad: "I joined her for a walk on the grounds and she was extremely quiet. Suddenly she stopped, looked down, and asked with all seriousness in a voice that sounded like a little girl's, 'Gene, do you like my voice?'" One thought in particular haunted MacDonald: when her own death came, there would be no children to mourn her. The prospect of never knowing if she had it in her to be as attentive and self-denying a mother as Anna unsettled her.

Anna's estate, including the house at 710 North Camden Drive, was valued at $100,000. Her will made bequests to each of her daughters and to her grandson, Earl. But after the funeral, when Elsie came to the Coast to visit, she told Blossom she felt she was not getting a fair share of their mother's personal effects. Without informing the others, Elsie snatched Anna's silk bedspread and brought it back to Philadelphia. Jeanette was furious and demanded its return. More than a bedspread was at issue. Anna's passing had reignited Jeanette's irrational anxiety about falling back into poverty. She wrote to her eldest sister on September 27:

> Dear Elsie,
>
> . . . I am sorry the question of the bedspread has come up, and feel that I had better straighten you out on the entire situation regarding the house and all of the household effects. . . .
>
> Except for the things that Mother's girlfriends gave her for Christmas and her birthday, such as writing paper, cocktail napkins and bonbon dishes, and handkerchiefs, etc., everything in the house was either mine or I gave Mother. All of the table linens, bed linens and household effects I either supplied for Mother or gave them to her from time to time, and so feel that, since I am planning on renting the house furnished, it is no more than right that it be completely furnished if I am to get any kind of rental price for it.
>
> As for the bedspread, that is my own, and if I report it to the insurance company it will create a great deal of fuss and investigation, so I think it will be better for you to return it. You see, Elsie, it was I who asked Mother to draw up a will, in the hope of eliminating any bickerings about who would get what. As you know, Mother left the jewelry (all of which I gave her, as you know) in accordance with our own requests for it. The bracelet which you asked for is the most valuable piece of all. It is valued at some $3500, so take good care of it. . . .
>
> Actually, I don't honestly feel I owe you an explanation, but, in view of the fact that you felt everything had been "tagged," I want you to know exactly what the situation is so there will be no hurt feelings on your part. After all, I do feel entitled to provide for my less productive years, and the house is something Mother and I had always talked of as a possible good provider against an indigent old age. . . .
>
> By now I suppose [your] re-drawn house agreement [with me] etc. is on its way back. Poor Blossie is still trying to get bids on the new house plans. She seems to be getting nowhere fast.
>
> Gene flew to Palm Springs today on business. It is plenty hot and I hope he survives the heat down there.
>
> Give our best love to Barney [Scheiter], and do let us hear from you.
>
> Your loving sister,
> Jeanette

Six months after Anna died of heart failure, MacDonald lost Ernst Lubitsch to the same disease. It was a grim irony in the Hollywood colony that the master of comic romance led a painfully sad life. When Ernst separated from his second wife, Vivian, in 1942, he seemed lonelier and more adrift than ever. For several years MacDonald and Mary Loos, Anita's niece, had been taking responsibility for Lubitsch's holidays. Each November, Jeanette would call Mary and ask, "Do you want him for Thanksgiving or do you want him for Christmas?" This year it was Thanksgiving at Twin Gables, where Ernst excitedly told everyone about his renewed plans to star Jeanette in a screen version of *Der Rosenkavalier*. Three days later he suffered cardiac arrest, reportedly while making love to a casual amour.

This new tragedy made MacDonald even more sensitive to her own mortality: "When at Lubitsch's funeral I sang, 'Beyond the blue horizon—waits a beautiful day,' the words seemed to take on a new and sweeter meaning for me . . . and I hoped for him, too." Gene was a pallbearer.

At Twin Gables, the winter holidays of 1947 were quiet and low-key. A small family gathering on Christmas Day included Jeanette's nephew, Earl, now an accomplished painter, and Earl's young daughter, Nanette. Nanette was a near image of her famous great-aunt, and she had inherited Jeanette's girlhood passion for entertaining relatives. As MacDonald watched the girl perform her latest steps learned at dancing school, she mused self-consolingly that Anna and Ernst, had they been present, would have clapped the loudest.

The loss of Anna and Ernst did not deter MacDonald from setting out on another grueling recital tour. Moments before her performance at Constitution Hall, on February 16, 1948, President Harry Truman and his family visited backstage. "I don't know how well I'll sing, Mr. President," Jeanette confessed. "I'm just over a cold, and I'm not sure whether I should go on or not. It seems . . . so far as the critics are concerned, I'm damned if I do and damned if I don't." First Lady Bess glanced at her husband: "I always say it's just the same thing with us, isn't it, Harry?" The president, grinning, counseled Jeanette to follow his special cold treatment: "I take two aspirins in one hand and a glass of whisky in the other. I throw the aspirins over my shoulder, drink the whiskey, and feel much better." MacDonald resisted this nostrum but doled out some wisdom of her own to Margaret, the president's daughter, who had recently given a concert to a skeptical audience at the Hollywood Bowl. "No matter how honest your intentions are," she told the young singer, "they'll be questioned. So go ahead and sing. You'll make a lot of people happy. The rest are probably Republicans, anyway!"

Hollywood and Washington were again locking horns. Months after MacDonald's return to MGM for *Three Daring Daughters*, the House Un-American Activities Committee began a full-scale probe into Communist influence in the motion picture industry. When this circus reached its first climax, MacDonald was off in Mexico for a broadcast to inaugurate radio station XEX, touted as the most powerful in the Western Hemisphere. For all her anti-Communist sentiment, Jeanette had no tolerance for the House Committee's inquisitorial methods. "Let he who is without sin cast the first stone," she told a Massachusetts reporter. For the record, Gene Raymond later stressed: "Throughout the HUAC hearings, Jeanette and I never thought of volunteering to appear before the Committee; nor were we ever subpoenaed to do so."

In mid-April 1948, MacDonald began what would be her final picture, *The Sun Comes Up*. Two years earlier, Metro's *The Yearling* had won two Oscars and a Special Academy Award for child actor Claude Jarman, Jr. To exploit the craze for sensitive tales about children and animals, MGM now cast Jarman and Lassie opposite MacDonald in an adaptation of a serial written by *The Yearling*'s author, Marjorie Kinnan Rawlings, for the *Saturday Evening Post*.

The Sun Comes Up presented MacDonald as an embittered, widowed concert singer who escapes to the Blue Ridge Mountains in order to forget her teenage son's tragic death, accidentally brought on by Lassie. Thanks to a winsome orphan boy, played with beautiful understatement by fifteen-year-old Jarman, she recovers her desire to live and love. *The Sun Comes Up* has its quota of corn. But, to the credit of MacDonald and Jarman, the picture projects a sincerity as moving today as in 1949.

Though Lassie is barely relevant to Jarman's unfolding love for MacDonald, the star dog was a nagging reminder of how removed Jeanette felt from her former rank. "I've come to this, working with a dog," she joked to cinematographer Charles Schoenbaum, who shot wardrobe tests. Claude Jarman, Jr., recalls MacDonald's ease on a "very congenial" production, much of which was shot amid the rolling bean and wheat fields of Santa Cruz. But Jarman also remembered Jeanette's distress when Lassie inadvertently threatened to ignite her allergies: "We had a makeup man named Lee Stanville, who was assigned incredibly to both MacDonald and Lassie. Lee stuck extra hair around Lassie's underside so that you couldn't tell whether he was male or female. One morning Jeanette said, 'Lee, do you make up Lassie?' He said, 'Yes.' 'Well, do you make Lassie up before you make me up?' He said, 'Yes, I do.' 'Well, from now on I think we ought to do it in reverse.'"

When the production wrapped, Jeanette gave Claude Jarman and Dwayne Hickman, who played the small part of her son, photos of herself with identical handwritten inscriptions: "If I had a son, I'd like him to be just like you!" Neither boy knew that the sentiment was co-exclusive. As with Wright and Forrest a decade earlier, another youth had a terrific impact on MacDonald's music. For two years André Previn had been part of MGM's army of music arrangers and orchestrators. A former Paris Conservatory student now attending Beverly Hills High, the worldly young Previn pooh-poohed most of MGM's chief composers while at the same time loving what he called the "peculiar fraternity" of movie musicians. When producer Robert Sisk asked him to compose the entire score for *The Sun Comes Up*, the eighteen-year-old prodigy was ecstatic. "What did I care," he recalled, "that it wasn't Dostoyevski? It was my own movie, my name was on it, and besides it was tailor-made for music, since the dialogue was sparse in favor of a lot of barking in picturesque meadows."

In his Hollywood memoir, *No Minor Chords,* Previn reported that "MacDonald sang two songs (Fauré and Puccini), and although her voice always had been a bit peculiar, she was the soul of kindness, she worked hard, and I liked her a lot." Actually, there was no Fauré in the picture. Along with the Puccini, Jeanette sang Dvořák's "Songs My Mother Taught Me" and joined in on "Cousin Ebenezer," a folksy Previn-arranged melody sung by the orphan boys on a bouncy car ride.

MacDonald's third piece, based on Anton Rubinstein's "Romance," was the last song she would ever sing on-screen. Wearing a white-and-green tailored dress, and accompanying herself at a living-room piano, MacDonald seems light-years removed from the vampish boudoir slitherings of "Dream Lover," her debut number in *The Love Parade.* Yet the lyrics of this final screen song express the same impulse that animated "Dream Lover" and that governed MacDonald's movie roles for the next two decades:

If you were mine to love,
Then I could have my true dream;

> If you were mine to love,
> I'd never want a new dream.
> . . . .
> If I could only say
> That magic was my power,
> I'd change all night and day
> To one romantic hour.

Midway through the story, Jarman has a heart-to-heart with Mac-Donald, explaining that when music touches him deeply his emotions swell "like the feeling you get when the sun comes up." Partly because she makes Rubinstein's "Romance" ache with longing and desire, Mac-Donald leaves us with an image of herself in middle age more muted but no less intensely romantic than the one we associate with her youthful years.

MacDonald proved she could still enthrall audiences in live perfor-mance when, shortly after *The Sun Comes Up* was completed, she gave her second Hollywood Bowl concert under the baton of Eugene Or-mandy. But she had no assurance she would ever work for MGM again. Nicholas Schenck had long become disenchanted with L. B. Mayer, and in July 1948, just days after *The Sun Comes Up* finished being shot, Dore Schary left RKO to become Metro's new head of pro-duction. With Mayer reduced to the honorific post of Vice-President in Charge of the Studio, Schary promised to stay committed to "good pic-tures about a good world" in the time-honored MGM tradition. Yet Schary, a liberal Democrat, was eager to produce "social problem" films like *Battleground*, the gritty war story with Van Johnson that be-came an immediate critical and commercial hit. Although Schary let Freed and Pasternak continue to operate their musical units semi-independently, Freed had no interest in MacDonald, and Pasternak had botched his costly attempt to revive her film career with *Three Daring Daughters.*

Nevertheless, MacDonald remained a radiant presence in the fa-mous portrait of fifty-eight stars and featured players that was pub-lished as part of MGM's Silver Jubilee in 1949. Sporting a brown-and-white checkered jacket, she is seated alphabetically in the fourth row, second from left, between deadpan Peter Lawford and décolleté Ann Miller. The photo discloses MGM's new crop of leading ladies: Arlene Dahl, Ava Gardner, Jennifer Jones. Except for Jeanette, the members of

Mayer's legendary roster of 1930s studio queens are gone—Garbo and Shearer into retirement; Colbert, Loy, and Crawford to other studios.

In contrast to the professionalism that Thalberg and Stromberg could always count on from MacDonald, in 1949 Freed and Pasternak were at wit's end with two of their best young singing stars. Judy Garland, not yet twenty-seven, was battling drug addiction, paranoia, and suicide attempts. After being dropped from *The Barkleys of Broadway* and replaced by Ginger Rogers, Garland was fired from *Annie Get Your Gun,* with the role going to Betty Hutton. Over at the Pasternak Unit, the robust tenor Mario Lanza was soon to enjoy phenomenal success in *The Great Caruso.* But Lanza, at Metro since 1947, plagued the studio with mood swings, weight fluctuations, and outré misconduct to equal Garland's. In her sixteen years at MGM, MacDonald had been caught up in political tensions and artistic differences. But she never brought scandal or embarrassment to the House of Mayer.

Released in May 1949, *The Sun Comes Up* lost $549,000 of its $1.6 million budget. In New York it played the Capitol, the site of Jeanette's greatest successes. Most reviewers labeled the picture family fare and agreed with A. H. Weiler of the *New York Times,* who called it "all very simple and sweet. Perhaps too sweet." *Daily Variety* was more upbeat: "Miss MacDonald's interpretation of the singer clearly proves that the industry has too long left this lovely and talented star off the screen."

As it turned out, the industry did not share *Variety*'s enthusiasm. Still, as MacDonald came to realize that *The Sun Comes Up* would be her final movie, she took comfort in the knowledge that no star of her generation had left pictures with more dignity and grace.

CHAPTER SIXTEEN

Distress Signals

The average male would find marriage to a woman like
Jeanette MacDonald a humbling—and somewhat
terrifying—experience.

JIMMIE FIDLER, 1943

"THERE JUST IS NO SCANDAL IN THEIR LIVES!" lamented
Hedda Hopper in a 1948 profile of the "notoriously congenial" Mac-
Donald-Raymond marriage. Off the record, however, Hopper knew that
after years of excessive praise, Hollywood's perennial honeymooners
were in trouble. Ever since Gene's return from the war, he and Jeanette
were at a loss to restore a sound balance between their professional and
private lives. MacDonald herself described the late 1940s and early
1950s as a time of "drifting" and "self-reproach," when "adjustment
problems" engulfed her and Gene in "a blizzard" of painful emotions.

Part of the problem was Gene's lagging career. RKO owed him two
films from a prewar agreement, but after assigning him to a paltry role
opposite Laraine Day in *The Locket* (1946), the studio lost interest and
bought out his contract. Gene then moved to Eagle-Lion, a B movie
outfit, where he honed a tough-guy image and made his directing debut
in 1948 with *Million Dollar Weekend*. Yet none of his postwar pictures—including *Sofia* (1948), a finely crafted cold war thriller—did
well at the box office. Gene had never expected to outshine his wife.
But faced with little work and no sense of purpose, he fell prey to depression and abandoned even his composing and scriptwriting projects.
"He lacked faith in himself at this stage," Jeanette reflected, "and I was
afraid to be too aggressive about it in case it seemed like nagging."

Soon Gene started chain-smoking, and his intake of booze escalated. His gift for showing Jeanette affection suffered.

MacDonald's movie prospects were no more certain than Gene's. But unlike him, she had her wildly popular recital tours to stroke her ego. Still, the tours added salt to their collective wounds. Jeanette gamely accepted Gene's refusal to accompany her on the road: "Trailing along on my tours would make him 'Mr. MacDonald,' a galling label for any self-respecting man. As it was, he was called Mr. Mac-Donald often enough to make me admire tremendously his good sportsmanship in taking it on the chin." Worse still were the people who called Gene "Nelson Eddy": "Of course we always laughed it off—sometimes Gene even obliged by signing Nelson's name—but no one will ever know the agonies I suffered on such occasions. More than anything else in the world in those days, I wanted to see him receive as much acclaim as I, to spare him these humiliations."

Gene's mother aggravated the rift by waging new assaults on Jeanette's character. If Gene was not thriving, Mrs. Kipling wrote, it was because he stupidly stayed married to the "prima donna." Kipling's cruelest jab came one Thanksgiving, when she sent Gene a holiday card depicting a family with children. Scrawled inside was a diatribe against Jeanette, who, Kipling said, had "never experienced motherhood" and "would never understand how a mother feels." Kipling didn't realize that the Raymonds' decision not to have children was continually reinforced by Kipling's own dirty tricks and by Gene's fear of repeating the upbringing he experienced at her hands.

In the thick of this turmoil, MacDonald received the original script of *Kiss Me Kate*. "Cole Porter had been out to California, and the idea was that I should star as Kate on Broadway. As I sat in my bedroom poring over the pages, I knew that if I returned to New York, an entirely different relationship would be created between Gene and me. Would our marriage stand the strain of more separated living? I wasn't sure. I couldn't take the risk. I turned down the show, to my subsequent regret, professionally, though both Gene and I were delighted when Patricia Morison, his co-star in *Sofia,* got the part." For years to come, one thought pestered MacDonald: "I never heard the music Cole Porter had written for *Kate*. Suppose I had listened to that entrancing score. Suppose I'd liked the script just a little bit more. Would I have gone to New York? I'll never know."

Jeanette opted for a new strategy. She was going to prove to herself—and to Mrs. Kipling—that she could be a "normal," stay-at-home wife. It wasn't easy. Throughout her life, MacDonald had let her mother or a servant oversee domestic matters. "Now I decided this should be my job. So I embarked on marketing sprees several times a week. My early childhood served me well. I tried experimenting with 'special dishes' from recipes I cut out of *Ladies' Home Journal* or *Good Housekeeping.*" On cook's days off, Jeanette made dinner: "It usually took me all day to cook a not-too-difficult meal, and Gene invariably kidded me about the mess the kitchen was in. But at least he kidded me, and *this* was progress."

A domestic calling, however, is hard to fake. It was obvious to Gene that his mate's new enthusiasm for gardening, golfing, and menu planning was forced. In truth, the more Jeanette pulled back from show business, the more Gene felt he was hampering her chances for renewal. His self-recriminations made Jeanette, in turn, feel guilty for blocking Gene's own chances for a better future. Jeanette adopted a new tactic. If time spent at home could not rescue her marriage, professional ventures that included Gene just might.

A first opportunity came with the 1949–50 holiday season. With Jeanette as the headliner, Gene was master of ceremonies in a touring variety show for U.S. Air Force troops and their families in Germany and Austria. "Just seeing and hearing her lifted [our spirits] . . . and made the world seem a better place," one sergeant in Heidelberg said of MacDonald. Yet there was no end of strife behind the scenes, mainly because Gene's abiding concern for Jeanette often outraged the second-string acts on the bill. When, for example, he found the acoustics in a Vienna venue "not to be complimentary to his wife's voice," he summarily canceled a radio broadcast of the entire show. In the course of the tour, one comedian complained: "Why didn't all the cast make a final curtain call rather than Miss MacDonald closing the show?" A dancer griped: "Why is the hair dresser assigned only to Mrs. Raymond?" "Why are the Raymonds getting all the publicity in local newspapers?" protested a cowboy actor. An air force official confirmed Gene's clout with the brass: "Mr. Raymond would at every station bypass the Project Officers and request in person of the Commanding Officers the things or favors he wanted done."

Back in the States, MacDonald made her long-deferred New York City recital debut at Carnegie Hall on October 16, 1950. It was to be, she said, "the biggest moment of my career." In spite of the hall's flawless acoustics, Jeanette feared that critics would slam her for the smallness of her voice. In a move that almost begged for criticism, she had a special band shell set up behind her on stage. The day before the performance she lunched with Ethel Merman, who had just opened to raves in Irving Berlin's *Call Me Madam.* "I don't know how I got into this," Jeanette told Ethel. "I get scared stiff, don't you?" Merman, who never had trouble with volume or stage fright, shot back matter-of-factly: "Why should I? I know my lines. What's there to be scared about?"

Tickets had sold out a week in advance. A few days prior to the recital, MacDonald pleaded in a New York paper that she had "won the right to be considered entirely on her merits as a musician, rather than as a visiting movie star." The critics didn't agree. In a review titled "Glamour Prevails at Carnegie Hall," Howard Taubman of the *New York Times* conceded that MacDonald was "not unaware of sound musical criteria." He praised her rendition of Grieg's "Ein Schwan" for conveying "something of the ecstasy and poetry the composer poured into it." But Taubman repeated the canard that MacDonald had been "taken in" by the brilliance of her "skillfully magnified" screen tones: "No one has the right to speak of this program as a musical evening pure and simple. . . . Framed against the dull gold of the small bandshell . . . she looked as if she were taking part in a triumphant sequence of a new film." The *Herald-Tribune*'s Francis D. Perkins described her voice as "pleasing, with a prevailing silvery quality" and found that her "initial vocal tension waned as the program progressed with songs by Strauss, Brahms, Grieg, and Wolf." Yet Perkins, like Taubman, begrudged MacDonald her arias by Bellini, Gounod, and Puccini, opining that "a somewhat less exacting program might give a more advantageous opportunity for the interpretative ability which she has shown in other allied fields."

As always, MacDonald lifted her audience to a state of adoring frenzy. "They applauded and shouted as if Jenny Lind, Adelina Patti, Mary Garden, and Geraldine Farrar, all rolled into one, had come to regale them in song," reported the *Times.* But no one anticipated the madness that followed her closing bow. As she walked off stage, arms laden with pink roses, a battalion of fans stormed the platform, knocked down the band shell, and cut her off as she headed toward her dressing room. "This is the only time the crowds really got me licked," said Emily Wentz. "I just gave up and managed to get Jeanette to safety. They finally had to call the police." Later that night, Harry "Buster" Mills, the J. C. Penney executive, and his wife, Yvonne, the Eastman Kodak heiress, gave a reception for Jeanette at their Park Avenue apartment.

A few weeks after the Carnegie Hall recital, MacDonald made her television debut on NBC's *The Voice of Firestone*. As a radio show, *The Voice of Firestone* had treated millions of Americans to a rich array of classical and semiclassical artists. Now it sought to appeal to the nation's eyes as well as its ears.

Live network TV was still in its infancy, and when MacDonald arrived for rehearsals in midtown Manhattan, the crude lighting and cheap sets astounded her. Her temper blew when she scoped her image on a monitor during a run-through of her waltz routine to "Will You Remember?" from *Maytime*. "I have not invested all this time in working out a dance number so that you can cut me at my thighs," she hollered at the camera operators. "I expect my feet to be seen!" Refusing to carry on, she summoned Gene and with his aid had the lights and camera setups readjusted to her standards. She also goaded the cameramen to improvise little stepladders so that they could reach the increased camera height she insisted they use for photographing her face. She even instructed the electricians to follow her with baby spotlights in order to diffuse ugly shadows. "There is no doubt that that was one of the great events in not only the *Voice of Firestone* progress, but also the television industry," observed Howard Barlow, conductor of the Firestone Orchestra, in an interview later that year. "We now have eye-lights on all the cameras . . . *and* we have stepladders and higher cameras. . . . MacDonald helped the entire industry on that particular day to make technical progress."

The telecast aired on November 13 with barely a glitch. Two male dancers nearly yanked Jeanette's arms from their sockets during "Italian Street Song," but she still managed to sustain her famous high note for twelve full seconds. In reviewing the show, *Variety* predicted that MacDonald's "looks and voice will fit excellently into television." But Jeanette found the new medium a nightmare. Except for guest spots on Ed Sullivan's *Toast of the Town,* Milton Berle's *Texaco Star Theater,* and a few game shows like *Masquerade Party* and *What's My Line?,* she declined most offers to return to the small screen until 1955. Particularly unpleasant was a run-in with comedian Jackie Gleason. At a rehearsal for *The Jackie Gleason Show* in February 1953, Emily Wentz, ever vigilant, peered through one of the cameras to check how Jeanette would be lit. Gleason caught sight of her and roared angrily, "Who is that dame? Get her off the stage!" Jeanette, angered by Gleason's boorishness, walked over to Emily and said, "Come on, we're *both* leaving." Gleason had little choice but to apologize. "By and large," Jeanette later reflected, "television seemed like small potatoes."

Three days following *The Voice of Firestone,* MacDonald was at work on her first LP for RCA, *Romantic Moments.* The conductor was Broadway's Robert Russell Bennett. "Everything was going well in Studio 2 on Twenty-fourth Street until she tried 'San Francisco,' " recalled John Pfeiffer, Victor's legendary producer. It was MacDonald's first commercial recording of the song she had introduced fourteen years earlier. "She just couldn't get the transition from one key to the next," Pfeiffer recounted. "We did several retakes, but Jeanette kept flubbing the modulation. Finally, she became furious with herself. She threw the music off the stand, rushed to the control room, and burst into tears. I really found it humorous that she overreacted in this way, so I laughed. Jeanette looked at me and realized it wasn't the end of the world. She smiled, and we tried it again. It went beautifully."

For Pfeiffer, MacDonald was unique among great Victor artists: "She had an aura about her, and singing was only a part of it. She represented beauty, simplicity, and vivacity that took us away from all the problems we had. It was like a mother's lullaby to hear her sing. You didn't associate her with the huge bombast of an opera singer. You associated her with security and comfort, with home and mother."

Yet, as with the Prince Umberto scandals of two decades past, MacDonald still affected some people in utterly bizarre ways. In early 1951, Heinrich Lang, a butcher in Graz, Austria, claimed he was Jeanette's actual father. Lang explained that his daughter, "Julie," had fled the family in 1925 after he and Frau Lang forbade her to enter the motion picture business. The couple had just rediscovered "Julie" at a screening of *The Merry Widow.* A front-page story in *Neue Illustrierte Wochenschau,* the *People* magazine of postwar Austria, set old Lang family photos side by side with famous stills of MacDonald. It quoted the aggrieved "mother" as saying she wanted nothing more than a sign of recognition from her famous daughter: "Or is it harmful to her career for her to acknowledge us as her parents?"

Less glitzy than the Prince Umberto fable, this hoax aroused little attention in this country, perhaps because there was no Bob Ritchie—or any other publicist—eager to exploit it. Only Louella Parsons ran a brief notice: "Not since the stories that Shirley Temple was actually a dwarf and wasn't a child actress, and that the real Mary Pickford had been dead for years and another actress was taking her place, have we had as ridiculous a fabrication as the one printed about Jeanette Mac-Donald. . . . [W]hoever started the Austrian parents' yarn certainly has a good imagination (or a bad one)."

In still another scheme to refocus both their marriage and their careers, Jeanette and Gene worked out a plan for a joint return to Broadway. The vehicle was Ferenc Molnar's *The Guardsman,* the classic tongue-in-cheek comedy about a Viennese husband so jealously in love with his flirtatious wife that he disguises himself as a Russian military man in order to test her fidelity. Alfred Lunt and Lynn Fontanne had popularized the play in the mid-1920s; Nelson Eddy and Risë Stevens had starred in MGM's 1941 musical version, *The Chocolate Soldier.* For the MacDonald-Raymond revival, the lead roles were changed from married actress and actor to concert diva and actor husband. Molnar himself rewrote the second act to allow MacDonald a minirecital. Ads for the show pledged: "JEANETTE SINGS AT EACH PERFORMANCE."

Gene appreciated the gamble Jeanette was taking by costarring with him. That Christmas, he wrote an impish note to her and their two eldest dogs, Tray and Misty:

> Thanks for all the good things you've given to us all through the years which don't come in boxes and bright ribbons—things like love, thoughtfulness, and comfort when things aren't going well. I love you all!
>
> O[ld]. M[an]. R[aymond].

The tryout tour began on January 25, 1951, at Buffalo's Erlanger Theater. A blizzard left the house half empty, but those present agreed that Jeanette looked glorious in faux-Viennese gowns designed for her by Cecil Beaton. The audience went wild when Gene delivered the aside, "How can I seduce my own *wife?*" Yet by the time the production reached Kansas City, a new director, Peter Godfrey, had to be rushed in to mend serious staging problems. Godfrey's tinkering helped. In an unannounced visit to Washington, D.C.'s New Gayety Theater on April 11, Harry and Bess Truman—hours after the president had fired General Douglas MacArthur, Supreme Commander for Allied Powers in the Pacific—enjoyed the show thoroughly. Lee Strasberg, the guiding force behind Method acting, told Gene following a performance in Philadelphia: "You know, you were better than I thought you'd be." Everywhere the notices were as mixed as Strasberg's backhanded compliment. This *Guardsman* was entertaining, but it was not the scintillating comic gem Jeanette and Gene had hoped for.

"Without a foolproof success," MacDonald later explained, "we knew the Broadway critics would slaughter us as a couple from Hollywood daring to emulate the beloved Lynn and Alfred." After four months on the road, she and Gene decided to close down *The Guardsman.*

For recreation, the Raymonds spent part of the summer in Italy, joining Constance Hope and her ophthalmologist husband, Milton Berliner, in Venice. Gene would have preferred a quiet fishing trip in the Canadian backwoods, but to avoid discord he bowed to Jeanette's desire for warm weather and lively company. The first leg of their trip, on the *ràpido* from Milan to Venice, was "like an unending nightmare excursion to Coney Island," recalled Jeanette: "Eight other people were crammed into our compartment, chewing sandwiches, sucking oranges, guzzling wine, piling in and out and on top of us with their luggage. For six or seven hours, I brooded guiltily: 'If anything can finish off our marriage, this is it, and it's all my fault.' I could see that Gene was thinking the trip was going to be every bit as bad as he'd anticipated—only worse."

Once bathed in the Old World elegance of the Hotel Lido, however, they both felt rejuvenated. Jeanette sent a postcard to Hedda Hopper: "Believe it or not, I have never been to Italy before. Will be home in September. Tonite my first gondola ride and full moon!! Ooh Gene." The vacation's real highlight was a motor trip to the French Riviera and Jeanette's rediscovery of Antibes. She later mused: "This was the territory I knew and loved in the days of glory and nonsense as a movie queen. . . . It was paradise regained."

Following her European holiday, MacDonald decided it was time to settle a remaining score on the American opera scene: she was going to prove she could hold her own in an East Coast operatic production. That December she sang *Faust* with the Philadelphia Civic Grand Opera Company. Giuseppe Bamboschek, who conducted the sold-out performance at the Academy of Music, recalled that MacDonald's "sincerity, like her enthusiasm, was infectious." West Philadelphia High School seized the occasion to give MacDonald its Distinguished Alumni Award.

The homecoming showed that middle age had not consumed MacDonald's beauty. One observer remarked: "Now in her forties, she can still snip off ten to fifteen years if she is in the mood. Her lustrous red-gold hair, [her] facial and body contours all give evidence of being great pals with youth." Still, MacDonald had no illusions about her future as a leading lady in musical films. Asked if she might costar on-screen with fellow Philadelphian Mario Lanza, she replied that "although our voices are of a blending timbre, I think the difference in our ages would rule out any chance of Mario and [me] appearing opposite each other." At the same time, MacDonald turned down screen roles judged unworthy of her diva status. When an offer came from Europe to join tenor Raoul Jobin in a Technicolor version of *Mârouf,* the French opera by Henri Rabaud based on a story from *The Thousand and One Nights,* MacDonald's reply was to the point: "I find it is nothing I would be interested in, as the role of Princess Fatima is not of stellar importance."

Still hopeful that their future lay with the Broadway stage, the Raymonds temporarily closed down Twin Gables in 1952 and moved to New York. At first they rented a stylish dwelling at 4 East Sixty-second Street, just off Fifth Avenue. Then they moved into a palatial apartment on the tenth floor of 888 Park Avenue, just above Seventy-eighth Street. Jeanette delighted in its vast dimensions: "With twelve rooms to rattle around in, the new apartment had the lofty ceilings every singer needs for practice; and the living room was more than big enough for parties, with space left over for my grand piano."

MacDonald's circle of East Coast friends included Yvonne Mills, Constance Hope, and the breakfast-cereal heiress Marjorie Merriweather Post. Chief stockholder in the General Foods Corporation, the statuesque Post was the grande dame of postwar American high society and epitomized the kind of woman MacDonald most respected: ladylike and strong. Jeanette also applauded Marjorie Post's taste in vintage movies. When Post and her third husband, Joseph E. Davies (FDR's ambassador to Moscow), yachted to the USSR on their honeymoon, they regaled guests on diplomatic calls with after-dinner screenings of *Naughty Marietta.* The actress Dina Merrill, Post's daughter by her second husband, stockbroker E. F. Hutton, recalled: "I think we saw that at least seven times when I was a little kid!"

Manhattan brought a fair amount of frustration. MacDonald's pet effort was to produce a Broadway version of *San Francisco,* in which she would star. This venture fell through, however, when MGM, still profiting from reissues of the picture, refused her the story rights. Equally disappointing was a first read-through for Sandy Wilson's stage musicalization of Cecil Beaton's satiric memoir, *My Royal Past.* Anita Loos had shaped this property with MacDonald in mind, but a new British import named Hermione Gingold got all the laughs. "We broke for coffee," Gingold recounted, "and Anita Loos surreptitiously took as many of the cast aside as she could and told them to stop laughing at me and start laughing at Jeanette." The reading of the second half went only slightly better, with the cast tittering politely at MacDonald's lines while continuing to roar at Gingold's. The next morning Jeanette withdrew from the project, effectively killing it.

MacDonald later admitted that she and Gene had been misguided in holding out for a Broadway show. "Agent after agent bustled in with proposals for one or the other of us to do a television series. But we were terribly choosy; we were very disdainful; we were utter fools." Yet, thanks to his appearances on network dramatic shows like *Pulitzer Prize Playhouse, Lux Video Theater,* and *Schlitz Playhouse of Stars,* Gene's popularity slowly bounced back. Three weeks after turning forty-five, he became series host of NBC's acclaimed *Fireside Theater.* MacDonald, now fifty, stayed underemployed: "I, who found guest shots nerve-wracking, wouldn't dream of taking on the fifteen-minute, twice-a-week singing programs I was offered. I couldn't fancy myself appearing in anything so unpretentious. Dinah Shore, who accepted a similar offer when it came along, showed better sense. Good for you, Dinah!"

National TV caught MacDonald off guard on November 12, 1952. "THIS IS YOUR LIFE, Jeanette MacDonald!" bellowed Ralph Edwards, host of a new weekly series that condensed famous lives into half-hour, emotion-crammed surprise salutes. Jeanette, in the midst of a recital tour, had been coaxed to Hollywood's El Capitan Theater on the pretext of presenting an award to Edwards from the International Optimists Society. Even when told by a parking attendant to place her car "right over there beside Nelson Eddy's," she was mainly unsuspecting. Besides Eddy, the parade of significant others featured Edna Clear, Jeanette's beloved seventh-grade English teacher; her sisters, Blossom and Elsie; Grace Adele Newell, just turned seventy-eight; and an ex-sailor who once jitterbugged with MacDonald at the Hollywood Canteen.

Early in the show, Jeanette exchanged long-distance banter with Gene, who was supposedly on a hookup from New York but soon popped out from behind the curtains, smiling broadly, to join her on the settee of honor. "You played it very well and very straight," Jeanette chided with obvious affection. Next came Nelson, who brought tears to Jeanette's eyes when he reprised "O Perfect Love," the hymn he had sung at her wedding. Even Reverend Willsie Martin showed up to extol Jeanette and Gene for embodying "in their life the philosophy of the holy bonds of matrimony." As the show raced to its finish, Edwards gave Jeanette an engraved Bulova diamond watch, a matched set of Amelia Earhart luggage, and a pledge from the sponsor, Hazel Bishop No Smear Lipstick, to provide fifty young voice students with tickets to her second recital at Carnegie Hall, scheduled for January 16, 1953. Edwards exclaimed once again: "Jeanette MacDonald, THIS IS YOUR LIFE!—a life that has been an inspiration to many and a joy to those who know and love you."

Jeanette was moved, and it showed. The program inspired more fan mail than any installment of Edwards's NBC series. But MacDonald, engrossed with strategies for her future, was not especially inclined to promote the nation's increasing nostalgia for prewar Hollywood. She told Ken Richards, a young actor and film buff who frequently pumped her for reminiscences: "This is very unhealthy, Ken. You should really be worrying more about your career and not my old pictures."

Washington's first Republican Inaugural Ball in twenty-four years was also its most extravagant. Milton Cross, the radio voice of the Metropolitan Opera, was about to introduce MacDonald to the celebrants jamming the National Guard Armory on the night of January 20, 1953. Minutes earlier, Jeanette had led the crowd in the national anthem, wearing a Philip Hulitar evening dress of red, white, and blue chiffon, with color-coordinated bra, slip, and panties. Now she had to change into white satin for her two arias, and no one could find the white underwear that went with the white gown. Emily normally oversaw such matters, but she was ill. Pinch-hitting was Mary Agresta, MacDonald's housekeeper. "Well," Jeanette told Mary, "I can't wear what I just took off. They'd show through the gown." So with a shrug of the shoulders, she decided: "I guess I'll have to go without panties. But heaven help me and Ike if I fall down the stairs!"

MacDonald first met Dwight Eisenhower in Denver before one of her concerts. She was his favorite singing star. After he and Mamie took tea with her, the future president walked Jeanette to her car. "Please give my warm regards to my comrade-in-arms," he said, referring to Major Gene Raymond. Ike's gentility charmed Jeanette. Along with fellow Republicans John Wayne, George Murphy, and Irene Dunne, she strenuously campaigned for the Eisenhower-Nixon ticket and grew particularly fond of Mamie's mother, Elivera Carlson Doud, whose quiet dignity reminded her of Anna's.

The early Eisenhower years saw a renewed popularity of semiclassical music. The vogue even struck neon-lit Las Vegas, where the latest "gimmick," as *Newsweek* put it, was "long-hair talent." Lauritz Melchior, Ezio Pinza, Robert Merrill, and the flamenco dancer José Greco constituted, with MacDonald, a new wave of concert artists who drew upon the stunning $6 million spent by the casino bosses on name entertainment in 1953. MacDonald had her usual jitters when she made her debut in the Hotel Sahara's Congo Room on March 10. She opened with "Beyond the Blue Horizon" and confessed her stage fright to a receptive audience. Her thirty-minute act, made up of songs from her films, had a format similar to that of her recitals. A touch defensively, she told the reporter Erskine Johnson: "Just because it's a night club, I don't feel I have to inject any tricks." It was MacDonald's view that "whether you sing in an auditorium, a saloon, a dive, or an air-raid shelter, good music will appeal."

And it did. Her Sahara gig played to capacity crowds. Still, when she came back for a three-week run at the Sands in October, MacDonald took the advice of Wilbur Clark, owner of the Desert Inn: "You've got to keep up with yourself or you're real dead here. You always need something Vegas hasn't ever seen before." This time Jeanette built her act around the kinship between older and newer music. To open, she segued from a special arrangement of Irving Berlin's "There's No Business Like Show Business" to Georges Bizet's "Ouvre ton coeur." One of her skits was a takeoff on the shift from radio to television. Later she paired Puccini's "Un bel dì vedremo" with a current pop tune, the lush "Ebb Tide" by Carl Sigman and Robert Maxwell. As a surprise finale, MacDonald joined dancers Bill Alcorn and Jack Mattis in an intricate romp to a medley of standards from her films and records. The routine brought down the house. When MacDonald took the act to the Cocoanut Grove in January 1954, the *Hollywood Reporter* certified it a "smash hit." Many ranked her legs, hidden from public display since *Broadway Serenade,* in a league with Dietrich's.

Smoky, rattly night clubs were not, however, MacDonald's cup of tea. She much preferred concert halls, where she could better control herself, her repertoire, and her audience. In truth, MacDonald's main purpose in subjecting herself to two shows nightly and three on Saturday was to prove her stamina and drawing power to potential Broadway investors. A younger generation of singer-comediennes—Florence Henderson, Julie Andrews, Gwen Verdon, Kaye Ballard—would soon bring new luster to the Great White Way. But Broadway could occasionally make room for Hollywood veterans, as Rosalind Russell had just shown by opening to acclaim in Leonard Bernstein's *Wonderful Town*. Even Bette Davis had recently made a Broadway comeback in the ill-fated musical revue *Two's Company*. Surely, MacDonald persisted in telling herself, there was a place on the boards for Hollywood's best-known and best-loved soprano.

Nelson Eddy, who debuted in nightclubs before MacDonald, thrived in cabarets. He jumped at the chance to spoof his wooden movie image and, unlike MacDonald, to do an act totally free of highbrow traces. Audiences reveled in Eddy's newfound zing. All but the most die-hard Jeanette-Nelson fans cheered Gale Sherwood, his young and shapely new partner. "I couldn't possibly have taken Jeanette's place," admitted Sherwood, who teamed with Eddy until his death. "Jeanette had it all. She was a better musician than I. When Jeanette and Nelson sang, it was perfect. Her voice was higher than mine. My B-flats were round and rich, but it was always hard for me to hit the high C's. So musically, Nelson and I did not fit as well together. Mine was a 'personality' type of voice, best in ballads and comedy songs. But I did sing 'Indian Love Call' in Nelson's key." Sherwood, who often wore skimpy harem or Indian maiden costumes, also gave an unexpected sexual buzz to Eddy's act.

Eddy's love affair with the café circuit dampened MacDonald's hope for a screen reunion. The prospect originated in 1948, when MGM producer Arthur Freed reunited Ginger Rogers and Fred Astaire in *The Barkleys of Broadway*. At that time Joe Pasternak announced a similar return vehicle for MacDonald and Eddy, titled *Emissary from Brazil*. The project ended up in smoke, however, after Dore Schary took over the studio. Jeanette vented her frustration in a letter to Hedda Hopper on October 26, 1954:

> . . . For so many years, since Nelson and I split up, I have been besieged by questions how, when, why, where, etc. etc.—from sales people, taxi drivers, to strangers on the street, and newspaper people et al, that a reunion became almost an obsession with me—certainly a conviction . . . I am sure he has been besieged as I . . . but my impression has been that he has not warmed to the idea as have I. His present set-up gives him the uncontested stellar position, which is always a happy booster for the male ego. And Hedda, he is damned good! I saw him at the Copacabana and enjoyed his act thoroughly. His leading lady, Gale Sherwood, is fine—she is pretty, sings well, has a lovely figure, so what more could he want?

MacDonald told Hopper how betrayed she felt by "the new studio regimes":

> . . . Didn't it seem strange to you that in the MGM anniversary telecast
> of Ed Sullivan's show, about a year ago, there was not one clip of a
> MacDonald-Eddy picture? Didn't it also seem strange to you that in a
> Romberg story [MGM's *Deep in My Heart,* 1954], they abandoned first
> the idea of having Nelson and me in a sequence, settling on using a part of
> one of our pictures, then ending up skipping the whole idea? . . . I know
> that years ago a sort of hands-off policy was established through subtle
> propaganda, and that undoubtedly settled the question of our possibly
> being used by any of the other studios.

Jeanette took the matter into her own hands. She arranged a tenta-
tive deal with the producer David Rose for a MacDonald-Eddy picture
to be shot in England and distributed through Warner Bros. This Technicolor musical, alternately titled *A Kiss in the Dark* and *Will You Remember?,* was to draw on two classic Victor Herbert scores, *The Only
Girl* and *The Princess Pat.* To give the project momentum, MacDonald
quietly invested her own money in developing the script. The story
dealt with an attractive widower (Eddy) who shelters his niece from
Broadway show people only to fall in love himself with a famous operetta star emerging from semiretirement (MacDonald). "I assure you,"
Jeanette confided to her attorney Louis Swarts, "that while I hold no
particular love for Nelson, I am fairly practical-minded, and feel that
both his and my careers need a good hypodermic, and this would
surely be it."

Eddy, however, was ambivalent about a screen reunion. Ted Paxson,
his longtime accompanist, reported that Nelson was "always looking
for a film that would be as successful as *Naughty Marietta,* but not one
in which he would have to share star billing." Pressed to signal his intentions, Nelson at first informed Gene Raymond that the proposed
screenplay was not up to scratch: "I'm convinced that if we had a good
script this or any other—we wouldn't *have* to go to England, but
could do it right in Hollywood!" Then, when Eddy learned that Mac-
Donald was a silent investor, he backed out completely. Jeanette later
told Mabel Willebrandt: "I was so damned mad at such an infantile attitude that I simply became disgusted with the whole deal. . . . Being
practical, like most women, I have no pride where my career is concerned, and think Nelson has been influenced too strongly by either—
1. his own male ego, or—2. Ann's jealousy all these years."

MacDonald was so intent on making movie history one more time
that she even considered replacing Eddy with Maurice Chevalier: the
picture's locale would change from Broadway to London's West End;

and Rouben Mamoulian would be brought in to direct. This inspired plan, however, came to naught, as did another Broadway scheme, in which Leo McCarey would have directed her in a stage version of *Love Affair* (McCarey's classic RKO romantic comedy with Irene Dunne and Charles Boyer) that would now feature unpublished songs by Jerome Kern.

This string of failed starts inevitably eroded MacDonald's optimism. "It is, apparently, as difficult to convince the wise guys around Broadway that I have talent, or that I have what the public wants, as it is to convince the great moguls in Hollywood," she told Louis Swarts sarcastically. "And while you recommend patience, my impatience invariably stems from my observation of the lack of talent one sees today on the stage, on television, and in motion pictures."

MacDonald found a welcoming new venue in summer stock: "The choice I had was strictly limited. My kind of show—or rather the kind of show I was identified with—was under a pall on Broadway. Operetta was in a decline. Raucous musical comedy was the favorite of the day. . . . So I took the plunge with Noël Coward's *Bitter Sweet*."

George Schaefer, who directed her at the Dallas State Fair Musicals Festival, recalled her electric impact: "In the first scene, you could just hear people in the audience saying, 'Oh my God, she's aged! Lord, oh Mercy!' Then she had that very quick change, where she whips off the wig and comes out looking a radiant eighteen—which goodness knows she was not. But in that huge auditorium, and with the proper lights, it was a breathtaking transition. The audience just gasped."

Strong reviews and exuberant ovations restored MacDonald's self-confidence. In less than no time she tracked down Noël Coward during his Las Vegas debut at the Desert Inn and asked if he would let her do a Broadway revival of *Bitter Sweet*. According to Coward's friend Cole Lesley, "With the breath taken right out of his body, Noël just managed to say, 'No,' very firmly." Jeanette was crushed. She immediately sent off a note to Gene that ended: "I'm only the best when you're around! I love you. Your Old Lady." Tucked in the envelope was her longhand transcription of a Robert Browning lyric, added as a "belated Valentine's offering":

> Grow old along with me!
> The best is yet to be,
> The last of life, for which the first
>   was made.

When MacDonald returned from her first summer on the straw-hat circuit, Gene was making another Hollywood comeback. Joe Pasternak had signed him for a featured role in MGM's CinemaScope remake of the Vincent Youmans musical *Hit the Deck*. Gene's good fortune thrilled Jeanette. But as she unpacked amid the splendor of her sprawling Park Avenue residence, Jeanette absurdly convinced herself she was a total failure. Gene's mother had once predicted her daughter-in-law would become "a bitter, catty, unfair, sour, has-been movie star." Jeanette suddenly believed Mrs. Kipling had guessed the truth. "I was alone. The anxieties of the day spilled over into the nights. I paced the floor, plagued by insomnia and hay fever, as usual, one aggravating the other. . . . My judgment was all mixed up, and I couldn't trust that sixth sense anymore. I asked myself, night after night, 'How many mistakes are you making? You know about some. What about the others? How many mistakes can you afford to make?' "

On Friday, September 17, 1954, in a late-summer heat wave, Mac-Donald went clothes shopping on Madison Avenue because, she recalled self-reproachingly, "I had nothing better to do." When she arrived back at the apartment, she felt "weary from the heat and, more than that, exhausted to the bone by anxiety that never slept." As in *Love Me Tonight*, but this time for real, she walked through her front door and dropped in a dead faint. Emily, unable to bring her round, phoned Milton Berliner, who rushed over with Dr. Shepard Aronson, an internist. "When he examined me," Jeanette recounted, "I was hanging somewhere between consciousness and shadows. . . . I had no idea of what they were all thinking, but in my heart I felt that I would die. What difference did it make, anyway?" Her temperature shot up to 105 degrees, and when she failed to respond to antibiotics, the doctors grew uncertain about her chances for recovery. They later informed her that in addition to an unidentifiable virus, she suffered from "anemia," "tension," and "nerves twisted to the point of breakdown."

Gene flew in from the Coast. Jeanette was still in a daze when he walked into their bedroom: "I opened my eyes, and he was suddenly there. I puzzled for a moment over how he had arrived, what he was doing, where we were." After grasping her hand and kissing her forehead, Gene said, "Hello, Bunko." Then, climbing onto the bed, he lifted her head to his shoulder and whispered: "As soon as we've pulled you through, I'm going to take you home, back to California and the old place." Jeanette, feeling cozy and comfortable, fell asleep in her husband's arms.

Gene's shooting schedule required him to race back to Los Angeles. A few days later, Jeanette mustered up the energy to write him a letter:

9/54

My dearest,

Before this past eventful week-end, I'd have been embarrassed for fear of your thinking it silly and sentimental to address you so. Now, I know that whatever is true could never be silly—and this is true so why should I be timid about expressing it?!

I know, too, that your being here with me when I needed you so terribly did more to restore my long abused and deflated ego than anything that's happened in several years. All of the professional success etc. meant exactly nothing when I was lying in bed with only half of me functioning. So, accordingly YOU *are* my better half!! Now I realize fully what that means, only it's no joke where we're concerned. The MDs are all fine and can surely treat the physical me—but where the spiritual and mental me is concerned you and God are my only medicine. I give you 1st billing you'll notice because "You're the Best!" I hope that isn't considered sacrilegious. Anyway, in my book. I think God will agree with me. I hated to see you leave but you left me with something so sweet that I now know the meaning of "Parting is such sweet sorrow." I felt as secure in our love as a bride—and as cherished! The *depth of our* caring. . . . Thank you Pappie and for having asked me to be your wife. I'm glad I said "yes."

I love you.

Convalescence was a condition MacDonald had little patience for, but ten weeks of rest and inactivity brought back her strength and an eagerness to resume work. Her first engagement was a command solo recital at the White House on the evening of December 1, 1954. That afternoon, thanks to a ticket secured from Vice President Richard Nixon, Gene sat in the Senate gallery and witnessed the historic debate over a resolution to condemn Joseph McCarthy for demagoguery. The nasty, noisy proceedings were in striking contrast to the smooth civility of that night's state dinner to honor the president's cabinet members and their spouses. The dinner menu featured turtle soup, filet mignon, corn pudding, and tutti-frutti ice cream, but MacDonald was duty-bound to protect her voice (she was to sing *after* the meal) and had to hold back from sampling even a morsel. At the end of her program, Eisenhower put in a request for an encore: "Italian Street Song."

Back in their hotel suite, Jeanette was famished and ordered room service to bring her creamed chicken on toast. As they laughed over this culinary anticlimax, Gene gently reminded Jeanette how fortunate she was. True, she might never get a Broadway show. Nor might she ever make another Hollywood picture. But she was once again healthy; she had just enthralled the president of the United States; and she was about to return to their beloved Twin Gables.

"I never felt better in my life," she later reflected. "Loved and wanted and secure."

CHAPTER SEVENTEEN

"Carve your name in human hearts"

Jeanette MacDonald had two great talents—
one for singing, the other for living.

Sound engineer MIKE MCLAUGHLIN, 1965

MACDONALD MAINTAINED HER JOIE DE VIVRE in the mid-to-late 1950s, while becoming just a bit cynical. She missed the nonstop limelight and bouquets, yet had little need to eye popularity polls for confirmation of her worth. She devoted more time to charities, especially the American Cancer Society and the Jewish Home for the Aged. She pursued her music as she understood it, arguing madly for melody. When one reporter tagged her "the great, popular woman singer of not-so-long ago," she accepted this truth with a cool head.

Though Jeanette and Gene still searched for joint ventures, they no longer felt driven. On New Year's Day 1956, they emceed the first Tournament of Roses Parade to be color telecast from Pasadena. A few weeks later Jeanette was seen in *Prima Donna*, a charming sitcom pilot written by Gene and aired as part of NBC's *Screen Directors Playhouse*. She also played the "real" aunt in a *Playhouse 90* production of the classic drag farce *Charley's Aunt,* with Art Carney as the female impersonator and Gene as Sir Francis Chesney. Arthur Penn directed. Around this time, Gene set to work on a movie script about a college music teacher whose students go bonkers for rock and roll—an idea that took root when Ithaca College awarded MacDonald an honorary doctor of music degree. Planned as her second big-screen comeback, this project stalled and then ran out of steam.

Hard-core MacDonald fans were still a force to be reckoned with, as Harry and Bess Truman discovered on August 20, 1956. The former First Couple were among the record-breaking crowd of 7,214 who cheered MacDonald's debut in *The King and I* at Kansas City's Starlight Theater. When the Trumans learned they had disappointed Jeanette by not coming to see her afterward, Bess accounted for the un-intended breach of manners:

Dear Miss MacDonald—

Mr. Truman and I greatly appreciate your nice note, especially *of course* the part about Margaret.

And I must tell you that we and our guests *expected* to ask if we might go backstage to speak to you *until* they announced there were two thousand MacDonald Club "fans" coming backstage after the show! We were fans but did not belong to the Club and felt it would be an imposition to add one more handshake.

"Your" show is by far the most outstanding one they have put on this year and we were so glad we came home in time to see it.

Sincerely,
Bess W. Truman

PLEASE do not answer this note as it is simply by way of explanation and I have some slight idea of what your mail must be.

Early in the Kansas City run of *The King and I,* near disaster struck. "I was in the wings," recalled Jack Lee, the show's associate music con-ductor. "Jeanette was starting the verse to 'Hello, Young Lovers,' when all of a sudden I heard her slur, *'When I think of To-ohhhhm.'* I ran on stage and found she had fainted in the arms of Terry Saunders, who was Lady Thiang. Jeanette's secretary passed smelling salts to the cho-rus girls and they got her back on a little bit. When she finished the scene, we dropped the lights so a doctor could examine her. For the rest of the run, we shortened 'Shall We Dance?' and cut out the monologue 'Shall I Tell Him What I Think of Him?' "

MacDonald let it be known that her collapse was due to heat pros-tration, though in fact she had suffered a mild heart attack. Her trouper mind-set alone would have pushed her to complete the show's two-week run. But Jeanette's I've-got-to-prove-it-to-the-skeptics men-tality was also operating. "When I first saw *The King and I* on Broad-way," she explained, "I fell in love with the role of Anna, the governess who goes to the Court of Siam. 'This is a show *I* could do,' I told myself delightedly. I envied Gertrude Lawrence the part. But Dick Rodgers and Oscar Hammerstein II, hearing about my aspirations, couldn't see me as Anna. It looked as though this would have to be one more ambition I wasn't going to fulfill." Faced with the prospect of conceding defeat in Kansas City, MacDonald chose to fight back, no matter the strain on her heart. "I retained enough of the snippy little girl from Philadelphia to crow to myself, 'See, Mr. Rodgers? I told you so, Mr. Hammerstein!'" The day Gene and Grace Newell flew in to catch the show, Jeanette insisted on performing "Shall We Dance?" and the monologue in their entirety.

Rare color footage of MacDonald in rehearsal confirms her absolute rightness for the role. Jack Lee, who directed many Annas, judged MacDonald's to be one for the ages: "Jeanette, Gertie Lawrence, and Risë Stevens all had one thing in common, a sense of humor. Most of the ladies who have played the role since then have been *just* singers. But Jeanette truly committed herself to being an actress. She had that little icy way of slapping her lines back at Leonard Graves, who played the King."

MacDonald's last major concert took place at Milwaukee's Blatz Temple of Music on July 16, 1957. Described by the local press as "indestructible and irrepressible," she drew a capacity crowd of eighty-five hundred. With the MacDonald-Eddy films now being aired on late-night TV, Jeanette suddenly enjoyed new popularity. Much of her fan mail, she noted with glee, came from "young people, who say they once regarded their parents as cornballs for talking about the good old Jeanette MacDonald movie days, but changed their attitude after seeing my films on television." TV's comic giants—from Sid Caesar and Imogene Coca through Danny Kaye, Carol Burnett, and Tony Randall—regularly indulged in shrewd but loving parodies of the MacDonald-Eddy classics. "When they *stop* burlesquing me or us, I'll feel we're *done!*" Jeanette prudently told her fans. To those who derided her old pictures as mushy, she retorted: "Have we become so self-sufficient that we can live without sentiment? Sentiment, after all, is basic. Without it there is no love, no life, no family."

Later that summer MacDonald took part in a nostalgic reunion with Maurice Chevalier, who in a blazing return to Hollywood musicals was shooting Alan Jay Lerner and Frederick Loewe's *Gigi* at MGM. To celebrate Chevalier's sixty-ninth birthday, Arthur Freed and Vincente Minnelli threw a party on the set and arranged for MacDonald to be the surprise guest. When Maurice caught sight of his former costar, he dashed to greet her and smacked a kiss on her familiar lips. The media played up this show of abiding affection, with no one recalling the old rivalry. At one point, however, Maurice asked Jeanette, not quite innocently: "Why don't you make films any more?" Without missing a beat, Jeanette pointed to Gene and replied: "Because for exactly twenty years I've played my best role, by his side. And I'm perfectly happy."

On September 25, 1957, MacDonald reunited with Nelson Eddy on Patti Paige's TV show, *The Big Record.* In a medley of songs from *Naughty Marietta* Jeanette sounded under par, but she clung to the final high note in "Italian Street Song" for an amazing seventeen seconds. RCA responded to the public's renewed interest in the team by producing *Jeanette MacDonald and Nelson Eddy Favorites in Hi-Fi,* in both mono and stereo versions. The album featured remakes of four of their best-known movie duets plus a newly recorded solo for MacDonald, Ernesto Lecuona's "The Breeze and I." Within a year the record soared onto *Billboard*'s Best Selling LPs chart, placing the Singing Sweethearts in competition with Elvis Presley and Ricky Nelson. *Favorites in Hi-Fi* eventually went gold.

MacDonald never made peace with the musical revolution brought about by Presley, Bill Haley, and Chuck Berry. "I find nothing sustaining or beautiful in much of the so-called pop music of today," she asserted, issuing a warning that a steady diet of "noise" and "nervous beat" would result in an "undernourishment of America's soul for fine music." MacDonald deplored the record industry's efforts to segregate the youth market and to deprive most teens of what she called "the thrill of wonderful lyrics and the meaning of great melodies." In the late 1950s a few classical musicians with dazzling charisma, such as Leonard Bernstein, Maria Callas, and Van Cliburn, were enjoying mass adulation to rival that of MacDonald in her heyday. But except for the occasional operetta revival, pops concert, or supper club tribute to Herbert, Romberg, or Friml, semiclassical artists had few venues open to them. "I feel a little sorry for the young generation of serious singers," MacDonald told Edward R. Morrow on the TV show *Person to Person.* "You know, they have no outlet; everything is geared for popular music, and the operettas have sort of gone by the board."

Five weeks after the MacDonald-Eddy TV reunion, Louis B. Mayer died of leukemia at age seventy-two. Howard Strickling phoned Jeanette to ask if she would sing for the memorial service at the Wilshire Boulevard Temple on October 31. Unlike many attending the funeral, MacDonald participated out of genuine grief, not duty: "One

of the greatest sadnesses of life is to realize how much you owe someone when it's too late to express any gratitude. . . . I admired [L. B.
Mayer] to the end." Before two thousand mourners, Jeanette sang the
old man's favorite song, "Ah, Sweet Mystery of Life!" "I think he
would have been pleased," she later reflected. "It recalled the faraway
times he represented."

After an absence of over twenty-five years, Gene briefly returned to
the Broadway stage the following winter, playing a State Department
official accused of Communist espionage in Sol Stein's *A Shadow of
My Enemy,* based on the notorious Alger Hiss trial. In late November
1957, Jeanette had joined Gene for his opening tryouts in Washington,
D.C., and suddenly developed abdominal pains. Despite her protest
that it was simply a post-Thanksgiving stomachache, she was rushed to
Georgetown University Hospital, where Dr. James E. Fitzgerald performed an emergency appendectomy on December 1. Tokens of concern poured into her hospital room, including flowers from the Eisen-
howers and the Nixons and a note from Greer Garson that especially
perked up Jeanette: "Good gracious! Imagine two openings in the family in one week. Good luck to Gene and his play."

Luck, however, was not on the Raymonds' side. *A Shadow of My
Enemy* closed after five New York performances, and as a result of her
appendix surgery Jeanette came down with hepatitis. She and Gene re-
cuperated in Palm Springs.

That summer MacDonald applauded *Gigi* at its Hollywood premiere and called the film "quite poignant." A few weeks later, the *Saturday Evening Post* juxtaposed half-page photos of her and Chevalier
together, one from *The Merry Widow* in 1934 and another from
Chevalier's sixty-ninth birthday fete. Clearly, time had dealt kindly
with both. On the night *Gigi* grabbed nine Academy Awards, Chevalier
won a Special Oscar for "contributions to the world of entertainment
for more than half a century." Jeanette was overjoyed for Maurice, and
claimed not to envy Hermione Gingold their witty *Gigi* duet, "I Remember It Well." Yet in discussing her ex-partner's aptitude for grand-
fatherly roles, MacDonald was not immune from vanity. She told interviewer Tony Thomas: "Maurice—and I say this with all modesty—is
much, much older than I. . . . And of course, I'm by no means ready for
that!" (Chevalier was in actuality fifteen years MacDonald's senior;
Gingold, only six. But Hollywood, then as now, could be kinder to its
aging male stars: a man of almost seventy was venerated for smirking
at pubescent girls; a woman in her midfifties was used goods.)

Like Chevalier, MacDonald never stopped thriving on live contact with the public. In March 1959, she traveled east to Atlantic City to launch what was supposed to be a concert tour of fifteen small cities. Unwisely, she had arranged *An Evening with Jeanette MacDonald* with no business representation other than her personal lawyer. When she and conductor Robert Armbruster arrived at the Warren Theater, they discovered that Imperial Attractions, Inc., the tour's New York–based producer and booking agent, had not printed tickets and posters until forty-eight hours prior to the Sunday concert. The upshot was inevitable: barely four hundred people showed up in a house that held three thousand. Worse, staffing was so inadequate that minutes before curtain time Jeanette herself was setting lights and giving cues. After the performance, her promoters declared themselves unable to meet MacDonald's guaranteed fee. Jeanette saw no way out but to withdraw from the tour at once. Three days later, *Variety* reported the story under a page-two headline: "INEXPERTLY CONTRACTED AND MANAGED: JEANETTE MACDONALD NOT PAID OFF IN ATLANTIC CITY." MacDonald went on to sue Imperial for $14,000. "It was quite a disastrous experience," she confessed to a friend.

Except for chronic allergies, Jeanette had enjoyed impeccable fitness most of her life. The viral infection and nervous exhaustion in 1954, as well as the cardiac incident two years later, were anomalies. By early 1960, however, MacDonald's health was tottering. On a weekend retreat at Harry and Yvonne Mills's estate in Rye, New York, Jeanette suddenly found herself short of breath and unable to speak. Terrified, she scribbled a note to a servant: "Please call Mrs. Mills—tell her to [instruct] Mr. Raymond to come here right away—I am sick." A few hours later, on Sunday, March 27, 1960, MacDonald was admitted to Manhattan's Presbyterian Hospital, where she remained for the next four weeks. The diagnosis was bronchial pneumonia. The following year Jeanette learned she had valvulitis, a rheumatic heart disease. Because cardiac arrest had caused the deaths of her mother and father, MacDonald rightly feared that she, too, would succumb to this killer. On orders from her physician, she canceled all plans for travel and public appearances.

It was around this time that MacDonald was drawn to the Church of Religious Science, a California-based spiritual movement. Having long ceased to identify as a Presbyterian, Jeanette was ripe for embracing an alternative religion. "I'm not sure whether I believe in God or not," she once wrote. "But let me qualify that statement. I mean the fire and brimstone sort of religion that tends to make us more superstitious than pious." Her attraction to Religious Science lay in its belief that one need not fear judgment in the afterlife, since God is love and the soul is "forever and ever expanding." Soon, practitioners of Religious Science made frequent visits to Twin Gables. Along with counseling Jeanette when she was ill, they gave instruction to Gene and Emily, who joined Peggy Lee, Fernando Lamas, and Jeanette's friends Lloyd Nolan and Leon Ames as disciples.*

Wavering health gave new impetus to MacDonald's decision to write her autobiography. When she started the project in the mid-1950s, she hired a succession of ghost writers but wound up firing them all. One, she reported, was too "mushy"; a second distorted truth for the sake of drama; she described the third as "too fond of the cocktail hour." Finally Jeanette took solo control of the manuscript. "It's a real chore," she told one interviewer. "I'm up to my neck in me and my past and past pictures and what I've done until I could almost scream. . . . Thank heavens I have only *one* life to give to my country."

Many expected MacDonald to call her memoir *The Iron Butterfly.* Her own preference, *No Royal Road to Song,* got vetoed by her New York publisher, Julian Messner, Inc. Another working title was *Do Re Mi,* whose hidden meaning she later divulged: "I came to Hollywood frankly for the DOUGH; when I was a star, I met the RAY—Gene—and we were married; and then, as Mrs. Raymond, I really found ME." MacDonald hoped the book would persuade readers she was not "the angelic creature that I seemingly represent to a certain group of people." The manuscript candidly described her romantic entanglements with Jack Ohmeis and Bob Ritchie and Ernst Lubitsch as well as with Gene: "I think those romances, in their fashion, will help young people who are going through the same problems that I had to go through when I was trying to mix a career and romance."

Before the book's planned publication in December 1960, MacDonald's editors required her to obtain releases from those who figured prominently in her story. In a letter to Bob Ritchie, MacDonald assured her ex-consort he would "come off extremely well." Ritchie, who still

---

*Unlike Christian Science, Religious Science promotes healing through the mind *in conjunction with* established medical practice. MacDonald always sought out the finest MDs available to her.

carried a torch for Jeanette and was miffed at having been excluded from her *This Is Your Life* telecast, replied:

Dear Shorty—

Enclosed herewith!

Re my "coming off extremely well"—[that's] certainly not a world-shaking statement. How else could I "come off"?

And you know it better than anybody does—but on occasion you've taken a very funny way of showing it.

And still with only your best interests in mind—don't let anybody rush you to a dead-line. You've missed the Xmas market, so why?

If there is any way I can help, aid, assist, abet, etc., let me know—because it could be a helluva book—and should be!

As the fellow says, "as if you didn't know."

Bob

MacDonald asked Nelson Eddy to approve her anecdote about a never-completed sculpture he once did of her. Eddy answered wittily:

[September] 14 [1960]

Dear Jeanette,

Sure, it's okay.

Thanks for asking.

I'm only sorry that you can't add that *your* bust did you justice, instead of being a bust!

Hope the Book is a bang.

Best to you and Gene from me and all,

Nelson

The book never got printed. It hit a fatal snag when the publisher rejected MacDonald's final draft as too genteel and insisted she spice it up with celebrity bedroom gossip. MacDonald refused. In a letter to a correspondent, she explained:

. . . I am sorry to report that for the time being I have abandoned [my memoir] because of publisher difficulties. They, seemingly, were not satisfied with the rewrite, and I became disgusted with their attitude, inasmuch as they, apparently, want something more controversial than I could give them. They published *Peyton Place* and *The Return to Peyton Place*—both, as you know, full of "smut." I just cannot reshape my life to please their kind of readers.

So until I find the right publisher, I am putting it completely out of my mind, and trying to get some much-needed sleep!

Although she kept tinkering with her manuscript, MacDonald never resubmitted it. When she owned up that the book might never see the light, she took solace in recalling a Presbyterian minister's words she had memorized in childhood: "Marble and granite are perishable monuments, and their inscriptions may be seldom read. Carve your names in human hearts; they alone are immortal."

The early 1960s brought tantalizing ideas for new MacDonald projects. Harold Prince, decades before hiring Glenn Close, imagined Jeanette as the perfect choice to star in a staged musicalization of *Sunset Boulevard*. "I had what I still think is a marvelous idea," the producer said in 1991 while reworking the property with composer Andrew Lloyd Webber. "And that was to star Jeanette MacDonald as Norma Desmond and Nelson Eddy as Max, her former co-star who had become her chauffeur." Prince and his partner Robert Griffith, who had just coproduced the Pulitzer Prize–winning *Fiorello,* met with MacDonald at Twin Gables in December 1960. Prince reminisced: "It was a beautiful house, and she was a beautiful woman. More beautiful in person, I believe, than on film. Her coloring was exquisite. She invited me to their library to make us each a martini, and she gave an excellent impersonation of a glamorous and seductive star. I was lost—*until* she asked me what I intended to call the musical. I replied, *The Iron Butterfly*. Rather coldly, she replied, 'That is what *some* people in Hollywood called me.' 'I know,' I said." Though MacDonald had reservations about playing a delusional Hollywood has-been, Hal Prince stayed optimistic: "In truth, I think she would have done it, but, if my not always accurate memory serves me, she died before we got to write the show."

Another show in which MacDonald would have played a faded star was *A Little Night Music,* a dreamy concoction conceived for her and the young Liza Minnelli by composer Hugh Martin and librettist Marshall Barer. Other overtures came from the movie producer Ross Hunter, who wanted MacDonald for *The Thrill of It All,* his spoof of TV starring Doris Day, and from Frank Loesser, the stage composer who had blended musical comedy, operetta, and opera in *The Most Happy Fella* and who now wooed MacDonald for a part in *Greenwillow,* his new musical set in bygone rural America. MacDonald claimed to be tempted by the Mother Abbess, written for contralto, in Rodgers and Hammerstein's *The Sound of Music.* When director Robert Wise cast the screen version a few years later, MacDonald's name cropped up, but according to Saul Chaplin, the film's associate producer, "she was never under serious consideration for the role." TV mogul Aaron Spelling was more aggressive in pursuing her—and Nelson Eddy—for an episode of *Burke's Law*, "Who Killed Rigoletto?," but ultimately to no avail.

Most of MacDonald's energies went toward custom-designing vehicles of her own. After buying the rights to "When the Wood Grows Dry," a *Ladies' Home Journal* story by Gladys Taber, she hired DeWitt Bodeen, the screenwriter of *I Remember Mama*, to adapt it into a teleplay called *The Rosary*. (L. B. Mayer, who always wept at renditions of Ethelbert Nevin's fin de siècle love ballad "The Rosary," often told MacDonald that *The Rosary* would make a great title for a movie starring her.) When *Playhouse 90* turned down *The Rosary* because of "technical impracticability," MacDonald tried without success to get Frank Capra, fresh from his own comeback with *A Hole in the Head* and *Pocketful of Miracles*, to direct it for the large screen. Another ambitious idea, developed with scriptwriter Donn Mullally, was a series of TV docudramas on famous figures in music and the people who influenced them. Inspired partly by Leonard Bernstein's *Young People's Concerts*, MacDonald conceived of the series as helping to make television a friendlier medium for classical music. Her outline of thirty installments, registered with the Writers Guild, included profiles of Jascha Heifetz, Lotte Lehmann, and Gian Carlo Menotti, and stories from the past, such as George Sand's affair with Chopin and the inspirational loves of Puccini. Jeanette saw herself as hosting the programs and capping each with a celebrity interview.

MacDonald was now at a stage in life where tributes began piling up. One memorable salute occurred in February 1960, when she won the Woman of the Year award from the Philadelphia Club of Advertising Women. It was the first time this honor, given for exceptional "achievement and womanhood," went to an entertainer and a native daughter. Prior recipients had been Elizabeth Arden, from business; Ivy Baker Priest, from government; and "Babe" Didrickson Zaharias, from sports. As the festivities unfolded in the Crystal Room of the Benjamin Franklin Hotel, a telegram arrived from President Eisenhower:

BEFORE LEAVING FOR SOUTH AMERICA, I WOULD LIKE TO SEND GREETINGS TO THE MEMBERS AND GUESTS OF THE PHILADELPHIA CLUB OF ADVERTISING WOMEN GATHERED IN HONOR OF MISS JEANETTE MACDONALD. I UNDERSTAND THAT MISS MACDONALD IS BEING HONORED FOR HER EXEMPLARY CITIZENSHIP AND FOR HER SPLENDID RECORD

OF COMMUNITY SERVICE. THE WORK SHE HAS DONE FOR THE
ARMY EMERGENCY RELIEF FUND IS DESERVING OF SPECIAL
ATTENTION. PLEASE GIVE HER MY PERSONAL CONGRAT-
ULATIONS AND BEST WISHES. DWIGHT D. EISENHOWER

Also read was a bon mot from Nelson Eddy:

> . . . As an old-time Philadelphia advertising man, allow me to join you in
> your salute to Miss Jeanette MacDonald, of whom all Philadelphia is
> proud.
>   I am honored to have been associated with her in motion pictures and
> proud of our record of eight happy marriages therein.
>   I wish her continued success and give her my continuous
>
> Sincerity,
> Nelson Eddy

From Beverly Hills, Blossom wired:

PLEASE TELL JEANETTE MCDONALD [*sic*] NO MATTER HOW
MANY MILES SEPARATE US I AM THINKING OF HER TONIGHT.
IF I HAD MY VERY OWN NEWSPAPER I'D PRINT A SPECIAL
EDITION WITH HEADLINES READING JEANETTE MAC RAYMOND
WINS ANOTHER AWARD — FOR BEING THE NICEST KID SISTER
IN THE WHOLE WIDE WORLD. LOVE. BLOSSOM.

For quite a while Jeanette had been keeping the wolf from Blossom's
door. When her husband, Rocky, now night manager of the Beverly
Hills Hotel, developed terminal cancer of the esophagus, Blossom had
what Jeanette called "a complete breakdown, due, no doubt, to anxiety
and overwork." A few months before Rocky's death in July 1960,
Jeanette wrote to her sister:

> Dear Blossie,
>
> It's difficult to say some things without becoming emotional—(for both of
> us perhaps), so I want to write to you what I really want to say—(as your
> little sister taking a *big* sister's attitude).
>   I want you to *take back the money* that you so *conscientiously* paid back
> to me on that [$5,000] loan—I *do not need* it and *you do*. It will relieve
> you of some of the anxiety about where Rocky's nurse's monies are coming
> from. If you recall, I gave you a note saying if anything happened to me—
> to *forget* the loan entirely—NOW let's forget the loan until you are *all* well
> and able to work again—and the doctor *assures* me (& you too) that you
> can work again after your current problem's solved. *Please* let me help you
> solve it!! Remember, we've always been very close and these are times when
> we need each other. So please help me as I want to help you. (Understand—
> this is only a loan!) Now maybe that will make you feel better. I took out

$1,728.33. Imagine I didn't take it out—for it is all YOURS—and that will take care of plenty of nurses and doctors!

So STOP worrying about money. Remember God supplies us with plenty when we believe and trust in "him." You go ahead and pay the bills on *your* checking acct so as not to get too involved, but I will simply put the money in it to replenish it. No problem at all.

Your loving sister,
Jimmee

P.S. No arguments! please!

Despite her generosity, MacDonald continued to frown at needless spending. For nearly seven years she was content to drive a white-and-green no-frills 1955 Buick. Gene ended this austerity when, in June 1962, he surprised her with a silver-blue Jaguar for their twenty-fifth wedding anniversary. Jeanette squawked at the extravagance and roguishly reciprocated by having Gene's Golden Hawk Studebaker painted silver. Gene found a more frugal way to touch her when, on the day of the anniversary, he sent Jeanette a single pink rose of the variety that had adorned their wedding ceremony a quarter century earlier. She conveyed her feelings in a note:

Dearest Pappie—

The sweetest thing you could have done this year was to remember "Joanna Hill" Day—not so much that it was June 16 but "J. H."—In our world of fading sentiment an occasional lapsing into the tenderness of "early love" is the most reassuring thing I can think of for reviving "faith"—

Thank you—and in turn—

All my love,
O[ld]. L[ady]. R[aymond].

That same month marked the silver anniversary of the Jeanette Mac-Donald International Fan Club. Clara Rhoades, the editor of the club's newsletter, was a schoolteacher from Topeka, Kansas, who had met MacDonald in 1940 and developed a good friendship with the star during the years that followed. To celebrate the club's twenty-five years, Rhoades joined MacDonald in planning a get-together in Los Angeles. Jeanette, who thought of her fans as an extended family, dubbed their conclave a "Clan Clave," and there have been Clan Claves each June ever since. During that first Clave, the Raymonds hosted dinner for forty members at the Luau, a Polynesian restaurant, and with MacDonald's blessing the group descended upon Twin Gables and got to roam at will. "It's really quite amazing," Jeanette told reporter Bob Thomas. "You don't see [their] kind of loyalty very often." MacDonald also arranged for the faithful to visit and eat lunch at MGM, where they watched *Smilin' Through*—the winning title of a club preference poll. Until Lorimar Productions took over the Culver City lot in 1987, studio publicist Dore Freeman each year arranged for the Clan to watch two classic pictures of their choice in an MGM screening room. Norma Shearer Thalberg was the only other party regularly accorded this privilege.

In summer 1981, nineteen years after the first Clan Clave, *Variety* observed: "With the tone set by Gene Raymond, . . . warmth and humor—not mawkish posthumous drooling—marked the forty-fourth anniversary banquet of the Jeanette MacDonald International Fan Club at the Beverly Hilton last week. . . . Those present represented a fraction of the club's all-time high membership of 1,800—a 300 increase over 1980."

It was tempting for MacDonald to use her fan club as a platform for her politics. During Richard Nixon's unsuccessful 1962 bid for the California governorship, she and Gene made public appearances "to convince people that this man is really a great man." Yet in a message "to those of you in our Club who are Democrats," Jeanette insisted: "I hope this will not make any difference in your feelings toward us. After all, the one thing I think we must all be grateful for is that we still have the right to believe and vote as our conscience dictates." That Thanksgiving, as President John F. Kennedy stood strong against Nikita Khrushchev and the buildup of Soviet missiles in Cuba, MacDonald told club members: "These days, one lives from day to day hoping that the Cuba crisis will be met with good American traditional determination not to allow ourselves to be pushed around by a couple of crackpots like Castro and company."

On the day of the Kennedy assassination, MacDonald coincidentally was in Texas, recovering from surgery for a blocked artery. Troubled by blackout spells, she had flown to Houston's Methodist Hospital on November 1, 1963, to consult with her new physician, the pioneering Michael DeBakey of Baylor College of Medicine. "She was having symptoms resulting from a stenotic lesion in the right carotid artery," recalled Dr. DeBakey, who had recently perfected a procedure to ease this ailment. DeBakey advised surgery for Tuesday morning, November 5, and performed "a right carotid endarterectomy to relieve the obstructed blood flow to the brain on that side."

According to DeBakey, the operation produced "a very good result." Within a week, however, MacDonald came down with pleurisy and as a consequence remained at the Houston hospital through mid-January. Gene, whose mother had died of cardiac arrest earlier that year, took a room in Methodist Hospital and remained at Jeanette's bedside until New Year's Day, when he had to head home to shoot Ross Hunter's *I'd Rather Be Rich,* a Sandra Dee comedy. Blossom pinch-hit for Gene until she, too, had to race to Los Angeles for an appearance on the *Phil Silvers Show.*

When MacDonald left the hospital on January 19, 1964, she didn't return to Twin Gables. The previous summer she and Gene had sold the Bel-Air house to Gene's business manager, Bo Roos, largely because climbing stairs was putting excessive strain on Jeanette's heart. "Gene and I . . . are trying to simplify our living," MacDonald explained to a friend just before vacating her twenty-one-room estate. In late August the Raymonds moved into a large double apartment on the eighth floor of the Wilshire Comstock, a luxury high-rise in Westwood. Emily Wentz, after two decades of virtual cohabitation, now had her own address on Olympic Boulevard in a Beverly Hills apartment building, which she managed for its owners—Gene and Jeanette.

"The Times They Are a-Changin'," sang Bob Dylan on his first hit album in 1964. The mood of America was indeed shifting from complacency to soul-searching, from orderliness to public turmoil. A nation grieving for its dead president had witnessed the assassin's murder on TV. As African Americans marched on Washington to protest institutionalized racism, President Lyndon Johnson was tightening screws on the Vietcong, student demonstrators were being arrested in Berkeley, and Betty Friedan was sparking women's liberation with her bestseller, *The Feminine Mystique.* Old assumptions about entertainment were also falling by the wayside. ABC's *Peyton Place* pushed the bounds of prime-time TV sex to new extremes. Barbra Streisand—who would burlesque MacDonald on Mike Douglas's TV show—conferred glamour upon in-your-face ethnicity. Caged go-go girls set the pace for jerky disco dancing. Nancy Sinatra and Joey Heatherton were hailed, prematurely, as star vocalists. The TV appearance of the Beatles on *The Ed Sullivan Hour* gave notice to the world in January 1964 that the sound and style of popular music would never be the same.

A few weeks after the Fab Four took New York by storm, *The Judy Garland Show,* which followed Sullivan on Sunday evenings, featured

Judy and guest star Jack Jones in a medley of songs from MacDonald-Eddy movies. After Judy's intense rendition of "Lover, Come Back to Me," the twenty-six-year-old son of Allan Jones remarked: "You know, Jeanette MacDonald didn't make *all* her pictures with Nelson Eddy." Pretending this was news to her, Judy responded: "Oh, you can't be serious; why, the next thing you'll be telling me is there's no Santa Claus!" In homage to Jack's father, the pair segued into a swingy duet of "The Donkey Serenade" from MacDonald's *The Firefly*.

Jeanette, recuperating at home, watched the Garland show with small satisfaction. The segment, she thought, was a hopeful reminder that "her" music might yet survive through effective jazz and pop treatments. But it was also clear to her that Jack, Judy, and jazz were themselves old hat in a pop-music business now dominated by the Beach Boys and the Supremes.

Still, MacDonald's MGM movies provided a secure frame of reference for those left cold by contemporary trends. The year before her arterial surgery, MacDonald gave a talk at the Colorado Theater in Pasadena, where *Sweethearts* was part of a screen operetta retrospective. Afterward, one spectator informed the management: "We want love and trust and understanding and courage and faith and honor. Like Miss MacDonald said the other evening, we want to leave the theater feeling good, and happy to be numbered among the human race." Later that year, Jeanette introduced a revival of *Maytime* at the Picwood Theater in Westwood. "I couldn't be more flattered," she told the packed house,

> having you all come here tonight, and it really makes me feel good to know that you all have supported these pictures, that this is the kind of moving picture you all like—to feel good, even though maybe a little sad, when you leave the theater; and you do like to have the kind of music that Nelson and I and some of the others have tried to offer you.

Mike McLaughlin, MacDonald's sound engineering wizard, was in the audience that night. After asking him to stand and accept applause, Jeanette paid tribute to another "great guy" who was present:

> Now they always say that a woman likes to have the last word. I don't know who *they* are, but *they* say women like to have the last word. I don't always agree with them, do you girls? However, tonight I'm going to pass up this great privilege of having the last word and I'm going to pass it on to someone else. Now perhaps this young man doesn't take any credit for recording my voice, or maybe my singing, but I must say he should take credit for *living* with a prima donna all these years. He survived, and I might

add, his disposition is very, very good through it all. So I thought maybe you would like to meet the gentleman I like to call my better half—Gene Raymond.

Gene quipped, "I might as well make the most of this—it's very seldom it happens," and went on in a humorous vein:

> I really don't know what I am doing up here because I didn't even play a bit in this picture. Of course, I could use the opportunity to clear up one misconception that has prevailed in certain circles of the population through the years, and that is, despite what it says on our marriage certificate, Jeanette is really in actuality married to Nelson Eddy! As a matter of fact, through the years, you know, Nelson and I have cultivated quite a sense of humor about this because he's frequently mistaken for me, and I'm frequently mistaken for him. . . . I don't know why this should be because in actuality Nelson and I don't look anything alike. He's big and robust, and handsome, and magnetic, and I'm not even a robusto baritone. But we've survived over the years, and it's really, I think, solely because of Jeanette that this mistaken identity occurred. . . .
>
> This particular picture is my favorite of all her beautiful performances. And of course it's sort of a milestone in our career together because it was made during the time we were courting, and maybe I should say that I *do* have a part in this picture, because all the beautiful adrenaline you see flowing on the screen had to do with my performance off screen!
>
> At any rate, I just want to make my tribute to Jeanette for making so many beautiful things. She does all things well. As a matter of fact, as I have said before, she's the only woman in my family that ever made a brilliant marriage! Enjoy the picture, as I will.

Although she rarely ventured out for new films now, the big-screen debut of Hollywood's new soprano sensation, Julie Andrews, enticed MacDonald to go see *Mary Poppins*. Afterward, she wrote a fan letter to the film's other star, Dick Van Dyke:

> September 16, 1964
>
> My dear Mr Van Dyke,
>
> (Although, actually, it is hard to call you Mr. Van Dyke, since I feel I know you so well from your television series, which I see regularly.)
>
> I am sure the Walt Disney Studios are taking care of the stacks of fan mail you are, undoubtedly, receiving as a result of MARY POPPINS, which my husband (Gene Raymond) and I saw last week at Grauman's Chinese.
>
> My chief concern is my curiosity as to your lineage. You see, W. S. Van Dyke, whom I called Van or Woody, was my favorite director at Metro, and directed at least half of my most successful pictures. . . . My curiosity has been aroused by the fact that your wife, in your series, is named Laura. You see, my mother and Mrs. Van Dyke, Sr., were very close friends, attended book readings together, and, by a strange coincidence, Mrs. Van

Dyke's name was Laura. If, by any chance, your mother was Ruth, then she was Van's wife, and if this is so it is ironical.

Van had no patience with music, and I am particularly amused when I see what a truly magnificent dancer and musician you are. The main facets of your career certainly come to the fore in MARY POPPINS.

I am intruding on your personal address, I know, but I felt I had to get this off my chest, and to congratulate everyone concerned in the making of the picture. And I bless Walt Disney's genius for combining his wonderful talents and his loyalty in giving the oldtimers, such as Reggie Owens and Ed Wynn, opportunities to make brilliant come-backs.

Thank you again for your brilliant performance, and I know that you have just begun an even more brilliant future career.

Sincerely,
Jeanette MacDonald Raymond*

Around this time, Vivien Leigh was in Hollywood to film what would be her last picture, Stanley Kramer's *Ship of Fools*. Leigh coaxed reporter Radie Harris into setting up a brunch or tea with her idol, but MacDonald, too weak to accept, asked for a rain check. The next day Leigh received a photo inscribed by Jeanette with a message of reciprocal admiration, which Leigh proudly displayed on her dressing table. The two legends would never meet face-to-face and would die within thirty months of each other.

Now seven years older than her father had been when he fell victim to heart failure at age fifty-four, MacDonald felt her days were numbered. On October 1, 1964, the day Grace Newell turned ninety, Jeanette wrote to her hale and hearty teacher:

Dearest Gracie,

I want to explain something to you so you can enjoy life and not feel you must economize (the habits are hard to break). But last year I made a new will (morbid thought but important) and BEFORE any other bequests or arrangements are made, YOU will be taken care of for the REST OF YOUR life—no matter what the circumstances will be. You will have an income of $500.00 a month (6,000.00 per year). Now, dear Grace, I tell you this only because I'm sure as time goes on you have some concern about your future. But I want you to have the most out of life you can, for certainly YOU have made it possible for me to have had the most out of my work, for which you *know* I shall be grateful always. *Now!* I want you to take taxis to and from—no busses—and I want you to continue to have the doctor check

*Dick Van Dyke is not related to Woody.

you *regularly*—and *I* want to feel secure *myself* that you are taking care of *yourself* and not letting me wonder about you.

    Please understand that if you were my *real* mother instead of my adopted mother, I'd want it this way. 'Cause I love you very sincerely even tho I am not the demonstrative type.

Always with my deepest devotion,
Jeanette

MacDonald's premonitions were well founded. Four days before Christmas 1964, she was rushed to UCLA Medical Center and underwent surgery for abdominal adhesions stemming from her appendectomy seven years earlier. The operation overexerted her heart, and for a while her condition was "touch and go," according to Emily Wentz. Emily had planned to host a Christmas meal for Jeanette, Gene, and Blossom, who was at last enjoying national celebrity through her role as Grandmama in *The Addams Family* TV show. "Gene managed to make it to dinner and then returned to the hospital immediately," Emily remembered.

Jeanette was released from the Medical Center on New Year's Eve, but the private nurse caring for her at home reported that "Mrs. Raymond remained very sick." Her condition stabilized for about a week, and then went from bad to worse. When she failed to gain strength and appetite, Dr. DeBakey, in consultation with MacDonald's specialists in Los Angeles, raised the possibility of open-heart surgery similar to that which he had performed on the duke of Windsor a few weeks earlier. At six in the morning on Tuesday, January 12, 1965, Gene phoned DeBakey's office and instructed the surgeon's assistant to reserve a hospital room for Jeanette and to have an ambulance meet them at the Houston airport. Mary Agresta, the Raymonds' housekeeper, accompanied them on the trip. To calm himself, Gene inscribed each task at hand in his date book.

The noonday Continental flight upset Jeanette's stomach. As the plane approached Houston, Air Control informed the captain that the hospital ambulance had not yet arrived on the tarmac. Gene, irritated, pressured the pilot to order another, and by touchdown a substitute vehicle was waiting. During the ride to the hospital Jeanette shivered beyond control, murmuring that she wanted only to fall sleep. "When I saw her," DeBakey related, "she was suffering from very severe congestive heart failure resulting from severe mitral and aortic valve disease." DeBakey immediately ordered tests and put Jeanette on intravenous feeding in the hope of improving her ability to survive surgery.

That evening Gene reminded Jeanette that the next day was the thirteenth, their good-luck number. Wednesday in fact turned out to be uneventful.

On the afternoon of Thursday, January 14, Jeanette was resting calmly. All of a sudden she told Gene her feet were cold. Slipping his hands under the bedcovers, Gene began to massage them. Jeanette smiled and whispered, "I love you." Gene replied, "I love you, too." He then heard a long, low sigh, and watched Jeanette's head drop. It was 4:32 P.M.

As two dispatchers wheeled MacDonald's body to the hospital morgue, Gene arranged for a private undertaker to prepare the remains for travel. He then phoned the news to Blossom and Elsie, and afterward called Helen Ferguson, who offered to help plan a funeral.

Gene needed fresh air. He exited the hospital and roamed, aimless, losing all sense of time. After several hours Mary Agresta tracked him down, and they flew back to Los Angeles with Jeanette.

CHAPTER EIGHTEEN

"Just the echo of a sigh"

Music, when soft voices die,
Vibrates in the memory.

PERCY BYSSHE SHELLEY, 1821

MACDONALD'S LEAVE-TAKING at Forest Lawn Memorial-Park had all the pomp and circumstance that defined MGM in its glory days. For *Newsweek,* it was "the funeral of the year"—though, for January 18, the judgment seemed hasty. Howard Strickling and studio publicity veterans helped orchestrate the event. Yet the glitz and splash in no way detracted from the intensity of real feeling. For the three hundred mourners inside the chapel as well as the estimated two thousand outside, this lavish Hollywood adieu was a fit expression of love and reverence for a movie queen who had touched their lives prodigiously, in a unique and indelible way.

To attend the service, high on a hill, one passed slopes with names that still conjure up Jeanette MacDonald musicals—Whispering Pines, the Mystery of Life Garden, Everlasting Love. The church itself looks as if it emerged from MacDonald's *Smilin' Through.* Gene Raymond had gallantly arranged for select members of the Jeanette MacDonald International Fan Club to attend the service inside the church. For the benefit of those outside—some had traveled from as far as Montreal and Manila—he had the proceedings carried over a loudspeaker. "Jeanette would want it that way," Gene was heard to say.

Deep within the church stood an open bronze casket lined with pink tufted satin. MacDonald was laid out in silver brocade embroidered with flowers. Covering her body from the waist down was a blanket of pink roses, an echo of her wedding. William Tuttle, MGM's chief makeup artist, lovingly restored luster to her complexion. Her manicured hands clasped a pink rose and the satin-and-gold prayer book she had carried at her marriage ceremony. Behind the bier were 140 floral pieces dominated by a huge cross of white roses and chrysanthemums signed "Ike and Mamie."

As mourners streamed into the chapel, an organist gently played melodies MacDonald had made famous. Strains of "Indian Love Call," "Zigeuner," "Wanting You," "Will You Remember?," and "Vilia" evoked memories, smiles, and tears. Cramming the pews were many of Jeanette's screen costars, including Allan Jones, Spencer Tracy, Lew Ayres, Jack Oakie, and José Iturbi. In the front-left rows were the pallbearers: Senator Barry Goldwater (recently defeated in his run for the presidency), NATO Supreme Military Commander General Lauris Norstad (his presence a tribute to Gene's participation in the Army Air Force Reserves), composer Meredith Willson, conductor Robert Armbruster, and actors Lloyd Nolan and Leon Ames. Honorary casket bearers included, from politics, former presidents Harry Truman and Dwight Eisenhower, Senator George Murphy, Chief Justice Earl Warren, former vice president Richard Nixon, and future governor and president Ronald Reagan; from music, Lauritz Melchior, Wilfred Pelletier, Collins Smith, and Giuseppe Bamboschek; and from the movies, Joe E. Brown, Maurice Chevalier, Alfred Hitchcock, Joe Pasternak, and Hunt Stromberg. Befitting the occasion, Hollywood's royal Mary Pickford made one of her last public appearances. The most sought-after figure in the chapel was Nelson Eddy, still a charismatic presence though reportedly suffering from a hernia condition.

Dr. Gene Emmet Clark of the Church of Religious Science, Beverly Hills, officiated. "Jeanette," he declaimed, "is one of the loveliest forms of expression that God's life has ever taken. That life lived *in* this body. Jeanette is one of the ways God expressed the beauty of His Spirit." He concluded by voicing gratitude, on the congregation's behalf: "Thank you, Jeanette, for putting something beautiful into our lives that we shall always cherish." Suddenly MacDonald's voice could be heard singing "Ave Maria." A leak to the press blunted the surprise for many, but still the effect was stunning.

Lloyd Nolan, a close friend of the Raymonds who had acted with MacDonald in *The Sun Comes Up*, delivered the eulogy: "We know that her glorious voice brought joy and delight to whole generations of people. Kings, princes, presidents—all sat entranced by the beauty of her song. Cameramen, grips, laborers—they listened and a strange transformation took place. They became kings, princes, and presidents under the spell of her magnificent voice. . . . Now, we must ask why? There were other voices, other lovely faces. What was different about Jeanette? Why is hers the voice and the face we shall always remember?" The answer, Nolan went on to say, was that when Jeanette sang "there was more than music": "There was warmth in her heart and in her song—magic in her voice—tenderness and affection for all mankind. She sang to you—to you alone—and to you she sent her message of love."

MacDonald's voice again filled the church, this time in "Ah! Sweet Mystery of Life." As the organist broke into "I'll See You Again," family and friends filed past Jeanette's coffin in a last farewell. Many had been to her wedding twenty-seven years before.

Newsweek rated the whole affair a "larger-than-life" demonstration of "what many Americans still consider the ultimate in funerals." The magazine also reported with a wink that when celebrities exited the church the "unbidden bereaved" rushed forward en masse, and "out came the autograph books." Many who were present contest this observation, calling it a reporter's fantasy. Still, it's a fan response that would not have displeased MacDonald.

On January 25, MacDonald's remains were placed in a pink-marble double vault at the Sanctuary of Heritage, a magnificent crypt within Forest Lawn's Freedom Mausoleum. The vault is on the right wall, two rows from the top, adjacent to those of singer Nat "King" Cole and comedians George Burns and Gracie Allen.

A report circulated that Nelson Eddy had inherited MacDonald's private copy of *Rose Marie*, but the information proved bogus. Jeanette never owned prints of her films. The memento she willed to Eddy was a silver plate etched with a scene from *Rose Marie*. Allan Jones received a similar gift, with a scene from *The Firefly*.

MacDonald left the bulk of her estate to Gene Raymond, who received half of it outright and the remainder as a trust fund. Upon Gene's death, monies from the trust are to go to the Motion Picture Country House and Hospital in Woodland Hills, California. Much of

MacDonald's jewelry went to friends and relatives, with Blossom and Elsie inheriting the more valuable pieces. Along with a lifetime annuity and Jeanette's Jaguar Mark II, Emily Wentz was left a matching brooch and necklace made up of a star sapphire, 120 baguette diamonds, 222 round diamonds, and 29 square ones. Nanette Wallace, Jeanette's grandniece, was the beneficiary of a trust account. Nanette later married Val Danneskiold, and they had a son. Their marriage ended in divorce.

In honor of her coach and fellow singer Lotte Lehmann, MacDonald willed her opera gowns, wigs, and costume jewelry to the Music Academy of the West, in Santa Barbara, for use in student productions. She bequeathed her leather-bound volumes of stills from her movies to the Hollywood Museum Associates for a planned museum.

In 1966, John and Michelle Philips of the newly hot vocal group the Mamas and the Papas purchased Twin Gables. Pioneers in hippie counterculture, the Philipses painted the mansion's interior woodwork black, stuck a billiard table at the center of the dining room, and set up a hookah in the living room. Their marriage dissolved a few months later. Subsequent owners have preserved the Tudor feel of the exterior and grounds, and as a result the estate looks very much today as it did when the Raymonds moved in.

Jack Ohmeis, MacDonald's first beau, died in 1967. Jeanette saw him for the last time in 1959, in Manhattan.

After MacDonald's death, Nelson Eddy continued working nightclubs and often mused on his perennial pairing with Jeanette in the public imagination. "The world has done me the honor to associate my name with hers," he affirmed soon after the funeral. To the end, Eddy remained grateful to MacDonald for the fabulous turn his career had taken in 1935. In 1967, when he returned from a tour of Australia, Eddy opened at the Sans Souci in Miami, on March 5. In the middle of his act he became disoriented and was unable to find the words to a song he was singing. His accompanist, Theodore Paxson, had to help him off the stage. Eddy died the next morning of a cerebral hemorrhage.

Eddy's burial took place at Hollywood Memorial Park, adjacent to Paramount Studios. When the ceremony was over, his widow, Ann, walked toward Gene Raymond, who was a pallbearer. After kissing him, Ann said to Gene: "Now they will sing beautiful music together again." Ann Franklin Eddy died on August 28, 1987.

When Maurice Chevalier learned of MacDonald's passing, he wrote admiringly: "The consolation that can give strength to Gene Raymond is that she has never been replaced and there is no greater conclusion for an artist." Chevalier's last on-screen performance was in a 1967 Disney production, *Monkeys, Go Home!* After making a stupendous farewell tour with his one-man stage show in 1968, Chevalier retired from public life at age eighty. Two and a half years later, he slashed his wrists in a suicide attempt. In the months that followed, Maurice spoke endlessly about his mother and about Jeanette MacDonald. On January 1, 1972, at age eighty-three, Chevalier died of natural causes.

Bob Ritchie left show business after World War II and for a few years prospered as a sales executive with Stephen Leedom Carpet Company in New York City. When he died of cancer on July 15, 1972, Ritchie was broke and had considerable debts. Because Bob left no will, the government "moved in and took his few possessions," noted Ritchie's nephew John.

Grace Adele Newell outlived her star pupil by fourteen months, dying of pneumonia at age ninety-two. Though Grace often joked about wanting her ashes to be scattered over the racetrack at Santa Anita, they are buried under a pepper tree in Westwood Memorial Park.

Jeanette's eldest sister, Elsie, died of a stroke and heart attack at age seventy-six in Wayne, Pennsylvania, on October 2, 1970, and was buried near her parents in Mount Peace Cemetery, Section M, Lot 242. Among her survivors was Bernard J. Scheiter, her husband of thirty years.

Blossom's fame, brought on by *The Addams Family,* was short-lived. After suffering a stroke in 1966 that deprived her of speech, she retired to the Motion Picture Country House. As if to ratify Jeanette's belief in the mystical force of the number thirteen, Blossom died on January 14, 1978—thirteen years to the day after her younger sister's death. Blossom, too, was interred at Forest Lawn.

Emily Wentz remained an independent woman well into her nineties. She died in her sleep on December 10, 1996. Gene Raymond offered a tribute to Emily's years of devotion and friendship at a memorial service in the chapel of Westwood Cemetery. Jeanette's recording of "Ah! Sweet Mystery of Life" was played.

Gene Raymond acted on stage and TV in the years following Jeanette's death. His final professional appearance, in March 1974, was as an aging coach on the television series *Apple's Way*. From 1966 to 1969, Gene was a trustee of the Academy of Television Arts and Sciences. His efforts on behalf of the Air Force Reserves in the early years of the Vietnam War brought him a Legion of Merit award. In the late 1960s Gene kept company with the actress Jane Wyman, and there was talk of a marriage. But in September 1974, Gene wed Mrs. Bentley Hees of Pacific Palisades. By an extraordinary coincidence, Mrs. Hees's first name was Nelson. "Nels" died of Alzheimer's disease on March 19, 1995.

After Nels's death, Gene continued to live at home, by the ocean, in Pacific Palisades. His primary business was real-estate investments. He never stopped carrying in his wallet the four-leaf clover wrapped in cellophane that Jeanette had given him when he went to war.

Gene Raymond's last public appearance was on June 27, 1997, at the Beverly Wilshire Hotel, for the sixtieth anniversary banquet of the Jeanette MacDonald International Fan Club. On May 3, 1998, he died of pneumonia at Cedars-Sinai Medical Center in Los Angeles. Gene's remains lie alongside Jeanette's at Forest Lawn, in the Freedom Mausoleum.

The City of Brotherly Love continues to embrace MacDonald. The house in which she was born and raised stands intact at 5123 Arch Street, West Philadelphia. Except for the front vestibule, the interior configuration is exactly as it was when the MacDonalds lived there. The current occupants are leaders in a community effort to revitalize the neighborhood. Three blocks away, the stone building that was Thomas Dunlap Elementary School is now a dwelling for seniors and the disabled, and has been designated a historic structure. West Philadelphia High School, on Forty-seventh and Walnut Streets, still flourishes. Shortly after MacDonald's death, the surviving alumnae of the Class of '22 contributed $150 in her memory to the Children's Heart Hospital of Philadelphia. "We did remember and admire her!" said Louise Horner a few weeks before the group's seventieth anniversary reunion in 1992.

In the spring of 1965, the Free Library of Philadelphia mounted a two-month commemorative exhibition, "Jeanette MacDonald: Girl from Philadelphia." Twenty-three years later, on March 31, 1988, the Philadelphia Music Alliance, in Gene Raymond's presence, dedicated a bronze plaque in Jeanette's honor on its Walk of Fame, a stretch of pavement on South Broad Street that runs in front of the Academy of Music and the Shubert Theater. Other musical greats enshrined for their ties to the city are Leopold Stokowski, Marian Anderson, Anna Moffo, Ethel Waters, Dizzy Gillespie, Nelson Eddy, Mario Lanza, and Frankie Avalon.

The prime keepers of MacDonald's flame are the two women who lovingly head the Jeanette MacDonald International Fan Club—Clara Rhoades and Tessa Williams of Topeka, Kansas. In 1962, MacDonald handpicked Rhoades to serve as the club's president, and she has functioned in that capacity ever since. Two months after Jeanette's death, Gene Raymond urged the club not to disband: "When [Jeanette] spoke of you she radiated pride and wonderment. . . . I propose we accept and maintain our common bond and stay united." This exceptional fan club is now in its sixty-first year of devotion to its star. It continues to honor MacDonald's request that the club help those in need, particularly crippled children.

The club motto is "Let us work with love."

Afterword

A people which loses contact
with its past becomes culturally psychotic.

American critic DWIGHT MACDONALD, 1962

When a cousin found out I was writing this book, she phoned from Vancouver to voice her excitement. As if to claim a bond rarer than blood, Barbara Rand admitted she was a longtime MacDonald fan and urged me to dedicate the biography "to all those who sing 'Italian Street Song' in the shower and aim to hit the high note." Like me, Barbara is too young to have known Jeanette's movies and music at their original release. Her surprise confession was a reminder that, to this day, Jeanette MacDonald maintains a grip on people's hearts, minds, and, in some cases, vocal cords.

All of MacDonald's Metro films are now available on video through Ted Turner's MGM/UA Home Entertainment Group, Inc. American Movie Classics often celebrates MacDonald's birthday in June with screenings of her early Paramount pictures, and Turner Classic Movies and TNT regularly showcase her MGM musicals. *Jeanette MacDonald in Performance,* a tape of her half-hour television debut on *The Voice of Firestone,* is in distribution from Video Artists International. The hour-long documentary *Nelson and Jeanette: America's Singing Sweethearts,* produced by WTTW-TV of Chicago and narrated by Jane Powell, airs frequently on PBS stations, and Ralph Edwards's biographical tribute, *This Is Your Life, Jeanette MacDonald,* is a favorite cable rerun.

MacDonald's enduring status as a cultural icon is further attested by fin de siècle retrospectives, such as James Clive's *Fame in the Twentieth*

Century; the TV game show *Jeopardy* (most recently under the Famous
Women category); National Public Radio (pop artist Roy Lichtenstein
told an interviewer on *Fresh Air* that MacDonald and Nelson Eddy
were key influences on his early sensibilities); and *Entertainment
Tonight,* which has highlighted the still-active Jeanette MacDonald International Fan Club. The star's seductive presence can be felt sublimi-
nally each time Bell Atlantic lures telephone credit-card users with
promos that read, "When I'm Calling You—oo—oo—ooh—oo—oo—
oooh," or when magazine ads for Godiva Chocolatier show heart-
shaped bonbons positioned as notes on a musical staff above the words
"Sweetheart, Sweetheart, Sweetheart."

Yet a countercurrent also persists. Early in my research, I surveyed
how media critics and historians had treated MacDonald and film operetta over the decades. I was struck by the fact that most of the
strongly visceral attacks on her persona and singing emanated from
men, not women, and that their main target was her romantic films
with Nelson Eddy, not her boudoir farces with Maurice Chevalier—
which these same writers often praised no end. As I made contact with
flesh-and-blood MacDonald fans, I saw that they, too, often have a
lopsided attachment to the oeuvre, but in a reverse direction. As one
woman told me, "I confess that my recollections center almost exclusively on the movies made with Nelson Eddy. Even today my heart
beats a little faster at the memory!"

I eventually wrote an essay that dealt with this paradox from a psychological perspective.* My main claim was that most male viewers
are at ease with the MacDonald-Chevalier films because they reinforce
fantasies of men's potency and superiority. Even the songs in these pictures support male dominance, since Chevalier's bouncy, half-spoken
showstoppers tend to overpower MacDonald's delicate soprano lyricism. In her films with Eddy, by contrast, MacDonald expresses sentiment and desire through unrestrained operatic-style singing—sometimes solo, sometimes in duet, but never outclassed by her partner's
robust baritone. Moreover, when Eddy doesn't sing, his image seems
unfinished and vulnerable. The MacDonald-Eddy movies thus upset
routine expectations. They call upon viewers to acknowledge MacDon-

---

*Edward Baron Turk, "Deriding the Voice of Jeanette MacDonald: Notes on Psycho-
analysis and the American Film Musical," *Camera Obscura,* nos. 25–26 (spring 1991):
225–49. The essay was reprinted, in a slightly revised form, in Leslie C. Dunn and
Nancy A. Jones, eds., *Embodied Voices: Representing Female Vocality in Western Culture* (Cambridge: Cambridge University Press, 1994), 103–19.

ald as the more active, determining agent in a revised scheme of male-female relations. These films evoke defensive and derisive responses in some men, I proposed, because the unleashed soprano voice, while capable of producing extreme pleasure, may also be experienced on a deep level as a fierce acoustic assault. In such instances, the viewer may subconsciously perceive MacDonald as an awesome female demon. She will then, like the Sirens in Homer's *Odyssey,* imperil men's sense of control and dominance. Take another look at Eddy's nightmare sequence at the climax of the team's swan song, *I Married an Angel.* It's a dramatic display of how the voice of MacDonald's unangelic character, coupled with her independent pursuit of fleshly pleasures, can provoke terror in men.

More obvious factors affect how people respond to MacDonald and her music today. While glamorous lyric sopranos are not entirely absent from ordinary experience, opera and operetta are increasingly peripheral to dominant tastes. During the Reagan-Bush era, Madison Avenue seemed confident that strains of Renata Tebaldi singing "Un bel dì" from *Madama Butterfly* would make consumers rush to buy DuPont stain-resistant carpet. By the start of the 1990s, dozens of TV commercials were using snatches of opera to lend status to their products. The yuppy ascendancy also saw Hollywood movies like *Moonstruck, Pretty Woman,* and *The Godfather Part III* unfold fantasies of grand romance within opulent opera houses. Still, the prevailing vocal sound of our second half century—raw and growling, nasal and metallic—stands far distant from the refinement of tone usually associated with classical vocal convention. In the mid-1960s, Julie Andrews ruled the silver screen. Yet Andrews's lacy lyric style was simply an end point in the tradition of genteel cinematic vocalism. The pop sounds of Barbra Streisand and Liza Minnelli, along with the honeyed whispers of Diana Ross, would dominate the 1970s. Since the mid-1980s singers like Carly Simon, Linda Ronstadt, Michael Feinstein, and Mandy Patinkin have tried to revive a pre-rock style of vocal lushness. But their retro-spiced sound remains steeped in up-to-date sensibilities that take "sweetness," "beauty," and "clarity of tone" as suspect terms.

Perhaps the only mainstream havens for the trained soprano voice today are Disney animated features and Andrew Lloyd Webber stage extravaganzas. In these venues, however, electronic sequencers, synthesizers, and mega-amplification have virtually stripped expansive singing—soprano and otherwise—of its prior links to ideals of delicacy and charm. The performances of Sarah Brightman in *Phantom of the*

Opera, Glenn Close in *Sunset Boulevard,* and Madonna in *Evita* show that the female stars of most contemporary blockbuster musicals have little chance to project vocal freshness or idiosyncrasy. Be it on stage or screen, they often wind up sounding like disembodied dubbings. The opera critic Will Crutchfield notes with regret that current sound technology in virtually all branches of popular musical entertainment has bred the "perverse perception that the singing that . . . sounds most 'natural' is the kind requiring electronic enhancement to be heard." For all the hullabaloo about how the sound engineers at Paramount and Metro boosted the volume of her voice, MacDonald never failed to generate vital presence in both the movie house and the concert hall.

Of course, the range of contemporary musical idioms is by no means trifling. Variants of heavy metal, folk-rock, punk, and rhythm and blues vigorously compete with classic rock; the club scene accommodates assorted trends like house, techno, acid jazz, and hip-hop. Although no style dominates the field, many composers of classical music increasingly favor a neo-romantic manner as they strive to capture the allegiance of audiences that rejected much of the atonal, experimental music of the postwar avant-garde. Ours is also a time of lively cross-fertilization. Opera stars record Broadway musicals and the Great American Songbook, while pop icons have a go at writing opera and art songs. The jazz pianist Keith Jarrett unveils a gift for performing Bach, and Barry Manilow attempts jazz. The Three Tenors—Luciano Pavarotti, Plácido Domingo, and José Carreras—conclude their colossal operatic concerts with such popular chestnuts as "O sole mio," "Cielito lindo," "La vie en rose," and Webber's "Memory" (from *Cats*). From the Who's *Tommy* (1969) to Jonathan Larson's *Rent* (1996) and beyond, hip composers and theatrical producers labor—like alchemists searching for the philosophers' stone—to achieve a perfect high-tech fusion of rock, opera, and Broadway.

But classical operetta—the type of music MacDonald sang better than anyone and to which she owes most of her fame—has proven too singular and fragile to survive well when borrowed or tinkered with. Stage works by Stephen Sondheim, Andrew Lloyd Webber, and Claude-Michel Schönberg have overhauled the genre in assorted ways. Yet the mixed results of recent East Coast revivals of Lehár's *The Merry Widow,* Romberg's *The Desert Song,* and Herbert's *Naughty Marietta* attest to the daunting standards of vocal technique, diction, interpretive subtlety, and emotional honesty performers must adhere to *as a complete package* if operetta is to avoid camp or hoity-toity affectation. MacDonald wielded that package in spades, but few of her successors have come even close.*

Jeanette MacDonald's great romantic films can help us set fresh standards for fantasies of impassioned love. However, viewers must revisit MacDonald free of the myths of virginal innocence and treacly sentimentality that often attach to the very mention of her name nowadays. On the contrary, MacDonald's pertinence for our times stems in large part from her repeated portrayal of strong women in pursuit of deep emotional fulfillment despite failed first marriages (*Love Me Tonight, The Merry Widow, Broadway Serenade, Three Daring Daughters*), in defiance of marital custom (*Monte Carlo, One Hour with You, Naughty Marietta, Maytime, Bitter Sweet*), and with self-assured disregard for popular opinion (*The Vagabond King, Oh, for a Man!, The Cat and the Fiddle, The Firefly, Girl of the Golden West, Smilin' Through*). This swerve from orthodoxy makes her work especially fascinating today.

Moreover, erotic yearning in MacDonald's pictures takes on a fullness rarely matched in movie musicals. A lingering myth in film history holds that while the MGM/Freed Unit musicals of Judy Garland, Gene Kelly, and Fred Astaire ooze sophistication, those of MacDonald belong to a simpler, less complicated era. This is true only if we equate sophistication with self-conscious theatricality. Freed films like *Summer Stock* (1950), *Singin' in the Rain* (1952), and *The Band Wagon* (1953) deliberately offer an exuberant, adolescent-like toying with feeling. While exploring in depth the machinery of show business, they make light of the consequences of emotional attachments. MacDonald's MGM musicals, by contrast, confer urgency and complexity upon mature, all-consuming emotion. Ira Siff, better known as Madam Vera Galupe-Borszkh, founding diva of the all-male La Gran Scena Opera Company, unintentionally pinpointed the distinctive trait of MacDonald's movies when he described how "emotional commitment" sets opera apart from the other arts: "It's standing-on-the-ledge-about-to-jump emotionalism. It's why something that isn't even sung can be operatic."

*The acclaimed revival of Rodgers and Hammerstein's *Carousel,* directed by Nicholas Hytner at the Vivian Beaumont Theater in 1994, exposed the startling gap between operetta's demands and the capabilities of most singing actors today. To those who recalled the vocal luster of John Raitt, Gordon MacRae, Jan Clayton, Shirley Jones, and Barbara Cook in the leads, the *New York Times* theater critic David Richards warned that in this new edition the music was "indifferently sung," with "gorgeous singing matter[ing] less . . . than the proletarian authenticity of the characters" (March 25, 1994, p. C1).

MacDonald's unflamboyant offscreen love life probably hampers her long-run celebrity. Unlike Garbo, Dietrich, Crawford, and Garland, she has not inspired an endless stream of Peeping Fan biographies— though a few fanatics continue to manufacture stories of a secret liaison between MacDonald and Nelson Eddy. Such make-believe speaks to the ever-present demand for salacious celebrity gossip, but it surely is not the key for arousing new interest in Jeanette MacDonald.

The best case for MacDonald's contemporary worth must, I think, focus on her place in the history of cultural taste. MacDonald was the embodiment of cultured WASP-dom in mid-twentieth-century America. Whether she sang Charles Gounod, Rudolf Friml, Stephen Foster, or Nacio Herb Brown, she promised uplift and refinement to a nation of immigrants who craved legitimacy and social approval. For a large part of the population, she provided a first and defining encounter with the pleasures of classical music. The artistic avant-garde had already turned to Africa, China, Egypt, and Mexico for reinvigoration. MacDonald, however, championed American middlebrow. Despite the vaguely exotic issues of gender raised by her films, MacDonald's appeal to the masses lay largely in her staunch allegiance—expressed through her music—to the Protestant ethic that facilitated America's material growth: ambition, hard work, civic-mindedness, self-discipline. Her virtuosic singing was a sign of uncommon achievement. But MacDonald packaged it in a democratic manner, believing that all people could learn to understand, admire, and even emulate her success. She was confident that most people wanted to.

World War II somewhat altered American attitudes toward "legit" singing. The United States had always been ambivalent about embracing cultured traditions over more humble ones. Though MacDonald was an outstanding favorite among millions of civilians and recruits throughout the war, her vocal style suddenly appeared to some as a pinch too reminiscent of Old World notions of aristocratic breeding and polish. The War Department, in ringing the praises of the common citizen, set the stage for the heightened popularity of screen singers who unambiguously projected down-to-earth American values, like Garland, Kelly, Betty Hutton, Alice Faye, and Betty Grable. By 1942 the hottest moneymaking team in movie musicals was no longer Mac-Donald and Eddy, but comics Bud Abbott and Lou Costello. The latter's cavorting in MGM's remake of the operetta *Rio Rita* relegated Kathryn Grayson, the picture's "cultivated" warbler, to the background. Judy Garland enshrined the new populism by belting "The

Joint Is Really Jumpin' Down at Carnegie Hall" in MGM's 1943 army-camp spectacular, *Thousands Cheer.* The Fight for Democracy, the entertainment industry seemed to proclaim, called for music that could energize the nation easily and swiftly. Pop, swing, and boogie-woogie became instant allies. Operetta—high-flown and less plainly native—aroused a dab of suspicion.

Rock and roll pushed MacDonald and semiclassical music still further from the core of popular taste. Yet throughout the 1950s MacDonald remained a huge draw in her concerts, summer stock performances, and television work. Of all TV programs, *The Ed Sullivan Show*—for which MacDonald served as occasional summer host—perhaps best reflected the middlebrow variety of the Eisenhower years. On Sullivan, all arts were safe and consoling, and MacDonald fit in as cozily as Maria Callas or Sophie Tucker, the Bolshoi Ballet or an army drill team. Intellectual snobs derided such homogenization as ersatz culture, or "kitsch," echoing art critic Clement Greenberg's classic definition of this term as "the epitome of all that is spurious in the life of our times." By the late 1950s, Dwight Macdonald fine-tuned a trendier put-down, Midcult, which he vilified as "a tepid ooze" of "trivial and comfortable cultural products" that is "spreading everywhere" and that pretends with "alarming ambiguity" to respect the standards of High Culture while vulgarizing and watering them down for the masses. Among those indicted were John Steinbeck, Pearl Buck, *Omnibus,* Rodgers and Hammerstein's *South Pacific,* Sir Edward Elgar, and the Book-of-the-Month Club.

Middlebrow culture of the kind represented by MacDonald would soon run out of gas. "The music I have sung and have been identified with does not occupy center stage in our contemporary world," she conceded in the early 1960s. Still, as high priestess of Midcult, MacDonald clung to its articles of faith until her death in 1965: "I will not sing any song for the sake of singing. . . . I've kept my integrity reasonably intact so far and I see no reason to throw it out the window now."

In the months that followed her death, MacDonald's guiding principles suffered their rudest pounding. Race riots, campus unrest, and opposition to the war in Vietnam called into radical doubt the old verities of American culture. A median range of acceptable taste, once viewed as socially progressive, would now be ridiculed as exclusionist and reactionary. The core beliefs that had given meaning and mission to MacDonald's life and work—cultural cohesiveness, reverence for tradition, lofty ambition, high standards of quality—would now be construed by many as repressive Establishment tools. To be sure, this topsy-turvy tumult ushered in a quarter century of unprecedented social awareness and tolerance for diverse subcultures. Yet in an ironic turn, the middlebrow musical tradition that once eased the entry of millions of Americans into the cultural mainstream became itself a marginalized minority voice.

Jeanette MacDonald was committed to ideals of true inclusivity and human connection. She tried to speak to the whole country, not just to those already hooked on opera and operetta. She carved out a common ground on which the masses and the privileged could share deep, emotional experience and dignified pleasures. As our democracy enters the new millennium, we are perhaps most in need of new cultural forms that can reconnect us with that sense of encompassing community.

On January 16, 1965, the *Chicago Daily News* concluded its editorial on MacDonald's death with resignation: "The older folks will mourn and remember Miss MacDonald and the young will never know what they missed." It's time to make up for our youthful ignorance by reclaiming MacDonald as an exemplary part of our American heritage.

Stage Credits

This is the first detailed listing of Jeanette MacDonald's stage work to be published. I include childhood performances only when print documentation survives, and even in these cases the available information is often fragmentary. Cast members are listed in their order of general importance, with the exception of MacDonald, whose role I specify at the head of each cast list, regardless of her actual billing.

CHARITY   A children's opera. February 19, 1909. Academy of Music, Philadelphia. Producer: Management Charity Opera Company. Stage director: James H. Littlefield. Music director: Caroline D. Littlefield. Assistant stage director: Clem Harris Congdon. Costumes: Minnie S. Barry.

Cast: Jeanette MacDonald (Mother Hubbard), Florrie Dorn (a fairy, Charity, a beggar girl), Clem Harris Congdon (a bear, a prince), Blossom MacDonald (a Scots dancer), Elsie MacDonald (a grenadier doll), Anna Pennington (Wilhelmina). [Sixteen-year-old Pennington shortened her first name and went on to become the dimple-kneed dancer who popularized "The Black Bottom" in *George White's Scandals of 1926*.]

MacDonald sang: "A Real Scotch Song by a Real Scotch Lassie," "The Plight of Old Mother Hubbard," "Maybe It's a Bear."

"POP" SHOW   A children's revue. December 25, 1909. Pennsylvania Railroad YMCA, Philadelphia.

MacDonald sang: "Take Me Up with You, Dearie," "A Real Scotch Song by a Real Scotch Lassie."

SIX SUNNY SONG BIRDS   A vaudeville kiddie act. Circa 1911–1913. Played vaudeville houses in and around Philadelphia, Harrisburg, and Reading, Pennsylvania, and southern New Jersey. Producer and director: Al White.

Cast: Membership changed over time; on the reverse side of an undated photo of the Song Birds, MacDonald Archive, are listed: Jeanette MacDonald, Edward Delany, Charles Speece, Bessie Cole, Charles Kleeman, and Joseph Schramm.

MacDonald often sang "A Little Love, a Little Kiss" (m. Lao Silèsu, Fr. w. Nilson Fysher, Eng. w. Adrian Ross), a number she would revive in MGM's *Smilin' Through* in 1941.

AL WHITE'S ANNUAL CHILDREN'S CARNIVAL   A showcase for young Philadelphia talent. 1913. Broad Street Theater, Philadelphia. Producer and director: Al White.

MacDonald sang: "Won't You Come Out and Play With Me?," "Up the Rickety Stairs." In a special effect at the climax of another child's solo number, "A Trip to Mars in a Flying Machine," MacDonald "flew" onstage in a miniature airship as a chorus welcomed her with the song "Come Take a Trip in My Flying Machine."

SEVEN MERRY YOUNGSTERS   A vaudeville act. Circa 1914. Played vaudeville houses in and around Philadelphia, Trenton, Newark, and New York City. Producer and director: Elwood Wolf.

NED WAYBURN'S DEMI TASSE REVUE   A movie-palace prologue. New York opening: October 24, 1919, Capitol Theater. Producers: Messmore Kendall and Edward Bowes. Producing director: Ned Wayburn. Music director: Cass Freeborn. Conductor: Arthur Pryor. Dance coach: Walter Baker. Electrical effects: New York Calcium Light Company, with Frank Schmieder.

Cast: Janette McDonald [*sic*] (an Indian girl, a twinkling star), Blossom McDonald [*sic*] (a silhouette, a bronco buck dancer), Mae West [dropped after two performances], Muriel De Forrest, Lucille Chalfant, Paul Frawley, Will Crutchfield.

MacDonald sang and danced in Will Crutchfield's production number "In Arizona" and in the revue's finale, "Come to the Moon," featuring Paul Frawley and Lucille Chalfant; she also understudied Lucille Chalfant. Between October and late December 1919, a new scene was added every two weeks; as of January 1920, the revue's title became SONG SCENES, and MacDonald took part in the numbers "A Little Bit o' Scotch" and "Say It with Flowers."

THE NIGHT BOAT   "A Musical Comedy." New York opening: February 2, 1920, Liberty Theater. Producer: Charles Dillingham. Music: Jerome Kern. Book and lyrics: Anne Caldwell, from a French farce by Alexandre Bisson. Stage director: Fred G. Latham. Dance director: Ned Wayburn. New York run: 148 performances.

Cast: Jeannette McDonald [*sic*] (a dancer and singer in the ensemble), John E. Hazzard (Bob White), Louise Groody (Barbara), Stella Hoban (Hazel White), Ada Lewis (Mrs. Maxim), Ernest Torrence (Robert White), Hal Skelly (Freddie Ives).

MacDonald played in the show until August 1920; she danced and incidentally sang in the numbers "Some Fine Day," "Left All Alone Again Blues,"

"Good Night Boat," and "Catskills, Hello"; she understudied Louise Groody and Stella Hoban.

IRENE   "A Musical Comedy." New York opening: November 18, 1919, Vanderbilt Theater. Producers: Carle Carlton and Joseph McCarthy. Music: Harry Tierney. Lyrics: Joseph McCarthy. Book: James Montgomery. Director: Edward Royce. New York run: 670 performances.

MacDonald played Eleanor Worth, the second ingenue lead, in a road company that starred Helen Shipman and played Boston in August–September 1920, and Philadelphia in October–December 1920. She sang "Hobbies" and "Castles of Dreams."

TANGERINE   "A Musical Comedy." New York opening: August 9, 1921, Casino Theater. Producer: Carle Carlton. Music: Monte Carlo and Alma M. Sanders. Lyrics: Howard Johnson. Book: Guy Bolton, from a play by Philip Bartholomae and Lawrence Langner. Stage directors: George Marion and Bert French. Music directors: Gus Kleinicke, Jean Salzer, and Max Steiner. New York run: 318 performances.

Cast: Jeanette MacDonald (Kate Allen, a divorcée who tracks down her alimony-evading husband), Julia Sanderson (Shirley Dalton), John E. Hazzard (King Home-Brew), Frank Crumit (Dick Owens), Allen Kearns (Lee Loring), Becky Cauble (Elsie Loring), Gladys Wilson (Mildred Floyd), Jeannetta Methven (Noa).

MacDonald joined the show in mid-September 1921 (replacing Edna Pierce) and sang and danced "Man Is the Lord of It All"; she understudied Julia Sanderson until leaving the show in April 1922.

A FANTASTIC FRICASSEE   "A Revue in Fifteen Courses." New York opening: September 11, 1922, The Greenwich Village Theater. Producer: Marguerite Abbott Barker. Music director: Roy Shields. Dance director: Edwin Strawbridge. Scenic director: André Chotin. New York run: 124 performances.

Cast: Jeanette MacDonald, "Bobby" Edwards, Jocelyn Burke, Jimmy Kemper, Mabel Rowland, Gretchen Hood, Jean White, Remo Bufano's Marionette Theater.

MacDonald joined the revue in October 1922 and sang "Waiting for You" (W. Franke Harling), "A Heart That's Free" (R. J. Robyn and T. Railey), and "Maman, dites-moi" (French folk song, arr. Jean-Baptiste Weckerlin).

THE MAGIC RING   "A Musical Comedy." New York opening: October 1, 1923, Liberty Theater. Producer: Henry W. Savage. Music: Harold Levey. Book and lyrics: Zelda Sears. Stage director: Ira Hards. Music director: Dave Bennett. Scenery: Castle. Prologue settings and costumes: Adrian. New York run: 96 performances.

Cast: Jeannette [*sic*] MacDonald (Iris Bellamy, a rival for the hero's affections), Mitzi (Polly Church), Boyd Marshall (Tom Hammond), Sydney Greenstreet (Henry Brockway), Janet Murdock (Phoebe Brockway), Phoebe Crosby (Mrs. Bellamy), Ed Wakefield (a policeman), John Lyons (a policeman), Wait Until You See Her [a trained monkey] (Minnie), Adrian Rosley (Moe Bernheimer), Estelle Birney (Stella).

MacDonald sang: "Keepsakes," "Milaiya," "Broken Hearts," "Deep in Someone's Heart." After the show's New York run, she traveled with the national road company through May 26, 1925.

TIP-TOES   "A Musical Comedy." New York opening: October 28, 1925, Liberty Theater. Producers: Alex A. Aarons and Vinton Freedley. Music: George Gershwin. Lyrics: Ira Gershwin. Book: Guy Bolton and Fred Thompson. Stage director: John Harwood. Dance director: Sammy Lee. Sets: John Wenger. New York run: 194 performances.

Cast: Jeannette [*sic*] MacDonald (Sylvia Metcalf, a Palm Beach flapper socialite), Queenie Smith ("Tip-Toes" Kaye), Allen Kearns (Steve Burton), Robert Halliday (Rollo Metcalf), Amy Revere (Peggy Schuyler), Andrew Tombes (Hen Kaye), Gertrude McDonald (Binnie Oakland), Lovely Lee (Denise Marshall).

MacDonald sang: "Nice Baby," "It's a Great Little World," "Sweet and Low Down."

A 1978 revival at the Goodspeed Opera House in Haddam, Connecticut, had Georgia Engel (of *The Mary Tyler Moore Show*) in the title role; Marti Rolph (who originated Young Sally in Stephen Sondheim's *Follies*) revived MacDonald's part.

BUBBLING OVER   "An Effervescent Musical Comedy." Tryout start: August 2, 1926, Garrick Theater, Philadelphia. Producer: Edward Royce. Music: Richard Myers. Lyrics: Leo Robin. Book: Clifford Grey. Stage director: Edward Royce. Costumes: Ada Peacock. Sets: George Vail.

Cast: Jeannette [*sic*] MacDonald (Geraldine Gray, in love with Monty); Cecil Lean (Monty Baxter), Bubbles Clayton (Cleo Mayfield), Jack Thompson (Archie Vanderpool), Hugh Cameron (Rawles), John Henshaw (Colonel Drew), Imogene Coca (Jane), Brenda Bond (Barbara Drew), James Darling (Captain Jim).

MacDonald sang: "Dreams Never Die," "I'm a One-Man Girl," "Shake Me and Wake Me," "Montezuma," "In an Old Rose Garden," "Bubbling Over." She left the show in the middle of its Boston tryouts and was replaced by Gloria Foy; *Bubbling Over* then hobbled into Werba's Brooklyn Theater on October 4, 1926, for a one-week run, and closed for good after two weeks at the Selwyn Theater in Chicago.

YES, YES, YVETTE   "A New Musical Comedy." New York opening: October 3, 1927, Sam H. Harris Theater. Producer: H. H. Frazee. Music: Philip Charig and Ben Jerome. Lyrics: Irving Caesar. Book: James Montgomery and William Cary Duncan, from James Montgomery's farce *Nothing But the Truth*. Dance director: Sammy Lee. Stage director: Frederick B. Manatt. Sets: P. Dodd Ackerman. Costumes: Milgrim. New York run: 40 performances.

Cast: Jeanette MacDonald (Yvette Ralston, a fiancée stunned to learn the truth from her intended), Jack Whiting (Robert Bennett), Charles Winninger (S. M. Ralston), Brenda Bond (Ethel Clark), Virginia Howell (Mrs. Ralston), Arnold Lucy (Bishop Doran), Joseph Herbert (Mr. Van Dusen), Roland Woodruff (Dick Donnelly). [During the year-long tryout tour Lynne Overman and Bernard Granville variously played the part of Robert; Amy Revere was Ethel.]

MacDonald sang: "My Love, My Life, My Lady," "Yes, Yes, Yvette," "How'd You Like To?"

THE STUDIO GIRL "A Parisian Musical Romance." Tryout start: October 31, 1927, Shubert Theater, Newark. Producers: J. J. and Lee Shubert. Music: William Ortmann. Lyrics: J. Keirn Brennan. Book: Edward Locks, from George Du Maurier's novel *Trilby*. Stage director: J. C. Huffman. Dialogue director: M. H. Varnel. Music director: Leon Rosebrook. Dance director: Carl Randall. Sets: Watson Barratt.

Cast: Jeanette MacDonald (Trilby, a young concert singer mesmerized by Svengali), Max Figman (Svengali), Lloyd Garrett (Little Billie), Arthur Lipson (Gecko), Rose Winter (Mrs. Bagot), Wessley Pierce (Dodor), Hazel Harris (Mme. Dodor), Carl Randall (Duc de la Rochemartel, aka "Zouzou"), Annie Pritchard (Duchesse de la Rochemartel, aka "Mme. Zouzou"), Laura Lee (Sally Sloane). [*The Studio Girl* had already tried out in Newark and Brooklyn when MacDonald joined it in Philadelphia on November 14, 1927, replacing Florence Misgen of the Chicago Opera Company. The show closed two weeks later.]

MacDonald sang: "Trilby O'Farrell's Me Name," "Moonlight and Love and All," "Way Down in Barbizon," "Somewhere."

SUNNY DAYS "A New Musical Comedy." New York opening: February 8, 1928, Imperial Theater. Producer: Hassard Short. Music: Jean Schwartz and Eleanor Dunsmuir. Book and lyrics: Clifford Grey and William Cary Duncan, from Maurice Hennequin and Pierre Veber's French farce *The Kiss in a Taxi*. Stage director: Hassard Short. Dance director: Ralph Reader. Sets: Watson Barratt. New York run: 109 performances.

Cast: Jeanette MacDonald (Ginette Bertin, a florist shop girl who after many complications winds up a happy bride), Frank McIntyre (Leon Dorsay), Billy B. Van (Rudolph Max), Lynne Overman (Maurice Vane), Carl Randall (Paul Morel), Bob Lively (Inspector Bergeot), Claire Hooper (Countess d'Exmore), Audrey Maple (Madame Dorsay), Masie Yorke (Marie), Charlotte Ayres (première danseuse), Maurice Holand (Victor Duval), Margery Finley (Nanine), Rosalie Claire (Angèle Larue).

MacDonald sang: "Trample Your Troubles," "Really and Truly," "Sweet Daddy," "Because He Loves Her."

ANGELA "A Comedy with Music." New York opening: December 3, 1928, Ambassador Theater. Producers: J. J. and Lee Shubert. Music: Alberta Nichols. Lyrics: Mann Holiner. Book: Fanny Todd Mitchell, from Captain Robert Marshall's play *A Royal Family*. Stage director: George Marion. Dance director: Chester Hale. Sets: Watson Baratt. Orchestrations: Emil Gerstenberger. New York run: 41 performances.

Cast: Jeanette MacDonald (Princess Alestine Victorine Angela, obliged to wed a prince who is fated to save the kingdom), Eric Blore (Louis VII, King of Arcacia), Audrey Maple (Queen Consort of Arcacia), Alison Skipworth (Queen Ferdnande), Meeka Aldrich (Countess Carini), Gattison Jones (Duke of Berascon), Oscar Figman (Baron von Holdenson), Peggy Cornell (Bijou), Roy Hoyer

(Count Bernadine), Gus Alexander (Phileon Button), Arthur Cole (Mr. Sneck-kenberger), Jane Manners (the girl from London).

MacDonald sang: "Love Is Like That," "The Baron, the Duchess, and the Count," "I Can't Believe It's True," "Maybe So," "You've Got Me Up a Tree."

BOOM-BOOM   "A New Musical Comedy." New York opening: January 28, 1929, Casino Theater. Producers: J. J. and Lee Shubert. Music: Werner Janssen. Lyrics: Mann Holiner and J. Keirn Brennan. Book: Fanny Todd Mitchell, from Louis Verneuil's French farce *Mademoiselle, ma mère*. Stage director: George Marion. Dance directors: John Boyle and Jack Donahue. Sets: Watson Barratt. Costumes: Orry Kelly. New York run: 72 performances.

Cast: Jeanette MacDonald (Jean, a young woman who finds herself step-mother to the man she loves), Frank McIntyre (Worthington Smith), Stanley Ridges (Tony Smith), Archie Leach [Cary Grant] (Reggie Phipps), Nell Kelly (Tilly McGuire), Kendall Capps (Skippy Carr), Eddie Nelson (Texas), Laurette Adams (Gussie), Richard Lee (Sigmund Squnk), Marcella Swanson (Marcella La Tour), Harry Welsh (the headwaiter).

MacDonald sang: "What Could I Do?," "Nina."

JEANETTE MACDONALD, EN PERSONNE   A specialty revue attraction. Paris opening: September 4, 1931, Empire Theater. Producers: Oscar Dufrenne and Henri Varna. Stage director: Francis A. Mangan. Music director: Lucien Rémond. Costumes: Molyneux and Jenny Dolly. Paris run: two weeks.

Cast: Jeanette MacDonald, with the Mangan-Tiller Girls.

MacDonald sang: "Dream Lover" (m. Victor Schertzinger, w. Clifford Grey), "Un Jour" ("Some Day," m. Rudolf Friml), "Beyond the Blue Horizon" (m. Richard Whiting and W. Franke Harling, w. Leo Robin), "Reviens" (Harry Fragson), "Marche des Grenadiers" ("March of the Grenadiers," m. Schertzinger).

JEANETTE MACDONALD, IN PERSON   A specialty revue attraction. London opening: September 21, 1931, Dominion Theater. London run: two weeks. [Essentially the same as MacDonald's act at the Empire in Paris.]

JEANETTE MACDONALD, DANS UNE CREATION SCENIQUE   A specialty revue attraction. Paris opening: February 3, 1933, Rex Theater. Producer: Jacques Haïk. Stage director: Francis A. Mangan. Music director: Pierre de Cailloux. Dance director: Ethel Holliwell. Costumes: Molyneux and Zanel. Paris run: two weeks. [In the weeks that followed, MacDonald took this act to Lille, Lyons, Marseilles, Strasbourg, Amsterdam, Rotterdam, Brussels, Geneva, and Lausanne.]

Cast: Jeanette MacDonald, with Mary Honer, Betty Ann, the New Wayburn Rhythm Dancers, the Rex Appeal Girls, and the Mangan-Tillerex Dancers.

MacDonald sang: "Aimez-moi ce soir" ("Love Me Tonight," m. Richard Rodgers), "Reviens" (Fragson), "Parlez-moi d'amour" ("Speak to Me of Love," Jean Lenoir), "N'est-ce pas poétique?" ("Isn't It Romantic?," m. Richard Rodgers), "La Chanson de Vilia" ("Vilia," m. Franz Lehár, w. André Hornez), "J'aime d'amour" ("I'm in Love," m. Lehár, w. Hornez), "Marche des Grenadiers" (m. Schertzinger).

JEANETTE MACDONALD, IN RECITAL First U.S. tour started on March 16, 1939, at Kansas State Teachers College, Pittsburg, Kansas. Accompanist: Giuseppe Bamboschek. Impresario: Charles L. Wagner. Repeated in 20 cities.

MacDonald's 1939 recital repertoire included: "Lehn' Deine Wang an Meine Wang" (A. Jensen), "Du bist wie eine Blume" (R. Schumann), "Das Madchen Spricht" (J. Brahms), "Ich Liebe Dich" (E. Grieg), "Old Kentucky Home" (S. Foster), "El tra la la y el punteado" (E. Granados), "Maman, dites-moi" (adap. J.-B. Weckerlin), "Jeunes Fillettes" (adap. J.-B. Weckerlin), "Comin' Thro' the Rye" (arr. G. H. Clutsam), "The Jewel Song" from *Faust* (Ch. Gounod), "Sempre Libera" from *La traviata* (G. Verdi), "J'ai pleuré en rêve" (G. Hüe), "Ouvre tes yeux bleus" (J. Massenet), "Le Papillon" (F. Fourdrain), "Till I Wake" (A. Woodforde-Finden), "From the Land of the Sky-Blue Water" (C. W. Cadman), "Awake It Is Day" (F. Barbour), "Daddy's Sweetheart" (L. Lehmann), "Lullaby" (C. Scott), "When I Have Sung My Songs" (E. Charles).

Other major recital tours: spring 1940 (30 cities); fall 1940 (11 cities); winter 1941 (13 cities); fall 1942, for the Army Emergency Relief Fund (14 cities); summer 1943 (7 cities); fall 1943 (20 cities); spring 1944 (14 cities); fall 1944 (10 cities); fall 1945 (17 cities); summer 1946, in England, Scotland, and Wales (7 cities); spring 1948 (18 cities); winter 1949–50, U.S. Air Force Holiday Variety Show (Western Europe, 16 cities); spring 1950 (13 cities); fall 1950 (7 cities); fall 1952, in U.S. and Canada (14 cities). Principal accompanists: Giuseppe Bamboschek, from 1939 through 1942; Collins Smith, thereafter. Principal impresarios: Charles L. Wagner, through 1943; James A. Davidson and Sol Hurok, thereafter.

MacDonald's later recital repertoire often included: "I'm a Merry Zingara" (M. W. Balfe), "Ah! non credea mirarti" from *La sonnambula* (V. Bellini), "Morgen" (R. Strauss), "Er Ist's" (H. Wolf), "O, Charlie Is My Darling" (Scottish anon.), "The Last Rose of Summer" (old Irish air), "Fantoches" (C. Debussy), "Beau soir" (C. Debussy), "Le Miroir" (G. Ferrari), "L'Eventail" (J. Massenet), "Depuis le jour" from *Louise* (G. Charpentier), "Recuerdo" (M. Castelnuovo-Tedesco), "Silent Strings" (G. Bantock), "The Daisies" (S. Barber), "Midsummer" (A. Worth), "Release" (G. Raymond), "Mr. Nobody" (E. Remick Warren), "Down in the Glen" (E. Remick Warren).

ROMEO ET JULIETTE Opera in 5 acts. MacDonald's debut: May 8, 1943, His Majesty's Theater, Montreal. Music: Charles Gounod. Libretto: Jules Barbier and Michel Carré, from Shakespeare's tragedy. Producer: Armand Vincent and Canadian Entertainments Company. Conductor: Wilfred Pelletier. Stage director: Désiré Defrère. MacDonald's costumes: Adrian.

Cast: Jeanette MacDonald (Juliette, a star-crossed lover), Armand Tokatyan (Roméo), Ezio Pinza (Friar Laurent), Lionel Daunais (Mercutio), Alessio de Paolis (Tybalt), John Gurney (Capulet), Gérard Gélinas (Gregorio), Alice Howland (Stéphano, the page), Jeanne Desjardins (Gertrude, the nurse), George Cehanovsky (Duke of Verona), Tortoléro (Paris).

This production was repeated in Montreal (on May 10, 1943) and then traveled to Quebec City, Capital Theater (May 12); Ottawa, Auditorium (May 15, 17); Toronto, Massey Hall (May 20, 22); Windsor, Arena (May 24).

JEANETTE MACDONALD, IN CONCERT   First major appearance as a concert soloist: August 10, 1943, Emil Blatz Temple of Music (Milwaukee), Music Under the Stars Symphony Orchestra, Jerzy Bojanowski, conductor.

MacDonald's first concert program included: "Le Roi de Thulé" from *Faust* (Ch. Gounod), "The Jewel Song" from *Faust* (Ch. Gounod), "The Waltz Song" from *Roméo et Juliette* (Ch. Gounod), "Les Filles de Cadiz" (L. Delibes), "Badinage" from *Sweethearts* (V. Herbert).

Other major concerts: August 9, 1945, the Hollywood Bowl, Hollywood Bowl Symphony Orchestra, Leopold Stokowski, conductor; August 18, 1948, the Hollywood Bowl, Hollywood Bowl Symphony Orchestra, Eugene Ormandy, conductor; January 13, 1949, War Memorial Opera House (San Francisco), San Francisco Symphony Orchestra, Pierre Monteux, conductor; July 27, 1950, Robin Hood Dell (Philadelphia), Philadelphia Orchestra, Vladimir Golschmann, conductor; July 19, 1951, Lewisohn Stadium (New York City), Stadium Concerts Symphony Orchestra, Alexander Smallens, conductor; July 26, 1951, Robin Hood Dell, Philadelphia Orchestra, Erich Leinsdorf, conductor; July 14, 1952, Robin Hood Dell, Philadelphia Orchestra, Erich Leinsdorf, conductor; July 2, 1954, Red Rocks Theater (Denver), Denver Symphony Orchestra, Saul Caston, conductor; July 16, 1957, Emil Blatz Temple of Music (Milwaukee), Music Under the Stars Orchestra, John Anello, conductor.

MacDonald's later concert repertoire often included: "Il est doux, il est bon" from *Hérodiade* (J. Massenet), "Ouvre ton coeur" (G. Bizet), "The Jewel Song" from *Faust* (Ch. Gounod), "Un bel dì" from *Madama Butterfly* (G. Puccini), "Summertime" from *Porgy and Bess* (G. Gershwin), "Zigeuner" from *Bitter Sweet* (N. Coward).

ROMEO ET JULIETTE   November 4, 1944, Chicago Civic Opera House. Producer: Chicago Opera Company. Conductor: Louis Hasselmans. Stage director: Lothar Wallerstein. Chorus master: Konrad Neuger. Ballet master: Boris Romanoff.

Cast: Jeanette MacDonald (Juliette), Marine Capt. Michael Bartlett (Roméo), Nicola Moscona (Friar Laurent), Stephan Ballarini (Mercutio), Henry Cordy (Tybalt), Jean Fardulli (Capulet), Wilfred Engelman (Gregorio), Lucielle Browning (Stéphano, the page), Doris Doe (Gertrude, the nurse), Alexander Kulpak (Duke of Verona), Algerd Brazis (Paris).

This production was repeated in Chicago on November 11 and in Milwaukee on November 9, 1944.

FAUST   Opera in 5 acts. MacDonald's debut: November 15, 1944, Chicago Civic Opera House. Producer: Chicago Opera Company. Music: Charles Gounod. Libretto: Jules Barbier and Michel Carré, from Johann Wolfgang von Goethe's poem. Conductor: Fausto Cleva. Stage director: Lothar Wallerstein. Chorus master: Konrad Neuger. Ballet director: Ruth Page.

Cast: Jeanette MacDonald (Marguerite, the object of Faust's affections), Raoul Jobin (Faust), Ezio Pinza (Méphistophélès), Francesco Valentino (Valentin), Lucielle Browning (Siebel), Doris Doe (Martha), Wilfred Engelman (Wagner).

ROMEO ET JULIETTE   Cincinnati Zoological Gardens Pavilion, July 10, 1945, with Armand Tokatyan and Nicola Moscona; Fausto Cleva conducted.

FAUST   Cincinnati Zoological Gardens Pavilion, July 15 and 25, 1945, with Armand Tokatyan and Nicola Moscona; Fausto Cleva conducted. Chicago Civic Opera, October 27 and November 3, 1945, with Nino Martini and Nicola Moscona; Fausto Cleva conducted. Philadelphia Civic Grand Opera, December 12, 1951, with David Poleri and Raffaele Arie; Giuseppe Bamboschek conducted.

THE GUARDSMAN   A revival of Ferenc Molnar's comedy. Tryout start: January 25, 1951, Erlanger Theater, Buffalo, New York. Producers: Richard Aldrich and Richard Myers in association with Julius Fleischmann. New adaptation: Ferenc Molnar. Stage director: Sam Wanamaker. Scenery: Herbert Gahagan. MacDonald's gowns: Cecil Beaton.

Cast: Jeanette MacDonald (Singer, flirtatious and married), Gene Raymond (Actor), Josephine Brown ("Mama"), Gwen Vandam (Maid), Herbert Berghof (Critic), Maurice Shrog (Creditor), Collins Smith (Concierge and Piano Accompanist).

MacDonald sang: "The Jewel Song" from Gounod's *Faust;* "The Last Rose of Summer" (old Irish air), "Italian Street Song" (m. Victor Herbert, w. Rida Johnson Young), "Clair de Lune" (m. Claude Debussy, w. Gene Raymond).

This production played in twenty-three northeastern and midwestern cities between January 25 and June 2, 1951; it closed before reaching Broadway.

JEANETTE MACDONALD AT THE SAHARA   A nightclub act. Las Vegas opening: March 10, 1953, Congo Room, Hotel Sahara. Producers: Milton Prell and Stan Irwin. Stage director: George Moro. Conductor: Cee Davidson. Las Vegas run: two weeks.

Supporting acts: Mickey Sharp (comic), Yvonne Moray (singer), the Sa-Harem Dancers.

MacDonald sang: from her films, "Beyond the Blue Horizon," "Will You Remember?," "Smilin' Through," "Ah! Sweet Mystery of Life," "Indian Love Call," "Giannina Mia," "Italian Street Song"; also "The Waltz Song" from Gounod's *Roméo et Juliette,* "Nicolette" (m. Maurice Ravel).

THE FIRST LADY OF SONG, JEANETTE MACDONALD   A nightclub act. Las Vegas opening: October 28, 1953, Copa Room, Sands Hotel. Producer: Jack Entratter. Conductor: Ray Sinatra. Dance director: Al White. Gowns: Countess Alexander. Las Vegas run: three weeks.

Supporting acts: the Nicolas Brothers (dancers), Eddie Garson (comic), the Girls of the Sands.

MacDonald sang: "There's No Business Like Show Business" (Irving Berlin), "Ouvre ton coeur" (m. Georges Bizet), "Indian Love Call," "Giannina Mia," "Chansonette," "The Donkey Serenade," "Ebb Tide" (m. Robert Maxwell, w. Carl Sigman), "Un bel dì" from Puccini's *Madama Butterfly.* As a finale, MacDonald danced with Bill Alcorn and Jack Mattis to a medley of songs from her movies.

MacDonald brought this act to the Cocoanut Grove, Hotel Ambassador, Los Angeles, on January 20, 1954, for a two-week run. For the Grove show, she replaced "Giannina Mia" with a Paris medley that included "April in Paris" (m. Vernon Duke, w. E. Y. Harburg), "I Love Paris" (Cole Porter), and "C'est Magnifique" (Cole Porter); Benny Strong conducted.

BITTER SWEET   Summer stock productions of Noël Coward's operetta. Opening: July 19, 1954, Iroquois Amphitheater, Louisville, Kentucky, for five performances. Subsequent runs: Iroquois Amphitheater, Louisville, July 27–August 2, 1954; Pitts Stadium, Pittsburgh, August 9–14, 1954; Fox Valley Playhouse, St. Charles, Illinois, August 31–September 12, 1954; State Fair Auditorium, Dallas, July 4–17, 1955; Packard Music Playhouse Hall, Warren, Ohio, August 11–17, 1959; Cass Theater, Detroit, Michigan, September 15–27, 1959. *Following data for Dallas production only:* Producer: Charles R. Meeker, Jr., for State Fair Musicals, Inc. Stage director: George Schaefer. Music director: Franz Allers [who soon left Dallas to conduct the opening of *My Fair Lady* on Broadway]. Dance director: Edmund Balin. Art director: Peter Wolf. Costumes: Vivian Faucher, with Joe Crosby.

Cast [*in Dallas*]: MacDonald (Sarah Millick/Sari Linden/the Marchioness of Shayne), Glenn Burris (Carl Linden), Virginia Oswald (Manon), Andrew Gainey (Captain August Lutte), Mildred Trares (Dolly Chamberlain), John H. Jones (Vincent Howard), Pat Remick [Lee Remick's mother] (Mrs. Millick), Patricia Dell Moore (Lady Devon), Paul Ukena (the Marquis of Shayne and Lord Henry Jekyll), Rosemary Harris (Mrs. Devon), William Le Massena (the Hon. Hugh Devon and Herr Schlick).

MacDonald sang: "The Call of Life," "I'll See You Again," "What Is Love?," "Eeny, Meeny," "Should Happiness Forsake Me," "Evermore and a Day," "Dear Little Café," "I'll Follow My Secret Heart," "Zigeuner."

THE KING AND I   Summer stock production of Rodgers and Hammerstein's musical. Opening: August 20, 1956, Starlight Theater, Kansas City, Missouri, for two weeks. Producer: Richard H. Berger, for the Starlight Theater Association of Kansas City. Stage director: Glenn Jordan. Music director: Ronald Fiore. Associate music conductor: Jack Lee. Dance director: James Jamieson. Sets: G. Philippe de Rosier.

Cast: Jeanette MacDonald (Anna Leonowens), Leonard Graves (the King), Ronnie McLaren (Louis Leonowens), Glenn Burris (Lun Tha), Dorothy Coulter (Tuptim), Terry Saunders (Lady Thiang), Jack Edelman (Phra Alack), Fred Harper (Sir Edward Ramsey), Ted Beniades (the Kralahome), Mark Hykin (Prince Hulalongkorn).

MacDonald sang: "I Whistle a Happy Tune," "Hello, Young Lovers," "Getting to Know You," "Shall I Tell You What I Think of You?," "Shall We Dance?"

JEANETTE MACDONALD, ENCORE AT THE SAHARA   A nightclub act. June 12–17, 1957. [With one day's notice, MacDonald stepped in to replace headliner Teresa Brewer, who had fallen ill.]

Film Credits

In addition to principal cast and credits, I list songs, Academy Awards and nominations, and, when known, the number of production days, production costs, domestic and foreign earnings, and the profit or loss for each of Jeanette MacDonald's films. Production and financial figures for the MGM pictures come from Edgar J. "Eddie" Mannix, ledger of the profits and losses on all MGM releases between 1924 and 1963, Howard Strickling Collection, Herrick Library, Academy of Motion Picture Arts and Sciences, Beverly Hills; discrepancies between the difference between cost and earnings, on one hand, and profits, on the other, result from the omission of advertising and distribution expenses in MGM's method of accounting for production costs; moreover, profit figures may have been deliberately manipulated for tax and accounting purposes. For films adapted from stage musicals, all songs are by the original composer and lyricist unless otherwise noted. I list films in their order of production. Principal cast members are listed in their order of general importance.

THE LOVE PARADE   (Paramount Famous Lasky, 1929). Producer: Ernst Lubitsch. Director: Ernst Lubitsch. Screenplay: Ernst Vajda and Guy Bolton, from Leon Xanrof and Jules Chancel's play *The Prince Consort*. Music direction: Victor Schertzinger, with Nathaniel Finston. Songs: (m.) Schertzinger, (w.) Clifford Grey. Sound: Franklin Hansen. Cinematography: Victor Milner. Art direction: Häns Dreier. Costumes: Travis Banton. Editor: Merrill White. Running time: 110 minutes. New York premiere: November 19, 1929, Criterion Theater.

Cast: Jeanette MacDonald (Queen Louise of Sylvania, a monarch in search of a husband), Maurice Chevalier (Count Alfred), Lillian Roth (Lulu), Lupino Lane (Jacques), Eugene Pallette (minister of war), Edgar Norton (major domo), Lionel Belmore (prime minister), Albert Roccardi (foreign minister), Carl Stockdale (admiral), E. H. Calvert (Sylvanian ambassador), Russell Powell (Afghan ambassador), Margaret Fealy (first lady-in-waiting), Virginia Bruce (lady-in-waiting), Ben Turpin (cross-eyed lackey), Jean Harlow (extra in theater audience), Yola d'Avril (Paulette), André Chéron (Paulette's husband).

MacDonald sings: "Dream Lover," "Anything to Please the Queen," "My Love Parade," "March of the Grenadiers." Other songs: "Champagne," "Paris, Stay the Same," "Let's Be Common," "Nobody's Using It Now," "The Queen Is Always Right."

Academy Award nominations: Best Picture, Actor, Directing, Cinematography, Art Decoration, Sound Recording.

THE VAGABOND KING (Paramount Publix, 1930). Producers: B. P. Schulberg and J. G. Bachmann. Director: Ludwig Berger. Screenplay: Herman J. Mankiewicz, from Justin Huntly McCarthy's novel *If I Were King* and Rudolf Friml's operetta *The Vagabond King*, book by Brian Hooker, Russell Janney, and W. H. Post, lyrics by Hooker. Music direction: Nathaniel Finston. Sound: Franklin Hansen. Cinematography: Henry Gerrard and Ray Rennahan. Technicolor consultant: Natalie Kalmus. Art direction: Häns Dreier. Costumes: Travis Banton. Editor: Merrill White. Running time: 104 minutes. New York premiere: February 19, 1930, Criterion Theater. Cost: $1,200,000.

Cast: Jeanette MacDonald (Katherine de Vaucelles, niece of King Louis and inspiration for the beggar-poet who fights to defend France), Dennis King (François Villon), O. P. Heggie (King Louis XI), Lillian Roth (Huguette), Warner Oland (Grand Marshall Thibault), Arthur Stone (Oliver, the barber), Thomas Ricketts (astrologer), Lawford Davidson (Tristan), Christian J. Frank (executioner), Gene Wolff ("Death March" singer).

MacDonald sings: "Some Day," "Only a Rose," "Love Me To-night." Other songs: "King Louie" (m. Sam Coslow and Newell Chase, w. Leo Robin), "If I Were King" (m. Coslow and Chase, w. Robin), "What France Needs" (m. Chase, w. Robin), "Song of the Vagabonds," "Huguette's Waltz," "Mary, Queen of Heaven" (m. Coslow and Chase, w. Robin), "Death March" (m. Chase, w. Robin).

Academy Award nomination: Art Direction.

[The UCLA Film and Television Archive unveiled its long-awaited restoration of a 35mm Technicolor print of *The Vagabond King,* supervised by preservation officer Robert Gitt, on July 21, 1991, at UCLA's Melnitz Theater. The surviving nitrate print (six reels) was donated to the Archive by Paramount Studios in December 1975, with the cooperation of the film's copyright owner, MCA/Universal. In striking a new "internegative" and a new 35mm print, the preservationists utilized one reel with sharper color donated by Miles Kreuger, president of the Institute of the American Musical, Inc., Los Angeles.]

THE LOTTERY BRIDE (United Artists for Artcinema Associates, 1930). Producer: Arthur Hammerstein. Presented by Joesph M. Schenck. Supervised by John W. Considine, Jr. Director: Paul L. Stein. Screenplay: Horace Jackson and Howard Emmett Rogers, from Herbert Stothart's story "Bride 66." Music direction: Hugo Riesenfeld. Songs: (m.) Rudolf Friml, (w.) J. Keirn Brennan. Sound: P. P. Reed and Frank Maher. Black-and-white cinematography: Karl Freund. Color cinematography: Ray Rennahan and Ray June. Art direction: William Cameron Menzies, with Park French. Costumes: Alice O'Neill. Editor: Robert J. Kern. Running time: 85 minutes. New York premiere: October 25, 1930, Rialto Theater.

Cast: Jeanette MacDonald (Jenny Trondson, a young Norwegian whose boyfriend's brother wins her in a mail-order marriage lottery), John Garrick (Chris Svenson), Joe E. Brown (Hoke Curtis), ZaSu Pitts (Hilda), Robert Chisholm (Olaf Svenson), Joseph Macaulay (Alberto), Harry Gribbon (Bjork), Carroll Nye (Nels Trondson), Max Davidson (marriage broker), Frank Brownlee (guard), Paul Hurst (lottery agent), Robert E. Homans (miner).

MacDonald sings: "Yubla," "My Northern Light." Other songs: "Come Drink to the Girl That You Love," "Round She Whirls," "Shoulder to Shoulder," "High and Low," "Napoli," "Two Strong Men," "You're an Angel," "I'll Follow the Trail."

LET'S GO NATIVE (Paramount Publix, 1930). Producer: Paramount Pictures, Inc. Director: Leo McCarey. Screenplay: George Marion, Jr., and Percy Heath. Songs: (m.) Richard A. Whiting, (w.) George Marion, Jr. Sound: Harry D. Mills. Dance direction: David Bennett. Cinematography: Victor Milner. Montage sequences: Slavko Vorkapich. Running time: 75 minutes. New York premiere: August 29, 1930, Paramount Theater.

Cast: Jeanette MacDonald (Joan Wood, a New York career girl who gets stranded on a tropical island), Jack Oakie (Voltaire McGinnis), Kay Francis (Constance Cooke), Richard "Skeets" Gallagher (king of the island), Eugene Pallette (Deputy Sheriff Careful Cuthbert), James Hall (Wally Wendell), Virginia Bruce (Grandpa Wendell's secretary), William Austin (Basil Pistol), Charles Sellon (Grandpa Wendell), David Newell (Chief Officer Williams), Rafael Storm (an Argentine), Charlie Hall (a mover), E. H. Calvert (diner eating duck), Grady Sutton (diner), John Elliott (captain), Oscar Smith (cook), the King's Men (singers).

MacDonald sings: "My Mad Moment," "It Seems to Be Spring." Other songs: "Let's Go Native," "I've Gotta Yen for You," "Joe Jazz."

PARAMOUNT ON PARADE (Paramount Publix, 1930). Producer: Paramount Pictures, Inc. Supervisor: Elsie Janis. Directors: Dorothy Arzner, Victor Heerman, Ernst Lubitsch, Edward Sutherland, Otto Brower, Lothar Mendes, Edmund Goulding, Rowland V. Lee, Victor Schertzinger, Frank Tuttle, Edwin H. Knopf. Cinematography: Harry Fischbeck and Victor Milner. Dance direction: David Bennett. Sets: John Wenger. Running time: 101 minutes. New York premiere: April 20, 1930, Paramount Theater.

Cast: Jeanette MacDonald, Maurice Chevalier, and, in alphabetical order, Richard Arlen, Jean Arthur, William Austin, George Bancroft, Clara Bow, Evelyn Brent, Mary Brian, Clive Brook, Virginia Bruce, Nancy Carroll, Ruth Chatterton, Gary Cooper, Leon Errol, Stuart Erwin, Kay Francis, Skeets Gallagher,

Harry Green, Mitzi Green, James Hall, Phillips Holmes, Helen Kane, Dennis King, Abe Lyman Band, Fredric March, Nino Martini, Mitzi Mayfair, David Newell, Jack Oakie, Warner Oland, Zelma O'Neal, Eugene Pallette, Joan Peers, William Powell, Charles "Buddy" Rogers, Lillian Roth, Stanley Smith, Fay Wray.

[MacDonald appeared only in some Spanish-language releases of *Galas de la Paramount* and sang "Music in the Moonlight" (m./w. Newell Chase and Sam Coslow). An episode entitled "It's Tough to Be a Prima Donna," filmed for the English-language edition but then dropped, had MacDonald singing a medley of themes taken from "Il Bacio" (m. Luigi Arditi, w. Gottardo Aldighieri), *The Mikado* (m. Arthur Sullivan, w. W. S. Gilbert), "That's My Weakness Now" (w./m. Bud Green and Sam H. Stept), and *Rhapsody in Blue* (George Gershwin). Materials housed in the Institute of the American Musical, Inc., Los Angeles, show that the mistress of ceremonies for *Galas de la Paramount* was not MacDonald, as is often asserted, but Rosita Moreno. Virtually all footage of MacDonald's participation has been lost.]

MONTE CARLO (Paramount Publix, 1930). Producer: Ernst Lubitsch. Director: Ernst Lubitsch. Screenplay: Ernst Vajda, from Hans Müller's play *Die Blaue Küste* and Booth Tarkington's novel *Monsieur Beaucaire*. Additional dialogue: Vincent Lawrence. Music direction: Nathaniel Finston. Songs: (m.) Richard Whiting and W. Franke Harling, (w.) Leo Robin. Sound: Harry D. Mills. Cinematography: Victor Milner. Art direction: Häns Dreier. Running time: 90 minutes. New York premiere: August 27, 1930, Rivoli Theater.

Cast: Jeanette MacDonald (Countess Helene Mara, a runaway bride who falls in love with a count disguised as a hairdresser), Jack Buchanan (Count Rudolph Farriere), Claud Allister (Duke Otto von Liebenheim), ZaSu Pitts (Berthe), Lionel Belmore (Count Gustave von Liebenheim), Tyler Brooke (Armand), John Roche (Paul), Albert Conti (Otto's companion), Sidney Bracy (hunchback), Donald Novis (Monsieur Beaucaire), Helen Garden (Lady Mary), Billy Bevan (conductor), Frances Dee (receptionist).

MacDonald sings: "Beyond the Blue Horizon," "Give Me a Moment Please," "Whatever It Is, It's Grand," "She'll Love Me and Like It," "Always in All Ways." Other song: "Trimmin' the Women."

OH, FOR A MAN! (Fox, 1930). Producer: Sol Wurtzel. Director: Hamilton MacFadden. Assistant director: Sam Wurtzel. Screenplay: Philip Klein, from Mary T. Watkins's story "Stolen Thunder." Dialogue: Lynn Starling. Music direction: Arthur Kay. Sound: E. Clayton Ward. Cinematography: Charles G. Clarke. Art direction: Stephen Goosson. Costumes: Sophie Wachner. Editor: Al De Gaetano. Running time: 86 minutes. New York premiere: November 29, 1930, Fox Theater (Brooklyn).

Cast: Jeanette MacDonald (Carlotta Manson, a temperamental diva who falls for a singing burglar), Reginald Denny (Barney McGann), Alison Skipworth (Laura, Carlotta's maid), Bela Lugosi (Frescatti, the impresario), Albert Conti (Peck), Warren Hymer (Pug Morini), Marjorie White (Totsy Franklin), André Chéron (Costello, the voice coach), William Davidson (Kerry Stokes), Bodil Rosing (masseuse).

MacDonald sings: "Liebestod" from Richard Wagner's *Tristan und Isolde,* "On a Summer Night" (m. William Kernell). Other songs: "Believe Me If All Those Endearing Young Charms" (m. traditional, w. Thomas Moore), "I'm Just Nuts About You" (m. Kernell).

DON'T BET ON WOMEN (Fox, 1931). Producer: Sol Wurtzel. Associate producer: John W. Considine. Director: William K. Howard. Staging: Henry Kolker. Screenplay: Lynn Starling and Leon Gordon, from William Anthony McGuire's story "All Women Are Bad." Sound: Albert Protzman. Cinematography: Lucien Andriot. Art direction: Duncan Cramer. Costumes: Sophie Wachner. Editor: Harold Schuster. Running time: 70 minutes. New York premiere: March 6, 1931, Roxy Theater.

Cast: Jeanette MacDonald (Jeanne Drake, a woman whose husband inadvertently prods her to seek out extramarital pleasures), Edmund Lowe (Roger Fallon), Roland Young (Herbert Drake), Una Merkel (Tallulah Hope), Louise Beavers (the maid), J. M. Kerrigan (Chipley Duff), Henry Kolker (Butterfield), Helene Millard (Doris Brent), Cyril Ring (a guest).

MacDonald does not sing.

ANNABELLE'S AFFAIRS (Fox, 1931). Producer: Sol Wurtzel. Associate producer: William Goetz. Director: Alfred L. Werker. Assistant director: Horace Hough. Screenplay: Leon Gordon and Harlan Thompson, from Clare Kummer's play *Good Gracious Annabelle.* Sound: Al Bruzlin. Cinematography: Charles G. Clarke. Editor: Margaret Clancy. Art direction: Duncan Cramer. Costumes: Dolly Tree. Running time: 79 minutes. New York premiere: June 26, 1931, Roxy Theater.

Cast: Jeanette MacDonald (Annabelle Leigh, a New York playgirl who fails to recognize a Montana millionaire as her estranged husband), Victor McLaglen (John Rawson), Roland Young (Roland Wimbledon), Louise Beavers (Ruby, the maid), Sam Hardy (James, the butler), William Collier, Sr. (Wickham), Ruth Warren (Lottie, the maid), Joyce Compton (Mabel), Sally Blane (Dora), George André Béranger (Archer), Walter Walker (Gosling), Ernest Wood (McFadden), Jed Prouty (Bolson), Hank Mann (Summers), Wilbur Mack (Vance, assistant hotel manager).

MacDonald does not sing. [Only Reel 3 survives and is housed at the UCLA Film and Television Archive. The final shooting script in the Twentieth-Century Fox Collection, Doheny Library, USC, calls for MacDonald to sing the lullaby "Other Eyes" to tipsy Roland Young during a scene aboard a yacht. *Motion Picture Herald,* on May 30, 1931, specifies that "she has only one song"; *Variety,* on June 30, 1931, writes that she gets "a chorus of a song." Yet no nontrade reviewer refers to her singing, and *Picturegoer Weekly* (London), on December 19, 1931, states explicitly that "she does not sing." One can conclude that the song was cut from release prints because screen singing continued to be unpopular with audiences that year.]

ONE HOUR WITH YOU (Paramount Publix, 1932). Producer: Ernst Lubitsch. Director: Ernst Lubitsch, supervising George Cukor. Screenplay: Samson Raphaelson, from Lothar Schmidt's play *Nur ein Traum (Only a Dream).* Music direction: Nathaniel Finston. Songs: (m.) Oscar Straus, (w.) Leo Robin.

Interpolated music: Richard A. Whiting. Sound: M. M. Paggi. Cinematography: Victor Milner. Art direction: Häns Dreier. Costumes: Travis Banton, with Edith Head. Sets: A. E. Freudeman. Editor: William Shea. Running time: 80 minutes. New York premiere: March 25, 1932, the Rivoli and Rialto Theaters.

Cast: Jeanette MacDonald (Colette Bertier, wife of a Paris doctor with a roving eye), Maurice Chevalier (Dr. André Bertier), Genevieve Tobin (Mitzi Olivier), Charlie Ruggles (Adolph), Roland Young (Professor Olivier), George Barbier (police commissioner), Josephine Dunn (Mlle. Martel), Donald Novis (singer at party), Richard Carle (detective), Charles Judels (policeman), Barbara Leonard (Mitzi's maid), Charles Coleman (Marcel, the butler), Eric Wilton (butler), George Davis (cab driver), Kent Taylor (a guest).

[*Une heure près de toi*, with dialogue by Léopold Marchand and lyrics by André Hornez, premiered at Paris's Paramount Theater on June 1, 1932. In addition to MacDonald and Chevalier, the principals of the French-language cast were: Lili Damita (Mitzi Olivier), Pierre Etcheparé (Adolphe), Ernst Ferny (Professor Olivier), André Chéron (police commissioner), Josephine Dunn (Mlle. Martel), Richard Carle (detective).]

MacDonald sings: "What a Little Thing Like a Wedding Ring Can Do," "(Day After Day) We Will Always Be Sweethearts," "One Hour with You," "It Was Only a Dream Kiss." Other songs: "Three Times a Day," "Oh, That Mitzi," "(Now I Ask You) What Would You Do?"

Academy Award nomination: Best Picture.

LOVE ME TONIGHT (Paramount Publix, 1932). Producer: Rouben Mamoulian. Director: Rouben Mamoulian. Screenplay: Samuel Hoffenstein, Waldemar Young, and George Marion, Jr., from Léopold Marchand and Paul Armont's play *Tailor in the Chateau*. Music direction: Nathaniel Finston. Songs: (m.) Richard Rodgers, (w.) Lorenz Hart. Sound: M. M. Paggi. Cinematography: Victor Milner. Art direction: Häns Dreier. Costumes: Edith Head. Editor: William Shea. Running time: 104 minutes. New York premiere: August 11, 1932, Rivoli Theater. Cost: $1,000,000.

Cast: Jeanette MacDonald (Princess Jeanette, a young depressed widow whose doctor advises her to get a husband, soon), Maurice Chevalier (Maurice Courtelin), Charlie Ruggles (Vicomte Gilbert de Vareze), Charles Butterworth (Count de Savignac), Myrna Loy (Countess Valentine), C. Aubrey Smith (the Duke), Elizabeth Patterson (an aunt), Ethel Griffies (an aunt), Blanche Frederici (an aunt), George "Gabby" Hayes (grocer), Joseph Cawthorn (Dr. Armand de Fontinac), Robert Greig (Major Domo Flamond), Ethel Wales (Madame Dutoit), Bert Roach (Emile), Tyler Brooke (composer), Rolfe Sedan (taxi driver), Gordon Westcott (collector), Clarence Wilson (shirtmaker), William H. Turner (bootmaker), Tony Merlo (hatmaker), Mary Doran (Madame Dupont), Edgar Norton (valet), Cecil Cunningham (laundress), Rita Owin (chambermaid), Mel Kalish (chef).

MacDonald sings: "Isn't It Romantic?," "Lover," "A Woman Needs Something Like That," "Love Me Tonight." Other songs: "That's the Song of Paree," "How Are You?," "Mimi," "The Poor Apache," "The Son of a Gun Is Nothing But a Tailor."

THE CAT AND THE FIDDLE (Metro-Goldwyn-Mayer, 1934). Producer: Bernard H. Hyman. Director: William K. Howard. Assistant director: Lesley Selander. Screenplay: Samuel and Bella Spewack, from Jerome Kern's operetta *The Cat and the Fiddle,* book and lyrics by Otto Harbach. Music direction: Herbert Stothart. Sound: Douglas Shearer. Black-and-white cinematography: Harold Rosson and Charles G. Clarke. Color cinematography: Ray Rennahan. Technicolor consultant: Natalie Kalmus. Art direction: Alexander Toluboff. Sets: Edwin B. Willis. Costumes: Adrian. Editor: Frank Hull. Running time: 92 minutes. New York premiere: February 16, 1934, Capitol and Loew's Metropolitan Theaters. Production days: 74. Cost: $843,000. Earnings: domestic $455,000; foreign $644,000; total $1,099,000. Loss: $142,000.

Cast: Jeanette MacDonald (Shirley Sheridan, an aspiring American songwriter who makes it big in Europe), Ramon Novarro (Victor Florescu), Frank Morgan (Jules Daudet), Vivienne Segal (Odette Brieux), Charles Butterworth (Charles), Jean Hersholt (Professor Bertier), Irene Franklin (Lotte Lengel), Herman Bing (drum major), Paul Porcasi (café proprietor), Leonid Kinsky (violinist), Sterling Holloway (messenger), Frank Conroy (theater owner), Henry Armetta (taxi driver), Adrienne D'Ambricourt (concierge), Yola d'Avril (maid), Armand Kaliz (leading man), Leo White (stage manager), Billy Dooley (electrician), Joseph Cawthorn (Rudy Brieux), Earl Oxford (singer), the Albertina Rasch Ballet (dancers).

MacDonald sings: "The Night Was Made for Love," "She Didn't Say 'Yes,' " "I Watch the Love Parade," "Try to Forget," "A New Love Is Old," "Long, Long Ago" ("Poor Pierrot"), "One Moment Alone." Other songs: "The Breeze Kissed Your Hair," "Don't Tell Us Not to Sing," "Hh! Cha Cha!"

THE MERRY WIDOW (Metro-Goldwyn Mayer, 1934 [retitled THE LADY DANCES for television following MGM's 1952 remake, but available again as THE MERRY WIDOW on video]). Producer: Irving Thalberg [uncredited]. Director: Ernst Lubitsch. Assistant directors: Joseph Newman and Joseph Lefert. Screenplay: Samson Raphaelson, Ernst Vajda, and Lorenz Hart, from Franz Lehár's operetta *Die Lustige Witwe,* libretto and lyrics by Victor Leon [pseud. Victor Hirschfeld] and Leo Stein [pseud. Leo Rosenstein]. Music adaptation and direction: Herbert Stothart. New lyrics: Lorenz Hart and Gus Kahn. Sound: Douglas Shearer. Dance direction: Albertina Rasch. Cinematography: Oliver T. Marsh. Art direction: Cedric Gibbons and Frederic Hope. Sets: Edwin B. Willis, with Gabriel Scognamillo. Men's costumes: Ali Hubert. Women's gowns: Adrian. Editor: Frances March. Running time: 110 minutes. New York premiere: October 11, 1934, Astor Theater. Production days: 88. Cost: $1,605,000. Earnings: domestic, $861,000; foreign, $1,747,000; total, $2,608,000. Loss: $113,000. [In view of the picture's cost, *The Merry Widow* was not the "flop" many later claimed it to have been.]

Cast: Jeanette MacDonald (Sonia, aka Fifi, the world's richest widow, who sets out for the pleasures of Paris), Maurice Chevalier (Captain Danilo), George Barbier (King Achmed), Una Merkel (Queen Dolores), Edward Everett Horton (Ambassador Popoff), Sterling Holloway (Mischka, who lip-synchs to Allan Rogers's tenor), Akim Tamiroff (manager of Maxim's), Herman Bing

(Zizipoff), Leonid Kinsky (shepherd), Jason Robards, Sr. (arresting officer), Minna Gombell (Marcelle), Ruth Channing (Lulu), Henry Armetta (Turk), Barbara Leonard (maid), Donald Meek (valet), Lucien Prival (Adamovitch), Katherine Burke (prisoner), Richard Carle (defense attorney), Morgan Wallace (prosecuting attorney), Frank Sheridan (judge), Arthur "Pop" Byron (doorman), Matty Roubert (newsboy), Ferdinand Munier (jailer), Hector Sarno (gypsy leader), Bela Loblov (gypsy violinist [miming to Louis Kaufman's solo violin]), Jan Rubini (violinist), Albert Pollet (head waiter), Rolfe Sedan (Gabrilovitch), Jacques Lory (goatman), Barbara Barondess (a Maxim's girl), Dorothy Granger (a Maxim's girl), Eleanor Hunt (a Maxim's girl).

[*La Veuve joyeuse,* with lyrics by André Hornez and dialogue by Marcel Achard, premiered at Paris's Madeleine Theater on February 4, 1935. In addition to MacDonald and Chevalier, the principals of the French-language cast were: André Berley (King), Danièle Parola (Queen), Marcel Vallée (ambassador), George Davis (Mischka), Fifi d'Orsay (Marcelle), Pauline Garon (Lulu), Emile Dellys (Zizipoff), André Chéron (judge), Lya Lys (a Maxim's girl), Jean Perry (valet), Alice Ardell (Kiki). (The Mannix cost/profit ledger does not include separate financial figures for this version.)]

MacDonald sings: "Vilia," "Tonight Will Teach Me to Forget [The Diary Song]," "Melody of Laughter," "Maxim's," "The Merry Widow Waltz," "If Widows Are Rich." Other song: "Girls, Girls, Girls!"

[Richard Rodgers and Lorenz Hart wrote three new songs for the movie, but they were not used: "It Must Be Love" (for Chevalier), "A Widow Is a Lady" (for MacDonald), and "Dolores" (for Chevalier). Although Rodgers shared screen credit, Hart alone was responsible for all of the English-language lyrics, with the exception of "Tonight Will Teach Me to Forget," by Gus Kahn.]

Academy Award: Art Decoration (Cedric Gibbons and Frederic Hope).

NAUGHTY MARIETTA (Metro-Goldwyn-Mayer, 1935). Producer: Hunt Stromberg. Director: W. S. Van Dyke II. Assistant director: Eddie Woehler. Screenplay: Frances Goodrich, Albert Hackett, and John Lee Mahin, from Victor Herbert's operetta *Naughty Marietta,* book and lyrics by Rida Johnson Young. Music direction: Herbert Stothart. New lyrics: Gus Kahn. Sound: Douglas Shearer. Cinematography: William Daniels. Art direction: Cedric Gibbons, with Arnold Gillespie and Edwin B. Willis. Costumes: Adrian. Editor: Blanche Sewell. Running time: 106 minutes. New York premiere: March 29, 1935, Capitol Theater. Production days: 44. Cost: $782,000. Earnings: domestic $1,058,000; foreign $999,000; total $2,057,000. Profit: $407,000. [Reissues in 1936–37 and 1944–45 brought profits of $92,000 and $297,000, respectively.]

Cast: Jeanette MacDonald (French princess Marie de Namours de la Bonfain, who escapes an arranged marriage and, as Marietta Franini, joins a shipload of auction-brides headed for colonial New Orleans), Nelson Eddy (Captain Richard Warrington), Frank Morgan (Governor Gaspard d'Annard), Elsa Lanchester (Madame d'Annard), Douglass Dumbrille (Marie's uncle, prince de Namours de la Bonfain), Joseph Cawthorn (Herr Schuman), Greta Meyer (Frau Schuman), Helen Shipman (Marietta Franini), Cecilia Parker

(Julie), Walter Kingsford (Don Carlos de Braganza), William Burress (Bouget), Delos Jewkes (priest on dock), Akim Tamiroff (Rudolpho), Harold Huber (Abe), Edward Brophy (Zeke), Dr. Edouard Lippe [Nelson Eddy's vocal coach] (landlord), Olive Carey (Madame Renavent), Guy Usher (ship's captain), Ed Keane (Major Cornell), Roger Gray (sergeant).

MacDonald sings: "Chansonette," "Italian Street Song," "Ship Ahoy," "Ah! Sweet Mystery of Life." Other songs: "Tramp, Tramp, Tramp," "The Owl and the Bob Cat," "'Neath the Southern Moon," "I'm Falling in Love with Someone," "Antoinette and Anatole."

Academy Award: Sound Recording (Douglas Shearer). Academy Award nomination: Best Picture.

ROSE MARIE (Metro-Goldwyn-Mayer, 1936 [retitled INDIAN LOVE CALL for television following MGM's 1954 remake, but available again as ROSE MARIE on video]). Producer: Hunt Stromberg. Director: W. S. Van Dyke II. Assistant director: Joseph Newman. Screenplay: Frances Goodrich, Albert Hackett, and Alice Duer Miller, from Rudolf Friml and Herbert Stothart's operetta *Rose-Marie,* book and lyrics by Otto Harbach and Oscar Hammerstein II. Music direction: Herbert Stothart. Staging of opera scenes: William von Wymetal. Sound: Douglas Shearer. Dance direction: Chester Hale. Dance staging for opera sequences: Val Raset. Cinematography: William Daniels. Montage effects: Slavko Vorkapich. Art director: Cedric Gibbons, with Joseph Wright and Edwin B. Willis. Costumes: Adrian. Editor: Blanche Sewall. Running time: 113 minutes. New York premiere: January 31, 1936, Capitol Theater. Production days: 51. Cost: $875,000. Earnings: domestic $1,695,000; foreign $1,820,000; total, $3,515,000. Profit: $1,488,000. [A reissue in 1938–39 brought profits of $54,000.]

Cast: Jeanette MacDonald (Marie de Flor, an opera star who falls for the Canadian Mountie tracking down her brother; aka Rose Marie), Nelson Eddy (Sergeant Bruce), James Stewart (John Flower), David Nivens [*sic*] (Teddy), Allan Jones (Romeo/Mario Cavaradossi), Reginald Owen (Myerson), Halliwell Hobbes (Mr. Gordon, opera manager), Alan Mowbray (premier of Québec), Una O'Connor (Marie's maid), George Regas (Boniface), Herman Bing (Mr. Danielle), Gilda Gray (Belle), Robert Greig (café manager), James Conlin (piano player), Lucien Littlefield (storekeeper), Dorothy Gray (Edith), Mary Anita Loos [Anita Loos's niece] (Corn Queen), Milton Owen (stage manager), Matty Roubert (newsboy), Agostino Borgato (opera fan), Adrian Rosley (opera fan), Delos Jewkes (butcher), Paul Porcasi (Emil, the chef), Olga Dane (*Roméo et Juliette* singer).

MacDonald sings: "Juliette's Waltz" and the death scene from Charles Gounod's *Roméo et Juliette* (libretto by Jules Barbier and Michel Carré), "Pardon Me, Madame" (m. Stothart, w. Gus Kahn), "Dinah" (m. Harry Akst, w. Sam Lewis and Joe Young), "Some of These Days" (Shelton Brooks), "Three Blind Mice" (traditional), "Indian Love Call," scenes from act 3 of Giacomo Puccini's *Tosca* (libretto by Giuseppe Giacosa and Luigi Illica). Other songs: "The Mounties," "Rose Marie," "Totem Tom Tom," "Serenade Just for You" (m. Stothart, Friml, w. Gus Kahn).

SAN FRANCISCO (Metro-Goldwyn-Mayer, 1936). Producers: Bernard H. Hyman and John Emerson. Director: W. S. Van Dyke II. Assistant director: Joseph Newman. Screenplay: Anita Loos, from an original story by Robert Hopkins. Music direction: Herbert Stothart. Songs: (m.) Bronislaw Kaper and Walter Jurmann, (w.) Gus Kahn; (m.) Nacio Herb Brown, (w.) Arthur Freed. Sound: Douglas Shearer. Dance direction: Val Raset. Opera direction: William von Wymetal. Cinematography: Oliver T. Marsh. Art direction: Cedric Gibbons, with Harry McAfee and Edwin B. Willis. Costumes: Adrian. Special effects: Arnold Gillespie and James Basevi. Montage effects: John Hoffman. Editor: Tom Held. Running time: 115 minutes. New York premiere: June 26, 1936, Capitol Theater. Production days: 52. Cost: $1,300,000. Earnings: domestic $2,868,000; foreign $2,405,000; total $5,273,000. Profit: $2,237,000. [Reissues in 1938–39 and 1948–49 brought profits of $124,000 and $647,000, respectively.]

Cast: Jeanette MacDonald (Mary Blake, a parson's daughter with a gift for opera who falls in love with a lusty saloon keeper), Clark Gable (Blackie Norton), Spencer Tracy (Father Tim Mullin), Jack Holt (Jack Burley), Jessie Ralph (Maisie Burley), Ted Healy (Matt), Margaret Irving (Della Bailey), Harold Huber (Babe), Al Shean (Professor), William Ricciardi (Signor Baldini), Kenneth Harlan (Chick), Roger Imhof (Alaska), Frank Mayo (dealer), Charles Judels (Tony), Russell Simpson (Red Kelly), Bert Roach (Freddy Duane), Warren B. Hymer (Hazeltine), Edgar Kennedy (process server), Shirley Ross (Trixie), Tandy MacKenzie (Faust), Tudor Williams (Mephistopheles), Saint Luke's Choristers (choir), Allen Churchill (boy soloist), Long Beach Boys' Choir (choir), Delos Jewkes ("Battle Hymn" singer), Homer Hall ("Battle Hymn" singer).

MacDonald sings: "Love Me and the World Is Mine" (m. Ernest R. Ball, w. Dave Reed), "San Francisco" (m. Kaper and Jurmann, w. Kahn), "A Heart That's Free" (A. J. Robyn and T. Railey), "The Holy City" (Stephen Adams and F. E. Weatherly), "Would You" (m. Brown, w. Freed), scenes from Charles Gounod's *Faust* (libretto by Jules Barbier and Michel Carré) and Giuseppe Verdi's *La traviata* (libretto by Francesco Maria Piave), "Nearer, My God, to Thee" (m. Lowell Mason, w. Sarah F. Adams), "The Battle Hymn of the Republic" (m. William Steffe, w. Julia Ward Howe).

Academy Award: Best Sound Recording (Douglas Shearer). Academy Award nominations: Best Picture, Best Actor (Spencer Tracy), Best Director, Best Assistant Director, Best Original Story.

[Producers Martin L. Marcus, Marvin Krauss, and Nica Burns were reportedly developing a Broadway musical version of *San Francisco* in 1992, with book by Tim Prager and music and lyrics by Geoff Morrow.]

MAYTIME (Metro-Goldwyn-Mayer, 1937). Producer: Hunt Stromberg. Director: Robert Z. Leonard. Assistant directors: Joseph Newman and Marvin Stuart. Screenplay: Noel Langley and Claudine West, from Sigmund Romberg's operetta *Maytime*, book and lyrics by Rida Johnson Young. Music direction: Herbert Stothart. Special lyrics: Bob Wright and Chet Forrest. Opera direction: William von Wymetal. Assistant dance directors: Paul Foltz and Harvey Karels.

Special French libretto: Gilles Guilbert. French choral arrangements: Léo Arnaud. Sound: Douglas Shearer. Dance direction: Val Raset. Cinematography: Oliver T. Marsh. Makeup: Jack Dawn. Montage effects: Slavko Vorkapich. Art direction: Cedric Gibbons, with Frederic Hope and Edwin B. Willis. Costumes: Adrian. Editor: Conrad A. Nervig. Running time: 132 minutes. New York premiere: March 17, 1937, Capitol Theater. Production days: 60. Cost: $2,126,000. Earnings: domestic $2,183,000; foreign $1,823,000; total $4,006,000. Profit: $594,000.

Cast: Jeanette MacDonald (Miss Morrison, an elderly recluse who recounts her tragic life as the diva Marcia Mornay), Nelson Eddy (Paul Allison), John Barrymore (Nicolai Nazaroff), Tom Brown (Kip), Lynne Carver (Barbara Roberts), Herman Bing (August Archipenko), Leonid Kinsky (student in bar), Rafaela Ottiano (Ellen, the maid), Charles Judels (cab driver), Paul Porcasi (Trentini), Sig Rumann (Fanchon), Anna Demetrio (Madame Fanchon), Guy Bates Post (Emperor Louis Napoleon), Iphigenie Castiglioni (Empress Eugenie), Frank Puglia (orchestra conductor), Harry Davenport (opera director), Frank Sheridan (O'Brien, the director), Maurice Cass (opera house manager), Douglas Wood (hotel manager), Bernard Suss (assistant hotel manager), Henry Roquemore (publicity man), Paul Weigel (prompter), Paul Cremonesi (opera critic), Adia Kuznetzoff (Dubrovsky, the Czaritza's minister), Mariska Aldrich (opera contralto), the Don Cossack Chorus (for "Le Régiment de Sambre et Meuse"), Nan Merriman (chorus member for *Les Huguenots*), George London (chorus member for *Les Huguenots*), Joan Le Sueur [Joan Crawford's three-year-old niece] (maypole dancer), Russell Hicks (voice teacher), M. Marova (contralto in *Czaritza*), Tudor Williams (bass in *Les Huguenots*), Ludovico Tomarchio (tenor in Saint-Cloud festival).

MacDonald sings: "Les Filles de Cadiz" (m. Léo Delibes, w. Alfred de Musset), "Le Régiment de Sambre et Meuse" (m. Robert Planquette, w. Paul Cezano), "Carry Me Back to Old Virginny" (James A. Bland), "Nobles seigneurs, salut" and "Une dame noble et sage" from Giacomo Meyerbeer's *Les Huguenots* (libretto by Eugène Scribe and Emile Deschamps), "Santa Lucia" (Neapolitan folk song), "Will You Remember?" (m. Sigmund Romberg, w. Rida Johnson Young), passages from Verdi's *Il trovatore* and *La traviata*, Gounod's *Faust*, Wagner's *Tristan und Isolde*, Michael William Balfe's *The Bohemian Girl*, Friedrich von Flotow's *Martha*, and Donizetti's *Lucia di Lammermoor*, scenes from the ersatz opera *Czaritza* (m. Herbert Stothart, Chet Forrest, and Bob Wright from Pëtr Ilich Tchaikovsky's Fifth Symphony, French lyrics by Gilles Guilbert). Other songs: "Plantons la vigne" (traditional Breton folk song), "Vive l'Opéra," "Ham and Eggs" (a pastiche of melodies from Verdi, Rossini, Wagner, Gounod, and Donizetti, compiled by Stothart, Wright, and Forrest).

Academy Award nomination: Music Score (Herbert Stothart).

THE FIREFLY (Metro-Goldwyn-Mayer, 1937). Producer: Hunt Stromberg. Director: Robert Z. Leonard. Assistant director: Joseph Newman. Screenplay: Ogden Nash, Frances Goodrich, and Albert Hackett from Rudolf Friml's operetta *The Firefly*, book and lyrics by Otto Harbach, and August Ludolf

Friedrich Schaumann's novel *On the Road with Wellington*. Music direction: Herbert Stothart. Songs: (m.) Rudolf Friml and Herbert Stothart, (w.) Robert Wright and Chet Forrest. Sound: Douglas Shearer. Dance direction: Albertina Rasch. Cinematography: Oliver T. Marsh. Montage effects: Slavko Vorkapich. Art direction: Cedric Gibbons, with Edwin B. Willis and Paul Groesse. Technical adviser: George Richelavie. Costumes: Adrian. Editor: Robert J. Kern. Running time: 138 minutes. New York premiere: September 1, 1937, Astor Theater. Production days: 61. Cost: $1,495,000. Earnings: domestic $1,244,000; foreign $1,430,000; total $2,674,000. Profit: $163,000.

Cast: Jeanette MacDonald (Nina Maria Azara, a Spanish spy who helps free her country from Napoleon's clutches while falling in love with a French spy), Allan Jones (Don Diego Manrique de Lara, aka Captain François André), Warren William (Colonel de Rougemont), Douglass Dumbrille (Marquis de Melito), Belle Mitchell (Lola), Leonard Penn (Etienne), Billy Gilbert (innkeeper), Tom Rutherford (King Ferdinand), Henry Daniell (General Savary), George Zucco (St. Clair), Manuel Alvarez Maciste (Pedro, the coach driver), Robert Spindola (Juan, the driver's son), Zeni Vatori (waiter), John Picorri (café proprietor), Maurice Black (pigeon vendor), Maurice Cass (strawberry vendor), Stanley Price (Joseph Bonaparte), Matthew Boulton (Duke of Wellington), Edward Keane (chief of staff), Victor Adams (jail guard), Jason Robards, Sr. (Spanish patriot), David Tihmar (Madrid café dancer), Robert Z. Leonard (Bayonne café extra), Albertina Rasch (Bayonne café extra), St. Luke's Choristers, St. Brendan's Boys Choir, and Our Lady of the Angels Choir (choirs).

MacDonald sings: "Love Is Like a Firefly," "He Who Loves and Runs Away," "Sympathy," "When a Maid Comes Knocking at Your Heart," "Giannina Mia," "The Donkey Serenade." Other songs: "A Woman's Kiss," "Para la salud" (arr. Stothart), "Ojos rojos" (Argentine folk song).

THE GIRL OF THE GOLDEN WEST (Metro-Goldwyn-Mayer, 1938). Producers: William Anthony McGuire and Robert Z. Leonard. Director: Robert Z. Leonard. Assistant directors: Robert A. Golden and George Yohalem. Screenplay: Isabel Dawn and Boyce DeGaw, from David Belasco's play *The Girl of the Golden West*. Music director: Herbert Stothart. Songs: (m.) Sigmund Romberg, (w.) Gus Kahn. Dialogue coach: Dave Weber. Sound: Douglas Shearer. Dance direction: Albertina Rasch. Cinematography: Oliver T. Marsh. Costumes: Adrian. Art direction: Cedric Gibbons, with Eddie Imazu and Edwin B. Willis. Montage effects: Slavko Vorkapich. Editor: W. Donn Hayes. Running time: 120 minutes. New York premiere: March 24, 1938, Capitol Theater. Production days: 57. Cost: $1,680,000. Earnings: domestic $1,597,000; foreign $1,285,000; total $2,882,000. Profit: $243,000.

Cast: Jeanette MacDonald (Mary Robbins, a saloon keeper who discovers her lover to be a notorious bandito from Mexico), Nelson Eddy (Ramerez, aka Lieutenant Dick Johnson), Walter Pidgeon (Sheriff Jack Rance), Buddy Ebsen (Alabama), Leo Carrillo (Mosquito), H. B. Warner (Father Sienna), Cliff Edwards (Minstrel Joe), Leonard Penn (Pedro), Monty Wooley (Governor), Priscilla Lawson (Nina Martinez), Ynez Seabury (Wowkle), Brandon Tynan

(Professor), Bob Murphy (Sonora Slim), Noah Beery, Sr. (the General), Bill Cody, Jr. ("Gringo," Ramerez as a boy), Jeanne Ellis (Mary, as a girl), Charles Grapewin (Uncle Davy), Chief Big Tree (Indian chief), Olin Howland (Trinidad Joe), Hal LeSueur (adjutant), St. Luke's Choristers and Father Machaias Lanis Choir (choirs), Carlos Ruffino ("Mariachie" soloist), Rodolfo Hayos ("Mariachie" soloist).

MacDonald sings: "Shadows on the Moon," "The Wind in the Trees," "Liebestraum" (m. Franz Liszt, w. Gus Kahn), "Ave Maria" (m. J. S. Bach and Ch. Gounod), "Mariachie" (w. Carlos Ruffino, Kahn), "Who Are We to Say?," "Señorita." Other songs: "Sun-up to Sundown," "Soldiers of Fortune," "The West Ain't Wild Anymore."

SWEETHEARTS (Metro-Goldwyn-Mayer, 1938). Producer: Hunt Stromberg. Director: W. S. Van Dyke II. Assistant directors: Hugh Boswell, Charles O'Malley, and Ted Stevens. Screenplay: Dorothy Parker and Alan Campbell. Music direction: Herbert Stothart, from Victor Herbert's operetta *Sweethearts,* book by Harry B. Smith and Fred De Gressac, lyrics by Robert B. Smith. New lyrics: Bob Wright and Chet Forrest. Sound: Douglas Shearer. Musical presentation: Merrill Pye. Dance direction: Ray Bolger and Albertina Rasch. Cinematography: Oliver T. Marsh and Allen Davey. Technicolor consultants: Natalie Kalmus and Henri Jaffa. Costumes: Adrian. Art direction: Cedric Gibbons, with Joseph Wright and Edwin B. Willis. Editor: Robert J. Kern. Running time: 114 minutes. New York premiere: December 22, 1938. Production days: 47. Cost: $1,966,000. Earnings: domestic $2,017,000; foreign $1,230,000; total $3,247,000. Profit: $120,000.

Cast: Jeanette MacDonald (Gwen Marlowe, the First Lady of the Broadway musical theater), Nelson Eddy (Ernest Lane), Frank Morgan (Felix Lehman), Ray Bolger (Hans), Florence Rice (Kay Jordan), Mischa Auer (Leo Kronk), Herman Bing (Oscar Engel), Reginald Gardiner (Norman Trumpett), Terry Kilburn (Gwen's brother, Junior), Betty Jaynes (Gwen's understudy, Una Wilson), Douglas McPhail (Ernest's understudy, Harvey Horton), Alan Joslyn (Dink Rogers), Raymond Walburn (Orlando Lane), Lucille Watson (Mrs. Marlowe), Kathleen Lockhart (Aunt Amelia Lane), Gene Lockhart (Augustus Marlowe), Berton Churchill (Sheridan Lane), George Barbier (Benjamin Silver), Olin Howland (Appleby), Margaret Irving (Madame), Dalies Frantz (pianist), Ralph W. and Rollin B. Berry (the twin Bogardus lawyers), Chester L. and Walter E. Bcrolund (the twin Butterfield lawyers), Fay Holden (Hannah, the dresser), Paul Kerby (orchestra conductor).

MacDonald sings: "(Nanette and Her) Wooden Shoes," excerpt from "Angelus" (w. Robert B. Smith), "Every Lover Must Meet His Fate," "Sweethearts," "Auld Lang Syne" (w. Robert Burns), "Pretty as a Picture," "Mademoiselle," "The Message of the Violet," "Keep It Dark," "Summer Serenade" (from Herbert's piano piece "Badinage"), "Little Gray Home in the West" (m. Hermann Löhr, w. D. Eardley-Wilmot). Other song: "On Parade."

Special Academy Award: Color Cinematography (Oliver Marsh and Allen Davey). Academy Award nominations: Sound Recording (Douglas Shearer), Scoring (Herbert Stothart).

BROADWAY SERENADE   (Metro-Goldwyn-Mayer, 1939). Producer: Robert Z. Leonard. Director: Robert Z. Leonard. Assistant director: Marvin Stuart. Screenplay: Charles Lederer, from a story by Lew Lipton, John Taintor Foote, and Hans Kraly. Music direction: Herbert Stothart. New songs: (m.) Herbert Stothart and Edward Ward, (w.) Bob Wright and Chet Forrest. Musical presentation: Merrill Pye. Sound: Douglas Shearer. Dance direction: Seymour Felix and Busby Berkeley. Cinematography: Oliver T. Marsh. Montage effects: John Hoffman. Art direction: Cedric Gibbons, with Joseph Wright. Sets: Edwin B. Willis. Costumes: Adrian, with Valles. Makeup: Jack Dawn. Editor: Harold F. Kress. Running time: 113 minutes. New York premiere: April 6, 1939, Capitol Theater. Production days: 49. Cost: $1,284,000. Earnings: domestic $617,000; foreign $617,000; total $1,234,000. Loss $511,000.

Cast: Jeanette MacDonald (Mary Hale, a singer whose success ruins her marriage), Lew Ayres (Jimmy Seymour), Ian Hunter (Larry Bryant), Frank Morgan (Cornelius Collier, Jr.), Rita Johnson (Judith), Virginia Grey (Pearl), Al Shean (Herman), Wally Vernon (Joey the Jinx), William Gargan (Bob, the press agent), Katharine Alexander (Miss Ingalls), Franklin Pangborn (Gene, the choreographer), Esther Dale (Mrs. Olson), Kenneth Stevens (stage singer), Ken Darby's Octet and Six Hits and a Mix (singers), Mary Kent (contralto).

MacDonald sings: "Yip-I-Addy-I-Ay" (John H. Flynn and Will D. Cobb), "Rufus Rastus Johnson Brown" (m. Harry von Tilzer, w. Andrew B. Sterling), "Hearts Win, You Lose" (Andrew B. Sterling), "Love's Old Sweet Song" (m. J. L. Molloy, w. G. Clifton Bingham), "A Tisket, a Tasket" (nursery rhyme), "Here We Go 'Round the Mulberry Bush" (nursery rhyme), "No Time to Argue" (m. Sigmund Romberg, w. Gus Kahn), "For Ev'ry Lonely Heart" [aka "Broadway Serenade"] (m. Stothart and Edward Ward, from Tchaikovsky's "None But the Lonely Heart," w. Wright and Forrest and Kahn), "High Flyin'," "One Look at You," "Un bel dì" from Giacomo Puccini's *Madama Butterfly* (libretto by L. Illica and G. Giacosa), "Italian Street Song" (m. Herbert, w. Young), "Les Filles de Cadiz" (m. Delibes, w. Musset), "Musetta's Waltz Song" from Puccini's *La Bohème* (libretto by Illica and Giacosa). Other songs: "The Farmer in the Dell" (nursery rhyme), "Time Changes Everything" (m. Walter Donaldson, w. Gus Kahn), "Musical Contract" (m. Stothart and Ward, w. Wright and Forrest).

NEW MOON   (Metro-Goldwyn-Mayer, 1940). Producer: Robert Z. Leonard. Director: Robert Z. Leonard. Assistant directors: Marvin Stuart and Hugh Boswell. Screenplay: Jacques Deval and Robert Arthur, from Sigmund Romberg's operetta *The New Moon*, book by Oscar Hammerstein II, Frank Mandel, and Laurence Schwab, lyrics by Oscar Hammerstein II. Music direction: Herbert Stothart. Sound: Douglas Shearer. Dance direction: Val Raset. Cinematography: William Daniels, with Clyde de Vinna. Art direction: Cedric Gibbons, with Eddie Imazu and Edwin B. Willis. Gowns: Adrian. Men's costumes: Gile Steele. Makeup: Jack Dawn. Editor: Harold F. Kress. Running time: 104 minutes. New York premiere: July 18, 1940, Capitol Theater. Production days: 65. Cost: $1,487,000. Earnings: domestic $1,290,000; foreign $1,237,000; total $2,527,000. Profit: $211,000.

Cast: Jeanette MacDonald (Marianne de Beaumanoir, an aristocrat who arrives to take charge of a Louisiana plantation on the eve of the French Revolution), Nelson Eddy (Charles Michon, né Charles-Henri, duc de Vidier), Mary Boland (Valerie de Rossac), George Zucco (Vicomte de Ribaud), H. B. Warner (Father Michel), Richard Purcell (Alexander), Stanley Fields (Tambour), John Miljan (Pierre Brugnon), Bunty Cutler (Julie, the maid), George Irving (ship captain), Grant Mitchell (Governor of New Orleans), Cecil Cunningham (Governor's wife), Warren Rock [MacDonald's brother-in-law] (a mate).

MacDonald sings: "Stranger in Paris," "The Way They Do It in Paris," "One Kiss," "Wanting You," "Lover, Come Back to Me," "Marianne." Other songs: "Dance Your Cares Away," "Shoe Shine Song" "Softly, As in a Morning Sunrise," "Troubles of the World" (Negro spiritual), "No More Weeping and Wailing" (Negro spiritual), "Stouthearted Men," "La Marseillaise" (Claude Rouget de Lisle).

BITTER SWEET (Metro-Goldwyn-Mayer, 1940). Producer: Victor Saville. Director: W. S. Van Dyke II. Assistant director: Hugh Boswell. Screenplay: Lesser Samuels, from Noël Coward's operetta *Bitter Sweet*. Music direction: Herbert Stothart. Musical presentation: Merrill Pye. Sound: Douglas Shearer. Dance direction: Ernst Matray and Maria Solveg Matray. Cinematography: Oliver Marsh and Allen Davey. Technicolor consultants: Natalie Kalmus and Henri Jaffa. Art direction: Cedric Gibbons, with John S. Detlie. Sets: Edwin B. Willis. Gowns: Adrian. Men's costumes: Gile Steele. MacDonald's hairstyles: Sydney Guilaroff. Makeup: Jack Dawn. Editor: Harold F. Kress. Running time: 94 minutes. New York premiere: November 21, 1940, Radio City Music Hall. Production days: 39. Cost: $1,098,000. Earnings: domestic $972,000; foreign $1,292,000; total $2,264,000. Profit: $285,000.

Cast: Jeanette MacDonald (Sarah Millick, called Sari, a young woman who jilts her pompous fiancé and runs away with her voice teacher), Nelson Eddy (Carl Linden), Ian Hunter (Lord Shayne), George Sanders (Baron von Tranisch), Felix Bressart (Max), Curt Bois (Ernst), Edward Ashley (Harry Daventry), Fay Holden (Mrs. Millick), Diana Lewis (Jane), Charles Judels (Herr Wyler), Lynne Carver (Dolly), Sig Rumann (Herr Schlick), Janet Beecher (Lady Daventry), Veda Ann Borg (Manon), Herman Bing (market keeper), Greta Meyer (Mama Luden), Armand Kaliz (headwaiter), Hans Conreid (Rudolph, at Mama Luden's), Warren Rock [MacDonald's brother-in-law] (Wyler's secretary), Pamela Randall (singer at Schlick's), Muriel Goodspeed (singer at Schlick's), Paul Oman (onstage gypsy violinist), Dalies Frantz (Roger), Delos Jewkes (singer).

MacDonald sings: "I'll See You Again," "What Is Love?," "Dear Little Café" (new lyrics by Gus Kahn), "If You Could Only Come with Me," "Kiss Me," "Ladies of the Town," "Zigeuner." Other song: "Tokay."

[MacDonald prerecorded "If Love Were All," but this number was used only as orchestral background music.]

Academy Award nominations: Color Cinematography (Oliver T. Marsh and Allen Davey), Color Art Direction (Cedric Gibbons and John S. Detlie).

SMILIN' THROUGH (Metro-Goldwyn-Mayer, 1941). Producers: Victor Saville and Frank Borzage. Director: Frank Borzage. Assistant director: Lew

Borzage. Screenplay: Donald Ogden Stewart and John Balderston, from Jane Cowl and Jane Murfin's play *Smilin' Through*. Music direction: Herbert Stothart. Sound: Douglas Shearer. Cinematography: Leonard Smith. Technicolor consultants: Natalie Kalmus and Henri Jaffa. Art direction: Cedric Gibbons, with Daniel B. Cathcart. Sets: Edwin B. Willis. Gowns: Adrian. Men's costumes: Gile Steele. Makeup: Jack Dawn, with William Tuttle. Special effects: Roy Newcombe. Montage effects: Peter Ballbusch. Editor: Frank Sullivan. Running time: 100 minutes. New York premiere: December 4, 1941, Capitol Theater. Production days: 50. Cost: $1,105,000. Earnings: domestic $868,000; foreign $1,536,000; total $2,404,000. Profit: $364,000.

Cast: Jeanette MacDonald (Moonyean Clare, a bride shot to death at her wedding by a jilted lover, and Kathleen, Moonyean's niece, who falls in love with the murderer's son); Brian Aherne (Sir John Carteret, Moonyean's widower), Gene Raymond (Jeremy Wayne, Moonyean's murderer, and Kenneth Wayne, Kathleen's suitor), Ian Hunter (Rev. Owen Harding), Jackie Horner (Kathleen, as a child), Frances Robinson (Ellen), Patrick O'Moore (Willie), Wyndham Standing [Sir John Carteret in the 1922 version] (doctor), Emily West [later MacDonald's private secretary] (a chorus singer).

MacDonald sings: "The Kerry Dance" (L. J. Molloy), "Drink to Me Only with Thine Eyes" (m. anon., w. Ben Jonson), "A Little Love, a Little Kiss" (m. Leo Silèsu, w. Adrian Ross), "Ouvre ton coeur" (m. Georges Bizet), "Smilin' Through" (Arthur Penn), "There's a Long, Long Trail" (m. Alonzo Elliott, w. Stoddard King), "Land of Hope and Glory" (m. Edward Elgar, w. A. C. Benson).

I MARRIED AN ANGEL (Metro-Goldwyn-Mayer, 1942). Producer: Hunt Stromberg. Director: Major W. S. Van Dyke II. Assistant director: Marvin Stuart. Screenplay: Anita Loos, from the Richard Rodgers and Lorenz Hart stage adaptation of Janos Vaszary's play *Angyalt Vettem Feleségül*. Songs: (m.) Rodgers, (w.) Hart. Music direction: Herbert Stothart. Special lyrics: Bob Wright and Chet Forrest. Sound: Douglas Shearer. Dance direction: Ernst Matray. Cinematography: Ray June, with Len Smith. Art direction: Cedric Gibbons, with John S. Detlie, Motley, and Vincente Minnelli. Sets: Edwin B. Willis. Special effects: Arnold Gillespie and Warren Newcombe. Costumes: Motley. Gowns: Kalloch. Hairstyles: Sidney Guilaroff. Makeup: Jack Dawn. Editor: Conrad A. Nervig. Running time: 98 minutes. New York premiere: July 9, 1942, Capitol Theater. Production days: 62. Cost: $1,492,000. Earnings: domestic $664,000; foreign $572,000; total $1,236,000. Loss: $725,000.

Cast: Jeanette MacDonald (Anna Zador, a mousy secretary in love with her playboy boss, and Brigitta, a beauteous angel who comes to the playboy in his dreams), Nelson Eddy (Count Willie Palaffi), Binnie Barnes (Peggy), Mona Maris (Marika), Edward Everett Horton (Peter), Reginald Owen (Herman Rothbart, aka "Whiskers"), Inez Cooper (Iren), Douglass Dumbrille (Baron Szigetti), Leonid Kinsky (Zinski), Anne Jeffreys (Polly), Marion Rosamond (Dolly), Odette Myrtil (modiste), Esther Dale (Mrs. Gherkin), Grace Hayle (Mrs. Gabby), Gertrude W. Hoffman (Lady Gimcrack), Florence Auer (Mrs. Roquefort), Walter Soderling (Mr. Kipper), Dick Elliott (Mr. Scallion),

Oliver B. Prickett (Mr. Gherkin), Almira Sessions (Mrs. Scallion), Lon Poff (Mr. Dodder), Charles Brabin (Mr. Fairmind), Anita Bolster (Mrs. Kipper), Beryl Wallace (Fifi), Cecil Cunningham (Mrs. Fairmind), Jack Lipson (Mr. Roquefort), Janis Carter (Sufi).

MacDonald sings: "Caprice Viennois" (Fritz Kreisler), "I Married an Angel," "Spring Is Here," "Villanelle" (Eva dell Acqua), "A Twinkle in Your Eye," "Chanson Bohème" from Bizet's *Carmen* (libretto by Henri Meilhac and Ludovic Halévy), "Anges purs, anges radieux" from Gounod's *Faust,* "Aloha Oe" (Princess Liliuokalani). Other songs: "Surprise at Party," "Tira Lira La," "I'll Tell the Man in the Street," "May I Present the Girl."

CAIRO (Metro-Goldwyn-Mayer, 1942). Producer: Metro-Goldwyn-Mayer. Director: Major W. S. Van Dyke II. Assistant director: Marvin Stuart. Screenplay: John McClain, from an idea by Ladislas Fodor. Music direction: Herbert Stothart. Music conductor: George Stoll. Sound: Douglas Shearer. Choreography: Sammy Lee. Cinematography: Ray June. Art direction: Cedric Gibbons, with Lyle Wheeler. Sets: Edwin B. Willis, with Richard Pefferis. Gowns: Kalloch. Editor: James E. Newcom. Running time: 101 minutes. New York premiere: November 5, 1942, Capitol Theater. Production days: 33. Cost: $924,000. Earnings: domestic $616,000; foreign $581,000; total $1,197,000. Loss: $131,000.

Cast: Jeanette MacDonald (Marcia Warren, an ex–movie diva whose high Cs undo a Nazi plot to bomb a U.S. warship), Robert Young (Homer Smith), Ethel Waters (Cleo), Reginald Owen (Philo Cobson), Mona Barrie (Mrs. Morrison), Dooley Wilson (Hector), Lionel Atwill (Teutonic gentleman), Eduardo Ciannelli (Ahmed Ben Hassan), Dennis Hoey (Colonel Woodhue), Cecil Cunningham (Madam Laruga), Cecil Stewart (pianist), Louise Bates (Mrs. Woodhue), the King's Men (singers).

MacDonald sings: "Les Filles de Cadiz" (m. Delibes, w. Musset), "The Waltz Is Over" (m. Arthur Schwartz, w. E. Y. Harburg), "A Heart That's Free" (R. J. Robyn and T. Railey), "Il Bacio" (m. L. Arditi, w. Gottardo Aldighieri), "Sextet" from Donizetti's *Lucia di Lammermoor* (libretto by Salvatore Cammarano), "To a Wild Rose" (Edward MacDowell), "From the Land of the Sky-Blue Water" (m. Charles Wakefield Cadman, w. Nelle Richmond Eberhart), "Beautiful Ohio" (m. Mary Earl, w. Ballard MacDonald), "Waiting for the Robert E. Lee" (m. Lewis F. Muir, w. L. Wolfe Gilbert), "Avalon" (B. G. DeSylva, Al Jolson, Vincent Rose), "Home Sweet Home" (Harry Bishop), "Keep the Light Burning Bright" (m. Arthur Schwartz, w. Howard Dietz and E. Y. Harburg), "Cairo" (m. Schwartz, w. Harburg). Other songs: "We Did It Before and We Can Do It Again" (m. Cliff Friend, w. Charles Tobias), "Buds Won't Bud" (m. Harold Arlen, w. Harburg).

FOLLOW THE BOYS (Universal, 1944). Producer: Charles K. Feldman. Associate producer: Albert J. Rockett. Director: Eddie Sutherland. Assistant director: Howard Christie. Screenplay: Lou Breslow and Gertrude Purcell. Music direction: Leigh Harline. Dance direction: George Hale. Cinematography: David Abel. Special effects: John Fulton. Editor: Fred R. Feitshans, Jr. Running time: 122 minutes. New York premiere: April 25, 1944, Loew's Criterion. Cost: $1,291,352.

Cast: Jeanette MacDonald (as herself), John Meredith (homesick blinded soldier), George Raft (Tony West), Vera Zorina (Gloria Vance), Grace McDonald (Kitty West), Charley Grapewin (Nick West), Charles Butterworth (Louie Fairweather), Elizabeth Patterson (Annie), and, as themselves: Orson Welles, Marlene Dietrich, Dinah Shore, Donald O'Connor, W. C. Fields, the Andrews Sisters, Artur Rubinstein, Sophie Tucker, Louise Beavers, Susanna Foster, Andy Devine, Randolph Scott.

MacDonald sings: "Beyond the Blue Horizon" (m. Whiting and Harling, w. Robin), "I'll See You in My Dreams" (m. Isham Jones, w. Gus Kahn).

THREE DARING DAUGHTERS (Metro-Goldwyn-Mayer, 1948). Producer: Joseph Pasternak. Director: Fred Wilcox. Assistant directors: Dolph Zimmer and Jack Mackenzie. Screenplay: Albert Mannheimer, Frederick Kohner, Sonya Levien, and John Meehan, from Fredrick Kohner and Albert Mannheimer's play *The Bees and the Flowers.* Music direction: George Stoll. Sound: Douglas Shearer. Cinematography: Ray June. Technicolor direction: Natalie Kalmus and Henri Jaffa. Art direction: Cedric Gibbons, with Preston Ames. Sets: Edwin B. Willis, with Arthur Krams. Costumes: Irene, with Shirley Braker. Makeup: Jack Dawn. Editor: Adrienne Fazan. Running time: 119 minutes. New York premiere: February 12, 1948, Capitol Theater. Production days: 78. Cost: $2,538,000. Earnings: domestic $2,659,000; foreign $1,351,000; total $4,010,000. Loss: $136,000 [per Mannix ledger, but dubious in light of cost and earnings].

Cast: Jeanette MacDonald (Louise Morgan, a divorced magazine editor whose children rebel when she falls in love with a famous concert pianist), José Iturbi (himself), Jane Powell (Tess Morgan), Ann E. Todd (Ilka Morgan), Mary Eleanor Donahue (Alix Morgan), Edward Arnold (Robert Nelson), Harry Davenport (Dr. Cannon), Moyna Macgill [Angela Lansbury's mother] (Mrs. Smith), Larry Adler (himself), Kathryn Card (Jonesy), Amparo Iturbi (specialty pianist), Dorothy Porter (specialty singer).

MacDonald sings: "The Dickey-Bird Song" (m. Sammy Fain, w. Howard Dietz), "Where There's Love" (based on themes from Richard Strauss's *Der Rosenkavalier,* w. Earl Brent), "You Made Me Love You" (m. Jimmy Monaco, w. Joe McCarthy), "Sweethearts" (m. V. Herbert, w. B. Wright and C. Forrest), "Springtide," (m. Edward Grieg, w. Earl Brent). Other songs: "Alma Mater" (m. George Stoll, w. Billy Katz), "Fleurette" (m. Herbert, w. Ralph Freed), "The Waltz Song" from Gounod's *Roméo et Juliette,* "Route 66" (Bobby Troup).

THE SUN COMES UP (Metro-Goldwyn-Mayer, 1949). Producer: Robert Sisk. Director: Richard Thorpe. Screenplay: William Ludwig and Margaret Fitts, from Marjorie Kinnan Rawlings's short story "A Mother in Mannville" and six-part serial fiction, *Mountain Prelude.* Music: André Previn. Sound: Douglas Shearer. Cinematography: Ray June. Art direction: Cedric Gibbons, with Randall Duell. Sets: Edwin B. Willis, with Hugh Hunt. Gowns: Irene. Editor: Irving Warburton. Running time: 94 minutes. New York premiere: May

12, 1949, Capitol Theater. Production days: 45. Cost: $1,659,000. Earnings: domestic $1,280,000; foreign $764,000; total $2,044,000. Loss: $549,000.

Cast: Jeanette MacDonald (Helen Lorfield Winter, a concert singer who searches for solitude after her teenage son is accidentally killed), Claude Jarman, Jr. (Jerry), Lassie (himself), Dwayne Hickman (Hank Winter), Percy Kilbride (Mr. Willie B. Williegoode), Lewis Stone (Arthur Norton), Lloyd Nolan (Thomas Chandler), Margaret Hamilton (Mrs. Golightly), Ida Moore (Mrs. Sally), Teddy Infuhr (Junebug), Barbara Billingsley [*Leave It to Beaver*'s June Cleaver] (nurse).

MacDonald sings: "Tes Yeux" (René Alphonse Rabey), "Un bel dì vedremo" from Puccini's *Madama Butterfly,* "Songs My Mother Taught Me" (m. Antonin Dvořák, w. Natalie MacFarren), "Cousin Ebenezer" (m. André Previn, w. William Katz), "Romance" (m. Anton Rubinstein and André Previn, w. William Katz).

Principal Recording Sessions

Jeanette MacDonald recorded exclusively for RCA Victor and its international affiliates. A compact disc, *"San Francisco" and Other Jeanette MacDonald Favorites* (RCA Gold Seal 09026-60877-2), features twenty-two recordings the soprano made between 1929 and 1950. A CD from France, *Jeanette MacDonald, 1929–1939* (Chansophone 141), includes several of the singer's previously inaccessible French-language titles. A private label, OASI, has issued two comprehensive CDs, *A Tribute to Jeanette MacDonald*, volumes 1 and 2 (OASI 7007 and 7011); unlike the RCA disc, the sound quality varies because source materials were unavailable. During the LP era, RCA issued many albums featuring the soprano, including *Romantic Moments* (RCA LM-62), *Favorites* (RCA LM-73), *Jeanette MacDonald and Nelson Eddy in Hi-Fi/Stereo* (RCA LPM-1738/LSP-1738), *Smilin' Through* (Camden CAL-325), *Jeanette MacDonald Sings Songs of Faith and Inspiration* (Camden CAL-750), *Jeanette MacDonald and Nelson Eddy* (Vintage Series) (RCA LPV-526), *Jeanette MacDonald Opera and Operetta Favorites* (RCA LM-2908), and *Jeanette MacDonald Sings "San Francisco" and Other Silver Screen Favorites* (RCA Vic-1515). The last three titles were released soon after MacDonald's death.

In the chronology that follows, I give the dates, sites, vocal collaborators, conductors, and song titles (with last names of composers and lyricists) for MacDonald's principal commercial, nonfilm recording sessions. The term "unreleased" after a title indicates that no take of that title was published at the time; I do not list sessions from which there were never any published takes. This listing is based in large part on archival documents kindly made available to me by Bernadette Moore of BMG/RCA Music and on an unpublished MacDonald discography compiled by Bill Park, whose diligence and generosity I acknowledge with gratitude.

December 11, 1929. Liederkranz Hall, New York City. With the Revelers. Conductor: Nathaniel Shilkret. "March of the Grenadiers" (Schertzinger-Grey), "Dream Lover" (Schertzinger-Grey).

January 19, 1930. Hal Roach Studios, Culver City, California. Conductor: Leroy Shield. "Dream Lover" (Schertzinger-Grey) [unreleased].

August 4, 1930. Hollywood Recording Studio, Los Angeles. Conductor: Leroy Shield. "Always in All Ways" (Whiting-Harling-Robin).

August 5, 1930. Hollywood Recording Studio, Los Angeles. With the Rounders Quartet. Conductor: Leroy Shield. "Beyond the Blue Horizon" (Whiting-Harling-Robin).

September 25, 1931. Kingsway Hall, London [label: His Master's Voice]. Conductor: Ray Noble. "Dear, When I Met You" (Von Tilzer-Brown), "Reviens" (Fragson), "Good Night" (Abrahám), "Pardon, Madame" (Abrahám).

April 24 and April 27, 1932. Hollywood Recording Studio, Los Angeles. Conductor: Nat Finston. "One Hour with You" (Whiting-Robin), "Une heure près de toi" ("One Hour with You") (Whiting-Hornez), "We Will Always Be Sweethearts" (O. Straus–Robin), "Coeur contre coeur" ("We Will Always Be Sweethearts") (O. Straus–Hornez).

July 5, 1932. Hollywood Recording Studio, Los Angeles. Conductor: Nat Finston. "Love Me Tonight" (Rodgers-Hart), "Veux-tu m'aimer?" ("Love Me Tonight") (Rodgers-Hornez), "Isn't It Romantic?" (Rodgers-Hart), "N'est-ce pas poétique?" ("Isn't It Romantic?") (Rodgers-Hornez).

February 27, 1933. Paris [label: Disque Gramophone]. Conductor: M. Bervily. "Only a Rose" (Friml-Hooker) [unreleased], "Chanson de Vilya" (Lehár-Caillavet–de Flers), "J'aime d'amour" ("The Merry Widow Waltz") (Lehár-Caillavet–de Flers).

August 14, 1934. Hollywood Recording Studio, Los Angeles. Conductor: Herbert Stothart. "Merry Widow Waltz" (Lehár-Hart), "J'aime d'amour" ("The Merry Widow Waltz") (Lehár-Caillavet–de Flers) [unreleased], "Vilia" (Lehár-Hart), "Chanson de Vilya" (Lehár-Caillavet–de Flers).

August 30, 1934. Hollywood Recording Studio, Los Angeles. Conductor: Herbert Stothart. "To-Night Will Teach Me to Forget" ("The Diary Song") (Lehár-Stothart-Kahn), "Mon coeur est las, mon coeur est lourd" ("Tonight Will Teach Me to Forget") [unreleased].

September 20, 1934. Hollywood Recording Studio, Los Angeles. Conductor: Herbert Stothart. "Try to Forget" (Kern-Harbach), "Essayons d'oublier" ("Try to Forget") (Kern-Salesmon) [unreleased].

March 20, 1935. Hollywood Recording Studio, Los Angeles. Conductor: Herbert Stothart. "Italian Street Song" (Herbert-Young), "Chanson italienne"

("Italian Street Song") (Herbert) [unreleased], "Ah! Sweet Mystery of Life" (Herbert-Young), "Mélodie du rêve" ("Ah! Sweet Mystery of Life") (Herbert) [unreleased].

September 19, 1936. Hollywood Recording Studio, Los Angeles. With baritone Nelson Eddy. Conductor: Nathaniel Shilkret. "Indian Love Call" (Friml-Stothart-Harbach-Hammerstein), "Ah! Sweet Mystery of Life" (Herbert-Young).

September 21, 1936. Hollywood Recording Studio, Los Angeles. With baritone Nelson Eddy. Conductor: Nathaniel Shilkret. "Farewell to Dreams" (Romberg-Young), "Will You Remember?" (Romberg-Young), "Song of Love" (Romberg-Donnelly) [unreleased until 1965, on RCA LPV-526].

September 11, 1939. Hollywood Recording Studio, Los Angeles. Piano accompanist: Giuseppe Bamboschek. "When I Have Sung My Songs" (Charles), "Do Not Go, My Love" (Hageman), "Annie Laurie" (Scott-Douglas), "Comin' Through the Rye" (traditional), "From the Land of the Sky-Blue Water" (Cadman-Eberhart), "Let Me Always Sing" (Raymond).

September 13, 1939. Hollywood Recording Studio, Los Angeles. Conductor: Giuseppe Bamboschek. "Ave Maria" (Bach-Gounod), "Les Filles de Cadix" (Delibes-Musset), "Depuis le jour" (Charpentier) [unreleased].

September 15, 1939. Hollywood Recording Studio, Los Angeles. Conductor: Giuseppe Bamboschek. "Il était un roi de Thulé" (Gounod-Barbier-Carré), "Air des bijoux" ("The Jewel Song") (Gounod-Barbier-Carré), "Je veux vivre dans ce rêve" ("Juliette's Waltz Song") (Gounod-Barbier-Carré).

September 16, 1939. Hollywood Recording Studio, Los Angeles. Conductor: Giuseppe Bamboschek. "Depuis le jour" (Charpentier), "Lover, Come Back to Me" (Romberg-Hammerstein), "One Kiss" (Romberg-Hammerstein). With piano accompanist Gene Raymond: "From the Land of the Sky-Blue Water" (Cadman-Eberhart) [unreleased], "Let Me Always Sing" (Raymond) [unreleased].

October 5, 1939. Hollywood Recording Studio. Piano accompanist: Gene Raymond. "From the Land of the Sky-Blue Water" (Cadman-Eberhart) [unreleased], "Let Me Always Sing" (Raymond) [unreleased].

September 22, 1941. Hollywood Recording Studio. Conductor: Herbert Stothart. "Drink to Me Only with Thine Eyes" (traditional–Ben Jonson), "Smilin' Through" (Penn), "The Kerry Dance" (Molloy), "Ouvre ton coeur" (Bizet), "A Little Love, a Little Kiss" (Silèsu-Ross), "Land of Hope and Glory" (Elgar-Benson).

January 29 and January 31, 1945. RCA Studio 2 [155 East 24th Street], New York City. Conductor: Maximillian Pilzer. "Agnus dei" (Bizet), "Panis angelicus" ("O Lord Most Holy") (Franck), "Summer Serenade" (Herbert-Wright-Forrest), "Italian Street Song" (Herbert-Young). With mixed chorus: "Abide with Me" (Monk-Lyte), "The Holy City" (Adams-Weatherly), "Nearer My God to Thee" (Mason-Adams), "Battle Hymn of the Republic" (Steffe-Howe).

February 3, 1945. Lotos Club, New York City. Conductor: Robert Russell Bennett. "Carousel in the Park" (Romberg-Fields), "It Doesn't Cost You Anything to Dream" (Romberg-Fields). With baritone Robert Merrill: "Close as

Pages in a Book" (Romberg-Fields), "The Fireman's Bride" (Romberg-Fields).

April 16, 1946. Lotos Club, New York City. Conductor: Russ Case. "They Didn't Believe Me" (Kern-Rourke), "Giannina Mia" (Friml-Harbach).

April 18, 1946. Lotos Club, New York City. Conductor: Russ Case. "Smoke Gets in Your Eyes" (Kern-Harbach), "Sweetheart Waltz" (Herbert-Smith), "Romany Life" (Herbert-Smith), "Donkey Serenade" (Friml-Stothart-Wright-Forrest).

August 23, 1946. Lotos Club, New York City. With nonsinging supporting cast. Conductor: Russ Case. *Cinderella.* [MacDonald narrates, performs the title role, and sings all four sings in this musicalization of the children's fairy tale, adapted by Michael Martin, with music by William Provost and lyrics by Lee Rogrow.] "I Wish I May, I Wish I Might," "Look at Me, Look at Me," "Dancing the Waltz Tonight," "Today I've Found Prince Charming."

October 11, 1946. Lotos Club, New York City. Conductor: Frieder Weissmann. "Mi chiamano Mimì" (Puccini-Giacosa-Illica), "Un bel dì vedremo" (Puccini-Giacosa-Illica).

December 17, 1947. Hollywood Recording Studio, Los Angeles. Conductor: Robert Armbruster. "I'll See You Again" (Coward), "Romance" (Debussy-Bourget-Carman), "Beau soir" (Debussy-Bourget-Chapman), "I Love You Truly" (C. Jacobs–Bond), "A Perfect Day" (C. Jacobs–Bond).

December 18, 1947. Hollywood Recording Studio, Los Angeles. Conductor: Robert Armbruster. "Springtide" (Grieg-Vinje-Dole), "Where There's Love" (R. Strauss–Brent), "Summertime" (G. Gershwin–I. Gershwin–Heyward), "The Man I Love" (G. Gershwin–I. Gershwin), "Zigeuner" (Coward).

May 18, 1949. Hollywood Recording Studio, Los Angeles. Conductor: Robert Armbruster. "Tes yeux" (Rabey), "Vilia" (Lehár-Ross), "If You Were Mine" (Rubinstein-Previn-Katz), "Songs My Mother Taught Me" (Dvořák-MacFarran).

August 2, 1950. RCA Studio 2, New York City. Conductor: Robert Russell Bennett. "Only a Rose" (Friml-Hooker), "Les Filles de Cadiz" (Delibes-Musset), "The Old Refrain" (Kreisler-Mattullath).

August 4, 1950. RCA Studio 2, New York City. Conductor: Robert Russell Bennett. "Beyond the Blue Horizon" (Whiting-Harlan-Robin), "Ciribiribin" (Pestalozza-Taylor), "One Night of Love" (Schertzinger-Kahn), "Indian Love Call" (Friml-Stothart-Harbach-Hammerstein).

November 9, 1950. RCA Studio 2, New York City. Conductor: Robert Russell Bennett. "When You're Away" (Herbert-Blossom), "One Alone" (Romberg-Harbach-Hammerstein), "Parlez-moi d'amour" (Lenoir).

November 16, 1950. RCA Studio 2, New York City. Conductor: Robert Russell Bennett. "Will You Remember?" (Romberg-Young), "Ah! Sweet Mystery of Life" (Herbert-Young), "San Francisco" (Kaper-Jurmann-Kahn).

September 27, 1957. Webster Hall, New York City. With baritone Nelson Eddy. Conductor: Lehman Engel. "Ah! Sweet Mystery of Life" (Herbert-Young), "Indian Love Call" (Friml-Stothart-Harbach-Hammerstein), "Wanting You" (Romberg-Hammerstein), "Will You Remember?" (Romberg-Young).

June 5, 1958. Radio Recorders Studios, Hollywood. Conductor: David Rose. "Giannina Mia" (Friml-Harbach), "Beyond the Blue Horizon" (Whiting-Harling-Robin), "Italian Street Song" (Herbert-Young), "The Breeze and I" (Lecuona-Stillman).

Abbreviations

AFI	American Film Institute
auto.	Jeanette MacDonald's unpublished autobiography, MacDonald Archive, Topeka, Kansas
BG	*Boston Globe*
BH	*Boston Herald*
biog.	biography
CS	*Chicago Sun*
CT	*Chicago Tribune*
CUOHC	Columbia University Oral History Collection, Butler Library, New York, New York
DL	Doheny Library, University of Southern California, Los Angeles, California
EBT	Edward Baron Turk
EHW	*Exhibitors Herald-World*
FD	*Film Daily*
FLP	Free Library of Philadelphia
FW	*Film Weekly* (London)
HL	Margaret Herrick Library, Academy of Motion Picture Arts and Sciences, Beverly Hills, California
HR	*Hollywood Reporter*
HS	*Hollywood Spectator*

JAM	Jeanette Anna MacDonald
JMIFC	Jeanette MacDonald International Fan Club, Topeka, Kansas
LAE	*Los Angeles Examiner*
LAH	*Los Angeles Herald*
LAHE	*Los Angeles Herald-Examiner*
LAN	*Los Angeles News*
LAT	*Los Angeles Tribune*
MacD Archive	Jeanette MacDonald Archive, Jeanette MacDonald International Fan Club Headquarters, Topeka, Kansas
MPH	*Motion Picture Herald*
MT	*Morning Telegraph* (London)
n.	number
n.d.	undated
NYA	*New York American*
NYC	New York City
NYDM	*New York Daily Mirror*
NYDN	*New York Daily News*
NYEP	*New York Evening Post*
NYEW	*New York Evening World*
NYH	*New York Herald*
NYHTr	*New York Herald-Tribune*
NYJ	*New York Journal*
NYJA	*New York Journal-American*
NYM	*New York Mirror*
NYS	*New York Sun*
NYSH	*New York Sun-Herald*
NYT	*New York Times*
NYTr	*New York Tribune*
NYWJTr	*New York World-Journal-Tribune*
NYWT	*New York World-Telegram*
NYWTS	*New York World-Telegram & Sun*
PBI	*Philadelphia Bulletin-Inquirer*

PCA	Production Code Administration
PCAC	Production Code Administration Collection, Herrick Library, Academy of Motion Picture Arts and Sciences, Beverly Hills, California
PEB	*Philadelphia Evening-Bulletin*
PEBP	*Philadelphia Evening Bulletin-Post*
PEL	*Philadelphia Evening Ledger*
PEN	*Philadelphia Evening News*
PI	*Philadelphia Inquirer*
PPG	*Pittsburgh Post Gazette*
pub.	publicity
RHC	Regional History Collection, University of Southern California, Los Angeles, California
RRC	Robert Ritchie Collection, Myrtle Beach, South Carolina
SA	Shubert Archive, New York, New York
SEP	*Saturday Evening Post*
SFC	*San Francisco Chronicle*
SMUOHC	Southern Methodist University Oral History Collection on the Performing Arts, DeGolyer Library, Dallas, Texas
TM	*Theatre Magazine*
UCLAOHC	UCLA Oral History Collection, Los Angeles, California
WP	*Washington Post*
WS	*Washington Star*
WSJ	*Wall Street Journal*
WTH	*Washington Times-Herald*

Notes

CHAPTER 1. "NOW EVERYBODY'S GOT TO CLAP!"

"She used to say" JAM, auto., I, 7.
"You always were impatient" Daniel MacDonald, in JAM, auto., I, 7.
"fabulous creature" Anita Loos, transcript, CUOHC, 14 July 1971, 8.
"very distinguished . . . Dr. MacDonald" JAM, auto., I, 12.
"one of Philadelphia's leading contractors" JAM, in Sonia Lee, "Jeanette MacDonald Warns the High-Hatters," *Screenplay,* June 1935.
"We had our share of" JAM, auto., I, 19.
"silently prayed for a . . . feminine disappointment" JAM, auto., I, 7–8.
"near the railroad tracks" Blossom MacDonald, in "Grandma, How Weird You Are!" *PEB,* 2 August 1964.
"well cared for, small" JAM, auto., I, 9.
"Iceman! Iceman! . . . come back later!" Daniel and Anna MacDonald, in JAM, auto., I, 17.
"What a lovely back" Daniel MacDonald, in JAM, auto., I, 17.
"I've often wondered" JAM, auto., I, 11.
"our morning drink" JAM, auto., I, 11.
"I was constantly pestering" JAM, auto., I, 13.
"an extrovert, who needed" JAM, auto., I, 26.
"only served to make me" JAM, auto., I, 13–14.
"I paused ever so" JAM, auto., I, 21.
"Get the hook! . . . in a week!" Charles A. Wright, "My Little Cousin— Who Became a Movie Star," *Pennsylvania Magazine,* Spring 1985, 29.
"I could imitate any" JAM, auto., I, 27.
"the knockout" Cecil E. "Teet" Carle, interview with EBT, North Hollywood—Boston, 4 November 1991.
"When my memory failed" JAM, auto., I, 37.

"The real wonder of" Unreferenced review in JAM, auto., I, 30. MacDonald refers only to a "faded clipping" that was "written by one of Philadelphia's leading music critics" and found among her mother's belongings "many years afterward" (I, 29). The *Philadelphia Public Ledger* ran a review of the performance on February 20, 1909, but it did not mention MacDonald. In "Jeanette M'Donald Scared by Big Bear," *PEB*, 11 April 1932, Mrs. Minnie Barry, who costumed the show, recounted the colorful but unlikely story that Jeanette was so scared by the bear that she "dashed clear off the stage in the middle of her refrain."

"marked . . . spit in their eyes" JAM, auto., I, 29.

CHAPTER 2. SCANDALS

"I had a quirk . . . of our family" JAM, auto., I, 9–10.
"You're always so mean . . . give you this?" JAM, Elsie MacDonald, and Earle Schmidt, in JAM, auto., I, 31.
"Perhaps if I'd kicked" JAM, auto., I, 31.
"had deceived her, and" JAM, auto., I, 32.
"I want you to promise" Anna MacDonald, in JAM, auto., I, 32.
"On Arch Street" JAM, auto., I, 33.
"I patted him, tickled" JAM, auto., I, 35.
"that which is truly . . . own sunlight" Enoch Pearson, "What Music in the Public Schools Is Accomplishing," *Etude*, March 1915, 177.
"She looked so radiantly" JAM, auto., I, 27.
"I was constantly struggling" JAM, auto., I, 56.
"I used to come home" JAM, auto., I, 56.
"I had no more" JAM, auto., I, 71.
"you couldn't trust girls . . . at feminine hands" JAM, auto., I, 57–58.
"Dance doesn't necessarily mean" Al White, unreferenced newspaper clipping, Al White biog. file, Theatre Collection, FLP.
"lascivious attractions and salacious seductions" Theodore Ledyard Cuyler, *A Model Christian* (Philadelphia: Presbyterian Board of Publication and Sabbath-School Work, 1903), 65.
"the most complete happiness" JAM, auto., I, 40.
"It gave me a sense" JAM, auto., I, 41.
"vaudeville's best juvenile act . . . the troupe" "The 'Six Little Songbirds [sic]' Rapturously Received by the Audience," unreferenced newspaper clipping, MacD Archive.
"Dear Rachel . . . a BASTARD!" Joseph Armstrong and JAM, in JAM, auto., I, 48.
"Miss [Morley], there are . . . dedicated woman!" Daniel MacDonald and Sallie Morley, in JAM, auto., I, 48. Perhaps out of a belated sense of deference, MacDonald's memoir refers to the school's principal as "Miss Morrison." The annual *Hand Book[s] of the Board of Public Education, First School District of Pennsylvania*, list Sallie Gilbert Morley, not "Miss Morrison," as Thomas Dunlap's principal between 1907 and 1917; in a phone conversation with me (Hockessin, Del.—Boston, 5 May 1992),

MacDonald's classmate Louise Horner confirmed that there was no Miss
Morrison at Dunlap during this period. (Curiously, "Miss Morrison" is the
adopted name of MacDonald's incognita character in the film *Maytime*.)
"Now when I whale . . . same thing myself" Daniel and Anna MacDonald,
in JAM, auto., I, 50.
"in a mood to . . . report him and you!" JAM and Daniel MacDonald, in
JAM, auto., I, 58–59.
"So long as my" JAM, auto., I, 25.
"Isn't it funny how" JAM, auto., I, 43.
"brazen, objectionable child" Miss Held, in JAM, auto., I, 44.
"There she is . . . appear in court" Detectives, JAM, and Anna MacDonald,
in JAM, auto., I, 61.
"To a proud and sensitive" JAM, auto., I, 61.
" 'The Jewel Song' is just like any other" JAM, auto., I, 64.
"Her disapproval shot invisibly" JAM, auto., I, 65.
"It was inconceivable . . . standing up to do so." JAM, auto., I, 66–67.
"I was too excited" JAM, auto., I, 38–39.

CHAPTER 3. TWINKLING STARS AND FOUR-LEAF CLOVERS

"a part usually given only" Virginia Henderson, in "Jeanette M'Donald
Almost a 'Steno,' " *PEB*, 9 April 1932.
"the official assessor" JAM, auto., I, 67.
"no evidence that Daniel" James Kimpson, Personnel Department,
Philadelphia Municipal Services Building, verbal report to EBT
(Philadelphia—Boston, 8 June 1992) following our eight-week effort to
find documentation of Daniel Mc/MacDonald's alleged public service.
"He was in his" JAM, auto., I, 69.
"an inborn air of" Ned Wayburn, "Show Girls Yesterday and Today," *TM*,
December 1916, 362.
"to the romantic and the beautiful" Ned Wayburn, "The Chorus Girl—Old
and New," *TM*, May 1920, 404.
"For Mother and Father" JAM, auto., I, 73.
"While we strive to" Michael H. Lucey, *The Blue Bird: 1913–24* (special
celebration issue of Julia Richman High School literary magazine, 1924), 24.
"la Jeanette. . . . felt terrible" Jerome Kern and Betty Kern, in Gerald
Bordman, *Jerome Kern: His Life and Music* (New York: Oxford University
Press, 1980), 351, 352.
"commendable absence of offensiveness" Patterson James, "The Night
Boat," *Billboard*, 21 February 1920.
"a bit naughty" *NYSH*, 3 February 1920.
"She impressed all of" Louise Horner, interview with EBT, Hockessin,
Del.—Boston, 5 May 1992.
"I was invited with" JAM, auto., II, 19.
"Had it been necessary" JAM, "If You Hope for a Film Career," *Etude*,
November 1953, 16.

"I bet you sweated plenty" Unnamed theatrical agent, in Gene Raymond, interview with EBT, Beverly Hills, 8 August 1991.

"I wanted to prove myself . . . drink like a fool" JAM, auto., I, 92–94.

"nervous but well-possessed" Herbert Ohmeis, "Jeanette MacDonald," typescript, 1978, MacD Archive.

"I am going to star" JAM, auto., I, 89.

"an uncooked mess" C. P. S. " 'Fantastic Fricassee' an Uncooked Mess," *NYEP,* 12 September 1922.

"all gravy and no meat . . . have been in vain" Patterson James, "A Fantastic Fricassee," *Billboard,* 11 November 1922.

"Debussy gone sour . . . delirium tremens" Alan Dale, "Village Theatre Has Curious Offering," *NYA,* 12 September 1922.

"cute as a bug's ear" Henry Savage, in JAM, auto., I, 96.

"I wanted men to" JAM, auto., I, 98.

"appearance and voice . . . merits of the evening" "Mitzi Fine in New Role," *NYT,* 2 October 1923.

"pleasing voice and pellucid personality" Alan Dale, "Mitzi, and Mitzi, and Mitzi, Little Else in 'Magic Ring,' " *NYA,* 4 October 1923.

"pretty and refreshingly naive" "Mitzi Charms Anew in 'The Magic Ring,' " *NYH,* 2 October 1923.

"The blonde beauty of" B. F., " 'The Magic Ring' and Mitzi at the Liberty," *NYTr,* 2 October 1923.

"the first time in history" "Mitzi Charms Anew in 'The Magic Ring,' " *NYH,* 2 October 1923.

"voice of unusual quality" "Mitzi Charms Anew in 'The Magic Ring,' " *NYH,* 2 October 1923.

"Look, you have a" Phoebe Crosby, in JAM, auto., II, 11.

"Lei è come un venticello primaverile!" Ferdinand Torriani, quoted by Ann Torri Arndt, phone interview with EBT, NYC, 8 March 1992.

"I can do a lot for your voice" Ferdinand Torriani, quoted in JAM, auto., II, 12–13.

"There were no phoney" JAM, auto., II, 12.

"an unhinging and excessive" Patterson Greene, "Miss M'Donald Wins Success," *LAE,* 31 March 1948.

"To hear this was" JAM, auto., II, 13.

"a geography of the" JAM, paraphrased in press release by Charles Emerson Cook, *Yes, Yes, Yvette* file, Theatre Collection, FLP.

"Very early in my" JAM, auto., II, 15.

"cultured, discriminating taste" Muriel Stafford, "Handwriting Never Lies," unreferenced syndicated column, c. 1943, MacD Archive.

"purpose . . . bubbling vivacity" Shirley Spencer, "Quirks of Pen Vivid Even Tho Name Vanishes," *CT,* c. 1944, MacD Archive.

"In the darkness I . . . Father died" JAM, Daniel MacDonald, and Jack Ohmeis, in JAM, auto., II, 5–7.

"He lay with his" JAM, auto., II, 7A.

"I followed Mother up" JAM, auto., II, 7A.

"greatest regret" JAM, "My Frankest Confession," *Screenland,* January 1940, 81.

CHAPTER 4. A FAIR PRINCESS ON BROADWAY

"It would be unfair" JAM, auto., II, 16.

"For all the years" JAM, birthday note to Grace Adele Newell, c. 1961, MacD Archive.

"MacDonald is never satisfied" Albertina Rasch, in John Woolfenden, press release, n.d., Hedda Hopper Collection, HL.

"lithe and resilient . . . abundant vitality" Albertina Rasch, in Frank W. D. Ries, "Albertina Rasch: The Concert Career and the Concept of the American Ballet," *Dance Chronicle* 7, n. 2 (1984): 167.

"The day I called" JAM, auto., II, 17.

"brutally cretinous" Lorenz Hart, letter to Ira Gershwin, January 1926, in Frederick Nolan, *Lorenz Hart: A Poet on Broadway* (New York: Oxford University Press, 1994), 73.

"unusually ingratiating" Don Carle Gillette, "Tip-Toes," *Billboard,* 9 January 1926.

"truly beautiful" " 'Tip Toes' Here with Tunes," *NYT,* 29 December 1925.

"And Jeannette [sic] MacDonald" D. D. M., " 'Tip-Toes' Has, Well, It Has Everything," *Newark Star,* 1 December 1925.

"Beautiful and true as" Ira Gershwin, in David Ewen, *George Gershwin: His Journey to Greatness* (New York: Ungar, 1986), 105–6.

"Perhaps the greatest mistake" JAM, "Operetta and the Sound Film," *Etude,* June 1938, 359.

"One afternoon on our" Amy Revere McCauley, interview with EBT, Menlo Park, CA—Boston, 9 February 1992.

"In those days I" Imogene Coca, letter to EBT, 14 March 1991.

"And what a pretty" C. Pannill Mead, "Davidson [Theater] Has Sparkling Hit with 'Yvette,'" *Newark Star,* 24 May 1927.

"wifehood and motherhood . . . outside the home" "Heroine of *Yes, Yes, Yvette* Predicts the 'New' Woman Will Be Old-Fashioned," unreferenced newspaper clipping, *Yes, Yes, Yvette* file, Theatre Collection, FLP.

"One evening when we" Amy Revere McCauley, interview with EBT, Menlo Park, CA—Boston, 9 February 1992.

"wanted Youmans to compose" Irving Caesar, interview with William Bass, in Bass, "Jeanette MacDonald: The Triumphant Voice," 96, MacD Archive.

"If Jeanette would come" H. H. Frazee, in JAM, auto., II, 18.

"lousy dramatic shows" J. J. Shubert, in Brooks McNamara, *The Shuberts of Broadway: A History Drawn from the Collections of the Shubert Archive* (New York: Oxford University Press, 1990), 155.

"My association with J. J." JAM, transcript, CUOHC, June 1959, 15.

"and should you attempt . . . dressing room—ALONE" Contract between JAM and Shubert Theatre Corporation, 7 November 1927, SA. (Although

MacDonald's name is typed "Miss Janet MacDonald," her signature reads
    "Jeanette.")
"The cast is about"   Waters, "The Studio Girl," *Variety,* 23 November 1927.
" 'I'm so glad to have Lux' "   *New Yorker,* 19 May 1928, 45.
"beautiful"   John J. Daly, "Phantasmagoria of Color in New Musical
    Comedy," *WP,* n.d.; "easy on the eyes" Robert Coleman, " 'Sunny Days'
    Delightful," *NYM,* 9 February 1928; "command[ing] an orchidlike
    daintiness" Burns Mantle, "Another Peppy Music Play Thrills Crowd at
    the Imperial," *NYDN,* 9 February 1928.
"We shall provide you"   Shubert Theatre Corporation, letter to JAM, 12
    March 1928, MacDonald contract file, SA.
"very happy . . . has been deducted"   J. W. Ashley, letter to Mr. Kaye, c/o
    Shubert Office, 20 March 1928, MacDonald contract file, SA.
"Jeanette MacDonald has been"   "Broadway Openings and Closings,"
    Billboard, 27 March 1928, 9.
"In the darkened projection"   JAM, auto., II, 30.
"Why should we help"   J. J. Shubert, in Sheilah Graham, "Ups and Downs
    of Jeanette MacDonald's Career," *BG,* 9 November 1938.
"I knew what I"   JAM, auto., II, 22.
"never indulged . . . Once, after Yes, Yes"   Irving Caesar, in Bass, "Jeanette
    MacDonald," 103.
"I didn't think my"   JAM, auto., II, 22.
"Girls get Itchy"   Anonymous, "Poem for Bob," Scrapbook n. 2, RRC.
"Dear Shorty, By the"   Bob Ritchie, letter to JAM, in JAM, auto., II, 24.
    Although MacDonald refers in her text to the other woman as "Florence,"
    a telegram from Ritchie to his parents on 4 October 1928 (RRC) specifies
    that he married that morning Gertrude Laird in Portchester, New York;
    Gertrude was the daughter of Charles Laird of Boston.
"Although I could never"   JAM, auto., II, 27.
"a very feminine desire . . . makes any sense"   JAM, auto., II, 28–29.
"Oddly enough, while I"   JAM, auto., II, 29.
"unchallenged title . . . fair princesses"   Donald Mulhern, *Brooklyn Standard
    Union,* 5 December 1928.
"redeeming feature"   Burns Mantle, " 'Angela' Familiar Royal Romance,"
    NYDN, 4 December 1928.
"Thank you, but we"   Fox representatives, in JAM, auto., II, 34.
"Yessah—I likes my girls light . . . is it not?"   Fanny Todd Mitchell, *Boom-
    Boom,* Act II, typescript, 14 February 1929, SA.
"Most actors and actresses"   J. J. Shubert, in JAM, transcript, CUOHC, 14.
"This is the rottenest"   JAM, auto., II, 33.
"If you don't open"   J. J. Shubert, in JAM, auto., II, 32.
"INDIGNANT STAR HALTS SHOW"   *Newark Ledger,* 22 January 1929.
"Jeanette MacDonald in her"   S. B., "The New Musical Show," *WSJ,* 29
    January 1929.
"Dear Mr. Shubert, Please"   JAM, letter to J. J. Shubert, MacDonald
    contract file, SA.
"You're going to be"   Bob Ritchie, in JAM, auto., II, 34–35.

CHAPTER 5. LUBITSCH AND CHEVALIER

"Show me some old . . . found the queen!" Ernst Lubitsch, in Leonard Hall, "The Prima Donna and the 'Old Man,' " *Photoplay,* February 1931, 63.

"Meine Liebling, you are" Lubitsch, in JAM, auto., II, 35.

"the only difference between" Robert Benchley, "A Possible Revolution in Hollywood," *Yale Review,* September 1931, 102.

"Never in my life" JAM, auto., II, 38.

"The wonder is that" JAM, auto., II, 40.

"Right and left that" JAM, auto., II, 50.

"I think you're . . . thought is mutual?" Louella Parsons and JAM, in JAM, auto., II, 85.

"I want to see . . . checking" Hedda Hopper, in JAM, auto., II, 50.

"Paramount touches the lives" *Variety,* 7 August 1929, special Paramount-sponsored issue.

"When he directed, he" JAM, auto., II, 45.

"There were no outward" JAM, auto., II, 42–43, 44.

"You notice your chair? . . . a bitch yourself!" Ernst Lubitsch and JAM, in JAM, auto., II, 43–44.

"Is it true that . . . married before" Lubitsch and JAM, in JAM, auto., II, 44–45.

"I stood there berserk . . . never figure how" JAM, auto., II, 46–47.

"What name? . . . open my mouth—" JAM, Lubitsch, and Greta Garbo, in Jessie Henderson, "Greta Garbo Finds Joker at Dinner," *PBI,* 14 August 1930.

"They would get in" JAM, transcript, CUOHC, 33.

"Please send word back" JAM, transcript, CUOHC, 33.

"outdo Cecil B. De Mille" "Hollywood Chatter," *Variety,* 17 July 1929, 73.

"fragile, fluttery, and every" "Hollywood Styles," *Variety,* 10 July 1929, 41.

"the boudoir warbler" "Jeanette's Top Tunes," *Variety,* 23 February 1933, 4.

"stretch" and *"patch"* Nathaniel Finston and Merill Pye, in Bass, "Jeanette MacDonald," 175.

"engaged" *Variety,* 11 September 1929, 6.

"We are not engaged" JAM, in "Miss MacDonald Denies Betrothal to Her Manager," *LAE,* 10 October 1929.

"I had just traveled" Dorothy Rodgers, interview with EBT, NYC, 30 November 1990.

"ninety-nine percent in" Helene Lubitsch, in "Lubitsches Are Divorced," *NYT,* 24 June 1930.

"He took hold of " JAM, auto., II, 55.

"I am too important . . . go along with it" Ernst Lubitsch, in JAM, auto., II, 56–57.

"Neither [of us] gave" JAM, auto., II, 57.

"Ironically, Lubitsch got fewer"   JAM, auto., II, 58.

"I've often been asked"   Maurice Chevalier, *Ma Route et mes chansons,*
   volume 2 (Paris: Julliard, 1947), 220.

"Splendid, Maurice! Marvelous!"   Chevalier, *Ma Route et mes chansons,*
   volume 2, 152.

"The Screen's Greatest Lovers . . . fifty-fifty"   Ernst Lubitsch, "Maurice and
   Jeanette: The Screen's Greatest Lovers," *Singapore Free Press,* 1 May 1933.

"who all but steals the picture"   Ohar., "The Love Parade," *Variety,* 27
   November 1929.

"informal and Parisian"   "The New Pictures," *Time,* 2 December 1929, 39.

"Nothing in her past"   Richard Watts, Jr., "On the Screen," *NYHTr,* 20
   November 1929.

"clear and true voice"   Edwin Schallert, " 'Love Parade' Gay and Clever,"
   LAT, 24 January 1930.

"Jeanette MacDonald is no"   W. H. Brenner, "The Voice of the Industry,"
   EHW, 24 May 1930, 56.

"What outsiders thought about"   JAM, auto., II, 49.

"almost one third of"   "Third of Audience Seeing 'Love Parade' Again,
   Ushers Learn," *EHW,* 8 March 1930.

CHAPTER 6. ONLY A NOSE

"The Vagabond King will not"   Arch Reeve, "As the Picture Goes into
   Production," press release, *The Vagabond King* file, PCAC.

"a series of beautiful"   "An Extraordinary Film; 'The Vagabond King'
   Attains a New High Point in Movie Art," *PEB,* 20 February 1930.

"was a heavy-handed German"   JAM, auto., II, 52.

"After I'd set the"   Ray Rennahan, quoted in Bass, "Jeanette MacDonald,"
   391.

"the gorgeous beauty and"   Arch Reeve, "As the Picture Goes into
   Production," press release, *The Vagabond King* file, PCAC.

"musical comedies . . . not educated as yet"   "Musicals and Operettas,"
   Variety, 25 June 1930.

"[The industry] must offer"   Dr. Herbert T. Kalmus, in *Film Daily Yearbook:
   1931,* 552.

"the future medium of"   Igor Stravinsky, in "Screen for Music and Masses,"
   Variety, 28 May 1930, 1.

"grand opera on the"   Bruno Walter, in "Great Future for Opera in Sound
   Films Is Opinion of Bruno Walter," *EHW,* 2 November 1929, 39.

"musical genius which otherwise"   Oscar Straus, "And So to Hollywood:
   Notes on a Pilgrimage to the Sound Studios," *TM,* April 1930, 40.

"romantic drama with music"   "Belasco's Starring Offer to Jeanette
   MacDonald," *Variety,* 14 May 1930.

"When Ritchie was in"   Cecil E. "Teet" Carle, interview with EBT, North
   Hollywood—Boston, 4 November 1991.

"in the near future"   "Jeanette MacDonald Engaged," *NYT,* 21 December
   1930.

"the longest engagement in Hollywood" Louella Parsons, "Most Spectacular Film Events of 1935," *LAE,* 30 December 1935.

"Heretofore the rumors had" Walter Winchell, reprinted in "Report Jeanette a Bride," *PEB,* 13 May 1933.

"So I should" JAM, in Jack Grant, "Winchell was Wrong!—says Jeanette MacDonald," unreferenced magazine article, January 1935, MacD Archive.

"He, of course, was" Chevalier, in Gene Ringgold and Dewitt Bodeen, *Chevalier: The Films and Career of Maurice Chevalier* (Secaucus, N.J.: Citadel Press, 1973), 42.

"We always heard in" John Ritchie, interview with EBT, Myrtle Beach, SC, 11 January 1993.

"I got your sweet sentimental" JAM, letter to Bob Ritchie, 11 February 1931, RRC.

"You know why I'm" JAM, letter to Bob Ritchie, 13 February 1931, RRC.

"It's the difficult things" JAM, letter to Bob Ritchie, 24 February 1931, RRC.

"They tell me she" Louella Parsons, *LAE,* 4 February 1930.

"only saving grace was" JAM, auto., II, 53.

"Something that even amateurs" *Variety,* 3 December 1930, 14.

"There are songs in" *Publix Opinion,* 1 August 1930.

"abnormally long" George Gerhard, *NYEW,* 20 November 1929.

"I'm sorry, but one" JAM, in Bass, "Jeanette MacDonald," 240.

"I was frequently challenged" Jack Buchanan, in Boze Hadleigh, *The Vinyl Closet: Gays in the Music World* (San Diego: Los Hombres Press, 1991), 173.

"I felt a very arresting" Jack Buchanan, in Bass, "Jeanette MacDonald," 225.

"If it were not for" *Variety,* 3 September 1930.

"Meritorious Deeds" "Good Deeds of 1930 Series," *Film Daily Annual: 1931,* 17.

"took me out of the doldrums" Gene Raymond, transcript, SMUOHC, 28.

"When I count the" JAM, letter to Bob Ritchie, 3 February 1931, RRC.

"I am awfully tired" JAM, letter to Bob Ritchie, 21 February 1931, RRC.

"the subtlest, sexiest, super-sophisticated" Garvey, pub. packet, *Oh, for a Man!* file, PCAC.

"What the people at" JAM, auto., II, 57.

"I sweated blood learning" JAM, auto., II, 58.

"The musicians must have" JAM, auto., II, 58.

"We had a report . . . the cans with them?" Sol Wurtzel and JAM, in JAM, auto., II, 58–59.

"She liked to go" Charles G. Clarke, in Christopher Finch and Linda Rosenkrantz, *Gone Hollywood* (Garden City, N.Y.: Doubleday, 1979), 31.

"I found that to" Charles G. Clarke, *Highlights and Shadows* (Metuchen, N.J.: Scarecrow Press, 1989), 132.

"There is no question" JAM, letter to Bob Ritchie, 23 February 1931, RRC.

"Over my dead body!" JAM, in Dora Albert, "You've Got to Be Temperamental!" *Movie Mirror,* 1931, 72.

"hilariously funny . . . undresses well"   "Cinema," *Time,* 26 July 1931, 20.
"a shock for the boys . . . on the Coast"   "Annabelle's Affairs," *Variety,* 30 June 1931, 15.

CHAPTER 7. VIVE LA FRANCE!

"I am afraid that now"   Ernst Lubitsch, letter to JAM, 31 May 1931, MacDonald scrapbooks, n. 1, Department of Special Collections, University Library, UCLA.
"the preposterous story . . . embarrassment"   "Cinema," *Time,* 6 July 1931, 20.
"tarnished a Belgian Princess"   Jean Variot, "Pour l'honneur du journalisme: L'affaire Janette [*sic*] MacDonald," *Nation Belge,* 21 April 1931.
"Mademoiselle, Paris can very"   Jean de Rovéra, "Lettre ouverte à Mlle Jeanette MacDonald," *Comoedia,* 8 August 1931.
"In under fifteen minutes"   O. P., "Jeanette MacDonald reçoit," *Candide,* 8 September 1931.
"a practical assurance of success"   Wolf Kaufman, "Few International Stars," *Variety,* 29 December 1931, 13.
"The moment this radiant"   Henry Fleurance, *L'Echo de Paris,* 8 September 1931.
"Jeanette MacDonald is not"   "Silhouettes: Jeanette MacDonald," *Courrier Cinématographique,* 23 May 1931.
"I hereby declare my"   E. G., in Paul Achard, *Jeanette MacDonald* (Paris: Nouvelle Librairie Française, 1932), 48–49. Archard's book, part of the series "Collection Hollywood," is the first monograph written on MacDonald and covers her life and films through *One Hour with You* (1932). Earlier titles in the series treat Garbo, Chaplin, Dietrich, Annabella, and Lilian Harvey.
"Yes, this is her!"   Chevalier, in Achard, *Jeanette MacDonald,* 48.
"men so bizarrely made"   Chevalier, *Ma route et mes chansons,* volume 1, 92.
"From my observation of"   Cukor, interview with Bill Bass, in Bass, "Jeanette MacDonald," 249.
"as large as Chevalier's . . . as Chevalier's"   Paramount legal officer, in James Cunningham, "Asides and Interludes," *MPH,* 2 April 1932, 19.
"Maurice and I made"   JAM, auto., II, 72–73.
"charm and magnetism distinguish"   Regina Crewe, *NYA,* 26 March 1932.
"The industry has . . . listened"   B. P. Schulberg, in "Comparison of X and Y Proves Simple Dramatic Picture Pays," *MPH,* 16 April 1932, 9.
"Do anything you want"   Adolph Zukor, in Rouben Mamoulian, transcript, SMUOHC, 31.
"Art for art's sake"   Rouben Mamoulian, transcript, CUOHC, December 1958, 108.
"Rouben, we are supposed"   JAM, auto., II, 73.
"I think Myrna was"   Joseph Youngerman, interview with EBT, Los Angeles, 3 July 1991.

"took the whole thing" Rouben Mamoulian, transcript, SMUOHC, 33.
"washed up . . . a flop" *MPH,* 17 and 31 December 1932.
"AA" to "H" "133 Film Names Have B.O.," *Variety,* 23 August 1932.
"I don't think my" JAM, in Nancy Pryor, "No More Nighties for Jeanette," *Motion Picture,* February 1933, 27.
"Marriage to Monsieur Chevalier" JAM, auto., II, 75.
"ALL TOGETHER THIS EVENING" JAM, Paul and Henriette Chevalier, telegram to Maurice Chevalier, 28 December 1932, RRC.
"ANOTHER SONG ANOTHER TRIUMPH" Lawrence Tibbett, telegram to JAM, 3 February 1933, MacD Archive.
"[MacDonald] gave the Parisians" Didier Daix, "La Rentrée de Jeanette MacDonald," *L'Intransigeant,* 8 February 1933.
"I was handed a" JAM, auto., II, 76.
"sick of the tripe" Ernst Lubitsch, in "Films Can't Figure Public," *Variety,* 1 April 1931, 20.
"I felt like a hypocrite" JAM, auto., II, 79.

CHAPTER 8. MR. MAYER AND THE WIDOW

"your friend, counselor, and guide" Louis B. Mayer, in JAM, auto., II, 80.
"One day I had to" Sam Marx, interview with EBT, Los Angeles, 13 August 1990.
"Mr. Mayer, you simply . . . great picture" JAM and L. B. Mayer, in JAM, auto., II, 87.
"L. B. Mayer was a . . . 'know that aria!'" John Green, transcript, 17–21 July 1975, SMUOHC, 98–99.
"You can say what" Allan Jones, interview with EBT, NYC, 8 December 1990.
"Seconds after Dick struck" Sam Marx, interview with EBT, Los Angeles, 13 August 1990.
"the sanctity of the . . . religious faith" Association of Motion Picture Producers, Inc., and Motion Picture Producers & Distributors of America, Inc., "A Code Regulating Production of Motion Pictures," *EHW,* 5 April 1930, 12–13.
"blasphemous and sacrilegious . . . profane" Joseph Breen, letter to L. B. Mayer, 2 February 1935, *I Married an Angel* file, PCAC.
"I just think that's" JAM, in Bass, "Jeanette MacDonald," 274.
"a bluff sea captain" JAM, auto., II, 82.
"a musical episode must" Herbert Stothart, "Through the Years: Mr. Stothart Talks About the Techniques He Helped Develop," *NYT,* 7 December 1941.
"My mother used to" Herbert Stothart II, interview with EBT, Pacific Palisades, 26 July 1990.
"Hello, Viv, have you . . . cast me after that" JAM (as quoted by Segal) and Segal, in Tony Slide, "Vivienne Segal," *Film Fan Monthly,* October 1972, 26. Segal speaks directly, and even more harshly, against MacDonald in her SMUOHC interview with Ronald L. Davis, n. 224, 23 September 1981; Segal specified, however, that no one may quote from that transcript.

"Vivienne Segal is in"   Louella Parsons, *LAE,* 31 October 1933.

"After The Cat and*"*   William Tuttle, interview with EBT, Pacific Palisades—Brentwood, 22 August 1990.

"She was so kind"   Kitty Carlisle Hart, interview with EBT, NYC, 22 January 1991.

"There was an oboe player"   Virginia Majewski, interview with EBT, Los Angeles—Provincetown, 30 December 1991.

"One of the bits"   JAM, auto., II, 80.

"particularly absurd . . . present ending ride"   JAM and Eddie Mannix, in JAM, auto., II, 81–82.

"with a cauliflower ear . . . in his body"   Unattributed description of Mannix, in Gary Carey, *All the Stars in Heaven: Louis B. Mayer's M-G-M* (New York: Dutton, 1981), 124.

"The hell with budget"   Eddie Mannix, in JAM, auto., II, 82.

"The trouble with Jeanette"   Eddie Mannix, in JAM, auto., II, 82.

"Dear Jeanette: I have"   Louis B. Mayer, letter to JAM, 12 May 1934, MacD Archive.

"When you play Marietta . . . in your hands"   Louis B. Mayer and JAM in JAM, auto., II, 83. Other versions of this famous episode are found in Bosley Crowther, *The Lion's Share* (New York: Dutton, 1957), and James Robert Parish, *The Jeanette MacDonald Story* (New York: Mason/Chartier, 1976). A *New Yorker* profile on Mayer from 28 August 1936 situates the event after *The Merry Widow;* a *Fortune* profile on Loew's, Inc., from August 1939 places it after *Maytime;* Charles Higham, in *Merchant of Dreams: Louis B. Mayer, MGM and the Secret Hollywood* (New York: Donald I. Fine, 1993), 231, asserts that the story has "no truth." Sidney Guilaroff, in *Crowning Glory: Reflections of Hollywood's Favorite Confidant* (Los Angeles: General Publishing Group, 1996), claims he was present at the event, but he undermines his credibility by situating the moment during the production of *Smilin' Through* (1941). Gene Raymond corroborated MacDonald's account in an interview with me on 15 August 1992.

"made in heaven"   Frederick L. Collins, "Sweethearts of the Film," *Good Housekeeping,* May 1933, 191.

"boudoir conqueror"   Chevalier, paraphrased in Edwin Schallert, "Feud Flam: *Merry Widow* Warry Musical," *LAT,* 18 September 1933, 8.

"I can only think . . . that"   Lubitsch, in Louella Parsons, "So Chevalier Is Annoyed? Ask Lubitsch," *LAE,* 9 October 1933.

"I COULD NEVER SAY"   Chevalier, telegram to Irving Thalberg, quoted in Louella O. Parsons, "Merry Widow Row Denied by Chevalier," *LAE,* 15 October 1933.

"I am greatly surprised"   Irving Thalberg, letter to Ernst Lubitsch, quoted in Louella Parsons, "Merry Widow Row Denied by Chevalier," *LAE,* 15 October 1933.

"Painfully surprised to receive"   Maurice Chevalier, letter to Bob Ritchie, 16 September 1933, RRC.

"You have only one"   Joan Crawford, in JAM, auto., II, 84.

"moose"   Otis Ferguson, "Love Me Some Other Time," *New Republic*, 24 July 1935, 308.

"Time for Jeanette MacDonald"   Louella Parsons, *LAE*, 19 December 1933.

"amiable worldliness, her beautiful"   "Hollywood Soprano," *Vanity Fair*, December 1933.

"No matter what Irving"   Louis B. Mayer, in JAM, auto., II, 86–87.

"He really gave me"   JAM, auto., II, 87.

"a hundred percent romantic . . . modern flavor"   Ernst Lubitsch, quoted in "A Production Landmark," MGM *Merry Widow* press kit, 1934, HL.

"It is unfortunately true"   Lubitsch, in Molly Hollywood, "No Romance in Life Today," *LAE*, 12 August 1934.

"They picked it up"   Joseph Newman, interview with EBT, Los Angeles, 9 July 1991.

"Mr. Thalberg will reshoot"   Joe Breen, memo to the file, 13 August 1934, *Merry Widow* file, PCAC.

"I am on the side . . . intelligent people"   Ernst Lubitsch, in André Sennwald, "A Word with Ernst Lubitsch," *NYT*, 25 November 1934.

"Boys, I'm on my own!"   JAM, in Regina Crewe, "Merry Widow in New York to Make Merry by Herself," *LAE*, 30 September 1934.

"purely a matter of"   JAM, paraphrased by Herbert Ohmeis in "Jeanette MacDonald," MacD Archive.

"the Easter eggs of Fabergé . . . widow herself"   Sir Cecil Beaton, *Cecil Beaton's Scrapbook* (London: Batsford, 1937), 51.

"seem like amateurs"   Louella Parsons, *LAE*, 30 November 1934.

"the cool chrysalis . . . love and life"   Regina Crewes, "Acting in *Merry Widow* as Brilliant as Direction," *NYA*, 12 October 1934.

"What I'm most pleased"   JAM, in "The *Merry Widow* Again," *NYEP*, 6 October 1934.

"out of step with modern America"   Herman J. Brown, "What the Picture Did for Me," *MPH*, 5 January 1935, 60.

"the few high-brows we got to see it"   Bert Silver, "What the Picture Did for Me," *MPH*, 2 February 1935, 88.

"Let me again assure"   Herman J. Brown, "What the Picture Did for Me," *MPH*, 5 January 1935, 60.

CHAPTER 9. AN ALL-AMERICAN TEAM

"No question about it"   JAM, auto., II, 102.

"another Lawrence Tibbett . . . Tibbett?"   Mark Sandrich and Merian Cooper, in Edwin Lester, transcript, UCLAOHC, 52.

"I remember seeing Nelson"   JAM, auto., II, 90.

"Dear Miss MacDonald, Thank"   Nelson Eddy, letter to JAM, 7 November 1934, MacD Archive.

"I was all prepared"   Nelson Eddy, quoted by JAM in Roger Carroll, "Jeanette Confesses About Nelson Eddy," typescript interview, spring 1938, Nelson Eddy scrapbooks, volume 7, DL.

"I resent simpering idiots"   Woody Van Dyke, guest column for "Walter Winchell on Broadway," *NYDM,* reprinted in Robert Cannom, *Van Dyke and the Mythical City of Hollywood* (Culver City: Murray and Gee, 1948), 296.

"Well, that's just dandy"   Woody Van Dyke, in Cannom, *Van Dyke and the Mythical City of Hollywood,* 323.

"fast apologizing"   Eddie Mannix, in JAM, auto., II, 91.

"Now may I come"   JAM, in Cannom, *Van Dyke and the Mythical City of Hollywood,* 325.

"When he reached my"   JAM, auto., II, 92.

"To Naughty Marietta"   Woody Van Dyke, note to JAM, in JAM, auto., II, 92.

"That established our relationship"   JAM, auto., II, 92.

"Yes . . . TURN 'EM!"   JAM and Woody Van Dyke, in Cannom, *Van Dyke and the Mythical City of Hollywood,* 328.

"I've handled Indians, African natives"   Woody Van Dyke, in Cannom, *Van Dyke and the Mythical City of Hollywood,* 325–26.

"They told me you . . . as well as sing"   Louis B. Mayer, in *Newsweek,* 30 March 1935, 29.

"a potent force"   Woody Van Dyke, in Cannom, *Van Dyke and the Mythical City of Hollywood,* 336.

"Excellent, that's the word . . . situation"   S. H. Rich, "What the Picture Did for Me," *MPH,* 3 August 1935.

"The public is getting"   O. Ingmar Oleson, *MPH,* 30 November 1935, 82.

"Suddenly I had a"   JAM, auto., II, 102.

"I wanted to write"   JAM, in "Lovely Singer Sparkles Despite Run in Stocking," *Rochester Democrat and Chronicler,* 25 November 1940.

"the women got so"   Theodore Paxson, in Paul Cranston, "Nelson Eddy Still Hunts Ideal Girl," *PEB,* 13 April 1935.

"he-man . . . ZaSu Pitts"   Frances Holmes, "Knocks and Boosts," unreferenced newspaper clipping, MacD Archive.

"I think what attracted"   Kitty Carlisle Hart, interview with EBT, NYC, 22 January 1991.

"Together they're a world rarity!"   Mike McLaughlin, in "Hollywood's Ace Sound Mixer Plans Hobby: Deep-Sea Diving," unreferenced newspaper clipping, MacD Archive.

"more human, more sympathetic . . . reveled in it"   JAM, auto., II, 102–3.

"I liked myself on"   JAM, in W. H. Mooring, " 'Marietta Made Me Happy' Says Jeanette MacDonald," *Kine Weekly* (London), 12 April 1935.

"stand on their tails . . . grunion are running!"   Elsa Lanchester, *Charles Laughton and I* (New York: Harcourt, Brace, 1938), 149–50.

"unbelievable personal strength . . . frozen custard"   Nelson Eddy, "Categorically Speaking: Jeanette as Seen by Nelson Eddy," *Photoplay,* 6 June 1940, 91.

"a platinum-plated steam shovel"   JAM, "Categorically Speaking: Nelson as Seen by Jeanette MacDonald," *Photoplay,* 6 June 1940, 23.

"They were always friendly" Joseph Newman, interview with EBT, Los Angeles, 9 July 1991.

"Dad told us one" Virginia Eddy Brown, phone interview with EBT, 21 October 1994.

"One day Mrs. Eddy" JAM, auto., II, 93.

"Perhaps I should not . . . are in love" JAM, "So I'm in Love with Nelson Eddy!" *Hollywood,* June 1935, 26.

"The truth of the" JAM, auto., II, 93.

"Darlings, how nice of" Roszika Dolly, quoted by JAM in Elizabeth Wilson, "MacDonald's Merry Romance," *Screenland,* November 1936, 77. MacDonald gave a similar version in 1952, on the TV show *This Is Your Life.* Gene Raymond recalled his first encounters with Jeanette in his SMUOHC transcript, 28–29.

"young god's physique" JAM, auto., II, 101.

"Do you always turn" Gene Raymond, remarks at JMIFC banquet, Beverly Wilshire Hotel, 29 June 1993.

"that mysterious tingle" JAM, auto., II, 94.

"Well, I seem to . . . tomorrow night?" Gene Raymond, remarks at JMIFC banquet, Beverly Wilshire Hotel, 29 June 1993.

"the most gorgeous thing" George Sydney, interview with EBT, Boston, 1 October 1989.

"He was always around" Betty Lasky, interview with EBT, Los Angeles, 4 July 1991.

"an introvert in a" JAM, auto., II, 142.

"living up to expectations" Gene Raymond, in Charles Grayson, "Indifferent to Girls," *Motion Picture,* November 1932.

"bucking against the entire industry" Gene Raymond, in Frederick Russell, "Gene Raymond's Secret Ambition," *Film Pictorial* (London), 23 March 1935, 24.

"knew what they were doing" Gene Raymond, transcript, SMUOHC, 20–21.

"Are you so bored . . . birthday!" Gene Raymond and JAM, in JAM, auto., II, 104.

"Jeanette was the only" Gene Raymond, remarks at JMIFC banquet, Beverly Wilshire Hotel, 29 June 1991.

"I had to stay on" JAM, auto., II, 115.

"not wanting marriage" JAM, auto., II, 105.

"indifferent to girls . . . domestic life" Gene Raymond, in Charles Grayson, "Indifferent to Girls," *Motion Picture,* November 1932.

"forced to protect themselves" JAM, auto., II, 141.

"I'm afraid she hasn't . . . realize my feelings" Gene Raymond and JAM, in JAM, auto., II, 109–10.

"had done more" JAM, auto., II, 110.

"Being wealthy means nothing" Gene Raymond, in Jack Smalley, "An Open Letter to Jeanette MacDonald," *Photoplay,* February 1937, 84.

"a gift I thought" JAM, auto., II, 110.

"How dare you send"   Mary Kipling, in JAM, auto., II, 111.

"The scenery here is"   JAM, letter to Bob Ritchie, 11 September 1935, RRC.

"That 'Rose Marie' song"   JAM, letter to Bob Ritchie, dated "Tuesday," RRC.

"shook so much . . . scarcely speak"   JAM, auto., II, 117.

"One morning, it was"   Joseph Newman, interview with EBT, Los Angeles, 9 July 1991.

"in all the time"   JAM, auto., II, 118.

"design for living"   Doris Warner, in JAM, auto., II, 119.

"This romance hadn't quite"   JAM, auto., II, 105, 116.

"Well, it won't be"   JAM, letter to Bob Ritchie, 16 September 1935, RRC.

"Fine thing . . . effect on him"   Nelson Eddy and JAM, in JAM, auto., II, 116.

"Here I sit in"   JAM, letter to Gene Raymond, 23 September 1935, MacD Archive.

"I am so full"   JAM, letter to Gene Raymond, 23 September 1935, MacD Archive.

"Bob arrives tomorrow at"   JAM, letter to Gene Raymond, 21 September 1935, MacD Archive.

"OH MORPHEUS MY MORPHEUS"   JAM, telegram to Gene Raymond, 4 October 1935, MacD Archive.

"If report [is] true"   Louella Parsons, *LAE,* 8 October 1935.

"Robert Ritchie and Jeanette"   Walter Winchell, *NYDM,* 11 December 1935.

"Hollywood is completely mystified"   Louella Parsons, *LAE,* 15 December 1935.

"Dear Bub, They're just"   JAM, letter to Bob Ritchie, c. early February 1936, RRC.

"We had the boys"   B. A. McConnell, "What the Picture Did for Me," *MPH,* 7 March 1936.

"Popsie my sweet, Just"   JAM, letter to Bob Ritchie, 24 August 1935, RRC.

"at the head of"   *Variety,* 12 February 1936, 66.

"It is not too"   W. J. Henderson, "Music and Musicians," *NYS,* 15 February 1936.

"For the death scene"   Allan Jones, interview with EBT, NYC, 8 December 1990.

"How does it feel . . . telling me!"   Woody Van Dyke and Nelson Eddy, in Gail Lulay, *Nelson Eddy: America's Favorite Baritone* (Wheeling, Ill.: Goldfleet Publishing), 60.

"[Nelson and I] never"   JAM, remarks to Patti Paige, *The Big Record,* CBS TV, 25 September 1957.

CHAPTER 10. THE IRON BUTTERFLY

"Halfway ambition can be"   JAM, "I Shouldn't Tell This, But I Will!," *Screenland* April 1936.

"San Francisco! Earthquake! MacDonald"   Robert Hopkins, in Samuel Marx, interview with EBT, Los Angeles, 13 August 1990.

"a woman of great"   Anita Loos, transcript, CUOHC, 14 July 1971, 8.

"Hell, when she starts"   Clark Gable, in JAM, auto., II, 126.

"Filmgoers today want credibility*"*   JAM, in "Jeanette MacDonald Sees Trouble Ahead for Hollywood Producers," *Film Weekly,* 15 February 1936.

"Dear Felix, This will"   JAM, letter to Felix F. Feist, 20 March 1935, MacD Archive.

"MY DEAR JEANNETTE [sic]"   Felix F. Feist, telegram to JAM, 22 March 1935, MacD Archive.

"I literally felt the"   JAM, auto., II, 119.

"Why are you trying . . . without letting you know"   Mary Kipling and JAM, in JAM, auto., II, 121–22.

"Why don't we pray"   JAM, auto., II, 125.

"$140,000 poorer"   JAM, auto., II, 126.

"Gable is a mess!*"*   JAM, letter to Bob Ritchie, 27 February 1936, RRC.

"good friendship and companionship"   Margaret Irving, letter to JMIFC, *The Petite Comet,* Spring 1979.

"mismatch in routine"   Joseph Newman, interview with EBT, Los Angeles, 9 July 1991.

"They were not kindred spirits"   Emily Torchia, transcript, SMUOHC, 22–23.

"Why did you want . . . and insulted"   Clark Gable and JAM, in JAM, auto., II, 127.

"How do you suppose . . . you will find out"   JAM and Spencer Tracy, in JAM, auto., II, 127.

"BORED"   Gene Raymond, telegram to JAM, in JAM, auto., II, 127.

"Your face is getting"   Oliver Marsh, in JAM, auto., II, 125.

"One wonders why she"   J. A. H., "Eddy in New Film, *Rose Marie,*" *Musical America,* 10 February 1936, 11.

"a little bit too . . . necessary stamina"   Wilhelm von Wymetal, in Joseph Newman, interview with EBT, Los Angeles, 9 July 1991.

"She's had many offers"   Grace Adele Newell, in Katharine Hartley, "Jeanette Was the Unwanted Girl," *Screenbook,* June 1937, 99.

"An American composer would"   Bronislaw Kaper, transcript, Louis B. Mayer/AFI Film History Program, July–October 1975, Louis B. Mayer Library, AFI, 84.

"At the close of"   J. A. Reynolds, "What the Picture Did for Me," *MPH,* 12 December 1936, 57.

"We are not *mawkish"*   Greg Gallipau, in Merla Zellerbach, "Do We Need a New Song?" *SFC,* 25 March 1974, 16.

"a glint in Judy's"   Hugh Martin, letter to EBT, 21 July 1993.

"I think I should"   JAM, to Ken Richards, 1962, in Richards, interview with EBT, NYC, 28 April 1990.

"acting with her teeth"   "The New Pictures," *Time,* 6 July 1936, 48.

"It is impossible to"   "San Francisco," *Hollywood Spectator,* 4 July 1936, 12.

"a near-perfect illustration"   Frank S. Nugent, "San Francisco," *NYT,* 27 June 1936, 21.

"five to fifteen cents"   Russell Sanjek, *American Popular Music and Its Business,* volume 3 (New York: Oxford University Press: 1988), 128.
"just once . . . stand for!"   JAM, *Lux Radio Theatre,* 29 June 1936, reel-to-reel tape recording and typed transcript, HL.
"I've been waiting for"   Gene Raymond, in JAM, auto., II, 130.
"Lucky dog. She always"   JAM, letter to Bob Ritchie, c. June 1935, RRC.
"a square deal in"   JAM, in "Star Engaged Five Years: Jeanette MacDonald Would Marry Only After Successful Career," *PEB,* 28 November 1934.
"It would be most"   Gene Raymond, interview with EBT, Los Angeles, 14 July 1993.
"I believe a man"   JAM, "The Modern Husband," *PEL,* 10 February 1936.
"It is unwise to"   JAM, in Charles Darnton, "Does Hollywood Defy Romance?" *Hollywood,* 1937, 60.
"inconsiderate to flaunt jewelry"   JAM, "My Frankest Confession," *Screenland,* January 1940, 80.
"I am the happiest . . . we are"   Gene Raymond and JAM, in "Jeanette MacDonald Engaged to Gene Raymond," *PEB,* 21 August 1936.
"This could really wipe"   Louella Parsons, in JAM, auto., II, 132.
"When would you like . . . very much"   JAM, auto., II, 132.
"vicious influence"   Mary Kipling, in JAM, auto., II, 131.
"I am engaged to"   Gene Raymond, letter to Mary Kipling, 18 October 1936, in JAM, auto., II, 132–33.
"the true artistic"   "Phi Beta Honors Jeanette MacDonald," *LAT,* 7 November 1936.

CHAPTER 11. HOLLYWOOD DIVA

"look and act their"   Edward Johnson, in "Met Opera's S.[ex] A.[ppeal] Grief," *Variety,* 5 February 1936, 57.
"in deepest admiration for"   Ferdinand Schumann-Heink, note to JAM, reprinted in Louella Parsons, *LAHE,* 9 January 1938.
"chatter[ing] like schoolgirls together"   Edwin McArthur, *Flagstad: A Personal Memoir* (New York: Knopf, 1965), 61.
"breadth of human understanding . . . every other thought"   JAM, "No Royal Road to Song" (MGM-published pamphlet), MacD Archive.
"Thalberg envisioned a romantic"   Joseph Newman, interview with EBT, Los Angeles, 9 July 1991.
"The scenes themselves and"   Hunt Stromberg, memo, 19 September 1936, *Maytime* file, MGM Collection, DL.
"undisputed evidence . . . remembrance of ecstasy"   Stromberg, story notes, 12 October 1936, 2–3, *Maytime* file, MGM Collection, DL.
"Both MacDonald and I"   Hunt Stromberg, story notes, 15 October 1936, 4–5, *Maytime* file, MGM Collection, DL.
"one of the most"   JAM, auto., II, 130A.
"The Red Volcano"   Robert Z. Leonard, in "Jeanette MacDonald: Remembrance," *Hollywood Studio,* November 1977, 6.

"come sweeping *into the room"* Robert Z. Leonard, in *Maytime* press packet, MacD Archive.

"to cut to the minimum" Joseph Breen, letter to L. B. Mayer, 31 October 1936, *Maytime* file, PCAC.

"You may as well know . . . the Fifth Symphony" JAM, Eddy, Bob Wright, Chet Forrest, in Bob Wright and Chet Forrest, interview with EBT, NYC, 25 February 1990.

"John, you're not drinking . . . any alcohol*"* Joseph Newman, interview with EBT, Los Angeles, 9 July 1991.

"It's been a nightmare" JAM, letter to Bob Ritchie, 12 January 1937, RRC.

"Unfortunately, Barrymore couldn't remember . . . poise and assurance!" JAM, John Barrymore, Robert Z. Leonard, in JAM, auto., II, 130C–130D.

"If you wave that" John Barrymore, in John Kobler, *Damned in Paradise: The Life of John Barrymore* (New York: Atheneum, 1977), 308.

"busy roaming" JAM, quoted by Clara Rhoades, interview with EBT, Topeka, Kansas, 18 January 1992.

"a good and powerful" "*Maytime* Gets Credit for Altar Rush," *NYJ,* 8 April 1937.

"It is a temptation" *HR,* 4 March 1937, 3.

"She does a job of" Louella Parsons, "Love Wafts Jeanette MacDonald to Zenith of Fame," *LAE,* 14 March 1937.

"comes just a little" "A Little Long but Lovely," *HS,* 13 March 1937.

"miracle . . . sound controls" Frank S. Nugent, *NYT,* 28 March 1937.

"film actress . . . soprano" Oscar Thompson, ed., *The American Singer: A Hundred Years of Success in Opera* (New York: Dial, 1937), 383, 386, and index. (Thompson grants bona fide "baritone" status to Nelson Eddy because he, unlike MacDonald, had already worked on the opera stage.)

"hodgepodge of arias" Howard Barnes, "The Screen: Full Speed in Musicals," *NYTr,* 28 March 1937.

"syrupy . . . overdrawn" Howard Barnes, "The Screen: Full Speed in Musicals," *NYTr,* 28 March 1937.

"A pain in the neck" L. V. Bergtold, "What the Picture Did for Me," *MPH,* 26 February 1938.

"Too much Italian [sic] opera!" C. A. Jordan, "What the Picture Did for Me," *MPH,* 25 September 1937.

"More than a part" JAM, transcript of remarks, Picwood Theater, Los Angeles, 2 April 1963, MacD Archive.

"one of those silly'" Nelson Eddy, in Paul Meskil, "Nelson Eddy Didn't Like His Motion Picture Image," *NYWJTr,* 6 March 1967.

"human ideals" Willsie Martin, in Kolma Blake, "A Minister Looks at Hollywood," *Modern Screen,* February 1951, 29.

"the most sacred" JAM, letter to Editor, *Life,* 21 November 1938, 2.

"Hollywood's most colossal" "Raymonds Hiding After Wedding," *PEB,* 17 June 1937.

"Princess and Prince Charming" Robert Z. Leonard, in Harrison Carroll, "Screen Teams," *LAHE,* 4 December 1936, 3.

"From the beginning"   Nelson Eddy, "Gene Raymond Is a Lucky Guy,"
   Screenplay, January 1937, 20.
"Dear Jeanette, Sure I'll"   Nelson Eddy, letter to JAM, 15 April 1937, MacD
   Archive. MacDonald stapled to this letter a handwritten note that read: "I
   want to keep this in my bride's book."
"Yes, on June 16"   Gene Raymond, in Dorothy Manners, *LAHE,* 6 June
   1937, V5.
"It was the most moving"   Chet Forrest, interview with EBT, NYC, 25
   February 1990.
"a kind of crush"   JAM, transcript, CUOHC, 36.
"I am much more"   Jean Harlow, in Elza Shallert, [article on Harlow],
   Motion Picture, November 1936, 32.
"She was rather like"   Anita Loos, transcript, CUOHC, 1959, 18–19.
"a young, naive, nice . . . sweet young impulse"   JAM, transcript, CUOHC,
   35–36.
"Dear Bub, Your letter"   JAM, letter to Bob Ritchie, 14 June 1937, RRC.
"My dearest one—With"   JAM, note to Gene Raymond, 15 June 1937,
   MacD Archive.
"I don't blame Lily"   JAM, auto., II, 136.
"This taffeta underskirt is"   JAM, auto., II, 137.
"wait up all night"   James P. Cunningham, "Asides and Interludes," *MPH,*
   26 June 1937.
"super-musical comedy"   "Musical in Technicolor," *Life,* 24 October 1938,
   29.
"really a simple . . . a MacDonald!"   JAM, letter to Editor, *Life,* 21
   November 1938, 2. (Although she signed her letter "Jeanette MacDonald
   Raymond," *Life* dropped the "Raymond"—which reportedly left
   MacDonald infuriated.)
"This is no usual"   Louella Parsons, "Jeanette Becomes Bride of Raymond,"
   LAE, 17 June 1937, 3.
"Louella, you and that"   JAM, in Louella Parsons, *NYJA,* 20 January 1965.
"It's in case anybody . . . pay for it?"   Gene Raymond and JAM, in
   Raymond, transcript, SMUOHC, 26 August 1986, 31.
"I thought it remarkable"   Fay Wray, interview with EBT, Los Angeles, 22
   July 1991.
"My mouth sagged open"   JAM, auto., II, 138, 140.
"one for each of us"   Gene Raymond, in JAM, auto., II, 130.
"If the governor of"   Gene Raymond, in "Jeanette, Gene Back; Her Joy Boils
   Over," unreferenced newspaper clipping, 6 August 1937, Gene Raymond
   file, RHC.
"I reported every morning"   JAM, auto., II, 137.
"in love. . . . name on it!"   Rudolf Friml, transcript, CUOHC, 30 June 1971,
   1, 12.
"ZOT IS NOT FRIML!"   Rudolf Friml, quoted by Bob Wright, interview with
   EBT, NYC, 25 February 1990.
"The first day on"   Allan Jones, interview with EBT, NYC, 8 December
   1990.

"her best work"   Allan Jones, transcript, SMUOHC, 22.
"Jeanette MacDonald was never"   "The Firefly," *FD*, 2 September 1937.
"lightly amusing"   "The Firefly," *FW*, 20 October 1937, 27.
"dashing and manly"   Flin., "The Firefly," *Variety*, 28 July 1937.
"size . . . screaming eagle"   Flin., "The Firefly," *Variety*, 28 July 1937.
"pretentious"   Kate Cameron, *The Firefly* Glows on the Astor Screen,"
    NYDN, 2 September 1937.
"excessive"   A. E. Hancock [Columbia Theater, Columbia City, Indiana],
    "What the Picture Did for Me," *MPH*, 8 January 1938.
"a little high-class for the hillbillies"   B. Hollenbeck [Rose Theatre, Sumas,
    Washington], "What the Picture Did for Me," *MPH*, 5 March 1938.
"the great essential is"   Hunt Stromberg, "The Producer," in Stephen
    Watts, ed., *Behind the Screen: How Films Are Made* (New York: Dodge,
    1938), 1.
"a montage sequence of"   William Weaver, "The Firefly" [review of preview
    cut], *MPH*, 24 July 1937.

CHAPTER 12. MIDDLEBROW MUSE

"Radio, in my opinion . . . taste of the nation"   JAM, in "Opportunity
    Knocks: Always Room for Real Talent, Declares Famous Singing Star,"
    NYWT, 20 November 1937.
"a treat for all . . . artist's dignity"   Bob Landry, "Jeanette MacDonald,"
    Variety, 29 September 1937.
"All day Sunday . . . grim experience"   JAM, auto., II, 146.
"an attack of ptomaine poisoning"   "Jeanette MacDonald Ill," *PEB*, 20
    December 1937.
"the greatest development"   Bob Landry, "Radio's H'Wood Headaches,"
    Variety, 29 September 1937.
"complete merger of radio"   Louis B. Mayer, in "MGM's Studio Gives First
    Radio Show," *MPH*, 13 November 1937.
"favorite actress"   Result of a poll conducted in July 1937 and reported in
    Fortune, November 1939, 176.
"top musical magnet"   "Top Pix and Stars of 1937," *Variety*, 5 January
    1938, 54.
"I could feel the"   JAM, auto., II, 153.
"I went to argue"   JAM, auto., II, 154.
"You're going to have . . . with another one?!"   Nelson Eddy and Allan
    Jones, in Jones, interview with EBT, NYC, 8 December 1990.
"Come on, now. Let's"   Nelson Eddy, in Roger Carroll, "Jeanette Confesses
    about Nelson Eddy," Nelson Eddy scrapbooks, volume 7, DL.
"the ice between them"   Vera Matthews Gebbert, letter to EBT, 11 March
    1995.
"Nelson was the team's"   Bob Wright, interview with EBT, NYC, 25
    February 1990.
"ten best movies"   "What Are the Women of America Thinking?," *Ladies'
    Home Journal*, February 1939, 64.

"Mr. Raymond's 'getting hot' . . . don't sing!"   "Gene Raymond and the Alligators," *Variety,* 25 May 1938.

"stiff and unsociable"   Amy Revere McCauley, interview with EBT, Menlo Park, California—Boston, 9 February 1992.

"Gene Raymond was very"   Fay Wray, interview with EBT, Los Angeles, 22 July 1991.

"I think the two"   Lew Ayres, interview with EBT, Los Angeles, 28 July 1990.

"the most thoughtfully generous . . . McGillicutty"   JAM, auto., II, 140.

"a kind of secrecy . . . hard to bear"   JAM, auto., II, 142.

"I'm mighty proud of"   Gene Raymond, letter to JAM, in JAM, auto., II, 145.

"radiantly happy . . . suffered as a husband"   JAM, auto., II, 143.

"Dad, Dad, Dad!"   Gene Raymond, in JAM, auto., II, 144.

"I had to try"   JAM, auto., II, 144.

"Writing for films"   Dorothy Parker, in "Are Film Writers Workers?," *Pacific Weekly,* 29 June 1936, 371.

"sophistication . . . type of writing"   Hunt Stromberg, story notes, 29 December 1937, *Sweethearts* file, MGM Collection, DL.

"Our scenes must have"   Hunt Stromberg, story notes, 13 November 1937, *Sweethearts* file, MGM Collection, DL.

"He would much rather"   Hunt Stromberg, story notes, 29 October 1937, *Sweethearts* file, MGM Collection, DL.

"Nelson Eddy comes to"   Walter Winchell, "On Broadway," *NYDM,* 25 December 1938.

"bold . . . accented"   Adrian, in Gwenn Walters, "Fashion Letter," *Photoplay,* October 1938, 78.

"a good scene for Jeanette"   Stromberg, story conference notes, 23 January 1938, *Sweethearts* file, MGM Collection, Doheny Library, USC.

"A dream of ribbons"   Bosley Crowther, *NYT,* 23 December 1938.

"It really is too much"   "Too Much of a Good Thing," *HS,* 24 December 1938, 16.

"The production numbers are"   Kate Cameron, *NYDN,* 23 December 1938.

"pleasantly coy . . . old-fashioned musicals"   "Musical in Technicolor: Sweethearts," *Life,* 24 October 1938, 29.

"all very much like"   *NYS,* 23 December 1938.

"Marriage is the tax"   Nelson Eddy, in Boze Hadleigh, *The Vinyl Closet: Gays in the Music World* (San Diego: Los Hombres Press, 1991), 72.

"[Eddy] didn't want a"   Noël Coward, in Axel Madsen, *The Sewing Circle: Hollywood's Greatest Secret* (New York: Birch Lane Press, 1995), 18.

"slept in a double"   Sidney Franklin, Jr., phone interview with EBT, 15 December 1994.

"Ann was very protective"   Virginia Eddy Brown, phone interview with EBT, 21 October 1994.

"Rock of Gibraltar . . . normal person"   Gale Sherwood, phone interview with EBT, 20 October 1994.

"it was just like"   Nelson Eddy, in Gale Sherwood, phone interview with EBT, 20 October 1994.

"long, expensive talks . . . lettuce, then"   JAM and unnamed hypnotherapist, in JAM, auto., II, 148–49.
"You must wonder why . . . evening progressed"   JAM, auto., II, 149.
"There are two kinds"   Charles L. Wagner, in Elizabeth Elliot, "Sincerity Termed Keynote of MacDonald's Character," *Roanoke (Virginia) World-News*, 25 January 1941.
"To be honest"   JAM, auto., II, 147.
"the charming way . . . meaning of the words"   "Salt Lake Fans Mob Singing Star, Husband," *Salt Lake City Telegram*, 29 April 1939; "Singer Charms 3,000 in Coliseum Concert; Police Guard Needed," *Daily Argus-Leader* (Sioux-Falls, SD), 22 April 1939.
"Anyone who keeps abreast"   Walter A. Hansen, "Jeanette MacDonald," *Fort Wayne (Indiana) News Sentinel*, 15 April 1939.
"It put me into"   JAM, auto., II, 150B.
"Dear Howard: Have been"   JAM, letter to Howard Strickling, 11 April 1939, MacD Archive.
"Remind them that [Claudette] . . . bigger cash elsewhere"   JAM, letter to Louis Swarts, 9 April 1939, MacD Archive.
"confidant, guide . . . out of my office!"   Louis Swarts and Louis B. Mayer, in JAM, auto., II, 155.
"And if I quit . . . I don't believe this"   Louis B. Mayer and Nicholas Schenck, in JAM, auto., II, 154–55.
"That's showing off"   JAM, notes to Sylvia Grogg, 16 August 1939, MacD Archive.
"I do not hold myself"   JAM, letter to Louis Swarts, 9 April 1939, MacD Archive.
"sad . . . sour"   *Variety*, 12 April 1939; 3 May 1939; 19 April 1939.
"a so-called better . . . opportunity for me"   Lew Ayres, interview with EBT, Los Angeles, 28 July 1990.
"After a few days"   Lew Ayres, remarks at JMIFC banquet, Beverly Hilton Hotel, 23 June 1990.

CHAPTER 13. THE SOPRANO MILITANT

"I want to be"   Gene Raymond, in Ida Zeitlin, "Jeanette Sends Her Man to War," *Photoplay*, June 1942.
"my air fiend"   JAM, interview with Edward R. Morrow, *Person to Person*, CBS TV, 31 October 1958.
"Like most people in"   JAM, auto., II, 145.
"While I do not"   Robert Z. Leonard, letter to JAM, 16 February 1940, MacD Archive.
"a welcome antidote"   "*New Moon* Again," *Newsweek*, 1 July 1940, 41.
"As at any focal"   JAM, in Hope Ridings Miller, "Jeanette MacDonald Charms Guests at Mrs. Willebrandt's Gay Reception," *WP*, 28 February 1940.
"The Washington audience was"   JAM, letter to Ida Koverman, 8 March 1940, MacD Archive.

"volume" Glenn Dillard Gunn, "Miss MacDonald Heard by Packed House," *WTH,* 29 February 1940.

"emotional depth" Alice Eversman, "Jeanette MacDonald Proves Glamorous in Recital," *WS,* 29 February 1940.

"strange tonal flurry" Bruno David Usher, "MacDonald in Recital," *LAN,* 26 April 1940.

"smaller, less secure, but" Claudia Cassidy, "On the Aisle," *Chicago Journal of Commerce,* 30 March 1940.

"like a million bucks" Hugh Martin, interview with EBT, Encinitas, California, 19 August 1990.

"Damned if I wasn't . . . with reservations" JAM, letter to Ida Koverman, 8 March 1940, MacD Archive.

"It really is frightening . . . suitcase" Noël Coward, *The Noël Coward Diaries,* ed. Graham Payne and Sheridan Morley (Boston: Little Brown, 1982), 59.

"not particularly happy having" Pamela Randall, interview with EBT, West Hills—Los Angeles, 15 June 1991.

"I had to move" JAM, in Elinor Hughes, "Jeanette MacDonald, Here for Boston Debut, Discusses Contrast Between Concert and Films," *BH,* 29 November 1940.

"nervous indigestion" Assistant Director's Report, 9 September 1940, *Bitter Sweet* file, MGM Script Collection, DL.

"I sing for Democrats . . . favorite son" JAM, in June Mull, "Glamorous Singing Star of Screen Arrives in City," *Muncie Star,* 19 November 1940.

"France, at least the" JAM, in "Miss MacDonald Foresees Filming of American Opera," *Buffalo News,* 23 November 1940.

"Many things German are" JAM, in June Mull, "Glamorous Singing Star of Screen Arrives in City," *Muncie Star,* 19 November 1940.

"De política nada, señores" JAM, in François Baguer Marty, "Jeanette MacDonald, la Famosa Estrella del Cinema Sonor, es Hoy Huésped de la Habana," unreferenced newspaper clipping, Cuba, 2 February 1941, recital scrapbooks, MacD Archive.

"frozen silence . . . flattery" R. C. B., "Miss MacDonald in First Recital Here," *NYWT,* 5 December 1940.

"truth . . . unreal schmaltz" Donald Ogden Stewart, *By a Stroke of Luck* (New York: Paddington Press, 1975), 195.

"Any actor or actress" JAM, in Gladys Hall, "Most in Love Couple in Hollywood," *Silver Screen,* October 1941, 70.

"I'm just the 'forgotten man'" Frank Borzage, *Morning Telegraph* (New York), 11 June 1941.

"You can believe love" JAM, in Gladys Hall, "Most in Love Couple in Hollywood," *Silver Screen,* October 1941, 70.

"He didn't need any" JAM, in Gladys Hall, "Most in Love Couple in Hollywood," *Silver Screen,* October 1941, 71.

"I didn't see eye" Gene Raymond, transcript, SMUOHC, 27. (The transcript erroneously refers to "Joe" Schenck, Nicholas's brother and head of Twentieth Century-Fox.)

"to face the kind" JAM, auto., II, 157.

"Although I saw it" Subject "50A," in J. P. Mayer, *British Cinemas and Their Audiences* (London: Dennis Dobson, 1948), 238.

"you know what . . . on the jaw" Walter Winchell, JAM, and Gene Raymond, in JAM, auto., II, 152.

"I have always thought" Gene Raymond, notes appended to a copy of his song "It's All Over," MacD Archive.

"That's when everyone got" Vera Kackley, "Thousands Attend Memorial Rites for War Victims," unreferenced newspaper clipping, 23 February 1942, MacD Archive.

"I'll keep 'em flying" Gene Raymond, interview with EBT, Beverly Hills, 9 August 1991.

"My sweetheart, This is" JAM, letter to Gene Raymond, 13 March 1942, MacD Archive.

"It's high time for" JAM, in Elizabeth Wilson, "A Message from Jeanette MacDonald to Other American Women Whose Men Are in Service," hand-corrected typewritten press release, spring 1942, MacD Archive.

"Yes, Jeanette and all" Anna MacDonald, letter to Sally Thurber, 4 August 1942, MacD Archive.

"of somewhat classical . . . singing with her" Ronald Reagan, *Where's the Rest of Me?* (New York: Hawthorn, 1965), 112.

"Just give me a sound" JAM, in Bill Wickersham, "Soldiers Applaud Singer," *LAE,* 16 August 1942.

"militant diva . . . more style" John Mosher, "The Current Cinema: Blue Blues," *New Yorker,* 13 December 1941, 120.

"I'm going to be" Bud Bittler, letter to his mother, in Elizabeth Wilson, "Jeanette Sings for the Soldiers," press release, MacD Archive.

"You give to the" JAM, in "Star-spangled Singer," unreferenced fan magazine article, MacD Archive.

"Without dramamine—which hadn't" JAM, auto., II, 158.

"Looking around me at" JAM, auto., II, 160.

"I think I missed" JAM, in Frank Brookhouser, "Jeanette MacDonald Home on a Visit," *Sunday Philadelphia Bulletin,* 28 February 1960, TB6.

"Dearest Bunk: That evening" Gene Raymond, letter to JAM, 10 September 1942, MacD Archive.

"She wouldn't come to . . . you're loved" JAM, letter to Gene Raymond, 23 August 1942, MacD Archive.

"IT FEELS TERRIFIC WONDERFUL" JAM, cablegram to Gene Raymond, 21 September 1942, MacD Archive.

"While you think I've" JAM, auto., II, 161.

"give this meeting . . . plea to you" Sam Jaffe, letter to JAM, 9 October 1942, MacD Archive.

"Dear Mr. Jaffe, In" JAM, letter to Sam Jaffe, 12 October 1942, MacD Archive.

"comrades" Chaplin, in "Artists Give Rally for Second Front," *NYT,* 17 October 1942.

"This was probably the"   Richard Rodgers, transcript, CUOHC, 148–49.
"one of the greatest"   Hunt Stromberg, letter to Jeff Shurlock, 18 September
   1941, *I Married an Angel* file, PCAC.
"sex suggestiveness"   Production Code Administration, letter to Louis B.
   Mayer, 22 September 1941, *I Married an Angel* file, PCAC.
"any attempt to parallel"   Production Code Administration, letter to Louis B.
   Mayer, 6 August 1941, *I Married an Angel* file, PCAC.
"streamlined siren"   Anita Loos, incomplete screenplay, 18 September 1941,
   I Married an Angel file, MGM Collection, DL.
"if any story ever"   Hunt Stromberg, letter to Jeff Shurlock, 18 September
   1941, *I Married an Angel* file, PCAC.
"loved the material . . . as they had been"   Bob Wright, interview with EBT,
   NYC, 25 February 1990.
"Kid, I've used up"   George Sidney, interview with EBT, Boston, 1 October
   1989.
"The Monday after Pearl Harbor"   Bob Wright, interview with EBT, NYC,
   25 February 1990.
"hated . . . credit to nobody"   JAM, auto., II, 159.
"The critics really walloped"   Ed Sullivan, "Little Old New York," *NYDN,*
   14 July 1942.
"Something Different!"   Title card, trailer, *I Married an Angel* file, MGM
   Collection, DL.
"a horrible mess"   Nelson Eddy, in Gail Lulay, *Nelson Eddy: America's
   Favorite Baritone* (Wheeling, Ill.: Goldfleet, 1990), 129.
"These asses of movie"   JAM, letter to Gene Raymond, 21 December 1942,
   MacD Archive.
"I didn't dream there"   JAM, in Marjory Adams, "Jeanette MacDonald Will
   Sing Army Camps' Favorite Tonight," *BG,* 1 October 1942.
"I can't imagine any"   Ken Jessamy, "Headlines, Footlights," *The People's
   Voice,* 19 December 1942.

CHAPTER 14. BATTLES OPERATIC

"Why not enroll in"   Edward Johnson, in JAM, auto., II, 165.
"Buying my debut is"   JAM, auto., II, 165.
"Looking back, I realize"   JAM, auto., II, 164.
"there [is] no contract . . . box-office draw"   Edward Johnson, paraphrased
   in "Concert and Opera," *NYT,* 21 February 1943, X7.
"submit her qualifications to"   "Jeanette in Opera? Canadians to Decide,"
   Toronto Daily Star, 10 May 1943.
"When [Jeanette] walked into"   Constance Hope, "Jeanette MacDonald,"
   unpublished liner notes for JAM's RCA LP *Opera and Operetta Favorites,*
   RCA-Victor LM-2908, 1967, MacD Archive.
"Keep your fingers crossed"   JAM, in "Arrives for Opera Debut,"
   unreferenced newspaper clipping, JAM scrapbook, UCLA.
"I knew I was"   JAM, auto., II, 166.

"ne'er saw true beauty" William Shakespeare, *Romeo and Juliet*, I, v, 52.

"perfect . . . tremendous charm" Wilfred Pelletier, *Une Symphonie inachevée* (Ottawa: Editions Leméac, 1972), 231.

"It was a great" Wilfred Pelletier, letter to Clara Rhoades, 14 October 1965, MacD Archive.

"Oh, cut it out!" JAM, quoted by Gene Raymond, interview with EBT, Beverly Hills, 9 August 1991.

"UNDERSTAND YOUR ROMEO AND" Mark Woods, telegram to JAM, 21 May 1943, MacD Archive.

"THANK YOU FOR YOUR" JAM, telegram to Mark Woods, 22 May 1943, MacD Archive.

"one more crashing mistake" JAM, auto., II, 172.

"I settled the bills" JAM, auto., II, 173.

"Darling, if I ever" Gene Raymond, in JAM, auto., II, 169.

"He would be flying" JAM, auto., II, 174.

"It naturally is not" Gene Raymond, letter to JAM, 18 October 1943, MacD Archive.

"You—on toast—will" Gene Raymond, letter to JAM, 24 July 1943, MacD Archive.

"Many More Happies" Ann and Nelson Eddy, in MacRaymond guest book, 17 June 1944, MacD Archive.

"I was really curious . . . than Jeanette" Lotte Lehmann, sidebar liner notes to JAM's *Opera and Operetta Favorites,* RCA-Victor LM-2908, 1967.

"He is convinced that" JAM, letter to Lotte Lehmann, 8 August 1944, MacD Archive.

"There is nothing" Lotte Lehmann, letter to JAM, 11 August 1944, MacD Archive.

"I screamed and fought . . . a souvenir" JAM and unidentified assailant, in "Jeanette MacDonald Ambushed by Bellhop," *LAT,* 16 July 1944.

"Dearest Jeanette, It sounded" Lotte Lehmann, letter to JAM, 5 September 1944, MacD Archive.

"particularly stupid . . . so much" JAM, letter to Lotte Lehmann, 19 October 1944, MacD Archive.

"Dearest Jeanette, Don't blame" Lotte Lehmann, letter to JAM, 22 October 1944, MacD Archive.

"It takes real flexibility" Felix Borowski, "Miss M'Donald Brings Small Voice to Opera," *CS,* 5 November 1944.

"an exquisite performance" Claudia Cassidy, "Miss M'Donald Stars; Faust Superbly Sung," *CT,* 16 November 1944.

"a beautiful musical rapport . . . in a flash" JAM, auto., II, 176.

"beautifully sung with . . . as a bass solo" Claudia Cassidy, "Miss M'Donald Stars; Faust Is Superbly Sung," *CT,* 16 November 1944.

"I cannot tell you . . . Good idea!!!" Lotte Lehmann, letter to JAM, 21 November 1944, MacD Archive.

"Hollywood intrusion" JAM, auto., II, 174.

"We believe the [San Francisco]"   Unidentified spokesperson for the San Francisco Opera Company, in JAM, auto., II, 178. In a letter to EBT, 31 August 1994, Koraljka Lockhart, publications editor of the San Francisco Opera, wrote: "I can neither substantiate nor deny Maestro Merola's offer. No archives for those years exist around here." Nor can a record of the offer be found among the holdings of the San Francisco Performing Arts Library and Museum.

"I do not wish to"   JAM, letter to Edward Johnson, n.d., in JAM, auto., II, 178.

"If external influences could"   Edward Johnson, letter to JAM, n.d., in JAM, auto., II, 179. The original for this letter was long held to have disappeared. However, on 4 May 1998, Robert Tuggle, head archivist of the Metropolitan Opera Association, faxed EBT a copy of the full draft of Johnson's letter, dated 19 October 1943; MacDonald's quotation matches Johnson's carbon copy word for word.

"Patrice Munsel is pretty"   Irving Kolodin, "Romeo Revived at Metropolitan," *NYS*, 4 December 1945.

"too intelligent to let"   George Cukor, interview with William Bass, unpublished note, MacD Archive.

"This lovely star, who"   Robert Merrill, *Once More from the Beginning* (New York: Macmillan, 1965), 111.

"Thank you, ladies and"   JAM, "V-E Day Hollywood Victory Special," CBS Radio, Hollywood, 8 May 1945.

"When you hear my songs"   JAM, letter to Lotte Lehmann, 1 May 1945, MacD Archive.

"perfect . . . like that on the program"   Lotte Lehmann, letter to JAM, April 1945, MacD Archive.

"There was at no"   JAM, letter to Lotte Lehmann, 19 July 1945, MacD Archive.

"Won't you please sing"   Unidentified fan, quoted by JAM in Hershel Brown, "Jeanette Going to Call Again," *PPG*, 29 April 1950.

"I am quite sure"   Lotte Lehmann, sidebar liner notes to JAM's *Opera and Operetta Favorites*, 1967.

"I have never heard"   JAM, auto., loose page numbered "151 (Rewrite)."

"dramatic focus . . . his money's worth"   Claudia Cassidy, *CT*, 28 October 1945.

"I didn't dare take"   JAM, auto., II, 176.

"She just couldn't take"   Emily Wentz, letter to Helen Ferguson, 29 October 1945, MacD Archive.

"cease to talk about"   Lotte Lehmann, letter to JAM, 21 November 1945, MacD Archive.

"Opera takes too much"   JAM, in Hershel Brown, "Jeanette Going to Call Again," *PPG*, 29 April 1950.

CHAPTER 15. A GRACEFUL EXIT

"pass her the bag"   Collins Smith, interview with EBT, NYC, 23 January 1991.

"I'm a living argument" JAM, letter to Erskine Johnson, 25 June 1946, MacD Archive.

"The problem of the" *Daily Express* (London), 1 July 1946.

"Londoners have the sturdy" JAM, letter to Erskine Johnson, 25 June 1946, MacD Archive.

"She jist spoke awa' . . . aboot" Balfron villager, in Christina Stewart, "Jeanette Has to Dodge Hay Fever," *People's Journal* (Dundee, Scotland), 13 July 1946.

"totally without interest . . . aggressive" Claude Briac, "Les Films Nouveaux: Amants," *Paris-Matin,* 8 June 1946.

"No actress can afford" JAM, in Louella Parsons, "Louella O. Parsons in Hollywood," *LAE,* 23 May 1948.

"disloyalty . . . never thought about that" L. B. Mayer and JAM, in JAM, auto., II, 189.

"It's a wonderful feeling" JAM, in Paul Marsh, "Jeanette Reconsiders," *Silver Screen,* August 1947.

"The only difference is" JAM, in "Jeanette MacDonald Back in Groove Once More," *PEN,* 11 November 1946.

"She knew what she" Jane Powell, transcript, SMUOHC, 8.

"anti-social . . . serious criticism" Joseph I. Breen, letter to L. B. Mayer, 22 October 1946, *Three Daring Daughters* file, PCAC.

"Just between you and" JAM, letter to Hedda Hopper, 26 October 1954, Hedda Hopper Collection, HL.

"ruin his concert career" Sol Hurok, in Bronislaw Kaper, transcript, Louis B. Mayer/AFI Oral History Program in Motion Picture History, L. B. Mayer Library, AFI, 80.

"At one point [Iturbi]" Unreferenced newspaper clipping, *NYWT,* MacD Archive.

"lovely and friendly . . . pushing me down!" Elinor Donahue, interview with EBT, Los Angeles, 16 August 1990.

"amazingly competent in a role" Edwin Schallert, "Silly Story Well Glossed in *Daughters,*" *LAT,* 3 March 1948.

"Jeanette, I have to" Emily Wentz, in JAM, auto., II, 186.

"I remembered Father in" JAM, auto., II, 187.

"I joined her for" Gene Raymond, interview with EBT, Beverly Hills, 16 August 1991.

"Dear Elsie, . . . I am" JAM, letter to Elsie MacDonald Scheiter, 27 September 1947, MacD Archive.

"Do you want him" MacDonald, in Scott Eyman, *Ernst Lubitsch: Laughter in Paradise* (New York: Simon and Schuster, 1993), 333.

"When at Lubitsch's funeral" JAM, auto., II, 188.

"I don't know how . . . probably Republicans, anyway!" JAM, Harry Truman, and Bess Truman, in JAM, auto., II, 202–3.

"Let he who is" JAM, in "Enthusiastic Fan Club Follows Jeanette MacDonald on Current Tour," *Springfield Union,* 8 May 1950.

"Throughout the HUAC hearings" Gene Raymond, interview with EBT, Beverly Hills, 14 July 1993.

"I've come to this"   Charles Schoenbaum, quoted by his daughter Vera
Matthews Gebbert, interview with EBT, Washington, D.C.—Boston, 3
March 1992.
"very congenial . . . 'do it in reverse' "   Claude Jarman, Jr., interview with
EBT, San Francisco, 3 May 1991.
"If I had a son"   Claude Jarman, Jr., and Dwayne Hickman, in separate
interviews with EBT, San Francisco, 3 May 1991, and Santa Monica, 16
June 1991.
"peculiar fraternity . . . liked her a lot"   André Previn, *No Minor Chords: My
Days in Hollywood* (New York: Doubleday, 1991), 22.
"good pictures about a good world"   Dore Schary, in Schatz, *The Genius of
the System,* 454.
"all very simple and"   A. H. Weiler, "The Sun Comes Up," *NYT,* 13 May 1949.
"Miss MacDonald's interpretation of "   "Trade Show: *The Sun Comes Up,"*
Daily Variety, 31 December 1948.

CHAPTER 16. DISTRESS SIGNALS

"There just is no . . . congenial"   Hedda Hopper, "MacDonald-Raymond
Marriage Defies Hollywood Traditions," *LAT,* 28 November 1948.
"drifting . . . a blizzard"   JAM, auto. II, 180.
"He lacked faith in"   JAM, auto., II, 185.
"Trailing along on my . . . these humiliations"   JAM, auto., II, 181–82.
"prima donna . . . a mother feels"   Mary Kipling, in Gene Raymond,
interview with Clara Rhoades, June 1986.
"Cole Porter had been . . . I'll never know"   JAM, auto., II, 195.
"Now I decided this . . . this was progress"   JAM, auto., II, 195–96.
"Just seeing and hearing"   Sgt. Pauline Moore, "At the Air Force Variety
Show in Heidelberg, Germany," press release, MacD Archive.
"not to be complimentary . . . local newspapers?"   Unnamed complainants,
in Captain H. P. Psomas, memo to Lt. Col. Goetz, 11 January 1950, Hedda
Hopper Collection, HL.
"Mr. Raymond would at"   Captain H. P. Psomas, USAF, memo to Lt. Col.
Goetz, 11 January 1950, Hedda Hopper Collection, HL.
"the biggest moment of my career"   JAM, in "Goal Near," *LAT,* 30
September 1950.
"I don't know how . . . scared about?"   JAM and Ethel Merman, in JAM,
auto., II, 201–2.
"won the right to"   JAM, in William Hawkins, "Jeanette Sings into Gotham
at Last," *NYWTS,* 3 October 1950.
"not unaware of sound . . . of a new film"   Howard Taubman, "Glamour
Prevails at Carnegie Hall," *NYT,* 17 October 1950, 39.
"pleasing, with a prevailing . . . allied fields"   Francis D. Perkins, "Concert
and Recital: Jeanette MacDonald," *NYHTr,* 17 October 1950.
"They applauded and shouted"   Taubman, "Glamour Prevails at Carnegie
Hall," *NYT,* 17 October 1950.

"This is the only time" Emily Wentz, interview with EBT, Los Angeles—Topeka, 20 January 1992.

"I have not invested" JAM, in Gene Raymond, interview with EBT, Beverly Hills, 9 August 1991.

"There is no doubt" Howard Barlow, transcript, CUOHC, 1950, 196.

"looks and voice will" "Tele Follow-Up Comment," *Variety,* 15 November 1950.

"Who is that dame . . . both leaving" Jackie Gleason and JAM, in Emily Wentz, interview with EBT, Los Angeles—Topeka, 20 January 1992.

"By and large, television" JAM, auto., II, 200.

"Everything was going well . . . home and mother" John Pfeiffer, interview with EBT, NYC, 9 January 1992.

"Or is it harmful" "Das Rätsel um Jeanette Macdonald," *Neue Illustrierte Wochenschau,* 7 January 1951, 1.

"Not since the stories" Louella Parsons, *LAE,* 22 February 1951.

"Thanks for all the" Gene Raymond, in JAM, auto., II, 197.

"You know, you were" Lee Strasberg, in Collins Smith, interview with EBT, NYC, 23 January 1991.

"Without a foolproof success" JAM, auto., II, 198.

"like an unending nightmare" JAM, auto., II, 198–99.

"Believe it or not" JAM, postcard to Hedda Hopper, 16 August 1951, Hedda Hopper Collection, HL.

"This was the territory" JAM, auto., II, 200.

"sincerity, like her enthusiasm" Giuseppe Bamboschek, letter to Clara Rhoades, 1 April 1965, MacD Archive.

"Now in her forties" Marion Kelley, "Jeanette MacDonald Wants to Stay Awhile on Stage," *PI,* 22 April 1951.

"although our voices are" JAM, in Mary Jane Hope, "Jeanette MacDonald Has Subtle Glamor," *PEB,* 15 July 1952.

"I find it is" JAM, letter to Raoul Jobin, 25 May 1951, MacD Archive.

"With twelve rooms to" JAM, auto., II, 201.

"I think we saw" Dina Merrill, letter to EBT, 23 July 1992.

"We broke for coffee" Hermione Gingold with Anne Clements Eyre, *How to Grow Old Disgracefully* (New York: St. Martin's Press, 1988), 120.

"Agent after agent . . . for you, Dinah!" JAM, auto., II, 200.

"This is very unhealthy" JAM, in Ken Richards, interview with EBT, NYC, 28 April 1990.

"Well, I can't wear . . . down the stairs!" JAM, in Clara Rhoades, interview with EBT, Topeka, 18 January 1992.

"Please give my warm" Dwight D. Eisenhower, in JAM, auto., II, 204.

"gimmick . . . long-hair talent" "The Desert Song," *Newsweek,* 24 August 1953, 48.

"Just because it's a" JAM, in Erskine Johnson, "Jeanette Defends Saloon Debut," *NYWTS,* 13 March 1953.

"whether you sing in" JAM, in "Miss MacDonald Wins Night Clubs with Good Music," *LAT,* 17 January 1954.

"You've got to keep up"   Wilbur Clark, in Richard English, "The Million-Dollar Talent War," *Saturday Evening Post,* 24 October 1953, 70.

"smash hit"   Les Yard, "Cocoanut Grove," *HR,* 22 January 1954.

"I couldn't possibly have"   Gale Sherwood, phone interview with EBT, 20 October 1994.

"For so many years . . . the other studios"   JAM, letter to Hedda Hopper, 26 October 1954, Hedda Hopper Collection, HL.

"I assure you that"   JAM, letter to Louis E. Swarts, 14 June 1954, MacD Archive.

"always looking for a"   Theodore Paxson, in Tessa Williams, interview with EBT, Topeka, 23 January 1991.

"I'm convinced that if"   Nelson Eddy, letter to Gene Raymond, 19 May 1951, MacD Archive.

"I was so damned"   JAM, letter to Mabel Walker Willebrandt, 15 February 1960, MacD Archive.

"It is, apparently, as"   JAM, letter to Louis E. Swarts, 10 July 1954, MacD Archive.

"The choice I had"   JAM, auto., II, 205.

"In the first scene"   George Schaefer, interview with EBT, Beverly Hills—Boston, 20 August 1991.

"With the breath taken"   Cole Lesley, *Remembered Laughter: The Life of Noël Coward* (New York: Knopf, 1976), 344.

"I'm only the best . . . 'the first was made'"   JAM and Robert Browning, in JAM, letter to Gene Raymond, 3 July 1954, MacD Archive.

"a bitter, catty, unfair"   Mary Kipling, in JAM, auto., I, 6.

"I was alone. The"   JAM, auto., II, 206.

"I had nothing better . . . point of breakdown"   JAM, auto., II, 206–7.

"I opened my eyes . . . the old place"   JAM and Gene Raymond, in JAM, auto., II, 207–8.

"My dearest, Before this"   JAM, letter to Gene Raymond, 23 September 1954, MacD Archive.

"I never felt better"   JAM, auto., II, 209.

CHAPTER 17. "CARVE YOUR NAME IN HUMAN HEARTS"

"the great, popular woman"   Mary Ann Callan, "Pop Tunes Meaningless to Jeanette MacDonald," *LAT,* 31 August 1955.

"Dear Miss MacDonald—Mr. Truman"   Bess Truman, letter to JAM, 23 August 1956, MacD Archive.

"I was in the wings"   Jack Lee, interview with EBT, NYC, 22 December 1990.

"When I first saw . . . Mr. Hammerstein!"   JAM, auto., II, 210.

"Jeanette, Gertie Lawrence, and"   Jack Lee, interview with EBT, NYC, 22 December 1990.

"indestructible and irrepressible" "Jeanette MacDonald Back Sunny as Ever for 'Stars,' " *Milwaukee Journal,* 16 July 1957.

"young people, who say" JAM, in Marie Torre, "Jeanette MacDonald in Quandary," *NYHTr,* 28 October 1958.

"When they stop burlesquing" JAM, handwritten response to JMIFC questionnaire, c. 1962, MacD Archive.

"Have we become so" JAM, in Marie Torre, "Jeanette MacDonald in Quandary," *NYHTr,* 28 October 1958.

"Why don't you make . . . perfectly happy" JAM and Maurice Chevalier, in unreferenced French movie magazine, September 1957, tr. *The Golden Comet* 45, n. 2 (summer 1982): 30.

"I find nothing sustaining . . . great melodies" JAM, in Mary Ann Callan, "Pop Tunes Meaningless to Jeanette MacDonald," *LAT,* 31 August 1955.

"I feel a little sorry" JAM, interview with Edward R. Morrow, *Person to Person,* CBS TV, 31 October 1958.

"One of the great sadnesses . . . he represented" JAM, auto., II, 213–14.

"Good gracious! Imagine two" Greer Garson, in JAM, auto., II, 213.

"quite poignant" JAM, handwritten response to JMIFC questionnaire, c. 1958, MacD Archive.

"Maurice—and I say" JAM, transcript, interview with Tony Thomas, c. 1959, MacD Archive.

"INEXPERTLY CONTRACTED AND MANAGED" *Variety,* 4 March 1959, 2.

"It was quite a disastrous experience" JAM, letter to Clara Rhoades, 9 March 1959, MacD Archive.

"Please call Mrs. Mills" JAM, handwritten note, [27 March 1960], MacD Archive.

"I'm not sure whether" JAM, "This I Believe," typescript, c. 1953, MacD Archive.

"forever and ever expanding" International Association of Religious Science Churches, "Origin, Organization, Objective, Declaration of Religious Science Principles," Los Angeles, n.d. [leaflet]; reprinted in J. Stillson Judah, *The History and Philosophy of the Metaphysical Movements in America* (Philadelphia: Westminster Press, 1967), 227.

"mushy . . . cocktail hour" JAM, in Clara Rhoades, interview with EBT, Topeka, 15 January 1992.

"It's a real chore" MacDonald, transcript, interview with Tony Thomas, c. 1959, MacD Archive.

"I came to Hollywood" JAM, in Dewitt Bodeen, "Jeanette MacDonald," *Films in Review,* March 1965, 140.

"the angelic creature . . . career and romance" JAM, transcript, interview with Tony Thomas, c. 1959, MacD Archive.

"come off extremely well" JAM, letter to Bob Ritchie, 17 October 1960, MacD Archive.

"Dear Shorty—Enclosed herewith!" Bob Ritchie, letter to JAM, c. late October 1960, MacD Archive.

"Dear Jeanette, Sure, it's" Nelson Eddy, letter to JAM, 14 September 1960, MacD Archive.

"I am sorry to report" JAM, letter to Mrs. William Baumgartner [of Greensburg, Indiana], 11 September 1961, MacD Archive.

"Marble and granite" Theodore Ledyard Cuyler, *A Model Christian* (Philadelphia: Presbyterian Board of Publication and Sabbath-School Work, 1903), 94.

"I had what I . . . write the show" Harold Prince, letter to EBT, 30 April 1991.

"she was never under" Saul Chaplin, interview with EBT, Los Angeles— Boston, 11 March 1991.

"technical impracticability" JAM, letter to Mabel Walker Willebrandt, 15 February 1960, MacD Archive.

"BEFORE LEAVING FOR SOUTH" Dwight D. Eisenhower, telegram to Irene C. Clough, 20 February 1960, MacD Archive.

"As an old-time Philadelphian" Nelson Eddy, letter to Irene C. Clough, 5 February 1960, MacD Archive.

"PLEASE TELL JEANETTE MCDONALD" Blossom Rock, telegram to JAM, 25 February 1960, MacD Archive.

"a complete breakdown, due" JAM, letter to Margaret Cloghessy, 27 July 1960, MacD Archive.

"Dear Blossie, It's difficult" JAM, letter to Blossom Rock, c. early 1960, MacD Archive.

"Dearest Pappie—The sweetest" JAM, note to Gene Raymond, c. mid-June 1962, MacD Archive.

"It's really quite amazing" JAM, in Bob Thomas, "Far-Flung Fans Loyal to Jeanette," *PEB*, 8 July 1962.

"With the tone set" Will Tusher, "44 Years of Adulation: Humor and Tone at Anni Recall of La MacDonald," *Variety*, 8 July 1981.

"to convince people that . . . Castro and company" JAM, letter to President Clara Rhoades and JMIFC membership, 14 November 1962, MacD Archive.

"She was having symptoms . . . very good result." Dr. Michael E. DeBakey, letter to EBT, 10 March 1994.

"Gene and I" JAM, letter to Clara Rhoades, 15 May 1963, MacD Archive.

"We want love and" Mrs. William F. Hannaford, letter to manager, Colorado Theater, Pasadena, 25 January 1963, Hedda Hopper Collection, HL.

"I couldn't be more . . . picture, as I will" MacDonald and Gene Raymond, transcript, remarks at Picwood Theater, Westood, Los Angeles, 2 April 1963, MacD Archive.

"My dear Mr. Van Dyke" JAM, letter to Dick Van Dyke, 16 September 1964, MacD Archive.

"Dearest Gracie, I want" JAM, note to Grace Adele Newell, 1 October 1964, MacD Archive.

"touch and go . . . hospital immediately" Emily Wentz, letter to Clara Rhoades, 28 December 1964, MacD Archive.

"Mrs. Raymond remained very sick"   Susan Cosak Nelson, interview with
   Helen F. Crawford, Covina, California, 26 February 1994.
"When I saw her"   Dr. Michael E. DeBakey, letter to EBT, 10 March 1994.
"I love you . . . you, too"   JAM and Gene Raymond, in Gene Raymond,
   interview with EBT, Beverly Hills, 27 July 1990.

CHAPTER 18. "JUST THE ECHO OF A SIGH"

"the funeral of the year"   "California: Funeral of the Year," *Newsweek,*
   1 February 1965, 22.
"Jeanette would want it that way"   Gene Raymond, in Roberta L. Reynolds,
   "Music and Praise Honor Jeanette's Memory," *Golden Comet,* special
   memorial issue, 1965, 116.
"Jeanette is one of . . . always cherish"   Dr. Gene Emmet Clark, transcript,
   funeral oration, 18 January 1965, MacD Archive.
"We know that her . . . message of love"   Lloyd Nolan, transcript, eulogy, 18
   January 1965, MacD Archive.
"larger-than-life . . . autograph books"   "California: Funeral of the Year,"
   Newsweek, 1 February 1965, 22.
"The world has done"   Nelson Eddy, letter to Clara Rhoades, 23 January
   1965, MacD Archive.
"Now they will sing"   Ann Eddy, in Gene Raymond, letter to Clara Rhoades,
   18 March 1967, MacD Archive.
"The consolation that can"   Maurice Chevalier, letter to Clara Rhoades, 6
   April 1965, MacD Archive.
"moved in and took"   John Ritchie, interview with EBT, Myrtle Beach, SC,
   12 January 1993.
"We did remember and"   Louise Horner, letter to EBT, 13 April 1992.
"When [Jeanette] spoke of you"   Gene Raymond, letter to Clara Rhoades, 31
   March 1965, MacD Archive.

AFTERWORD

"I confess that my"   Mary Komidar, letter to David Lapin and EBT, 24
   September 1988.
"perverse perception that the"   Will Crutchfield, "Crutchfield at Large,"
   Opera News, 55, n. 3 (1990): 68.
"emotional commitment . . . can be operatic"   Ira Siff, in Lawrence O'Toole,
   "Opera, the Fairest One of All," *New York Times,* 11 July 1993, H1.
"the epitome of all"   Clement Greenberg, "Avant-Garde and Kitsch,"
   Partisan Review 6, n. 5 (fall 1939): 39, 40.
"a tepid ooze . . . alarming ambiguity"   Dwight MacDonald, "Masscult and
   Midcult" in *Against the American Grain* (New York: Random House,
   1962), passim.
"The music I have . . . window now"   JAM, auto., II, 215.

Bibliography

Listed here are the principal books, manuscripts, and articles that were useful in my research for *Hollywood Diva*. Of the innumerable pieces on MacDonald in fan magazines and daily newspapers, I include only those of special value.

BOOKS AND BOOK-LENGTH MANUSCRIPTS ON MACDONALD

Achard, Paul. *Jeanette MacDonald*. Paris: Nouvelle Librairie Française, 1932.

Bass, William. "Jeanette MacDonald: The Triumphant Voice." c. 1978. Unfinished book manuscript, 306 typescript pp. MacDonald Archive. Jeanette MacDonald International Fan Club Headquarters, Topeka, Kansas.

Castanza, Philip. *The Films of Jeanette MacDonald and Nelson Eddy*. Secaucus, N.J.: Citadel Press, 1978.

Hamann, G. D., ed. *Jeanette MacDonald in the 30's*. Hollywood: Filming Today Press, 1995. A compilation of articles, notices, and film reviews culled from eight Los Angeles newspapers.

Jeanette MacDonald's Favorite Operatic Airs and Songs. New York: G. Schirmer, 1940.

Knowles, Eleanor. *The Films of Jeanette MacDonald and Nelson Eddy*. Cranbury, N.J.: A. S. Barnes, 1975. Film credits by John Robert Cocchi; music credits and discography by J. Peter Bergman.

MacDonald, Jeanette. "Jeanette MacDonald Autobiography." 1957–61. Unpublished autobiography, 318 typescript pp., with handwritten corrections and annotations. MacDonald Archive. Jeanette MacDonald International Fan Club Headquarters, Topeka, Kansas.

Parish, James Robert. *The Jeanette MacDonald Story.* New York: Mason/ Charter, 1976.

Privat, Henri. *Jeanette MacDonald?* Paris: Les Documents Secrets, 1931.

Rhoades, Clara, and Tessa Williams, eds. and comps. *Lookin' In! and Cookin' In! with the MacRaymonds at Twin Gables.* Topeka, Kans.: Jeanette MacDonald International Fan Club, copyright 1984; published 1991.

Stern, Lee Edward. *Jeanette MacDonald.* New York: Jove, 1977.

Tierney, Tom. *Jeanette MacDonald and Nelson Eddy: Paper Dolls in Full Color.* Mineola, N.Y.: Dover, 1992.

ARTICLES ON MACDONALD

Balling, Fredda Dudley. "The Love Song Is Ended." *Motion Picture,* April 1965, 39–40, 63–66.

Beatty, Jerome. "The Girl Who Sang in the Bathtub." *American Magazine,* July 1937, 32–33, 138–41.

Bodeen, Dewitt. "Jeanette MacDonald." *Films in Review,* March 1965, 129–44.

Bull, Clarence Sinclair. "Angel Face and Angel Voice." In *The Faces of Hollywood.* South Brunswick, N.J.: A. S. Barnes, 1968, 59.

Driscoll, F. Paul. "I Dream of Jeanette." *Opera News,* March 1995, 50.

Hall, Leonard. "The Prima Donna and the Old Man." *Photoplay,* February 1931, 63, 108.

Harvey, James. "Jeanette MacDonald." In *Notable American Women,* edited by Barbara Sicherman and Carol Hurd Green, 446–47. Cambridge, Mass.: Harvard University Press, 1980.

Howe, Herb. "Jeanette Takes Paris!" *The New Movie Magazine,* February 1932, 34–35, 106–8.

Knowles, Eleanor. "Jeanette MacDonald: Comedienne Lost." *Films of the Golden Age,* Spring 1996, 16–19.

Lockhart, Freda Bruce. "And So One Star Was Born." *Film Weekly* (London), 23 October 1937, 29–31.

Lubitsch, Ernst. "Maurice and Jeanette: The Screen's Greatest Lovers." *Singapore Free Press,* 1 May 1933.

MacDonald, Jeanette. "If You Hope for a Film Career," *Etude,* November 1953, 16, 64.

———. "Jeanette MacDonald." Transcript. June 1959, 62 pp. Columbia University Oral History Collection. Butler Library, Columbia University, New York.

———. "Ma Carrière de chanteuse." *Aujourd'hui* (Paris), 3 June 1934.

———. "My Frankest Confession," *Screenland,* January 1940, 33, 80–81.

———. "No Royal Road to Song." Pamphlet, 4 pp. Culver City: MGM, c. 1937. Abridged rprt. in *Better Homes and Gardens,* 27 September 1941, 27.

———. "Operetta and the Sound Film," *Etude,* June 1938, 359–60.

MacKay, Harper. "*Roméo* and Jeanette" *Opera News,* 13 April 1991, 12.

Ohmeis, Herbert. "Jeanette MacDonald." Typescript. 1978. MacDonald Archive. Jeanette MacDonald International Fan Club Headquarters, Topeka, Kansas.

Parish, James Robert, and Michael R. Pitts. "Jeanette MacDonald." In *Hollywood Songsters: A Biographical Dictionary,* 417–24. New York: Garland, 1991.

Peary, Danny. "Jeanette MacDonald." In *Cult Movie Stars,* 345–46. New York: Simon and Schuster, 1991.

Pryor, Nancy. "No More Nighties for Jeanette." *Motion Picture,* February 1933, 27, 97.

Raymond, Gene. "Gene Raymond." Transcript. 26 August 1986, 42 pp. Oral History Collection on the Performing Arts in America. DeGolyer Library, Southern Methodist University, Dallas.

Rhoades, Clara, and Tessa Williams. "Jeanette MacDonald Super Star." Parts 1, 2. *American Classic Screen,* August 1978, 8–11; November–December 1978, 37–42.

Ritchie, Robert. "The Jeanette MacDonald I Know!" *Film Pictorial* (London), June 1935.

Rutledge, Fred. "Make Way for Melody." Parts 1, 2, 3, 4. *Radio Mirror,* December 1936, 12–14, 60; January 1937, 32–33, 66; February 1937, 36–38, 84–85; March 1937, 38–39, 86–87.

Shipman, David. "Jeanette MacDonald." In *The Great Movie Stars: The Golden Years,* 367–69. London: Macdonald, 1989.

Shute, Nerina. "Jeanette MacDonald—by Bob Ritchie." *The Sunday Referee* (London), 11 June 1933.

Sullivan, Ed. "Hermits of Hollywood: MacDonald and Eddy." *Chicago Sunday Tribune,* 22 October 1939, graphic section, 1, 3.

Sunshine, Linda. "Sentimental Love: MacDonald and Eddy." In *Lovers,* 81–87. Atlanta: Turner Publishing.

Turk, Edward Baron. "Deriding the Voice of Jeanette MacDonald: Notes on Psychoanalysis and the American Film Musical." *Camera Obscura,* nos. 25–26 [spring 1991]: 225–49. Reprt. in *Embodied Voices: Representing Female Vocality in Western Culture,* edited by Leslie C. Dunn and Nancy A. Jones, 103–19. Cambridge: Cambridge University Press, 1994.

———. "Jeanette Anna MacDonald." In *American National Biography,* edited by John A. Garraty and Mark C. Carnes. Cary, N.C.: Oxford University Press, forthcoming.

Waller, George L. "Jeanette MacDonald, Film Star, W.P.H.S. Grad, Talks on Talkies." *The Western News* [West Philadelphia High School newspaper], 23 January 1930, 1, 6.

Wlaschin, Ken. "Jeanette MacDonald." In *Opera on Screen: A Guide to 100 Years of Films and Videos Featuring Operas, Opera Singers, and Operettas,* 311–12. Los Angeles: Beachwood Press, 1997.

Wright, Charles A. "Jeanette M'Donald 9 Hours in Bathtub." *Philadelphia Evening Bulletin,* 23 July 1932.

———. "My Little Cousin Who Became a Movie Star." *Pennsylvania Magazine,* Spring 1985, 28–29.

———. "Regal Roles Fit Miss M'Donald." *Philadelphia Evening Bulletin,* 28 July 1932.

Zillner, Dian. "Jeanette MacDonald (with Nelson Eddy)." In *Hollywood Collectibles,* 134–41. West Chester, Pa.: Schiffer Publishing, 1991.

OTHER SOURCES

Altman, Rick. *The American Film Musical.* Bloomington: Indiana University Press, 1987.

Atkinson, Brooks. *Broadway.* New York: Macmillan, 1970.

Bailey, Margaret J. *Those Glorious Glamour Years: Hollywood Costume Design of the 1930s.* Secaucus, N.J.: Citadel Press, 1982.

Balio, Tino. *Grand Design: Hollywood As a Modern Business Enterprise, 1930–39.* New York: Scribner's, 1993.

Barrios, Richard. *A Song in the Dark: The Birth of the Musical Film.* New York: Oxford University Press, 1995.

Basinger, Jeanine. *A Woman's View: How Hollywood Spoke to Women.* New York: Knopf, 1993.

Beaton, Cecil. *Sir Cecil Beaton's Scrapbook.* London: Batsford, 1937.

Behlmer, Rudy, ed. *Memo from David O. Selznick.* New York: Viking, 1972.

———. *W. S. Van Dyke's Journal: "White Shadows in the South Seas" (1927–1928) and Other Van Dyke on Van Dyke.* Lanham, Md.: Scarecrow Press, 1996.

Behr, Edward. *The Good Frenchman: The True Story of the Life and Times of Maurice Chevalier.* New York: Villard Books, 1993.

Bergan, Ronald. *The United Artists Story.* New York: Crown, 1986.

Blitzstein, Marc. "Popular Music—An Invasion: 1923–1933." *Modern Music,* January–February 1933, 96–102.

Bloom, Ken. *Broadway: An Encyclopedic Guide to the History, People and Places of Times Square.* New York: Facts on File, 1991.

Bogdanovich, Peter. "Hollywood." [On Ernst Lubitsch.] *Esquire,* November 1972, 82, 86.

———. "Leo McCarey." Transcript. 1968–69. Louis B. Mayer/American Film Institute Oral History Program in Motion Picture History. Louis B. Mayer Library, American Film Institute, Los Angeles.

Bookspan, Martin, and Ross Yockey. *André Previn.* Garden City, N.Y.: Doubleday, 1981.

Bordman, Gerald. *American Musical Comedy.* New York: Oxford University Press, 1982.

———. *American Musical Revue.* New York: Oxford University Press, 1985.

———. *American Musical Theatre: A Chronicle.* 2nd ed. New York: Oxford University Press, 1986.

———. *American Operetta.* New York: Oxford University Press, 1981.

———. *Jerome Kern: His Life and Music.* New York: Oxford University Press, 1980.

Bordwell, David, Janet Staiger, and Kristin Thompson. *The Classical Hollywood Cinema: Film Style and Mode of Production to 1960.* New York: Columbia University Press, 1985.

Brenson, Michael. "Is 'Quality' an Idea Whose Time Has Gone?" *New York Times,* 22 July 1990, H1, 27.

Brown, Virginia Eddy. "In Defense of Nelson Eddy." *Yankee,* June 1995, 14.

Caffin, Caroline. *Vaudeville.* New York: Mitchell Kennerly, 1914.

Cannom, Robert C. *Van Dyke and the Mythical City of Hollywood.* Culver City, Calif.: Murray and Gee, 1948.

Carey, Gary. *All the Stars in Heaven: Louis B. Mayer's MGM.* New York: Dutton, 1981.

———. *Anita Loos.* New York: Knopf, 1988.

Cendrars, Blaise. *Hollywood: Mecca of the Movies.* Berkeley: University of California Press, 1995. Tr. from orig. French edition, 1936.

Chevalier, Maurice. *Ma Route et mes chansons.* 3 vols. Paris: René Julliard, 1946–48.

Chierichetti, David. *Hollywood Costume Design.* New York: Harmony Books, 1975.

Cohen-Stratyner, Barbara. "The Dance Direction of Ned Wayburn: Selected Topics in Musical Staging, 1901–1923." Ph.D. diss., New York University, 1980.

Colton, Helen. "Top Dog in Hollywood: Canine Star Lassie." *New York Times,* 27 February 1949.

Copland, Aaron. "Second Thoughts on Hollywood." *Modern Music,* March–April 1940, 141–45.

Crowther, Bosley. *Hollywood Rajah: The Life and Times of Louis B. Mayer.* New York: Holt, Rinehart and Winston, 1960.

———. *The Lion's Share.* New York: Dutton, 1957.

Cukor, George. "George Cukor." Transcript. 22 June 1971. Oral History Collection. Butler Library, Columbia University, New York.

———. "George Cukor." Transcript. 27 May 1977. Oral History Collection on the Performing Arts. DeGolyer Library, Southern Methodist University, Dallas.

———. "Recollections of George Cukor." Transcript. 28 September 1968. Oral History of the Motion Picture in America Project. University Library, University of California, Los Angeles.

Daly, Maury. "Gene Raymond: Renaissance Man." *Classic Images,* November 1995, 12–13, 50–51.

Davis, Ronald L. *Opera in Chicago: A Social and Cultural History, 1850–1965.* New York. Appelton-Century, 1966.

Dewey, Donald. *James Stewart.* Atlanta: Turner Publishing, 1996.

Dizikes, John. *Opera in America.* New Haven, Conn.: Yale University Press, 1993.

Eames, John Douglas. *The MGM Story.* New York: Crown, 1982.

———. *The Paramount Story.* New York: Crown, 1985.

Eddy, Nelson. "Success in Voice Study." *Etude,* November 1939, 695–96, 754.

Eyman, Scott. *Ernst Lubitsch: Laughter in Paradise.* New York: Simon and Schuster, 1993.

Farber, Manny. "Movies in Wartime." *New Republic,* 3 January 1944, 16–20.

Fields, Armond, and L. Marc Fields. *From the Bowery to Broadway: Lew Fields and the Roots of American Popular Theater.* New York: Oxford University Press, 1993.

Freedland, Michael. *Maurice Chevalier.* New York: Morrow, 1981.

Friedrich, Otto. *City of Nets: A Portrait of Hollywood in the 1940s.* New York: Harper and Row, 1986.

Gabler, Neal. *An Empire of Their Own: How the Jews Invented Hollywood.* New York: Crown, 1988.

Gardner, Gerald. *The Censorship Papers: Movie Censorship Letters from the Hays Office, 1934 to 1968.* New York: Dodd, Mead, 1987.

Gershwin, George. "Our New National Anthem." *Theatre Magazine,* May 1925, 30.

Gerson, Robert A. *Music in Philadelphia.* Philadelphia: Theodore Presser, 1940.

Glass, Beaumont. *Lotte Lehmann: A Life in Opera and Song.* Santa Barbara, Calif.: Capra Press, 1988.

Green, Stanley. *Broadway Musicals: Show by Show.* New York: Hal Leonard, 1990.

———. *Encyclopedia of the Musical Film.* New York: Oxford University Press, 1981.

Hammerstein, Oscar, II. "Voices Versus Feet." *Theatre Magazine,* May 1925, 14, 70.

Harding, James. *Maurice Chevalier: His Life, 1888–1972.* London: Secker and Warburg, 1982.

Hart, Dorothy. *Thou Swell, Thou Witty: The Life and Lyrics of Lorenz Hart.* New York: Harper, 1976.

Hart, Lorenz. "Running Up a Score." *New York Times,* 29 October 1939.

Harvey, James. *Romantic Comedy in Hollywood, from Lubitsch to Sturges.* New York: Knopf, 1987.

Hay, Peter. *MGM: When the Lion Roars.* Atlanta: Turner Publishing, 1991.

Hayes, Helen, with Katherine Hatch. *My Life in Three Acts.* Orlando, Fla.: Harcourt, Brace, Jovanovich, 1990.

Hemming, Roy. *The Melody Lingers On: The Great Songwriters and Their Movie Musicals.* New York: Newmarket Press, 1986.

Hench, William Martin. "Trends in the Size of Industrial Companies in Philadelphia from 1915 through 1930." Ph.D. diss., University of Pennsylvania, 1938.

Higham, Charles. *Merchant of Dreams: Louis B. Mayer, M.G.M., and the Secret Hollywood.* New York: Douglas I. Fine, 1993.

Hirschhorn, Clive. *The Hollywood Musical.* New York: Crown, 1981.

Hoffmeister, Harry P. "The Story of Music." In *History of the West Philadelphia High School Prepared on the Occasion of Its Fiftieth Anniversary, 1912–1962.* Philadelphia: West Philadelphia High School Alumni Association, 1962.

Hoopes, Roy. *When the Stars Went to War: Hollywood and World War II.* New York: Random House, 1994.

Horowitz, Joseph. *Understanding Toscanini: How He Became an American Culture-God and Helped Create a New Audience for Old Music.* Minneapolis: University of Minnesota Press, 1987.

Jablonski, Edward. *Gershwin: A Biography.* Garden City, N.Y.: Doubleday, 1987.

Jellinek, George. "On the Home Front: Opera and World War II." *Opera News,* July 1995, 30–33.

Johnston, Alva. "Lord Fauntleroy in Hollywood." [On Woody Van Dyke.] *New Yorker,* 28 September 1935, 20–24.

Jones, Robert Edmond. "The Crisis of Color." *New York Times,* 19 May 1935, X3.

———. "The Problem of Color." *New York Times,* 27 February 1938, X4.

Judah, J. Stillson. *The History and Philosophy of the Metaphysical Movements in America.* Philadelphia: Westminster Press, 1967.

Kiner, Larry F. *Nelson Eddy: A Bio-discography.* Metuchen, N.J.: Scarecrow Press, 1992.

Knight, Arthur. "All Singing! All Talking! All Laughing!" *Theatre Arts Monthly,* September 1949, 33–40.

Kobal, John. *People Will Talk.* New York: Knopf, 1985.

Kobler, John. *Damned in Paradise: The Life of John Barrymore.* New York: Atheneum, 1977.

Koestenbaum, Wayne. *The Queen's Throat: Opera, Homosexuality, and the Mystery of Desire.* New York: Poseidon, 1993.

Koppes, Clayton R., and Gregory D. Black. *Hollywood Goes to War.* New York: Free Press, 1987.

Kreuger, Miles, ed. *The Movie Musical from Vitaphone to 42nd Street: As Reported in a Great Fan Magazine.* New York: Dover, 1975.

Lambert, Gavin. *Norma Shearer: A Life.* New York: Knopf, 1990.

Laroche, Robert. "Les Veuves au cinéma." *L'Avant-Scène Opéra,* Autumn 1982, 99–103.

Lasky, Jesse L., with Don Weldon. *I Blow My Own Horn.* New York: Doubleday, 1957.

Lawler, Harrison. "Opera on the Screen." *Etude,* May 1936, 283–84.

Lesley, Cole. *Remembered Laughter: The Life of Noël Coward.* New York: Knopf, 1976.

Levy, Emanuel. *George Cukor, Master of Elegance.* New York: Morrow, 1994.

Liebling, A. J. "The Boys from Syracuse." [On J. J. and Lee Shubert.] Parts 1, 2, 3. *New Yorker,* 18 November 1939, 26–30; 25 November 1939, 23–39; 2 December 1939, 33–37.

Loos, Anita. "Afterword." *San Francisco: A Screenplay.* Edited by Matthew J. Bruccoli. Carbondale: Southern Illinois University Press, 1979.

———. *Cast of Thousands.* New York: Grosset and Dunlap, 1977.

———. *Kiss Hollywood Good-by.* New York: Viking, 1974.

Loy, Myrna, with James Kotsilibas-Davis. *Myrna Loy: On Being and Becoming.* New York: Knopf, 1988.

Lulay, Gail. *Nelson Eddy: America's Favorite Baritone.* Wheeling, Ill.: Goldfleet Publishing, 1990.

Macdonald, Dwight. *Dwight Macdonald on Movies.* Englewood Cliffs, N.J.: Prentice-Hall, 1969.

———. "Masscult and Midcult." In *Against the American Grain.* New York: Random House, 1962, 3–75.

MacKay, Harper. "Going Hollywood." *Opera News,* 31 April 1991, 10–13, 48, 54.

Maeder, Edward, ed. *Hollywood and History: Costume Design in Film.* Los Angeles: County Museum of Art, 1987.

Maltin, Leonard. *The Great American Broadcast: A Celebration of Radio's Golden Age.* New York: Dutton, 1997.

Marion, John Francis. *Within These Walls: A History of the Academy of Music in Philadelphia.* Philadelphia: Academy of Music, 1984.

Marx, Samuel. *Mayer and Thalberg: The Make-Believe Saints.* New York: Random House, 1975.

Mast, Gerald. *Can't Help Singin': The American Musical on Stage and Screen.* Woodstock, N.Y.: Overlook Press, 1987.

Mayer, J. P. *British Cinemas and Their Audiences.* London: Dennis Dobson, 1948.

McArthur, Edwin. *Flagstad: A Personal Memoir.* New York: Knopf, 1965.

McGilligan, Patrick. *George Cukor: A Double Life.* New York: Saint Martin's Press, 1991.

McNamara, Brooks. *The Shuberts of Broadway.* New York: Oxford University Press, 1990.

Merrill, Robert, with Sanford Pody. *Once More from the Beginning.* New York: Macmillan, 1965.

Mordden, Ethan. *Demented: The World of the Opera Diva.* New York: Franklin Watts, 1984.

———. *The Hollywood Musical.* New York: St. Martin's Press, 1981.

———. *The Hollywood Studios.* New York: Knopf, 1988.

Nasaw, David. *Going Out: The Rise and Fall of Public Amusements.* New York: Basic Books, 1993.

Nolan, Frederick. *Lorenz Hart: A Poet on Broadway.* New York: Oxford University Press, 1994.

Parish, James R. "Gene Raymond." In *Hollywood Players: The Thirties.* New Rochelle, N.Y.: Arlington House, 1976.

Pasternak, Joe, with David Chandler. *Easy the Hard Way.* New York: Putnam, 1956.

Pelletier, Wilfred. *Une Symphonie inachevée.* Ottawa: Editions Leméac, 1972.

Peters, Margot. *The House of Barrymore.* New York: Knopf, 1990.

Pleasants, Henry. "New Note on a Familiar Theme." *Modern Music,* January–February 1940, 84–86.

Ponselle, Rosa, with James Drake. *Ponselle: A Singer's Life.* Garden City, N.Y.: Doubleday, 1982.

Previn, André. *No Minor Chords: My Days in Hollywood.* New York: Doubleday, 1991.

Raphaelson, Samson. "Freundschaft." [On Ernst Lubitsch.] *New Yorker,* 11 May 1981, 38–62.

Ringgold, Gene, and Dewitt Bodeen. *Chevalier: The Films and Career of Maurice Chevalier.* Secaucus, N.J.: Citadel Press, 1973.

Riva, Maria. *Marlene Dietrich.* New York: Knopf, 1993.

Rockwell, John. "Opera Gives Its Regards to Broadway." *New York Times,* 15 November 1987, 1, 18.

Rodgers, Richard. *Musical Stages.* New York: Random House, 1975.

Roosevelt, Felicia Warburg. *Doers and Dowagers.* Garden City, N.Y.: Doubleday, 1975.

Rubin, Joan Shelley. *The Making of Middlebrow Culture.* Chapel Hill: University of North Carolina Press, 1992.

Rubin, Martin. *Showstoppers: Busby Berkeley and the Tradition of Spectacle.* New York: Columbia University Press, 1993.

Salles, Jacques. *L'Empire, un temple du spectacle.* Paris: S.F.P. and Jacques Salles, 1975.

Sanjek, Russell. *American Popular Music and Its Business: The First Four Hundred Years.* Vol. 3, *From 1900 to 1984.* New York: Oxford University Press, 1988.

Sarris, Andrew. "Lubitsch in the Thirties." Parts 1, 2. *Film Comment,* Winter 1971, 55–57; Summer 1972, 20–21.

———. "Obbligato for the Operetta." *Village Voice,* 14 July 1987, 59.

Schatz, Thomas. *The Genius of the System: Hollywood Filmmaking in the Studio Era.* New York: Pantheon, 1988.

Scherer, Laurence Barrymore. "A Night in Venice with Naughty Marietta on the H.M.S. Pinafore." *Opera News,* August 1995, 12–16.

Schuller, Gunther. *The Swing Era: The Development of Jazz, 1930–1945.* New York: Oxford University Press, 1989.

Schwartz, Nancy. "Lubitsch's Widow: The Meaning of a Waltz." *Film Comment,* March–April 1975, 13–17.

Seldes, Gilbert. "Jazz, Opera, or Ballet?" *Modern Music,* January–February 1926, 10–16.

Sennett, Ted. *Hollywood Musicals.* New York: Abrams, 1981.

Shale, Richard. *The Academy Awards Index: The Complete Categorical and Chronological Record.* Westport, Conn.: Greenwood Press, 1993.

Sills, Beverly, and Lawrence Linderman. *Beverly: An Autobiography.* Toronto: Bantam, 1987.

Slide, Anthony. *The American Film Industry: A Historical Dictionary.* Westport, Conn.: Greenwood Press, 1986.

———. *The Encyclopedia of Vaudeville.* Westport, Conn.: Greenwood Press, 1994.

Smith, Jack. "*Rose Marie*'s Stout-Departed Men." *Los Angeles Times,* 27 July 1981.

Snyder, Robert W. *The Voice of the City: Vaudeville and Popular Culture in New York.* New York: Oxford University Press, 1989.

Soupault, Philippe. *Ecrits de cinéma: 1913–1931.* Paris: Plon, 1979.

Stagg, Jerry. *The Brothers Shubert.* New York: Random House, 1968.

Stenn, David. *Bombshell: The Life and Death of Jean Harlow.* New York: Doubleday, 1993.

Stine, Whitney. *Stars and Star Handlers: The Business of Show.* Santa Monica, Calif.: Roundtable Publishing, 1985.

St. Johns, Adela Rogers. "The Jean Harlow Story Hollywood Suppressed." *Photoplay,* August 1937, 19–21, 126.

Stowe, David W. *Swing Changes: Big-Band Jazz in New Deal America.* Cambridge, Mass.: Harvard University Press, 1994.

Thomas, Tony, and Jim Terry. *The Busby Berkeley Book.* Greenwich, Conn.: New York Graphic Society, 1973.

Traubner, Richard. *Operetta: A Theatrical History.* Garden City, N.Y.: Doubleday, 1983.

Tynan, Kenneth. "The Genius and the Girls." [On George Cukor.] *Holiday,* February 1961, 99–107.

Vieira, M. Laffite. *West Philadelphia Illustrated: Early History of West Philadelphia, Its People and Its Historical Points.* Philadelphia: Avil Printing, 1903.

Vieira, Mark A. *Hollywood Portraits: Classic Scene Stills 1929–41.* Greenwood, Conn.: Portland House, 1988.

———. *Hurrell's Hollywood Portraits.* New York: Abrams, 1997.

Vorkapich, Slavko. "Slavko Vorkapich." Transcript. 11 August 1975. Oral History Collection on the Performing Arts in America. DeGolyer Library, Southern Methodist University, Dallas.

Watts, Stephen, ed. *Behind the Screen: How Films Are Made.* New York: Dodge Publishing, 1938.

Wayburn, Ned. *The Art of Stage Dancing.* New York: Ned Wayburn Studios, 1925.

Weaver, Wallace. *West Philadelphia: A Study of Natural Social Areas.* Philadelphia: University of Pennsylvania, 1930.

Weinberg, Herman G. *The Lubitsch Touch.* 3rd ed. New York: Dover, 1977.

Weygandt, Cornelius. *Philadelphia Folks: Ways and Institutions In and About the Quaker City.* New York: D. Appleton-Century, 1938.

Wind, Herbert Warren. "Another Opening, Another Show." [On Robert Russell Bennett.] *New Yorker,* 17 November 1951, 46–73.

Wolf, Edwin. *Philadelphia: Portrait of a City.* Philadelphia: Stackpole Books, 1975.

Woll, Allen L. *The Hollywood Musical Goes to War.* Chicago: Nelson Hall, 1983.

Wood, Robin. "Democracy and Shpontanuity: Leo McCarey and the Hollywood Tradition." *Film Comment,* January–February 1976, 7–15.

Photo Credits

Index

Compositor:	Impressions Book and Journal Services, Inc.
Text:	10/13 Sabon
Display:	Bickham Script
Printer and Binder:	Edwards Brothers, Inc.